Experiencing
Intercultural
Communication

Experiencing Intercultural Communication

An Introduction

Fourth Edition

Judith N. Martin
Arizona State University

Thomas K. Nakayama
Northeastern University

McGraw Hill

Connect
Learn
Succeed™

Published by McGraw-Hill, an imprint of The McGraw-Hill Companies, Inc., 1221 Avenue of the Americas, New York, NY, 10020. Copyright © 2011. All rights reserved. No part of this publication may be reproduced or distributed in any form or by any means, or stored in a database or retrieval system, without the prior written consent of The McGraw-Hill Companies, Inc., including, but not limited to, in any network or other electronic storage or transmission, or broadcast for distance learning.

This book is printed on acid-free paper.

1 2 3 4 5 6 7 8 9 0 DOC/DOC 0 9

ISBN: 978-0-07-340679-4
MHID: 0-07-340679-1

Vice President, Editorial: *Michael Ryan*
Senior Sponsoring Editor: *Gina Boedeker*
Executive Marketing Editor: *Pamela Cooper*
Managing Editor: *Meghan Campbell*
Development Editor: *Craig Leonard*
Production Editor: *Aaron Downey, Matrix Productions, Inc.*
Manuscript Editor: *John Kavouras*
Cover Design: *Laurie Entringer*
Cover Photo: *Jenny Robbins/Getty Images, Inc.*
Manager, Photo Research: *Brian J. Pecko*
Senior Production Supervisor: *Laura Fuller*
Compositor: *10/12 Janson Text here by MPS Limited, A Macmillan Company*
Printing: *RR Donelley & Sons*

Credits: The credits section for this book begins on page C-1 and is considered an extension of the copyright page.

Library of Congress Cataloging-in-Publication Data
Martin, Judith N.
   Experiencing intercultural communication: an introduction / Judith N. Martin, Thomas K. Nakayama.—4th ed.
      p. cm.
ISBN 978-0-07-340679-4
   1. Intercultural communication. I. Nakayama, Thomas K. II. Title.
HM1211.M37 2011
303.48'2—dc22
                                                        2009050745

The Internet address listed in the text were accurate at the time of publication.
The inclusion of a Web site does not indicate an endorsement by the authors or
McGraw-Hill, and McGraw-Hill does not guarantee the accuracy of the information
presented at these sites.

www.mhhe.com

Brief Contents

Contents

Part III Intercultural Communication in Everyday Life

Preface

As we continue to teach and write about intercultural communication, we are struck by the continued need for information covering the practical aspects of communicating across cultures. When we look back on international and intercultural situations at the time we began writing this book, we recognize how rapidly the world has changed and the increasing need for intercultural communication scholars and practitioners. The current global economic downturn, the volatile price of fuel, and the impact these changes have had on travel and business costs point to new international relationships. Changes such as these are likely to influence the shape of intercultural communication. Natural disasters, such as the typhoon in Myanmar and earthquakes in China, and ongoing conflicts, like that in Darfur, have summoned a variety of positive responses, including tremendous caring and compassion across intercultural and international divides, but these tragedies also exacerbated enduring social group inequities. Regional identities continue to challenge national identities, such as in Belgium, for example, which appears closer than ever to dissolution along the lines of linguistic identities.

In addition, the increasing use of communication technologies, such as the Internet and burgeoning Social Networking Sites (SNS), and more mobile communication devices (e.g., cell phones) have made intercultural interactions that may once have seemed distant or peripheral to our lives far more immediate. These changes emphasize the increasing interconnectedness of nations in a global economy—showing that our lives and jobs depend more and more on intercultural communication skills.

How can we use our intercultural skills to help enrich our lives and the lives of those around us? Can intercultural communication scholars promote a better world for all? Are there general intercultural communication skills that can be used in a variety of cultural contexts? Is there culture-specific information that can help us become better intercultural communicators? Is there a way to tap into information on the Internet to provide useful guidelines for intercultural communication? We wrote this book to address these questions and issues.

As in our earlier books, we have tried to use information from a variety of approaches, drawing from traditional social psychological approaches, as well as from ethnographic studies and more recent critical media studies. However, the emphasis in this book is on the practical, experiential nature of intercultural communication. We still acknowledge that there are no easy answers to many intercultural situations. However, we attempt to give solid practical guidelines while noting the complexity of the task facing the student of intercultural communication.

FEATURES OF THE BOOK

This book addresses the core issues and concerns of intercultural communication by introducing a group of general skills in Chapter 1 and emphasizing the concepts and the skills of communicating interculturally throughout the text. This textbook

- Includes a balanced treatment of skills and theory. The skills focus is framed by the presentation of the conceptual aspects of culture and communication. Each chapter has a section called "Building Intercultural Skills" that provides guidelines for improving the reader's intercultural communication.

- Provides a framework for understanding intercultural communication, focusing on four building blocks (culture, communication, context, and power) and four barriers (ethnocentrism, stereotyping, prejudice, and discrimination).

- Focuses on personal experiences by including students' narratives and the authors' personal experiences highlighted throughout the text.

- Presents the material in a student-friendly way. There are four types of thoughtful and fun bits of information in the margin provided for student interest. This edition contains new updated examples and websites:

   "What Do You Think?" includes information and questions that challenge students to think about their own culture and communication styles.

   "Surf's Up" suggests websites that students can visit for more information about culture and communication.

   "Pop Culture Spotlight" presents examples of culture and communication from today's popular culture.

   "Info Bites" provides fun facts and figures that illustrate issues related to intercultural communication.

- Includes separate chapters on history and identity, with sections on Whiteness and assisting European American students in exploring their own cultural issues.

- Focuses on popular culture, both in a separate chapter and in examples woven throughout the book.

- Applies concepts to real-life contexts; the book includes four chapters on how intercultural communication works in everyday settings in tourism, business, education, and health.

NEW TO THE FOURTH EDITION

This edition includes updated material addressing recent challenges of intercultural communication, including increased worldwide religious and ethnic conflict, the impact of political context on intercultural encounters, and technological challenges. For example, in Chapter 4 we expand our discussion of religious identity to include new material on the varying boundaries of religious identities, and discuss how religious identities influence attitudes and behaviors. In Chapter 9 we describe how generational differences in religious beliefs among immigrants play a role in encouraging or discouraging intercultural romantic relationships. In Chapter 12 we describe the rising influence of religious educational institutions.

We also recognize the continuing importance of political and socioeconomic issues in intercultural contexts. For example, Chapter 1 discusses the domestic and international impacts of the recent election of Barack Obama—the first biracial president of the United States—and the impact of the worldwide economic downturn on intercultural encounters. In Chapter 2, we consider the historical impact of capitalism on contemporary intercultural encounters. Chapter 8 emphasizes that conflict is not simply due to cultural differences but also can be due to economic conditions.

To continue to recognize the increasing role technology plays in intercultural human communication, we once again update our discussion and statistics concerning the "digital divide" in Chapter 1. In Chapter 4 we added new material on how social class influences young people's choice of Social Networking Sites (SNS). In Chapter 9 we describe the worldwide impact of SNS on opportunities to develop and maintain intercultural relationships.

OVERVIEW OF THE BOOK

The first chapter focuses on the changing dynamics of social life and global conditions that provide a rationale for the study of intercultural communication, suggesting that intercultural learning is not just transformative for the individual, but also benefits the larger society and other cultural groups in our increasingly interdependent world. In this edition we provide updated statistics and examples.

Chapter 2 outlines a framework for the book and identifies four building blocks of intercultural communication—culture, communication, context, and power, as well as four attitudinal and behavioral barriers to effective intercultural communication: ethnocentrism, stereotyping, prejudice, and discrimination. In this edition, we provide an expanded discussion of the role of perception in intercultural communication, and we include examples of hate speech in an expanded discussion of discrimination/prejudice in intercultural communication.

Chapter 3 focuses on helping students see the importance of history in understanding contemporary intercultural communication issues and a discussion of how postcolonial histories intertwine with today's practices of outsourcing and global business. This edition provides an expanded discussion of political, intellectual, and social histories as well as clarifies the role of the grand narrative in contemporary intercultural encounters.

Chapter 4 discusses issues of identity and intercultural communication. In this chapter we address a number of identities [gender, age, race, and ethnicity (including White identity), physical ability, religion, class, national and regional identity]. We also discuss issues of multicultural identity—people who live on the borders—and issues of crossing borders and cultural shock and adaptation. This edition includes expanded discussions of the role of religious, social class, and national identities in contemporary intercultural encounters.

Chapter 5 addresses verbal issues in intercultural communication, describing cultural variations in language and communication style, attitudes toward speaking, writing and silences, as well as issues of power and language. The chapter presents several models of effective intercultural communication. This edition includes a discussion of the political contexts of language including language policies (e.g., Ebonics) and racial labels.

Chapter 6 focuses on the role of nonverbal behavior in intercultural interaction, describing universal and culture-specific aspects of nonverbal communication, and the ways nonverbal behavior can provide a basis for stereotyping and prejudice. This chapter also addresses cultural space and its dynamic, changing nature, and a discussion of cyberspace as cultural space. This edition includes new material on cultural variations of paralinguistic behaviors and an expanded discussion on cultural uses of silence.

Chapter 7 addresses popular culture and intercultural communication. We define pop culture and discuss the ways in which pop culture forms our images of culture groups and the ways in which we consume (or resist) popular culture products. This edition includes new examples of international popular cultural product controversies, (i.e. the celebration of Barbie's 50th birthday and the release of the award-winning movie *Slumdog Millionaire*).

Chapter 8 discusses the role of culture and conflict. The chapter identifies characteristics of intercultural conflict, describes both personal and social/political aspects of conflict, and examines the role of religion in intercultural conflict and the ways conflict management varies from culture to culture. This edition includes an expanded discussion of the role economic conditions and social inequities play in intercultural conflict.

Chapter 9 focuses on intercultural relationships in everyday life. It identifies the challenges and benefits of intercultural relationships, examining how relationships may differ across cultures and exploring a variety of relationship types: friendship, gay, dating, and marriage relationships. In this edition, we expand our discussion of conflict negotiation in various types of relationships, and add new material on online intercultural relationships.

Chapters 10 through 13 focus on intercultural communication in specific contexts. Chapter 10 addresses issues of intercultural communication in the tourism industry, exploring various ways in which hosts and tourists may interact, the ways varying cultural norms may affect tourist encounters, language issues and communication style, and the sometimes-complex attitudes of hosts toward tourists. In this edition, we include discussions of the impacts of the recent economic downturn, political instability, health risks, and environmental disasters (earthquakes, hurricanes) on touristic encounters; new material on medical tourism; and expanded discussion on sustainable tourism projects.

Chapter 11 focuses on intercultural communication in business contexts, identifying several communication challenges (work-related values, differences in management styles, language issues, and affirmative action) in both domestic and international contexts, and the social and political contexts of business. We also provide a discussion of how power relations affect intercultural business encounters—both interpersonal relationships and larger system impacts. This edition includes new sections on intercultural negotiations and intercultural relationship building in global business contexts.

Chapter 12 explores intercultural communication and education, discussing different kinds of educational experiences (e.g. study abroad, culture-specific settings) and communication challenges (e.g. varying roles for teachers and students, grading, and power); addressing social concerns and the role of culture in admissions, affirmative action, and standardized tests; and examining the challenges of educating immigrants. This edition includes new discussions of the role of culture in religious educational institutions and expanded discussion of the challenges of language education.

Chapter 13 addresses intercultural communication and health care, focusing on intercultural barriers to effective health care, the historical treatment of cultural groups, and the ways power dynamics, religious beliefs, and language barriers influence communication in health care settings. It also includes a discussion of alternative and complementary medicine as other ways of thinking about health care. This edition includes a stronger focus on family inclusion in patient care as well as a discussion of ethics in medical care, for example the controversy over the "Octomom" case.

CourseSmart
Learn Smart. Choose Smart.

This text is available as an eTextbook at www.CourseSmart.com. At CourseSmart you can save up to 50% off the cost of a print textbook, reduce your impact on the environment, and gain access to powerful web tools for learning. CourseSmart has the largest selection of eTextbooks available anywhere, offering thousands of the most commonly adopted textbooks from a wide variety of higher education publishers. CourseSmart eTextbooks are available in one standard online reader with full text search, notes and highlighting, and email tools for sharing notes between classmates. For further details contact your sales representative or go to www.coursesmart.com.

ACKNOWLEDGMENTS

As always, we owe a great deal to our colleagues in the Hugh Downs School of Human Communication, College of Liberal Arts and Sciences, at Arizona State University as well as to our colleagues outside our school. Our colleagues at

ASU helped us work though our ideas and shared insights from their lives and the lives of their students. Our students have contributed a great deal to this book; they willingly shared examples and stories from their own lives and enthusiastically supported this project.

Special thanks go to our editorial assistants: Charee Mooney and Patrick McDonald, who found new margin material for us, worked competently, creatively, and—perhaps most importantly—with extreme good nature under almost impossible deadlines. We especially appreciate these students' assistance, given the many demands in their own lives and work.

Many other Communication colleagues contributed, including Professor Anneliese Harper (Scottsdale Community College) who gave us the idea of writing this book by pointing out the need for more context-specific and experientially based materials in the intercultural communication curriculum. Professor Shelley Smith (University of Minnesota–Duluth), Professor Dawn Braithwaite (University of Nebraska) and Professor Denis Leclerc (Thunderbird School of Global Management) provided us with resources and suggestions for framing the "contexts" chapters in the first edition. Thanks also to Robert Barr, M.D. of the Mecklenburg Radiology Associates in Charlotte, North Carolina, for the helpful tips on health communication.

Thanks to the fine team at McGraw-Hill who make it all happen. Thanks to senior sponsoring editor Katie Stevens who skillfully guided us through the McGraw-Hill publishing process. We also want to acknowledge the fine work of production editor Aaron Downey and copyeditor John Kavouras, and give special thanks to development editor Craig Leonard, who so patiently and competently—once again—kept us on track. Thanks also to marketing manager Pamela Cooper and managing editor, Meghan Campbell.

In addition, we want to thank the reviewers and readers, whose thoughtful and insightful comments led to careful revisions and a much-improved manuscript: James Bostick, Bakersfield College; Michael Daniels, University of Wisconsin, Milwaukee; Gloria Galanes, Missouri State University; Wenshan Jia, Chapman University; Priya Kapoor, Portland State University; Susan Kilgard, Anne Arundel Community College; David Lapakko, Augsburg College; Barrie Mason, North Central College; Michele Mega, California State University, Northridge; Nan Peck, Northern Virginia Community College; Jim Reed, Glendale Community College; and William Scott, Green River Community College.

To those friends and colleagues who enrich our lives and our scholarship by helping us understand what it means to live interculturally, we are grateful: Dr. Amalia Villegas, Laura Laguna, Cruzita and Aurelio Mori, Lucia Madril and family, many of the faculty, staff, and participants at the Summer Institute for Intercultural Communication in Portland, Oregon, and Jean-Louis Sauvage (Université de Mons-Hainaut). Finally, we thank our partners, Ronald S. Chaldu and David L. Karbonski for hanging in there with us once again!

About the Authors

Judith Martin grew up in Mennonite communities, primarily in Delaware and Pennsylvania. She has studied at the Université de Grenoble in France and has taught in Algeria. She received her doctorate at the Pennsylvania State University. By background and training, she is a social scientist who has focused on intercultural communication on an interpersonal level and has studied how people's communication is affected as they move or sojourn between international locations. She has taught at the State University of New York at Oswego, the University of Minnesota, the University of New Mexico, and Arizona State University. She enjoys gardening, reading murder mysteries, traveling, hanging out with her large extended family, and she does not miss the harsh midwestern winters.

Tom Nakayama grew up mainly in Georgia, at a time when the Asian American presence was much less than it is now. He has studied at the Université de Paris and various universities in the United States. He received his doctorate from the University of Iowa. By background and training, he is a critical rhetorician who views intercultural communication in a social context. He has taught at California State University at San Bernardino, Arizona State University, the University of Iowa, and the Université de Mons-Hainaut. He has guest lectured at many institutions, including the University of Maine, Centre Universitaire (Luxembourg), University of Southern California, University of Georgia, and Centre National de la Recherche Scientifique (Paris). He watches TV—especially baseball games—and lifts weights. Having just relocated to the Northeast, he enjoys the New England autumns.

CHAPTER ONE

Studying Intercultural Communication

CHAPTER OUTLINE

STUDY OBJECTIVES

After reading this chapter, you should be able to:

1. Describe the peace imperative for studying intercultural communication.

2. Identify and describe the economic and technological imperatives for studying intercultural communication.

3. Describe how the changing demographics in the United States and the changing worldwide immigration patterns affect intercultural communication.

4. Explain how studying intercultural communication can lead to increased self-understanding.

5. Understand the difference between a universalistic and relativist approach to the study of ethics and intercultural communication.

6. Identify and describe characteristics of an ethical student of culture.

KEY TERMS

assimilable	globalization
class structure	heterogeneous
cosmopolitans	immigration
cross-cultural trainers	*maquiladoras*
demographics	melting pot metaphor
diversity	relativist position
enclaves	self-awareness
ethics	self-reflexivity
global village	universalist position

1

On Election Day, men and women who had once fought for the right to vote stood in line for hours to elect a black president. At the Obama victory rally, when asked to explain the tears running down his cheek, the Rev. Jesse Jackson said he was thinking of all the martyrs who had given their lives to make the moment possible. Television footage from across the country showed people crying and hugging each other, evoking images of the spontaneous celebrations at the end of World War II. A new day seemed to be dawning. Once again America was leading by example, giving hope to all who believe in the possibilities of democracy.

—John Dittmer, Professor Emeritus of History
at DePauw University.[1]

When Barack Obama was elected President of the United States in November 2008, people around the world watched and commented on this election. In Kenya, a national holiday was declared, and many Kenyans celebrated the outcome of the election.[2] The worldwide reaction (see Box 1.1) highlights the tightly knit world we live in. The United States and its economy are very important globally, so many people saw this election as an opportunity to foster more positive international relationships with the United States.

This election promoted positive intercultural and international relations; but the Southern Poverty Law Center reported that this election also fueled a rise in hate groups.[3] For example, three men in Springfield, Massachusetts, according to authorities, "bitter about the election of the nation's first black president and furious in their belief that minorities would gain more rights, torched the partially built church of a black congregation just hours after Barack Obama's landmark victory."[4] These kinds of reactions only increase intercultural tensions, rather than more positive relations. In the first few weeks after the election, "From California to Maine, police have documented a range of alleged crimes, from vandalism and vague threats to at least one physical attack."[5]

We live in a rapidly changing world. The worldwide financial crisis has underscored how tightly connected we are to others around the world. The current crisis is not limited to Wall Street and the United States, but has been felt around the world. Iceland's leaders have been struggling to keep their economy from collapsing; Russia's economy has been hard hit, as has the European Union. While these close economic connections highlight our global economy, these relationships also point to the large numbers of people who communicate every day with people from around the world. Some of this communication is face-to-face with business travelers, tourists, migrants, and others. Some of this

Surf's Up!

Yahoo! travel guide gives you the backgrounds, facts, and statistics of any place and people that you are interested in learning about. Visit the website to see how intercultural your experience is (http://sg .travel.yahoo.com/guide).

BOX 1.1

Worldwide reaction to the election of Barak Obama highlights the close connections that nations around the world have with each other. Note the various reactions to President Obama's election by leaders of other nations.

Australia

"Forty-five years ago Martin Luther King had a dream of an America where men and women would be judged not on the color of their skin but on the content of their character. Today, what America has done is turn that dream into a reality."

—*Prime Minister Kevin Rudd*

France

"With the world in turmoil and doubt, the American people, faithful to the values that have always defined America's identity, have expressed with force their faith in progress and the future."

—*President Nicolas Sarkozy*

Germany

"The world faces significant challenges at the start of your term. I am convinced that Europe and the United States will work closely and in a spirit of mutual trust together to confront new dangers and risks and will seize the opportunities presented by our global world."

—*Chancellor Angela Merkel*

India

Obama's "extraordinary journey to the White House will inspire people not only in [the United States] but also around the world."

—*Prime Minister Manmohan Singh*

Indonesia

"Indonesia especially hopes that the U.S., under new leadership, will stand in front and take real action to overcome the global financial crisis, especially since the crisis was triggered by the financial conditions in the U.S."

—*President Susilo Bambang Yudhoyono*

Israel

"This is a mark of merit for American democracy. During Barack Obama's recent visit to Israel, and especially during the tour we conducted together in the city of Sderot, the people of Israel were impressed by his commitment to the peace and security of Israel. Israel looks forward to continued close strategic cooperation with the new administration, the new president,

(Continued)

BOX 1.1 (Continued)

and the U.S. Congress, in order to continue to strengthen the lasting special relationship between our two countries."

—*Foreign Minister Tzipi Livni*

Kenya

"We the Kenyan people are immensely proud of your Kenyan roots. Your victory is not only an inspiration to millions of people all over the world, but it has special resonance with us here in Kenya."

—*President Mwai Kibaki*

Russia

"We hope that our partners—the new U.S. administration—will make a choice in favor of fully-fledged relations with Russia."

—*President Dmitry Medvedev*

From: Emling, S. (2008, November 6). World cheers Obama election. *The Daily Reflector.* Retrieved February 2, 2009 from: http://www.reflector.com/news/nation/elections/world-cheers-obama-election-226706.html

communication is online through the internet, texting, or other communication media.

Many larger forces drive people to interact with others who are culturally different. Economics are one important force, but there are many other reasons that people come into intercultural contact. Wars or other violent conflicts drive some people to leave their homelands to seek a safer place to live. Natural disasters can drive people to other areas where they can rebuild their lives. Some people seek a better life somewhere else, or are driven by their own curiosity to seek out and visit other parts of the world. People often fall in love and build families with people in another country. Can you think of other reasons that drive people to interact across cultural differences?

What do you as a student of intercultural communication need to learn to understand the complexities of intercultural interaction? And how can learning about intercultural communication benefit you?

It is easy to become overwhelmed by that complexity. However, not knowing everything that you would like to know is very much a part of the learning process, and this inability to know everything is what makes intercultural communication experiences so exciting. Rather than being discouraged by everything that you cannot know, think of all the things you can learn from intercultural communication experiences.

Why is it important to focus on intercultural communication and to strive to become better at this complex form of interaction? There are many reasons why you might want to learn more about intercultural communication. Perhaps you want to better serve a diverse clientele in your chosen occupation; perhaps members of your extended family are from different races or religions, or have physical abilities that you would like to understand better. Perhaps you want to better understand the culturally diverse colleagues in your workplace. Or perhaps you want to learn more about the people you come into contact with through the Internet, or to learn more about the countries and cultures that are in the daily news: Iraq, racial tensions on university campuses, hate crimes in cities large and small. In this chapter we discuss the following imperatives—reasons to study intercultural communication: peace, economic, technological, demographic, self-awareness, and ethical. Perhaps one or more will apply to your situation.

THE PEACE IMPERATIVE

The key issue is this: Can individuals of different genders, ages, ethnicities, races, languages, and religions peacefully coexist on the planet? The history of humankind, as well as recent conflicts in the Middle East, Iraq, North Korea, Iran, India, Pakistan, and Ireland, are hardly grounds for optimism. Contact among different national groups—from the earliest civilizations until today—often leads to disharmony. According to the Center for Systemic Peace, of the approximately 75 armed conflicts in the world between 1990 and 2004, only 10 have been traditional international conflicts. The rest have arisen between ethnic or political groups within a country—for example, in Cyprus, Russia, Turkey, Kashmir, Ethiopia, Bosnia, and Sudan.[6] Consider the ethnic struggles in Bosnia and in the former Soviet Union, the conflict between the Indonesians and East Timorese, and the racial and ethnic tensions in various U.S. cities. Some of these conflicts represent a legacy of colonialism around the world, in which European powers forced diverse groups—differing in language, culture, religion, or identity—together to form one state. For example, the union of Bangladesh, Pakistan, and India was imposed by the British; eventually, Pakistan won its independence from India, as did Bangladesh from Pakistan. The United States had colonial interests in the Philippines and in Hawaii. The tremendous diversity—and historical antagonisms—within many former colonies can be better understood in the context of colonialism.

Some of the conflicts are also tied to economic disparities and economic colonialism. The tremendous influence of U.S. technology and media is seen as a positive benefit by some people and as a cause for resistance by others. Communication scholar Fernando Delgado describes these tensions:

> Such cultural dominance, though celebrated at home, can spark intercultural conflicts because it inhibits the development of other nations' indigenous popular culture products, stunts their economic development, and foists U.S. values and perspectives on other cultures. These effects, in turn, often lead to resentment and conflict.[7]

He goes on to cite the claim of Canadian leaders that a Canadian cultural identity is almost impossible due to the dominance of American media. Delgado recognizes the complexity of this issue. He recounts noticing anti-American sentiments in graffiti, newspapers, and TV programs during a recent trip to Europe.

What Do You Think?

A group of prominent Canadian international figures have called for a "Department of Peace" or "Ministries of Peace" that would promote and utilize nonviolent methods of resolving conflicts around the world. What do you think would be the major functions of a Department of Peace? What kind of person is capable of becoming a Minister of Peace?

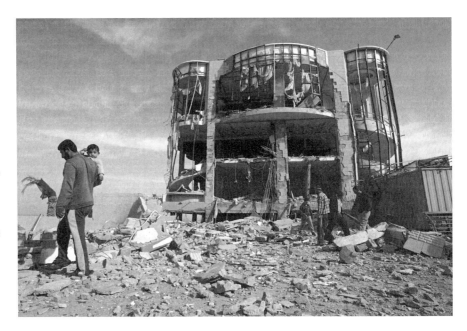

People are often caught in devastating consequences of conflicts they neither started nor chose. In this photo, victims of the Gaza conflict search through the rubble of buildings destroyed by war. While communication skills cannot solve all political conflicts, they are vital in dealing with intercultural strife.

But U.S. influences also were evident in youth music, television, film, and cars. He observed that locals were amazed and resentful at the same time at the penetration of U.S. popular culture. It would be naive to assume that simply understanding something about intercultural communication would end war and intercultural conflict, but these problems do underscore the need for us to learn more about groups of which we are not members. We need to remember as well that individuals often are born into and are caught up in conflicts that they neither started nor chose and that are impacted by the larger societal forces.

THE ECONOMIC IMPERATIVE

You may want to know more about intercultural communication because you foresee tremendous changes in the workplace in the coming years. This is one important reason to know about other cultures and communication patterns. In addition, knowing about intercultural communication is strategically important for U.S. businesses in the emerging transnational economy. As noted by writer Carol Hymowitz of the *Wall Street Journal*, "If companies are going to sell products and services globally, then they will need a rich mix of employees with varied perspectives and experiences. They will need top executives who understand different countries and cultures."[8]

The Workplace

Given the growing cultural diversity in the United States, businesses necessarily must be more attentive to diversity issues. As the workforce becomes more diverse, many businesses are seeking to capitalize on these differences: "Once organizations learn to adopt an inclusive orientation in dealing with their members, this will also have a positive impact on how they look at their customer base, how they develop products and assess business opportunities, and how they relate to their communities."[9] Benefiting from cultural differences in the workplace involves not only working with diverse employees and employers but also seeing new business markets, developing new products for differing cultural contexts, and marketing products in culturally appropriate and effective ways. From this perspective, diversity is a potentially powerful economic tool for business organizations. We will discuss diversity issues further in Chapter 11.

The Global Economy

Businesses all around the world are continually expanding into overseas markets in a process of **globalization.** This recent trend is shown dramatically in the report of a journalist who asked a Dell computer manager where his laptop is made. The answer? It was codesigned by engineers in Texas and Taiwan; the microprocessor was made in one of Intel's factories in the Philippines, Costa

Multicultural work environments are becoming increasingly common in the 21st century. In many of these situations, working in small groups is especially important. Given this trend, workers need to learn to deal with cultural differences.

Rica, Malaysia, or China; the memory came from factories in Korea, Germany, Taiwan, or Japan. Other components (keyboard, hard-disk drive, batteries, etc.) were made by Japanese, Taiwanese, Irish, Israeli, or British firms with factories mainly in Asia; and finally, the laptop was assembled in Taiwan.[10]

Increasingly, businesses find that they need to sell globally in order to compete. Wal-Mart Stores just launched a major expansion into China and plans to hire 150,000 people there in the next five years, five times the number it currently employs in the United States.[11] However, more common are the Chinese products being sold to Americans. Our trade deficit with China is enormous. According to the U.S. Department of Commerce, in 2007 the trade deficit with China grew by $23.7 billion—or 10.2 percent—to $256.3 billion. The imbalance is getting bigger every year.[12]

What is the ultimate impact of globalization on the average person? Some people defend it, saying the losses are always offset by the gains in cheaper consumer prices. However, many working people, seeing their jobs outsourced to cheap labor in India, China, and Malaysia, feel threatened. For example, Dell, the world's top PC maker, has outsourced many jobs and currently employs thousands in its plants in India. Some estimate that U.S. workers lost 900,000 jobs to Mexico and Canada as a result of free trade agreements.[13]

An increasing number of economists are skeptical about the benefits of globalization to U.S. workers. One of the world's leading economists, Paul Samuelson, argues that consumer gains of cheaper products are offset by income losses. As globalization causes many American workers to suffer lower wages, America as a whole loses. Some also argue that globalization is the cause of growing poverty and inequality around the world.[14] At the world level, the top 20 percent now has 82 times as much wealth as the bottom 20 percent, compared to a 30-to-1 ratio 50 years ago. Half the world's people live on less than $2 a day, and one-fifth live on less than $1 a day. Also, 800 million are chronically hungry, and new evidence shows that the World Bank (responsible for some of these figures) has, if anything, underestimated the numbers of the destitute. These kinds of inequalities can lead to resentment, despair, and ultimately to intercultural conflict.[15] Economist Samuelson argues that the answer to globalization is not to resign from the world trading system but rather to understand how and why the big winners from globalization, the Asian nations, are gaining and to learn from them, just as in the past they learned from us.[16]

In addition, there are other considerations in understanding the global market. Moving operations overseas to take advantage of lower labor costs has far-reaching implications for corporations. One example is the ***maquiladoras***—foreign-owned plants that use domestic labor—just across the U.S.-Mexican border. The U.S. companies that relocate their plants there benefit from lower labor costs and lack of environmental and other business regulations, while Mexican laborers benefit from the jobs. But there is a cost in terms of environmental hazards. Because Mexico has less stringent air and water pollution regulations than the United States, many of these *maquiladoras* have a negative environmental impact on the Mexican side of the border. Because the two

International trade is one of the driving forces in interactions between cultures. However, as shown by these people protesting at the G-20 meeting in London in April, 2009, there is some concern that growing poverty and inequality resulting from globalization may lead to increased intercultural conflict.

nations are economically and environmentally interdependent, they share the economic and environmental impact. Thus, these contexts present intercultural challenges for Mexicans and Americans alike.

To help bridge the cultural gap, many companies employ **cross-cultural trainers,** who assist people going abroad by giving them information about and strategies for dealing with cultural differences; such trainers report that Japanese and other business personnel often spend years in the United States studying English and learning about the country before they decide to build a factory or invest money here. By contrast, many U.S. companies provide little or no training before sending their workers overseas and expect business deals to be completed very quickly. They seem to have little regard for cultural idiosyncrasies, which can cause ill will and mistrust, enhance negative stereotypes, and result in lost business opportunities.

In the future, economic development in Japan and other Asian countries (including Singapore, Taiwan, South Korea, and China), as well as in Latin America, will create even more demand for intercultural communication. Economic exchanges will drive intercultural interactions. This development will create not only more jobs but also more consumers to purchase goods from around the world—and to travel in that world.

THE TECHNOLOGICAL IMPERATIVE

In the 1960s, media guru Marshall McLuhan coined the term **global village** to describe a world in which communication technology, such as TV, radio, and news services, brings news and information to the most remote parts of the world.[17]

Today, people are connected—through text messaging, e-mail, bulletin boards, blogs, and websites on the Internet, as well as through older technology like voice mail and fax machines—to other people whom they have never met face-to-face. It's possible not only to communicate with other people but also to develop complex relationships with them through such technology.

Technology and Human Communication

These monumental changes have affected how we think of ourselves and how we form intercultural relationships. In his book *The Saturated Self*, psychologist Kenneth Gergen describes the changes that occur as technology alters patterns of communication.[18] In past centuries, social relationships typically were circumscribed by how far one could walk, but they evolved with each technological advance—whether it be the railroad, automobile, telephone, radio, TV, or movies. These relationships have now expanded exponentially. We can be "accessed" in many ways, including e-mail, text messaging, phone, and express mail, and be involved simultaneously in many different relationships, all without face-to-face contact.

The wireless and mobile "revolution" has also impacted our communication. Sometimes when we're in face-to-face contact with others, we are not interacting, because we can "hide" behind cell phone conversations, for example, in order to not communicate with those around us.[19] Some fear that mobile communication may result in a psychological "emptying out" of public space, where people's bodies are present, but personalities are engaged elsewhere.[20]

Most of us cannot imagine life without the Internet, which is now estimated to include more than a billion websites. As of October 2008, about 75 percent of adults and 91 percent of young people in the United States use the Internet. The ability to access and use these communication technologies depends, among other things, on one's age, income, geographical location, race, and ethnicity. Access is an important issue discussed later in this chapter. Internationally, the use of English continues to dominate the Internet. In a recent study, University of Guelph professor Manish Raizada found that about 70 percent of the material on the Internet is in English and most people who are searching for information use their native languages rather than English; therefore, they miss most of the information available. The study also "found that 80 to 90 percent of food- and health-related institutions don't translate their websites into multiple languages, including information related to crisis situations".[21] The early fears of English taking over the Internet seem to be somewhat fulfilled. The move should be toward more multilingualism—rather than toward a global English Internet.[22] This means that global businesses need to adapt to local languages to sell their products. They could hire translating services or work directly with local and regional organizations. Marketing should take place in the language of the target market. Willy Brandt, the former German chancellor, put it this way: "If I'm selling to you, I speak your language. If I'm buying, *dann müssen Sie Deutsch sprechen* [then you must speak German]."[23]

Surf's Up!

Do you know the proper procedure for exchanging business cards in Japan? How should you dress when conducting business in Denmark? In India, when is the word *Namaste* used? Globalization has changed the face of business. The manner by which we conduct business in the United States is often very different from other countries. What should you know about different cultural practices to become an international business traveler? Check out www.buzzle.com/chapters/travel-and-tourism_business-and-executive-travel_etiquette-and-related-issues.asp for information on conducting business in other countries.

What does this have to do with intercultural communication? Through high-tech communication, we come into contact with people who are very different from ourselves, often in ways we don't understand. The people we talk to on e-mail networks and blogs may speak languages different from our own, come from different countries, be of different ethnic backgrounds, and have had many different life experiences. America Online, for example, hosts the "Bistro," which brings people in contact via e-mail in various languages. As AOL notes, "The purpose of the Bistro is to bring people of differing cultural and ethnic backgrounds together to speak in their native language, discuss international topics, and learn more about the world we live in." Blogging provides another opportunity for intercultural contact, especially for young people. People 12–32 are more likely than older users to read other people's blogs and to write their own[24] and there are now about 70 million blogs worldwide in many different languages.[25] People blog for many reasons: to document their lives; to express opinions or commentary; to test ideas or "muse"; and as a community forum or religious expression and connection.[26] Technology has increased the frequency with which many people encounter multilingual situations; they must decide which language will be used. Contrast this situation with the everyday lives of people 100 years ago, in which they rarely communicated with people outside their own villages, much less people speaking different languages. The use of e-mail for intercultural communication is yet another reason to study this topic. People seek out intercultural communication for many different reasons, including the use of other languages to express their thoughts and feelings.

One of the issues of interest to those who study intercultural communication is the "digital divide" that exists between those who have access to technologies like the Internet and those who do not.

Studies show that in the United States the people most likely to have access to and use the Internet are young or middle age, have a college degree or are students, and have a comfortable income. Race and ethnicity doesn't seem to play a role, if we compare similar levels of education and income.[27] While the digital divide is shrinking, certain groups still lag behind—those with low incomes and less education. Even more important than income, education, or access to a home computer, "Internet connectedness" also depends on one's social environment. People are more likely to use the Internet if they have family and friends who also use the Internet, can help them resolve Internet-related problems, and who see the Internet us playing an important role in their lives (e.g. getting in touch with people when looking for a job, gaining skills for career development, getting work done, providing amusement, etc.).[28]

Even larger inequities exist outside the United States. While there is high Internet usage in the high-tech countries in Asia, most of Western Europe, and North America, there are many countries, especially in Africa, where Internet usage and even telephone service are almost nonexistent. There are pockets of low Internet use all over the world (Albania 13 percent, Bolivia 6 percent, India 5 percent, Laos 1.5 percent and Somalia 1 percent).[29]

Pop Culture Spotlight

The movie *My Big Fat Greek Wedding* (2002) tells the story of an intercultural marriage between a Greek American woman and a White U.S. American college professor from a low-key New England family. She is the rather reserved, devoted daughter in a big Greek American family. Working in her father's restaurant, one day she finds herself pouring coffee for him; they get to know each other, he inspires her to change her life, and they fall in love and plan to get married. When their two families meet and get to know each other, there are many (humorous) cross-cultural misunderstandings. While we can learn a lot about cultures and the challenges of intercultural relationships, movies can also present and reinforce cultural stereotypes. How can you know whether a culture is presented in a realistic way in a particular movie or as a harmful stereotype?

These inequities have enormous implications for intercultural communication. In the global information society, information is an important commodity. Everybody needs it to function. This ability is especially important in an increasingly "networked" society. It is easy to see how without these skills and knowledge one can feel marginalized and disconnected from the center of society.[30]

THE DEMOGRAPHIC IMPERATIVE

Demographics refers to the general characteristics of a given population. The demographics of the United States will change dramatically during your lifetime—the next 50 years. The workforce that you enter will differ significantly from the one that your parents entered. These changes come from two sources: changing demographics within the United States and changing immigration patterns.

Changing U.S. Demographics

According to the U.S. Population Reference Bureau, the nation's Hispanic and Asian populations are expected to triple by 2050, while non-Hispanic Whites are expected to grow more slowly to represent about one-half of the nation's population. People of Hispanic origin (who may be of any race) will increase from 36 million to 103 million. The Asian population is projected to triple, from 11 million to 33 million. The Black population is projected to grow from 36 million to 61 million in 2050, an increase of 71 percent. That change will increase Blacks' share of the nation's population from 13 percent in 2000 to 15 percent in 2050.

The population representing "all other races"—a category that includes American Indians, Alaska Natives, Hawaiian and other Pacific Islanders, as well as those who indicated two or more races on census forms—is also expected to triple between 2000 and 2050, growing from 7 million to about 22 million.[31] The integration of the new workers with the current ones will provide both opportunities and challenges for American businesses, as well as for the country as a whole.

Another interesting fact is the increase in multicultural people. The 2000 Census was the first that allowed persons to categorize themselves as "two or more races," and 2.4 percent of respondents did just that. Most of them live in the southern and western regions of the United States, regions with the most ethnic and racial diversity. Based on Census 2000 information, where you live determines to some extent how much opportunity you have to interact with people who are different from you ethnically or racially. According to the 2000 Census, the 10 states with the most ethnically diverse populations are California, Nevada, Arizona, New Mexico, Texas, Louisiana, Mississippi, Georgia, Florida, and Illinois. In fact, in California, the 2000 Census data showed that no single racial or ethnic group, including non-Hispanic Whites, makes up more than 50 percent of the state population. Minorities, both citizens and noncitizens, are now the majority in Miami, Los Angeles, Houston, and San Francisco. New York and Washington will join the list soon.[32] This presents special challenges and opportunities for intercultural understanding.[33]

Changing Immigration Patterns

The second source of demographic change is **immigration.** There are two contradictory faces to the story of immigration in the United States. The United States often is described as a nation of immigrants, but it is also a nation that established itself by subjugating the original inhabitants of the land and that prospered economically while forcibly importing millions of Africans to perform slave labor. It is important to recognize the many different experiences that people have had in the United States so that we can better understand what it means to be a U.S. American. We cannot simply think of ourselves as a nation of immigrants if we want to better understand contemporary U.S. society.

Current patterns of immigration are having a significant effect on the social landscape. Prior to the 1960s, most of the immigrants to the United States came from Europe, compared to only 14 percent today. According to the U.S. Census Bureau, the vast majority (about 80 percent) of today's immigrants come from Latin America (52 percent) and Asia (25 percent). These immigrants also tend to settle in particular areas of the country. They are more likely to live in the western part of the United States and are more likely to live in the central locations of metropolitan areas, adding to the diversity of these areas. These immigration changes, along with increasing domestic diversity, clearly show that the United States is becoming more **heterogeneous,** or diverse.[34]

These demographic changes present many opportunities and challenges for students of intercultural communication and for society. Tensions among different racial and ethnic groups, as well as fear on the part of politically dominant groups, must be acknowledged. However, intercultural conflict is not necessarily a consequence of **diversity.** As we'll see in Chapter 9, intercultural encounters in certain types of conditions can lead to very positive outcomes, including reduced prejudice and positive intergroup relationships. Diverse college campuses, for example, can provide opportunities for the type of intercultural contact in which intercultural friendships can flourish—opportunities for extensive contact in a variety of formal and informal settings that promote communication that fosters relationship developments.[35] In fact, not surprisingly, the more diverse a campus is, the more likely students are to develop intercultural friendships—these friendships provide opportunities to expand our horizons linguistically, politically, and socially, as various lifestyles and ways of thinking come together.[36] We often profit from being exposed to different ways of doing things and incorporate these customs into our own lifestyles.

Historical Overview   To get a better sense of the sociocultural situation in the United States today, let's take a look at our history. As mentioned, the United States has always been a nation of immigrants. When Europeans began arriving on the shores of the New World, an estimated 8 to 10 million Native Americans were already living here. The outcome of the encounters between these groups—the colonizing Europeans and the native peoples—is well known. By 1940, the

Info Bites

International student enrollment in the United States reached 565,039 in 2004–2005, recovering from a 3-year decrease since the September 11, 2001, terrorist attacks. The Council of Graduate Schools (CGS) released a report warning that this decline in the numbers of international students hurt the balance sheet of many institutions of higher learning, and was threatening the country's long-term competitiveness in research and development. Again, in 2007–2008 the number of international students jumped to 623,805, up 7 percent from previous years. (SOURCES: Jim Lobe, November 14, 2005, *Inter Press Service* [http://www.cqsnet.org/portals/Q/pdf/N_pr_GED2005.pdf]; 2008 IIE Open Doors Report, http://opendoors.iienetwork.org/)

Info Bites

Marketing education is a big business in many industrialized countries. For example, in Australia, foreign students now contribute 14 percent of university revenue. They make up one in five of the total numbers enrolled. According to IDP Australia, the marketing organization owned by Australia's universities, demand for an Australian education will increase ten-fold in 20 years. (SOURCE: "International Education in Australia," IDP Education website [http://www.idp .com/research/fastfacts/ default.asp])

Native American population of the United States had been reduced to an estimated 250,000. Today, there are about 2.5 million American Indians, from 542 recognized tribes, living in the United States.[37]

African Americans are a special case in the history of U.S. immigration because they were brought to this country involuntarily. Some Europeans and Asians also arrived in the country as indentured or contract labor. However, by the middle of the seventeenth century this system of indenture was stopped because it was not economically viable for farmers and did not solve the problem of chronic labor shortage.[38] Landowners needed captive workers who could neither escape servitude nor become competitors. The answer was slavery. Native Americans were not a good choice, given that they could always escape back to their own lands, but Africans were. In fact, Europeans and Africans were already in the slave business, and so America became a prime market. The slave trade lasted about 350 years, during which time 9 to 10 million Africans reached the Americas (the vast majority died in the brutal overseas passage).[39] As James Baldwin has suggested, slavery is what makes U.S. history and current interracial relations different from those in Europe.[40]

Historically, slavery presented a moral dilemma for many Whites, but today a common response is to ignore history. Many Whites say that because not all Whites owned slaves we should simply forget it and move on. For most African Americans, however, this is unacceptable. Rather, as Cornel West, a professor of Afro-American studies and the philosophy of religion at Harvard University, suggests, we should begin by acknowledging the historical flaws in American society and recognizing the historical consequences of slavery.[41] The continuing controversy over the Confederate flag flying above the South Carolina state capitol building reflects a desire to remember that past in a different way. It is also interesting to note that there are several Holocaust museums in the United States, but only recently has there been official national recognition of the horrors of slavery—with the proposals for two new museums—the Smithsonian National Museum of African-American History and Culture in Washington, DC, and the United States National Slavery Museum in Fredericksburg, Virginia.[42]

Relationships between residents and immigrants—between old-timers and newcomers—often have been contentious. In the nineteenth century, Native Americans sometimes were caught in the middle of U.S. and European rivalries. During the War of 1812, for example, Indian allies of the British were severely punished by the United States when the war ended. In 1832, the U.S. Congress recognized Native Americans' right to self-government, but an 1871 congressional act prohibited treaties between the U.S. government and Indian tribes. In 1887, Congress passed the Dawes Severalty Act, terminating Native Americans' special relationship with the U.S. government and paving the way for the removal of Native Americans from their land.

As waves of immigrants continued to roll in from Europe, the more firmly established European—mainly English—immigrants tried to protect their way of life, language, and culture. James Banks has identified various conflicts throughout the nation's history, many of which were not uniquely American but were imported from Europe.[43] In 1729, for example, an English mob prevented a group of Irish immigrants from landing in Boston. A few years later, another mob destroyed a new Scotch-Irish Presbyterian church in Worcester, Massachusetts. Subsequently, as immigrants from northern and western Europe came to dominate American culture, immigrants from southern, central, and eastern Europe were expected to assimilate into the so-called mainstream culture—to jump into the "melting pot" and come out "American."

In the late nineteenth and early twentieth centuries, an anti-immigrant, nativistic movement promoted violence against newer immigrants. For example, in 1885, 28 Chinese were killed in an anti-Chinese riot in Wyoming; in 1891, a White mob attacked a Chinese community in Los Angeles and killed 19 people; in 1891, 11 Italian Americans were lynched in New Orleans.

The anti-immigrant, nativistic sentiment was well supported at the government level as well. In 1882, Congress passed the Chinese Exclusion Act, officially prohibiting Chinese from immigrating to this country. In 1924, the Johnson-Reed Act and the Oriental Exclusion Act established strict quotas on immigration and completely barred the immigration of Asians. According to Ronald Takaki, these 1924 laws "provided for immigration based on nationality quotas: the number of immigrants to be admitted annually was limited to 2 percent of the foreign-born individuals of each nationality residing in the United States in 1890."[44] The underlying rationale was that economic and political opportunities should be reserved for Whites, native-born Americans or not. Thus, the dominance of Whites in the United States is not simply the result of more Europeans wanting to come here; the U.S. government designed our society in this way.[45]

Info Bites

Could the slave trade be the first organization in world history? The United Nations Educational, Scientific and Cultural Organization (UNESCO) holds a project called the Slave Trade, launched in 1994 with the goal of maintaining a commitment to peace, historical truth, intercultural dialogue, and human rights and development. UNESCO cultural programs aim to improve global intercultural dialogues.

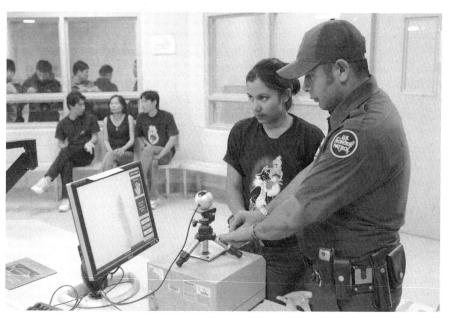

An immigration officer in San Ysidro, California, compares an immigrant's fingerprints against those shown on a green card. Immigration, especially from Asia and Latin America, will only serve to increase the intercultural experiences of many U.S. Americans.

Pop Culture Spotlight

If you haven't seen it yet, check out the feature film that received 10 Academy Award nominations in March 2003, *Gangs of New York*. The film underscores the conflicts that often arise between immigrant residents and immigrant newcomers. It also reflects the history of New York's Ellis Island, a famous port of entry into the United States for many immigrants in the early 1900s. The film features such popular actors as Leonardo DiCaprio, Daniel Day-Lewis, and Cameron Diaz.

By the 1930s, immigrants from southern and eastern Europe were considered **assimilable,** or able to become members of White American society, and the concept of race assumed new meaning. All of the so-called White races were now considered one, so racial hostilities were directed toward members of non-White ethnic groups, such as Asian Americans, Native Americans, and Mexican Americans; this bias was particularly devastating for African Americans.[46] In the growing but sometimes fragile economy of the first half of the twentieth century, only White workers were assured a place. White immigrants may have earned relatively low wages, but they were paid additional "psychological" wages in the form of better schools, increased access to public facilities, and more public deference.

Economic conditions make a big difference in attitudes toward foreign workers and immigration policies. Thus, during the Great Depression of the 1930s, Mexicans and Mexican Americans were forced to return to Mexico to free up jobs for White Americans. When prosperity returned in the 1940s, Mexicans were welcomed back as a source of cheap labor. In 2006, many businesses as well as the government favored a "guest worker program" with Mexico—which would allow Mexican workers to temporarily reside in the United States. In fact, this occurs all over the world. North African workers are alternately welcomed and rejected in France, depending on the condition of the French economy and the need for imported labor. The resulting discontent and marginalization of these immigrants were seen in weeks of rioting in French cities in the fall of 2005.[47] Guest workers from Turkey have been subjected to similar uncertainties in Germany. Indian workers in Kenya, Chinese immigrants in Malaysia, and many other workers toiling outside their native lands have suffered from the vagaries of fluctuating economies and inconsistent immigration policies.

The Current Situation   The tradition of tension and conflict between cultures continues to this day. The conflicts that occurred in Southern California in the 1990s have their roots in the demographic changes in the United States. In fact, the situation in greater Los Angeles is a prime example of the problems associated with intercultural communication in twenty-first-century America. The 2005 movie *Crash* showed the complexity of these problems. In the movie, the lives of a racially and economically diverse group of people (a Black police detective, a White district attorney and his pampered wife, a Persian shopkeeper, a Latino locksmith, an Asian businessman) collide with one another in interesting and sometimes tragic ways. The characters show how racism is not a simple issue—individuals who feel victimized by any number of situations (economic, bureaucratic, racist, etc.) sometimes perpetrate their own ignorance and stereotypes on the next racially different person they encounter.

The tensions in Los Angeles among Latinos/as, African Americans, Korean Americans, and European Americans can be examined on a variety of levels. Some of the conflict is due to different languages, values, and lifestyles. Some African Americans resent the success of recent Korean immigrants—a common reaction throughout history. The conflict may also be due to the pattern of settlement that results in cultural **enclaves**—for example, Latinos/as in Inglewood and East Los Angeles, Koreans in the "Miracle Mile" section west of downtown Los Angeles, and Whites on the west side of the city. As in other parts of the country, the majority of White suburban Americans live in neighborhoods that are overwhelmingly White.[48]

Some of the conflict may be due to the economic disparity that exists among these different groups. To understand this disparity we need to look at issues of economic class. Most Americans are reluctant to admit that a **class structure** exists, let alone admit how difficult it is to move up in this structure. But the fact is that most people live their lives in the same economic class into which they were born. In addition, the U.S. cultural myth that anyone can move up the class structure through hard work, known as the Horatio Alger myth, is not benign. Rather, it reinforces middle- and upper-class beliefs in their own superiority and perpetuates a false hope among members of the working class that they can get ahead. And there are just enough success stories—for example, Ross Perot, Roseanne, and Madonna—of easy upward mobility to perpetuate the myth.

How have economic conditions changed for the various classes, and what might the future hold? Workers' salaries are suffering as U.S. firms struggle to compete against cheaper products produced overseas by downsizing, moving jobs to other countries, or filing for bankruptcy. Typical examples are Delphi's (a large auto parts manufacturer) recent decision to cut costs by closing 24 factories employing thousands of workers, and General Motors's decision to cut thousands of jobs.[49]

This trend has caused the middle and working class to lose ground in salaries while the CEOs of many corporations, like in the oil industry, have reaped record salaries. According to the U.S. Census Bureau figures, since 1999, the income of the poorest fifth of Americans has dropped 8.7 percent in inflationary-adjusted dollars. In 2004 alone, 1.1 million were added to the 36 million already on the poverty rolls.[50] The recent collapse of the U.S. economy has drawn attention to executive compensation, particularly for those financial institutions that are receiving federal financial help. For example, the New York and North Carolina attorneys general have asked Bank of America for the names of the people who received $3.6 billion in bonuses from Merrill Lynch just before it was purchased by Bank of America.[51] The public anger points to an important shift in how people feel about the class structure in the United States, and a reflection of this shift has been President Obama's efforts at trying to rein in executive compensation, in response to "growing populist outrage over sky-high pay among the banks and other companies now on the public dole."[52] Changing these differences will not be easy, but how will they influence our intercultural interaction?

Increasingly diverse groups mostly come in contact during the day in schools, businesses, and hospitals, but they bring different languages, histories, and economic backgrounds to these encounters. This presents a challenge for our society and for us as individuals to look beyond the Hollywood stereotypes,

Pop Culture Spotlight

The film *Spanglish* (2004) features the life of a Mexican immigrant mother and daughter in the United States. The mother is hired to care for the children of a wealthy White family, eventually asked to sacrifice the care of her own daughter in order to spend more time with her employers' children. It shows the current debates over multiculturalism and immigration policies. The interactions between a White family and the immigrant family present the complexity of intercultural communication. However, both sides do their best to adapt to each other in spite of language barriers and cultural differences.

to be aware of this diversity, and to apply what we know about intercultural communication. Perhaps the first step is to realize that the **melting pot metaphor**—in which all immigrants enter and blend into American society—probably was never viable. That is, not all immigrants could be assimilated into the United States in the same way.

The legacy of the tensions over immigration remains today. With the downturn in the economy, many U.S. Americans are not in favor of additional immigration; they see immigrants as additional competition for jobs. One area where this debate has taken place is over the immigration of highly skilled workers. These workers are typically given H-1B visas to work in the United States. Yet with a flagging economy, highly skilled workers may not choose to remain in the United States. A senior research associate at Harvard Law School observes:

> As the debate over H-1B workers and skilled immigrants intensifies, we are losing sight of one important fact: The U.S. is no longer the only land of opportunity. If we don't want the immigrants who have fueled our innovation and economic growth, they now have options elsewhere. Immigrants are returning home in greater numbers. And new research shows they are returning to enjoy a better quality of life, better career prospects, and the comfort of being close to family and friends.[53]

What impact will changes in immigration make to our society? How will the loss of highly skilled workers impact our ability to recover economically and technologically? And how will these changes impact how we interact with others?

Fortunately, most individuals are able to negotiate day-to-day activities in schools, businesses, and other settings in spite of cultural differences. Diversity can even be a positive force. Demographic diversity in the United States has provided us with tremendous linguistic richness and culinary variety, has given us the resources to meet new social challenges, and has created domestic and international business opportunities.

THE SELF-AWARENESS IMPERATIVE

One of the most important reasons for studying intercultural communication is to gain an awareness of one's own cultural identity and background. This **self-awareness** is one of the least obvious reasons. Peter Adler, a noted social psychologist, observes that the study of intercultural communication begins as a journey into another culture and reality and ends as a journey into one's own culture.[54]

Examples from the authors' own lives come to mind. Judith's earliest experiences in public school made her realize that not everyone wore "coverings" and "bonnets" and "cape dresses," the clothing worn by the females in her Amish/Mennonite family. She realized that her family was different from most of the others she came in contact with. Years later, when she was teaching high school in Algeria, a Muslim country, she realized something about her own religious identity as a Protestant. December 25 came and went, and she taught

What Do You Think?

Information about others often helps us see ourselves in a different way. Of the 10 tallest buildings in 2009, only two were in the United States—the Empire State Building in New York City and the Sears Tower in Chicago. Currently, the world's tallest building is the Burj Dubai, in Dubai. Additionally, the bridge with the longest span is in Hyogo, Japan. The longest bridge in the United States is the Verrazano-Narrows Bridge in New York City, which comes in at number eight on the list. Do these facts surprise you or make you think about the United States in a different way?

classes with no mention of Christmas. Judith had never thought about how special the celebration of Christmas was or how important the holiday was to her. She recognized on a personal level the uniqueness of this particular cultural practice.

When Tom, who is of Japanese descent, first started elementary school, he attended a White school in the segregated American South. By the time he reached the fourth grade, schools were integrated, and some African American students were intrigued by his very straight black hair. At that point, he recognized a connection between himself and the Black students, and he began to develop a kernel of self-awareness about his identity. Living in an increasingly diverse world, we can take the opportunity to learn more about our own cultural backgrounds and identities and about how we are similar to and different from the people we interact with. However, it is important to recognize intercultural learning is not always easy or comfortable. What you learn depends on your social and economic position in society. Self-awareness through intercultural contact for someone from a racial or minority group may mean learning to be wary and not surprised at subtle slights by members of the dominant majority— and reminders of their place in society. For example, an African American colleague has remarked that she notices some White cashiers avoid touching her hand when they return her change.

If you are White and middle class, intercultural learning may mean an enhanced awareness of your privilege. A White colleague tells of feeling uncomfortable staying in a Jamaican resort, being served by Blacks whose ancestors were brought there as slaves by European colonizers. On the one hand, it is a privilege that allows travelers like our colleague to experience new cultures and places. On the other hand, one might wonder if we, through this type of travel, are reproducing those same historical postcolonial economic patterns.

Self-awareness, then, that comes through intercultural learning may involve an increased awareness of being caught up in political, economic, and historical systems not of our own making.

THE ETHICAL IMPERATIVE

Living in an intercultural world presents challenging ethical issues that can be addressed by the study of intercultural communication. **Ethics** may be thought of as principles of conduct that help govern the behavior of individuals and groups. These principles often arise from communities' views on what is good and bad behavior. Cultural values tell us what is "good" and what "ought" to be.

Ethical Judgments and Cultural Values

Ethical judgments focus more on the degrees of rightness and wrongness in human behavior than do cultural values.[55]

Some judgments are stated very explicitly. For example, the Ten Commandments teach that it is wrong to steal, tell a lie, commit murder, and so on. Many

Surf's Up!
Did you know that in China, bribery is called "gray money," and is often accepted as a form of payment to low-paid government officials? Visit the website of Transparency International (www .transparency.org/), a global organization that monitors and tracks various bribery practices in businesses around the world.

Americans are taught the "Golden Rule"—do unto others as you would have them do unto you. Laws often reflect the cultural values of dominant groups. For instance, in the past, many states had miscegenation laws prohibiting interracial marriage. Contemporary debates about legalizing same-sex marriage reflect the role of cultural values in laws. Many other identifiable principles arise from our cultural experience that may be less explicit—for example, that people should be treated equally and that they should work hard.

Several issues come to mind in any discussion of ethics in intercultural communication. For example, what happens when two ethical systems collide? While the desire to contribute to the development of a better society by doing the right thing can be an important motivation, it is not always easy to know what is "right" in more specific situations in intercultural communication. Ethical principles are often culture-bound, and intercultural conflicts arise from varying notions of what constitutes ethical behavior.

Another ethical dilemma involves standards of conducting business in multinational corporations. The U.S. Congress and the Securities and Exchange Commission consider it unethical for corporations to make payments to government officials of other countries to promote trade. Essentially, such payment smacks of bribery. However, in many countries, such as China, government officials are paid in this informal way instead of being supported by taxes. What is ethical behavior for personnel in multinational subsidiaries?

This book stresses the relativity of cultural behavior; no cultural pattern is inherently right or wrong. Is there any universality in ethics? Are any cultural behaviors always right or always wrong?

The answers depend on one's perspective.[56] According to the **universalist position,** we need to identify those rules that apply across cultures. A universalist might try, for example, to identify acts and conditions that most societies think of as wrong, such as murder, treason, and theft. Someone who takes an extreme universalist position would insist that cultural differences are only superficial, that fundamental notions of right and wrong are universal. Some religions take universal positions—for example, that the Ten Commandments are a universal code of behavior. But Christian groups often disagree about the universality of the Bible. For example, are the teachings of the New Testament mainly guidelines for the Christians of Jesus's time, or can they be applied to Christians in the twenty-first century? These are difficult issues for many people searching for ethical guidelines.

By contrast, according to the **relativist position,** any cultural behavior can be judged only within the cultural context in which it occurs. This means that only a community can truly judge the ethics of its members. Intercultural scholar William S. Howell explains the relativist position:

Ethical principles in action operate contingently. Circumstances and people exert powerful influences. . . . The environment, the situation, the timing of an interaction, human relationships—all affect the way ethical standards are applied. Operationally, ethics are a function of context. . . .

Info Bites

In London, it is unlawful to kiss in a movie theater. It is taboo, or forbidden, for Greenland Eskimos to mention their own names. Donald Duck comic books were banned from libraries in Finland because authorities felt that it wasn't good to show children a hero who ran around without pants on. (SOURCE: *It Is Illegal to Quack Like a Duck and Other Freaky Laws,* by Barbara Seuling and Gwen Seuling, 1988, New York: Penguin Group [USA])

> All moral choices flow from the perceptions of the decision maker, and
> those perceptions are produced by unique experiences in one person's life,
> in the context in which the choices are made.[57]

These are not easy issues, and philosophers and anthropologists have struggled
to develop ethical guidelines that are universally applicable but that also reflect
the tremendous cultural variability in the world.

Scholar David W. Kale has proposed a universal code of ethics for intercultural communicators. This code is based on a universal belief in the sanctity
of the human spirit and the desirability of peace.[58] While we may wish to assume
that universal ethical principles exist, we must be careful not to assume that our
ethical principles are shared by others. When we encounter other ethical principles in various situations, it is often difficult to know if we are imposing our
ethical principles on others and whether we should. There are no easy answers
to these ethical dilemmas.

Like David Kale, philosopher Kwame Appiah agrees that there are, and
should be, values such as tolerance that are universal. He discusses how the mis-
placed belief of "my values are the only right ones" can lead to intolerance, cru-
elty, and even murder by both Christians and Muslim fundamentalists (e.g.,
bombings of abortion clinics or other buildings). He addresses the difficult question of how we can maintain universal values and still respect cultural distinctness.
His answer is that we must all become **cosmopolitans**—citizens of the world—
taking seriously the value of not just human life, but particular human life, never
forgetting that each human being has responsibilities to every other.[59]

The study of intercultural communication should not only provide insights
into cultural patterns but also help us address these ethical issues involved in
intercultural interaction. Appiah and other contemporary scholars stress the
importance of dialogue and "conversations across differences," suggesting that
as part of coordinating our lives with each other as world citizens, we critique
existing norms together and arrive at more acceptable ethical standards.[60] First,
we should be able to judge what is ethical and unethical behavior given variations in cultural priorities. Second, we should be able to identify guidelines for
ethical behavior in intercultural contexts where ethics clash.

Another ethical issue concerns the application of intercultural communication scholarship. Everett Kleinjans, an international educator, stresses that intercultural education differs from some other kinds of education: Although all
education may be potentially transformative, learning as a result of intercultural
contact is particularly so in that it deals with fundamental aspects of human
behavior.[61] Learning about intercultural communication sometimes calls into
question the very core of our assumptive framework and challenges existing
beliefs, values, and patterns of behavior.

Becoming an Ethical Student of Culture

Part of learning about intercultural communication is learning about cultural
patterns and identities—your own and those of others. Four skills are important

Pop Culture Spotlight

Intercultural communica-
tion can take place in
unexpected places. For
example, *Second Life*, an
Internet-based game that
touts itself as the
"Internet's largest user-
created 3D virtual world
community" allows play-
ers to assume any iden-
tity and speak with
anyone from around the
world. In February 2009,
Second Life recorded
that nearly 1.4 million
users logged on to the site
within the past 60 days.
Although completely
virtual and touted as a
world community,
increases in contact with
other cultures and ethnic
groups has led to cases of
"virtual" racism.
Shouldn't the ability to
assume any identity
actually lessen racism?
Or does the anonymity
provided by virtual
settings, like *Second Life*,
make racism more likely?

here: practicing self-reflexivity, learning about others, listening to the voices of others, and developing a sense of social justice.

***Practicing Self-Reflexivity*   Self-reflexivity** refers to the process by which we "look in the mirror" to see ourselves. In studying intercultural communication, you must understand yourself and your position in society. When you learn about other cultures and cultural practices, you often learn much about yourself as well. And the knowledge that you gain from experience is an important way to learn about intercultural communication. Intercultural experiences teach you much about how you react and interact in different cultural contexts and help you evaluate situations and deal with uncertainty. Self-reflection about your intercultural experiences will go a long way toward helping you learn about intercultural communication. When you consider ethical issues in intercultural communication, you need to recognize the strengths and limitations of your own intercultural experiences. Many immigrants have observed that they never felt so much like someone of their nationality until they left their homeland. As part of the process of self-reflexivity, when you gain more intercultural experiences, your views on ethics may change. For example, you may have thought that arranged marriages were misguided and unethical until you gained more experience with people in successful arranged marriages, which have very low divorce rates in comparison with traditional "romantic" marriages.

Many cultural attitudes and ideas are instilled in you and are difficult to unravel and identify. Discovering who you are is never a simple matter; rather, it is an ongoing process that can never fully capture the ever-emerging person. Not only do you grow older, but your intercultural experiences change who you are and who you think you are. When Judith compares her intercultural experiences in France and in Mexico, she notes that, while the two experiences were similar, her own reactions to these intercultural encounters differed markedly because she was younger and less settled into her identity when she went to France.

It is also important to reflect on your place in society. By knowing what social categories—groups defined by society—you fill and what the implications of those categories are, you will be in a better position to understand how to communicate. For example, your status as a male or female may influence how certain messages are interpreted as sexual harassment. Or your identification as a member of some groups may allow you to use certain words and humor, but using other words or telling some jokes may get you in trouble. Many Belgians, for example, are well aware that French sometimes tell *blagues belges*, or jokes about Belgians. Yet if the same joke is told by a Belgian, it has a different tenor. It is important to recognize which social categories you belong to, as well as which ones you are perceived by others as belonging to, as it influences how your message may be interpreted.

***Learning about Others*   It is important to remember that the study of cultures is actually the study of other people. Never lose sight of the humanity of the topic of study. Try not to observe people as if they are zoo animals. Remember that you are studying real people who have real lives, and your conclusions about them may have very real consequences for them and for you.

When Tom was growing up, he was surprised to hear from an older woman that the first time she saw a Japanese or Chinese person was in the circus when she was a little girl. Judith remembers feeling uneasy watching White tourists at the Navajo Nation fair in Window Rock, Arizona, intrusively videotaping the Navajo dancers during their religious ceremonies. In each case, people who were different were viewed and treated as if their cultural practices were for the display and entertainment of others and there was no real attempt to understand them or their culture.

Cultural studies scholar Linda Alcoff discusses the ethical issue involved when students of culture try to describe cultural patterns of others.[62] She acknowledges the difficulty of speaking "for" and "about" people from different cultures. Instead, she claims, students of culture should try to speak "with" and "to" people. Rather than merely describe other people from afar, it's better to listen to and engage them in a dialogue about their cultural realities.

Listening to the Voices of Others   We learn much from real-life experiences. Hearing about the experiences of people who are different from you can lead to different ways of viewing the world. Many differences—based on race, gender, sexual orientation, nationality, ethnicity, age, and so on—deeply affect the everyday lives of people. Listening carefully as people relate their experiences and their knowledge helps us learn about other cultures.

Communication scholars Starosta and Chen suggest that a focus on mutual *listening*, instead of talking, forms the core of successful intercultural understanding. They suggest that good intercultural listeners are receptive to "life stories" from a wide range of culturally different individuals, as a way of understanding and explaining the world around them. These listening skills are built on a foundation of openness, curiosity, and empathy.[63]

Japanese scholar Ishii suggests that the very core of intercultural communication is listening. The effective intercultural communicator, sensitive to the other person, listens *carefully* before speaking. He or she hears the message from the other person, considers it, then reconsiders it, trying on different possible interpretations—trying to understand the speaker's possible intent. When the listener believes she has understood the point being made, she may respond, always in a nonthreatening manner.[64] The point here is that we can only really understand another person when we have listened to him or her carefully.

Developing a Sense of Social Justice   A final ethical issue involves the responsibility that comes with the acquisition of intercultural knowledge and insights. What constitutes ethical and unethical applications of intercultural knowledge? One questionable practice concerns people who study intercultural communication in order to proselytize others without their consent. For example, some religious organizations conduct Bible study sessions on college campuses for international students under the guise of English conversation lessons. Another questionable practice involves cross-cultural consultants who misrepresent or exaggerate their ability to deal with complex issues of prejudice and racism in brief, one-shot training sessions. Another way of looking at ethical responsibility suggests that intercultural learning is not just transformative for the individual, but should also benefit the larger society and other cultural groups in the increasingly interdependent world. The first step in working for social justice is acknowledging that oppression and inequities exist. As we have tried to point out, cultural differences are not just interesting and fascinating; they exist within a hierarchy where some are privileged and set the rules for others.

As you learn about yourself and others as cultural beings, as you come to understand the larger economic, political, and historical contexts in which interaction occurs, is there an ethical obligation to continue learning? We believe that as members of an increasingly interdependent global community, intercultural communication students have a responsibility to educate themselves, not just about interesting cultural differences, but also about intercultural conflicts, the impacts of stereotyping and prejudice, and the larger systems that can oppress and deny basic human rights—and to apply this knowledge to the communities in which they live and interact.

SUMMARY

In this chapter, we identified six reasons for studying intercultural communication: the peace imperative, the economic imperative, the technological imperative, the demographic imperative, the self-awareness imperative, and the ethical imperative. Perhaps you can think of some other reasons. We stressed that the situations in which intercultural communication takes place are complex and challenging.

BUILDING INTERCULTURAL SKILLS

So what are the skills necessary to communicate effectively across cultures? It isn't easy to come up with specific suggestions that will always work in every situation. Communication is much too complex. However, we can identify several general skills that can be applied to the various aspects of intercultural communication covered in this book: (1) understanding cultural identity and history, (2) improving verbal and nonverbal communication, (3) understanding the role of popular culture in intercultural communication, and (4) building relationships and resolving conflicts.

Throughout the book, we'll focus on cultivating and improving the following communication skills:

1. Become more conscious of your communication. This may sound simple, but how often do you really think about your communication and whether it is working? Much of your communication, including intercultural communication, occurs at an unconscious level. A first step in improving your intercultural communication is to become aware of the messages you send

and receive, both verbal and nonverbal. You can't really work on improving your communication until you become aware of it on a conscious level.

2. Become more aware of others' communication. Understanding other people's communication requires the important intercultural skill of empathy—knowing where someone else is coming from, or "walking in his or her shoes." This is no easy task, but by doing things such as improving your observational skills and learning how to build better intercultural relations you can accomplish it.

3. Expand your own intercultural communication repertoire. This involves experimenting with different ways of looking at the world and of communicating, verbally and nonverbally. Building this skill may require that you step outside your communication comfort zone and look at things in a different light. It may require that you question ideas and assumptions you've not thought about before. All this is part of expanding your communication options.

4. Become more flexible in your communication. Closely related to the previous skill—and perhaps the most important one—this involves avoiding what has been called "hardening of the categories."

5. Be an advocate for others. This is something that isn't often included in lists of communication skills. To improve intercultural communication among groups, however, everybody's voice must be heard. Improving relations among groups of people—whether based on ethnicity, race, gender, physical ability, or whatever difference—is not just about improving individual communication skills; it is also about forming coalitions with others.

It is important to remember that becoming a better intercultural communicator is not achieved quickly but rather is a lifelong process. In each of the following chapters, we invite you to take up the challenge of continuing to build these skills.

ACTIVITIES

1. *Intercultural encounters:* Describe and analyze a recent intercultural encounter with someone of a different age, ethnicity, race, religion, and so on.

   a. Describe the encounter. What made it "intercultural"?

   b. How did you feel after the encounter? Why do you think you felt as you did?

   c. Based on this experience, identify some characteristics that may be important for successful intercultural communication.

2. *Intercultural imperatives:* There are many reasons to study intercultural communication, including the six discussed in this chapter. What other imperatives can you identify?

3. *Household products:* Look at the products in your home. How many different countries do they come from? How might your purchases increase intercultural contact?

ENDNOTES

1. Dittmer, J. (2008, November 9). What it meant. *Boston Globe*. Retrieved March 2, 2009 from: http://www.boston.com/bostonglobe/ideas/articles/2008/11/09/what_it_meant/

2. Hubert, T. (2008, November 5). Kenya celebrates Obama win in US election. *France 24*. Retrieved March 2, 2009 from: http://www.france24.com/en/20081105-celebrate-celebrations-obama-kenyans-kenya-wins-elections-usa

3. United Press International. (2009, February 29). Obama election inspires racist hate groups. UPI.com. Retrieved March 2, 2009 from: http://www.upi.com/Top_News/2009/02/26/Obama_election_inspires_racist_hate_groups/UPI-58811235688959/

4. Saltzman, J. & Ballou, B. (2009, January 19). Church arson tied to racism. *Boston Globe*. Retrieved March 2, 2009 from: http://www.boston.com/news/local/massachusetts/articles/2009/01/17/church_arson_tied_to_racism/

5. Obama election spurs race threats, crimes. (2008, November 15). *MSNBC*. Retrieved March 2, 2009 from: http://www.msnbc.msn.com/id/27738018/

6. Marshall, M. G. (2006). *Major episodes of political violence 1946–2005*. Retrieved from http://members.aol.com/cspmgm/warlist.htm

7. Delgado, F. (2002). Mass-mediated communication and intercultural conflict. In J. M. Martin, T. K. Nakayama, & L. A. Flores (Eds.), *Readings in intercultural communication* (pp. 351–360). Boston: McGraw-Hill, p. 353.

8. Hymowitz, C. (2005, November 14). The new diversity. *The Wall Street Journal*, p. R1.

9. Pacelle, M. (2003, June 12). U.S. banks vie for big postwar roles—Financial reconstruction may include J. P. Morgan, Citigroup, Bank of America. *The Wall Street Journal (Europe)*, p. A3.

10. Friedman, T. L. (2005). *The world is flat: A brief history of the twenty-first century*. New York: Farrar, Straus & Giroux.

11. Wal-Mart poised for major China expansion. (2006, March 19). CNNMoney.com. Retrieved from http://money.cnn.com/2006/03/19/news/companies/walmart_china.reut/index.htm

12. Scott, R. E. (2008, February 15). International picture. Economic Policy Institute. Retrieved March 3, 2009 from http://www.epi.org/publications/entry/indicators_intlpict_20080215

13. Dell plans to double Indian headcount to 20,000. (2006, March 20). Reuters. Retrieved from http://today.reuters.com/news/newsArticle.aspx?type=technologyNews&storyID=2006-03-20T133909Z_01_BNG267009_RTRUKOC_0_US-INDIA-DELL.xml; Dobbs, L. (2005, April 4). The wrong trade czar. *U.S. News and World Report*. Retrieved from http://www.usnews.com/usnews/opinion/articles/050404/4dobbs.htm

14. Samuelson, R. J. (2005). Think locally, act globally [Editorial and Opinion]. *The New York Sun*, p. 9.

15. George, S. (n.d.). *Why globalization is pernicious*. European Business Forum. Retrieved from http://www.ebfonline.com/at_forum/at_forum.asp?id=292&linked=288

16. Maital, S. (2005, May 26). Globalization is a two-way street: It's time we started taking ideas from China and India. *Global News Wire—Asia Africa Intelligence Wire*. Retrieved from LexisNexis database.

17. McLuhan, M. (1967). *The medium is the message*. New York: Bantam Books.

18. Gergen, K. (1991). *The saturated self: Dilemmas of identity in contemporary life*. New York: HarperCollins/Basic Books.

19. Gergen, K. J. (2002). The challenge of absent-presence. In J. Katz & M. Aakhus (Eds.), *Perpetual contact: Mobile communication, private talk, public performance* (pp. 223–227). Cambridge, UK: Cambridge University Press.

20. Katz, J. E. (2007). Mobile media and communication: Some important questions. *Communication Monographs*, 74(3), 389–394.

21. Internet information not reaching non-English users. (2007, August 13). University of Guelph. Retrieved on March 2, 2009 from: http://www.uoguelph.ca/news/2007/08/internet_inform.html

22. Dor, D. (2004). From Englishization to imposed multilingualism: Globalization, the Internet, and the political economy of the linguistic code. *Public Culture, 16*, 97–118.

23. Global Reach website, http://www.glreach.com/eng/ed/art/rep-eur21.php3

24. Jones, S., & Fox, S. (2009). Generations online in 2009. Pew Internet & American Life Project. Retrieved February 2, 2009 from: http://www.pewinternet.org/pdfs/PIP_Generations_2009.pdf

25. State of the Blogosphere/2008. (2008). Technorati.com. Retrieved December 13, 2008 from http://technorati.com/blogging/state-of-the-blogosphere/

26. Cheong, P., & Poon, J. (In press). Weaving webs of faith: Examining Internet use and religious communication among Chinese Protestant transmigrants. *Journal of International and Intercultural Communication*; Nardi, B. A., Schiano, D. J., & Gumbrecht, M. (2004) *Blogging as social activity, or, would you let 900 million people read your diary?* Proceedings of the 2004 ACM conference on computer supported cooperative work (pp. 222–231). Chicago, Illinois. Retrieved February 2, 2009 from http://home.comcast.net/~diane.schiano/CSCW04.Blog.pdf

27. Demographics of internet users (2008, October). Pew Internet and American Life Project. Retrieved February 1, 2009 from http://www.pewinternet.org/trends/User_Demo_10%2020%2008.htm; Fox, S., & Livingston, G. (2007). Latinos online. Pew Internet & American Life Project. Retrieved February 2, 2009 from http://www.pewinternet.org/pdfs/Latinos_Online_March_14_2007.pdf

28. Jung, J-Y. (2008). Internet connectedness and its social origins: An ecological approach to postaccess digital divides. *Communication Studies, 59*(4), 322–339.

29. World Internet Usage Statistics (2008). Retrieved February 2, 2009 from http://www.internetworldstats.com/stats.htm; Wray, R. (2007, June 14). China overtaking US for fast internet access as Africa gets left behind. *The Guardian*, retrieved February 2, 2009 from http://www.guardian.co.uk/money/2007/jun/14/internetphonesbroadband.digitalmedia

30. van Dijk, J. (2004). Divides in succession: Possession, skills, and use of new media for societal participation. In E. P. Bucy & J. E. Newhagen (Eds.), *Media access: Social and psychological dimensions of new technology use* (pp. 233–254). Mahwah, NJ: Erlbaum; Rojas, V., Straubhaar, J., Roychowdhury, D., & Okur, O. (2004). Communities, cultural capital, and the digital divide. In Bucy & Newhagen, pp. 107–130.

31. Scommegna, P. (2003). U.S. growing bigger, older and more diverse. Population Reference Bureau website, http://www.prb.org/

32. Hutcheson, R. (2006, April 3). A nation of immigrants, with mixed feelings. *Philadelphia Inquirer*, p. A01.

33. Brewer, C. A., & Suchan, T. A. (2001). *Mapping Census 2000: The geography of U.S. diversity* (U.S. Census Bureau, Census Special Reports, Series CENSR/01-1). Washington, DC: U.S. Government Printing Office.

34. Gibson, C., & Jung, K. (2006). *Historical census statistics on the foreign-born population of the United States: 1850–2000*. Washington, DC: U.S. Census Bureau.

35. Fischer, M. J. (2008). Does campus diversity promote friendship diversity? A look at interracial friendships in college. *Social Science Quarterly, 89*(3), 631–655.

36. Gurin, P., Nagda, B. A., & Lopez, G. E. (2004). Benefits of diversity in education for democratic citizenship. *Journal of Social Issues, 60*(1), 17–34.

37. U.S. Bureau of the Census website, http://www.census.gov/prod/2002pubs/c2kbr01-15.pdf. The American Indian and Alaskan Native Population: 2000.

38. Webster, Y. O. (1992). *The racialization of America*. New York: St. Martin's Press.

39. Curtin, P. D. (1969). *The Atlantic slave trade: A census*. Madison: University of Wisconsin Press.

40. Baldwin, J. (1955). *Notes of a native son*. Boston: Beacon Press.

41. West, C. (1993). *Race matters*. Boston: Beacon Press.

42. Carroll, J. (2006, February 6). A homecoming. *The Boston Globe*, p. A13; Samuels, A. (2006, February 20). Learning to give—New Black history museums need cash. *Newsweek*, p. 67.

43. Banks, J. (1991). *Teaching strategies for ethnic studies*. Needham, MA: Allyn & Bacon.

44. Takaki, R. (1989). *Strangers from a different shore*. New York: Penguin Books, p. 209.

45. Roediger, D. R. (2005). *Working toward Whiteness: How America's immigrants became White*. New York: Basic Books.

46. Roediger, D. R. (1991). *The wages of Whiteness: Race and the making of the American working class*. New York: Verso.

47.   Hoagland, J. (2005, November 9). French lessons. Washingtonpost.com. Retrieved from http://www.washingtonpost.com/wp-dyn/content/article/2006/03/31/AR2006033101713 .html?sub=new

48.   Logan, J. R., Stults, B. J., & Farley, R. (2004). Segregation of minorities in the metropolis. *Demography, 41,* 1–22.

49.   Clanton, B. (2006, March 31). UAW: Delphi to shed 14 of its U.S. plants. *Detroit News,* p. 01A; Industrial job implosion. (2006, April 3). *The Providence Journal.* Retrieved from http://www .projo.com/cgi-bin/bi/gold_print.cgi

50.   Scheer, R. (2005, September 6). The real costs of a culture of greed. *Los Angeles Times,* p. B11.

51.   Bernard, S., & Augstums, I. M. (2009, February 27). Bank CEO Ken Lewis keeps lips sealed. *BusinessWeek.* Retrieved March 2, 2009 from: http://www.businessweek.com/ap/financialnews/ D96JNOIG0.htm

52.   Labaton, S., & Bajaj, V. (2009, February 4). In curbing pay, Obama seeks to alter corporate culture. *New York Times.* Retrieved March 2, 2009 from: http://www.nytimes.com/2009/02/05/ us/politics/05pay.html?_r=1

53.   Wadhwa, V. (2009, March 2). Why skilled immigrants are leaving the U.S. *BusinessWeek.* Retrieved March 2, 2009 from: http://www.businessweek.com/technology/content/feb2009/ tc20090228_990934.htm

54.   Adler, P. S. (1975). The transition experience: An alternative view of culture shock. *Journal of Humanistic Psychology, 15,* 13–23.

55.   Johannesen, R. L. (1990). *Ethics in human communication* (3rd ed.). Prospect Heights, IL: Waveland Press.

56.   Evanoff, R. J. (2004). Universalist, relativist, and constructivist approaches to intercultural ethics. *International Journal of Intercultural Relations, 28,* 439–458.

57.   Howell, W. S. (1982). *The empathic communicator.* Belmont, CA: Wadsworth.

58.   Kale, D. W. (1994). Peace as an ethic for intercultural communication. In L. Samovar & R. E. Porter (Eds.), *Intercultural communication: A reader* (7th ed., pp. 435–441). Belmont, CA: Wadsworth.

59.   Appiah, K. A. (2006). *Cosmopolitanism: Ethics in a world of strangers.* New York: Norton.

60.   Appiah (2006); Evanoff (2004); Kidder, R. M. (2006, April 4). Values for citizens of a flat world. *Christian Science Monitor,* p. 17.

61.   Kleinjans, E. (1975). A question of ethics. *International Education and Cultural Exchange, 10,* 20–25.

62.   Alcoff, L. (1991/1992). The problem of speaking for others. *Cultural Critique, 20,* 5–32.

63.   Starosta, W. J., & Chen, G.-M. (2005). Intercultural listening: Collected reflections, collated refractions. In W. J. Starosta & G.-M. Chen (Eds.), *Taking stock in intercultural communication: Where to now?* (pp. 274–285). Washington, DC: National Communication Association.

64.   Ishii, S. (1984). *Enryo-sasshi* communication: A key to understanding Japanese interpersonal relations. *Cross Currents, 11,* 49–58.

CHAPTER TWO

Intercultural Communication

BUILDING BLOCKS AND BARRIERS

STUDY OBJECTIVES

After reading this chapter, you should be able to:
1. Define culture.
2. Define communication.
3. Discuss the relationship between culture and communication.
4. Describe the role that context and power play in intercultural interactions.
5. Identify and define ethnocentrism.
6. Identify and describe stereotyping.
7. Identify and describe prejudice.
8. Identify and describe discrimination.
9. Explain the ways in which ethnocentrism, stereotyping, prejudice, and discrimination act as barriers to effective intercultural communication.

KEY TERMS

color-blind approach
communication
context
culture
discrimination
embodied ethnocentrism
ethnocentrism
hate speech
individualism
intercultural
  communication
long-term versus short-
  term orientation

masculinity/femininity
perceptions
power
power distance
prejudice
stereotypes
uncertainty avoidance
values
worldview

Surf's Up!

To see photos and a first-hand account of Josh Miller's extraordinary journey to the annual Festival Au Desert in Timbuktu, Mali, visit www.jambase.com /headsup.asp?storyID= 8319. It was also a trip "home" for Josh, who lived in Mali for 2 years while serving in the Peace Corps several years ago.

Timbuktu is home to the "Blue People" of the Sahara—the guardians of the desert—the Tuareg, . . . a proud people who still ride into the city on their camels, dressed in their indigo-dyed clothes (the dye rubs onto their skin giving them the blue skin they are named for) and brandishing the swords you might see in a Sinbad movie.

For the past eight years, in the town of Timbuktu (yes, there really is such a place!), in Mali, Africa, musicians from all over the world gather for a yearly world festival of music.[1] Organized by the Touareg (Tuareg in Arabic)—a nomadic group—headliners have included Robert Plant of Led Zepplin, the French group LoJo, a native Indian group from Arizona, and leading musicians from Mali such as Oumou Sangare and Fantani Toure. One attendee describes this intercultural event:

> The Touaregs came on their bedecked camels from villages far and wide, and also outsiders from the United States and Europe. . . . Apart from camel-hide tents for musicians and visitors, a main concert-stage and a canopy for after-noon events, it was just an ocean of sand. There were no seats and that was fine with everyone as the natural setting was an attraction in itself. As the sun disappeared in the sandy horizon, the main stage started to become active. . . . Sixty groups performed over three days. The music played was not just entertainment but an artistic expression of their culture and tradition.[2]

This intercultural event in Timbuktu represents a joyous sharing of music, art, and culture, possible only in today's global world. Other intercultural events in our world are more challenging. Consider the "Day without Immigrants" event on Monday, May 1, 2006, when immigrants and their supporters took to the streets of all major American cities to protest proposed immigration laws and boy-cotted businesses to express their economic power. These protesters encountered people from other groups who did not agree with them. The discussions between various ethnic, racial, and socioeconomic groups regarding immigration policies represent the complexity of intercultural interactions in today's society.[3]

While these events represent intercultural interaction on a global and national scale, intercultural interactions are also a part of your everyday life—from your encounters with diverse groups of students in your classes, to your interactions with your parents (from a different generational culture!), as well as your interaction with friends of opposite genders and sexual orientations.

Groups of people everywhere are coming together, sometimes with enor-mous differences in cultural backgrounds, beliefs, lifestyles, economic resources, and religions. This illustrates that intercultural communication does not happen in a vacuum. History, economics, and politics play an important role in how var-ious people and groups react when they encounter each other in specific con-texts and engage in intercultural communication. What are some of the specific building blocks and barriers of intercultural communication? The answer to that question is the focus of this chapter.

Intercultural communication occurs when people of different cultural backgrounds interact, but this definition seems simplistic and redundant. To properly define intercultural communication, it's necessary to understand the

In today's global world, groups of people everywhere come together, sometimes with enormous differences in cultural backgrounds, beliefs, lifestyles, economic resources, and religion—like these people participating in the Toureg dance performance at the annual Festival in the Desert in Essakane, Mali.

two root words—*culture* and *communication*—that represent the first two building blocks. In addition, communication always happens in a particular situation or context, our third building block. Our fourth building block concerns the element of power, something that is part of every intercultural interaction. We first define and describe culture and communication and then discuss how these two interact with issues of context and power to form our understanding of intercultural communication.

BUILDING BLOCK 1: CULTURE

Culture is often considered the core concept in intercultural communication. One characteristic of culture is that we may not think about it very much. Trying to understand one's own culture is like trying to explain to a fish that it lives in water. Often, we cannot identify our own cultural backgrounds and assumptions until we encounter people from other cultures, which gives us a frame of reference. For example, consider our student, Ann, who participated in a study-abroad program in Mexico. She told us that she thought it was strange that many young Mexicans lived with their parents even after they had graduated from college and were working. Gradually, she recognized that Mexicans tend to have a stronger sense of family responsibilities between children and parents than Americans do. Thus, young people often live at home and contribute to the

What Do You Think?

Rank-order the following in terms of their importance in defining "American culture": hamburgers, movies, corn, apple pie, pizza, baseball, hot dogs, milkshakes, french fries, and big cars. Did you know that only three of those things actually are indigenous to the United States (corn, baseball, milkshakes), while the other seven are from Europe? What does this say about the ideas and values of U.S. culture?

family income. Older parents rarely go to retirement communities, but are cared for within the family. While volunteering in a senior citizens' home, Ann was impressed by how few people lived in the facility.

Culture has been defined in many ways. For some people, it means the opera or classical music, but for the purposes of this book, we define **culture** as learned patterns of perception, values, and behaviors, shared by a group of people, that are dynamic and heterogeneous. Culture also involves our emotions and feelings. Let's look at what this definition actually means.

Culture Is Learned

First, culture is learned. While all human beings share some universal habits and tendencies—we all eat, sleep, seek shelter, and share some motivations to be loved and to protect ourselves—these are not aspects of culture. Rather, culture is the unique way we have learned to eat, sleep, and seek shelter because we are American or Japanese, male or female, and so on. For example, most Americans eat holding a fork in one hand, but when they use a knife, they shift the fork to their other hand. Europeans think this is clumsy; they simply eat with fork in one hand and knife in the other. While Americans and Japanese share a need to be loved, Americans tend to express feelings of love more overtly, whereas Japanese are taught to be more restrained. When we are born, we don't know how to be a male or female, American or Mexican, and so on; we are taught. We have to learn how to eat, walk, talk, and love like other members of our cultural groups—and we usually do so slowly and subconsciously, through a process of socialization. Think of how young children learn to be male or female. Young boys imitate their fathers and other grown men, while young girls learn to talk and act like their mothers and other women. The same is true for other groups we belong to. For example, an American child adopted by a Finnish family will embrace Finnish cultural values; likewise, a Korean child raised by a German family will exhibit German cultural values.

When we move into new cultures, we learn new cultural patterns. For example, when Chinese students first arrive in the United States they are surprised to see car drivers motioning with their hand to pedestrians to let them pass first. In China, this gesture is used only when a person gets frustrated or irritated at another person! Gradually Chinese students learn the meaning of this gesture—that the driver is actually being polite—and then use it themselves when driving.

Culture Involves Perception and Values

What do cultural groups learn and share? First, they share **perceptions,** or ways of looking at the world. Culture is sometimes described as a sort of lens through which we view the world. All the information we receive in a given day passes through this perceptual lens. The process of perception is composed of three phases: selection, organization, and interpretation. Our cultural experiences influence every phase of the perception process and ultimately determine how

Many cultural groups value family relationships, but how and how often families interact may depend on the particular cultural norms. How often does your extended family get together and what are the expectations for the interaction?

we make sense of the world and how we respond to the people, places, and things in it. During the *selection* process, we are only able to give attention to a small fraction of all the information available to our senses. What we choose to pay attention to is based upon features of stimuli (size, intensity, etc.) as well as what we perceive to be important and relevant to us. In the *organization* phase we categorize the information into recognizable groups. Last in the perception process is *interpretation*, the ways in which we assign meaning to the information we have organized.[4]

Consider the following scenario: Towanda and Matthew are walking across campus discussing a problem that Matthew is having with his sociology course project. In the distance another group of students wearing deerskin clothing, soft moccasins, and carrying feathers is walking toward an open area of campus. Matthew is engrossed in his thoughts and does not even perceive the group of students, and even when he notices them he does not perceive them as Towanda does. Towanda grew up close to the Dineh nation and organizes the perception of these individuals into a known cognitive category and says, "The American Indian student group is practicing for their dance competition. I have a friend in the competition; let's go watch the practice." She selected, organized, and interpreted the sights and sounds of the students because of her familiarity with them. Matthew, on the other hand, does not see them at first, and then he notices but does not interpret any special meaning. This scenario shows how individuals may be exposed to the same stimuli, but because of differences in cultural backgrounds (age, gender, race, ethnicity, nationality) may select, organize, and interpret things very differently. Each cultural group has a different "prescription" for its "lenses."

What Do You Think?

What kind of cultural values are embraced by children in multiracial families, such as golf star Tiger Woods, who calls himself "Cablinasian," meaning Caucasian, Black, American Indian, and Asian? What about the Hollywood movie star Keanu Reeves, who is "Eurasian," being White, Chinese, and Hawaiian? He was born in Lebanon and grew up in Canada and America. With such family backgrounds, might multiracial kids be more interculturally competent?

Surf's Up!

Take a test to assess your own cross-cultural competence at www.maec.org /cross/table1.html. The 20 questions listed assess a person's knowledge of the relationships among culture, communication, and language.

The difficulty is in trying to understand our own cultural perceptions—like trying to look at our own glasses without taking them off.

The perception process is laden with opportunities for us to compare ourselves and our culture to others. Later in the chapter, we'll show that categorization and interpretation processes *can* lead to overgeneralizations, stereotypes, and prejudice, which can have negative consequences.

Another metaphor for culture is a computer program in that culture, in a sense, serves as a "program of the mind" that every individual carries within himself or herself. These programs of the mind, or patterns of thinking, feeling, and potential acting, work just like computer software. That is, they tell people (subconsciously) how to walk, talk, eat, dance, socialize, and otherwise conduct their lives.[5]

Culture Involves Feelings

Culture is experienced not only as perceptions and values but also as feelings. When we are in our own cultural surroundings we *feel* a sense of familiarity and a certain level of comfort in the space, behavior, and actions of others. We might characterize this feeling as a kind of **embodied ethnocentrism,** which is normal.[6] (Later on we'll discuss the negative side of ethnocentrism.) This aspect of culture has implications for understanding adaptation to other cultural norms and spaces. The stronger your identification with a particular space or cultural situation, the more difficult it might be to change spaces without experiencing a lot of discomfort—actual psychological and physiological changes. For example, dining in a formal Japanese restaurant, with flat tables, rice-paper walls, silence, and low light, would probably give U.S. Americans a feeling of mild unfamiliarity, compared to experiences in most U.S. restaurants. However, experiencing new cultural situations on a daily basis can give a stronger *feeling* of disorientation. (We'll discuss this more when we talk about culture shock in Chapter 10.)

U.S. students studying in France described their feelings in coping with the French language. Their self-esteem dropped and they became very self-conscious. Their whole bodies were entrenched in this effort of trying to communicate in French; it was a laborious and involved process that was connected to all aspects of themselves—a feeling of being out of their cultural comfort zone.[7] We should not underestimate the importance of culture in providing us a feeling of familiarity and comfort.

Culture Is Shared

Another important part of our definition of culture is that cultural patterns are shared. The idea of a culture implies a group of people. These cultural patterns of perceptions and beliefs are developed through interactions with different groups of individuals—at home, in the neighborhood, at school, in youth groups, at college, and so on. Culture becomes a group experience because it is shared with people who live in and experience the same social environments. Our perceptions are similar to those of other individuals who belong to the same cultural groups. In class, the authors sometimes put students in same-gender groups to highlight how many men share many similar perceptions about being male and similar attitudes toward women; the same seems to hold true for women. For example, men sometimes share a perception that women have power in social situations. Women sometimes share a perception that men think badly of women who go out with a lot of guys. This same pattern of shared perceptions is evident in polls of attitudes of African Americans and Whites. White Americans seem to share a perception that things are getting better for African Americans and that racial attitudes and interactions are improving. By contrast, many African Americans share a perception that, while equality between races has improved, there is still a long way to go. For example, in a recent poll, Blacks and Whites polled after Hurricane Katrina in fall 2005 drew very different lessons from the Katrina tragedy. Seven-in-ten Blacks (71 percent) said the disaster showed that racial inequality remains a major problem in the country, compared to only 32 percent of Whites. More striking was the disagreement over whether the government's response to the crisis would have been faster if most of the storm's victims had been White; 66 percent of African Americans express that view, compared to 17 percent of Whites.[8]

Our membership in cultural groups ranges from involuntary to voluntary. Many of the cultural groups we belong to—specifically, those based on age, race, gender, physical ability, sexual orientation, and family membership—are involuntary associations over which we have little choice. We belong to other cultural groups—those based on professions, political associations, and hobbies—that are voluntary associations. And some groups may be involuntary at the beginning of our lives (those based on religion, nationality, or socioeconomic status) but become voluntary associations later on. Some experts argue that involuntary memberships, like gender or race, are more consequential than voluntary ones in impacting on our communication. People often respond to us on the basis of physical characteristics that define these identities, which can, as we'll see later in the chapter, lead to stereotyping and prejudice.[9]

Culture Is Expressed as Behavior

Our cultural lens or computer program influences not only our perceptions and beliefs but also our behaviors. For example, Ann's belief in (or lens on) the importance of individual independence, or individualism, is reflected in her behavior. She was expected to become increasingly independent when growing up and to be on her own after college, and she was socialized to make her own decisions about dating, marriage, and career. By contrast, the young people she met in Mexico were socialized to the cultural value of collectivism. They were expected to be more responsible for caring for other family members and to take their wishes into consideration in marriage and career decisions.

It is important to understand that we belong to many different cultural groups and that these groups collectively help determine our perceptions, beliefs, and behavior. These patterns endure over time and are passed on from person to person. Therefore, just as Ann was socialized to be individualistic, she'll probably pass on these same beliefs and behaviors to her own children.

Surf's Up!

Although individualism and collectivism are culture-specific value orientations, some cultures seem to favor one or the other as a barometer for proper living. Check out the websites for the Individualist Research Foundation (http://home.earthlink.net/~whm/) and Enter Stage Right (www.enterstageright.com/). Do these groups equate individuality with liberty and freedom? How might these groups adapt to life among collectivist cultures like the Diné (Navajo) or the Thai?

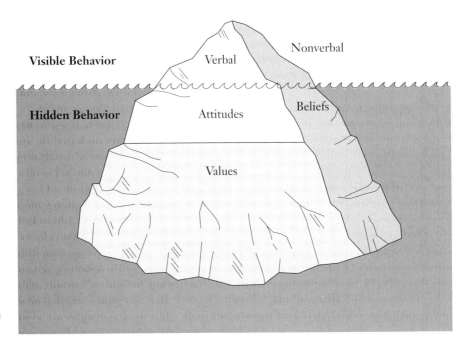

The visible and hidden layers of culture.

Culture Is Dynamic and Heterogeneous

Another crucial feature of culture is that it is dynamic, or changing, and can often be a source of conflict among different groups.[10] It is important to recognize that cultural patterns are not rigid and homogeneous but are dynamic and heterogeneous. A good example of cultural heterogeneity is the varying opinions among Latinos/as regarding U.S. immigration policies. During the spring 2006 protests regarding proposed immigration legislation, many Latinos/as stressed that they did not agree with the protesters. For example, one Latino war veteran said that, while he understands the contribution immigrants have made to the United States, "We're all here today to tell all those protesters, 'You do not speak for me.'" It is important to remember that members of cultural groups do not all think or behave in the same way.[11] Sometimes there is conflict over cultural patterns and meanings. For example, who gets to define what "Native American" means? The government has one definition: a person who has proven Native American ancestry and is enrolled in a particular tribe. But some people feel that a Native American can be anyone who follows Native American cultural and spiritual traditions and practices.

Table 2.1 shows some cultural behaviors that are widely shared in some cultures around the world. Note that these are shared, collective cultural behaviors, rather than individual characteristics.

Viewing culture as dynamic is particularly important for understanding the struggles of various groups—Native Americans, Asian Americans and Pacific Islanders, African Americans, Latinos/as, women, gays and lesbians, working-class

TABLE 2.1 Interesting Cultural Behaviors

Thailand: Thai people greet each other with a wai greeting—hold your hands together at the chest like a prayer and give a light bow.

Egypt: Using the left hand alone to exchange an item with an Egyptian is considered rude.

France: The French expect promptness. They are not accustomed to standing in line.

Germany: Germans often bang their fists on the table to show their appreciation at the end of a meeting.

Japan: When you are offered a gift, you must first refuse it once, modestly and serenely. Then you should accept it using both hands.

Israel: When Israelis invite someone to their home, it is an important gesture. It is appropriate to bring a book as a gift.

Spain: After a meal, you must place your utensils together on the plate. Otherwise, your Spanish host would think that you were not satisfied.

French Polynesia: It is not necessary to tip. People usually give small gifts instead.

Source: Selling Destinations: Geography for the Travel Professional, 4th ed., by M. Mancini, 2003, Clifton Park, NY: Thomson/Delmar Learning.

people, and so on—as they try to negotiate their relationships and ensure their well-being within U.S. society. By studying the communication that arises from these ongoing struggles, we can better understand several intercultural concerns. Consider, for example, Proposition 227, passed by California voters in 1998, which eliminated public funding for bilingual education. The controversy surrounding the passage of this proposition illustrates the concerns of many different cultural groups. Some Whites and long-term immigrants wanted to eliminate public funding for any programs for more recent immigrants. Others felt that providing bilingual education was a good investment and that failing to do so sent a message of hostility to new immigrants.

Seeing culture as dynamic and heterogeneous opens up new ways of thinking about intercultural communication. After all, the people from a particular culture are not identical, and any culture has many intercultural struggles. For instance, when we speak of Chinese culture or French culture, we ignore the diversity that resides in that culture. That "Chinese culture" may refer to the mainland Chinese; or to the inhabitants of the island of Taiwan, who speak Taiwanese or Mandarin; or to the Chinese from Hong Kong, who speak Cantonese. The label "Chinese" thus obscures incredible diversity. Similarly, "French culture" could refer to the "Pieds Noirs" (North Africans of French descent), or to Vietnamese of French descent, or to the Bretons, who live in northwestern France and speak their own language.

Yet, cultures are not heterogeneous in the same way everywhere. How sexuality, race, gender, and class function in other cultures is not necessarily the same as or even similar to how they do in the United States. For example, there are

Pop Culture Spotlight

We can see the dynamism of changing culture in American movies, especially with remakes. In the original *Father of the Bride* with Spencer Tracy, from the 1950s, his wife is a housewife in high heels. In the Steve Martin version in the 1980s, she has a career. Bela Lugosi's *Dracula* movies from the 1930s only hint at sexuality. In the Christopher Lee films of the 1960s, there are half-naked female vampires in Dracula's castle. And the Gary Oldman version from the 1990s is even more graphic.

poor people in most nations. The poor in the United States are often viewed with disdain, as people to be avoided; in many European countries, by contrast, the poor are seen as a part of society, to be helped by government programs. Likewise, gender issues are not framed the same way in all countries. In the United States, gender equality is defined in terms of equal pay and career opportunities. In some Middle Eastern countries, women may be seen to have equality because they have tremendous power within the home and family but less influence in public arenas. In short, by viewing any culture as heterogeneous, we can understand the complexities of that culture and become more sensitive to how people in that culture live.

BUILDING BLOCK 2: COMMUNICATION

Communication, our second building block, is also complex and may be defined in many ways. For our purposes we define **communication** as a symbolic process whereby meaning is shared and negotiated. In other words, communication occurs whenever someone attributes meaning to another's words or actions. In addition, communication is dynamic, may be unintentional, and is receiver-oriented. Let's look more closely at what this means.

First, communication is symbolic. That is, the words we speak and the gestures we make have no meaning in themselves; rather, they achieve significance only because people agree, at least to some extent, on their meaning. When we use symbols, such as words or gestures, to communicate, we assume that the other person shares our symbol system. If we tell someone to "sit down," we assume that the individual knows what these two words (symbols) mean. Also, these symbolic meanings are conveyed both verbally and nonverbally. Thousands of nonverbal behaviors—gestures, postures, eye movements, facial expressions, and so on—involve shared meaning.

Think about the symbolic meaning of some clothing. Why is it that many people value Ralph Lauren clothing more than clothes from J. C. Penney? It has to do with the symbolic meaning associated with the clothing, rather than anything intrinsically special about the clothing. Sometimes we mistakenly assume that the other person shares our symbol systems. When Jenny, a Canadian, moved to the United States as a child, she knew Canadian money and American money did not look alike, but thought they at least would be called the same things. She was very confused when she found out that in the United States, one-dollar bills or coins were not called Loonies and two-dollar bills or coins not called Toonies. In America, she couldn't even find a two-dollar bill or coin!

People also disagree over the meaning of powerful verbal and nonverbal symbols—like the flag and the national anthem. Consider the recent controversy over the singing of the national anthem in Spanish. For some people, the anthem symbolizes the diversity of the United States: singing it in any language is acceptable. For others, the anthem symbolizes the unity of the United States and should be sung only in English. Another good example is the controversial practice of flying the Confederate flag over the South Carolina Statehouse.

Surf's Up!

Learn more about the disability culture and how it exemplifies the five elements of this textbook's definition of culture at www.disabilityculture.org. To learn the characteristics of the American deaf culture, go to www.deafculture.com. Think abut whether the disability culture is a full-fledged culture and how it is similar to or different from an ethnic culture.

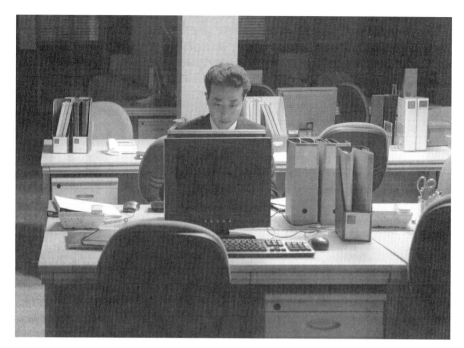

An important U. S. value revolves around keeping busy and achieving things in life. Unlike people in many cultures, most Americans prefer to work longer hours for extra money rather than work less and have more time to spend with family and friends.

Obviously, the flag has tremendous symbolic meaning for many people. For some Whites, the flag symbolizes the rich legacy of the South and the gallant fight in the Civil War. For some African Americans, the same flag is a negative reminder of slavery, oppression, segregation, and prejudice. A more recent example is the lawsuit regarding the placement of the granite Ten Commandment monument in a courthouse in Alabama during the summer of 2003. For those in favor, the monument represented the strength of the Protestant role in U.S. history and politics. For those opposed (who eventually won the lawsuit), the placement violated the First Amendment—separation of church and state. The monument was a powerful symbol for both groups.[12]

Second, communication is a process involving several components: people who are communicating, a message that is being communicated (verbal or nonverbal), a channel through which the communication takes place, and a context. People communicating can be thought of as senders and receivers—they are sending and receiving messages. However, communication does not involve tossing "message balls" back and forth, such that one person sends a single message and the other person receives it. Rather, it is more akin to clicking on a website and being bombarded by many different messages at once.

Third, communication involves sharing and negotiating meaning. People have to agree on the meaning of a particular message, but to make things more complicated, each message often has more than one meaning. For example, the message "I love you" may mean, "I want to have sex with you tonight," "I feel guilty about what I did last night without you," "I need you to do me a favor," "I have a good time when I'm with you," or "I want to spend the rest of my life with you." When we communicate, we assume that the other person takes the meaning that we intend. But for individuals from different cultural backgrounds and experiences, this assumption may be wrong and may lead to misunderstanding and a lack of shared meaning. Often, we have to try harder in intercultural communication to make sure that meaning is truly shared.

Fourth, communication is dynamic. This means that communication is not a single event but is ongoing, so that communicators are at once both senders and receivers. For example, when a teacher walks into the classroom, even before she starts speaking, communication messages are flying all around. The students are looking at her and interpreting her nonverbal messages: Do her attire, her bearing, her facial expressions, and her eye movements suggest that she will be a good teacher? A hard teacher? Someone who is easy to talk with? The teacher in turn is interpreting the nonverbal messages of the students: Are they too quiet? Do they look interested? Disruptive? When we are communicating with another person, we take in messages through our senses of sight, smell, and hearing—and these messages do not happen one at a time, but rather simultaneously. When we are communicating, we are creating, maintaining, or sharing meaning. This implies that people are actively involved in the communication process. Technically, then, one person cannot communicate alone—talking to yourself while washing your car in the driveway does not qualify as communication.

Fifth, communication does not have to be intentional. Some of the most important (and sometimes disastrous) communication occurs without the sender knowing a particular message has been sent. During business negotiations, an American businessman in Saudi Arabia sat across from his Saudi host showing the soles of his feet (an insult in Saudi society), inquired about the health of his wife (an inappropriate topic), and turned down the offer of tea (a rude act). Because of this triple insult, the business deal was never completed, although no insult was intended. The American returned home wondering what went wrong.

Finally, communication is receiver-oriented. Ultimately, it is the person who assigns meaning who determines the outcome of the communication situation. That is, the Saudi businessman who misinterpreted the American's messages determined the outcome of the interaction—he never signed the contract. It didn't matter that the American didn't intend this outcome. Similarly, if someone interprets your messages as prejudicial or sexist or negative, those interpretations have much more influence over future interactions than does your intended meaning. What can you do when people interpret your communication in ways you don't intend? First, you need to realize that there is a possibility, particularly in intercultural encounters, that you will be misunderstood. To check whether others are understanding you, you can paraphrase or ask questions ("What did you think I meant?"), or you can observe closely to see if others are giving nonverbal cues that they are misinterpreting your messages. We'll address this issue of how to communicate more effectively throughout this textbook.

Info Bites

By 2008, the top five Internet languages were English, Chinese, Spanish, Japanese, and French. The top five countries with the highest Internet usage were China, the United States, Japan, India, and Germany. Think about the differences in online communication and the influence it brings to our daily communication. Do you visit websites in a language other than your own? (Source: http://www.internetworldstats.com/stats7.htm)

CULTURE AND COMMUNICATION

Communication, Cultural Worldviews, and Values

As already noted, culture influences communication. All cultural groups influence the ways in which their members experience and perceive the world. Members of a culture create a worldview, which, in turn, influences communication. For Judith, growing up in an Amish/Mennonite culture meant that she thought war was absolutely wrong. Tom, growing up in an Asian American, academic family, did not share that particular perception but learned other values.

Values, you will recall, have to do with what is judged to be good or bad, or right or wrong. They are deeply felt beliefs that are shared by a cultural group and that reflect a perception of what ought to be, not what is. Equality, for example, is a value shared by many people in the United States. It is a belief that all humans are created equal, even though we acknowledge that in reality there are many disparities, such as in talent, looks, and access to material goods. Collectively, the values of a cultural group represent a **worldview,** a particular way of looking at the world. Table 2.2 highlights some interesting cultural patterns from around the world. How do these cultural patterns reflect cultural values? Let's look more closely at specific conceptions of values.

Kluckhohn and Strodtbeck's Value Orientation   To more fully explain the concept of values, two anthropologists, Fred Strodtbeck and Florence Kluckhohn, studied how the cultural values of Hispanics, Native Americans, and European

Info Bites

In order to communicate effectively in another culture, people need to understand that a culture's worldview affects every aspect of its communication style. Here are some tips to improve intercultural communication competence with the French. French people do not smile frequently because they are reserved in terms of using facial expressions. French people are more prone to interrupt and engage the speaker in a dialogue or debate because they think this type of relationship creates a greater exchange of ideas. For more information, visit http://fits.depauw.edu/mkfinney/culturale resumes/france/new france/improve.htm.

TABLE 2.2 Interesting Cultural Patterns

Ireland: Irish are very proud of their histories.

Jordan: People are proud of their Arab heritage and are tremendously hospitable to their guests.

Fiji: Time is informal and it may be acceptable to arrive quite late.

Singapore: Punctuality for meetings is expected.

Egypt: Building trust is the most important aspect of any relationship. You should try to engage in extended conversation and coffee before starting a meeting.

Turkey: When you are doing business with Turks, it is important to deal with the person who has the most authority.

Mexico: "Mañana" (putting off a task until tomorrow) is a prevalent norm. This does not indicate Mexicans are lazy, but shows that their pace is more relaxed than in other places.

Tahiti: It is polite to taste a little bit of every food offered with your fingers in a Tahitian's home.

Source: Selling Destinations: Geography for the Travel Professional, 4th ed., by M. Mancini, 2003, Clifton Park, NY: Thomson/Delmar Learning.

Americans differ.[13] They suggested that members of all cultural groups must answer these important questions:

- What is human nature?
- What is the relationship between humans and nature?
- What is the relationship between humans?
- What is the preferred personality?
- What is the orientation toward time?

There are three possible responses to each question, and each cultural group has one or possibly two preferred responses. The range of answers to these questions is shown in Table 2.3. It is important to remember that value orientations are deeply held beliefs about the way the world should be, and not necessarily the way it is. These questions and responses help us understand broad cultural differences among various cultural groups—national groups, ethnic groups, and groups based on gender, class, and so on.

The Nature of Human Nature   As shown in Table 2.3, there are three "solutions." The solution to the issue of human nature is related to dominant religious and legal practices. One solution is a belief in the basic goodness of human nature. Legal systems in a society holding this orientation would emphasize rehabilitating those who violate the law; jails would be seen as places to train violators to rejoin society as contributing citizens. Some religions, such as Buddhism and Confucianism, focus on the perceived natural goodness of humans.

A second solution involves a combination of goodness and evil in human nature. We could argue that many groups within the United States hold to this orientation and that there has been a shift in this value orientation in the past 50 years.

TABLE 2.3 Value Orientation

	RANGE OF VALUES		
Human Nature	Basically good	Mixture of good and evil	Basically evil
Relationship between Humans and Nature	Humans dominate	Harmony between the two	Nature dominates
Relationships between Humans	Individual	Group-oriented	Collateral
Preferred Personality	"Doing": stress on action	"Growing": stress on spiritual growth	"Being": stress on who you are
Time Orientation	Future-oriented	Present-oriented	Past-oriented

Source: Adapted from *Variations in Value Orientations,* by F. Kluckhohn and F. Strodtbeck, 1961, Chicago: Row & Peterson.

In terms of religious beliefs, there is less emphasis on the fundamental evil of humanity than in, say, colonial America. However, with regard to the criminal justice system, there seems to be an increasing emphasis on incarceration and punishment ("three strikes" legislation) and less talk about rehabilitation and reform. The United States currently has a higher proportion of citizens incarcerated than any other Western nation.

According to a third solution, humans are essentially evil. Societies holding to this orientation would more likely punish criminals than rehabilitate them. For example, the strict laws and codes of Islam seem to reflect this orientation toward human nature, as do some forms of Christianity. While he lived in Belgium, Tom was particularly struck by the images of punishment and torture on display in the Counts of Flanders Castle in Ghent. He often wondered if he would better understand these cultural practices if he accepted the Christian view of humanity as essentially evil and born with sin.

The Relationship between Humans and Nature   In most of U.S. society, humans seem to dominate nature. For example, clouds are seeded in an attempt to bring rain. Rivers are rerouted and dammed to make way for human settlement, to form lakes for recreation, and to provide power. Conception is controlled by drugs and birth control devices. Of course, not everyone in the United States agrees that humans should dominate nature. Conflicts between environmentalists and land developers often center on disagreements over this value orientation. For example, there is an ongoing debate in Arizona between astronomers who want to build more telescopes on Mount Lemon (near Tucson) for scientific exploration and environmentalists who want to block construction in order to protect a rare species of squirrel.

By contrast, in a society that emphasizes the domination of nature over humans, families may be more accepting of the number of children that are born naturally. There is less intervention in processes of nature and fewer attempts to control what is seen as the natural order. An example might be people who live in floodplains; they often face floods and devastation, but they accept that relationship with nature. The same can be said of some people in the United States who keep repairing homes built too close to flooding rivers.

Many Native American groups, and also the Japanese, believe in the value of humans living in harmony with nature, rather than one dominating the other. Some Native Americans even consider living animals to be their brothers or sisters. In this value orientation, nature is respected and plays an important role in the spiritual and religious life of the community. Thus, for example, a hawk may be considered a messenger that guides humans in decision making and brings messages from God. And some societies, including many Arab cultural groups, emphasize aspects of both harmony with and domination of nature.

The Relationship between Humans   As the example of Ann and her Mexican friends showed, some cultural groups value individualism, while others are more group-oriented and value collectivism. **Individualism,** a key European American

Surf's Up!

Could it be possible for people in various countries to develop a similar system of cultural values? See what efforts UNESCO is making through its Universal Ethics Project (www.unesco.or.kr/front/business/asianvalues/yersu_kim.htm). The website notes, "In a multipolar world of heightened individualism and a possibly unprecedented splintering of perceptions, it is more than ever necessary to look for the acknowledgment, or rather the emergence of a common substratum of values which would make economically, ecologically, socially and culturally viable coexistence possible on a world-scale."

(and Canadian and Australian) value, places importance on the individual rather than the family or work team or other group. By contrast, people from more collectivist societies—such as those of Central and South America, many Arab groups, and the Amish and some Chicano and Native American communities in the United States—place a great deal of importance on extended families. For example, many collectivists believe that after children leave home they should still be in frequent contact with parents. This family bond extends even to in-laws. In some collectivist countries, like China, when you marry, you are expected to call your spouse's parents "mom" and "dad" and respect them as if they were your own parents. This stands in contrast to many people's attitudes in the United States. A Yugoslav student comments:

> When I told my friends that my grandmother from Yugoslavia was going to visit my family for a couple of months, the only person who thought that was great was my Chinese friend. All my other (American) friends felt bad for my mother because she had to deal with her mother-in-law for a couple of months.

Some collectivist cultural groups share a collateral value, a connection to ancestors even after they are no longer living. While relatives may be dead, they are believed to influence present-day relationships and family relationships continue. During the *Dia de los Muertos* (Day of the Dead) celebrations at the beginning of November, many Mexicans and Mexican-American families visit the gravesites of deceased relatives and communicate concerns and events of the past year, often through humorous stories, remembering and honoring family members who have died. The Vietnamese similarly revere their departed ancestors. As scholar Lana Lebozec describes it:

> They believe that those souls will never be destroyed and their ancestors will continue to watch over them; so, unless they give due respect to the dead, through the offering of foods and paper money, during the special family events, such as births, weddings, funerals, anniversaries, etc., their lives will be unfavorably influenced. . . . On the anniversary of the ancestor's death, everyone in the family is expected to be present . . . through family offerings, the ancestors are kept informed of any events of the family.[14]

Values may also be related to economic class or rural/urban distinctions. In the United States, for example, working-class people may be more collectively oriented than members of the middle or upper classes, given that working-class people reportedly give a higher percentage of their time and money to helping others.

These cultural values may influence how people communicate. For example, people who value individualism tend to value more direct forms of communication and conflict resolution. People in collectivist societies may employ less direct communication and more avoidance-style conflict resolution. For example, a Japanese student describes how her less direct Japanese style conflicts sometimes with the more direct U.S. communication style:

When I was talking with an American friend, he pointed out that I nodded too much during our conversations and didn't respond to him verbally. That's because when Japanese listen, they nod a lot to show that they are paying attention and being good listeners. My American friend told me that during conversations, Americans would rather ask questions, respond verbally, and say something instead of nodding quietly to show that they're listening. Even though I know it, it is hard for me to change my behavior.

It is important to remember that people may belong to cultural groups that hold contradictory values. For example, most work contexts in the United States require highly individualistic behavior, which may conflict with a more collectivist family/ethnic background. Some workers may find it hard to live with these competing values. For example, Phyllencia, a Navajo student, told us that she often feels a conflict between her more family-oriented life at home and the individualistic life expected of college students. She's expected to return home to participate in family and community activities; but she feels torn because she knows she'll be penalized for missing classes and not submitting schoolwork. Many students like Phyllencia, who live "between" two cultures, struggle to meet the demands of both cultures—meeting as many family and cultural obligations as possible while still succeeding in the academic and work worlds. This bicultural existence is akin to swinging on a trapeze. We'll talk more about bicultural identities in Chapter 4.

The Preferred Personality   The most common form of activity in the United States seems to involve a "doing" orientation. Thus, being productive and keeping busy are highly valued in many contexts—for example, in the workplace, most employees have to document what they "do" (number of sales made, number of clients seen, and so on). The highest status is usually given to those who "do" (sports figures, performers, physicians, lawyers) rather than those who mostly "think" (philosophers, priests, scholars).

By contrast, a "growing" orientation places importance on the spiritual aspects of life. This orientation seems to be less common than the other two; the main practitioners are Zen Buddhists. Some societies, such as Japan, are said to combine a doing and a growing orientation, emphasizing both action and spiritual growing.

A final orientation revolves around "being." In this process of self-actualization, "peak experiences," in which the individual is fused with the experience, are most important. This orientation can be found in Central and South America, and in Greek and Spanish cultural groups. For example, one of our Spanish students told us that his mother worked for an American company in Spain. The company was behind in production and asked the employees to work overtime, offering a good bonus as an incentive. The company was surprised when all the employees turned it down, saying they would rather have their usual five weeks of summer vacation than the additional money. This illustrates a being value orientation, whereby it is more important to spend time interacting with family and friends than to work (doing) for financial gain.

Surf's Up!

If culture is sometimes about making spaces to resist the dominant culture, Native American cultures are good examples of this. A website that seeks to further this resistance is On This Date in North American Indian History (http://american indian.net). What happened on today's date?

This school, attended by Ulysses S. Grant in the early 1800s, was demolished several years ago. The lack of concern for saving "historical" buildings and areas reflects a U.S. American value system that emphasizes newness and innovation rather than preservation of the old.

Info Bites

Different cultures have different sayings that often reflect their particular values. For example, an Italian proverb says "A closed mouth catches no flies." A Chinese saying goes "A man may dig his grave with his teeth." One Spanish proverb is "Who knows most speaks least." These sayings reflect cultural views on the relative importance of speaking or not speaking. (Source: *Brain Candy Quotations* [http://www.corsinet.com/braincandy/proverb.html])

The Orientation to Time   Most U.S. cultural communities—particularly European American and middle-class ones—seem to emphasize the future. This is evident in practices such as depositing money in retirement accounts that can be recovered only in the distant future and having appointment books that can reach several years into the future. A seeming contradiction is the heavy debt load carried by many Americans, indicating a lack of planning and a desire to live in the present. Perhaps this reflects a sense of optimism about the future, an assumption that things will get better—the future will be "new and improved!" This same optimism about the future can also be seen in the relative lack of concern about saving "historical" buildings and areas. Many old buildings in the United States have been destroyed and replaced with newer—and sometimes less well constructed—buildings, whereas in Europe and South America buildings are constantly being refurbished.

Other societies (Spain, Greece, Mexico) seem to emphasize the importance of the present, recognizing the value of living in the here and now, and the potential of the current moment. Many European societies (France, Germany, Belgium) and Asian societies (Japan, Korea, Indonesia) place a relatively strong emphasis on the past, believing that history has something to contribute to an understanding of contemporary life. And some cultures emphasize the present but also recognize the importance of the past. When Judith was in language school in Mexico, her professors would always answer questions about contemporary society with a story about history. For instance, there were regional elections going on at the time. If students asked about the implications of the campaign platform of one of the candidates, the professors would always answer by describing what had happened in the region 50 or 100 years earlier.

TABLE 2.4 Hofstede Value Orientations

Power Distance
    Low power distance   High power distance
    Less hierarchy better   More hierarchy better

Femininity/Masculinity
    Femininity   Masculinity
    Fewer gender-specific roles   More gender-specific roles
    Value quality of life, support for   Value achievement, ambition,
       unfortunate   acquisition of material goods

Uncertainty Avoidance
    Low uncertainty avoidance   High uncertainty avoidance
    Dislike rules, accept dissent   More extensive rules, limit dissent
    Less formality   More formality

Long-Term/Short-Term Orientation
    Short-term orientation   Long-term orientation
    Truth over virtue   Virtue over truth
    Prefer quick results   Value perseverance and tenacity

Source: Adapted from *Cultures and Organizations: Software of the Mind*, 2nd ed., by G. Hofstede and G. J. Hofstede, 2004, Boston: McGraw-Hill.

Hofstede's Value Dimensions   Dutch social psychologist Geert Hofstede has identified several additional cultural values that help us understand cultural differences: (1) power distance, (2) masculinity/femininity, (3) uncertainty avoidance, and (4) long-term versus short-term orientation to life.[15] (See Table 2.4.) These values also affect communication.

    Power distance refers to the extent to which less powerful members of institutions and organizations within a country expect and accept that power is distributed unequally. Societies that value low power distance (Denmark, Israel, New Zealand) believe that less hierarchy is better and that power should be used only for legitimate purposes. For example, in organizational settings in the United States, the best bosses are those who play down power differences by telling subordinates to call them by their first names, by accepting subordinates' suggestions as important and worthwhile, and so on. By contrast, in societies that value large power distance (Mexico, Philippines, India), boss-subordinate relationships and decision-making processes are more formalized. Thus, bosses are expected to provide answers and to give orders. For example, an American working in India got into trouble when he tried to use an egalitarian approach and let the workers decide how to sequence their work. The workers thought he was insincere and incompetent because he didn't act the way a boss should act in India, and failed to emphasize the status difference between himself and his subordinates.

    The **masculinity/femininity** dimension refers to (1) the degree to which gender-specific roles are valued and (2) the degree to which a cultural group

Pop Culture Spotlight

Do we learn our values through children's stories? Think of what Kluckhohn and Strodtbeck and Hofstede might say about your favorite characters from the universes of Winnie the Pooh, Bugs Bunny, Mickey Mouse, Scooby Doo, Sesame Street, the Muppets, Marvel superheroes, Teenage Mutant Ninja Turtles, and even the Teletubbies, Pokémon, and the Power Rangers.

values "masculine" (achievement, ambition, acquisition of material goods) or "feminine" (quality of life, service to others, nurturance) values. People in Japan, Austria, and Mexico seem to prefer a masculine orientation, expressing a general preference for gender-specific roles. In these countries, certain roles (wage-earner) should be filled by men, and other roles (homemaker, teacher) by women. By contrast, many people in northern Europe (Denmark, Norway, Sweden, the Netherlands) seem to prefer a feminine orientation, reflecting more gender equality and a stronger belief in the importance of quality of life for all. In the United States, we tend to prefer gender-specific roles, though not as rigid as in Japan, Austria, or Mexico; but we also tend toward a masculine orientation, with a high value placed on competition and acquisition.

Uncertainty avoidance describes the degree to which people feel threatened by ambiguous situations and try to ensure certainty by establishing more structure. Relatively weak uncertainty-avoidance societies (Great Britain, Sweden, Ireland, Hong Kong, the United States) share a preference for a reduction of rules and an acceptance of dissent, as well as an increased willingness to take risks. By contrast, strong uncertainty-avoidance societies (Greece, Portugal, Japan) usually prefer more extensive rules and regulations in organizational settings and more consensus concerning goals.

Hofstede acknowledged and adopted the **long-term** (Confucian) **versus short-term orientation** to life, which originally was identified by a group of Asian researchers.[16] This value has to do with a society's search for virtue versus truth. Societies with a short-term orientation (the United States, Canada, Great Britain, the Philippines, Nigeria) are concerned with "possessing" the truth (reflected in Western religions like Judaism, Christianity, and Islam). The emphasis is on quick results in endeavors, and social pressure exists to "keep up with the Joneses" even if it means overspending. Societies with a long-term orientation (China, Hong Kong, Taiwan, Japan, South Korea, Brazil, India) are more concerned with virtue (reflected in Eastern religions like Confucianism, Hinduism, Buddhism, and Shintoism). The emphasis is on perseverance and tenacity in whatever is attempted regardless of how long it takes, as well as on thrift.

Intercultural conflicts often result from differences in value orientations. For example, past-oriented people may feel strongly that it is important to consider how things were done in the past. For them, the past and tradition hold answers. Values often conflict in international assistance projects, such as fertilizing crops or improving infrastructures, in which future-oriented individuals (such as many Americans) may show a lack of respect for traditional ways of doing things. For another example, individualist-oriented people often value direct confrontation to solve problems, while collectivists prefer more nonconfrontative ways. One American student talks about her experience with her roommate:

> One of my college roommates is a girl from South America. I can recall one incident when she was upset with me and instead of confronting me about the problem, she left a note hanging on our bedroom door. It was so irritating to me that she would do that. The girl was very nonconfrontational. She

never told me when she was upset. She probably thought it was better for our relationships if we didn't have confrontation; however, from my individualistic upbringing, I didn't see it that way!

Conflicts may be even more complex when power differentials are factored in. Often, certain values are privileged over others. For example, most U.S. workplaces reward extremely individualistic relationships and "doing" behaviors at the expense of more collaborative, but equally productive, efforts. Individual employees frequently are recognized for achieving the most sales or issuing the most reports, but awards rarely are given for being a good team member or for helping someone else achieve a departmental goal.

Limitations of Value Frameworks While identifying cultural values helps us understand broad cultural differences, it is important to remember that not everyone in a given society holds the dominant value. We shouldn't merely reduce individuals to stereotypes based on these value orientations. After all, not all Amish or Japanese are group-oriented, and not all Americans and Australians are individualistic. While people in small rural communities may be more collectively oriented, or more willing to help their neighbors, we cannot say that all people in big cities ignore those around them.

One of the problems with these and similar cultural frameworks is that they tend to "essentialize" people. In other words, people tend to assume that a particular group characteristic is the essential characteristic of given group members at all times and in all contexts. But this ignores the heterogeneity within any population. For example, one could characterize the current debate about health care in the United States as a struggle between "masculine" and "feminine" value orientations. Some people believe that each person should be able to take care of himself or herself and should be responsible for paying for his or her own medical care. Others, representing a more feminine position, believe that everyone should sacrifice a little for the good of the whole, that everyone should be assured equal access to health care and hospitalization.

Value heterogeneity may be particularly noticeable in a society that is undergoing rapid change. Japan, for example, was defeated militarily and was in economic ruin only 50 years ago. It now has one of the world's strongest economies. This rapid social and economic change influenced traditional values. While many of the older folk in Japan hold to the traditional values of collectivism, giving undying loyalty to their companies and elders, this is not so true of the younger generation. They are moving toward more individualism, showing less loyalty to their families and companies—causing somewhat of a rift between the generations in contemporary Japanese society.[17] This could be compared to the way that the hippie generation of the 1960s altered some of the traditional values held by previous generations.

Although people may differ with respect to specific value orientations, they may hold other value orientations in common. For example, individuals may hold different views on the importance of individual or group loyalty but share

What Do You Think

How many holidays can you name for other cultures? Which culture celebrates "namedays"? Which culture celebrates the *Quinceañera* when a girl enters womanhood? Which culture celebrates *Summerfest*? How does this knowledge about other cultures help us better communicate with their people?

a deep belief in the goodness of human nature and in certain religious observances. While these group-related values tend to be relatively consistent, people are dynamic, and their behavior varies contextually. That is, people may be more or less individualistic or group-oriented depending on the context. For example, both Judith and Tom find that they are more individualistic (more competitive, more self-oriented) in work settings than in family settings.

In this sense, there are no easy lists of behaviors that are key to "successful" intercultural interaction. Instead, it's important to understand the contexts when interacting with Asian Americans, or persons with disabilities, or men or women, for that matter. A trip to the library or Internet research on a particular group may be helpful, but always remember that exceptions can and do occur. The value orientations discussed here are general guidelines, not rigid rules, to help you in your intercultural communication. Your own learning and behavior and experience with others will make a difference in your intercultural experiences.

Communication and Cultural Rituals

What Do You Think?

How do people learn about indigenous cultures? The Alaska Native Knowledge Network (ANKN, www.ankn.uaf.edu/index.html) serves as a resource for compiling and exchanging information concerning the Alaska native knowledge systems and their ways of knowing. They try to preserve and understand the experiences of Alaska natives. What do you know about the aborigines of Australia, Maori of New Zealand, Saami of Scandinavia, native Indians and Hawaiians of America? How might you learn about them?

Even as culture influences communication, communication influences and reinforces culture. This means that the way we communicate in cultural contexts often strengthens our sense of cultural identity. For example, participating in communication rituals such as prayers in a church or synagogue may strengthen our religious identity and sense of belonging to a religious community. Participating in a daily communication greeting ritual ("Hi, how are you?" "Fine, and you?") may strengthen our sense of who we are in our friendship networks.

An example of a communication ritual is the "griping" that takes place among middle-class Israelis. The griping topic in the Israeli ritual usually concerns some event in daily life, such as getting a vehicle emissions test. The purpose of the griping is not to solve the problem but to vent pent-up tensions. By participating in this ritual, Israelis feel more "Israeli"; their communication reinforces their sense of belonging to a cultural group. Like all rituals, the griping ritual follows a predictable sequence: Someone voices a complaint, others comment on the opener, and the griping continues until the end, when everyone sighs and agrees that it is a problem. "It's no joke; things are getting worse all the time," the participants might say. Although individuals belonging to other cultural groups certainly gripe about things, the activity may not be done in this systematic cultural way and may not fill the same function.[18]

Many White, middle-class U.S. residents participate in a similar communication ritual in which people who have a problem often acknowledge the problem and negotiate a solution.[19] These U.S. and Israeli communication rituals are similar in that they both revolve around problems and both provide a means of venting frustrations. However, they are different rituals. Whereas the U.S. ritual holds expectation that some solutions will be presented and discussed, the Israeli ritual focuses more on the venting and complaining. But in its own way, each ritual contributes to a sense of community identity.

There are other examples of how people's communication behavior reinforces their cultural identity and worldviews. For example, in many White working-class communities in the United States, men express their gender roles in many contexts by engaging in conversation with their peers, but not with women or children.[20]

As another example, consider the differences in how people in the United States and Colombia persuade others to do something for them.[21] The pattern in each country reflects and reinforces different value orientations. That is, people in the United States tend to be careful in telling someone what to do in order not to infringe on that person's rights—reflecting a value of individualism. In Bogotá, Colombia, however, with its more collectivistic orientation, giving orders must be negotiated within relationships. There has to be enough *confianza* (respect) or authority (whereby one person is required by the hierarchy to do the other's bidding). A close friend or family member may easily persuade someone else to do something, or a boss may easily give a direct order to a secretary. In each case, there is enough respect or authority to make the persuasion successful.

Communication and Resistance to the Dominant Culture

Another way to look at culture and communication is to think about how people may use their own space to resist the dominant culture. For example, we might study the floating bars in New York City—warehouses where people meet, clandestinely and illegally, for a night or two, exchange money, party, and then disappear. Because the "bar" does not obtain a liquor license or pay taxes, the people are circumventing the system. Similarly, workers often find ways to resist the extreme individualism and competition of the workplace. For example, flight attendants sometimes work together to protect each other from the critical gaze of supervisors. We can interpret these behaviors as resistance to the dominant cultural system.

BUILDING BLOCK 3: CONTEXT

A third building block of intercultural communication is **context**—the physical or social situation in which communication occurs. For example, communication may occur in a classroom, a bar, or a church; the physical characteristics of the setting influence the communication. People communicate differently depending on the context. You probably communicate differently when hanging out with friends than you do when talking with one of your instructors. Context often plays a significant role in determining how we communicate, and the same context may call for different behavior in different cultures. For example, one American student went to Scotland with his father to play golf—in celebration of his high school graduation. He loved to play golf and since Scotland is the birthplace of golf, he was very excited about the trip. When he and his father arrived at the golf club, they were dressed in golf hats and golf spikes, ready to start playing. To their surprise they received no assistance and were eventually asked to leave the building, although they had not yet played the course. Finally they realized that in Scotland, it is rude and not acceptable to wear golf hats or spikes in the clubhouse.

Context may consist of the physical, social, political, and historical structures in which the communication occurs. Consider the controversy over the Calvin Klein underwear ads that use adolescents as models. The controversy takes place in a social context that says that pedophilia is perverse or immoral. This means that any communication that encourages or feeds that behavior or perspective, including advertising, is deemed wrong by the majority of residents. However, pedophilia has not been considered wrong in all societies in all periods of history. To really understand the Calvin Klein ads, we have to know something about the current attitudes toward and meanings attached to pedophilia wherever the ads are displayed.

The political context in which communication occurs includes those forces that attempt to change or retain existing social structures and relations. For example, to understand the acts of protesters who throw blood or red paint on people who wear fur coats, we must consider the political context. In this case, the political context would be the ongoing informal debates about animal rights and animals farmed for their fur. In other countries or in other times, the protesters' communicative act would not make sense or would be interpreted in other ways.

We also need to examine the historical context of communication. For instance, African Americans and Whites in the United States might have more trouble communicating with one another than Whites and Blacks in Europe because the legacy of slavery influences these interactions even today.

BUILDING BLOCK 4: POWER

Power is always present when we communicate with each other although it is not always evident or obvious. We often think of communication between individuals as being between equals, but this is rarely the case. In every society, a social hierarchy exists that gives some groups more power and privilege than others. The groups with the most power determine, to a great extent, the communication system of the entire society.[22] This is certainly true in intercultural communication. For example, straight people often have more power than gays or lesbians, males more power than females, and nondisabled people more power than those with disabilities. Those in power, consciously or unconsciously, create and maintain communication systems that reflect, reinforce, and promote their own ways of thinking and communicating.

There are two types of group-related power. The first involves membership in involuntary groups based on age, ethnicity, gender, physical ability, race, and sexual orientation and is more permanent in nature. The second involves membership in more voluntary groups based on educational background, geographic location, marital status, and socioeconomic status and is more changeable.[23] The key point is that the dominant communication systems ultimately impede others who do not have the same ways of communicating. Arguably, the communication style most valued in college classrooms is a traditional White, middle-class male style—with emphasis on competition (the first person who raises a hand gets to speak)—a style that is not as comfortable for many women and members of minority groups. By contrast, the call-and-response style of African Americans is not the norm in corporate boardrooms or classrooms. However, some hip-hop cultural norms, such as baggy jeans worn low and caps worn backward, have entered American youth culture.

Power also comes from social institutions and the roles people occupy in those institutions. A college is such an institution. For example, in the classroom, there is temporary inequality, with the instructor having more power. He or she sets the course requirements, gives grades, and determines who speaks. In this case, the power rests not with the individual instructor but with the role that he or she is enacting.

Power is not a simple one-way proposition but is dynamic. Students in a classroom, for example, are not powerless; they may assert and negotiate their power. After all, one cannot be a teacher without students. Also, the typical power relationship between instructor and student often is not perpetuated beyond the classroom. There are, however, also issues of power in broader societal contexts. For example, in contemporary society, cosmetics companies have a vested interest in a particular image of female beauty that involves purchasing and using makeup. Advertising encourages women to feel compelled to participate in this cultural definition. But what happens if a woman decides not to buy into this definition? Regardless of her reasons for not participating, other people are likely to interpret her behavior in ways that may not match her own motivation. What her unadorned face communicates is understood against a backdrop of society's definitions—that is, the backdrop developed by the cosmetics industry.

Power in this sense should be thought of in broad terms. Dominant cultural groups attempt to perpetuate their positions of privilege in many ways. For example, one could speculate that the delay in providing assistance to the 2005 Hurricane Katrina victims might be related to the power structures. Many (not all) of the people affected were relatively poor and their voices did not seem to be heard. It is hard to imagine the same thing happening in a White, affluent area. Subordinate groups can resist this domination in many ways, too. For example, cultural groups can use political and legal means to maintain or resist domination. But these are not the only means of invoking power relations. Groups can negotiate their various relations to culture through economic boycotts, strikes, and sit-ins. Individuals can subscribe or not subscribe to specific magazines or newspapers, change TV channels, write letters to government officials, or take other action to influence power relations. For example, the European clothing distributor Benetton recently launched an ad campaign showing women with scarred breasts. The purpose was to draw attention to the problem of breast cancer. However, some advertisers found the ads offensive and refused to display them, in this way resisting the advertisements.

The disempowered may negotiate power in many ways. Employees in a large institution, for example, can reposition themselves to gain power. Or students might sign their advisors' signatures on their registration schedules if they don't have time to see their advisors or their advisors didn't have time for them.

Surf's Up!

How globally literate are you? Do you know where the show *Ugly Betty* originated? How about how many major military conflicts are going on in the world today? Take *Newsweek*'s globlal literacy quiz at: www .newsweek.com/id/ 143584.

Power is complex, especially in relation to institutions or the social structure. Some inequities, such as those involving gender, class, or race, are more rigid than those resulting from temporary roles like student or teacher. The power relations between student and teacher, for example, are more complex if the teacher is a woman challenged by male students. In short, we really can't understand intercultural communication without considering the power dynamics in the interaction.

BARRIERS TO INTERCULTURAL COMMUNICATION

Ethnocentrism

Ethnocentrism is the belief that one's own cultural group—usually equated with nationality—is superior to all other cultural groups. Believing that one's own country and culture are good is not bad in itself. After all, it is necessary to believe in one's country and group in order to pass along the values that are seen as important. One interesting place to see ethnocentrism is in world maps produced in different places. Most show their own country and culture centered in the middle of the world. One Chinese teaching assistant reported:

> When I asked my students to draw a world map in one intercultural communication class, we were all amazed to see that everybody started from different places. American students started from the map of the United States, Mexican students started from Mexico, and Chinese students

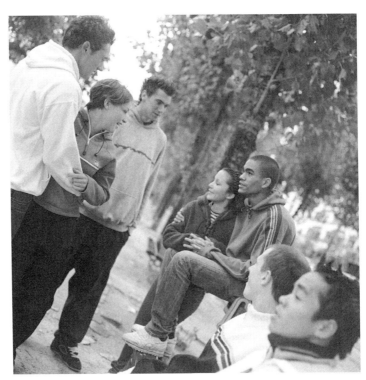

Intercultural communication may involve groups whose members differ in terms of gender, age, ethnicity, and physical ability, among other things.

started from China. Students are often confused about the locations of other countries or continents, partly because on the maps they are familiar with their own countries are always in the middle!

But ethnocentrism can also be extreme, to the point that one cannot believe that another culture's values are equally good or worthy. Ethnocentrism becomes a barrier when it prevents people from even trying to see another's point of view, through another's "prescription lens."

It can be very difficult to see our own ethnocentrism. Often, we see it best when we spend extended time in another cultural group. One of our students, Sara, described her realization of her own ethnocentrism:

> When I was 22 years old, I joined the Peace Corps and lived for two years in a remote, rural part of West Africa. I experienced first-hand a culture that was so entirely different from my own and yet had its own sensible, internal logic, that the complacency and arrogance of my U.S. American ethnocentrism was shaken to its core. I came to realize not only that other societies had valid worldviews and important wisdom but that it would take a special kind of attention to take in and understand these other ways of seeing the world.

Learning to see her own ethnocentrism helped Sara to be more receptive to learning about other cultures and to be more curious about other people's ways of living and experiencing the world.

Stereotyping

Another barrier to intercultural communication is stereotypes, which develop as part of our everyday thought processes. In order to make sense out of the overwhelming amount of information we receive every day, we categorize and generalize from this information. **Stereotypes** "are widely held beliefs about a group of people" and are a form of generalization—a way of categorizing and processing information we receive about others in our daily life. For example, Tom and Judith hold some generalizations about students. We assume that students don't want to study too much but that they want to know what will be on the tests we give. These generalizations, or mental shortcuts, help us know how to interact with students. However, generalizations become potentially harmful stereotypes when they are held rigidly. Thus, if we thought that all students were lazy or unwilling to study on their own, and we interacted with students based on this belief, we would hold a negative stereotype. A Korean student encountered negative stereotypes while shopping with his wife:

> My wife and I went to a shopping mall to buy some cosmetics. After comparing several products, my wife decided to buy a brand which is kind of expensive. When she went to pay for the cosmetic, the salesclerk saw our Asian faces and we also probably looked like students. She said, "You can't buy this. This is over one hundred dollars." We bought the lotion but did not want to return to her counter again. She communicated her negative stereotypes of Asian people and especially Asian students—as being very poor.

Surf's Up!

Discriminatory practices often go unnoticed by those who are responsible for them. We tend to perceive ourselves as fair, good-hearted human beings, unaware that there are hidden biases ingrained in us based on our cultural upbringing or socialization. Our cultural biases may be based on such factors as religion, race, class, gender, sexual orientation, age, disability, or even body image. Test yourself to explore your hidden biases, and reflect on what you can do to fight hate and prejudice in society (www.tolerance.org /hidden_bias).

Stereotypes also may be positive. For example, some people hold the stereotype that all attractive people are also smart and socially skilled. Even positive stereotypes can cause problems for those stereotyped. Attractive individuals may feel excessive pressure to fit the stereotype that they are competent at something they're not, or they may be hired on the basis of their appearance and then find out they cannot do the job.

Why do we hold stereotypes? One reason is that stereotypes help us know what to expect from and how to react to others. However, stereotypes, once adopted, are not easily discarded. In fact, people tend to remember information that supports a stereotype and to not retain information that contradicts the stereotype.

We pick up stereotypes in different ways. The media, for example, tend to portray cultural groups in stereotypic ways—for example, older people as needing help, or Asian Americans or African Americans as followers or background figures for Whites. Sometimes stereotypes persist because the media choose to not pass along information that would contradict stereotypes. Consider the many recent stereotypes about Muslim people and their religion of Islam. Western portrayals of Islam often omit the fact that Judaism, Christianity, and Islam are closely related—called "the three sisters of Abrahamic religions" by theologians. All three religions are monotheistic and absolutists (in contrast to the Asian religions that have many gods and are more relative in their dictates about right and wrong). Both Islam and Christianity accept Jesus as the messiah, accept the virgin birth, and recognize Jesus's sacred mission on earth—in contrast to Judaism. However in other aspects, Islam and Judaism are closer; for example, they emphasize a God of justice rather than love, hold to dietary laws, and require male circumcision.[24]

Other stereotypes portray Muslims as sexist and violent. The stereotype of Muslim women in Western media is usually drawn from a small minority of Muslim societies and does not represent the vast majority of Muslim people. The media neglect to tell us that when Canada had its first female prime minister, three different Muslim countries already had female prime ministers and one also had a woman leader of the opposition. Pakistan, Turkey, and Bangladesh have had women as chief executives, whereas the United States has had no woman president, Australia no woman prime minister, and Russia no woman president.

What about stereotypes of Islam and violence? It might depend on how we look at peace and violence. Consider Tehran, a city of 10 million people, about the size of New York City. Ali Muzrui writes that in the 1990s he often saw women and children picnicking in public parks at 10 P.M. or later. In four different Iranian cities, he observed mothers at night with their children, sometimes without men, walking the streets seemingly without fear of being mugged or sexually assaulted. These are not images we see on American television. The author goes on to explain,

> On the one hand, Iranians are a people capable of collective and purposeful political violence. They have engaged in revolution and war. On the other hand, Iranians seemed to be less prone to petty interpersonal violence such as mugging and rape, than Americans in big cities. . . . Cairo [Egypt] is a

Pop Culture Spotlight

Popular cultural products often deal with stereotypes, prejudice, and discrimination toward another cultural group. Films like *True Lies* (1994) and *The Siege* (1998) depict Middle Easterners as terrorists or extremists. The film *Guess Who* (2005) satirizes the stereotypes about intercultural relationships between U.S. Blacks and Whites. *Brokeback Mountain* (2005) exposes the prejudice and discrimination against the gay population. How do these films influence the way you think of individuals from other cultures? What are the different ways that popular culture deals with stereotypes, prejudice, and discrimination?

city of 15 million people and yet, has only a fraction of the crime rate of Washington, D.C., a much smaller metropolis. Again, much of the explanation is cultural, with Islam playing an important role. By some definitions of *peace*, Islam is a more peaceful tradition than American culture.[25]

We may learn stereotypes in our family. As one young man reported:

So I grew up with my dad particularly being really racist—he didn't really say much about any other group except Black people. The N word was a common word in my family. I knew there was the black side of town, there was the black neighborhood, and then the rest was white, and that's what I grew up in . . . but we never had any personal interactions with anybody from the black neighborhood.[26]

Stereotypes can also develop out of negative experiences. If we have unpleasant contact with certain people, we may generalize that unpleasantness to include all members of that particular group, whatever group characteristic we focus on (race, gender, sexual orientation).

Because stereotypes often operate at an unconscious level and are so persistent, people have to work consciously at rejecting them. This process involves two steps: (1) recognizing the negative stereotypes (we all have them), and (2) obtaining individual information that can counteract the stereotype. For another student, Jenni, an experience working at a homeless shelter helped break some stereotypes. She was amazed at the strength and adaptability of the children who lived there—and then realized that she must have expected something negative. She also realized "that it doesn't matter what race you are, you could end up being down on your luck or homeless. It really broke a stereotype for me personally. As much as I hate to admit it, I always thought of homeless people as lazy and usually not white."

Just as parents can perpetuate stereotypes, they can also help break them. Armstrong Williams, a *Los Angeles Times* reporter, recounts how his father resisted the impulse to stereotype:

My father told us that the men who burned down our farm were not three white men. They were individuals with jealousy and hatred in their hearts. He implored us not to label or stereotype anyone based on the color of their skin.[27]

Prejudice

Prejudice is a negative attitude toward a cultural group based on little or no experience. It is a prejudgment of sorts. Whereas stereotypes tell us what a group is like, prejudice tells us how we are likely to feel about that group. Why are people prejudiced? One answer might be that prejudice fills some social functions.[28]

One such function is the adjustment function, whereby people hold certain prejudices because it may lead to social rewards. People want to be accepted and liked by their cultural groups, and if they need to reject members of another group to do so, then prejudice serves a certain function. Another function is the

Surf's Up!

There are many barriers to intercultural communication. Read the frequently asked questions page *American Misconceptions About Japan* (www.faqs.org/faqs/japan/american misconceptions/). How many of these stereotypes do you believe in?

ego-defensive function, whereby people may hold certain prejudices because they don't want to admit certain things about themselves. For example, an instructor who does not feel successful as a teacher may find it easier to blame students and hold prejudices against them than to admit shortcomings as a teacher. Finally, people hold some prejudices because they help reinforce certain beliefs or values—the value-expressive function. For example, part of belonging to some religious groups might require holding certain prejudices against other religious groups. Our student Ron's family belonged to an evangelical Protestant church. When he was growing up, his parents made disparaging remarks about the Catholic religion. In his family, part of being a good church member meant being prejudiced against Catholics.

Prejudice may also arise from a personal need to feel positive about one's own group and negative about others, or from perceived or real threats.[29] These may be genuine threats that challenge a group's existence or economic/political power, or symbolic threats in the form of intergroup value conflicts and the accompanying anxieties. For example, one of our students from a multicultural family told us about the prejudice that his mother experienced. His mother is a middle-aged White woman and his father is Latino. When his mom was running for superior court judge in a predominantly Hispanic county, she encountered much prejudice because the Latino/a population generally thinks that White officials are not sensitive to the needs of minority populations. They didn't want to vote for a White woman judge since they saw her as a source of the problems facing their people. In addition, if someone has already had negative intercultural contact and is anxious about future contact, particularly if there are inequalities and perceived threats, prejudice likely will develop. This was probably true for the interactions between the residents of a small, largely White community of Lewiston, Maine, and the several thousand Somalis who moved there—for economic opportunities and to escape a brutal civil war in their home country.[30] The influx of almost 2,000 Muslim Somalis into life in French Canadian Catholic Lewiston has not been easy. There have been culture clashes and economic challenges. Some of the White residents saw the Somalis as an economic threat (taking jobs in an already economically depressed area), and some saw the Muslim Somalis as presenting a symbolic threat to their Catholic values. These conditions, combined with the White residents' previously held prejudices and lack of experience with racial diversity, probably reinforced some prejudice toward the Somalis. As one Somali student said, "The Somalis are in the limelight in two ways. They're Muslim, and they're black, which is the hardest position for a person to be in the United States today."[31]

It is also helpful to think about in different kinds of prejudice. The most blatant prejudice is easy to see but is less common today. It is more difficult, however, to pinpoint less obvious forms of prejudice. For example, "tokenism" is a kind of prejudice shown by people who do not want to admit they are prejudiced. They go out of their way to engage in unimportant but positive intergroup behaviors—showing support for other people's programs or making statements like "I'm not prejudiced" to persuade themselves and others that they are not prejudiced.

Pop Culture Spotlight

Bruce Lee was to be the star of the 1970s *Kung Fu* television series. He'd been a famous martial art star and to some extent created the idea for the series. But the producers and network didn't think people would want to see an Asian American hero, so David Carradine got the role. One implication was that the White man knew more about Asian cultures than Asian Americans do.

"Arms-length" prejudice is when people engage in friendly, positive behavior toward members of another group in public and semiformal situations (casual friendships at work, interactions in large social gatherings or at lectures) but avoid closer contact (dating, attending intimate social gatherings).[32]

These subtle yet real forms of prejudice often go hand-in-hand with a **color-blind approach** to intercultural relations. Many of us were taught that the best way to improve race relations was to not notice color, as comments from two students show:

> The message I got from teachers at the school and other people was that the way not to be racist was to just pretend that you don't see any differences between people. And so everyone had feelings about race, but nobody talked, there was no place to talk about those things. And you only have to treat everybody as an individual and everything will be fine.
>
> In my high school class, I asked a question about the Civil rights movement and racism. The answer I got was basically that everything was fine.[33]

Many experts think that this approach is counterproductive to the improvement of U.S. race relations—for many reasons. First, it's not possible. We *do* notice color in the United States and our race and ethnicity is often an important part of our identities. Clarence Page, an African American journalist, remarks: "Too much has been made of the virtue of 'colorblindness.' I don't want Americans to be blind to my color as long as color continues to make a profound difference in determining life chances and opportunities. Nor do I wish to see so significant a part of my identity denied."[34]

Second, a color-blind approach discourages any meaningful conversations about race relations—in our families, schools, churches, and synagogues. Psychologist Beverly Tatum illustrates how White children learn this at an early age:

> A young child asks his mother why the man in the grocery store is so dark. Instead of answering, his mother tells him to be quiet, which tells the child it's not OK to discuss differences.[35]

Third, a color-blind approach allows people to ignore, deny, disregard, and therefore continue to support (actively or passively) the status quo—existence of racial inequalities.[36] It allows blame to be placed on the minorities of lagging economically behind Whites. If discrimination is over, then Blacks' plight is because of their cultural deficiencies (laziness, lack of good values, etc).[37]

Ignoring race and not discussing it will not make problems disappear; as a Yale Law School professor cautions: "to not notice race is to miss one of the central ways in which power, position, and material well-being are distributed in our society."[38]

Like stereotypes, prejudice, once established, is very difficult to undo. Because it operates at a subconscious level (we often aren't really aware of our prejudice), there has to be a very explicit motivation to change our ways of thinking. One Lewiston, Maine, resident explained how she had to examine her own reactions as she was tempted to agree with others' prejudicial statements about Somalis,

Info Bites

A recent report revealed that temporary employment agencies in California show significant preference for White applicants by 3:1 over African Americans in undercover paired tests conducted by the Discrimination Research Center (DRC). By ratios of 4:1 in Los Angeles and more than 2:1 in San Francisco, agencies favored White job applicants over slightly higher qualified African American applicants. African Americans seeking temporary work received less consideration in the form of fewer offers and less desirable jobs. While it may be subtle or unconscious, this preference blocks the path of equal employment opportunity for African Americans.

As examples of preference, the White job applicants were more likely to be

- Offered a temporary or permanent job while the African American partner testers were not.
- Granted an interview while the African Americans were not.

(continued)

Info Bites (cont.)

· Offered a job with a higher salary or for a longer duration.
· Offered a job more quickly than the African American applicants.
· Were not required to follow the standard application procedure, given access to job opportunities that the African American applicants were not.
· Offered coaching on how to present them-selves, not offered to the African American applicants.

To read the full report, visit www.impactfund .org.

such as "They don't speak English. They don't work. They're uneducated." She thought about this, noted that most not only speak English but also speak three or four other languages, and wondered, "Now who's uneducated?" She also recognized that most Somalis worked very hard; they moved to Lewiston because they wanted work and a better life than they had before. Her sister also noted that it took some time and effort to not just unthinkingly adopt the prejudices expressed by those around her. "We were frustrated because we didn't know their culture," she says. "But we asked questions. You have to be able to talk to people."[39]

Discrimination

The behavior that results from stereotyping or prejudice—overt actions to exclude, avoid, or distance oneself from other groups—is called **discrimination.** Discrimination may be based on racism or any of the other "isms" related to belonging to a cultural group (sexism, ageism, elitism). One way of thinking about discrimination is that power plus prejudice equals "ism." That is, if one belongs to a more powerful group and holds prejudices toward another, less powerful group, resulting actions toward members of that group are based on an "ism" and so can be called discrimination.

Discrimination may range from very subtle nonverbal (lack of eye contact, exclusion of someone from a conversation), to verbal insults and exclusion from job or other economic opportunities, to physical violence and systematic elimination of the group, or genocide.

The connection between prejudice and extreme discrimination is closer than you might think. The famous psychologist Gordon Allport showed how, when no one speaks out initially, prejudice against a group of people can develop into scapegoating, which, in turn, can escalate into systematic elimination, or genocide, of a people.[40] This kind of ethnic cleansing has been seen recently in the former Yugoslavia and in Rwanda and Darfur, as well as in Nazi Germany in the 1930s and 1940s. He makes a powerful case for why it is important to speak up whenever we see prejudice or discrimination. **Hate speech** is a partic-ular form of verbal communication that can lead to (or reflect) prejudice and discrimination. It is legally defined as speech that is "intended to degrade, intimidate, or incite violence or prejudicial action against a person or group of people based on their group membership: race, gender, age, ethnicity, nationality, religion, sexual orientation, gender identity, disability, language ability, moral or political views, socioeconomic class, occupation or appearance (such as height, weight, and hair color), mental capacity and any other distinction-liability."[41]

There has been an attempt by some organizations, like universities and col-leges, to ban hate speech based on the assumption that such speech is the first point on Allport's scale, which measures prejudice in a society, and that it ultimately leads to illegal actions (discrimination) against certain groups. Other groups, like the ACLU, assert that forbidding certain types of speech is not the way to go on cam-puses, "where all views are entitled to be heard, explored, supported or refuted." They counter that "when hate is out in the open, people can see the problem.

Then they can organize effectively to counter bad attitudes, possibly change them, and forge solidarity against the forces of intolerance."[42]

Discrimination may be interpersonal, collective, and/or institutional. In recent years, interpersonal racism seems to be much more subtle and indirect but still persistent.[43] Institutionalized or collective discrimination—whereby individuals are systematically denied equal participation or rights in informal and formal ways—also persists. Sometimes institutional discrimination is very blatant. Consider, for example, the case of supervisors at a hospital outside Philadelphia who violated their antidiscrimination policy when they barred all African American employees from entering a patient's room. The White patient's husband had demanded that no Black employees assist in the delivery of her child.[44] Sometimes it is less blatant and only revealed after systematic study. For example, recently the U.S. Justice Department found that Black, Latino/a, and White motorists are equally likely to be pulled over by police, but Blacks and Latinos/as are much more likely to be searched, handcuffed, arrested, and subjected to force or the threat of it. Handcuffs were used on higher percentages of Black (6.4 percent), and Latino/a motorists (5.6 percent) than White (2 percent). Also, Blacks (2.7 percent) and Latinos/as (2.4 percent) were far more likely than Whites (0.8 percent) to report that police used force or the threat of force.[45]

A more frequent example of discrimination occurs in the hiring process. Consider the following scenario. Two men apply for a low-paying, entry-level job. One man is White and admits to having served 18 months in prison for possession of cocaine with intent to sell. The other is Black and has no criminal record. Which man is more likely to get called back? In a carefully crafted experiment in which college students posed as job applicants visiting 350 employers, the White ex-con was called back 17 percent of the time and the crime-free Black applicant only 14 percent of the time. This shows a graphic example of discrimination in the United States: the disadvantage carried by a young Black man applying for a job as a dishwasher or a driver is equivalent to forcing a White man to carry an 18-month prison record on his back. The researcher, who won an award for his study, concluded:

> In these low-wage, entry-level markets, race remains a huge barrier. Affirmative action pressures aren't operating here. . . . Employers don't spend a lot of time screening applicants. They want a quick signal whether the applicant seems suitable. Stereotypes among young black men remain so prevalent and so strong that race continues to serve as a major signal of characteristics of which employers are wary.[46]

In another study, researchers responded in writing to help-wanted ads in Chicago and Boston, using names likely to be identified by employers as White or African American. Applicants named Greg Kelly or Emily Walsh were 50 percent more likely to be called for interviews than those named Jamal Jackson or Lakisha Washington. The researchers concluded that having a White-sounding name on an application is worth as much as an extra eight years of work experience. These examples show how easily stereotypes about race can lead to discrimination.[47]

A young White man, Jordon, tells of an experience he had in his early teens:

We were hungry one morning, so we walked over to a donut shop. While in the restaurant, a couple of black kids, a little younger than ourselves, walked in and ordered breakfast themselves. At that time the donut chain was running a promotion for free donuts and coffee. The contest consisted of scratch-off tickets that were given to you for each item that you bought. While eating, I noticed that one of the black kids had apparently won a free donut. However, the lady at the counter refused to give the boy his prize because she said he scratched off a part that he was not supposed to. I went over to him and asked what was going on. After he explained what happened, he asked if I would try to redeem his ticket. I agreed but did not think she would accept it from me. To my dismay, they did not even question the ticket. I was totally shocked and outraged that this happened. After we confronted these women and I gave my new buddy the prize, I apologized on the employer's behalf. He said it was no big deal and that this kind of stuff happens to him and his friends all the time.[48]

It is particularly important that young people, like Jordon, understand and actively work to eradicate prejudice, racism, and discrimination. Much of the prejudice is more subtle—though still pervasive—than in earlier generations. At the same time, there has been a rise in violent racial acts committed by young White men. Finally, because of the changing U.S. demographics, young people will have more contact with diverse groups of people than did their parents and grandparents; they will likely have more impact on changing attitudes than older generations.[49]

SUMMARY

In this chapter, we identified and described the four building blocks of intercultural communication: culture, communication, context, and power. Culture can be viewed as learned, shared perceptions and values involving emotions, expressed as behaviors, that are dynamic and heterogeneous. Communication is a symbolic process whereby meaning is shared and negotiated. In addition, communication is dynamic, may be unintentional, and is receiver-oriented. The relationship between culture and communication is complex because (1) culture influences communication, (2) communication reinforces culture, and (3) communication is a way of resisting the dominant culture.

The context—the physical and social setting in which communication occurs, or the larger political, societal, and historical environment—affects that communication. The fourth building block, power, is pervasive and plays an enormous, though often hidden, role in intercultural communication interactions. Power relationships—determined largely by social institutions and roles—influence communication.

We also identified attitudinal and behavioral barriers to intercultural communication. Ethnocentrism is the belief that one's own culture is superior to all others. Stereotyping is the process of rigidly categorizing others; stereotypes may be negative or positive. Prejudice is the negative prejudging of others on the basis of little or no experience. Attitudes like stereotyping and prejudice may lead to behavioral barriers such as discrimination.

Now that we have laid the foundation of our approach to intercultural communication, the next step is to examine the role of history in intercultural communication.

BUILDING INTERCULTURAL SKILLS

1. Become more conscious of the identity groups you belong to, both voluntary and involuntary. Which are most important to you? Also become more conscious of the cultural values of your family. What sayings did your mother and father repeat to you ("Just because so-and-so does something doesn't mean you have to do it too!")? Which values were emphasized and communicated in your family? How do you think these values influenced the way you perceive other cultural groups? How did they influence your communication with others who are different from you?

2. Become more aware of your own communication in intercultural encounters. Think about the message you are sending, verbally and nonverbally. Think about your tone of voice, your posture, your gestures, and your eye contact. Are you sending the messages you want to send?

3. Notice how diverse your friends are. Do you have friends from different age groups? From different ethnic groups? Do you have friends with disabilities? Of both genders? From different socioeconomic classes? Whose first language is not English? Think about why you have or don't have diverse friends and what you can learn from seeing the world through their "prescription lenses."

4. Become more knowledgeable about different cultures by reading local ethnic newspapers and seeing foreign films.

5. Notice how different cultural groups are portrayed in the media. If there are people of color or other minority groups represented, what roles do they play? Major roles? Background? Comic relief?

6. When speaking about other groups, try to use tentative words that don't reflect generalizations—like "generally," or "many times," or "it seems to me," or "in my experience."

7. Practice speaking up when someone tells a joke that is hurtful toward another group. A simple "What do you mean by that?" or "Why is that funny?" or "I really don't think that's very funny" can prod the joketeller into thinking twice about telling racist or sexist jokes around you.

ACTIVITIES

1. *Cultural values:* Look for advertisements in popular newspapers and magazines. Analyze the ads to see if you can identify the societal values that they appeal to.

2. *Cultural groups and communication:* Identify the various cultural groups you belong to, both voluntary and involuntary. Choose two of these groups, and think about each group and your membership in that group. Then try to describe how belonging to that group influences your perceptions. For example, how is your worldview influenced by belonging to your family? By being a female or male? By being Asian American, or White, or an international student? Finally, describe how your communication with others is influenced by your membership in these two groups.

ENDNOTES

1. *Festival au Desert* (2008). Retrieved February 9, 2009 from http://www.festival-au-desert.org/
2. Desert rhythms. (2003, December 28). *The Hindu.* Retrieved from http://www.hinduonnet.com/thehindu/mag/2003/12/28/stories/2003122800440200.htm
3. Thousands march for immigrant rights. (2006, May 1). CNN.com. Retrieved from http://www.cnn.com/2006/US/05/01/immigrant.day/index. html
4. Singer, M. R. (1998). *Perception and identity in intercultural communication.* Yarmouth, ME: Intercultural Press.
5. Hofstede, H. (1997). *Cultures and organizations: Software of the mind* (Rev. ed.). New York: McGraw-Hill, p. 3.
6. Bennett, M. J., & Castiglioni, I. (2004). Embodied ethnocentrism and the feeling of culture. In D. Landis, J. M. Bennett, & M. J. Bennett (Eds.), *Handbook of intercultural training* (3rd ed., pp. 249–265). Thousand Oaks, CA: Sage.
7. Kristjánsdóttir, E. S. (2009). U.S. American student sojourners' lived experience in France: Phenomenological inquiry of cross-cultural adaptation. *Howard Journal of Communications, 20* (2).
8. Gilman, N. (2005, September 14). *What Katrina teaches about the meaning of racism.* Social Science Research Council. Retrieved from http://understandingkatrina.ssrc.org/Gilman/; http://peoplepress.org/reports/pdf/255.pdf
9. Singer (1998).
10. Hall, S. (1992). Cultural studies and its theoretical legacies. In L. Grossberg, C. Nelson, & P. Treichler (Eds.), *Cultural studies* (pp. 277–294). New York: Routledge.
11. Thousands march (2006).
12. House rebuffs court on 10 commandments. (2003, July 31). WorldNetDaily.com. Retrieved from http://www.worldnetdaily.com/news/article.asp?ARTICLE_ID=33843
13. Kluckhohn, F., & Strodtbeck, F. (1961). *Variations in value orientations.* Chicago: Row, Peterson.
14. Lebozec, L. (2001, October 6). *Vietnam: the extended family,* Retrieved October 4, 2008 from http://www.suite101.com/article.cfm/vietnam/81880.
15. Hofstede (1997). Note that Hofstede's research can be criticized. He conducted his initial research only in countries where IBM subsidiaries were located, ignoring many African and Middle Eastern countries in developing his value framework. In addition, his masculine/feminine orientation has been criticized for its stereotypical definitions of masculinity and femininity.
16. Chinese Culture Connection. (1987). Chinese values and the search for culture-free dimensions of culture. *Journal of Cross-Cultural Psychology, 18,* 143–164.
17. Matsumoto, D. (2002). *The new Japan: Debunking seven cultural stereotypes.* Yarmouth, ME: Intercultural Press.
18. Katriel, T. (1990). "Griping" as a verbal ritual in some Israeli discourse. In D. Carbaugh (Ed.), *Cultural communication and intercultural contact* (pp. 99–112). Hillsdale, NJ: Erlbaum.
19. Katriel, T., & Philipsen, G. (1990). What we need is communication: "Communication" as a cultural category in some American speech. In Carbaugh, pp. 77–94.
20. Philipsen, G. (1990). Speaking like a man in "Teamsterville": Culture patterns of role enactment in an urban neighborhood. In Carbaugh, pp. 11–12.

21. Fitch, K. L. (1994). A cross-cultural study of directive sequences and some implications for compliance-gaining research. *Communication Monographs, 61,* 185–209.

22. Orbe, M. O. (1998). *Constructing co-cultural theory: An explication of culture, power, and communication.* Thousand Oaks, CA: Sage.

23. Loden, M., & Rosener, J. B. (1991). *Workforce American! Managing employee diversity as a vital resource.* Homewood, IL: Business One Irwin.

24. Muzrui, A. A. (2001). Historical struggles between Islamic and Christian worldviews: An interpretation. In V. H. Milhouse, M. K. Asante, & P. O. Nwosu (Eds.), *Transcultural realities* (pp. 109–119). Thousand Oaks, CA: Sage.

25. Muzrui (2001), p. 114.

26. Chesler, M. A., Peet, M., & Sevig, T. (2003). Blinded by Whiteness: The development of White college students' racial awareness. In A. W. Doane & E. Bonilla-Silva (Eds.), *White out: The continuing significance of racism* (pp. 215–230). New York: Routledge, p. 222.

27. Mazel, E. (1998). *And don't call me racist: A treasury of quotes on the past, present and future of the color line in America.* Lexington, MA: Argonaut Press, p. 81.

28. Brislin, R. (1999). *Understanding culture's influence on behavior* (2nd ed). Belmont, CA: Wadsworth.

29. Hecht, M. L. (1998). Introduction. In M. L. Hecht (Ed.), *Communicating prejudice* (pp. 3–23). Thousand Oaks, CA: Sage.

30. Taylor, S. (2002, November 26). Diverse people stand united against hatred. *Lewiston Sun Journal.* Retrieved from http://sunjournal.com/story.asp?slg=112602diversity

31. Jones, C. (2003, February 7). Newcomers give old city a look at itself. *USA Today,* p. A13.

32. Brislin (1999).

33. Chesler, Peet, & Sevig (2003), p. 223.

34. Mazel (1998), p. 127.

35. Mazel (1998), p. 130.

36. Ditomaso, N., Parks-Yancy, R., & Post, C. (2003). White views of civil rights: Color blindness and equal opportunity. In Doane & Bonilla-Silva, pp. 189–198; McKinney, K., & Feagin, J. R. (2003). Diverse perspectives on doing antiracism: The younger generation. In Doane & Bonilla-Silva, pp. 233–252.

37. Gallagher, C. A. (2003). Playing the White ethnic card: Using ethnic identity to deny racial discrimination. In Doane & Bonilla-Silva, pp. 145–158.

38. Mazel (1998), p. 126.

39. Jones (2003, February 7).

40. Allport, G. (1970). *The nature of prejudice.* Reading, MA: Addison-Wesley.

41. Hate speech on campus (1994, December 31). American Civil Liberties Union website. Retrieved October 4, 2008 from http://www.aclu.org/studentsrights/expression/12808pub19941231.html

42. Hate speech on campus. (1994).

43. Maluso, D. (1995). Shaking hands with a clenched fist: Interpersonal racism. In B. Lott & D. Maluso (Eds.), *The social psychology of interpersonal discrimination* (pp. 50–79). New York: Guilford Press.

44. Pritchard, O. (2003, October 5). NAACP wants hospital supervisers punished. *The Philadelphia Inquirer.* Retrieved from http://www.philly.com/mld/inquirer/news/local/6928671.htm

45. Sniffin, M. J. (2005, August 24). Racc disparity seen during traffic stops. The Associated Press News Service.

46. Wessel, D. (2003, September 4). Studies suggest potent race bias in hiring. *Wall Street Journal,* p. A2.

47. Wessel (2003, September 4).

48. McKinney & Feagin (2003), p. 247.

49. McKinney & Feagin (2003).

CHAPTER THREE

History and Intercultural Communication

STUDY OBJECTIVES

After reading this chapter, you should be able to:

1. Understand the role of history in intercultural communication interactions. Describe some of the histories that influence our communication.

2. Explain the importance of "nonmainstream" histories and their relation to cultural identities. Explain why it is necessary to recover nonmainstream histories.

3. Understand the role of narratives in understanding various histories.

4. Understand the importance of history in contemporary intercultural relations.

5. Explain how diasporic histories influence intercultural interactions.

6. Explain how we can negotiate histories in interactions.

KEY TERMS

colonial histories
cultural group histories
diaspora
diasporic histories
ethnic histories
family histories
gender histories
grand narrative
Homo narrans
intellectual histories

national histories
political histories
postcolonialism
racial histories
religious histories
sexual orientation histories
social histories
socioeconomic class
  histories

I, Liliuokalani of Hawaii, *by the Will of God named heir-apparent on the tenth day of April, A.D. 1877, and by the grace of God Queen of the Hawaiian Islands on the seventeenth day of January, A.D. 1893, do hereby protest against the ratification of a certain treaty, which, so I am informed, has been signed at Washington by Messrs. Hatch, Thurston, and Kinney, purporting to cede those Islands to the territory and dominion of the United States. I declare such a treaty to be an act of wrong toward the native and part-native people of Hawaii, an invasion of the rights of the ruling chiefs, in violation of international rights both toward my people and toward friendly nations with whom they have made treaties, the perpetuation of the fraud whereby the constitutional government was overthrown, and, finally, an act of gross injustice to me.*

—Letter from Queen Liliuokalani to
President William McKinley, June 17, 1897[1]

Info Bites

Currently, numerous groups call for the independence of the Hawaiian state. While the groups seek political sovereignty, a response to years and years of what many call colonial rule, many also call for economic sovereignty. In other words, the groups seek to be less dependent on imports from mainland United States and subsequently gain an economic foothold in the Pacific Rim trade routes.

This is part of a letter written by the Queen of the Kingdom of Hawaii (Hawai'i) to the president of the United States in which she implores him not to allow ratification of a treaty that annexes Hawaii against the will of the native people and the monarchy. We know what happened in this situation. Hawaii today is one of the 50 states. But what does this history have to do with intercultural communication? How does this history play an important role in the cultural identities of those living in Hawaii today? How does this history give rise to a number of groups seeking Hawaiian sovereignty? Different perspectives on this history can sometimes come into conflict, as they have over the legality of the annexation of the Hawaiian islands.

It is not always immediately apparent what history has to do with culture, communication, or intercultural communication. In this chapter, we hope to show you the significance of history in forming cultural identities and in forming intercultural interactions.

The history that we know and our feelings about that history are strongly influenced by our culture. When people from differing cultural backgrounds encounter one another, these differences can form hidden barriers to communication. However, people often overlook this set of dynamics in intercultural communication. Although we typically think of "history" as something contained in history books, an awareness of history is important in understanding intercultural interaction.

History, of course, spans a long, long time. Many events have happened in the past that have created differences among cultural groups and then maintained those differences. It is not always easy to look back and deal with some of these events. Some people ask, "Why do we have to dwell on the past? Can't we all move on?" Other people say that it is impossible to understand them without understanding the history of their cultural group. These different viewpoints certainly can affect the intercultural communication among these people.

On a larger scale, we can see how history influences intercultural interaction in many different contexts. For example, Australia used to have what is often called a "White Australia" policy that guided their immigration restrictions. Australian immigration policy restricted non-Europeans from immigrating until the last of the racial restrictions was lifted in the 1970s.[2] When you imagine an "Australian" today, what do you envision? There are historical reasons why Australia is populated largely by people with European origins. History helps us understand why Australia looks the way it does today. The legacy of White Australia, and attempts to move toward "Multicultural Australia," laid the groundwork for cultural conflict between whites and ethnic minorities that flared up in December 2005. The important point here is that we do not escape history, because decisions made in the past continue to influence us today.

How we view the past directly influences how we view ourselves and others even here in the United States. Think about where you are from and what that might signify. What does it mean to be a midwesterner? A southerner? A Californian? A New Yorker? How do you know what these other regional identities mean, given that people's identities are rooted in different histories? In fact, this is the main theme of this chapter—that history is an important element in the experience of intercultural communication.

As you will see, culture and cultural identities are intimately tied to history, as they have no meaning without history. Yet there is no single version of history; the past has been recorded in many different ways. For example, your family has its own version of its history. Is it important to you to feel positively about who your forebears were and where they came from? We often feel a strong need to identify in positive ways with our past even if we are not interested in history. The stories of the past, accurate or inaccurate, help us understand why our families live where they do, why they own or lost land there, and so on. It helps us understand who we are and why we live and communicate in the ways we do.

In this chapter, we discuss the various histories that provide the contexts in which we communicate: political, intellectual, social, family, national, and cultural group. We then describe how these histories are intertwined with our various identities, based on gender, sexual orientation, ethnicity, race, and so on. Two identities have strong historical bases—diasporic and colonial. We pay particular attention to the role of narrating our personal histories. Finally, we explore how history influences intercultural communication. Throughout this chapter, you should think about the importance of history in constructing your own identity and how the relationship between the past and the present helps us understand different identities for others in different cultural groups.

FROM HISTORY TO HISTORIES

Many different kinds of history influence our understanding of who we are—as individuals, as family members, as members of cultural groups, as citizens of a nation. These histories necessarily overlap and influence one another. For example, think about the history of your family. How has your family history been influenced by your family's membership in certain cultural groups but not others? How has members' nationality been an important part of this history? How does your family history tie into the larger story of U.S. history? Identifying the various historical contexts is the first step in understanding how history affects communication.

Political, Intellectual, and Social Histories

Some people view "history" as only that information contained in documented events. When these types of history focus on political events, we call them **political histories.** Political histories are often the type of history taught in history courses. In these histories we learn about the past through politicians, such as Roman, Chinese, and other emperors, monarchs, as well as presidents and their decisions that helped shape the past. For example, the development of presidential libraries and the study of U.S. presidents focuses our understanding of U.S. history from the political history of the nation. With this focus on history, our attention is drawn to the political history as a way to understand how the United States came to be. When they focus on the transmission and development of ideas or ways of thinking, we call them **intellectual histories.** An intellectual history might trace the development of ideas about the unconscious or democracy. A focus on the history of capitalism points to the ideas that gave rise to this way of viewing the world. While the free exchange of goods for monetary gain had long been practiced, the term, "capitalism," did not emerge until the nineteenth century. An intellectual history would follow the discussions over the definition of "capitalism" and different conceptions of it from Adam Smith's *The Wealth of Nations* to Max Weber's *The Protestant Ethic and the Spirit of Capitalism.* Many of the key concepts in capitalism, such as production, consumption, the invisible hand of the market, and other terms would be traced to their contemporary usage and ideas today as people and governments try to correct the current economic situation. We could trace these ideas to their current expression by U.S. Federal Reserve Chairman Ben Bernanke and U.S. Secretary of the Treasury Tim Geithner, as they struggle with how much government intervention to recommend as they deal with the current financial crisis. And when they provide insight into the everyday life experiences of various groups in the past, we call them **social histories.** Social histories tell us about how we understand the past, but from a focus on the everyday lives of people. In contrast to political or intellectual history, social history draws our attention to the ways that people understood the world in the past. For example, social historians might focus on why eighteenth century French people massacred cats[3] and how they understood the need to do so. Others might focus on the

What Do You Think?

Did you know that Albert Einstein's wife was also a promising physicist? Before meeting Einstein, Mileva Maric was on the track to becoming a scientist of her own accord. She was the fifth woman to attend the ETH, an honored technical institute in Heidelberg, Germany, where she would later meet a younger Albert Einstein. The two were married in 1903 and thus began Einstein's most successful years as a theorist. Their divorce in 1919 marked the end of Einstein's most productive years. Is this mere coincidence? Historians now debate whether Mileva contributed to Albert's theories. How might we think of the history of science differently if we knew that Mileva contributed to Einstein's theories? Why must we consider the gendered dynamics of histories?

social meanings of smell and how they were regulated, constructed, and used.[4] How is smell used today?

This way of organizing and thinking about history may seem more manageable than the broad notion of history as "everything that has happened before now." But many different kinds of history influence our views of and knowledge about the past, and many historical events never get documented. For example, the strict laws that forbade teaching slaves in the United States to read kept many of their stories from being documented. The lack of a written record, of course, does not mean that the people did not exist, that their experiences do not matter, or that their history has no bearing on us. To consider such absent histories requires that we think in more complex ways about the past and the ways it influences the present and the future.

Family Histories

Family histories occur at the same time as other histories but on a more personal level. Often, they are not written down but are passed along orally from one generation to the next. Perhaps surprisingly, some people do not know which countries or cities their families emigrated from, or what tribes they belonged to, or where they lived in the United States. But other people place great emphasis on knowing that, say, their ancestors arrived on the *Mayflower*, or migrated to Utah with Brigham Young, or survived the Holocaust. Many of these family histories are deeply intertwined with ethnic group histories and religious histories, but the family histories identify the family's actual participation in these events. A key issue is whether it is possible or even desirable to escape from the history of one's family.

Sometimes the hidden histories of families are revealed through DNA testing. For Hispanics in the Southwest, DNA testing has helped many realize that they are likely descendants of Marranos (Sephardic Jews) who fled the Inquisition over 400 years ago. Some of these descendants reclaim their Jewish heritage, while others do not. "Modern science may not be shedding new light on the history of the crypto-Jews after molecular anthropologists recently developed a DNA test of the male or Y chromosome that can indicate an ancestral connection to the Cohanim, a priestly class of Jews that traces its origin back more than 3,000 years to Aaron, the older brother of Moses."[5] How might this knowledge about your family change your feelings about who you are? Given the history of the Inquisition with its persecution of Jews, it is clear why people would hide their Jewish identity, but how might people reconnect with Judaism today?

One of our students told us that his family immigrated to the United States from Warsaw, Poland, right before World War II. Because of their experiences there and the perceived anti-Jewish sentiment in Poland, his grandparents immediately quit speaking Polish upon arrival in the United States. Because of this family history, our student today does not speak Polish, as his parents and grandparents did not want to maintain that language in the family. Family histories can be very helpful in explaining who you are.

National Histories

Obviously, the **national history** of any nation—its great events and figures—is important to the people of that nation. U.S. national history typically begins with the arrival of Europeans in North America. U.S. citizens are expected to recognize the great events and the so-called great people (mostly men of European ancestry) who were influential in the development of the country. Thus, students are told stories, verging on myths, that give life to these events and people. For example, they learn about the Founding Fathers—George Washington, Benjamin Franklin, Thomas Jefferson, James Madison, and so on. They learn about Patrick Henry's "Give me liberty or give me death" speech, although the text of the speech was collected by a biographer who "pieced together twelve hundred words from scattered fragments that earwitnesses remembered from twenty years before."[6] And they learn about George Washington chopping down a cherry tree and then confessing his guilt, and about Abraham Lincoln helping to bind the nation's wounds with his stirring Gettysburg Address.

Yet, as you probably already know, traditionally, U.S. history textbooks "leave out anything that might reflect badly upon our national character."[7] They are written for White Americans. In his review of textbooks, James Loewen points to the importance of studying Native American Indian history since it "is the antidote to the pious ethnocentrism of American exceptionalism, the notion that European Americans are God's chosen people. Indian history reveals that the United States and its predecessor British colonies have wrought great harm in the world. We must not forget this—not to wallow in our wrongdoing, but to understand and to learn, that we might not wreak harm again."[8]

National history gives us a shared notion of who we are and solidifies our sense of nationhood. Although we may not personally fit into the national narrative, we are expected to know this particular telling of U.S. history so we can understand the many references used in communication. For example, when people talk about the "13 colonies," we are expected to know that the speaker is not referring to colonies in Africa or Asia. National history simply represents one way of constructing cultural discourses and cultural identities.

Yet U.S. students do not often learn much about the histories of other nations and cultures unless they are studying their languages. As any student of another language knows, it is part of the curriculum to study not only the grammar and vocabulary of the language but also the culture and history of the people who speak that language. Table 3.1 shows some of the name changes that places have undergone. Understanding the history of these places would help you understand why their names have changed.

Judith and Tom both studied French. Because we learned a great deal about French history, we were taught the French national narrative. The French have their own national history, centering on the evolution of France from a monarchy, to a dictatorship, to a republic. For example, French people know that they live in the Cinquième République (or Fifth Republic), and they know what this

TABLE 3.1 Dynamic Country Names

PRESENT NAME	PREVIOUS NAME
Benin	Dahomey
Burkina Faso	Upper Volta
Cambodia	Kampuchea Republic
Ghana	Gold Coast
Hawaii	Sandwich Islands
Iran	Persia
Myanmar	Burma
Québec	New France
Sri Lanka	Ceylon
Taiwan	Formosa

Surf's Up!

How do we investigate historical events such as parades, performances, political rallies, and protests? Moreover, how do we study these histories without actually participating in the events? The Hemispheric Institute, a group committed to making the political and social activities of the Americas accessible to publics, is working to answer these questions by electronically archiving key documents, videos, sound recordings, and photos of such events in Central, North, and South America. To view Cuban dance or to watch Tepeyac Television Service, a television project created by Mexican immigrant workers in New York City, go to http://hemi.nyu.edu/.

means within the grand narrative of French history. This history helps French citizens comprehend what it means to be French, as well as their country's relationships with other nations.

Cultural Group Histories

Although people may share a single national history, each cultural group within the nation may have its own history. The history may be hidden, but it also is related to the national history. These **cultural group histories** help us understand the identity of the group.

Consider, for example, the expulsion in the 1750s of many French-speaking Acadians from eastern Canada and their migration to Louisiana. These historical events are central to understanding the cultural traits of the Cajuns. For example, the popular saying "Laissez les bons temps roulez!" (Let the good times roll!) is spoken in French because of this history. The forced removal in 1838 of the Cherokees from their former nation, New Echota (located mostly in Georgia), to settlements in what eventually became the state of Oklahoma resulted in the death of one-fifth of the Cherokee population. This event, known as the Trail of Tears, explains much about the Cherokee Nation, including the split between the eastern and western Cherokees. The northward migration of African Americans in the early twentieth century helps us understand the settlement patterns and working conditions in northern cities like Cleveland, Detroit, Chicago, and New York. These cultural histories are not typically included in our national history, but they are important in the development of group identities, family histories, and the contemporary lives of individual members of these cocultures.

In this sense, history represents the many stories we tell about the past, rather than one ongoing story on a singular time continuum. Certainly, the events of families, cultural groups, and nations are related; even world events are

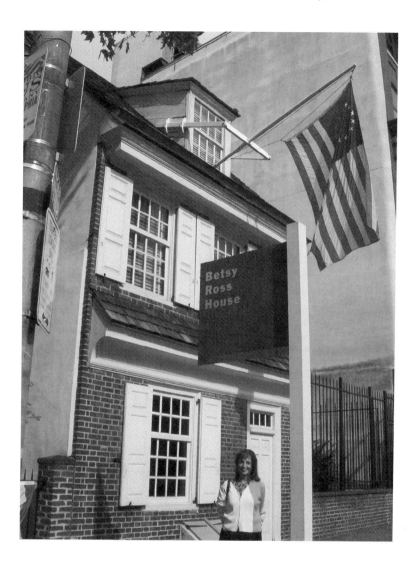

The Betsy Ross House in Philadelphia points to the importance of Ross's contributions to our national identity. She is often portrayed as the woman who created the first flag of the United States. What cultural myths do we tell ourselves about her? Pictured in front of the house is communication professor Roseann Mandziuk of Texas State University—San Marcos.

related. Ignorance of the histories of other groups makes intercultural communication more difficult and fraught with potential misunderstandings.

The Power of Other Histories

The past is very complex and people have attempted to understand history in a way that helps to make sense of this complexity. In order to do so, many cultures developed what is called a **"grand narrative"** to explain the past and, in part, the future. By telling a particular story about the past, the grand narrative brings coherence to everything that has happened before now. Some Christians, for example, believe in a more traditional narrative about the past that begins with

Adam and Eve. All history and all events are guided by our relationship with God. For Enlightenment historians, reliance on human reason and rational thought, society would progress morally, ethically, socially into the future. For Marxist historians, the past is explained by economics and class differences. There are many other ways to understand the past. And we can read the story of the past through any of these lenses to make sense of everything that has happened.

Many U.S. Americans were taught a particular grand narrative in which the founding fathers built a great nation that is based upon key principles, such as equality and freedom. The destiny of the nation was to move further west and expand into a great nation. The celebration of "American exceptionalism" and the upward trajectory of the United States, economically, socially, and geographically, is the grand narrative of this country. This grand narrative gives U.S. Americans a particular identity that is important to their notion of what it means to be an "American."

Since then, many other stories have arisen that have challenged the grand narrative. The traditional grand narrative left out many stories of the United States that did not demonstrate the values of equality and freedom. These other narratives have not necessarily displaced the grand narrative as much as they have created a more complex picture of the past. There are now many competing stories of the past.[9]

In place of the grand narrative are revised and restored histories that had been suppressed, hidden, or erased. The cultural movements that make this shift possible empower other cultural identities and enable the rewriting of the history of U.S. colonialism, slavery, immigration laws, and so on. Recovering various histories is necessary to rethinking what some cultural identities mean. It also helps us rethink the dominant cultural identity—what it means to be an "American."

Regardless of whether we choose to recognize the foundations for many of our differences, these inequalities influence how we think about others and how we interact. They also influence how we think about ourselves—our identities. These are important aspects of intercultural communication. It may seem daunting to confront the history of the world, and, indeed, there are many histories of the world. Nevertheless, the more you know, the better you will be positioned to engage in successful intercultural interactions.

HISTORY AND IDENTITY

In the previous chapter, we saw how individual identities develop. Here, we discuss the development of cultural identities, which is strongly influenced by history.

Histories as Stories

Faced with these many levels of history, you might wonder how we make sense of them in our everyday lives. Although it might be tempting to ignore them all and just pretend to be "ourselves," this belies the substantial influence that history has on our own identities.

Surf's Up!

Visit the History Channel website (www .historychannel.com/). What happened today in history?

According to communication scholar Walter Fisher, telling stories is fundamental to the human experience.[10] Instead of referring to humans as *Homo sapiens*, Fisher prefers to call them **Homo narrans,** because that label underscores the importance of narratives in human life. Histories are stories we use to make sense of who we are and who we think others are. However, it is important to recognize that a strong cultural element sometimes encourages us to try to forget history. As French writer Jean Baudrillard observes, "America was created in the hope of escaping from history, of building a utopia sheltered from history. . . . [It] has in part succeeded in that project, a project it is still pursuing today."[11]

The desire to escape history is significant in what it tells us about how our own culture negotiates its relation to the past and how we view the relation of other nations and cultures to their pasts. By ignoring history, we sometimes come to wrongheaded conclusions about others that reinforce particular stereotypes—for example, that "everybody loves Americans" in spite of many historical reasons they would not. The paradox is that we really cannot escape history even if we fail to recognize it or try to suppress it.

Nonmainstream Histories

For people whose histories are hidden from the mainstream, speaking out is an important step in the construction of personal and cultural identities. Telling our personal narratives offers us an entry into history and an opportunity to reconcile with the events of history. These stories help us understand how others negotiated the cultural attitudes of the past that have relevance for the present. Here, we identify some kinds of history that have the most influence on intercultural interaction.

Religious Histories   Different religious groups have had very different experiences throughout history. **Religious histories** emphasize the role of religions in understanding the past. Religious conflicts between Muslims and Christians have a very long history. This history, even if it is unimportant to some U.S. Americans, can be the cause of intercultural conflict. For example, when President George W. Bush was about to go to war in Iraq, he referred to this war as a "crusade." The use of this term evoked strong negative reactions in the Islamic world, due to the history of the Crusades nearly 1,000 years ago. Even if the Crusades carry little or no historical weight in the United States, this may not be true among other cultural groups around the world. The Crusades are a very important historical event in the religious identity of Muslims. The *Boston Globe* noted the following: "President Bush calls it a 'crusade,' a war against a new kind of evil. But using such a term, loaded with historical baggage about religious wars, could alienate moderate Muslims that the United States needs, some experts caution."[12] While President Bush may not have knowingly wanted to frame the Iraq invasion as a religious war against Muslims, the history of the Crusades may make others feel that it is.

What Do You Think?

Did you know that until 1990 gays and lesbians were legally barred from immigrating to the United States? In her book *Entry Denied: Controlling Sexuality at the Border,* Eithne Luibhéid (2002) explains that while the law changed in 1990, the practice of denying gays and lesbians access still continues. Why do the histories of laws continue well beyond the actual law? Why must we examine legal history to understand the way certain groups are treated in the present? (SOURCE: *Entry Denied: Controlling Sexuality at the Border,* by Eithne Luibhéid, 2002, Minneapolis: University of Minnesota Press)

When Brigham Young, who led the Mormons to Utah, first crossed the Wasatch Mountains and saw the Salt Lake Valley, he proclaimed, "This is the place." Today, a state park and monument mark "the place." This historic site is a significant part of Mormon identity.

Pop Culture Spotlight

In Octavia Butler's *Kindred,* a modern African American woman is mysteriously sent back in time to the 1850s South, where she must learn to adapt to the horrid conditions of slavery to survive. She makes it back to her own time with a new sense of her people's history and struggle. What movies or books have caused you to rethink who you are and where you come from?

For Jewish people, remembering the Holocaust is crucial to their identity. A Jewish colleague recalls growing up in New York City in the 1950s and 1960s and hearing stories of Nazi atrocities. Survivors warned that such atrocities could happen again, that persecution and victimization were always a possibility. Recent attempts by revisionists to deny that the Holocaust happened have been met with fierce opposition and a renewed effort to document that tragedy in grim detail. The Holocaust Museum in Washington, DC, is a memorial to that history for all of us.

Mormons also have experienced a turbulent history. In the early nineteenth century, Mormons were not welcomed in many U.S. communities, moving from New York to Ohio to Illinois, where they founded the town of Nauvoo (Hebrew for "beautiful place"). After the murder of Mormon leader Joseph Smith in 1844, however, Brigham Young decided to take the Mormons west, on what today is known as the Mormon Trek. Eventually, after crossing the pass into the Salt Lake Basin, Young is purported to have claimed, "This is the place!" Without understanding this history, you may not understand why so many Mormons today live in Salt Lake City and elsewhere in Utah.

Religious histories are never isolated; rather, they crisscross other cultural trajectories. Thus, we may feel placed in the role of victim or victimizer by historical events, or even both roles at the same time. Consider, for example, the position of German American Mennonites during World War II. They were punished as pacifists and yet also were seen as aggressors by Jewish Americans. It is often important to see the various ways that these histories make religious differences significant.

Gender Histories   Feminist scholars have long insisted that much of the history of women has been obliterated, marginalized, or erased. **Gender histories** emphasize the importance of gender in understanding the past, particularly the role of women. These histories are important in understanding how we live today, but they are often ignored. Historian Mei Nakano notes:

> The history of women, told by women, is a recent phenomenon. It has called for a fundamental reevaluation of assumptions and principles that govern traditional history. It challenges us to have a more inclusive view of history, not merely the chronicling of events of the past, not dominated by the record of men marching forward through time, their paths strewn with the detritus of war and politics and industry and labor.[13]

Although contemporary scholars are very much interested in women's history, they find it difficult to write that history due to the historical restrictions on women's access to public forums, public documents, and public records. For example, in the United States, women did not obtain the right to vote until 1920, so their participation in the nation's political history was restricted. And the attainment of women's suffrage has not followed the same pattern around the world, as the history of gender has been different in other cultures. For example, in 1893, New Zealand became the first nation to grant women the right to vote. Some nations recognized women's right to vote early in the twentieth century, such as Poland (1918), Mongolia (1924), Turkey (1930), Thailand (1932), Brazil (1934), and France (1944); others were slower to do so, such as Switzerland (1971), Jordan (1974), Iraq (1980), Liechtenstein (1984), and Samoa (1990). Yet women have played significant roles throughout history, even if it is difficult to recover that history.

It is important to note that contemporary life continues to be influenced by gender histories. Traditionally, many women were encouraged to focus on the home and on domestic concerns. Even today, many women in dual-career couples feel tremendous pressure to do the bulk of the housework, reflecting the influence of the past on the present. However, many people are working to overcome these historical legacies.

Sexual Orientation Histories   Interest in the history of sexuality is a fairly recent phenomenon that is beginning to challenge the ways that we think about the past. **Sexual orientation histories** emphasize the significance of sexuality in understanding the past and the present, yet these histories are often overlooked or silenced. If we do not listen to or cannot hear the voices of others, we will miss important historical lessons and create enormous misunderstandings about who we are. For example, Martin Duberman notes that "until recently the official image of the typical American was hysterically suburban: Anglo-Saxon, monogamous, heterosexual parents pair-bonded with two children and two cars—an image as narrow and propagandist as the smiling workers of China saluting the rice fields."[14] To correct this narrow view of the past, he wrote a partial history of gays and lesbians in the United States.

Info Bites

The influence of gender history can be seen in the rates of pay for men and women. In 2004, women's weekly earnings were around 80 percent of men's one year after college. According to the American Association of University Women Education Foundation, this gap grows to 69 percent ten years after college. Additionally, in 2009 the maximum salary for a member of the WNBA is $99,000 versus multi-million dollar contracts within the NBA.

What Do You Think?

In July 2005, two gay teenage boys were executed in Iran, having been accused of homosexuality. Iran has been highly criticized for these human rights violations. In an interview in 2008, Mahmoud Ahmadinejad, president of the Islamic Republic of Iran, said that his country did not have homosexuals like the United States (see www.youtube.com/ watch?v=4_3RUwAJ_MI for a clip of the interview). Contrast the treatment of homosexuals in your country. How has your country's history influenced the treatment of this and other cocultural groups?

The late Guy Hocquenghem, a gay French philosopher, lamented the letting go of the past because that made it difficult to avoid the lessons of history. He once observed: "I am struck by the ignorance among gay people about the past—no, more even than ignorance: the 'will to forget' the German gay holocaust. . . . But we aren't even the only ones who remember, we don't remember! So we find ourselves beginning at zero in each generation."[15]

How we think and what we know about the past contribute to building and maintaining communities and cultural identities. For example, stories of the treatment of gays and lesbians during World War II promote a common history and influence intercultural communication among gays and lesbians in France, Germany, the Netherlands, and other nations. Today, a monument in Amsterdam marks that history, helping to ensure that we remember that gays and lesbians were victims of the Nazi Holocaust as well.

Because these histories are so closely tied to our identities, many U.S. Americans were upset when they read about one historian's book that suggested that Abraham Lincoln may have engaged in same-sex activities.[16] As an important figure in U.S. history, the notion that president Lincoln may have engaged in homosexual relationships challenged many U.S. Americans' idea about their national identity. A writer for the *Christian Post* dismisses the book, noting that "a group of homosexual advocates has been ransacking history, looking for traces of homosexuality in major historical figures. Their agenda is clear—to argue for the normalization of homosexuality by suggesting that some of history's most preeminent figures were actually closeted (or not so closeted) homosexuals."[17] In contrast, commentator Andrew Sullivan chimes in: "The truth about Lincoln—his unusual sexuality, his comfort with male-male love and sex—is not a truth today's Republican leaders want to hear."[18] While we can never know for certain about Lincoln's complete sexual history, it is important to think about what difference it makes whether or not he did engage in homosexual relationships. It is also important to remember that our contemporary rigid categories of "homosexual" and "heterosexual" did not exist in Lincoln's era, so to identify him by these categories does not make sense.

Racial and Ethnic Histories   People from nonmainstream cultural groups often struggle to retain their histories. Theirs are not the histories that everyone learns about in school, yet these histories are vital to understanding how others perceive us, and why. Mainstream history has neither the time nor the space to include all **ethnic** and **racial histories,** which focus on the significance of race and ethnicity in understanding the past. Sometimes, the histories of such cultural groups seem to question, and even undermine, the celebratory nature of a national history.

The history of lynching in the United States reflects the brutality and horrific character of racism. Yet this history continues to return and its use in contemporary politics can raise objections, as in the 2005 election for Detroit's mayor.

A full-page newspaper advertisement depicting black corpses hanging from trees and likening media coverage of Mayor Kwame Kilpatrick to lynching has drawn criticism in the home stretch of his reelection campaign. . . . Detroit is about 80 percent black, and both candidates for mayor are black. But race and the issue of how much the city should cooperate with the surrounding suburbs have come up repeatedly in the campaign.[19]

This racial history can be used again and again to help shape how we view the world. The injustices done by any nation are often swept under the carpet. For example, in her book *The Rape of Nanking*, Iris Chang attempts to recover the history of the atrocities that occurred in the 1937 Japanese attack on Nanking, China—what she calls the "forgotten holocaust."[20] The millions killed in Kampuchea (Cambodia) after the Vietnam War, as well as the millions of Africans killed by European colonists in Africa and South America, are all reminders of the silencing of these histories. For example, the Royal Museum of Central Africa has little to say about the atrocities committed by the Belgians in the Congo.

In the United States, other histories have also been overlooked. In an attempt to bring attention to an understanding of the internment of Japanese Americans during World War II, former English professor John Tateishi collected the stories of some of the internees. He notes at the outset of his book that it "makes no attempt to be a definitive academic history of Japanese American internment. Rather it tries to present for the first time in human and personal terms the experience of the only group of American citizens ever to be confined in concentration camps in the United States."[21]

Although this collection of oral histories is not an academic history, it offers valuable insights into the experience of many Japanese Americans. Because this historical event demonstrates the fragility of the constitutional system and its guarantees in the face of rampant prejudice, it is not often discussed as a significant event in U.S. history. For Japanese Americans, however, it has been the most defining event in the development of their communities.

When Tom's parents meet other Japanese Americans of their generation, they are often asked, "What camp were you in?" This question makes little sense outside its historical context. We can see how this question is embedded in understanding a particular moment in history, a moment that is not widely understood. In the aftermath of that experience of internment, the use of that history as a marker has been important in maintaining cultural identity.

Diasporic Histories The international relationships that many racial and ethnic groups have with others who share their heritage and history often are overlooked in intercultural communication. These international ties may have been created by transnational migrations, slavery, religious crusades, or other historical events and forces. Because most people do not think about the diverse ways that people have connections to other nations and cultures, we consider these histories to be hidden. In his book *The Black Atlantic*, scholar Paul Gilroy emphasizes that, to understand the identities, cultures, and experiences of African descendants in Britain and the United States, we must examine the connections between Africa, North America, and Europe.[22]

What Do You Think?

What kind of history classes should be required in college? Should you take Western Civilization, or should you have the option of learning the history of other regions of the world? What might be the arguments on both sides?

The United States National Slavery Museum will open in Fredericksburg, Virginia. How does understanding the history of slavery help you better understand race relations in the United States? How does this history help us improve intercultural interactions today?

A massive migration, often caused by war, famine, enslavement, or persecution, that results in the dispersal of a unified group is called a **diaspora.** A cultural group (or even an individual) that flees its homeland is likely to bring along some old customs and practices to its new homeland. In fact, diasporic migrations often cause people to cling more strongly to their group's identity. Over the years, though, people become acculturated to some degree in their new homelands.

Consider, for example, the dispersal of eastern European Jews who migrated during or after World War II to the United States, Australia, Argentina, Israel, and other parts of the world. They brought with them their Jewish culture and their eastern European culture. But they also adopted new cultural patterns as they became U.S. Americans, Argentinians, Israelis, and so on. Imagine the communication differences among these people that have evolved over time. Imagine the differences between these groups and the dominant culture of their new homelands.

Diasporic histories help us understand the important cultural connections among people affected by diasporas and other transnational migrations. Yet we must be careful to distinguish between the ways that these connections are helpful or hurtful to intercultural communication. For example, some cultures tend to regard negatively those who have left the homeland. Many Japanese tend to look down on Japanese Canadians, Japanese Americans, Japanese Brazilians, Japanese Mexicans, and Japanese Peruvians. By contrast, the Irish tend not to look down on Irish Americans or Irish Canadians. Of course, we must remember as well that many other intervening factors might influence diasporic relationships on an interpersonal level.

Colonial Histories   As you probably know from history, many nations did not confine themselves within their own borders. Due to overpopulation, limited resources, notions of grandeur, or other factors, many people in recent centuries left their homelands to colonize other lands. It is important to recognize these **colonial histories,** which emphasize the important role of colonialism in understanding the past and its influence on the present, so we can better understand the dynamics of intercultural communication today.

Let's look at the significance of colonialism in determining language. Three of the most important colonizers were Britain, France, and Spain. As a result of colonialism, English is spoken in Canada, Australia, New Zealand, Belize, Nigeria, South Africa, India, Pakistan, Bangladesh, Zimbabwe, Hong Kong, Singapore, and the United States, among other places. French is spoken in Canada, Senegal, Tahiti, Haiti, Benin, Côte d'Ivoire, Niger, Rwanda, Mali, Chad, and the Central African Republic, among other places. And Spanish is spoken in most of the Western Hemisphere, from Mexico to Chile and Argentina, including Cuba, Venezuela, Colombia, and Panama.

Many foreign language textbooks proudly display maps that show the many places around the world where that language is commonly spoken. But the maps don't reveal why those languages are widely spoken in those regions, and they don't reveal the legacies of colonialism in those regions. For example, the United Kingdom maintains close relations with many of its former colonies through the Commonwealth of Britain—an organization of 54 nations, including Britain and its former colonies. The queen of England is also the queen of Canada, Australia, New Zealand, and the Bahamas.

Other languages have been spread through colonialism, including Portuguese in Brazil, Macao, and Angola; Dutch in Angola, Suriname, and Mozambique; and a related Dutch language, Afrikaans, in South Africa. Russian is spoken in the breakaway republics of Kazakhstan, Azerbaijan, and Tajikistan. But many nations have reclaimed their own languages in an effort to resist the influences of colonialism. For example, Arabic is spoken in Algeria, and Vietnamese is spoken in Vietnam; at one time, French was widely spoken in both countries. Today, in the newly independent Latvia, the ability to speak Latvian is a requirement for citizenship.

The reality is, we do not freely choose the languages we speak. Rather, we must learn the languages of the societies into which we are born. Judith and Tom, for example, both speak English, although their ancestors came to the United States from non-English-speaking countries. We did not choose to learn English among all of the languages of the world. Although we don't resent our native tongue, we recognize why many individuals might resent a language imposed on them. Think about the historical forces that led you to speak some language(s) and not others. Understanding history is crucial to understanding the linguistic worlds we inhabit.

The imposition of language is but one aspect of cultural invasion. Much colonial history is a history of oppression and brutality. To cast off the legacy, many people have looked toward **postcolonialism**—an intellectual, political, and cultural movement that calls for the independence of colonized states and

Info Bites

The Constitution and the Declaration of Independence are preserved in the National Archives in Washington, DC. Would you feel differently about your culture and history if someone came and took them away? What do you think happened to the history and cultures of the societies in Africa that had their artifacts taken by the British Museum?

for liberation from colonialist ways of thinking. Postcolonialism is a movement with many different emphases. In struggling with a colonial past, people have devised many ways of confronting that past. Because postcolonialism comes from the critical approach to intercultural communication, "it theorizes not just colonial conditions but why those conditions are what they are, and how they can be undone and redone."[23] It is not simply the study of colonialism, but the study of how we might deal with that past and its aftermath, which may include the ongoing use of the colonial language, culture, and religion. For example, many companies are locating parts of their businesses in India because of the widespread use of English as a former British colony. How should people in India deal with the ongoing dominance of English, the colonizer's language, but also the language of business?

As another example, Hispanics or Latinos/as share a common history of colonization by Spain, whether their families trace their origins to Mexico, Puerto Rico, Cuba, and so on. Although Spain is no longer in political control of these lands, how do those who live in the legacy of this history deal with that history? In what ways does it remain important, as a part of this cultural identity, to embrace the colonizer's language (Spanish)? The colonizer's religion (Catholicism)? And are there other aspects of Spanish culture that continue to be reproduced over and over again? Postcolonialism is not simply a call to make a clean break from that colonial past, but "to examine the violent actions and erasures of colonialism."[24] In this case, that interrogation might even mean reconsidering the category "Hispanic" that incorporates a wide range of groups that share a Spanish colonial history, but do not share other histories that constitute their cultures.

Socioeconomic Class Histories   Many U.S. Americans prefer to ignore class differences, but socioeconomic class has been a significant factor in the way people experienced the past. **Socioeconomic class histories** focus on the role of class in understanding these experiences. While we often overlook the importance of socioeconomic class as a factor in history, socioeconomic class helps explain why many people have immigrated to the United States. The poverty in nineteenth-century Ireland did much to fuel the flight of the Irish to the United States, so that today there are more Irish Americans than Irish.

Yet it is not always the socioeconomically disadvantaged who immigrate. After the Russian Revolution in 1917, a large number of fairly wealthy Russians moved to Paris. Similarly, after the Cuban Revolution in 1959, a large number of fairly wealthy Cubans fled Cuba. Today, Canada's sale of Canadian citizenship to those who can afford the fairly substantial price tag ensures that socioeconomic class will continue to inspire some migrations.

The point here is that these socioeconomic class distinctions often are overlooked in understanding the historical migrations and acculturation of groups around the world. The kinds of locations these migrants settled and the employment they found often were marked by the kinds of capital—cultural and financial—that they were or were not able to bring with them.

INTERCULTURAL COMMUNICATION AND HISTORY

So far, we have examined some interesting ways of thinking about the past and of viewing history. We are often uncomfortable in dealing with the past because we do not know how we should feel about or deal with many of the ugly things that have happened. Think, for example, about the history of the indigenous peoples in the United States. Native peoples throughout most of the United States were exterminated or removed to settlements in other regions, and many states now have few Native Americans and few, if any, reservations. The current residents had nothing to do with the events in their state's history, but they are the beneficiaries through the ownership of farms and other land. So, although contemporary U.S. Americans are not in a position of fault, they are, through these benefits, in a position of responsibility. In *Writing the Disaster*, Maurice Blanchot makes this important distinction between the position of fault and the position of responsibility.[25] Dealing with this past is not easy, but it is even more problematic simply to ignore it, because ignoring the past erases other cultural identities by pretending that we are all the same.

Our lives are entangled in the web of history from which there is no escape, only denial and silence. How should this influence the ways we think about intercultural communication? What does all of this have to do with intercultural interaction? There are various ways that we might think about history and intercultural communication. First, we can think about the ways that history helps us understand who we are—with all of our identities—and how we may feel constrained by those identities. Second, we can examine how various histories are negotiated in intercultural interaction.

Think about how history has determined, for example, what languages you do and do not speak. Many U.S. Americans no longer speak the language(s) of their forebears. Yet, languages may be an attraction or a repellent in intercultural interactions. Many U.S. Americans, for example, enjoy traveling to Britain, Australia, and Canada, where English is spoken. Many U.S. Americans also are hesitant to travel to non-English-speaking countries because of language differences, and popular movies may reinforce these fears.

Also consider what your identity positions mean to you. How do you feel about being an "American," if this is your national identity? How might non-Americans feel about Americans based on their historical knowledge of what U.S. Americans have and have not done to them and for them? Why do some people dislike U.S. Americans? Can you offer the same reflexive analyses of your other identities?

It is important to recognize that your identities—as a member of a racial or ethnic group, a nationality, a socioeconomic class, and so on—do not have the same meanings for you as they might for someone with differing identities. If you are "White," how might your racial identity have a different meaning for you than for someone who is not White? Is there a history to "Whiteness" that gives it different meanings for different groups of people? Conversely, what their identities mean to you may not be the same as what they mean for them.

Popular Culture Spotlight

Do you know the history of the popular 2004 movie *The Terminal* starring Tom Hanks? In a real-life intercultural predicament, Mr. Mehran Karimi Nasseri, an Iranian refugee, has been living in the Paris Charles de Gaulle Airport Terminal One since 1988. Nasseri has been taking showers in airport bathrooms, sleeping on benches, and accepting food vouchers from airport employees, making Terminal One his home. Nasseri finally was given documents to travel in France, but he refuses to use them. He claims that he has no identity so the terminal is the perfect place to live. Is this a typical life history for a refugee?

Not all history is hidden. Here we see an anniversary memorial service at the crash site of Flight 93—held on September 11, 2008. How might this commemoration help us, as U.S. Americans, think about our past?

For example, your notion of "Hawaiian" may differ significantly from that of Hawaiians. Questions about the legality of the overthrow of the Hawaiian monarchy, the Hawaiian sovereignty movement, and the history of the United States in Hawaii may create enormous differences in how these identities function in intercultural interactions.

Second, how can we balance the past and the present in our everyday intercultural interactions? Initially, it is important to recognize that each of us brings our histories (some known, some hidden) to interactions. We can try to evaluate the role that history plays for those with whom we interact. (Many tourist guidebooks offer a brief history of other countries to help tourists prepare for their trip there.)

Also, we should understand the role that histories play in our identities, in what we bring to the interaction. Communication scholar Marsha Houston says there are three things that White people who want to be her friends should never say: "I don't notice you're black," "You're not like the others," and "I know how you feel." In her opinion, each of these denies or rejects a part of her identity that is deeply rooted in history.[26]

Sometimes, it is unwise to ask people where they are "really from." Such questions assume that they cannot be from where they said they were, due to racial characteristics or other apparent features. Although she was born and raised in New York City, Geeta Kothari is often asked where she is from. She writes:

"Where are you from?" The bartender asks this as I get up from my table. It's quiet at the Bloomfield Bridge Tavern, home of the best pirogies in

Pittsburgh. . . . The man has no reason to ask me that question. We are not having a conversation, I am not his friend. Out of the blue, having said no other words to me, he feels that it is okay for him, a white man, to ask me where I am from. The only context for this question is my skin color and his need to classify me. I am sure he doesn't expect me to say New York. I look different, therefore it's assumed that I must be from somewhere, somewhere that isn't here, America. It would never occur to him to ask my boyfriend, who is white—and Canadian—where he's from.[27]

Although it may seem innocent to ask her where she is from, the question implies differences based on racial characteristics between those assumed to be "American" and those assumed to be from somewhere else. Recognizing a person's history and its link to his or her identity, as well as your own historical blinders and assumptions, is a first step toward establishing intercultural relationships.

Historical Legacies

Given these different histories—histories that we have been exposed to and histories that have remained hidden from us—what are the consequences of this past? How have they changed how we live, who we are, and what we hope for the future? We have already discussed how these different histories influence what languages we speak and what languages we do not speak.

At the outset of this chapter, we began with a look at the U.S. annexation of the Hawaiian islands. How does this history influence how we think about Hawaiians and their place in U.S. society? How does this history influence the ways U.S. Americans think about Hawaii and possibly spending a vacation there? In 1978, the State of Hawaii reestablished the Hawaiian language as an official language of Hawaii. How did the Hawaiian language become marginalized on the Hawaiian islands? Can it regain its dominant position again? In 1993, on the 100th anniversary of the overthrow of the Hawaiian monarchy, President Clinton signed a formal apology on behalf of the United States which, in part, "apologizes to Native Hawaiians on behalf of the people of the United States for the overthrow of the Kingdom of Hawaii on January 17, 1893, with the participation of agents and citizens of the United States, and the deprivation of the rights of Native Hawaiians to self-determination."[28] Given the historical legacy that led to statehood for Hawaii, how can the United States correct its past mistakes in taking Hawaii? Should the United States grant independence to Hawaii? Would that solve the historical problems, or is it impossible to return Hawaii to how it might have been without U.S. intervention?

You can probably speculate on these and many more aspects of the legacy of the annexation of Hawaii by the United States. For example, the recent controversy over the birthplace of President Obama would be an entirely different discussion if Hawaii had not been annexed. If Hawaii were still a separate nation, the Kingdom of Hawaii, how would history be different today? If Hawaii does

Iolani Palace in Honolulu, Hawaii, is the only palace on U.S. soil. Although the Kingdom of Hawaii is now the state of Hawaii, debates about the historical events that led to the U.S. annexation of Hawaii continue today. The rise of the Hawaiian sovereignty movement reflects the unhappiness of many Hawaiians with this annexation.

gain its independence from the United States, would that change how people view President Obama? The history of Hawaii continues to be written. President Obama has indicated that he "has pledged to work for a bill to create a process for native Hawaiian self-government, if necessary."[29] Given the current challenges facing his administration, he has not given this bill a high priority. What is important to understand is that the past is not simply over; rather, we should consider all of the ways that the past has constructed how we live in the present and what we think should happen in the future. These are all influences in intercultural interaction and how we think about ourselves and others.

SUMMARY

In this chapter, we explored some of the dimensions of history in intercultural communication. Multiple histories are important for empowering different cultural identities. These include political, intellectual, social, family, national, religious, and cultural group histories.

History is constructed through narrative. Our understanding of the events that occur comes to us through our "telling" of the events. Histories that typically are not conveyed in a widespread manner are considered to be hidden. These include histories based on gender, sexual orientation, race and ethnicity, migration, colonialism, and socioeconomic class. All kinds of histories contribute to the success or failure of intercultural interaction.

We also looked at how history plays a role in intercultural interaction. The key is to balance the past and the present in intercultural encounters. As the controversy over the relationship between the United States and Hawaii shows, history certainly plays a central role in intercultural conflict.

BUILDING INTERCULTURAL SKILLS

1. Reflect on the limitations of your understanding of the past and how some of those histories have been marketed to you. What kinds of history would you want to include in a tourist guidebook for non-Americans who are visiting your state? What would you not include? Why? Whose histories would you include? Think about how history might shape people's understanding of a destination and what they want to see.

2. Think about how some of these histories are important to different people in different ways. Some tourist destinations are marketed based on their historical importance. How might you connect this history with what you expect to see, say, in Tombstone, Arizona; at the Magnolia Plantation in South Carolina; or in Williamsburg, Virginia? Why might some people want to visit the old slave auction block in Fayetteville, North Carolina, or German concentration camps, such as Auschwitz in Poland or Dachau in Germany?

3. Reflect on the history of your family. In what ways does this history connect you with members of some cultural groups and distance you from members of other cultural groups? How has your family history determined your culture—what language(s) you speak, what foods you eat, what holidays you celebrate, and so on?

4. Understand the relationship between identity and history. How does history help you understand who you are? Which kinds of history are most important in your identity? National? Family? Sexual orientation?

5. Develop sensitivity to other people's histories. Aside from "Where are you from?" what questions might strangers ask that can be irritating to some people? Should you know about how history has shaped other cultural group identities? Think about how their histories are intertwined with your histories.

ACTIVITIES

1. *Family history:* Talk to members of your own family to see how they feel about your family's history. Find out, for example, how the family history influences the way they think about who they are. Do they wish they

knew more about your family? What things has your family continued to do that your forebears probably also did? Do you eat some of the same foods? Practice the same religion? Celebrate birthdays or weddings in the same way? Often, the continuity between past and present is taken for granted.

2. *Cultural group history:* Individually or in groups, choose a cultural group in the United States that is unfamiliar to you. Study the history of this group, answering the following questions:

   a. What is the historical relationship between this group and other groups (particularly the dominant cultural groups)?

   b. What are some significant events in the group's history?

   c. Are there any historical incidents of discrimination?

   d. What are common stereotypes about the group, and how did they originate?

   e. Who are important leaders and heroes of the group?

   f. What are some notable achievements of the group?

   g. In what ways does the history of this group influence the identity of group members today?

ENDNOTES

1. Queen Liliuokalani. (1897). *Letter to President McKinley.* Retrieved from http://libweb.hawaii.edu/libdept/hawaiian/annexation/protest/liliu5.html
2. Department of Immigration & Multicultural & Indigenous Affairs, Public Affairs Section, Fact Sheet No. 8, *Abolition of the "White Australia" Policy,* November 6, 2002. Retrieved from http://www.immi.gov.au/facts/08abolition.htm
3. Darnton, R. (1985). *The Great Cat Massacre and other episodes in French cultural history.* New York: Vintage.
4. Corbin, A. (1988). *The Foul and the fragrant: Odor and the French social imagination.* Cambridge, MA: Harvard University Press.
5. Romero, S. (2005, October 29). Hispanics uncovering roots as Inquisition's "hidden" Jews. *The New York Times,* p. A17.
6. Thonssen, L., Baird, A. C., & Braden, W. W. (1970). *Speech criticism* (2nd ed.). New York: Ronald Press, p. 335.
7. Loewen, J. W. (1995). *Lies my teacher told me: Everything your American history textbook got wrong.* New York: Touchstone, p. 13.
8. Loewen (1995), p. 136.
9. Lyotard, J.-F. (1984). *The postmodern condition: A report on knowledge* (G. Bennington & B. Massumi, Trans.). Minneapolis: University of Minnesota Press, p. 37.
10. Fisher, W. (1984). Narration as a human communication paradigm: The case of public moral argument. *Communication Monographs, 51,* 1–22; Fisher, W. (1985). The narrative paradigm: An elaboration. *Communication Monographs, 52,* 347–367.
11. Baudrillard, J. (1988). *America* (C. Turner, Trans.). New York: Verso, p. 80.
12. Buzbee, S. (2001, September 17). Muslims fret over Bush's use of term 'crusade.' *Boston Globe.* Retrieved from http://www.boston.com/news/daily/17/bush_crusade.htm
13. Nakano, M. (1990). *Japanese American women: Three generations, 1890–1990.* Berkeley and San Francisco: Mina Press and National Japanese American Historical Society, p. xiii.
14. Duberman, M. B. (1991). Introduction to first edition (1986). *About time: Exploring the gay past.* New York: Penguin Books, p. xiii.

15. Hocquenghem, G., & Blasius, M. (1980, April). Interview. *Christopher Street, 8*(4), 40.

16. Tripp, C. A. (2005). *The intimate world of Abraham Lincoln.* New York: Free Press.

17. Mohler, R. A., Jr. (2006, February 20). Was Abraham Lincoln gay? Homosexuality and history. *The Christian Post.* Retrieved May 22, 2006, from http://dc.christianpost.com/article/editorial/43/section/was.abraham.lincoln.gay.homosexuality.and.history/1.htm

18. Sullivan, A. (2005, January 12). *Log cabin Republican: How gay was Lincoln?* Retrieved May 22, 2006, from http://www.andrewsullivan.com/main_article.php?artnum=20050112

19. Runk, D. (2005, October 30). "Lynching" ad roils Detroit race: Violent images used to criticize media coverage of mayor. *The Washington Post,* p. A9.

20. Chang, I. (1997). *The rape of Nanking: The forgotten holocaust of World War II.* New York: Basic Books.

21. Tateishi, J. (1984). *And justice for all: An oral history of the Japanese American detention camps.* New York: Random House, p. vii.

22. Gilroy, P. (1993). *The Black Atlantic: Modernity and double consciousness.* New York: Verso.

23. Shome, R., & Hegde, R. (2002). Postcolonial approaches to communication: Charting the terrain, engaging the intersections. *Communication Theory, 12,* 250.

24. Shome & Hegde (2002), p. 250.

25. Blanchot, M. (1986). *The writing of the disaster* (A. Smock, Trans.). Lincoln: University of Nebraska Press.

26. Houston, M. (1997). When Black women talk with White women: Why dialogues are difficult. In A. González, M. Houston, & V. Chen (Eds.), *Our voices: Essays in ethnicity, culture, and communication* (2nd ed., pp. 187–194). Los Angeles: Roxbury.

27. Kothari, G. (1995). Where are you from? In G. Hongo (Ed.), *Under Western eyes: Personal essays from Asian America* (p. 153). New York: Anchor/Doubleday.

28. U.S. Public Law 103-150, 103rd Congress, Joint Resolution 19, November 23, 1993.

29. Camire, D. & Yaukey, J. (2009, February 15). Obama would push Native Hawaiian bill. *The Honolulu Advertiser.* Retrieved March 5, 2009 from: http://www.honoluluadvertiser.com/article/20090215/NEWS21/902150380/1001

Identity and Intercultural Communication

STUDY OBJECTIVES

After reading this chapter, you should be able to:

1. Explain how identities are developed through our communicative interaction with others.

2. Identify some of the ways in which people communicate their identity.

3. Explain how the context of the larger society contributes to the formation of identity.

4. Identify some of the major social and cultural identities that are manifest in our communication.

5. Explain differences in how identities are developed for minority versus majority group members in the United States.

6. Explain identity development of multiracial people.

7. Describe the relationship between identity and language.

KEY TERMS

age identity
class identity
constructive identity
core symbols
culture shock
encapsulated identity
ethnic identity
gender identity
global nomads
hyphenated Americans
identity
intercultural personhood
labels
majority identity development
minority identity development
multicultural identity
national identity
norms
personal identity
physical ability identity
racial identity
regional identity
religious identity
self
sexual identity
third culture kids (TCK)
U-curve theory
Whiteness

My last name is Kennedy, an Irish Catholic name, which seems fitting for a pale freckled red head girl. However, I am also Jewish, not so fitting I suppose. For a long time I struggled greatly with my identity, who I really was. I didn't understand myself as a Jew; my brothers and sisters looked much more "the part" than I did. Contrast that with people having a look of shock when I would tell them my name, and when they would eventually learn my religion they would be both confused and angered. It was almost as if I had deceived them by presenting myself with a name Kennedy, looking the way I do, but then turning out to be Jewish.

After a while I learned to anticipate people's reactions to my "identity" and learned how to avoid it in a way. When I was with my Jewish family and friends, or at Synagogue or Sunday school, I would use my first name. Anything I could do to make me "normal" whatever that means. The same went for the other side of me; in school where there was a small Jewish representation I would downplay my Jewish heritage as much as possible, using my name Kennedy as a symbol of my normative background and acceptable self identity. I was silencing aspects of what I was wherever I went, it just depended on the context as to what I would or would not disclose.

After a few years, I realized that the different cultures and ethnicities that were embedded in my history made me who I was. As I began to learn more and more I would look back and wonder how I ever thought that any part of myself was something to be ashamed of, something to hide, and ultimately something to silence.

—Rachel

Surf's Up!
What does cultural identity look like? This is a difficult question to answer because we often rely on visual cues to reinforce stereotypes that we hold about certain people and groups. In a series on U.S. American images, PBS explores this question of cultural identity. For more information go to www.pbs.org/ktca/ americanphotography/ features/cultural.html.

Identity plays a key role in intercultural communication, serving as a bridge between culture and communication. As Rachel tells us, it is through communication (sometimes in complex ways) with our family, friends, and others (sometimes people from different cultures) that we come to understand ourselves and our identity. And it is through communication that we express our identity to others. Knowing about our identity is particularly important in intercultural interactions.

Conflicts may arise when there are sharp differences between who we think we are and who others think we are, as Rachel tells us. For example, Mario, one of our students, has been living on his own since he was a first-year student and considers himself an independent adult. But when he goes home, he says, his parents still treat him like he's a child, imposing curfews and questioning his lifestyle choices. Cassandra, a student with disabilities who is often in a wheelchair, tells us that she gets irritated when people ignore her in conversations and talk with other people she's with. And Sam, a fourth-generation Chinese American, informs us that he's not sure how to answer when people ask him, "Where are you really from?" He is American and has never been to China. In each case, the person's identity is not confirmed but is questioned or challenged in the interaction.

In this chapter, we examine the relationship between communication and identity, and the role of identity in intercultural communication. After we define identity, we focus on the development of specific aspects of our social and cultural identity including those related to gender, age, race or ethnicity, physical ability, religion, class, and nationality. We then turn our attention to culture shock and cultural adaptation, and to multicultural identity, which refers to individuals who live on the borders between several identities and cultures. Finally, we discuss the relationship between identity, language, and communication.

UNDERSTANDING IDENTITY

How do we come to understand who we are, our **self**? Our self is what we're born with, our gender, our physical characteristics; our **identity** is created by the development of the "self" (our self-concept), in spurts, through communication over a long period of time. Further, we have not merely one identity but multiple identities, which are influenced by society and are dynamic. And the way identities develop depends on one's cultural background. Let's look more closely at these six aspects of identities.

Identities Are Created through Communication

Identities emerge when communication messages are exchanged between persons; they are negotiated, cocreated, reinforced, and challenged through communication.[1] In some sense, we know who we are as a result of our communication and our relationships with others. As psychologist Kenneth J. Gergen says, "I am linked therefore I am."[2] This means that presenting our identities is not a simple process. Does everyone see you as you see yourself? Probably not. Janice, a student of ours from Canada, is proud to be Canadian and gets tired of students in the United States always assuming she is a U.S. American. Her interactions with these American students influence how she sees herself; in discussing with them her Canadian background and experiences, she has developed a stronger sense of her Canadian national identity.

Different identities are emphasized depending on whom we are communicating with and what the conversation is about. In a social conversation with someone we are attracted to, our gender or sexual orientation identity is probably more important to us than, say, our ethnic or national identities. And our communication is probably most successful when the person we are talking with confirms the identity we think is most important at the moment. For example, if you are talking with a professor about a research project, the interaction will be most successful if it confirms the relevant identities of professor and student rather than other identities—for example, those based on gender, religion, or ethnicity.

Gergen has also emphasized that recent mobile communication technologies influence our relationships and, consequently, our sense of identity. He thinks that when individuals are constantly texting and IM-ing, they avoid face-to-face encounters; their bodies may be present, but their personalities are engaged elsewhere, which can result in social isolation, the stress of always being somewhere else no matter where one might be, and a diminished sense of identity.[3]

Identities Are Created in Spurts

Identities are created not in a smooth, orderly process but in spurts. Certain events provide insights into who we are, but these are framed by long periods during which we may not think much about ourselves or our identities. Thus, we sometimes may feel that we know exactly who we are and our place in the world and at other times may be rather confused.

Communication is crucial to the development of identity. For instance, our student Amanda felt confident of her religious identity until she married into another faith. Following long discussions with her in-laws about issues of spirituality, she began to question this aspect of her identity. As this example suggests, we may occasionally need to take some time to think through identity issues. And during difficult times, we may internalize negative identities as we try to answer the question of who we are. For example, Judith didn't tell any of her friends in high school that she had an Amish background, because she was embarrassed and thought that her friends would look down on her if they knew. Not until she became an adult would she disclose her religious background. Similarly, our student Shawna didn't want her friends to know that her mother was White and her father was Black, because she was afraid it would affect the way they felt about her.

Identities Are Multiple

It makes more sense to talk about our identities than our identity. Because we belong to various groups, we develop multiple identities that come into play at different times, depending on the context. Thus, in going to church or temple, we may highlight our religious identity. In going to clubs or bars, we may highlight our sexual orientation identity. Women who join social groups exclusive to women, or men who attend social functions just for men, are highlighting their gender identity.

Identities Are Influenced by Society

Our identities are formed through communication with others, but societal forces related to history, economics, and politics also have a strong influence. To grasp this notion, think about how and why people identify with particular groups and not others. What choices are available to them? The reality is, we

What Do You Think?

Sherry Turkle argues that computers are making our identities more fluid and fragmented. She points out how people take on multiple identities while interacting with others on the Internet. Have you ever done this? Do you play *World of Warcraft* or a similar computer game? Do you have a *Facebook* or *MySpace* profile? How do you communicate differently in each of these different spaces?
(Source: Turkle, S. (1995). *Life on the screen: Identity in the age of the Internet.* New York: Simon & Schuster).

are all pigeonholed into identity categories, or contexts, even before we are born. Many parents give a great deal of thought to a name for their unborn child, who is already part of society through his or her relationship to the parents. Some children have a good start at being, say, Jewish or Chicana before they are even born. It is very difficult to change involuntary identities rooted in ethnicity, gender, or physical ability, so we cannot ignore the ethnic, socioeconomic, or racial positions from which we start our identity journeys.

To illustrate, imagine two children on a train that stops at a station. Each child looks out a window and identifies his or her location. One child says that she is in front of the door for the women's room; the other says that he is in front of the door for the men's room. Both children see and use labels from their seating position to describe where they are; both are on the same train but describe where they are differently. And, like the two children, where we are positioned—by our background and by society—influences how and what we see, and, most important, what it means.[4]

Many White students, when asked what it means to be an American, talk about the many freedoms they experience, but members of minority groups and international visitors may not have the same experience. As one of our Dutch students said, "I think that Americans think that being an American means having a lot of freedom. I must disagree with that. Measuring it with my own experiences, I found America not so free at all. There are all those little rules I don't understand the meaning of." By "rules," she meant all those regulations that U.S. Americans accept as normal but Europeans are surprised at—for example, enforced drinking ages, leash laws, prohibitions against topless bathing on most beaches, and no-smoking ordinances.

The identities that others assign to us are socially and politically determined. But how are certain identities created by popular culture? For example, the label "heterosexual" is a relatively recent invention, less than 100 years old.[5] The word originally referred to someone who engaged in sexual activity with a person of either sex; only relatively recently has it come to mean someone who engages in sexual activity only with members of the opposite sex. And the term has had different social and political meanings over the years. In earlier times, the rules governing heterosexual behavior emphasized procreation and female submissiveness and passivity. There were even rules about when sex could happen; it was a sin for a man to "love" his wife too much. In World War II, the military devised a series of tests to determine the "true" sexuality of men, and those who failed the test were rejected from service. In this way, sex became a fixed identity, like race, with political implications.

When we think about how society or other people create ideas about our identity, we might try to resist those attempts to pigeonhole us and thus try to assign other identities to ourselves. Agusia, a Polish student of ours, counters "Polish jokes" by educating joke-tellers about the origination of the term *Polack*, which simply means "Polish man." The negative connotation came about during a period of U.S. history when there was intense hostility toward immigrants from southern and eastern Europe. By educating people about

Pop Culture Spotlight

In the 2008 movie, *The Women*, Mary Haines (played by Meg Ryan) is a mother and housewife who lives a high-society lifestyle. When she finds out her husband is having an affair, Mary begins to reflect on what she really wants in life for herself. Sponsored by the Dove Campaign for Real Beauty, the story promotes "beauty" as being a good friend and being independent, rather than being physically beautiful.

Polish immigration history, Agusia "resists" the negative, stereotypic identity that society places on her.

Similarly, people with disabilities often have the experience of being stereo-typed as helpless. Many people with disabilities view themselves as public educators—determined to redefine people's perceptions concerning disabilities and resisting stereotypes. For example, they sometimes humorously refer to nondisabled persons as "TABs" (temporarily able-bodied), reminding people that no one is immune from disability, or they may redefine an assisting device, by calling a cane a "portable railing."[6]

One aspect of this education is helping nondisabled people understand when and how it is acceptable to assist a person who has a disability in opening doors, picking up something out of reach, carrying something, and so on. Nondisabled people are not always sure whether to offer assistance; and accept-ing assistance can make people with disabilities feel embarrassed and unneces-sarily dependent. It is important to realize that disabled people, like any cultural group, do not hold one unified opinion. In one study, about 50 percent of peo-ple with disabilities surveyed said they would accept help when offered; the other half were adamant that nondisabled people should wait until their help was requested. In another study, disabled people gave five guidelines for nondis-abled people who want to assist a disabled person:[7]

1. Make the request very general: "May I help you?" or "Do you need anything?"

2. Make the offer of help natural and casual, like assistance that might be given to any individual, disabled or not, rather than emphasizing the per-son's dependence. "I'm going to get another drink, would you like another one also?"

3. Ask before acting . . . do not just grab the wheelchair and push.

4. Don't get your feelings hurt if the disabled person rejects the offer. As one disabled person said, "I guess ideally I'd like to have all ablebodied people in the world trained to ask the question . . . 'can I assist you or something?'" As one disabled person said, "I think offering assistance is fine as long as you don't get the feeling you are going to hurt their feel-ings if you say 'no' . . . don't get personally invested in the request. It may be turned down, and it is not a personal affront to you."[8]

5. Follow the instructions of the person with the disability—especially with complicated tasks like folding a wheelchair in a car or helping him or her up if fallen. Not paying attention to instructions can lead to wasted time, frustration, physical harm to the disabled person, or even breaking expen-sive equipment.

How do societal influences relate to intercultural communication? Basically, they establish the foundation from which the interaction occurs. Recall Sam, a Chinese American student of ours, who is occasionally asked where he is from or whether he is Chinese. The question puts him in an awkward position. He does not hold Chinese citizenship, nor has he ever lived in China. Yet the questioner probably doesn't mean to address these issues. It sometimes seems to Sam that the person who is asking the question is challenging Sam's right to his identity as an American. In this sense, the questioner seems to imply that Sam holds some negative identity.

Identities Are Dynamic

The social forces that give rise to particular identities are always changing. For example, the identity of "woman" has changed considerably in recent years in the United States. Historically, being a woman has variously meant working outside the home to contribute to the family income or to help out the country when men were fighting wars, or staying at home and raising a family. Today, there are many different ideas about what being a woman means—from wife and mother to feminist and professional. Specific political forces can influence how identities are expressed. For example, a recent study found that some Arab women changed the expression of their identity after 9/11. Before September 11, 2001, the women referred to themselves mainly with their community identities as Arab, Palestinian, or Arab American. After September 11, they tended to emphasize their national identities.[9] Similarly, the emergence of the European Union has given new meaning to the notion of being "European." Some Europeans are embracing the idea of a European identity, while others are rejecting the notion; the idea is dynamic and changing. For example, some Europeans prefer to be identified as "French," "Italian," or "German," instead of "European" since "European" does not communicate their strongest feelings of identification. In the future, do you think that European may become more important than these national identities?

As another example, think about how identity labels have changed from "colored," to "Negro," to "Black," to "Afro-American," to "African American," with a significant number of people still preferring the label "Black." Although the labels seem to refer to the same group of people, the political and cultural identities associated with these labels are different.

Identities Are Developed in Different Ways in Different Cultures

In the United States, young people often are encouraged to develop a strong sense of identity, to "know who they are," to be independent and self-reliant. This stems from the value of individualism, discussed in Chapter 2. However, this individualistic emphasis on developing identity is not shared by all societies. In many African, Asian, and Latino/a societies, the experience of childhood and adolescence revolves around the family. In these societies, then, educational, occupational, and even marital choices are made with extensive family guidance. As Andrea, a Mexican American student, explains, "Family is the sole source behind what it means to be Hispanic. The role parents play in our lives is an ongoing process that never ends. It is the complete opposite of America where the child turns 18 and is free of restriction and authority. Family is the number-one priority and the basis of all that is to come." Thus,

What Do You Think?

Perhaps you are on *MySpace*? Or perhaps you have a *Facebook* account to keep up with your friends? Both *MySpace* and *Facebook* are popular sites for individuals to create their own electronic space for keeping in communication with old friends, meeting new people, and sharing information. Next time you are scanning your friends list, think about the ways your friendships have shifted since switching to the net. Does this shift to mediated interface impact the ways we experience our identities? How about the ways that we experience others?

identity development does not occur in the same way in every society. Many African, Asian, and Latino/a societies emphasize dependency and interdependency among family members. So, in some cultural contexts, it makes more sense to speak of a familial or relational self than the self-creation of one's personal identity.[10]

However, if the dominant idea of individual identity development is presented as the only alternative, it can make members of some cultural groups in the United States feel inferior or even question their psychological health. For example, Manoj, an Indian medical student in New York, attended a lecture on adolescent development by a very well-known scholar. In his lecture, the professor said that unless a person went through a rebellious stage as an adolescent, it was impossible to achieve a healthy identity. Manoj searched within himself for any sign of rebellion he had felt against either of his parents when he was growing up in India or against any other parent figure. When he couldn't recall any such experience, he concluded that he must be abnormal.[11]

SOCIAL AND CULTURAL IDENTITIES

People can identify with a multitude of groups based on such things as gender, age, and ethnicity, as well as on occupational interests, sports (as spectators or participants), leisure activities, and special abilities. One of our friends belongs to a special car club—all owners of 1960s and 1970s "muscle cars." All these groups help shape our identities and affect our communication to some degree. In this section, we identify those identities that most affect our cultural perceptions and influence how we communicate cross-culturally.

Gender Identity

We often begin life with gendered identities. When newborns arrive, they may be greeted with clothes and blankets in either blue or pink. To establish a **gender identity** for a baby, visitors may ask if it's a boy or a girl. But gender is not the same as biological sex. This distinction is important in understanding how our views on biological sex influence gender identities.

We communicate our gender identity, and popular culture tells us what it means to be a man or a woman. For example, some activities are considered more masculine or more feminine. Similarly, the programs that people watch on television—soap operas, football games, and so on—affect how they socialize with others and come to understand what it means to be a man or a woman.

As a culture changes, so do notions of what is masculine or feminine. Even the popular image of the perfect male body changes. In the 1860s, the middle-class view of the ideal male body type was lean and wiry. By the 1890s, however, the ideal male body type was bulky with well-defined muscles.[12] These popular notions of the ideal male (or female) body are largely determined by commercial interests, advertising, and other cultural forces. This is especially true for women. Advertisements in magazines and commercials on television tell us what it means, and how much it will cost, to be a beautiful woman. As one of our students

Pop Culture Spotlight

Have you seen the 1999 film *Boys Don't Cry*? In it actor Hilary Swank plays Teena Brandon, or Brandon Teena, an individual experiencing a gender identity crisis who befriends a group of strangers in a small midwestern town. Debates and attitudes about issues of sex, gender, and sexuality are highlighted in the film, which has often been labeled controversial, due to its use of language, depiction of drugs, and graphic scenes of rape and murder that occur near the end. If you witness discussions about the main character by people who have seen the film, you may find many argue about the "true" identity of Brandon/Teena. You might hear others refer to him/her as a cross-dresser, a lesbian, a woman posing as a man, and so on. Considering that experts say sex is biological or innate and gender is a social construct, discuss with a friend or group whether you think it is possible to have a "true" gender identity.

explained, "I must compete with my fellow Americans for external beauty. As an American, I am expected to project a beautiful appearance. Perfection is portrayed at every stage in life—whether it is a beautiful doll little girls are given to play with or perfect-looking supermodels in fashion magazines. It is no secret what is expected and accepted." Our expression of gender identity not only communicates who we think we are but also constructs a sense of who we want to be. We learn what masculinity and femininity mean in our culture, and we negotiate how we communicate our gender identity to others.

Consider, for example, the contemporary trend against body hair on men. Today, the ideal male body type is sleek, with little body hair. Many men view their own bodies in relation to this ideal and decide to change themselves accordingly. Of course, at one time, a hairy body was considered more masculine, not less.

Or think about the controversy over whether certain actresses, like Nicole Richie, are too thin. The female models appearing in magazine advertisements and TV commercials are very thin—leading young girls to feel ashamed of any body fat. It was not always so. In the mid-1700s, a robust woman was considered attractive. Our Japanese students tell us that full lips for women, considered so desirable in the United States, are not considered very attractive in Japan. And in many societies today, in the Middle East and in Africa, full-figured women are much more desirable than thin women. This shows how the idea of gender identity is both dynamic and closely connected to culture. Society has many images of masculinity and femininity; we do not all seek to look and act according to a single ideal. At the same time, we do seek to communicate our gendered identities as part of who we are.

There are implications for intercultural communication as well. Gender means different things in different cultures. U.S. students who travel abroad often find that their movements are more restricted. For example, single women cannot travel freely in many Muslim countries. And gender identity for many Muslim women means that the sphere of activity and power is primarily in the home and not in public.

Sexual Identity

Our **sexual identities** should not be confused with our gender identities. Sexual identity is complex, particularly since different cultures organize sexualities in different ways. While many cultures have similar categories for male/female and masculine/feminine, many cultures have very different definitions of sexualities. For example, in the United States today, we often think of the categories heterosexual, gay, lesbian, and bisexual; yet the development of these categories is largely a late nineteenth-century invention.[13]

The difficulty that researchers have had with sexual identity across cultures is reflected in their own difficulties categorizing and understanding other ways of organizing sexualities. Rudi Bleys has attempted to demonstrate the ways that Western researchers have attempted to understand sexualities across cultures and how those understandings have shifted over time. It is important to understand

Pop Culture Spotlight

In the fall of 2005 the American Broadcasting Company (ABC) released a new drama series titled *Commander in Chief.* Mackenzie Allen (played by Geena Davis) became the first woman president of the United States. Each episode portrayed President Allen juggling her role as leader of the nation and her role as mother. Although canceled after its first year, the series captured several awards and nominations. The show was also the most popular new series in households with $100,000+ annual incomes. Can you forecast the impact, if any, on the ways that women envision their identities as a result of this series?

that the ways we categorize sexualities today may not be the same as other cultures in other times may have organized sexualities.[14]

The way we organize sexuality, however, is central to the development of sexual identities. If nobody identifies as "gay," then there can be no "gay rights" movement. If nobody identifies as "heterosexual," then there can be no assumption that anyone is only attracted to members of the opposite sex.

The language we use to self-identify can also complicate sexual identity. For example, someone who has not yet engaged in any sexual activities with anyone might identify as "gay," while someone else may identify as "heterosexual" but occasionally sleeps with members of the same sex. How might these categories be more complex than they first appear?

Sexual attraction, of course, makes sexual identities even less categorizable. Not only are sexual desires quite complex, but they are also influenced by attraction to those of other cultures, racial/ethnic backgrounds, ages, and cultural identities. Our language is full of terms for people who desire others who are quite different from themselves. How do these terms communicate meaning about sexual identities? How do they communicate value judgments about other sexual identities?

As you encounter people from around the world, do not assume that your framework for sexual categories is universal. Nor should you assume that the ways that sexuality is handled in public is the same as in your hometown. Sometimes people from other countries are shocked that U.S. Americans speak so openly to strangers about being in their second marriage. Others do not understand the public interest and uproar over President Clinton's activities with Monica Lewinsky, which they may see as part of private—not public—life.

Age Identity

As we age, we tap into cultural notions of how someone our age should act, look, and behave; that is, we establish an **age identity.** The United States is an age-conscious society. One of the first things we teach children is to tell their age. Children will proudly tell their age—until about the mid-20s when people rarely mention their age. In contrast, people over 70 often brag about their age. Different generations often have different philosophies, values, and ways of speaking. For example, recent data show that the millennium generation (or Gen Y, those born 1982–2001) are more diverse and globally oriented and are more knowledgeable about computers and technology than any preceding generation. They are also more optimistic, more committed to contributing to society, and more interested in life balance between work and play than the previous Gen X group (those born 1961–1981).[15] This is also reflected in the way they learn and work (e.g., multitasking, use of multimedia, etc).

Certain ages have special significance in some cultures. Latino/a families sometimes celebrate a daughter's 15th birthday with a *Quinceañera* party—marking the girl's entry into womanhood. Some Jewish families celebrate with a Bat Mitzvah ceremony for daughters and a Bar Mitzvah for sons on their

13th birthday.[16] Even as we communicate how we feel about our age to others, we receive messages from the media telling us how we should feel. Thus, as we grow older, we sometimes feel that we are either too old or too young for a certain "look." These feelings stem from an understanding of what age means and how we identify with that age.

Some people feel old at 30; others feel young at 40. There is nothing inherent in age that tells you that you are young or old. Our notions of age and youth are all based on cultural conventions—the same cultural conventions that suggest that it is inappropriate to engage in a romantic relationship with someone who is far older or younger.

Our notions of age often change as we grow older ourselves. When we are quite young, a college student seems old. But when we are in college, we do not feel so old. The relative nature of age is only one part of the age identity process; social constructions of age are another. The meanings that our society holds for different ages is an important influence in age identity. Often these are intimately connected to gender identity. A recent study of U.S. Americans shows that almost "a third of unmarried American women in their 40s through 60s who date are going out with younger men."[17] Traditionally, men were expected to be the same age as or older than the women they dated. Does age play a role in your dating experiences? Gender and age also work together as we age. A male colleague of ours who is in his late 40s recently purchased a new silver convertible. A female colleague in her 40s colors her hair. How do these purchasing decisions help both of them negotiate their age identities? What do they communicate about their identities?

Age identity, however, is not simply about how you feel about your age. It is also about how others treat you based on your age. Due to the practice of discrimination against older workers, the U.S. government enacted the Age Discrimination in Employment Act of 1967, which protects people who are 40 and older from employment discrimination. Aside from employment, are there other areas in society where people are treated differently based on their age?[18]

Moreover, while in the United States old age is demeaned, in other societies it is revered. An example of this is in East Africa, where words for older persons are used endearingly to refer to any respected person in the community. These different views on aging have implications for intercultural communication. For example, in one cultural exchange program between the People's Republic of China and the United States, Chinese administrators were offended because the United States sent young adults as the first exchangees. The Chinese, wanting to include some of their best and most revered citizens, sent scholars in their 50s and 60s.

Racial and Ethnic Identity

Racial Identity   In the United States today, the issue of race seems to be pervasive. It is the topic of many public discussions, from television talk shows to talk radio. Yet many people feel uncomfortable discussing racial issues. Perhaps we can better understand the contemporary issues if we look at how the notion of race has developed historically in the United States.

What Do You Think?

What ethnic label do you prefer for yourself? In an essay in the collection *Our Voices,* Dolores Tanno describes what the labels "Spanish," "Mexican American," "Latina," and "Chicana" mean to her. She concludes by saying that each of these terms, with its own unique meaning, describes a part of her. Which aspects of yourself do your preferred terms describe? (Source: "Names, Narratives, and the Evolution of Ethnic Identity," by Dolores Tanno, in *Our Voices* (pp. 38-41) by A. González, M. Houston, and V. Chen (Eds.), 2004, Los Angeles: Roxbury).

The roots of current debates about race can be located in the fifteenth century, when European explorers encountered people who looked different from themselves. The debates centered on the religious question of whether there was "one family of man." If so, what rights were to be accorded to those who were different? Arguments about which groups were "human" and which were "animal" pervaded popular and legal discourse and provided a rationale for slavery. Later, in the eighteenth and nineteenth centuries, the scientific community tried to establish a classification system of race based on genetics and brain size. However, these efforts were largely unsuccessful.

Most scientists now agree that there are more physical similarities than differences among so-called races and have abandoned a strict biological basis for classifying racial groups.

Recent research tracing the genetic makeup of the human race concludes that there is more genetic variation within racial groups than between them, making traditional categories of race fairly meaningless.[19] Instead, experts now take a more social scientific approach to understanding race, emphasizing that racial categories like White and Black are constructed in social historical contexts.[20]

Several arguments have been advanced to refute the physiological basis for classifying racial groups. First, racial categories vary widely throughout the world. In general, distinctions between White and Black are fairly rigid in the United States, and many people become uneasy when they are unable to categorize individuals. By contrast, Brazil recognizes a wide variety of intermediate racial categories in addition to White and Black. This indicates a cultural, rather than a biological, basis for racial classification.

Cultural traditions like the celebration of Kwanzaa often strengthen groups' sense of ethnic and/or religious identity. Kwanzaa, a December holiday observed by many African Americans, promotes group solidarity, cooperation, unity, and harmony with nature.

Second, U.S. law uses a variety of definitions in determining racial categories. The 1982 Susie Phipps case in Louisiana reopened debates about race as socially created rather than biologically determined. When Susie Phipps applied for a passport, she discovered that under Louisiana law she was Black because she was one-thirty-second African. (Her great-grandmother had been a slave.) She then sued to be reclassified as White. Not only did she consider herself White, as she grew up among Whites and attended White schools, but she also was married to a White man. Because her children were one-sixty-fourth African, however, they were legally White. Although she lost her lawsuit, the ensuing political and popular discussions persuaded Louisiana lawmakers to change the way the state classified people racially. This legal situation does not obscure the fact that social definitions of race continue to exist.[21]

Third, as their fluid nature indicates, racial categories are socially constructed. As more and more southern Europeans immigrated to the United States in the nineteenth century, the established Anglo and German society initially tried to classify some of them (Greeks, Italians, Jews) as non-White. However, members of this group realized that according to the narrower definition they might no longer form a majority and therefore would lose some power. So the notion of who was White was expanded to include all Europeans, while non-Europeans were designated as non-White.[22]

Racial identities, then, to some extent are based on physical characteristics, but they are also constructed in fluid social contexts. The important thing to remember is that the way people construct these identities and think about race influences how they communicate with others.

Ethnic Identity One's **ethnic identity** reflects a set of ideas about one's own ethnic group membership. It typically includes several dimensions: self-identification, knowledge about the ethnic culture (traditions, customs, values, behaviors), and feelings about belonging to a particular ethnic group. Ethnic identity often involves a common sense of origin and history, which may link members of ethnic groups to distant cultures in Asia, Europe, Latin America, or other locations.[23]

Ethnic identity thus means having a sense of belonging to a particular group and knowing something about the shared experiences of group members. For example, Judith grew up in an ethnic community; her parents and relatives spoke German, and her grandparents made several trips back to Germany and often talked about their German roots. This experience contributed to her own ethnic identity.

For some Americans, ethnicity is a specific and relevant concept. These people define themselves in part in relation to their roots outside the United States—as **"hyphenated Americans"** (Mexican-American, Japanese-American, Welsh-American—although the hyphen often is dropped)—or to some region prior to its being part of the United States (Navajo, Hopi, Cherokee). For others, ethnicity is a vague concept; they see themselves as "American" and reject the notion of hyphenated Americans. (We'll discuss the issues of ethnicity for White people later in the chapter.)

Info Bites

Ethnicity, which refers to racial and cultural background, comes from the Greek words *ethnos* and *ethne.* These terms describe nations of people, linking them with the lands they are from, but they also were used to refer to heathens or pagans or other non-Christian individuals. Thus, even from the beginning, *ethnicity* was a judgmental, divisive term.

The question remains, What does "American" mean? And who defines it? It is important to determine what definition is being used by those who insist that we should all just be "Americans." If one's identity is "just American," how is this identity formed, and how does it influence communication with others who see themselves as hyphenated Americans?

Racial versus Ethnic Identity   Scholars dispute whether racial and ethnic identities are similar or different. Some scholars emphasize ethnic identity to avoid any racism inherent in a race-centered approach; others reject this interpretation. To illustrate the complexity of the distinction, even within the United States racial and ethnic categories have varied over time. The category "Hispanic" did not appear on the U.S. Census until 1980, and then it was listed as a racial category. In the 2000 Census, "Hispanic" was categorized as an ethnicity, which one could select in addition to selecting a racial identity. Therefore, one could be "Asian" and "Hispanic," or "White" and "Hispanic." Similarly, people from India were once labeled "non-white Caucasians," but today are categorized with "Asian Americans" on the U.S. Census.[24] These categorizations are important because historically people have been treated quite differently based upon these categories. While racial restrictions no longer remain, we continue to live with the consequences of their past existence. For example, though slavery ended almost 150 years ago, many institutions remain racially segregated, such as many churches, schools, and other social institutions, as described in Chapter 1. On the one hand, discussions about ethnicity tend to assume a "melting pot" perspective on U.S. society. On the other hand, discussions about race as shaped by U.S. history allow for racism. If we talk not about race but only about ethnicity, we cannot fully consider the effects and influences of racism.

For most White people, it is easy to comprehend the sense of belonging in an ethnic group. Clearly, for example, being Amish means following the *Ordnung* (community rules). Growing up in a German American home, Judith's identity was characterized by seriousness and a lack of expressiveness. This identity differed from that of her Italian American friends at college, who were much more expressive.

However, what it means to belong to the dominant, White culture is more elusive. It can be difficult to identify the cultural practices that link White people together. For example, we should think of Thanksgiving and the Fourth of July as primarily White holidays. And some White people feel a sense of loss as part of their ethnic identity. In order to "join" the White race and gain White privileges, many southern and eastern European immigrants had to give up their names and their heritage. While they gained many racial privileges, they gave up certain aspects of their ethnic identities. Our student describes his feelings about this loss:

My last name is Metz, as is my father's. However, for my father the same can't be said for his entire life. My father was born with the name Gerry Maceijczyk on his birth certificate, a Polish name pronounced Ma-chey-zyk. Granted this last name is a handful to spell and pronounce, therefore, shortly after my father's birth his parents decided to change their last name from Maceijczyk to Metz. So what does this have to do with identity? Well, now that I have had the chance to really think about this, it is my heritage that has been taken from me. I cannot relate my name to that of my ancestors, even though no blood line is lost, that line of heritage is lost through a name. I cannot say that I am in any way upset about the change because I do like my last name and at the same time it gives me and my family a chance to start a new saga of the family name Metz.

Our sense of racial or ethnic identity develops over time, in stages, and through communication with others. These stages seem to reflect phases in the development of our self-understanding. They also depend to some extent on the types of groups we belong to. For example, members of many ethnic or racial groups experience common forces of oppression and so adopt attitudes and behaviors consistent with the effort to develop a strong sense of self—and group—identity. For many groups, these strong identities have served to ensure their survival.

Physical Ability Identity

We all have a **physical ability identity** because we all have varying degrees of physical capabilities. We are all disabled in one way or another—by our height, weight, sex, or age—and we all need to work to overcome these conditions. And our physical ability, like our age, changes over a lifetime. For example, some people experience a temporary disability, such as breaking a bone or experiencing limited mobility after surgery. Others are born with disabilities, or experience incremental disability, or have a sudden-onset disability (waking up quadriplegic).

According to a 2007 report, an estimated 20 percent of U.S. adults, or 1 in 5 people, had some level of disability. According to a United Nations report, about 10 percent of the world's population, or 650 million people, live with disabilities.[25] In fact, people with disabilities see themselves as a cultural group and share many perceptions and communication patterns.[26] Part of this identity involves changing how they see themselves and how others see them. For people who become disabled, there are predictable stages in coming to grips with this new identity. The first stage involves a focus on rehabilitation and physical changes. The second stage involves adjusting to the disability and the effects that it has on relationships; some friendships will not survive the disability. The final stage is "stigma incorporation," when the individual begins to integrate being disabled into his or her own definition of self. As one woman said, "I find myself telling people that this has been the worst thing that has happened to me. It has also been one of the best things. It forced me to examine what I felt about myself. . . . [C]onfidence is grounded in me, not in other people."[27]

Communication related to issues of identity often is difficult between nondisabled people and those with disabilities. Nondisabled people may not make eye

What Do You Think?

In an essay titled "Stolen Bodies, Reclaimed Bodies," author Eli Clare (2001) proposes that there are four dominant ways that disabled bodies are viewed. First, the medical model sees disability as something that is broken and in need of fixing or a cure. Second, the charity model views disability as something that we need to give generously to in order to clear away personal guilt. Third, disability is framed through logics of the super crip model where we recognize those with disabilities as heroes for just living. Finally, disability is framed through the moral model, which views disability as a moral weakness. Clare argues that these communicative "frames" always construct non-able bodies as bad and broken, thus impacting the ways that persons

(continued)

contact and otherwise restrict their communication with people with disabilities. For their part, people with disabilities struggle to convey a positive identity, to communicate that their physical ability (as is true for everyone) is only one of their many identities. As one young man said, "We need friends who won't treat us as weirdo asexual second-class children or expect us to be 'Supercrips'. . . . We want to be accepted the way we are."[28]

Religious Identity

Religious identity is an important dimension of many people's identities, as well as a common source of intercultural conflict. Often, religious identity gets confused with racial/ethnic identity, which means it can be problematic to view religious identity simply in terms of belonging to a particular religion. For example, when someone says, "I am Jewish," does this mean that this person practices Judaism or views Jewishness as an ethnic identity? When someone says, "That person has a Jewish last name," does this confer a Jewish religious identity? Historically, Jews have been viewed as a racial group, an ethnic group, and a religious group. Drawing distinct lines between various identities—racial, ethnic, religious, class, national, regional—can lead to stereotyping. For example, Italians and Irish are often assumed to be Catholic, while Episcopalians are frequently seen as belonging to the upper classes.

Perhaps thinking about the various boundaries of religious identity can be helpful here. What are the criteria for being a member of a particular religion? Some religions are defined by national boundaries, as is the case for various Christian Orthodox churches (e.g. the Russian, Bulgarian, or Greek Orthodox church). Some religions are defined by biology, where one is a member by DNA (e.g. Judaism is matrilineal—passed down through the mother—or one may become a member by a special ritual of "rebirth." Other religions define membership by lineage—where a teacher, guru, or Master can initiate devotees into a "divine" line by instruction on the path to enlightenment (e.g. Hinduism, Buddhism). Very recently, religions may be defined virtually on the Internet. Here boundaries are very permeable—one's nationality, ethnicity, and gender are all negotiable. And increasing numbers of people, particularly immigrants, are turning to cyber contexts for religious expression and support.[29] However, most religions are defined by "culture" where anyone can join if they accept the beliefs (e.g., Catholic, Protestant). However, some boundaries are stronger or weaker than others. To be either a Catholic or a Protestant in Northern Ireland is almost like being a member of an ethnic (or in another way, a national) religion—and to negotiate religious identity across religious boundaries is very challenging.[30]

When one religion is acknowledged over other religions in public places, controversy can ensue.[31] Religion traditionally is considered a private issue, and there is a stated separation of church and state. However, as noted in some countries, religion and the state are inseparable, and religion is publicly practiced.

What Do You Think? (cont.)

with disability experience their bodies and identities. Do you notice these frames of language in popular discourse about ability? How might we think about and talk about ability in ways that don't *steal* bodies from the person who experiences his or her body daily? (SOURCE: "Stolen Bodies, Reclaimed Bodies: Disability and Queerness," by Eli Clare, 2001, *Public Culture, 13,* 359–365)

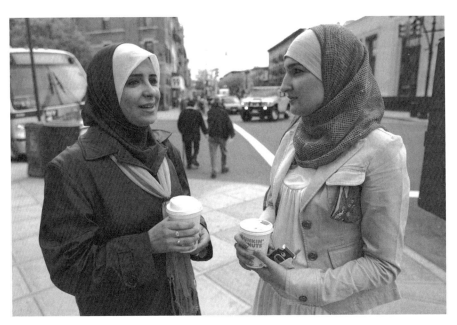

Some religious communities communicate and mark their religious identities through their dress. For example, some Muslim women wear head scarves to express commitment to their religious beliefs.

Intercultural communication among religious groups also can be problematic. Religious differences have been at the root of conflicts from the Middle East, to Northern Ireland, to India/Pakistan, to Bosnia-Herzegovina. In the United States as well, religious conflict forced the Mormons to migrate from New York to Ohio and Illinois and then to Utah. The traditional belief is that everyone should be free to practice whatever religion they want to, but conflict can result from the imposition of one religion's beliefs on others who may not share those beliefs. In 2003, Alabama Supreme Court Justice Roy Moore was found in violation of separation of church and state for his refusal to remove a monument to the Ten Commandments from the Alabama Supreme Court Building.

The influence of religious identities on Americans' attitudes was evidenced more recently in 2007 during Mitt Romney's (a Mormon politician) presidential campaign. A research study found that bias against Mormons was significantly more intense than bias against either African Americans or women, and that bias against Mormons was even more pronounced among conservative Evangelicals.[32]

Some religious communities communicate and mark their religious differences through their dress and other consumer practices. For example, Hassidic Jewish and Muslim women wear headscarves, and Jewish men similarly wear *yarmulkes* for religious expression. Among the Amish, the shape, color, or even size of men's hats, shirts, and trousers and the style of women's dresses or bonnets can mark subtle differences between groups. Food choices can also be religious expressions, (e.g. traditional Catholics not eating meat on Fridays; Muslims and Orthodox Jews not eating pork). Other religious expressions include clothing styles and grooming (e.g. Christians may wear jewelry with crosses) or purchase of household decorations and items like candles and ornaments that mark religious holidays.[33] In order to facilitate communication and show respect across religious groups, individuals need information about the various identity expressions. However, some religions express identities less obviously and everyday interactions may not invoke them.

Even though religious convictions (or the lack thereof) are viewed as private matters in the United States, they have implications for intercultural communication. One of our students described his experience in a discussion group made up of people of faith and those (like him) who considered themselves spiritual but had no particular religious convictions:

> It became very clear that many of the beliefs held were strong ones. It is as if two different cultures were meeting. The two groups act very differently and run their lives in very different ways. I have learned that many of the stereotypes that I have labeled religious people with are false, and I would hope that this group eliminated any stereotypes that religious people may have labeled someone like me with.

Class Identity

We seldom think about socioeconomic class as an important part of our identity—especially those in the middle class. As with race, there is invisibility associated with this dominant or normative **class identity.** Whereas members of the middle class rarely think about class, those in the working class are often reminded that they do not belong to the middle class. Class plays an important role in shaping our reactions to and interpretations of culture.

In our everyday language, terms like "trailer park trash" and "White trash" mark these class differences. Given their negative associations with members of the working class, not surprisingly, many Americans identify themselves as "middle class." But many people do not like to discuss class distinctions, as these conversations can range dangerously close to discussions of money—a topic to be avoided in "polite society."

Yet class identities are an important aspect of our identities in the United States, and even more so in some other societies. People use various strategies to locate individuals in the class hierarchy, as directly asking someone may be seen as impolite and may yield inaccurate information. Certain foods, for example, are viewed as "rich folks' food": lamb, white asparagus, brie, artichokes, goose, caviar. A lack of familiarity with these foods may reveal something about one's class background. People might ask where you went to college as a clue to your class background. Other signs of your class background include the words you use, the magazines you read, and the drinks you consume.[34]

Language and communication style also reflect class status. A communication scholar describes the language challenges he experienced in attending college as a working-class student: "I vividly recall coming to college saying things such as 'I seen that,' 'I ain't worried about that,' and 'that don't mean nothing to me.' I am glad my professors and friends helped me acquire a language that allowed me to succeed in mainstream American society." And the abstract philosophical conversations expected in class were very different from the working-class communication he was used to—more focused on everyday activities and getting things done.[35]

It may be that class identity can even be seen in the particular social network sites young people join. For example, *Facebook* tends to be accessed by youth from more educated affluent families, while *MySpace* is used by more working class individuals, those whose parents didn't go to college, those who get a job or go into the military immediately after high school.[36] The military sparked a controversy in Spring 2007 when it banned *MySpace* but not *Facebook*; officers, who were more likely to be on *Facebook*, could continue accessing their social network site while many soldiers, who were on *MySpace*, were prohibited.[37]

This lack of overt recognition of social class in the United States has several consequences. Despite evidence to the contrary, a popular belief in the United States, sometimes called the "mobility myth," is that with hard work and persistence any individual can improve his or her class status. The fact is that the United States has the most unequally distributed wealth and income in the world and few people change their class status in their lifetime. Specifically, the incomes of the poorest (bottom fifth) of U. S. families grew by an average of 19 percent ($2,660), over the past 20 years. Meanwhile, the incomes of the richest fifth of families grew by almost 60 percent ($45,100), and the top 1 percent skyrocketed—by 228 percent. Recent reports show that most workers have not benefitted from economic good times. The real wage of the typical male worker slid by 5 percent since 1979. Even before the recession started in 2008, the median income of working-age families was actually down 4.2 percent in real terms, a loss of $2,375 (2006 dollars). Poverty, at 12.3 percent, remains 1.0 percentage point above its 2000 trough.[38] One result of this mobility myth is that when poverty persists the poor are blamed. That is, they are poor because of something they did or didn't do, or were lazy, or didn't try hard enough, or were unlucky—a classic case of "blaming the victim." The media often reinforce these notions.

Working-class individuals who aren't upwardly mobile are often portrayed on TV shows (*The King of Queens, Everybody Loves Raymond, The Simpsons*) and in the movies as happy but unintelligent or unwilling to do what they have to do to better their lot in life. And members of the real working class, showing up increasingly as guests on talk shows like *Jerry Springer*, are urged to be contentious—verbally and sometimes even physically aggressive toward each other. Thus, the images of working-class people that are served up to the mass viewing audience are hardly positive.[39]

Race and class, and sometimes gender, identities are interrelated. For example, being born African American, poor, and female increases one's chances of remaining in poverty. At the same time, however, race and class are not synonymous; there are many poor Whites and increasing numbers of wealthy African Americans. It is important to see these multiple identities as interrelated but not identical. In any event, the lack of understanding about class differences and the stereotypes perpetuated in the media often make meaningful communication between classes difficult.

National Identity

Among our many identities is a national identity, which should not be confused with racial or ethnic identity. **National identity,** or nationality, refers to one's legal status in relation to a nation. Many U.S. citizens trace their family history to Latin America, Asia, Europe, or Africa, but their nationality, or citizenship, is with the United States.

What does it mean to be an American? When we ask our students this question, they respond in many ways. Some mention only positive things: freedom, the ability to do what one wants (within reason), economic opportunity, entertainment, and sports. Others mention unhealthy eating habits, obsession with diets, pressure to make lots of money, media determination of what is glamorous or accepted, more tax dollars spent on prisons and sports facilities than on education, and random violence on the highway and in the neighborhoods and schools. And yet, almost every student is proud of his or her national identity.

Our national identity certainly influences how we look at the world and communicate with people of other nationalities. As one of our students observed:

> The more I do to expand my cultural horizons, the more amazed I am at the way I look at life as a result of being American. There are so many things we take for granted as the only way of doing something or thinking. Like the whole individualism thing and all the behaviors and values associated with it. And there are types of people and personalities that I just never imagined before.

National identity is often influenced by how one's country is perceived on the world stage. For example, the enormous success of the Chinese 2008 summer Olympics resulted in an increased national pride and enhanced collective Chinese identity. The Chinese government went to great lengths to ensure that China presented a positive image to the world during this time. On the other hand, many people struggle with less than positive perceptions of their countries. Many Pakistanis resent the image of their country as one dominated by terrorists. Koreans see their powerful neighbors, China and Japan, perceived more positively while Korea (an economic and technological powerhouse) is the "by-passed country".[40]

National identity may be especially complicated when a nation's status is in doubt. For example, the Civil War erupted over the attempted secession in the mid-1800s of the Confederate States of America from the United States. More recently, bloody conflicts resulted when Eritrea tried to separate from Ethiopia, and Chechnya from Russia. Less bloody conflicts also involving nationhood led to the separation of Slovakia and the Czech Republic.

Contemporary nationhood struggles are being played out as Quebec attempts to separate from Canada, Corsica and Tahiti from France, Scotland from Great Britain, and Oaxaca from Mexico. Sometimes, nations disappear from the political map but persist in the social imagination and reemerge later; examples include Korea, Poland, the Ukraine, and Norway. In all of these cases, people identify with various ways of thinking about nationality.

What Do You Think?

Benedict Anderson has written a book called *Imagined Communities*, in which he argues that nations are fictions. That is, they are imaginary constructs not directly linked to the land that supposedly contains them. Thus, we base parts of our identities on these fictions. What parts of your identity may be based on fiction? (SOURCE: *Imagined Communities* by Benedict Anderson, 2006, New York: Verso)

Regional Identity

Closely related to national identity is the notion of **regional identity.** Many regions of the world have separate but vital and important cultural identities. For example, the Scottish Highlands region of northern Scotland is distinctly different from the Lowlands to the south, and regional identity remains strong in the Highlands.

Here in the United States, regional identities remain important. Southerners, for example, often view themselves and are viewed by others as a distinct cultural group. Texas advertises itself as "A Whole Other Country," promoting its regional identity. And people from New York are often stereotyped as brash and aggressive. These stereotypes based on regional identities often lead to difficult intercultural interactions. Our colleague Joyce's college roommate, Linda, was from southern Virginia. She told Joyce she had no desire to visit New York City because she had heard how unfriendly and aggressive people were there. After the two roommates got to know each other better, Joyce persuaded Linda to accompany her to the city. While the visit didn't dispel all her stereotypes, Linda did come to appreciate the energy and vitality of New York and New Yorkers.

Some regional identities can lead to national independence movements, but more often they are cultural identities that affirm distinctive cuisines, dress, manners, and sometimes language. These identities may become important in intercultural communication situations. For example, suppose you meet someone who is Chinese. Whether that person is from Beijing, Hong Kong, or elsewhere in China may raise important communication issues, because there are many dialects of the Chinese language, including Mandarin and Cantonese.

People in the United States are often proud of where they live—whether town, city, state, or region. As this sign portraying the tourist attractions of Michigan shows, these regional identities often are promoted in tourist publicity, like postcards and billboard signs.

Personal Identity

Many issues of identity are closely tied to one's notion of self. Each of us has a **personal identity,** but it may not be unified or coherent. While we are who we think we are, we are also who others think we are. In other words, if you think you are incredibly attractive, but others do not, are you attractive? Sometimes our personal identity is largely defined by outside forces.

At other times, how we behave and communicate to others helps construct our personal identity. If you are trustworthy and reliable, others may come to see you as trustworthy and reliable, which reinforces your personal identity.

Sometimes, however, our personal identity can come into conflict with other identities. For example, not all gay men are sharp dressers and knowledgeable about fine foods, yet they often feel as if they should be. Television shows like *Queer Eye for the Straight Guy* often reinforce these stereotypes. As another example, some people raised in very religious families may not feel similarly about their religious identity. They may feel caught between their family's traditional religious beliefs and their own personal identities. They may feel obligated to uphold their family's traditional ways, yet not feel comfortable with those beliefs. Along the Arizona–Utah border, a number of families belong to the Fundamentalist Church of Jesus Christ of Latter Day Saints. When members' personal identities do not match religious identities, conflicts often result:

> David Bateman, 19, said he had been in hot water with the church leadership since he stopped attending services two years ago. Word got out that he was going to movies in nearby St. George and listening to rock groups like Creed at home. "They really treat you bad if you don't conform to their way of thinking," Bateman said. "People drive by your house and flip you off. Others give you stares and dirty looks. I had two young kids on bicycles ride by me on the street. One of them yelled, 'Hey, faggot, what are you doing here?' The other one called me an SOB."[41]

The solution is often to be forced to choose.

Who we think we are is important to us, and often to those close to us, and we try to communicate that to others. We are more or less successful depending on how others respond to us. Sometimes those responses can be harsh. We use the various ways that identity is constructed to portray ourselves as we want others to see us.

IDENTITY DEVELOPMENT

Minority Identity Development

As mentioned previously, minority group members in the United States tend to develop a stronger sense of racial and ethnic identity than do majority group members. Whites tend to take their culture for granted; although they may develop a strong ethnic identity, they often do not really think about their racial identity.

What Do You Think?

British cultural studies scholar Stuart Hall explains how he thinks of his identity and the path he has taken in life. He explains: "Instead of asking what are people's roots, we ought to think about what are their *routes,* the different points by which they have come to be now; they are, in a sense, the sum of those differences." What are the routes that you and your family have taken that explain your identities? (Source: "A Conversation with Stuart Hall," Fall 1999, *Journal of the International Institute,* 7(1). Retrieved October 24, 2006, from http://www.umich.edu/ ~iinet/journal/vol7no1/ Hall.htm)

Surf's Up!

While President Obama has been hailed as the first African American president of the United States, some have questioned why he has not been characterized as biracial, since his mother was white. Listen to a group of biracial Americans discuss the importance of President Obama's identity: www.npr.org/templates/story/story.php?storyId=91375775.

In its four stages, **minority identity development** focuses on racial and ethnic identities but may also apply to other identities such as class, gender, or sexual orientation.[42] It is important to remember that, as with any model, this one represents the experiences of many people, but not everyone moves through these stages in exactly the same way. Some may spend more time in one stage, may experience a stage in different ways, or remain stuck in one of the early stages.

Stage 1: Unexamined Identity   This stage is characterized by the lack of exploration of ethnicity. Minority members may initially accept the values and attitudes of the majority culture, including negative views of their own group. They may have a strong desire to assimilate into the dominant culture, and they may express positive attitudes toward the dominant group. In this stage, their ideas about identity may come from parents or friends—if they have any interest in ethnicity. As one writer put it, "We were all color-blind in our relationships and remained so until our parents assigned the colors that were supposed to have meaning and made them ugly."[43]

Stage 2: Conformity   In this stage, individuals may have a strong desire to assimilate into the dominant culture and so internalize the values and norms of the dominant group. These individuals may have negative, self-deprecating attitudes toward themselves, as well as toward their group in general. One Jewish woman recalls that in college she had a real aversion to associating with Jewish women whom she believed fit the negative social stereotype of a "materialistic, whiny people."[44] Later she came to see this as her own buying into racism. People who criticize other members of their own group may be given negative labels such as "Uncle Toms" or "oreos" for African Americans, "bananas" for Asian Americans, "apples" for Native Americans, and "Tio Tacos" for Chicanos/as. Such labels condemn attitudes and behaviors that support the dominant White culture. This stage often continues until the person encounters a situation that causes him or her to question the dominant culture attitudes, which then starts the movement to the next stage: an ethnic identity search.

Stage 3: Resistance and Separatism   Many kinds of events can trigger the move to the third stage, including negative events, such as encountering discrimination or name calling. Sometimes, a growing awareness that not all the values of the dominant group are beneficial to minorities may lead to this stage. Suppose, for example, that someone who has been denying his or her racial heritage meets another person from that racial group who exhibits a strong cultural identity. A student of ours, Amalia, recounted her experience of going to college and meeting other Chicano/a students for the first time who had strong ethnic identities and were proud to be Mexican American. She hadn't thought about her heritage very much up to that point, so this was an important experience for her. She became interested in learning about the history of Mexican Americans in the United States, and she developed a stronger sense of her own identity. For Max, an African American, this awareness happened suddenly. He describes his

Group identities are often expressed and strengthened through communication. Which identities are expressed and affirmed by these college sorority sisters?

Info Bites

Chicano/a was once considered a derogatory term referring to immigrant farm workers. But due to the efforts of people like Cesar Chavez and other members of the farm workers' movement, the word has been redefined. Now, Mexican Americans use the term to help define their political struggle to participate fully in American society.

awareness that the Cinderella in his childhood coloring books was White. He was also deprived a part in a school play because of his color and was forced into pre-algebra class despite exceptional talent in math. This caused a rage and fury, and he became certain he was "destined for failure."[45]

This stage may be characterized by a blanket endorsement of one's group and all the values and attitudes attributed to it. At the same time, the person may reject the values and norms associated with the dominant group. For example, at this stage, individuals may find it important to join ethnic clubs like MEChA (*Movimiento Estudiante de Chicanos d'Aztlan*), the Black Students Union, or other groups where they can discuss common interests and experiences and find support.

Stage 4: Integration   According to this model, the ideal outcome of the minority identity development process is the last stage, an achieved identity. People who reach this stage have a strong sense of their own group identity (based on gender, race, ethnicity, sexual orientation, and so on) and an appreciation for other cultural groups. In this stage, individuals realize that racism and other forms of oppression occur but try to redirect any anger from the previous stage in more positive ways. A Latino writer describes how he entered this stage. It happened when he shared a college apartment with students from Taipei—persons who were foreign to the United States and its prejudices and who were interested in his background. "As I spoke to them of the history of my people—something I'd always known but never before thought about—I began to internalize that history. In a sense their curiosity sparked my own. Never again could I deny it, never again would I care to."[46] The end result is a confident and secure identity for a person who wants to eliminate all forms of injustice, not just oppression aimed at his or her own group.

Majority Identity Development

Two influential educators or scholars describe **majority identity development** for members of the dominant group. The following model differs somewhat from the minority identity model in that it is more prescriptive. That is, it doesn't represent exactly how White people's identities develop, but rather how they might move in unlearning the racism (and other "isms") that we unconsciously acquire as we grow up.[47]

Stage 1: Unexamined Identity   The first stage is the same as for minority individuals. People may be aware of some physical and cultural differences, but they do not fear other racial or ethnic groups or feel a sense of superiority. As our student Jenny said, "I remember in kindergarten my best friend was African American. We did everything together at school. We never even thought about the fact that we were of different races." Communication (and relationships) at this stage is not based on racial differences.

Stage 2: Acceptance   The second stage represents the internalization and acceptance of the basic racial inequities in society. This acceptance is largely unconscious, and individuals have no conscious identification with the dominant White culture. However, some assumptions, based on an acceptance of inequities in the larger society, are subtly racist (minority groups are culturally deprived and need help to assimilate; White culture—music, art, and literature—is "classical"; works of art by people of color are folk art or "crafts"). There is also an assumption at this stage that people of color are culturally different, whereas Whites are individuals with no group identity, culture, or shared experience of racial privilege. As a White student described it, "Where I grew up, it was all white and there was a clear sense that we were not like 'others.' Yes, we had it better, but that was because we worked harder—and the (people of color) simply did not. That was a given."[48]

At this stage, communication with minorities is either avoided or patronizing—or both. As one of our White students, Kortni, said, "I never thought about it until I took this class how I don't have any friends who aren't White. I came from a small town, and I just never really felt comfortable around people who weren't White."

Some people never move beyond this stage. If they do, it is usually the cumulative result of a number of events. Perhaps they become good friends with people of color, or they participate in a class or workshop that deals with issues of White privilege or racism. For our student Jenny, it was an undergraduate course in ethnic relations: "The professor had us read really interesting authors who talked about their experiences of growing up as people of color in the United States. I realized how little I knew about the experiences of those who aren't White." She described it as an eye-opening experience that prodded her to the next stage.

Stage 3: Resistance   This stage represents a major shift, from blaming minority members for their conditions to blaming the social system as the source of racial or ethnic problems. Resistance may be passive, with little behavioral change, or active—an ownership of racism. Individuals may feel embarrassed and ashamed at this stage, avoiding or minimizing their communication with other Whites and seeking out interactions with persons of color. This is what happened with Rina, a White student of ours who started dating an African American. According to one of her friends, "as she got to know this man she started to really reject the White culture that she was from. She criticized her family and any White person. She got an attitude that her Black friends had an exclusive right to anything that related to style or music or dance. She rejected her own culture and immersed herself in the culture she had discovered." She also started to speak up about racism when she saw it. Whites who resist are often criticized by other Whites, who may call them "race traitors" or "reverse oreos"; they may jokingly warn other Whites about dating African Americans, since "once you go Black, you never go back." This type of communication condemns attitudes and behaviors that resist dominant White culture.

Stage 4: Redefinition and Reintegration   In the fourth stage, as in minority identity development, people begin to refocus their energy to redefining Whiteness in nonracist terms and are finally able to integrate their Whiteness into all other facets of their identity. It is unclear why some Whites achieve this stage while others do not. Whites in this stage realize they don't have to accept the definition of White that society imposed on them. They can move beyond the connection to racism to see positive aspects of being European American and to feel more comfortable being White. They not only recognize their own identity as White but also appreciate other groups. Interestingly, at this stage there is no defensiveness about racism; individuals don't say "I'm not prejudiced." Rather, there is the recognition that prejudice and racism exist and that blame, guilt, or denial won't help solve the problem. There is also a recognition of the importance of understanding Whiteness and White identity. However, it is a big challenge to identify what White identity is for several reasons. First, because Whiteness has been the norm in U.S. society, it is often difficult to see. Next, what it means to be White in the United States is changing. As the U.S. population becomes more diverse, Whites are becoming more aware of their race and express this awareness in a variety of ways—from affinity for White supremacy groups to Wiggers (White youth adopting or co-opting Black culture) to those rejecting White privilege. These recent changes demonstrate that one single model of White identity development probably does not exist and presents a number of challenges for Whites in the United States.[49]

Characteristics of Whiteness

What does it mean to be White in the United States? What are the characteristics of a White identity? Does some unique set of characteristics define Whiteness, just like other racial identities? For most White Americans, being

White means rarely or never having to think about it. As one White student replied when asked what it is like being White:

> Whiteness to me is not having to think about being white. . . . I can make myself invisible in a majority of situations. . . . I could definitely tell my life story without mentioning race.[50]

What most Whites don't realize is that this perspective contrasts with the experiences of many people of color.

It may be difficult for most White people to describe exactly what cultural patterns are uniquely White. According to **Whiteness** experts (scholars who study inequalities among racial groups), there are at least three characteristics that many White people in the United States share: (1) an advantage of race privilege, (2) a standpoint from which White people view themselves, others, and society, and (3) a set of cultural practices, largely unrecognized by White people.[51]

The Advantage of Race Privilege

Many white people in the United States enjoy benefits of race privilege. Some are economic; for example, according to 2008 publications:

- In 2008, Black households earned 60 percent as much income as a White family; Latino households earned 70 percent.
- Poverty rates for Blacks are three times that for Whites and Asians (24 percent, 8 percent and 10 percent respectively.)[52]
- Three-fourths of White households own their own home compared to 50 percent of black and Latino households. While home ownership is near an all-time high in the United States, racial gaps have increased in the past 25 years.[53]

Some privileges involve better health and longer life expectancies:

- Whites and Asians are more likely than Blacks to rate their health as good or excellent (60 percent, 60 percent, and 44 percent respectively). Blacks are more than twice as likely as Whites to rate their health as fair or poor (21 percent and 10 percent respectively).[54]
- African Americans have the highest risk of all major ethnic groups in the United States of being diagnosed with and dying from cancer.[55]
- Black women are more than twice as likely to have stillborn infants (fetal deaths) than white women.[56]

Other privileges are more social:

- Whites can wander through stores and be fairly sure that no store employees will track their movements.
- Whites are rarely asked to speak for their entire race.
- Whites see people who look like themselves most places they go.[57]

As a result of taking a Racial/Ethnic Minorities class, a White student describes her realization of some of the privileges she enjoys:

> The class is opening my eyes to the inequalities the different races possess. The inequalities affect me in all that I do, and I am only beginning to recognize them for what they entail . . . these unspoken privileges that I have been given due to my race. From the moment I wake up in the morning and listen to a white broadcaster report the white men's successes of the day, until the time I go to bed listening to a white radio broadcaster playing predominantly white music. . . . Being born in a country where white is considered normative has put me in a position where I can encounter people of my race wherever I choose to go. I will generally feel welcome and feel comfortable in most situations . . . realizations like these weren't always in my conscious thought; it wasn't until recently I came to recognize these privileges.[58]

Most Whites rarely think about these privileges. A recent study surveyed 700 students asking them to indicate how strongly they agreed or disagreed with various statements regarding the meaning of Whiteness. Students who were not White tended to agree with the following statements, whereas Whites agreed less:

- "White people have privilege in the United States."
- "When people refer to 'Americans,' it is usually Whites they have in mind."
- "White people are regarded as superior to people of other racial groups."[59]

The study shows that while Whites may not perceive their racial privilege, it is quite clearly seen by those who are not White.

At the same time, while being White in the United States is linked with privilege, the two are not synonymous. All Whites do not have power and do not have equal access to power. At times during U.S. history, some White communities were not privileged and were viewed as inferior—for example, the Irish in the early twentieth century and German Americans during World War II. There was powerful and pervasive hostility against Italians (particularly those from southern Italy) in the early twentieth century. They were stereotyped in extremely negative ways by the writers of the time:

> They are impulsive and excitable; they would rather sit and sing all day than do any work and improve their surroundings. . . .
> . . . They huddle together in the cheapest tenements, sinking in the social scale but bearing children whom we must hope to inspire for better things. . . .
> . . . They do not keep their places clean . . . they bring the district into disrepute in many ways.[60]

Discrimination and violence against Italians were common. They were prevented from employment, and even subject to lynching. However, as bad as all

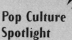

Pop Culture Spotlight

What is the ethnic identity of white rap artists like Eminem and Kid Rock? Are they simply confused? Or are they, as some critics have argued, merely the latest in a line of musicians, from Pat Boone, to Elvis Presley, to the Backstreet Boys, who have copied African American musical styles and movements? If ethnicity is not the same as race, how should we categorize these musicians?

this was, these forms of resistance were never as violent, organized, and relentless as those directed at African Americans. Because they were considered White, Italian Americans were never prevented from owning land, marrying freely, joining unions, serving on juries, or receiving other privileges reserved for Whites.[61] There are also many poor White people now in the United States who have no economic power.

There is an emerging perception that Whiteness is not equated with privilege, particularly as demographics change in the United States and as some Whites perceive themselves to be in the minority. For example, a Chicago college professor tells the story of how her students thought that 65 percent of the population near their university was African American. They based their estimate on their observations and anecdotes. When she corrected them, they were stunned. In fact, according to the 2000 U.S. Census, the percentage of Blacks in Chicago is only 37 percent. How could these students be so wrong? One reason might be the growing perception among Whites that racial and ethnic minority populations are exploding in growth and that Whites will soon be the new minority. They see their own numbers decreasing and are sometimes on the defensive. This perception has caused some to be very aware of their Whiteness and to see it as somewhat of a liability: They believe they are prejudged as racist, as being held responsible for conditions they did not create, and losing out on opportunities now given unfairly to minorities.[62]

In addition, as U.S. corporations downsize and more U.S. jobs are located overseas, increasing numbers of middle-aged White men fail to achieve the economic or professional success they had hoped for. They sometimes attribute their lack of success to immigrants who will work for less or to the increasing numbers of women and minorities in the workplace. In these cases, Whiteness is not invisible; it is an important aspect of the White individuals' identities. In fact, there is probably some fear that increasing demographic power of non-White immigrants will eventually translate into political, economic, and cultural power, and then what?

> Many whites fear that the result won't be a system that is more just, but a system in which white people become the minority and could be treated as whites have long treated non-whites. This is perhaps the deepest fear that lives in the heart of whiteness. . . . Are non-white people capable of doing to us the barbaric things we have done to them?[63]

The point is not whether these perceptions are accurate—and, indeed, many are not accurate. The reality is that most of the wealth, leadership, and power remains in the hands of Whites in the United States. Given that identities are negotiated and challenged through communication, and that people act on their perceptions and not on some external reality, perceptions related to racial identity make it difficult for Whites and Blacks to communicate effectively.

A Standpoint from Which to View Society   Some viewpoints are shared by many Whites, and opinion polls frequently reveal significant differences in how Whites and Blacks see many issues. According to a recent poll, 77 percent of Whites, but only 56 percent of Blacks, agreed that the position of Blacks in American society has improved in recent years. In addition, 63 percent of Whites (compared to 42 percent of Blacks) feel that Blacks who can't get ahead are mostly responsible for their own condition. The gaps on these issues have remained constant for the last decade.[64] How can the perception of race relations be so different for Whites and Blacks? Something about being White, and something about being African American, influences how people view the world and, ultimately, how they communicate.

In one research study, women were asked about their Whiteness and about White culture. Some reported that they viewed the culture as less than positive—as artificial and dominant, bland and sterile, homogeneous, and less interesting and rich than non-White culture. Others, however, viewed it as positive—as representing what was "civilized," as in classical music and fine art.[65] White identity often includes some ambivalence about being White. As these women note, there may be some elements of White culture to be proud of and others that are more problematic.

A Set of Cultural Practices Is there a specific, unique "White" way of viewing the world? As noted, some views held consistently by Whites are not necessarily shared by other groups. And some cultural practices and values, such as individualism, are expressed primarily by Whites and significantly less by members of minority groups. These cultural practices are most clearly visible to those who are not White, to those groups that do not share in the privileges enjoyed by Whites.[66] For example, the celebration of Snow White's beauty—emphasizing her pure white skin—is often seen as problematic by people who are not White. Perhaps it is easier to see why Snow White is offensive if one is not White.

MULTICULTURAL IDENTITY

Multicultural people, a group that is currently dramatically increasing in number, are those who live "on the borders" of two or more cultures. They often struggle to reconcile two very different sets of values, norms, worldviews, and lifestyles. Some have **multicultural identities** as a result of being born to parents from different racial, ethnic, religious, or national cultures, or they were adopted into families that are racially different from their own family of origin. Others are multicultural because their parents lived overseas and they grew up in cultures different from their own, or because they spent extended time in another culture as an adult or married someone from another cultural background. Let's start with those who are born into biracial or multiracial families.

Multiracial People

According to the U.S. Census Bureau, in 2000, the United States had an estimated 6.8 million multiracial people—that is, people whose ancestry includes two or more races—and this number is increasing.[67] Table 4.1 shows the U.S. states with the highest percentage of multiracial people. Why might these states

TABLE 4.1 Mixed Race: States with the Highest Percentage of People Who Self-Identified as More than One Race

1. Hawaii	6. Texas
2. Alaska	7. Florida
3. California	8. Illinois
4. Oklahoma	9. New Jersey
5. New York	10. Washington

Source: U.S. Census Bureau. Retrieved from http://www.census.gov/Press-Release/www/releases/archives/population/000441.html.

have the highest percentages? Which states might have the lowest percentages? The development of racial identity for multiracial children seems to be different from either majority or minority development.[68] These children learn early on that they are different from other people and that they don't fit into a neat racial category—an awareness-of-differentness stage.[69] Take our student Maureen, for example. Her mother is Korean and her father is African American. When she was 5, her family moved to a small town in northern New Mexico that was predominantly White. She recalled:

> I soon realized that I wasn't the only person who was different; the town had a large population of Hispanic and Native Americans. Yet, I also realized that I was still different from the rest of the children. It seemed that Hispanic children stayed with Hispanic children, White children with White children, Native American children with Native American children, and Asian children with Asian children. There weren't any Black children, and there definitely weren't any Black and Asian mixed children. The grouping of these children helped me realize that I was very different from all the children I went to school with. This realization left me confused and depressed.

Maureen's experience is typical of the first stage in the identity development of multiracial children.

The second stage involves a struggle for acceptance, in which these children experiment with and explore both cultures. They may feel as if they live on the cultural fringe, struggling with two sets of cultural realities and sometimes being asked to choose one racial identity over the other. This happened to Maureen. She was frustrated by the forms she had to fill out at school that asked her to indicate her ethnicity, because there was no space for multiracial ethnicity. She recalled, "It was explained to me that I needed to choose. I asked them if there was a possibility I could represent both, but I was firmly told that it would be a nuisance to try to identify with two different cultures for the rest of my life." As happens with some multiracial children in this stage, she chose one: "It was on this day that I officially became an African-American."

Whereas monoracial identity usually progresses toward one end state—one either resolves or doesn't resolve identity issues—biracial adolescents may resolve their identity status in several ways: they may identify with one group, both groups, or a new group (for example, biracial people). In the final stage, self-acceptance and assertion, these children find a more secure sense of self. This exposure to more than one culture's norms and values often causes difficulty for biracial children—they may find themselves rejected alternately by both groups (not Black enough or White enough). However, most biracial children want to embrace both parents' racial/ethnic groups, as expressed by one biracial child: "I am both white and black. I ought to be able to say I'm mixed. To not say so is a lie."[70]

The family and neighborhood play a huge role in biracial children's identity development. Strong family role models and a supportive neighborhood can lead to a flexible and adaptable sense of identity—a multicultural identity. Parents play an important role in helping their biracial children develop a healthy biracial identity. They can provide supportive communication by encouraging children to embrace both minority and majority racial/ethnic backgrounds. Beth described how her mother encouraged her:

> My mom is white and she said "I love you, but the world will see you as black because you have brown skin like your dad's. Don't let that label define you. You are black but you are also part of me."

Parents can also help children cope with prejudice and discrimination they might face. Beth recalls her mother's advice:

> She said "If someone calls you the 'N' word just tell them that their use of the word shows their ignorance." She wants me to be me, and I see myself as black but I am also part of my mom who happens to be white.[71]

As you might imagine, there are many positive aspects associated with having a biracial identity. Recent studies show that the majority of biracial children embrace the cultural backgrounds of both their parents, do not find it particularly difficult to manage their competing ethnicities or races, and do not necessarily feel marginalized.[72] Table 4.2 on page 122 summarizes the stages of minority, majority, and multiracial development.[73]

Global Nomads

Individuals develop multicultural identities for other reasons. For example, **global nomads** or **third culture kids** (TCKs) grow up in many different cultural contexts because their parents move around a lot (e.g. missionaries, international business employees, or military families). According to a recent study, these children have unique challenges and unique opportunities. They move an average of about eight times, experience cultural rules that may be constraining (e.g. in cultures where children have less freedom), and endure periods of family separation. At the same time, they have opportunities not provided to most

TABLE 4.2 Stages in Minority, Majority, and Multiracial Identity Development

| | STAGE | |
Minority	*Majority*	*Multiracial*
Unexamined identity	Unexamined identity	Awareness of difference
Conformity	Acceptance	Struggle for acceptance
Resistance and separatism	Resistance	Self-acceptance and assertion
Integration	Redefinition and reintegration	

people—extensive travel, living in new and different places around the world. As adults they settle down and often feel the need to reconnect with other global nomads (easier now through technologies such as the Internet).[74]

President Barack Obama is a good example of a global nomad (as well as a biracial individual). His father was an African exchange student and his mother a U. S. American college student. He spent his childhood first in Hawaii and then in Indonesia when his mother and his Indonesian stepfather moved there. Like many TCKs he was separated from his family during high school when he returned to Hawaii to live with his grandparents. His stepsister credits his ability to understand people from many different backgrounds to his many intercultural experiences as a child and adolescent—like many global nomads, these experiences "gave him the ability to . . . understand people from a wide array of backgrounds. People see themselves in him . . . because he himself contains multitudes."[75]

Just like biracial children, third culture kids/global nomads often develop resilience, tolerance, and worldliness, characteristics essential for successful living in an increasingly diverse and global social and economic world.[76]

Identity and Adaptation

People who maintain long-term romantic relationships with members of another ethnic or racial culture and children of foreign-born immigrants may also develop multicultural identities. Multicultural identities are often developed as a result of an extended stay in a foreign culture, where individuals are challenged to adapt to new ways of living. Let's examine the process of cultural adaptation.

There seem to be some common patterns of adaptation to a new culture, described as the **U-curve theory** of adaptation. In this model, migrants go through three fairly predictable phases in adapting to a new cultural situation. In the first phase, they experience excitement and anticipation, especially if they moved to the new culture voluntarily (study-abroad students, missionaries).

The second phase, culture shock (the bottom of the U-curve), happens to almost everyone in intercultural transitions. **Culture shock** is a relatively short-term feeling of disorientation, of discomfort due to the unfamiliarity of surroundings and the lack of familiar cues in the environment. However, people who are isolated from the new cultural context may experience culture shock minimally. For example, U.S. military personnel and diplomatic personnel often live in compounds overseas where they interact mainly with other Americans and have little contact with the indigenous cultures. Similarly, spouses of international students in the United States may have little contact with Americans. By contrast, corporate spouses may experience more culture shock, because they often have more contact with the host culture: placing children in schools, setting up a household, shopping, and so on.

During the culture shock phase, individuals experience disorientation and perhaps an identity crisis. Because our identities are shaped and maintained by our cultural contexts, experiences in new cultural contexts often raise questions about identities. One student in a study-abroad program in Mexico described her feelings of culture shock:

> I want to be at home—nothing feels familiar here—I'd like to be on a bus—in a theater—on a street—in a house—on the phone—ANYWHERE AND UNDERSTAND everything that's being said. I love my family and miss my friends. I'm lonely here—I'm unable to be me—conversations either elude me or make me sound like I'm 3 years old—I'm so different without my language. . . . I just ask for something simple—TO SPEAK—TO BE ME. Yet, as I think now, as I write, I see how much more than language it is—it's history—what's familiar—a lifetime—my lifetime—my home—and now I'm here—SO FAR AWAY.[77]

Notice that the challenge of language is often a big part of culture shock. The problem is the feeling that one can't really be oneself in another language—which is part of the identity crisis in cultural adaptation.

The third phase is adaptation, in which individuals gradually learn the rules and customs of the new cultural context. They may learn the language, figure out how much of themselves to change in response to the new context, and decide to change some aspects of their behavior. But they may also want to retain a sense of their previous cultural identities; each sojourner has to decide to what degree he or she wants to adapt. The student who wrote about her culture shock experiences later wrote, "Perhaps it was the rain—the downpour and the thunderstorm that preceded it. I feel good about Mexico now. The rainslick streets, the *torta Cubana* [a pastry]—the windy busride in the pitch-dark night. It's a peaceful beauty—I've regained a sense of self and space."

Although the U-curve seems to represent the experiences of many short-term sojourners, it may be too simplistic.[78] It might be more accurate to think of long-term cultural adaptation as a series of U-curves, where one alternates between feeling relatively adjusted and experiencing culture shock. Over time, the feeling of culture shock diminishes.

Culture shock occurs to almost all people who cross cultural boundaries, whether they have done so voluntarily or not. Most individuals then experience a long-term process of more or less adapting to the new culture. However, for many individuals, the long-term adaptation is not easy. Some actively resist

Info Bites
"The sun never set on the British Empire" because at one time Britain controlled enough colonies that it was always day somewhere in the Empire. How important is your national identity to you? Are you patriotic? Would your answer change if your nation was not a nation but a colony of another country?

What Do You Think?

Gloria Anzaldúa argues from what she calls the borderlands between two cultures. She also links this with racial issues involved in being *mestiza*, or of mixed heritage, as many Latinos and Latinas are. Other theorists have seized upon this notion of hybridity as something to be proud of; it also represents a rejection of years of denigration of biracial people. Do you experience living on cultural borderlands? (SOURCE: *Borderlands/La frontera: The New Mestiza* by Gloria Anzaldúa, 1987, San Francisco: Aunt Lute Books)

assimilation in the short term, as is the case with many immigrants. Others resist assimilation in the long term, as is the case with religious groups like the Amish and Hutterites. Some would like to assimilate but are not welcome in the new culture, as is the case with many Latin American immigrants to the United States. And some adapt to certain aspects of the new culture but not others. In short, many people who adapt to new cultural contexts also develop multicultural identities.

Living "On the Border"

The multicultural person is someone who comes to grips with multiple cultural realities, whether from being raised in a multiracial home or through adaptation to a new culture. This multicultural identity is defined not by a sense of belonging but by a new sense of self.[79] One of our students, Shannon, described how she has incorporated elements of Latino/a language and culture into her sense of self:

> I am white, American, raised middle class and female. All of these things make up the person I am. However, I have had the unique opportunity to be involved in numerous close relationships with people outside of my own race and ethnicity. I was engaged to a Mexican-American for nearly five years and I am also in a traditionally Latina sorority. All of my closest friends are Latino/a. As a result many of my feelings, attitudes, and my aspects of identity have changed. In particular, my language. I oftentimes use words in Spanish now because everyone around me does. For example, I'll refer to a stomach as a *panza*. This language has become a part of who I am although it does not necessarily reflect my ethnic identity.

Multicultural individuals may become "culture brokers" who facilitate intercultural interaction. However, it is important to recognize that there are stresses and tensions associated with being multicultural. These people may confuse the profound with the insignificant, lose sight of what is really important, feel fragmented, or feel a lack of authenticity.[80] Lucia, a Yaqui college student, described some of the challenges of living "on the border" between her Yaqui community and the college community:

> I get caught in the in-between. This is who I am: I'm Native American, and my belief system is to follow my Creator, walk the walk of the red road, and be aware of all things in nature around me. And then I look at the other—that is, going to school, which is geared more to the fast lane, a school of achievers. . . . When I go back to my village, I'm very special in one sense. In another sense, it makes me too smart. They still love me, but I notice I'm not like them anymore. I get sad, and it closes off communication; they don't talk to me. They think, "Now she's too intellectual."

Some people, trapped by their own multiculturalness, become "encapsulated"; others who seem to thrive on living on the border could be labeled "constructive."[81] Multicultural people with an **encapsulated identity** feel torn between different cultural identities. They have difficulty making decisions, are troubled by ambiguity, and feel pressure from both groups. They try to assimilate but never feel comfortable or "at home." As one multiracial student of ours said:

> In high school, I was the only Black student and was often left out, and when I got to college, I was thrilled that I was no longer the only Black girl, but I was different. I couldn't understand why they would want to exclude me. College has left me even more confused than elementary, junior high, or high school. I don't know if I will ever understand my culture since I am often left out of it, whatever it may be.

By contrast, multicultural people with a **constructive identity** thrive in their lives on the margins of two cultures. They see themselves, rather than others, as choice makers. They recognize the significance of being "in between," as many multicultural people do. April, a Korean American student of ours, explained:

> I still believe that I am, for lack of a better phrase, a hyphenated American because I grew up Korean in America. I am not truly Korean or American; I am somewhere in between. Yet I cannot deny that my beliefs about life stem from both my cultures. I hold many Korean notions very near my heart. Yet I am also very American.

Related to this idea of constructive identity is Communication scholar Young Yun Kim's notion of **intercultural personhood.** Kim suggests that more and more people, like April, who live on cultural borders undergo a gradual process of intercultural evolution—where one can see oneself and others as unique individuals (rather than as stereotypical categories) and at the same time as part of a larger common humanity. Furthermore, she notes that these intercultural persons are culture brokers who can "help fellow citizens see their collective 'blind spots' and to show a way of being in the world" which is much needed in today's increasingly integrated and globalized world.[82]

Even so, this identity is constantly being negotiated and explored; it is never completely easy. April went on to say, "My American selfishness fights with my Korean selflessness, my boisterous nature with my quiet contentment, my freedoms with my respect. I have had to find a way to mix those two very different cultures in my life."

Post-Ethnicity

Recently, a new approach to racial/ethnic identity called post-ethnicity has emerged. In the post-ethnic United States, identities are very fluid and driven by personal identity preferences. As two writers for the *Washington Post* recently observed, "Post-ethnicity reflects not only a growing willingness—and ability—to cross cultures, but also the evolution of a nation in which personal identity is

What Do You Think?

The debate about whether the Confederate flag should fly at the South Carolina Statehouse has been raging for years. For the supporters of the flag, it is a symbol of regional identity, a symbol of the spirit of Confederate rebellion. For African Americans, it is a symbol of a slave system enthusiastically supported by the South under that flag. What does the Confederate flag mean to you?

shaped more by cultural preferences than by skin color or ethnic heritage."[83] The freedom to cross cultures is a relatively recent phenomenon. As shown in Chapter 3, enormous social and legal barriers that prevent post-ethnicity are a part of everyday life in the United States. As these same two writers noted, however, "We aren't quite there yet."[84] What might be some reasons that we are not living in a post-ethnic society?

On October 7, 2003, California held an election in which most of the media coverage focused on the recall of then-California governor Gray Davis and the many candidates running to replace him. In that same election, however, voters had to decide on Proposition 54; if passed, it would forbid California cities, counties, and state agencies from collecting data on race and ethnicity. Opponents argued that the lack of data on racial/ethnic disparity would prevent schools, for example, from addressing financial inequities and disparities in performance. Two UCLA professors offered some examples of the value of collecting these data:

> [I]n 2002–03, high schools with predominately Latino and African American students had four times as many uncertified teachers and twice the proportion of new teachers as schools with the lowest concentration of these students. . . . Schools with majority Latino and African American students had greater shortages of textbooks and instructional materials.[85]

Why does race continue to reflect disparities in the allocation of resources? How far are we from really reaching a post-ethnic society?

IDENTITY, LANGUAGE, AND INTERCULTURAL COMMUNICATION

We express our identities to others through communication—in core symbols, labels, and norms. **Core symbols** tell us about the fundamental beliefs and central concepts that define a particular identity. For example, core symbols of African American identity might be positivity, sharing, uniqueness, realism, and assertiveness.[86] Individualism is often cited as a core symbol of European American identity.

Labels are a category of core symbols. They are the terms we use to refer to particular aspects of our own and others' identities (African American, Latina/o, White, European American). The labels that refer to particular identities are an important part of intercultural communication. Communication scholar Dolores Tanno describes her own multiple identities reflected in the various labels (Spanish, Mexican American, Latina, Chicana) applied to her.[87] The label "Spanish" was applied by her family and designates her ancestral origins in Spain. "Mexican American" reflects two important cultures that make up her identity. "Latina" reflects cultural and historical connectedness with others of Spanish descent, such as Puerto Ricans and South Americans, while "Chicana" promotes political and cultural assertiveness in representing her identity. She stresses that she is all of these, that each reveals a different facet of her identity: symbolic, historical, cultural, and political.

Stuart Hall, a West Indian writer, describes the variety of labels he's been given: "coloured," "West Indian," "Negro," "Black," "immigrant"—sometimes spoken in a friendly manner and sometimes in an abusive way. But he reminds us that, in fact, he is not one or another of these ways of representing himself but is all of them at different times and to varying degrees.[88] These and other terms construct relational meanings in communication situations. The interpersonal relationships between people are important, but so are such terms' social meanings. So there is no set, easy-to-understand identity that is "you." We have multiple identities that are dynamic and complex and that can only be understood in relation to the contexts and cultures in which we live.

Finally, some behavioral **norms,** or common patterns of behavior, are associated with particular identities. For example, women may express their gender identity by being more concerned about safety than men. They may take more precautions when they go out at night, such as walking in groups. People might express their religious identity by participating in activities such as church services or Bible study meetings.

Identity has a profound influence on intercultural communication processes. Sometimes, we assume knowledge about another person's identity, based on his or her membership in a particular cultural group. We may ignore the individual, but we need to recognize and balance both the individual and the cultural aspects of another's identity. As Tom put it: "The question here is one of identity: Who am I perceived to be when I communicate with others? . . . My identity is very much tied to the ways in which others speak to me and the ways in which society represents my interests."[89]

Think about the assumptions you might make about others based on their physical appearance. What do you "know" about people if you know they are from the South, or Mexico, or Australia, or Pakistan? Or think about the times that people have made erroneous assumptions about you based on limited information—assumptions that you became aware of in the process of communication. Focusing only on someone's nationality, birthplace, education, religion, and so on can lead to mistaken conclusions about the person's identity.

Given the many identities that each of us negotiates for ourselves in our everyday interactions, it is clear how our identities and those of others make intercultural communication problematic. It is important to remember that while identities are somewhat fixed they are also very dynamic. For example, the wide array of communication media available multiply the identities we must negotiate. Consider the relationships that develop by e-mail, for example. Some people even create new identities as a result of online interactions. We change who we are depending on the people we communicate with and the manner of our communication.

SUMMARY

In this chapter, we explored some of the facets of identity and the importance of identities in intercultural communication. Identities do not develop as a smooth process and are created through communication with others. Also, they are multiple and develop in different ways in different cultures. They are dynamic and may be created for us by existing social contexts and structures and in relation to group membership. When these created identities conflict with our sense of our own identity, we need to challenge, resist, and renegotiate those identities.

We also examined how identities are multiple and reflect gender, age, race, ethnicity, physical ability, religion, class, nationality, and other aspects of our society and culture. Identities develop in several stages in relation to minority and majority group membership as well.

Finally, we discussed multicultural identities, emphasizing both the benefits and the challenges of living on the border between two or more cultural realities. Identity is expressed through core symbols, labels, and norms of behavior. It is important to try to minimize making faulty assumptions about other people's identities in intercultural interactions. We need to remember that identities are complex and subject to negotiation.

BUILDING INTERCULTURAL SKILLS

1. Become more conscious of your own identities and how they relate to your intercultural communication. In what contexts and in which relationships do you feel most comfortable? Which aspects of your identity are most confirmed? Which identities do you most resist? Practice resisting those identities people assign to you that you're not comfortable with. Also practice communication strategies to tell people which identities are important to you and which are not.

2. Become more aware of how you assign identities to other people. What assumptions do you make about others' identities? About poor people? Older people? White people? People with disabilities? How do these assumptions influence your communication? Notice how you communicate with them based on your assumptions.

3. Practice communicating with others in ways that affirm their identities.

4. Talk about identities with your friends. Which identities are most important to them? Which identities do they resist? Which identities do they affirm?

ACTIVITIES

1. *Stereotypes:* List some of the stereotypes that foreigners have about Americans.
   a. Where do you think these stereotypes come from?
   b. How do these stereotypes develop?
   c. How do these stereotypes influence communication between Americans and people from other countries?

2. *Stereotypes and prime-time TV:* Watch 4 hours of television during the next week, preferably during evening hours when there are more commercials. During the commercials, record the number of representatives from different identity groups (ethnic, racial, gender, age, class, and so on) that are included

and the roles they are playing. Report on this assignment to the class, answering the following questions:

a. How many different groups were represented?

b. What groups were most represented? Why do you think this is so?

c. What groups were least represented? Why do you think this is so?

d. Were there any differences in the roles that members of the cultural groups played? Did one group play more sophisticated or glamorous roles than others?

e. In how many cases were people depicted in stereotypical roles, such as African Americans as athletes or women as homemakers?

f. What stereotypes were reinforced in the commercials?

g. What do your findings suggest about the power of the media and their effect on identity formation and intercultural communication?

ENDNOTES

1. Harwood, J. (2006). Communication as social identity. In G. J. Shepherd, J. St. John, & T. Striphas (Eds.), *Communication as . . . : Perspectives on theory* (pp. 84–90). Thousand Oaks, CA: Sage; Hecht, M. L. (1993). 2002—A research odyssey. *Communication Monographs, 60,* 76–82; Hecht, M L., Warren, J. R., Jung, E., & Krieger, J. L. (2005). A communication theory of identity: Development, theoretical perspective and future directions. In W. B. Gudykunst (Ed.), *Theorizing about intercultural communication* (pp. 257–278). Thousand Oaks, CA: Sage.

2. Gergen, K. J. (1985). The social construction movement in modern psychology. *American Psychologist, 40*(3), 266–275; Gergen, K. J. (2003). Self and community in the new floating worlds. In K. Nyíri (Ed.) *Mobile democracy: Essays on society, self and politics* (pp. 103–114). Vienna: Passagen Verlag.

3. Gergen, K. J. (2002). The challenge of absent-presence. In J. Katz & M. Aakhus (Eds.), *Perpetual contact: Mobile communication, private talk, public performance* (pp. 223–227). Cambridge, UK: Cambridge University Press.

4. Lacan, J. (1977). The agency of the letter in the unconscious or reason since Freud. In *Ecrits: A selection* (A. Sheridan, Trans.) (pp. 146–178). New York: Norton. (Original work published 1957)

5. Collier, M. J. (2005). Theorizing cultural identification: Critical updates and continuing evolution. In Gudykunst, pp. 235–256; Katz, J. (1995). *The invention of heterosexuality.* New York: Dutton.

6. Braithwaite, D. O., & Braithwaite, C. A. (2000). Understanding communication of persons with disabilities as cultural communication. In L. A. Samovar & R. E. Porter (Eds.), *Intercultural communication: A reader* (pp. 136–145). Belmont, CA: Wadsworth.

7. Braithwaite, D. O., & Eckstein, N. J. (2003). How people with disabilities communicatively manage assistance: Helping as instrumental social support. *Journal of Applied Communication Research, 31,* 1–26.

8. Braithwaite & Eckstein (2003), p.14.

9. Witteborn, S. (2004). Of being an Arab woman before and after September 11: The enactment of communal identities in talk. *Howard Journal of Communications, 15,* 83–98.

10. Roland, A. (2003). Identity, self, and individualism in a multicultural perspective. In E. P. Salett & D. R. Koslow (Eds.), *Race, ethnicity and self: Identity in multicultural perspective* (2nd ed., pp. 3–16). Washington, DC: National MultiCultural Institute.

11. Roland (2003), p. 8. Retrieved from http://www.vindy.com/print/296810619099445.shtml

12. Bederman, G. (1995). *Manliness and civilization: A cultural history of gender and race in the United States, 1880–1917.* Chicago: University of Chicago Press.

13. Miller, N. (1995). *Out of the past: Gay and lesbian history from 1869 to the present.* New York: Vintage.

14. Bleys, R. (1996). *The geography of perversion: Male-to-male sexual behavior outside the West and the ethnographic imagination, 1750–1918.* New York: New York University Press.

15. Strauss, W., & Howe, N. (2006). *Millennials and the pop culture.* Great Falls, VA: LifeCourse Associates.

16. Allen, B. J. (2004). *Difference matters: Communicating social identity.* Long Grove, IL: Waveland Press.

17. Crary, D. (2003, September 29). Generation gap? Older women dating younger men. *Chicago Sun Times.* Retrieved from http://www.suntimes.com/output/lifestyles/cst-nws-young29.html

18. U.S. Equal Employment Opportunity Commission. (1997, January 15). Facts about age discrimination. Retrieved from http://www.eeoc.gov/facts/age.html

19. Wells, S. (2002). The *journey of man: A genetic odyssey.* Princeton, NJ: Princeton University Press.

20. Allen (2004).

21. Hasian, M., Jr., & Nakayama, T. K. (1999). Racial fictions and cultural identity. In J. Sloop & J. McDaniels (Eds.), *Treading judgment.* Boulder, CO: Westview Press.

22. Roediger, D. R. (2005). *Working toward Whiteness: How America's immigrants became White.* New York: Basic Books.

23. Bernal, M. E., & Knight, G. (Eds.). (1993). *Ethnic identity.* Albany: State University of New York Press; Spindler, G., & Spindler, L. (1990). *The American cultural dialogue.* London: Falmer Press.

24. Koshy, S. (2004). *Sexual naturalization: Asian Americans and miscegenation.* Stanford, CA: Stanford University Press.

25. Reuters Health News (October 3, 2008). Retrieved October 6, 2008 from http://news.yahoo.com/s/nm/20081003/hl_nm/us_minorities_disabilities_1; also United Nations ENABLE Website. Retrieved October 6, 2008 from http://www.un.org/disabilities/default.asp?id=109:

26. Braithwaite, D. O., & Braithwaite, C. A. (2003). "Which is my good leg?": Cultural communication of persons with disabilities. In L. A. Samovar & R. Porter (Eds.), *Intercultural communication: A reader* (10th ed., pp. 165–176). Belmont, CA: Wadsworth.

27. Braithwaite & Braithwaite (2000), p. 141.

28. Pogrebin, L. C. (1992). The same and different: Crossing boundaries of color, culture, sexual preference, disability and age. In W. B. Gudykunst & Y. Y. Kim (Eds.), *Readings on communicating with strangers* (pp. 318–332). New York: McGraw-Hill.

29. Cheong, P. H., & Poon, J. (2009). Weaving webs of faith: Examining Internet use and religious communication among Chinese Protestant transmigrants. *Journal of International and Intercultural Communication, 2*(3), 189–207.

30. Barker, E. (2006). We've got to draw the boundaries somewhere: Exploration of boundaries that define locations of religious identity. *Social Compass, 53*(2), 201–213.

31. Gettleman, J. (2003, August 23). Alabama judge's colleagues order Ten Commandments removed. *International Herald Tribune.* Retrieved from http://www.iht.com/articles/107476.html

32. Luo, M. (2007, December 6). Crucial test for Romney in speech on his religion. *The New York Times*: Retrieved February 4, 2008, from http://www.nytimes.com; New Vanderbilt scientific poll reveals intense bias against Mormons (2007 December 4). Retrieved February 18, 2008 from http://www.vanderbilt.edu/news/releases

33. Cosgel, M. M., & Minkler, L. (2004). Religious identity and consumption. *Review of Social Economy, 60*(3), 339–350.

34. Fussell, P. (1992). *Class: A guide through the American status system.* New York: Touchstone Books. (Original work published 1983)

35. Engen, D. (2004). Invisible identities: Notes on class and race. In A. González, M. Houston, & V. Chen (Eds.), *Our voices: Essays in culture, ethnicity and communication* (pp. 250–255). Los Angeles: Roxbury, p. 253.

36. Boyd, D. (2007, June 24). Viewing American class divisions through Facebook and MySpace *Apophenia Blog Essay.* Retrieved February 18, 2008 from http://www.danah.org/papers/essays/ClassDivisions.html. Also Hargittai, E. (2007). Whose space? Differences among users

and non-users of social network sites. *Journal of Computer-Mediated Communication*, *13*(1), article 14. Retrieved February 18, 2008, from http://jcmc.indiana.edu/vol13/issue1/hargittai.html

37. DeRusha, J. (2007, May 14). Military bans *MySpace*, other web sites to soldiers. Retrieved February 18, 2008, from http://wcco.com/local/MySpace.Internet.Web.2.367379.html

38. Bernstein, J., & Mishel, L. (2007, September 3). *Economy's gains fail to reach most workers' paychecks*. Economic Policy Institute Briefing Paper #195. Retrieved February 18, 2008, from http://www.epi.org/content.cfm/bp195. Also Greenhouse, S. (2008). *The big squeeze: Tough times for the American worker*. Knopf; Mishel, L., Bernstein, J., & Allegretto, S. (2006). *The state of working America 2006/2007*. An Economic Policy Institute Book. Ithaca, N.Y.: ILR Press, an imprint of Cornell University Press.

39. Moon, D. G., & Rolison, G. L. (1998). Communication of classism. In M. L. Hecht (Ed.), *Communication of prejudice* (pp. 122–135). Thousand Oaks, CA: Sage.

40. Shim, Y-j., Kim, M-S, & Martin, J. N. (2008) *Changing Korea: Understanding culture and communication*. New York: Peter Lang.

41. Shaffer, M., & Reeves, J. A. (2003, September 28). "Foreigners in their own country." *The Arizona Republic*. Retrieved from http://www.azcentral.com/news/articles/0928polyg-males28.html

42. Ferguson, R. (1990). Introduction: Invisible center. In R. Ferguson, M. Gever, T. M. Trinh, & C. West (Eds.), *Out there: Marginalization and contemporary cultures* (pp. 9–14). New York and Cambridge, MA: New Museum of Contemporary Art and MIT Press.

43. Manjarrez, C. A. (1991). Mis palabras [my words]. In D. Schoem (Ed.), *Inside separate worlds*. Ann Arbor: University of Michigan Press, p. 51.

44. Hoare, C. H. (2003). Psychosocial identity development in the United States society: Its role in fostering exclusion of cultural others. In E. P. Salett & D. R. Koslow (Eds.), *Race, ethnicity and self* (2nd ed., p. 28). Washington, DC: National MultiCultural Institute.

45. Hoare (2003), p. 28.

46. Manjarrez (1991), p. 61.

47. Hardiman, R. (2003). White racial identity development in the United States. In Salett & Koslow, pp. 117–136; Helms J. G. (1995). An update of the Helms White and people of color racial identity models. In J. G. Ponterotto, J. M. Casas, L. A. Suzuki, & C. M. Alexander (Eds.), *Handbook of multicultural counseling* (pp. 181–198). Thousand Oaks, CA: Sage.

48. Chesler, M. A., Peet, M., & Sevig, T. (2003). Blinded by Whiteness: The development of White college students' racial awareness. In A. W. Doane & E. Bonilla-Silva (Eds.), *White out: The continuing significance of racism* (pp. 215–230). New York: Routledge, p. 223.

49. Hardiman (2003).

50. McKinney, K., Feagin, J. R. (2003). Diverse perspectives on doing antiracism: The younger generation. In Doane & Bonilla-Silva (pp. 233–252).

51. Frankenburg, R. (1993). *White women, race matters: The social construction of Whiteness*. Minneapolis: University of Minnesota Press.

52. Household income rises, poverty rate unchanged, number of uninsured down (2008, August 26) U. S. Census Bureau report, retrieved January 29, 2009 from http://www.census.gov/Press-Release/www/releases/archives/income_wealth/012528.html

53. Hilber, C. A. L., & Liu, Y. (2008), Explaining the black-white homeownership gap: The role of own wealth, parental externalities and locational preferences, *Journal of Housing Economics*, *17*(2), 152–174.

54. Centers for Disease Control (2008, October 3), *Report* 57(39), 1069 1073, retrieved January 29, 2009 from http://www.cdc.gov/mmwr/preview/mmwrhtml/mm5739a1.htm

55. DeLancey, J. O., Thun, M. J., Jemal, A., & Ward, E. M. (2008). Recent trends in Black-White disparities in cancer mortality. *Cancer Epidemiology Biomarkers & Prevention*, *17* (11), 2908–2912.

56. New report shows decline in stillbirths; racial disparities persist. (2007, February 21). Centers for Disease Control Report, retrieved January 29, 2009 from http://www.cdc.gov/media/pressrel/2007/r070221.htm?s_cid=mediarel_r070221_x

57. For lists of White privileges, see McIntosh, P. (1995). White privilege and male privilege: A personal account of coming to see correspondences through work in Women's Studies. In M. L. Andersen & P. H. Collins (Eds.), *Race, class, and gender: An anthology* (2nd ed., pp. 76–87). Belmont, CA: Wadsworth; Kivel, P. (1996). White benefits, middle class privilege. In *Uprooting racism: How White people can work for racial justice* (pp. 28–35). Gabriola Island, BC: New Society.
58. McKinney & Feagin (2003), p. 242.
59. Bahk, C. M., & Jandt, F. E. (2004). Being White in America: Development of a scale. *Howard Journal of Communications, 15,* 57–68.
60. Guglielmo, T. A. (2003). Rethinking Whiteness historiography: The case of Italians in Chicago 1890–1945. In Doane & Bonilla-Silva, pp. 49–61.
61. Guglielmo (2003).
62. Myers, K. (2003). White fright: Reproducing White supremacy through casual discourse. In Doane & Bonilla-Silva, pp. 129–144.
63. Jensen, R. (2005). *The heart of Whiteness: Confronting race, racism and White privilege.* San Francisco: City Lights, p. 5.
64. Allen (2004).
65. Frankenburg (1993).
66. Helms, J. (1994). *A race is a nice thing to have: A guide to being a White person.* Topeka, KS: Content Communication.
67. Jones, N. A., & Smith, A. S. (2001). The two or more races population. Census 2000 Brief (U.S. Census Bureau Publication No. C2KBR/01-6). Washington, DC: U.S. Government Printing Office.
68. See Miller, R. L., Watling, J. R., Staggs, S. L., & Rotheram-Borus, M. J. (2003). Growing up biracial in the United States. In Salett & Koslow, pp. 139–167.
69. Kich, G. K. (1992). The developmental process of asserting a biracial, bicultural identity. In M. P. P. Root (Ed.), *Racially mixed people in America* (pp. 304–317). Newbury Park, CA: Sage.
70. Newsome, C. (2001). Multiple identities: The case of biracial children. In V. H. Milhouse, M. K. Asante, & P. O. Nwosu (Ed.), *Transcultural realities: Interdisciplinary perspectives on cross-cultural relations* (pp. 145–169). Thousand Oaks, CA: Sage, p. 153.
71. Newsome (2001), p. 155.
72. Miller, R. L., Watling, J. R., Staggs, S. L., & Rotheram-Borus, M. J. (2003). Growing up biracial in the United States. In Salett & Koslow, pp. 139–168; Newsome (2001).
73. Miller, Watling, Staggs, & Rotheram-Borus (2003).
74. Ender, M. G. (2002). Beyond adolescence: The experiences of adult children of military parents. In M. G. Ender (Ed.) *Military brats and other global nomads* (pp. 83–100). Westport, CT: Praeger.
75. Obama's sister talks about his childhood. (2008, February 14). CBSNews.com. Retrieved May 1, 2008 from http://www.cbsnews.com/stories/2008/02/14/politics/main3831108.shtml
76. Ender, M. D. (1996). Recognizing healthy conflict: The postmodern self. *Global Nomad Perspectives Newsletter, 4*(1), 12–14.
77. From a student journal compiled by Jackson, R. M. (1992). *In Mexico: The autobiography of a program abroad.* Queretaro, Mexico: Comcen Ediciones, p. 49.
78. Berry, J. W. (1992). Psychology of acculturation: Understanding individuals moving between two cultures. In R. W. Brislin (Ed.), *Applied cross cultural psychology* (pp. 232–253). Newbury Park, CA: Sage.
79. Bennett, M. J. (1993). Towards ethnorelativism: A developmental model of intercultural sensitivity. In M. Paige (Ed.), *Education for the intercultural experience* (pp. 21–72). Yarmouth, ME: Intercultural Press. See also Kim, Y. Y. (2001). *Becoming intercultural.* Thousand Oaks, CA: Sage.
80. Adler, P. (1974). Beyond cultural identity: Reflections on cultural and multicultural man. *Topics in Culture Learning, 2,* 23–40.
81. Bennett, J. M. (1993). Cultural marginality: Identity issues in intercultural training. In Paige, pp. 109–136.

82. Kim, Y. Y. (2008). Intercultural personhood: Globalization and a way of being. *International Journal of Intercultural Relations, 32,* 359–368.

83. Kotkin, J., & Tseng, T. (2003, June 16–22). All mixed up: For young Americans, old ethnic labels no longer apply. *The Washington Post National Weekly Edition,* pp. 22–23.

84. Kotkin & Tseng (2003), p. 23.

85. Oakes, J., & Rogers, J. (2003, October 5). Who needs data on race? The schools for one. *Los Angeles Times.* Retrieved from http://www.latimes.com/news/opinion/sunday/commentary/la-op-oakes5oct05,1,7281774.story?coll=la-sunday-commentary

86. Hecht, M. L., Collier, M. J., & Ribeau, S. A. (1993). *African American communication: Ethnic identity and cultural interpretation.* Newbury Park, CA: Sage.

87. Tanno, D. (2000). Names, narratives, and the evolution of ethnic identity. In A. González, M. Houston, & V. Chen (Eds.), *Our voices: Essays in ethnicity, culture, and communication* (pp. 25–28). Los Angeles: Roxbury.

88. Hall, S. (1985). Signification, representation, ideology: Althusser and the post-structuralist debates. *Critical Studies in Mass Communication, 2,* 91–114.

89. Nakayama, T. K. (2000). Dis/orienting identities: Asian Americans, history, and intercultural communication. In González, Houston, & Chen, p. 14.

CHAPTER FIVE

Verbal Issues in Intercultural Communication

STUDY OBJECTIVES

After reading this chapter, you should be able to:

1. Identify and define the components of language.

2. Discuss the role that language plays within different cultures.

3. Describe ways that people deal with language and communication style differences.

4. Explain how language is related to power.

5. Discuss multilingualism and the process of moving between languages.

6. Discuss the complexities of language policies.

KEY TERMS

argot
back translation
bilingual
bilingualism
cocultural groups
code switching
communication style
Ebonics
equivalency
high-context
   communication
improvised performance
interlanguage
interpretation
language

language acquisition
language policies
low-context
   communication
multilingual
phonology
pragmatics
semantics
social positions
source text
syntactics
target text
third culture style
translation
verlan

It took me some time to get to know more about U.S. American culture and socialize with people around me. For example, during my first year in the States, going to parties was a challenging task, because I always brought the wrong stuff. My first party, after I came to the States, was a "potluck." I didn't know what a "potluck" was so I went there empty-handed. When I found out everyone else brought some food, I felt embarrassed. Soon after that another grad party took place and everyone was asked to bring their own beer. I saw something called "root beer" in a grocery store and brought several bottles to the party. Of course everyone laughed at me. The next party I made sure I took some real beer with me—something called "Blue Ribbon" or "PBR." My colleagues laughed again and told me it's an old fashioned beer favored by blue-collar old men.

—Mei, International student studying in the United States

As our student Mei discovered, intercultural communication involves more than just language skills, but language clearly cannot be overlooked as a central element in communication. Sometimes a very small misunderstanding of one simple sound or word can change the meaning in an interaction and present challenges for intercultural communicators. For example, consider our student Pat's experience in his job selling motorcycles. One day he received a call from a Japanese man looking for parts for his motorcycle:

> He told me the brand, which was a Honda, and the type. He asked if we had any "changes." I then proceeded to talk about the changes to that particular motorcycle. He politely said, after I spoke for a minute without interruption, "chains." I said "motorcycle chains?" He politely said "yes." I was embarrassed but apologized. He was very receptive to my apology. I told myself that I should have asked twice since I wasn't sure. We continued our conversation and I was able to get the parts he needed.

How can we begin to understand the important role of **language** in intercultural communication? The sheer number of languages spoken in the world today, about 6,000, is staggering. The top 10 languages (Chinese-Mandarin, English, Spanish, Bengali, Hindi, Portuguese, Russian, Japanese, German, and Arabic) are spoken by nearly half of the world's population.[1] (See Table 5.1 for the top 10 non-English languages most commonly spoken in the world.) How can people possibly communicate given all these different languages? What are some of

Info Bites

Consider the possibility that in the next century, over half of the world's approximately 6,000 languages could go extinct. When languages disappear so do significant aspects of cultural diversity. Because cultural diversity, biological diversity, and linguistic diversity are linked like clothing fibers, when you pull one thread the rest unravels.

(SOURCE: *Vanishing Voices: The Extinction of the World's Languages*, by D. Nettle and S. Romaine, 2000, New York: Oxford University Press)

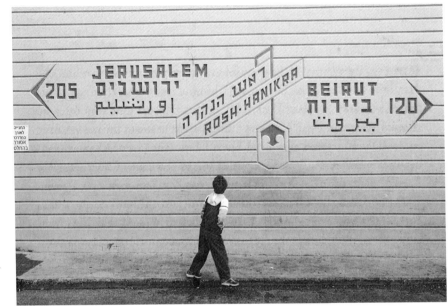

Language is an important aspect of intercultural communication, particularly when we travel internationally. People sometimes rely on universal symbols or meanings when crossing national borders.

Surf's Up!

Think about how politics and social events shape the words we use. In 2007, the American Dialect Society voted "subprime" as the word of the year and "green" as the most useful word of the year. In 2008, the word of the year was "bailout" and "Barack Obama" was the most useful word of the year. Can you think of other "hot" terms that gain rapid popularity based on current events? (SOURCE: http://www .americandialect.org/ index.php/amerdial/ categories/C178/)

the difficulties in translating and interpreting? How can we use language to become better intercultural communicators? Is it possible for two people to communicate effectively if they don't speak the same language? Should everyone learn a second or third language? These are some of the questions we explore in this chapter.

First we identify the components of language and explore the dynamic relationship between language, meaning, and perception. Next, we explore cultural variations of language and how people successfully communicate across these cultural variations. In the fourth section, we discuss the relationship between language and power. Finally, we examine multilingualism.

TABLE 5.1 Top 10 Non-English Languages Most Commonly Spoken in the World

1. Mandarin	6. Arabic
2. Spanish	7. Portuguese
3. Russian	8. Bengali
4. French	9. Japanese
5. Hindi	10. German

Learning another language, as some college students do, is never easy, but there are rewards. People have varying reasons for studying a language, including adapting to a new cultural context, getting a job, and traveling abroad.

THE STUDY OF LANGUAGE

The Components of Language

Are there any universal aspects shared by all languages? Can the same concept be expressed in any language? Or are there ideas that can only be expressed in particular languages? For answers to these questions, we turn to the discipline of linguistics. Linguistics usually divides the study of language into four parts: phonology, semantics, syntactics, and pragmatics. Let's look at each of these components.

Phonology   **Phonology** is the study of the sound system of language—how words are pronounced, which units of sounds (phonemes) are meaningful for a specific language, and which sounds are universal. Because different languages use different sounds, it is often difficult for nonnative speakers to learn how to pronounce some sounds.

French, for example, has no equivalent for the voiced "th" sound (as in *mother*) or the unvoiced "th" sound (as in *think*) in English. French speakers often substitute similar sounds to pronounce English words with "th." By contrast, English speakers often have a difficult time pronouncing the French "r" (as in *la fourrure*), which is produced further back in the mouth than in English. Similarly, many English speakers have trouble "rolling the r" in Spanish, pronouncing words like *carro* (car) or *perro* (dog). English speakers also have trouble pronouncing some Japanese words that contain a sound that is between the English "r" and "l" sounds—for example, the words *ramen* and *karaoke*. Also, in some African languages, sounds like "mba" and "njo" give English speakers problems because they are unfamiliar.

Languages such as Vietnamese that have tonal differences are also difficult for speakers of other languages. Vietnamese have six tones (level, high rising, low/falling, dipping-rising, high rising glotalized and low glotalized). This means that one word (ma) can have six different meanings: ghost, check, but, tomb, horse, and rice seedling, depending on the tone.[2]

Tones

1. level *(không dấu)* a ă â e ê i o ô ơ u ư y ma [mā] = ghost
2. high rising *(dấu sắc)* á ắ ấ é ế í ó ố ớ ú ứ ý má [má] = cheek
3. low/falling *(dấu huyền)* à ằ ầ è ề ì ò ồ ờ ù ừ ỳ mà [mà] = but
4. dipping-rising *(dấu hỏi)* à ằ ầ è ề ì ò ồ ờ ủ ừ ỳ mả [mả] = tomb
5. high rising glottalized *(dấu ngã)* ã ẵ ẫ ẽ ễ ĩ õ ỗ ỡ ũ ữ ỹ mã [má'] = horse
6. low glottalized *(dau nặng)* ạ ặ ậ ẹ ệ ị ọ ộ ợ ụ ự ỵ mạ [mà'] = rice seedling

What Do You Think?

Languages are in constant change as they require use to survive. In this way they might be considered "living" creations. What implications might establishing an official language such as English in the United States have on Native languages?

Semantics **Semantics** is the study of meaning—that is, how words communicate the meaning we intend to get across in our communication. For example, an international student ordered a cheeseburger at a fast-food restaurant, and the worker behind the counter asked him, "Is this for here or to go?" The international student understood the individual words—"for-here-or-to-go"—but not the meaning of the words strung together in that fashion.

Sometimes semantics focuses on the meaning of a single word. For example, what is a chair? Do we define a chair by its shape? Does a throne count as a chair? Do we define it by its function? If I sit on a table, does that make it a chair? Different languages have different words for the same object. Thus, the object that is called *a chair* in English is called *une chaise* in French and *la silla* in Spanish. Even different cultures that share a language, such as Great Britain and the United States, may have different words for the same object. The following list shows some differences between U.S. and British English:[3]

British	*U.S.*
jersey	sweater
pants	underwear
pumps	tennis shoes
trousers	pants
biscuit	cookie, cracker
chips	french fries
crisps	potato chips
twigs	pretzels
cooker	stove
rubber	eraser
loo	toilet
carrier bag	grocery sack

Similarly, in Mexico, a swimming pool is an *alberca*, but in Spain it is a *piscina*. Even within the United States there are semantic differences. For example, a *cabinet* in Rhode Island is often called a *milkshake* elsewhere. A *gumband* in Pittsburgh is called a *rubber band* in Phoenix.

Syntactics   **Syntactics** is the study of the structure of a language—the rules for combining words into meaningful sentences. One way to think of this is to consider how the order of the words in a sentence creates a particular meaning. For example, the word order in the sentence "The red car smashed into the blue car" makes a big difference in the meaning of the sentence. "The blue car smashed into the red car" means something else entirely.

In French, there is a difference between "Qu'est-ce que c'est?" and "Qu'est-ce que c'est que ça?" and "C'est quoi, ça?" Although all three questions mean "What is that?" they each emphasize something different. (Roughly translated, they mean "What's *that*?" "What *is* that?" and "That is *what*?") This illustrates that in French, meaning depends more on syntax than on the emphasis of single words in a sentence. This is often the case in English as well.

Each language has particular rules concerning the structure and expression of plurals, possessives, gender forms, subject-verb-object arrangement, and so on. For example, to express possession in English, we add an *'s* ("John's hat" or "the man's hat"). Other languages, such as Spanish, express possession through word sequence ("the hat of John" or "the hat of the man"). In English, the subject or actor is usually placed at the beginning of the sentence ("The girl ran"). By contrast, in Spanish, the subject is sometimes placed at the end of the sentence ("ran the girl"). Thus, learning a new language involves not only learning new words and their meaning but also the particular rules that govern that language. We'll give more examples of different syntactic rules in the next section.

Pragmatics   **Pragmatics** is the study of how language is actually used in particular contexts; the focus is on the specific purposes of language use. It is not enough to know the grammar and pronunciation of a language. We must also know how to use the language. For example, in the United States, we might ask someone, "Do you know what time it is?" A native speaker and member of that culture realizes that the correct answer is not a simple "yes."

Another example is the word "*inshallah*" (God willing) used in many Arabic-speaking cultures. Used traditionally as an expression of deep faith and a belief that all things occur (or don't occur) at God's will, the term is now used in many contexts. As one recent visitor to Egypt explained, *Inshallah* is now sometimes used as a response to the question "What's your name?". The response: "Muhammad, *inshallah*." Or in an elevator, when someone asks "Going down?" the response is "*inshallah.*" It is not enough to know the meaning and translation of the word, but a visitor would need to be familiar with the culture to know exactly how to use the word.[4]

We can employ more than one purpose for the same words. For example, if someone says "That's a lovely outfit," you might interpret it in different ways

What Do You Think?

One of the primary functions language serves is to communicate our feelings. Consider an experience that made you question if your words adequately express your emotions. What does this tell you about the limits of language? How might speaking many languages expand its potential to express feelings?

depending upon the way the speaker said it, your relationship with the speaker, and so on. The person might be making fun of your outfit, flirting with you, or simply giving you a compliment. So the meaning does not come from the words or the word order alone but depends on other things like nonverbal cues (facial expressions, vocal intonation), which we'll explore further in the next chapter.

Language and Perception

Our perceptions are shaped by our language. In a way, we communicate or paint pictures with words, and this may greatly influence how we see groups of people, ourselves, or important concepts. Our language has given us a variety of pictures complete with attitudes—and much of what we hold true is actually quite incorrect. For example, we might use the word "quaint" to describe the lifestyle of people in Switzerland. However, if we visit Zurich or Berne (cities in Switzerland), we might be surprised to see gleaming glass office buildings, everyone talking on cell phones, and a bustling metropolis. This happens sometimes when we meet people from another culture and are totally surprised as to how "nice" they are. When asked, "How many of these people do you actually know?" The answer comes back "Well I've heard . . .", showing that we may have (pre)conceptions of others based only on the language we've heard (or used) to describe them.

The "Power" Effects of Labels Another way to understand the way language and perception are intertwined is to think about how the labels we use to refer to other people and ourselves can impact perceptions. For example, in the 1960s the term "Negro" was replaced by "Black" during the civil rights movement because Black stood for racial pride, power, and rejection of the status quo. "Black is beautiful" and "Black power" became slogans during this time. In the late 1980s Black leaders proposed that "Black" be replaced with "African American," saying that this label would provide African Americans a cultural identification with their heritage and ancestral homeland.[5] The changes in these labels impact those who use and hear the terms—they have worked to strengthen group identity and facilitate the struggle for racial equality. Currently, both terms are used—depending on people's preference; "Black" is preferred by some because it shows commonality with people of African descent who are not U.S. American (e.g. Caribbean Islanders).[6]

However, sometimes people feel trapped or misrepresented by labels, when others use labels that we don't like or that we feel inaccurately describe us. Think about how you feel when someone describes you by terms that you do not like. Many times people use labels for others without any knowledge or understanding of their meanings, origin, or even current implications, and can demonstrate prejudicial feelings.[7] For example, many descendents of Spanish-speaking people living in the United States reject the term "Hispanic" since it was a census term created by the U. S. government in 1970 to identify a group of people; it was never used by people to describe themselves. Similarly, "Oriental" is a term rejected by many Asians and Asian Americans; and the word "homosexual" communicates negative characteristics about the speaker and establishes distance between the speaker and listener. Many indigenous people reject the term "Native American"—saying that it is only used by white people—preferring their more specific tribal name, or the terms American Indian or Indian. Many prefer "First Nations" people—to underscore the fact that tribes are in fact nations recognized by the U. S. government.[8]

More recently, we can see the power of labeling when some people are labeled as "terrorists" or "freedom fighters" or "patriots." What difference does it make? What kinds of responses might someone receive from others or the government if they are labeled as a "terrorist" or a "patriot"? But if we look historically, could we call Samuel Adams a "terrorist" instead of a "patriot"? Does it depend on our perspective?

Language use is closely linked to social structure, so the messages communicated through the use of labels depend greatly on the social position of the speaker. If the speaker and listener are close friends, then the use of certain labels may not be offensive or cause a rift in the relationship. But if the speaker and listener are strangers, then these same labels might invoke anger or close the lines of communication.

Sapir-Whorf Hypothesis How much of our perception is shaped by the particular language we speak? Do English speakers see the world differently from Arabic speakers? As a writer for *National Geographic* says, "More than a cluster of words or a set of grammatical rules, a language is a flash of the human spirit by which the soul of a culture reaches into the material world."[9] The idea that the particular language we speak determines our perception of reality is best represented by the Sapir-Whorf hypothesis. The hypothesis was developed by Edward Sapir and Benjamin Whorf, based on research they conducted on Native American languages. They proposed that language not only expresses ideas but also *shapes* ideas about and perceptions of the world.[10]

According to the Sapir-Whorf hypothesis, language defines our experience. For example, there are no possessives (his/her/our/your) in the Diné (Navajo) language; we might conclude, therefore, that Diné think in a particular way about the concept of possession. In contrast to English speakers, Diné may think that it's less important for individuals to own things; they may take a more communal approach to possession. The Penan people in Borneo have only one word for "he," "she," and "it," but they have six different words to express "we." This might suggest that social cooperation or collectivism is an important value for the Penan.[11]

A final example demonstrates the different ways various languages express formality and informality. English speakers do not distinguish between a formal and informal "you" (as in German, with *du* and *Sie*, and in Spanish, with *tu* and *usted*). This may mean that English speakers think about formality and informality differently than do German or Spanish speakers. And, indeed, people from outside the United States often comment on the informality of U.S. Americans, in social life, education, and business. As Geraldo, an exchange student of ours from Spain, observed, "It just amazes me how informal everyone is here—saying 'help yourself' to a guest in your home and meaning it! And everyone calling each other by first names, including teachers and students. This would never happen in my country."

How close is the relationship between language and perception? Probably not as close as suggested by the Sapir-Whorf hypothesis. For example, even though cultural groups may have different words for different colors, most can identify a particular color when asked. This means that we can "see" the same colors even if we have different words to describe them. A recent study looked at the Munduruku people in rural villages in Brazil. They have no formal schooling and speak a language that has few words describing geometrical or spatial concepts, and they have no rulers, compasses, or maps. Researchers showed them diagrams with containers of various shapes and then showed them the actual containers arranged in the same way. The researchers found that the Munduruku were easily able to relate the geometrical information on the diagram to the geometrical relationships on the ground. This shows, contrary to the Sapir-Whorf hypothesis, that language is not required to think about or perceive the world in a particular way.[12] Thus, a more moderate view, in which language is a tool to communicate rather than a mirror of perception, is probably more accurate. As these examples show, however, the language we speak has a tremendous impact on what and how we communicate every day.[13] This has important implications for intercultural communication. Perhaps it's not just languages that are different; rather, it may mean that members of cultural groups really experience the world very differently and, in a sense, live in very different perceptual worlds.

CULTURAL VARIATIONS IN LANGUAGE

Which is more important, being a good speaker or a good listener? Is it preferable to be effective at communicating verbally or nonverbally? Is it better to be direct and to the point in communicating, or is it better to take some time getting to the point? Is it more important to tell the truth or to make others feel good, even if it means being deceptive? As we'll see, different cultural groups have different answers to these questions. There are cultural variations in how language is used: differences in attitudes toward speech and silence, differences in whether meaning is more in the verbal or nonverbal communication, and differences in communication style. Let's look at each.

Attitudes toward Speaking, Writing, and Silence

In some cultural groups, including many U.S. speech communities, speaking is highly valued. It's also important to be articulate in many contexts (interpersonal, small-group, public speaking). For example, being a good political, business, or religious leader often depends on the ability to express oneself well, or to be "quick on one's feet." In these cultural groups, a secondary, or less important, mode of communication is listening. Silence is sometimes viewed negatively.

For example, people may feel bad or embarrassed if there are too many pauses or quiet moments in conversations, or they may feel that they aren't really connecting with people. Silence also can be interpreted as a sign of hostility or rejection, as when people are given "the silent treatment." It may even be interpreted as reflecting a lack of knowledge or a lack of verbal skills.[14]

By contrast, many cultural groups place a primary emphasis on silence and harmony and a secondary emphasis on speech. These groups may actually distrust speech, particularly public speech. The Amish, for example, are sometimes referred to as "the Quiet in the Land" due to their preference for silence, especially in public settings. Judith remembers being struck by the difference between her Amish friends and the non-Amish adolescents she saw in the malls in Lancaster, Pennsylvania. The non-Amish adolescents seemed so free and expressive as they roamed the malls.

The same is true for some Native American groups. Leon Rising Wolf, a member of the Blackfeet Indian Nation, describes the group's primary communication style as a "deeply communicative silence—active silence in which people share a communal silence."[15] Speaking is a secondary communication mode and is important for some Blackfeet people such as tribal leaders. But speaking is also seen as somewhat risky, because it might serve to undermine the communal connectedness.

Many East Asians not only distrust speech but also see the skillful use of silence as an important aspect of competent conversation; it shows the ability to read another person's mind intuitively, and it may even be a powerful way of controlling conversation. This emphasis on silence is based partly on religious teachings (Confucius rejected eloquent speaking and instead advocated hesitancy and humble talk in his philosophy of the ideal person) and partly on other cultural beliefs:

> Since ancient times, Japanese people have believed in *kotodama*, which literally means "the spirit living in words." This folk belief creates the superstition that a soul dwelling in words has a supernatural power to make anything happen simply by verbalizing it. Even in modern Japan, meaningless or careless utterance is not respected and valued.[16]

Other Asian cultures share this distrust of speech. As one of our Taiwanese students told us, "In America, sometimes students talk about half the class time. Compared to my classes in Taiwan, if a student asked too many questions or expressed his or her opinions that much, we would consider the person a show-off or insincere. Consequently, this is one of the difficulties I have experienced because of differences in culture."

Thus, it is clear that different views on silence can cause misunderstandings and even conflict in intercultural communication and that silence should be viewed as a legitimate conversational strategy. Since silence is a way of saying "no" for many cultural groups, knowing when *not* to talk in a particular cultural situation and knowing the meanings of silence is as important as knowing when and how to talk. For example, if European Americans, who think that a primary way

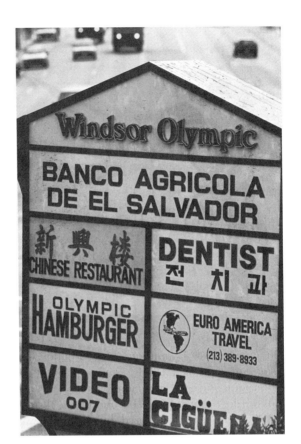

In our increasingly diverse world, many languages may be represented in a given area. This sign suggests that people from many cultural backgrounds live, work, and shop in the same neighborhood.

to connect with people is through verbal communication, try to befriend Native Americans, who use silence as a way to "get to know someone" and reserve talk for more intimate relationships, misunderstanding between the two groups is likely. See Table 5.2 for examples of attitudes toward speech and silence. We'll talk more about silence in the next chapter, on nonverbal communication issues.

TABLE 5.2 Attitudes toward Speech and Silence

Often, common phrases reveal cultural attitudes toward speaking and silence. Note the following examples:

It is what people say that gets them into trouble. (Japanese)

A loud voice shows an empty head. (Finland)

To be always talking is against nature. (Taoist saying)

One who speaks does not know. (Taoist saying)

The cat that does not mew catches rats. (Japanese)

Source: Non-Western Perspectives on Human Communication: Implications for Theory and Practice,
by Min-Sun Kim, 2002, Thousand Oaks, CA: Sage, pp. 135, 137.

The relationship between writing and speaking differs across cultures. In the United States (and other Western cultures), we often emphasize writing over speaking. Having something in writing, such as a written contract, is far more powerful than a verbal promise. We often ask, "Did you get that in writing?" to emphasize the importance of any agreement. Writing is clearly valued over speaking in these cultural contexts. In some cultures, however, oral communication is valued more highly than written communication. Publicly saying that you make a commitment is highly valued and seen as more significant than signing a paper. In the United States, remnants of valuing oral communication can be seen in the importance of saying "I do" when getting married, as opposed to signing a marriage license.

Variations in Communication Style

Communication style combines verbal and nonverbal elements. It refers to the way people use language, and it helps listeners understand how to interpret verbal messages. Recognizing different communication styles helps us understand cultural differences that extend beyond the words we speak. There are at least three distinct dimensions of communication style: high-/low-context, direct/indirect, and elaborated/understated.

High-/Low-Context Styles   A primary way in which cultural groups differ in communication style is a preference for **high-context** or **low-context communication.** A high-context communication style is one in which "most of the information is either in the physical context or internalized in the person, while very little is in the coded, explicit, transmitted part of the message."[17] This style of communication emphasizes understanding messages without directly stating the meaning in verbal communication. People in long-term relationships often use this style of communication, as the meaning is assumed to be understood by the other person.

In contrast, low-context communication places the majority of meaning and information in the verbal message. This style of communication, which emphasizes being explicit, is highly valued in many cultures where they feel it is better to get to the point, be explicit, and not leave things unstated. Consider this conversation:

ROBERT: What's for dinner?

PATRICIA: There's a great movie playing, and Barbara told me about this new Thai restaurant that's next to the Scottsdale 24-plex.

ROBERT: We could have the burritos we got the other night from Chili's.

PATRICIA: Whatever.

Patricia is using a high-context communication style. In this rather indirect style, most of the information is not in the verbal message; rather, the meaning is in the context or is internalized in the speaker.[18] This style emphasizes understanding messages without direct verbal communication. Often people in long-term

What Do You Think?
We often guess where people are from in the United States based on their "accent," especially the stronger ones such as those of a Bostonian or a New Yorker. Do you think you have an accent? Do you think it is possible not to have an accent? To find out what kind of accent you have, take this quiz: www.gotoquiz.com/what_american_accent_do_you_have.

relationships communicate in this style. For example, one partner may send a meaningful glance across the room at a party, and the other knows that it is time to go home.

In contrast, Robert's style is low-context communication, with most of the meaning contained in the spoken word. Low-context communication emphasizes explicit verbal statements ("What's for dinner?" "We could have the burritos . . ."). In most contexts in the United States, this style of communication is highly valued. For example, in business contexts, people are encouraged to value verbal communication, to make words "mean what they say." Interpersonal communication textbooks often stress that we should not rely on nonverbal, contextual information. It is better to be explicit than ambiguous.

By contrast, cultural groups around the world value high-context communication. In these groups, children and adolescents are encouraged to pay close attention to contextual cues (body language, environment), and not just the words spoken in a conversation. For example, a Japanese student told us how his mother encouraged him to try to understand what a neighbor was really saying when making a comment that they (the neighbors) would be going away for a while.[19] As the student recalled, he eventually understood that the neighbor actually was indirectly asking for help in caring for the yard while they would be away. The meaning was not in the words expressed, but in the context—the relationship between the two families, who had been neighbors for a long time.

Direct/Indirect Styles The indirect/direct dimension is closely related to high- and low-context communication. A direct communication style, like Robert's, is one in which verbal messages reveal the speaker's true intentions, needs, wants, and desires; the emphasis is on low-context communication. An indirect style, like Patricia's, is one in which verbal messages may obscure or minimize the speaker's true intentions, needs, wants, and desires; the emphasis is on high-context communication. For example, Patricia didn't directly tell Robert that she preferred to go out for dinner, but the implication was evident.

Many English speakers in the United States view the direct speech style as the most appropriate in most contexts. Although "white lies" may be permitted in some situations, the preference is for honesty, openness, individualism, and forthrightness, especially in business contexts:

> White male business executives tend to be clear, specific, and direct in their verbal communication, even if it means dealing with unpleasant realities. As they like to say: "Let's lay our cards on the table, shall we?" Or, "Let's stop beating around the bush and get to the point." [They] generally do not place a high value upon indirection or ambiguity, certainly not as much as some Asian Americans. Even in personal discussion, let alone a more impersonal business conversation, directness frequently is chosen over sensitivity toward feelings.[20]

By contrast, some cultural groups prefer a more indirect style, with an emphasis on high-context communication. Preserving the harmony of relationships has

Surf's Up!

The history of the English language stretches over a great amount of time and a number of countries. Go to www.wordorigins.org/index.php/site/comments/a_very_brief_history_of_the_english_language3/ for a glimpse at the evolutions it has gone through and diverse influences that the English language encompasses.

a higher priority than complete honesty. A speaker might look for a "soft" way to communicate that there is a problem in the relationship, perhaps providing contextual cues. For example, three Indonesian students living in the United States were invited by their advisor to participate in a cross-cultural training workshop. They did not want to participate, nor did they have the time. But they did not want to offend their professor, whom they held in high regard. Rather than tell him that they couldn't attend, they simply didn't return his calls and didn't show up for the workshop.

Fekri, a student of ours from Tunisia, had been in the United States for several months before he realized that if one was asked directions and didn't know the location of the place, one should tell the truth instead of making up an answer. He explained that he had been taught that it was better to engage in conversation, to give a person some response, than to disappoint the person by revealing that he didn't know.

Differing communication styles are responsible for many problems that arise between men and women and between persons from different ethnic groups. Many problems are caused by different priorities with regard to truth, honesty, harmony, and conflict avoidance in relationships. Perhaps you can think of times when you tried to protect someone's feelings by communicating indirectly but that person preferred a more direct style. Or perhaps you tend to be more direct, valuing honesty over relationship harmony. For example, our student Janelle has two roommates who both preferred a more indirect style of communicating. When there are conflicts among the three, Janelle tended to "tell it like it is," even if it meant saying negative things. It took her a while to realize that her roommates were offended by her direct, low-context way of speaking. And, of course, they didn't tell her they were offended because that would have required more direct communication, which they were uncomfortable with. They eventually solved their communication problem when Janelle learned to be more indirect and began to ask them if things were going OK, and her roommates learned to be a bit more direct with Janelle. We'll talk later about the importance of flexibility and adaptability in communicating effectively across cultures.

Elaborated/Understated Styles

This dimension refers to the quantity of talk that people value and is related to attitudes toward speech and silence. The elaborate style involves the use of rich, expressive language in everyday conversation. For example, Arabic speakers use many metaphorical expressions in everyday speech. In this style, a simple, assertive statement means little, and the listener might believe the opposite. Thus, if my host asks me if I've had enough to eat and I simply respond, "Yes," the host may not believe me; I need to elaborate.

By contrast, in the understated style, simple assertions and silence are valued. Amish people often use this style of communication. A common refrain is, "If you can't say anything good, don't say anything at all." Free self-expression is not encouraged. Silence is especially appropriate in ambiguous situations; that is, if one is unsure of what is going on, it is better to remain silent.

Info Bites

Verbal communication is often the source of misunderstandings in cross-cultural encounters. However, nonverbal communication is not without its potential for misunderstandings. When ordering something to drink in a restaurant in Germany, be sure to hold up your thumb for one drink because the index finger represents the number two in most German cities.

In international negotiations, visible differences in style can highlight these cultural variations. At the outset of the 2003 invasion of Iraq, or "Operation Iraqi Freedom," Saddam Hussein and George W. Bush each gave speeches to their own citizens that demonstrate these differences in communication styles. In his speech on March 20, 2003, George W. Bush used directness and succinctness:

> My fellow citizens. At this hour, American and coalition forces are in the early stages of military operations to disarm Iraq, to free its people, and to defend the world from grave danger.
>
> On my orders, coalition forces have begun striking selected targets of military importance to undermine Saddam Hussein's ability to wage war. These are the opening stages of what will be a broad and concerted campaign.[21]

Bush's speech stands in stark contrast to Hussein's:

> Oh great mojahed people.
> Oh sons of our glorious nation.
> Oh men, bearers of arms and the honor of resistance. God's peace be upon you as you confront the invaders, the enemies of God and humanity, the transient blasphemers with chests brimming with faith and the love of God. . . .
>
> Seize the opportunity, the pride of Iraq and the nation. It is the opportunity to become eternal and a long life for the living and glory unparalleled.
>
> Strike at them, fight them. They are aggressors, evil, accursed by God, the exalted. You shall be victorious and they shall be vanquished. . . .
>
> Fight them everywhere the way you are fighting them today and don't give them a chance to catch their breath until they declare it and withdraw from the lands of the Muslims, defeated and cursed in this life and the afterlife.[22]

These different uses of language communicate different things to their culturally different audiences. The same thing can happen in interpersonal communication. A Pakistani friend used the elaborate style when he thanked Judith for accompanying his young daughter to the doctor. He told Judith that she was "his angel of mercy to whom he was forever indebted." She remembers thinking (before she studied intercultural communication!) that the thanks seemed out of proportion and a bit insincere for a simple favor. It is not always easy to interpret language use from other people's perspectives.

Variations in Contextual Rules

While recognizing that there are differences in communication styles, we need to avoid stereotyping specific groups (such as Japanese or English speakers) in terms of style. No group uses a particular communication style all the time. It is also important to realize that the particular style we use may vary from context to context. Think of the contexts in which you communicate during the day—classroom, family, work, and so on—and about how you alter your communication

What Do You Think?
In the United States we are experiencing growth in the popularity and use of personal communication technologies such as text messaging. How do technologies such as this change or expand how you understand different communication styles?

to suit these contexts. For example, you may be more direct in your family contexts and less direct in classroom settings.

Let's look more closely at how different communication styles vary from context to context and may reflect the values of cultural groups. One example is the communication dynamics in many traditional Black churches in the United States. Many such congregations employ the call-response communication form, in which the minister proclaims and the audience gives a response. We can also see this call-response form in secular contexts, in the form of banter between the rapper and others in the social group. This form of call and response arises from the values or priorities identified in many African American communities: the importance of religion; the participatory, interrelatedness of people; the connectedness of spiritual and secular life. Also, public speaking is viewed as a communal event in which speakers are supported and reinforced.

Intercultural problems related to communication style can occur in Black–White communication. For example, when the Black person is speaking, the White person, because call-response is not part of his or her cultural heritage, likely will not engage in the response process. Instead, the White person might remain relatively passive, perhaps voicing an occasional, subdued, "uh-huh." Judging from the White person's seeming lack of involvement, the Black communicator might get the feeling that the White person isn't listening to him. And the White person might get the feeling that the Black person isn't listening because he keeps interrupting.[23]

Another example of different contextual rules for communication can be found in the classroom with Blackfeet students and White students. As we already explained, the primary mode of communication for Blackfeet is silence, whereas a White person's primary mode is speaking. In this case, a young female Blackfeet student was caught between several conflicting sets of contextual rules: (1) the Blackfeet primary mode, which called for proper connective silence, and the Whiteman's primary mode, which seemed to her a presumptuous verbal performance; (2) her Blackfeet heritage, which taught her to respect differences in people based on age and gender and to remain observant, and the White citizen's role, which called for her to speak out; and (3) the Blackfeet preference for a learning environment in which she could be a respectful listening student and the White people's expectation that she be a verbally active student. Table 5.3 summarizes the two modes of communication in this classroom setting.

As we've seen, people communicate differently in different cultural communities. Thus, the context in which the communication occurs is a significant part of the meaning. And while we might communicate in one way in one culture, we might change our communication style for another culture. People who live "on the border" between two different cultures often do this with ease. It's called **code switching.** A colleague of ours can always tell whether her daughter Shaquina is talking to her African American or White friends on the phone, because she uses a different language code. Many Spanish-speaking students do the same thing, speaking "Spanglish" among themselves and then code switching to Standard English when speaking to their professors in class. Native American

TABLE 5.3 Summary of Blackfeet and "Whiteman's" Models of Communication in a Classroom Setting

	BLACKFEET	"WHITEMAN"
Primary Mode	Silence→	Speaking→
Cultural Premise	Listener-active, interconnected	Speaker-active, constructive
Secondary Mode	Verbal speaking→	Silence→
Cultural Premise	Risky, rupture	Division
Social Position	Differences by gender and age	Commonality, equality
Typical Speaker	Elder male	Citizen
Cultural Persona	Relational connection	Unique individual
Values	Nature, heritage, modesty, stability	Upward mobility, change, progress

Source: "'I Can't Do That!' but I 'Can Actually See Around Corners': American Indian Students and the Study of Public 'Communication,'" by D. Carbaugh, in *Critical Perspectives on Communication Research and Pedagogy* (pp. 215–234), by J. Lehtonen and L. Lahtinen (Eds.), 1955, St. Ingbert, Germany: Rährig Universitätsverlag. With permission from the publisher and author.

students who travel between their nations and university campuses may also code switch, being more direct and personal in their university context and then being more indirect and contextual at home. Understanding the dynamics of various speech communities helps us see the range of communication styles.

COMMUNICATING ACROSS DIFFERENCES

Given all these differences in language use and communication styles, how can people successfully communicate with people from different cultures? Sometimes fear can get in our way. One of our students, Emily, described her nervousness in trying to communicate in French:

> Before leaving for France, I thought I was fully prepared for what to expect. I had, at that point, taken four years of French. When I was out to dinner with my "host" sister, one of her friends asked me in French, "What is your name?" I was so nervous and trying so hard to understand her native accent, but I couldn't make out her sentence. After asking me multiple times, slowly, she ended up asking me in English. Needless to say, it was embarrassing because it was one of the most elementary sentences and I couldn't understand!

Even when people speak the same language, there can be differences in communication style and language use. In this situation, which style should dominate? It probably depends on the context. In situations like Emily's, a foreigner is generally expected to adapt to the language and communication style of the host country. Usually both persons try to adapt somewhat to the language and style of the other—creating together what is sometimes called a **third culture style.** That is, when two people try to adapt to each other, they sometimes end up constructing a style that is not exactly like either of their styles![24]

Another way of thinking about intercultural interaction is as two people putting together an **"improvised performance."** In intercultural interaction, we don't have a ready-made conversation script (like we do in our familiar cultural contexts), and we might feel like we are just making up the performance as we go. As we become more skillful at intercultural communication, we can better "sense" where one person is going, and we try to follow and adapt, like a dance or an improvised performance. As we mentioned previously, this improvisation involves being flexible and adapting to the situation.

Mary Catherine Bateson, a famous anthropologist, gives an example of an intercultural improvisation when meeting her Armenian husband's extended family for the first time. She was uncertain about whom she should and should not kiss in greeting them. She assumed she should probably kiss the mother, the brother, and the sister, so she did. But should she kiss the sister's husband? the sister's husband's brother? She wasn't sure. She describes how they improvised:

> So I kissed the sister's husband, and I could feel in the set of his shoulder muscles that I had done the wrong thing, and at least I knew better than to kiss his brother. I was only a little off in this particular improvisation and there was good will to spare.[25]

We improvise verbally in similar ways. For example, if we are speaking to someone whose native language is not English, we might follow that person's lead and speak a little slower, using less slang. We might adapt to the speaker's use of gestures and eye contact (or lack of both), which might not exactly follow our own set of cultural rules.

LANGUAGE AND POWER

All language is social and powerful and complicates the view of intercultural interaction as third culture building or an improvised performance. The language that is used, the words and the meanings that are communicated, depends not only on the context but also on the social relations that are part of that interaction. For example, bosses and workers may use the same words, but the meanings that are communicated may differ. A boss and a worker may both refer to the company personnel as a "family." To the boss, this may mean "one big happy family," while to a disgruntled employee, it may mean a "dysfunctional family." To some extent, the difference is due to the power differential between boss and worker.

Language is powerful and can have tremendous implications for people's lives. For example, saying the words "I do" can influence lives dramatically. Being called names can be hurtful, despite the old adage "sticks and stones may break my bones, but words will never hurt me." In this section, we show how

Info Bites

Naming or labeling a person or group has important consequences. Consider the changing rates of heterosexual couples who hyphenate or creatively combine their last names upon marriage.

language is related to social position and is used by **cocultural groups**—groups that are not dominant within society's social structure.

Language and Social Position

Just as organizations have particular structures and specific job positions within them, societies are structured so that individuals occupy **social positions**—social constructs embedded with assumptions about gender, race, class, age, sexuality, and so on. Differences in social positions are central to understanding communication. For one thing, not all positions within society are equivalent; everyone is not the same. Thus, for example, when men whistle at a woman walking by, it has a different force and meaning than if women were to whistle at a man walking by.

Power is a central element, by extension, of this focus on differences in social position. When a judge in court says what he or she thinks freedom of speech means, it carries much greater force than when your neighbor who is not a judge gives an opinion about what this phrase means. When we communicate, we tend to note, however unconsciously, the group membership and positions of others.

Groups also hold different positions of power in society. Groups with the most power (Whites, men, heterosexuals)—consciously or unconsciously—use a communication system that supports their perception of the world. This means that cocultural groups (ethnic minorities, women, gays) have to function within communication systems that may not represent their lived experience. These nondominant groups find themselves in struggles: Do they try to adapt to dominant communication, or do they maintain their own styles?

There seem to be three general answers to this question of how cocultural groups can relate to the more powerful (dominant) groups. They can communicate nonassertively, assertively, or aggressively. Within each of these communication postures, cocultural individuals may emphasize assimilation—trying to become like the dominant group—or they can try to accommodate or adapt to the dominant group. They can also try to remain separate from the dominant groups as much as possible.[26] The point here is that there are both costs and benefits for cocultural members when they choose which of these strategies to use. Because language is structured in ways that do not reflect their experiences, they must adopt some strategy for dealing with the linguistic framework. For example, if Nick wants to refer to his relationship with James, does he use the word "boyfriend," "friend," "roommate," "husband," "partner," or some other word? If Nick and James are married where it is legal (e.g., Massachusetts, Canada, or Belgium), should they each refer to their "husband" when they are in places that explicitly say they do not recognize same-sex marriages from elsewhere (e.g., Arizona, Michigan, Texas, or Colorado)? What about at work? A party? A bar? What might the consequences be in each of these situations? Let's look at how these strategies might work and the costs and the benefits of them.

These three sets of orientations result in nine types of communication strategies. Which strategy is chosen depends on many things, including the

Pop Culture Spotlight

The crux of some of the most intense debates in the United States rests on the interpretation of words. At the heart of the gay-rights issue is the definition of marriage. Think about how opponents of gay marriage often cite the Bible as a basis for their interpretation of marriage as a union between one man and one woman. Gay marriage supporters argue that there is a difference between marriage as a religious institution and marriage as a civil union. How are other issues that affect us today framed by opposing sides?

TABLE 5.4 Cocultural Communication Orientations

	SEPARATION	ACCOMMODATION	ASSIMILATION
Nonassertive	Avoiding Maintaining interpersonal barriers	Increasing visibility Dispelling stereotypes	Emphasizing commonalities Developing positive face Censoring self Averting controversy
Assertive	Communicating self Intragroup networking Exemplifying strengths Embracing stereotypes	Communicating self Intragroup networking Using liaisons Educating others	Extensive preparation Overcompensating Manipulating stereotypes Bargaining
Aggressive	Attacking Sabotaging others	Confronting Gaining advantage	Dissociating Mirroring Strategic distancing Ridiculing self

Source: Constructing Co-Cultural Theory, by M. P. Orbe, 1998, Thousand Oaks, CA: Sage, p. 110.

desired outcome, perceived costs and rewards, and the context. Let's look at each of these orientations; Table 5.4 gives a summary.

Assimilation Strategies

Some cocultural individuals may use nonassertive assimilation strategies. These communication strategies emphasize trying to fit into and be accepted by the dominant group. Such strategies might emphasize commonalities ("I'm not that different"), be self-monitoring ("I'd better be careful about what I say in this organization to make sure I don't offend those in power"), and, above all, avoid controversy.

There are both costs and benefits for cocultural members who use these strategies. For example, women and members of ethnic minorities may use these strategies at work if they feel that their job success depends on not "making waves"—so they may benefit by keeping their job. For instance, they may keep quiet when they hear offensive or noninclusive remarks, such as a boss's use of "girls" to refer to female staff members. However, there are potential costs as well, for both cocultural members and the dominant group. The cocultural person may experience a lowering of self-esteem due to the feeling that he or she cannot be authentic. In addition, these kinds of strategies can foster an unhealthy communication climate that reinforces the dominant group's social and political power. For example, many African Americans have a distrust of primarily White-run medical institutions. There is a general feeling among communities of African Americans that these White institutions are not concerned with their well-being or how they feel.

What Do You Think?

Celebrations and festivals offer ways to preserve cultural diversity and work against assimilation. What cultural festivals have you been to? Were there elements such as food and dancing that were unique to particular cultures?

Assertive assimilation strategies also seek to downplay cocultural differences and promote a convergence into existing structures. But they do so more forcefully than the nonassertive strategies, not giving priority to others' needs ("I'll try to fit in, but I have to let people know how I feel from time to time"). However, these strategies may promote an us-versus-them mentality, and many people find it difficult to sustain them for long. Eventually, the cocultural member experiences burnout.

Aggressive assimilation strategies emphasize fitting in; cocultural members using these strategies go to great lengths to prove that they are like members of the dominant group. Some strategies are dissociating (showing that one is *not* like other cocultural group members), mirroring (dressing and behaving like the dominant group), or self-ridiculing. The benefits of these kinds of strategies are that the dominant group does not see the cocultural group members as "typical," but the costs sometimes involve ridicule from other cocultural members ("She's trying so hard to be White" or "male" or "straight"). So these individuals may find themselves constantly negotiating their position with the dominant group while being isolated from their own cocultural group.

Accommodation Strategies

Nonassertive accommodation strategies emphasize blending in with the dominant group but also tactfully challenging the dominant structure to recognize cocultural practices. Strategies include increasing visibility and dispelling stereotypes. For example, an African American manager might point out that she isn't particularly good friends with the one other African American in the organization; just because both workers are minorities doesn't mean they'll be good friends. The potential benefits for both dominant and cocultural groups are obvious. In this case the cocultural member is gently educating her colleagues and helping to change stereotypes of the cocultural group.

Also, using this strategy, the cocultural member may be able to influence group decision making while still showing loyalty to larger organizational goals. For example, a female business executive who shows that she's willing to work long hours, head up committees, and travel influences decision making while showing that she doesn't fulfill the stereotype of a working mother, for whom family always comes first. However, there are costs as well. Individuals with this orientation may be criticized by others for not being more aggressive in trying to change the dominant structures. Also, these communication strategies don't really promote major change in organizations to make them more inclusive and reflective of larger society.

Assertive accommodation strategies involve trying to strike a balance between the concerns of cocultural and dominant group members. These strategies involve communicating self, doing intragroup networking, using liaisons, and educating others. For example, using these strategies, African Americans may share information about themselves with their coworkers and educate others about phrases that are offensive, such as "working like a slave." Or gay colleagues may educate coworkers about how they feel excluded when so much of straight people's conversation focuses on heterosexual relationships and assumes that everyone is straight.

Aggressive accommodation strategies involve becoming a part of dominant structures and then working from within to promote significant changes, no matter how high the personal cost. Cocultural members who use these types of communication strategies may be seen as confrontational and self-promoting. However, they also reflect a genuine desire to work with and not against the dominant group members. For example, a Chicana colleague of ours uses this strategy in consistently reminding our department that affirmative action goals have to be integrated into the mission of the department and not seen as a separate goal—in which case people could compartmentalize their actions and only sometimes work for affirmative action. Similarly, a colleague with a disability consistently reminds the office staff that the facilities need to be more accessible—mailboxes that can't be reached, doors that do not open automatically, bathrooms that do not accommodate wheelchairs, and so on.

Cocultural members with this orientation may periodically use assertive as well as aggressive accommodation strategies and so may be perceived as genuinely committed to the larger group's good. In this way, they reap the benefits of being perceived positively by the dominant group and also have an impact on the organization. However, cocultural members who consistently use aggressive accommodating strategies may find themselves alienated from both other cocultural members and dominant group colleagues for being too confrontational.

Separation Strategies

Nonassertive separation strategies are employed by individuals who assume that some segregation is part of everyday life in the United States. Generally, people live, work, learn, play, and pray with people who resemble themselves. This is generally easier for the dominant group than for cocultural members. Some cocultural individuals regard segregation as a natural phenomenon but also use subtle communication practices to maintain separation from the dominant group. Perhaps the most common strategy is simply avoiding interaction with dominant group members whenever possible. Thus, gay people using this orientation may spend their social time with other gay people. Or women may prefer to use professional women's services (having a female doctor, dentist, and attorney) and socialize with other women.

Assertive separation strategies reflect a conscious choice to maintain space between dominant and cocultural group members. Typical strategies include communication practices such as stressing strengths and embracing stereotypes. Some assertive separation strategies, such as communicating self and intragroup networking, might also be employed by those wanting to assert separation. One of the benefits of assertive separation strategies, like the nonassertive strategies, is that they promote cocultural unity and self-determination. However, individuals might implement the strategies without having access to resources controlled by the dominant group.

Pop Culture Spotlight

In the film *The Wedding Banquet,* an Asian American is trying to figure out how to tell his traditional Chinese parents that he is gay, while his White lover is trying to learn Mandarin. In one very funny scene, the lover gives his partner's mother some beauty cream, but his Mandarin is so bad he describes it as cream for "old ladies." Are there things we can do to prepare for those inevitable mistakes?

Aggressive separation strategies are used by those for whom cocultural segregation is an important priority. These strategies include attacking and sabotaging others. Individuals using these strategies often criticize those who use assimilation or accommodation strategies. While cocultural members do not have the power base that members of the dominant group have, these strategies do enable cocultural members to confront pervasive discriminatory structures. However, they also risk retaliatory attacks by the dominant group.

It is useful to think about when it is effective to use these various strategies given that each may have some benefits and costs associated with it. For example, suppose Luis, the only minority group member, thinks that he is consistently "cut out of the loop" at work. He has just discovered that there was a meeting that impacts his projects that he was not told about. There are a number of ways that he might handle this situation. He could use an aggressive assimilation strategy and simply try as hard as he can to fit in and to be included. But this may not give him the outcome he wants and may lead to a perception that he doesn't have a strong ethnic identity. He could use an assertive accommodation strategy, reminding his coworkers that he needs to be included and explicitly pointing out when he is not included. This could produce the desired outcome and help the organization become more aware of its need for increased inclusiveness. Or he could adopt an aggressive accommodation strategy and march into the director's office, demanding to be included.

MOVING BETWEEN LANGUAGES

Multilingualism

People who speak two languages are considered **bilingual;** people who speak more than two languages are considered **multilingual.** Rarely, however, do bilinguals speak both languages with the same level of fluency. More commonly, they prefer to use one language over another, depending on the context and the topic.

Sometimes, entire nations are officially bilingual or multilingual. Belgium, for example, has three national languages: Dutch, German, and French. Canada recognizes English and French. Switzerland is a multilingual nation that has four official languages: French, German, Italian, and Romansh. And the United States has a growing number of speakers of English and Spanish as well as many other languages. Table 5.5 lists the 10 languages (other than English) that are most commonly spoken in U.S. homes. Laura, a college student, describes how it feels to be bilingual:

> Growing up bilingual, one must think before the words come out. If I am communicating with my boss at work, English is the common language. In a restaurant, depending on the person or friend, the language is determined: Is he or she English-speaking, Spanish-speaking, or bilingual? At home with family, it is natural to talk to them in Spanish. Growing up bilingual sometimes feels like a job. A job to be proud of.
>
> English I learned at school was second to Spanish. Growing up, it was normal to talk English to teachers and schoolmates at school, but at home,

TABLE 5.5 Top 10 Non-English Languages Most Commonly Spoken at Home in the United States

1. Spanish	6. Vietnamese
2. Chinese	7. Italian
3. French	8. Korean
4. German	9. Russian
5. Tagalog	10. Polish

Source: U.S. Census Bureau. Retrieved from http://www.census.gov/prod/2003pubs/c2kbr-29.pdf.

my grandmother and family spoke Spanish, and so did I. Spanish is what I heard and learned first growing up and raised by my grandmother. I feel comfortable and happy talking in Spanish. I feel I am the Spanish words that come out of my mouth.

I am proud to be bilingual. I talk like who I am, mestiza, mixed in my blood and in my language. There are many people who grew up like me, knowing two languages. A lot of the times as we talk we mix both Spanish and English together and come up with Spanglish, un mestizo. Spanglish is not a language on its own, it is a mix of two languages, English and Spanish, like our lives. I can communicate well with my boss and English-speaking friends. I can talk to my family and friends in Spanish. I can also combine both Spanish and English languages, and still others will understand me.

On either the individual or the national level, multilinguals must engage in language negotiation. That is, they need to work out, whether explicitly or implicitly, which language to use in a given situation. These decisions are sometimes clearly embedded in power-relations. For example, French was the court language during the reign of Catherine the Great, in 18th-century Russia. French was considered the language of culture, the language of the élite, whereas Russian was considered a vulgar language, the language of the uneducated.

Sometimes, a language is chosen as a courtesy to others. When Judith is with her bilingual friends (Spanish-English), they often speak English, because Judith's Spanish proficiency is low. Tom joined a small group going to see the fireworks display at the Eiffel Tower on Bastille Day one year. (Bastille Day is a French national holiday, celebrated on July 14, commemorating the storming of the Bastille prison and the beginning of the French Revolution.) One person in the group asked, "Alors, on parle français ou anglais?" ["Are we speaking French or English?"] Because one member was quite weak in English, French was chosen as the language of the evening.

The reasons people become bilingual reflect the trends we identified in Chapter 1 that drive the need for intercultural communication. **Bilingualism** results from these imperatives, as people move from one country to another, as businesses expand into international markets, and so on. More personal imperatives also drive people to become bilingual. Alice Kaplan, a French

What Do You Think?

What you name or label something has important cultural implications. Consider the fact that on most government-sponsored forms people of Latin heritage must check "Hispanic." What power differences are revealed through institutions' use of labels? What kinds of personal power are invoked when these populations write in labels like "Latina/o, Chicana/o, Cuban American, Dominican American, Mexican American," and so forth on government forms?

professor at Duke University, notes, "Speaking a foreign language is, for me and my students, a chance for growth, for freedom, a liberation from the ugliness of our received ideas and mentalities."[27] Many people use foreign languages to escape from the history of oppression in their own languages.

Perhaps it is easier to think of language as a "prisonhouse," since all of the semantic, syntactic, pragmatic, and phonetic systems are enmeshed in a social system from which there is no escape, except through the learning of another language. Consider the case of Sam Sue, a Chinese American born and raised in Mississippi, who explained his own need to negotiate these social systems—often riddled by stigmatizing stereotypes—by changing the way he speaks:

> Northerners see a Southern accent as a signal that you're a racist, you're stupid, or you're a hick. Regardless of what your real situation is. So I reacted to that by adapting the way I speak. If you talked to my brother, you would definitely know he was from the South. But as for myself, I remember customers telling my dad, "Your son sounds like a Yankee."[28]

Among the variations in U.S. English, the southern accent unintentionally communicates many negative stereotypes. Developing another accent is, for some, the only way to escape the stereotypes. When you hear different accents, what kinds of stereotypes do these accents invoke?

Aside from accents, cocultural groups often develop **argot,** a separate way of communicating. Argot often involves creating a way of communicating that distinguishes insiders from outsiders in a group. Insiders can understand what is being said, while outsiders cannot. In many ways, it is similar to learning another language. In French, one type of argot is called **verlan.** Verlan refers to the reversing of words in order to confuse those who do not understand verlan. It most often involves reversing syllables to create different words, thus "les pourris" (the rotten guys) becomes "les ripoux." Once these words are used enough, they become familiar terms and many French-speakers may use these words without realizing that they are verlan, such as the word "beur," which is verlan from "arabe." While verlan has existed since the beginning of the French language, it has become popular among poorer youth in the French suburbs.

Learning another language is never easy, but the rewards of knowing another language are immense. The reasons for studying intercultural communication that we discussed in Chapter 1 can also be applied to learning a second language. The demographic and economic imperatives are especially relevant, particularly in regions of the country where there is increasing ethnic and linguistic diversity. Our student Laura recently moved from Michigan to Arizona, where she works with many individuals who have recently moved there from Mexico. She comments, "It is sometimes hard, because you want to communicate, but do not always have the words. I do not speak much Spanish, so conversations can be difficult. However, where there's a will, there's a way. My friends and I make an effort to get our meanings across, and I have met some wonderful people as a result."

Surf's Up!

Artificial languages exist around the world. Consider Elvish, pig Latin, and Klingon, to name a few. Visit www.wikihow.com/ Create-a-Language to create your own language— from devising an alphabet to coming up with your own grammar rules.

Language acquisition simply refers to the process of learning another language. Language acquisition studies have shown that it is nearly impossible for someone to learn the language of a group of people they dislike. And learning another language can lead to respect for another culture. Our student Karla describes such an experience:

> As soon as I entered the seventh grade, I began to learn Spanish. It was very difficult and after speaking Spanish for many years I have a greater respect for bilingual people. (In fact, when I was little I always assumed that Mexicans were smarter than Americans because many of them spoke English and Spanish!) Once I began to advance in my Spanish classes, we learned more in depth about different cultures including Mexican and Spanish cultures. I had one teacher who realized that reading about other people was a hard way to relate to them. She designed an after-school group of teens that spoke English as their second language. As a class we would get together and talk with these students. This was a good opportunity to become friends with people I would never have met otherwise.

One interesting linguistic phenomenon that has implications for the teaching and learning of other languages is called **interlanguage.** Interlanguage refers to the type of communication that emerges when native speakers of one language are speaking in another language. The native language's linguistic structure often overlaps into the second language, which creates a third way of communicating. For example, many native English speakers might try to write in French "Je suis un Américain" in attempting to translate "I am an American." While we capitalize "American," it should not be capitalized in French. Also, the structure of the sentence reflects English grammar, as proper French would be "Je suis américain." Conversely, Sarah Turnbull, an Australian journalist, says that when she first met her French husband, Frédéric, his "English was sprinkled with wonderful expressions like 'foot finger' instead of toes."[29] The French often refer to toes as "doigts de pied" or literally "fingers of the foot" or "foot fingers." Frédéric's interlanguage caused him to overlap French structure into English, which creates a third way of communicating that is not exactly English, but certainly not French either.

People react differently to living in a multicultural world. Some work hard to learn other languages and other ways of communicating, even if they make a number of errors along the way. Others retreat into their familiar languages and customs. The tensions that arise over different languages and different meaning systems are played out around the world. And these tensions will never disappear but will always provide new challenges for intercultural communicators.

Translation and Interpretation

Intercultural communication scholars are also concerned with the role of translation and interpretation—that is, how people understand each other when they speak different languages. Because it is impossible to learn all of the languages in the world, we must rely on translation and interpretation—two distinct but important means of communicating across languages. The European Union (EU), for example, has a strict policy of recognizing all of the languages of its constituent members. Hence, a large number of translators and interpreters are hired to work by the EU to bridge linguistic differences.

Translation generally refers to the process of producing a written text that refers to something said or written in another language. The original-language text of a translation is called the **source text;** the text into which it is translated is called the **target text.** So, when *Gone with the Wind* is translated into Hungarian, the original text written by the author is the source text. The result of the translation, the Hungarian version, is the target text.

Interpretation refers to the process of verbally expressing what is said or written in another language. Interpretation can either be simultaneous, with the interpreter speaking at the same time as the original speaker, or consecutive, with the interpreter speaking only during the breaks provided by the original speaker.

Languages are entire systems of meaning and consciousness that are not easily translated into other languages word for word. The ways in which different languages convey views of the world are not equivalent, as we noted earlier. Remember the dilemma regarding color? The English word *brown* might be translated as any of these French words, depending on how the word is used: *roux, brun, bistre, bis, marron, jaune,* and *gris.*[30] For example, *brun* is used to describe brown hair, while *bis* is used to describe a brown pencil.

Issues of Equivalency and Accuracy   Some languages have tremendous flexibility in expression; others have a limited range of words. The reverse may be true, however, for some topics. This variation between languages is both aggravating and thrilling for translators and interpreters. The tradition of translation studies has tended to emphasize issues of accuracy and **equivalency**—the condition of being equal in meaning, value, quantity, and so on. That is, the focus, largely from linguistics, has been on comparing the translated meaning to the original meaning. Often, word-for-word translations that are not equivalent in meaning can yield amusing target texts, like the following signs in tourist spots around the world:[31]

- Is forbidden to steal hotel towels please. If you are not a person to do such thing is please not to read notice (Tokyo hotel).
- The lift is being fixed for the next day. During that time we regret that you will be unbearable (elevator in Bucharest, Romania).
- Please leave your values at the front desk (Paris hotel).
- Because of the impropriety of entertaining guests of the opposite sex in the bedroom, it is suggested that the lobby be used for this purpose (Zurich hotel).

- It is forbidden to enter a woman even a foreigner if dressed as a man (Bangkok temple).

- Specialist in women and other diseases (Rome doctor's office).

- The manager has personally passed all the water served here (Acapulco hotel).

In some instances, (e.g. translating research questionnaires) equivalency of meaning is very important. A special **back translation** technique can improve the translation's accuracy, and is often used in small amounts of text, like a questionnaire or an essay.[32] For example, Judith and Tom's colleague conducted a study comparing Japanese and U. S. students' conflict styles and used the back translation method. That is, he first developed a questionnaire in English and then translated it into Japanese. Then the translated Japanese text was translated back to English by another translator who had no prior knowledge of the text. The two texts were then compared—the original English text with the back translated text—and any discrepancies between the two versions were examined and resolved by a panel of multilingual experts. However, if the translation of the questionnaire was not acceptable, then this process (forward translation, back translation, discussion by the bilingual expert panel, etc.) would continue as many times as necessary until a satisfactory version is reached.[33]

There are some famous and very important "geopolitical" examples of bad translations creating problems. In June 1963, John F. Kennedy stood at the Berlin Wall and declared, *"Ich bin ein Berliner,"* which translates as "I am a cream bun." In December 1977, Jimmy Carter gave a speech in Poland which included the sentence, "I want to know the Polish people." When this was translated into Polish, the word "know" was mistranslated so that Carter was quoted as having said, "I want to have carnal knowledge of the Polish people."

For those interested in the intercultural communication process, the emphasis is not so much on equivalence but on the bridges that people construct to "cross" from one language to another.

Once when Tom was in Normandy, in northern France, a French police officer asked him to tell an English-speaking woman to get down from a wall that was high above the street. Tom called out to her that the officer wanted her to get down. She refused. The police officer became angry and began speaking louder and faster, repeating his request. Tom, too, began speaking louder and faster, giving the same request in English. The situation escalated until the woman hollered, "Tell him to go to hell!" At this point, Tom felt trapped, so he turned to the police officer and said, "Je ne comprends pas. Je ne parle pas français" ["I don't understand. I don't speak French"].

Tom tried to apologize and escape the situation. But the police officer interrupted him immediately and retorted, "Mais oui, tu peux parler français!" ["Oh yes, you can speak French!"] He continued barking angry commands at the woman. Throughout this situation, Tom never really expressed the nuances of the statements on either side. The officer, unless he understood English and refused to speak it, did not know the obscenities that were being hurled his way.

Pop Culture Spotlight

There are a great many versions or dialects of English spoken across the globe. Do any of these different types play a role in the television series that become part of your daily life? Consider the use of different dialects for comedic effects.

Nor did the woman understand the demeaning familiar forms of language used by the officer, or the significance of his demands as a police officer, a position of much more authority than in the United States.

The Role of the Translator or Interpreter We often assume that translators and interpreters are "invisible," that they simply render into the target language whatever they hear. The roles that they play as intermediaries, however, often regulate how they render what is said. Consider the previous example again. Because of the French police officer's position, it was nearly impossible for Tom to tell him what the woman was saying—even apart from the linguistic difficulty of translating profanity.

It is important that you acknowledge the role of an interpreter if you find yourself in that situation. Tom recently met with some journalists from China, and an interpreter who spoke Mandarin Chinese and English was brought along. Tom was sure to acknowledge her presence and asked her when and how he should stop speaking so she could interpret. He also ensured that she felt free to ask questions to clarify anything that might be interpreted in different ways. By doing this, the interpreter was given more flexibility and authority in interpretation, which hopefully assisted in the interpretation process.

We often assume that anyone who knows two languages can be a translator or an interpreter. Research shows, however, that a high level of fluency in two languages does not necessarily make someone a good translator or interpreter. The task obviously requires the knowledge of two languages. But that's not enough. Think about all the people you know who are native English speakers. What might explain why some of them are better writers than others? Knowing English, for example, is a necessity for writing in English, but this knowledge does not necessarily make a person a good writer. Because of the complex relationships between people, particularly in intercultural situations, translation and interpretation involve far more than linguistic equivalence, which traditionally has been the focus.

Language Politics and Policies

Some nations have multiple official languages. Here in the United States, there is no official, legal national language, although English is the de facto national language. There were discussions about language policy during the writing of the Constitution, as a number of languages were spoken by Europeans in the Americas at that time, including English, French, German, and Spanish. Ultimately, however, the Founding Fathers decided to not say anything in the Constitution with regard to language. However, some U.S. places have also declared two official languages, such as Guam (Chamorro and English), Hawaii (English and Hawaiian), New Mexico (English and Spanish), and Samoa (English and Samoan). And recently, the U.S. Senate debated establishing English as the national language of the United States. At the time of this writing, it isn't clear what will happen to this proposal, but the attempt to establish English as the national language "does not go as far as proposals to designate English the nation's official language, which would require all government publications and business to be in English."[34] Thus, if English is the national language of the United States, it might mean something different than the official language of the United States.

Laws or customs that emerge to determine which language is to be spoken where and when are referred to as **language policies.** These policies often emerge from the politics of language use. Historically, for example, European aristocrats spoke French. Recall that in the court of Catherine the Great of Russia, one heard and spoke French, not Russian. According to the language policies of the period, speaking Russian was seen as vulgar, or as they might have said, declassé. The French language, within those language policies, was closely tied to the politics of social and economic class. To illustrate, think about how you would feel if in the United States speaking English was a sign that you were "vulgar," while speaking French was a sign of high status.

Consider the controversy about **Ebonics**—an American English dialect spoken by some African Americans. A few years ago, the school board in Oakland, California, passed a resolution that recognized Ebonics as a separate language, not just a dialect. The resolution instructed teachers to "respect and embrace the language richness of Ebonics," but more important, it required schools to provide English as a Second Language instruction to students who spoke Ebonics as their first "language." A number of the teachers (and policy makers) viewed Ebonics as simply substandard English, not even a dialect, and were not willing to recognize Ebonics as a legitimate language nor provide funds for English language instruction.[35] This language controversy had far-reaching implications—involving not only the teachers and parents, but linguists and policymakers.

There are different motivations behind the establishment of language policies that guide the status of different languages in a place. Sometimes nations decide on a national language as part of a process of driving people to assimilate into the national culture. If the state wishes to promote assimilation, language policies that encourage everyone to speak the official language and conduct business in that language are promoted.

Sometimes nations develop language policies as a way of protecting minority languages so that these languages do not disappear. Welsh in Wales is one example, but Irish in Ireland and Frisian in Germany and the Netherlands are legally protected languages. Some language policies recognize the language rights of its citizens wherever they are in the nation. One example of this is Canada (English and French). Another is Kenya (Swahili and English). Government services are available in either language throughout the nation.

Other language policies are governed by location. In Belgium, Dutch (Flemish) is the official language in Flanders in the northern part of the country. French is the official language in Wallonia in the south, and German is the official language in the eastern Cantons bordering Germany. Thus, if you are boarding a train to go from Antwerp to Tournai, you would need to look for "Doornik" in the Antwerp train station. When you returned to the train station in Tournai to go back, you would look for the train to "Anvers." The signs would not be posted in both languages, except in the Brussels-Capital region (the only bilingual part of the nation).

Surf's Up!

Have you used any of the online translation web-based resources? Try experimenting with http://FreeTranslation.com. What happens when you attempt to translate a phrase such as "Don't hate me because I'm beautiful" from English to Spanish and then back again? Was the meaning conveyed? What does your experimenting tell you about the nature of communicating to someone who is a native speaker of a language other than your own?

Languages are entire systems of meaning and consciousness that are not easily translated into another language. This is also true for spoken language and sign language.

What Do You Think?

How many of your friends or family members are bilingual or multilingual? Did you grow up in a bi- or multilingual home? If so you may practice code switching, a concept that describes the combination of two or more languages while speaking or writing. What happens when people practice code switching in organizations like church, at work, or in study groups or sororities? Does code switching reveal differences among these organizations?

Sometimes language policies are developed with language parity, but the implementation is not equal. In Cameroon, for example, English and French are both official languages, although 247 indigenous languages are also spoken. Whereas Germany was the initial colonizer of Cameroon, Britain and France took over in 1916—with most of the territory going to France—and these "new colonial masters then sought to impose their languages in the newly acquired territory."[36] At independence in 1960, French Cameroon established French as its official language and English became the official language in the former British Cameroon areas once they joined together to form Cameroon. When united in 1961, Cameroon established both languages as official languages. Since French speakers are far more numerous than English speakers, "French has a de facto dominance over English in the areas of administration, education and the media. In fact, it is not an exaggeration to say that French influence as expressed in language, culture and political policy prevails in all domains."[37] So while Cameroon is officially bilingual, French dominates in nearly all domains, as most of the people are French speakers. Thus, "What appears to be a language policy for the country is hardly clearly defined, in spite of the expressed desire to promote English–French bilingualism and protect the indigenous languages."[38] European colonialism has left its mark in this African nation, and the language policy and language realities remain to be worked out.

We can view the development of language policies as reflecting the tensions between the nation's history and its future, between the various language communities, and between economic and political relations inside and outside the nation. Language policies can help resolve or exacerbate these tensions as in the case of China and the many languages spoken there (see Figure 5.1).

SINO-TIBETAN
☐ Mandarin
  1. Northern
  2. Eastern
  3. Southwestern
☐ Southern
  1. Wu
  2. Gan
  3. Xiang
  4. Min
  5. Hakka
  6. Yue
☐ Tibetan
  1. Amdo
  2. Khams
  3. Dbusgtsang
☐ Kam-Tai
☐ Miao-Yao
INDO-EUROPEAN
☐ Tajik
AUSTRO-ASIATIC
☐ Mon-Khmer
ALTAI
☐ Turkic
  1. Kazakh
  2. Uygur
  3. Kirghiz
☐ Mongolian
☐ Manchu-Tungus
☐ Korean

—— Province-level boundary

Figure 5.1 Linguistic maps show where different languages are spoken. This linguistic map shows where different dialects of Chinese are spoken in China. What might a linguistic map of other parts of the world look like?

Source: University of Texas at Austin Library. Retrieved from http://www.lib.utexas.edu/maps/middle_east_and_asia/china_ling_90.jpg.

In Canada today, many wonder about the bilingual future of the nation. Recently, the French magazine *L'Express* asked, "Is Canada always bilingual?" Suggesting that bilingualism will not last in Canada, the French-language Canadian magazine *L'actualité* responded, "the number of bilinguals is growing. They were 12 percent of the Canadian population in 1951. Fifty years later, they were 18 percent."[39] While we cannot know the future of Canada, the importance of language in Canada is not likely to go away anytime soon.

SUMMARY

In this chapter, we explored many dimensions of language in intercultural communication. Linguists study four basic components of language as they investigate how language works: (1) phonology, the study of the sound system, (2) semantics, the study of meaning, (3) syntax, the study of structure, and (4) pragmatics, the study of the purposes and contexts of language in use.

We also discussed the Sapir-Whorf hypothesis and how the particular language we speak influences our perception. Language is powerful, but it does not totally determine our perception. Languages exhibit many cultural variations, both in communication style and in the rules of context. Cultural groups may emphasize speech or silence, as well as the importance of verbal (low-context) or nonverbal (high-context) communication. Two types of communication styles are indirect/direct and elaborated/understated. The context in which the communication occurs is a significant part of the meaning. People bridge these different communication styles in intercultural interactions by together creating a "third culture style" and improvising a communication performance.

We also examined the role of power in language. Dominant groups, consciously or unconsciously, develop communication systems that require nondominant groups to use communication that doesn't fit their lived experience. We identified nine strategies that cocultural group members may use in communication with dominant group members. The effects of power are also revealed in the use of labels, with the more powerful people in a society labeling the less powerful. Individuals who occupy powerful positions in a society often don't think about the way their positions are revealed in their communication.

Next, we discussed multilingualism. Individuals learn languages for different reasons, and the process is often a rewarding one. The complexities of moving between languages is facilitated by interpretation and translation, in which issues of equivalency and accuracy are crucial. Being a good translator or interpreter requires more than just fluency in two languages.

Finally, we looked at the situations in Belgium, Cameroon, and Canada to explore some issues surrounding language policies and intercultural communication. The issue of what language should be spoken when, to whom, and why becomes quite complex.

BUILDING INTERCULTURAL SKILLS

1. Become more conscious of how you use language. Are you sending the messages you think you are sending? Sharpen your own skills by checking to see if people are interpreting messages the way you intend, particularly in intercultural situations. One way to do this is by asking others what they understood. If they didn't get your point, try paraphrasing.

2. Become more aware of others' verbal messages in intercultural encounters. Be aware of your own assumptions about others' language skills. For example, what kind of assumptions do you make when you hear accented English? Or a southern accent? Or an elaborated style? Or a succinct style? Practice your decoding skills. Check to see if others really meant to say what you understood. One way to do this is by asking others directly. However, remember that not everyone is comfortable with direct questions and answers. Practice other ways of trying to understand messages, such as observing or asking indirect questions.

3. Practice expanding your language repertoire in intercultural situations. When you speak with others whose first language is different from yours, speak more slowly, use easy-to-understand words and simple sentences, and avoid slang. If English isn't your first language, practice asking questions when you don't understand. And try to vary your own language patterns. If you tend to speak a lot, try listening. If you are often quiet, try speaking up.

4. Practice being flexible and adapting to others' language style in intercultural encounters. In formal situations, use more formal language. Or if someone uses a more indirect style, try using a more indirect style.

5. Practice using labels that are preferred by group members. Gay or homosexual? African American or Black? White or Caucasian? If you aren't sure, investigate using appropriate communication strategies—after making sure that you have the kind of relationship where you can ask freely.

ACTIVITIES

1. *Regional language variations:* Meet in small groups with other class members and discuss variations in language use in different regions of the United States (accent, vocabulary, and so on). Identify perceptions that are associated with these variations.

2. *"Foreigner" labels:* Meet in small groups with other class members, and come up with a list of general labels used to refer to people from other countries who come to the United States (such as immigrants, aliens, or foreigners). For each label, identify a general connotation (positive, negative, mixed). Discuss how the connotations of these words may influence our perceptions of people from other countries. Would it make a difference if we referred to them as *guests* or *visitors*?

ENDNOTES

1. Davis, W. (1999). Vanishing cultures. *National Geographic, 196,* pp. 62–89.
2. Omniglot, Writing Systems and Languages of the World. Retrieved January 29, 2009 from http://www.omniglot.com/writing/vietnamese.htm
3. Genzer, D. *The disorientation manual 1987–88.* (A guide for American students studying at the University of St. Andrews, Scotland). St. Andrews, Scotland: University of St. Andrews.
4. Slackman, M. (2008, June 20). With a word, Egyptians leave it all to fate. *The New York Times,* A9.
5. Smith, T. W. (1992). Changing racial labels: From "Colored" to "Negro" to "Black" to "African American." *The Public Opinion Quarterly, 56*(4), 496–514.
6. Sigelman, L., Tuch, S. A., & Martin, J. K. (2005). What's in a name? Preference for "Black" versus "African-American" among Americans of African descent. *Public Opinion Quarterly, 69,* 429–438; Why Black and not African American? (20 April 2007) Retrieved February 16, 2008 from http://theangryblackwoman.wordpress.com/2007/04/20/why-black-and-not-african-american/
7. Cruz-Janzen, M. (2002). Lives on the crossfire: The struggle of multiethnic and multiracial Latinos for identity in a dichotomous and racialized world. *Race, Gender & Class, 9* (2), 47–62.
8. Yellow Bird, M. (1999). What we want to be called. *American Indian Quarterly, 23*(2), 1–20.
9. Davis (1999), p. 65.
10. Hoijer, H. (1994). The Sapir-Whorf hypothesis. In L. Samovar & R. E. Porter (Eds.), *Intercultural communication: A reader* (pp. 194–200). Belmont, CA: Wadsworth.
11. Davis (1999), pp. 62–89.
12. Dehaene, S., Izard, V., Pica, P., & Spelke, E. (2006). Core knowledge of geometry in an Amazonian indigene group. *Science, 311,* 381–384; Kenneally, C. (2008, April 22). When language can hold the answer. *The New York Times,* p. F1.
13. Pinker, S. (1994). *The language instinct: How the mind creates language.* New York: HarperCollins, p. 72; Davies, I. R. L., & Sowden, P. T. (1998). A cross-cultural study of English and Setswana speakers on a colour triads task: A test of the Sapir-Whorf hypothesis. *British Journal of Psychology, 89,* 1–15.

14. Giles, H., Coupland, N., & Wiemann, J. (1992). Talk is cheap . . . but "My word is my bond": Beliefs about talk. In K. Bolton & H. Kwok (Eds.), *Sociolinguistics today* (pp. 218–243). New York: Routledge.

15. Carbaugh, D. (1995). "I can't do that!" But I "can actually see around corners": American Indian students and the study of public "communication." In J. Lahtonen & L. Lahtinen (Eds.), *Critical perspectives on communication research and pedagogy* (pp. 215–234). St. Ingbert, Germany: Rohrig Universitätsverlag.

16. Kim, M.-S. (2002). *Non-Western perspectives on human communication.* Thousand Oaks, CA: Sage, p. 135.

17. Hall, E. T. (1976). *Beyond culture.* Garden City, NY: Doubleday, p. 79.

18. Hall (1976), p. 79.

19. Gudykunst, W. B., & Ting-Toomey, S. (1988). *Culture and interpersonal communication.* Newbury Park, CA: Sage.

20. Kikoski, J. F., & Kikoski, C. K. (1999). *Reflexive communication in the culturally diverse workplace.* Westport, CT: Praeger, p. 67.

21. Bush, G. (2003, March 20). George Bush's address on the start of war. *The Guardian.* Retrieved from http://www.guardian.co.uk/Iraq/Story/0,2763,918031,00.html

22. Hussein, S. (2003, April 1). Strike at them, fight them. *The Guardian.* Retrieved from http://www.guardian.co.uk/Iraq/Story/0,2763,927647,00.html

23. Daniel, J. L., & Smitherman, G. (1990). How I got over: Communication dynamics in the Black community. In D. Carbaugh (Ed.), *Cultural communication and intercultural contact* (pp. 27–40). Hillsdale, NJ: Erlbaum.

24. Casmir, F. L. (1999). Foundations for the study of intercultural communication based on a third culture building model. *International Journal of Intercultural Relations, 23,* 91–116.

25. Bateson, M. C. (1993). Joint performance across cultures: Improvisation in a Persian garden. *Text and Performance Quarterly, 13,* 119.

26. Orbe, M. P. (1998). *Constructing co-cultural theory: An explication of culture, power, and communication.* Thousand Oaks, CA: Sage.

27. Kaplan, A. (1993). *French lessons: A memoir.* Chicago: University of Chicago Press, p. 211.

28. Sue, S. (1992). Growing up in Mississippi. In J. F. J. Lee (Ed.), *Asian Americans* (pp. 3–9). New York: New Press.

29. Turnbull, S. (2002). *Almost French: Love and a new life in Paris.* New York: Penguin, p. vii.

30. Vinay, J. P., & Darbelnet, J. (1977). *Stylistique comparée du français et de l'anglais: Méthode de traduction.* Paris: Marcel Didier, p. 261.

31. Lost in Translation. Retrieved January 29, 2009 from http://www.jnweb.com/funny/translation.html

32. Brislin, R. (1986). The wording and translation of research instruments. In W. J. Lonner & J. W. Berry (Eds.) *Field methods in cross cultural research* (pp. 137–164). Newbury Park, CA: Sage; Chang, A. M., Chau, J. P., & Holroyd, E. (1999). Translation of questionnaires and issues of equivalence. *Journal of Advanced Nursing, 29*(2), 316–322.

33. Shigenobu, T. (2007). Evaluation and usability of back translation for intercultural communication. In N. Aykin (ed.), *Usability and internationalization: Global and local user interfaces* (pp. 259–265). Berlin: Springer.

34. Hulse, C. (2006, May 19). Senate votes to set English as national language. *The New York Times,* p. A19.

35. Wolfram, W., Adger, C. T., & Christian, D. (1999). *Dialects in Schools and Communities.* Mahwah, NJ: Erlbaum.

36. Echu, G. (2003). Coping with multilingualism: Trends in the evolution of language policy in Cameroon. *PhiN, 25,* 34. Retrieved from http://web.fuberlin.de/phin/phin25/p25t2.htm#ech99b

37. Echu (2003), p. 39.

38. Echu (2003), p. 44.

39. Demetz, J.-M. (2006, February 23). Is Canada always bilingual? *L'Express,* pp. 42–45; Chartrand, L. (2006, May 1). Who defends bilingualism? *L'actualité,* p. 75. [Le nombre des bilingues s'accroît. Ceux-ci formaient 12% de la population canadienne en 1951. Cinquante ans plus tard, ils étaient 18%.]

CHAPTER SIX

Nonverbal Communication Issues

CHAPTER OUTLINE

Defining Nonverbal Communication
Comparing Verbal and Nonverbal Communication
What Nonverbal Behavior Communicates

Cultural Variations in Nonverbal Behavior
Nonverbal Codes
Cultural Variation or Stereotype?

Defining Cultural Space
Cultural Identity and Cultural Space
Changing Cultural Space
The Dynamic Nature of Cultural Spaces

Summary

Building Intercultural Skills

Activities

Endnotes

STUDY OBJECTIVES

After reading this chapter, you should be able to:

1. Define nonverbal communication.
2. Understand the difference between verbal and nonverbal communication.
3. Describe what nonverbal behavior communicates.
4. Identify cultural differences in nonverbal behavior.
5. Understand how nonverbal communication can reinforce cultural stereotypes.
6. Define and give examples of cultural space.
7. Describe the relationship between cultural identity and cultural space.
8. Describe the dynamic nature of cultural spaces.

KEY TERMS

adaptors	monochronic
contact cultures	neighborhood
cultural spaces	noncontact cultures
cyberspace	nonverbal communication
deception	paralinguistics
emblems	personal space
eye contact	polychronic
facial expressions	regionalism
gestures	regulators
home	relational messages
illustrators	silence
migration	status
MMOGs	traveling

What Do You Think?

How would you categorize gang signs in terms of nonverbal communication? What kinds of things do they communicate? Do they mean different things to different kinds of people? To new gang members? To rival gang members? To teachers and parents? To police officers?

Nonverbal communication, just like language, can vary dramatically across cultures. These differences can sometimes lead to misunderstandings. For example, a new coworker from Mexico, who is accustomed to closer spatial distances, stands closer to you than you are comfortable with and you back up to become comfortable. What does this action communicate to your coworker? While the consequences for this encounter may be a bit awkward, in some other instances, understanding nonverbal communication can be a key to survival. For example, when military investigators asked U.S. soldiers if they had shot at women and children in cars at checkpoints, one soldier answered, "Yes." Asked why, he replied, "They didn't respond to the signs [we gave], the presence of troops, or warning shots. Basically, we were at a checkpoint, we had two Arabic signs that said to turn around or be shot. Once [they passed] . . . the first sign, we fired a warning shot. If they passed the second sign, we shot the vehicle. Sometimes it bothers me. What if they couldn't read the signs?[1]

In this instance nonverbal signals were problematic. On the other hand, sometimes nonverbal communication can help us get our message across, when we don't understand a foreign language. For example, our student Yadira was camping with friends in Greece and wanted to ask permission to pitch their tent in a local farmer's meadow, but she didn't speak Greek. By drawing a picture of a tent and using lots of hand gestures, she was able to obtain permission.

You may never be in the military or be a tourist in Greece, but you certainly will find yourself in many intercultural communication situations (e.g. in a culturally diverse work situation). In this chapter, we discuss the importance of understanding nonverbal aspects of intercultural communication. We also explore specific nonverbal communication codes (personal space, gestures, facial expressions, and so on) and expressions of power in intercultural contexts. Finally, we investigate the concept of cultural space and the way people's cultural identities are shaped by the spaces (home, neighborhood, and so on) they occupy.

DEFINING NONVERBAL COMMUNICATION

What is not said is often as important as what is said. **Nonverbal communication** is communication through means other than language—for example, facial expression, personal space, eye contact, use of time, and conversational silence.[2] Nonverbal communication also involves the notion of cultural space. **Cultural spaces** are the contexts that form our identity—where we grow up and where we live (not necessarily the actual homes and neighborhoods, but the cultural meanings created in these places).

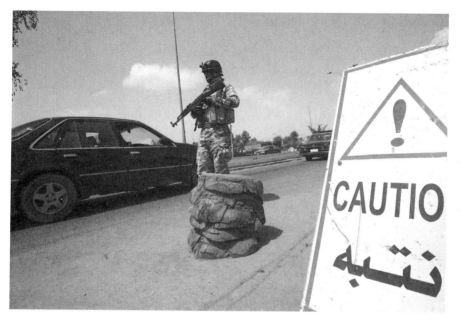

Understanding nonverbal communication can be a key to survival in some intercultural contexts, like Iraqis passing at this military checkpoint. Notice that the soldier's nonverbal communication is reinforced by words and international symbols on the sign in the foreground.

Comparing Verbal and Nonverbal Communication

Both verbal and nonverbal communication are symbolic, both communicate meaning, and both are patterned—that is, are governed by rules that are determined by particular contexts and situations. And just as different societies have different spoken languages, so they have different nonverbal languages. However, there are some important differences between nonverbal and verbal communication in any culture. Let's look at some examples of these differences.

The following incident happened to Judith when she was teaching public speaking to a group of Japanese teachers of English. She explained how to write a speech and gave some tips for presenting the speech. The teachers seemed attentive, smiling and occasionally nodding. But when the time came for them to present their own speeches, she realized that they had many questions about how to prepare a speech and had not really understood her explanations. What she learned was that it is customary for students in Japan to not speak up in class unless they are called upon. In Japan, a nod means that one is listening—but not necessarily that one understands. As this example illustrates, rules for nonverbal communication vary among cultures and contexts.

Let's consider another example. Two U.S. American students attending school in France were hitchhiking to the university in Grenoble for the first day of classes. A French motorist picked them up and immediately started speaking English to them. They wondered how he knew they spoke English. Later, they took a train to Germany. The conductor walked into their compartment and scolded them in English for putting their feet on the opposite seat. Again, they wondered how he had known that they spoke English. As these examples show, nonverbal communication includes more than gestures. Even our appearance can

Surf's Up!

John Bulwer was one of the first people to study nonverbal communication, way back in 1649. He is quoted as arguing that facial expressions are important to understand because "they are the neerest and immediate organs of the voluntaire or impetuous motions of the mind." Check out the website http://mambo.ucsc .edu/psl/bulwer.html to see some of Bulwer's early explorations into nonverbal communication. Do you agree that nonverbal communication reflects internal feelings? Are his ideas relevant in cross-cultural situations?

communicate loudly; in fact, the students' very appearance no doubt was a good clue to their national identity. As these examples also show, nonverbal behavior operates at a subconscious level. We rarely think about how we stand, what hand gestures we use, what facial expressions we're using, and so on. Occasionally, someone points out such behaviors, which brings them to a conscious level.

When misunderstandings arise, we are more likely to question our verbal communication than our nonverbal communication. We can use different words to explain what we mean, or look up words in a dictionary, or ask someone to explain unfamiliar words. But it is more difficult to identify and correct nonverbal miscommunications or misperceptions.

Learning Nonverbal Behavior Whereas we learn rules and meanings for language behavior in grammar and spelling lessons, we learn nonverbal meanings and behaviors more unconsciously. No one explains, "When you talk with someone you like, lean forward, smile, and touch the person frequently, because that will communicate that you really care about him or her." In the United States, these behaviors often communicate positive meanings.[3] But if someone does not display these behaviors, we are likely to react quite differently.

Sometimes we learn strategies for nonverbal communication. For example, you may have been taught to shake hands firmly when you meet someone, or you may have learned that a limp handshake indicates a person with a weak character. Likewise, many young women learn to cross their legs at the ankles and to keep their legs together when they sit. In this sense, we learn nonverbal behaviors as part of being socialized about appropriate behavior.

Coordinating Nonverbal and Verbal Behaviors Nonverbal behaviors can reinforce, substitute for, or contradict verbal behaviors. When we shake our heads and say "no," we are reinforcing verbal behavior. When we point instead of saying "over there," we are substituting nonverbal behavior for verbal communication. In the example of Yadira and the tent, Yadira's drawing and gestures substituted for verbal communication. When we tell a friend, "I can't wait to see you," and then don't show up at the friend's house, the nonverbal behavior is contradicting the verbal behavior.

Because nonverbal communication operates at a more subconscious level, we tend to think that people have less control over their nonverbal behavior. Therefore, we often think of nonverbal behaviors as containing the "real" message. Have you ever received a compliment from someone you thought was not being sincere? You may have thought the person insincere because her nonverbal communication contradicted the spoken words. Perhaps she did not speak very forcefully or was not smiling very much. Perhaps she was giving other nonverbal clues indicating that she did not really mean what she was saying.

What Nonverbal Behavior Communicates

Nonverbal behavior sends relational messages and communicates status and deception.[4] Although language is effective at communicating specific information, nonverbal communication often communicates **relational messages** about

Info Bites

In the United States we are concerned with making things smell pleasing to us—just think about all of the things you can buy that are scented: perfumes, colognes, candles, soaps, and even markers. According to World Watch Institute, the United States and Europe spend $12 billion a year on perfumes, when it would take $6 billion (in addition to current expenditures) to provide basic education for all people in developing nations. How do your spending habits reflect your cultural values? Do you think we have a responsibility to others in the world?

(Source: http://www .worldwatch.org/node/764)

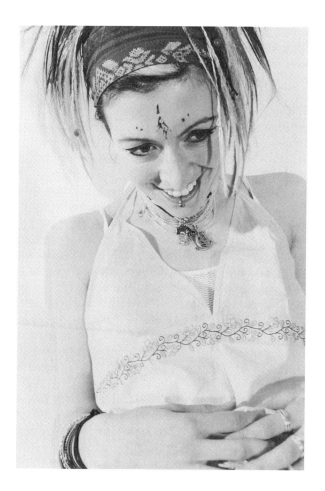

Tattoos and body piercing communicate different meanings to different audiences. Think about the inferences people can draw from these nonverbal communication markers about social status. For example, most of us would be shocked if the president was tattooed and pierced.

how we really feel about the person, and so on. For example, when you first meet someone, he may say "Glad to meet you," but he also communicates nonverbally how he feels about you. He may smile, make direct eye contact, and mirror your body language—all very positive messages in U.S. culture. Or perhaps he does not make direct eye contact, does not smile, and does not give any other nonverbal cues that indicate enthusiasm. One difficulty is that nonverbal clues are not always easy to interpret. And it is dangerous to assume that, every time someone doesn't smile or make direct eye contact, he is communicating lack of interest. It may be that he is preoccupied, and his nonverbal message is not meant the way you interpret it.

There are three guidelines to prevent hasty interpretations of nonverbal behaviors. The first is to think about the context. What is going on in the situation that might help you interpret someone's nonverbal message? For example, if someone has her arms folded and does not make eye contact after meeting you, it may mean that she is not enthusiastic about meeting you. But it also may mean that the room is cold or that she is focusing on something else at the moment. So always remember to think about the context.

Info Bites

Roger E. Axtell, in his book *Gestures: The Do's and Taboos of Body Language Around the World,* lists some nonverbal do's and don'ts in different cultures. Did you know that in Australia it is rude to place your hands in your lap during a meal? That in Turkey it is rude to have your hands in your pocket when conversing with someone? That in Iran people rarely exhibit signs of affection in public? Or that in Pakistan you can eat only with the right hand because the left hand is used for bodily hygiene and is considered unclean? Think about the important role of nonverbal behavior in communicating across cultures and the importance of learning nonverbal meanings as well as the language of various cultures.

The second guideline is to consider the person's other nonverbal behaviors. Don't interpret nonverbal behaviors in isolation. If the person has her arms folded but is also smiling, making direct eye contact, and leaning toward you, then she probably is sending a positive message. So, while each message carries some relational meaning, we must be cautious about being too hasty in interpreting this message.

A third guideline is to remember to consider the verbal messages along with the nonverbal messages. If a person is talking in a pleasant voice and standing with arms folded, the overall relationship message is likely positive. On the other hand, if the person is saying negative things to you, standing with arms folded, and averting eye gaze, then it is likely that the overall message is a more negative one. Thus, you really have to read the whole message and not just part of it.[5]

Nonverbal behavior also communicates **status**—the relative position a person occupies in an organizational or social setting. For example, a supervisor may be able to touch subordinates, but it usually is unacceptable for subordinates to touch a supervisor. Expansive gestures and control over space are associated with high status; conversely, holding one's body in a tight, clenched position communicates low status. For example, in meetings in most U.S. American business contexts, the people who make the grandest gestures and who take up the most space generally are the ones who have the highest status. This might be one reason women generally carry books close to their bodies and sit with their feet and legs together; by contrast, men generally carry books under their arms and tend to sprawl when sitting.

Nonverbal behavior also communicates **deception.** Early researchers believed that some nonverbal behaviors—such as avoiding eye contact and touching or rubbing the face—indicated lying. But more recent research examining hundreds of studies shows that it is very difficult—even for professional lie catchers, like police interrogators—to detect deception with accuracy better than chance. While liars have a tendency to speak with a higher pitched voice, include fewer details in their explanations, and make fewer gestures, there appears to be no one single nonverbal cue that is uniquely related to deception. And the clear cues of nervous behavior—such as avoiding eye contact and fidgeting—do not appear to be related. Each individual has his or her own distinct way of communicating deception.[6] It is important to remember that most nonverbal communication about relational messages, status, and deception happens at a subconscious level. For this reason, it plays an important role in intercultural interactions. We may communicate messages that we aren't even aware of—as in the examples at the beginning of this section.

CULTURAL VARIATIONS IN NONVERBAL BEHAVIOR

How do culture, ethnicity, and gender influence nonverbal communication patterns? How universal is most nonverbal communication? Do people in most countries communicate in the same way nonverbally? In this section, we look for cultural variations in nonverbal behavior that may serve as tentative guidelines to help us communicate better with others.

There is something very basic, and perhaps universal, about much of our nonverbal behavior—particularly our **facial expressions,** facial gestures that convey emotions and attitudes. For example, smiling and laughing probably fill a universal human need for promoting social connections or bonding—an attempt to influence others, to make them feel more positive toward the sender. Researchers point out that people in all cultures use these nonverbal behaviors to influence others and that, over time, these behaviors that contributed to positive relationships were favored and eventually became automatic and nonconscious.[7] The more researchers learn about animal behavior, particularly that of nonhuman primates like chimps and gorillas, the more similarities they find between them and humans, although animal communication appears to be less complex.[8] That is, humans are capable of many more gestures and facial expressions than are animals. Apparently, there are also some nonverbal behaviors that are innate, that we don't have to learn. For example, children who are blind usually make the same facial expressions as sighted children—even though they can't see to learn how to make these expressions.[9]

There are many universal facial gestures, including the eyebrow flash (raising the eyebrow to communicate recognition), the nose wrinkle (indicating slight social distancing), and the "disgust face" (sending a strong signal of social repulsion). In fact, at least six basic emotions—happiness, sadness, disgust, fear, anger, and surprise—are communicated by facial expressions in much the same way in most societies. The fact that facial expressions for these emotions are recognized by most cultural groups as having the same meaning seems to suggest some innate, universal basis for these behaviors.

However, nonverbal communication also varies in many ways from culture to culture. The evoking stimulus, or that which causes the nonverbal behavior, may vary from one culture to another. Smiling, for example, is universal. But what prompts a person to smile may be culture-specific. In some cultures, seeing a baby may cause people to smile; in other cultures, one is not supposed to smile a lot at babies. Judith's Diné (Navajo) friend told her that in the Navajo Nation the first person to cause a baby to smile has to throw a party for baby and family, so people don't always want to cause a baby to smile!

There are variations in the rules for nonverbal communication and the contexts in which it takes place. For example, people kiss in most cultures, but there is variation in who kisses whom and in what contexts. When French friends greet each other, they often kiss each other on both cheeks but never on the mouth. Friends in the United States usually kiss each other on greeting only after a long absence, and this is usually accompanied by a hug. The rules for kissing also vary along gender lines. In this section, we examine how nonverbal communication varies from culture to culture.

Surf's Up!

Take a look at the Automated Face Analysis website (www.cs.cmu .edu/~face/home.htm). Do you believe that these kinds of facial expressions not only are similar across cultures but also can be accurately deciphered by a computer?

Nonverbal Codes

Paralinguistics   **Paralinguistics** refer to the study of paralanguage—vocal behaviors that indicate *how* something is said, including speaking rate, volume, pitch, and stress, among others. Saying something very quickly in a loud tone of voice will be interpreted differently from the same words said in a quieter tone of voice at a slower rate. How would you likely respond to someone speaking in a loud voice if he or she were speaking a foreign language? There are two types of vocal behavior—voice qualities and vocalizations.[10]

Voice Qualities or the non-technical term, tone of voice, include speed, pitch, rhythm, vocal range, and articulation; these qualities make up the "music" of the human voice. We all know people whose voice qualities are widely recognized. For example, the voice of actor Fran Drescher, who starred in the TV sitcom *The Nanny*, has been frequently remarked upon. Her trademark whiny chuckle and nasal voice allow her to be recognized no matter where she is. Speakers also vary in how they articulate sounds; that is, how distinctly they pronounce individual words and sounds. We tend not to notice these paralinguistic features unless someone articulates very precisely or very imprecisely. Paralinguistics often leads people to negatively evaluate speakers in intercultural communication contexts even when they don't understand the language. For example, Chinese speakers often sound rather musical and nasal to English speakers; English speakers sound rather harsh and guttural to French speakers.

Vocalizations are the sounds we utter that do not have the structure of language. Tarzan's yell is one famous example. Vocalizations include vocal cues such as laughing, crying, whining, and moaning as well as the intensity or volume of one's speech. They also include sounds that aren't actual words but that serve as fillers, such as "uh-huh," "uh," "ah," and "er." The paralinguistic aspects of speech serve a variety of communicative functions. They reveal mood and emotion; they also allow us to emphasize or stress a word or idea, create a distinctive identity, and (along with gestures) regulate conversation. Paralanguage can be a confusing factor in intercultural communication. For example, Europeans interpret the loudness of Americans as aggressive behavior, while Americans might think the British are secretive because they talk quietly. The amount of silence in conversations and the speaking rate differ among cultures. For instance, the Finnish and Japanese are comfortable having pauses in their conversations, while most U.S. Americans talk rapidly and are pretty uncomfortable with silences.

Personal Space   **Personal space** is the "bubble" around each of us that marks the territory between ourselves and others. How big your bubble is depends on your cultural background. In some cultures, people stand very close together to talk, while in others, they feel a need to be farther apart when talking. This difference in personal space rules can cause misunderstandings and even some discomfort in intercultural interactions. For example, in one university there were reports of miscommunication between Arab and U.S. American students. The Arab students complained that the American students were distant and rude, while the U.S. American students characterized the Arab students as pushy, arrogant, and impolite. The problem was that the two groups were operating with different rules concerning personal space. The Arab students were accustomed to standing closer together when talking, while the U.S. American students had been raised to do just the opposite.

In fact, some cultural groups are identified as contact cultures, and others as noncontact cultures. **Contact cultures** are those in which people stand closer together while talking, make more direct eye contact, touch frequently, and speak in louder voices. Societies in South America and southern Europe are identified as contact cultures. By contrast, those in northern Europe, North America, East Asia, and the Far East are **noncontact cultures,** in which people tend to stand farther apart when conversing, maintain less eye contact, and touch less often.[11] Jolanta, a Polish student of ours, talked about her first experience abroad, as the guest of an Italian family, and being overwhelmed by the close physical contact and intense nonverbal behavior: "Almost every aspect of this family's interactions made me anxious and insecure. This included the extreme close personal distance, touching and speaking loudly, all of which was quite overwhelming." Figure 6.1 shows the "immediacy orientations" of selected countries and regions.

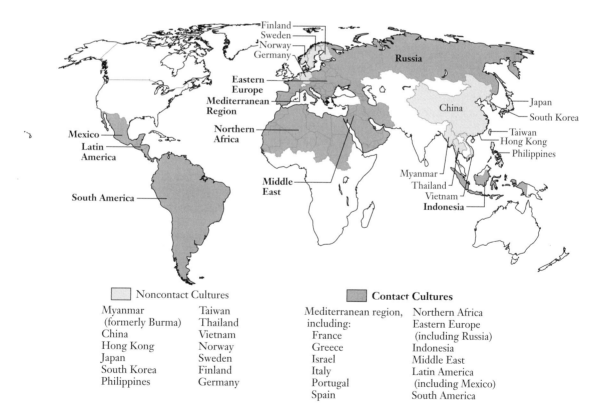

Figure 6.1 Immediacy orientations of selected countries and regions.

Is it possible that the degree of contact is affected by geography and climate? It is interesting that many high-contact cultures are in warmer places, located closer to the equator. In contrast, most low-contact cultures are in cooler climates. And even within many northern countries, southerners are more nonverbally expressive and interpersonally oriented than northerners. Think of the general impression of U.S. southerners as being warmer, hospitable, and open, whereas New Englanders have the reputation for being more reserved and less demonstrative. The same is true for people in the south and north of France. One explanation might be that where it's colder, people spend more time dressing, storing food, and planning for winter (being task-oriented), whereas people in warmer climates have access to each other all year round.[12]

Of course, we cannot say categorically that these patterns are found everywhere. Many countries in Asia, for example, have warm climates and are considered low contact. Here, the influence of Confucianism with emphasis on self-control and proper behavior may be a greater influence.

Of course, many other factors besides culture determine how close together or far apart people stand. Gender, age, ethnicity, the context of the interaction, and the topic of discussion all influence the use of personal space. For example, in Algeria (a contact culture), gender might be more important than nationality in determining amounts of personal space. Unmarried young women and men rarely stand close together, touch each other, or maintain direct eye contact with each other. However, young men commonly hold hands with their male friends, and young women will do the same with their female friends.[13] Similarly, in China (a noncontact culture) it's quite normal for girls to hold each other's hands or arms. As one of our Chinese students describes it:

> It's a sign of good friendship. I did it all the time with my good female friends when I was in China. After I came to the U.S., somehow I found out that people of the same sex don't do this unless they are in a romantic relationship. So I don't hold other girls' hands anymore, even with my Chinese friends here. What's more interesting is that when I go back to China on vacations, I am not used to holding other girls' hands anymore!

Eye Contact   **Eye contact** is often considered an element of personal space because it regulates interpersonal distance. Direct eye contact shortens the distance between two people, while a lack of eye contact increases the distance. Eye contact communicates meanings related to respect and status, and it often regulates turn taking in conversations.

Patterns of eye contact vary from culture to culture. In many societies, avoiding eye contact communicates respect and deference, although this may vary from context to context. For many Americans, maintaining eye contact communicates that one is paying attention or showing respect. But a Diné (Navajo) student told us that the hardest thing for her to learn when she left the Navajo Nation to study at Arizona State was to remember to look her professors in the eye. Her whole life, she had been taught to show respect by avoiding eye contact.

What Do You Think?

If you are text messaging someone you like, how would you let them know? Through our use of technologies we have adapted to a lack of visual cues by creating nonverbal codes that act as facial expressions for such things as kisses and other forms of affection. Many of us recognize signs such as :-) and :-X as "I'm smiling right now" or "I'm sending you a kiss." Think about the text messages, e-mails, and instant messages you send. Do you use these signs? How else do you convey emotion (other symbols, punctuation, and capitalization)? How does your use of signs and symbols change based on who you are messaging?

When they speak with others, most U.S. Americans look away from their listeners most of the time. They might look at their listeners every 10 or 15 seconds. And when a speaker is finished taking a turn, he or she looks directly at the listener to signal completion. However, some cultural groups within the United States use even less eye contact while they speak. For example, some Native Americans tend to avert their eyes during conversation.

Facial Expression   As noted previously, some facial expressions seem to express the same emotions all over the world. However, it's important to recognize that there is variation in many aspects of facial expressions. A smile may universally indicate pleasure and happiness, and a frown may indicate sadness, but there is a lot of variation in what causes someone to smile or frown. For example, in the United States, meeting someone for the first time may call for a smile, while in other cultures, it is better to look serious. By contrast, a snake may call for a facial expression of disgust in some cultural contexts, and in others may call for a smile at the prospect of a delicious meal.

The rules that regulate facial expressions also may vary. Thus, a greeting may call for a wide smile in some cultures and a much more subdued or less expressive smile in others. Europeans often remark that U.S. Americans seem to smile too much. Some Asians make the same observation of U.S. Americans. For them, smiling is even considered a bit "immature." As one of our Chinese students noted:

> Most of my American colleagues and friends have very vivid facial expressions most of the time. However, in China people usually don't display that much facial expression. What's more, it is seen as being more mature and experienced if you don't disclose your inner emotions through your facial expressions (especially for men!). However, I guess that would be considered a "poker face" by most Americans.

Gestures   **Gestures** are simply arm and hand movements that communicate nonverbally. There are at least four different kinds of gestures: emblems, illustrators, regulators, and adaptors.[14] **Emblems** are those gestures that have a specific verbal translation. For example, when you wave your hand as someone is leaving, it means good-bye. Or when you give "the finger," it is interpreted as an insult. There are at least a hundred identifiable gestures in our culture. Of course, other cultures have their own emblems. For example, in India, a slow shaking of the head means "yes" (not "no"). You might think that there are some universal gestures or at least some universal *categories* of gestures (e.g., every culture must have an obscene gesture), but this appears not to be true. There are a number of societies (e.g., the Netherlands, Norway, Switzerland) that have no obscene gesture.[15] And in some ways, emblems are the easiest gestures to understand cross-culturally, because they are easy to reproduce; when emblems have the same meaning cross-culturally, there is no problem. When people are in a foreign country and do not know the language, they often resort to emblems.

Surf's Up!

Take the quiz at www.kent .ac.uk/careers/interviews/ nvc.htm to learn how to manage your nonverbal communication in interviews. Think about how many of these suggestions apply only to a U.S. American context. Think about how you would manage your nonverbal interview behavior when applying for a position in a multinational corporation overseas.

For example, our student Dave was visiting in Mexico with some friends, none of whom spoke much Spanish. They were trying to find a hotel. "We were trying to communicate that we needed somewhere to stay and the man couldn't understand us and started acting very frustrated. We started using nonverbal gestures—showing signs of sleep—and he understood and showed us a place to stay. Everything turned out okay."

However, if an emblem varies slightly from culture to culture, there can be misunderstanding. For example, in Germany and many other European cultures, the gesture for "stupid" is a finger on the forehead; the American gesture for "smart" is nearly identical, but the finger is held an inch to the side, at the temple. If the emblem has a different meaning, it can be very confusing, as President George W. Bush discovered when he gave the "hook 'em horns" greeting to the University of Texas Longhorn marching band during his inauguration. In Norway, this gesture is considered a salute to Satan, and Norwegians were confused when they saw photos of this greeting at the inauguration.[16]

Even more difficult types of gesture to understand in intercultural communication are the illustrators and regulators. **Illustrators** are all those gestures that go along with our speech. Have you ever noticed that there seems to be a "flow" to people's verbal communication—when they are talking, their gestures are usually very synchronized? For example, when emphasizing a point by shaking a finger, the speaker stops shaking the finger at the end of the sentence. And it all seems very natural. In fact, symptoms of mental illness are sometimes revealed in people's gesturing behavior; their gestures may seem "jerky" or seem not to go with their speech.

Of course, different cultural groups use different types and amounts of illustrators. Italians are often characterized as "talking a lot with their hands," or using a lot of illustrators. Another student, Marjorie, who traveled to Italy, noticed this: "In watching people in the streets, it always seemed like they must be angry at each other—all the waving of hands and gesturing." Actually, it is merely the custom there to use a lot of illustrating gestures. Other cultural groups, like the Chinese, may use fewer illustrators. Of course, the number of illustrators used may also be related to a person's family background or individual preferences. The important thing to remember is that, if you encounter someone who uses many illustrators, it doesn't mean that he's angry; and if someone uses few illustrators, it doesn't mean that she's not into the conversation.

We rarely think about it, but much of our conversation is regulated by nonverbal gestures, called **regulators.** Thus, when someone tries to interrupt while we are talking, we may put out our hand, indicating that we aren't finished speaking. Greeting and leave-taking are usually indicated by regulating gestures. For example, when we greet someone, we may shake their hands or hug them. When we get ready to leave, we often gather our stuff together. It is important to remember that each language has a somewhat unique set of regulators. For example, in Japan, turn taking is regulated more by pauses than by gestures, so that a brief pause in the conversation indicates that the next person may talk. In fact, Japanese

Info Bites

Did you know that in Mexico it is considered a challenge when you put your hands on your hips? That in France, when you kiss someone's cheeks, you should start on the right side? That in Britain and Thailand, people point with their heads? That in Poland, it is acceptable for a stranger to join you at your restaurant table for dinner? That winking has no meaning in Japan? Or that yawning is considered rude in Argentina? (SOURCE: *The Complete Idiot's Guide to Cultural Etiquette*)

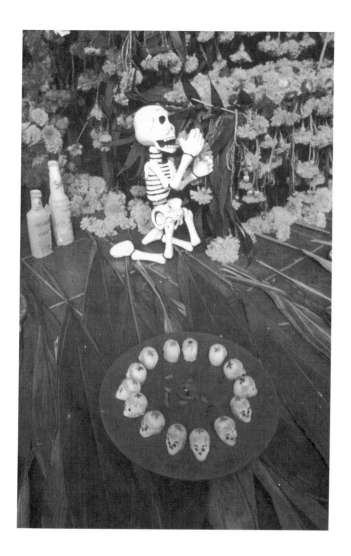

Holidays are often filled with nonverbal symbols that communicate important meanings to the participants. The objects in this Latino/a family's *offrenda* or altar are an important part of their "Dia de los Muertos" (All Souls Day) holiday and help them remember family members who have died. How does your family remember those who have died?

people remark that it is sometimes difficult to jump into an American conversation because they are waiting for the regulating "pause" that never comes.

The final type of gesture is **adaptors,** which are related to managing our emotions. For example, we may tap our feet or fingers when we're nervous, or rub our eyes when we feel like crying, or clench our fists when we're angry. Again, from a cultural perspective, it's important to recognize that the adaptors we use are part of our particular cultural upbringing, and that other people may use other types of adaptors to manage or reflect their emotions.

A researcher, after studying the many variations of gestures around the world, said he was amazed by the "power, nuances, and unpredictability of cultural differences" in nonverbal behavior. On a practical note, he urged travelers to practice "gestural humility": (1) assume that the familiar gestures of our home culture will not mean the same things abroad, and (2) do not assume that we can interpret the meaning of any unfamiliar gestures we observe in other cultures.[17]

Time Orientation   There are many cultural variations regarding how people understand and use time. One way to understand these variations is to look at the differences between monochronic and polychronic time orientations.[18] People who have a **monochronic** concept of time, like most people in the United States, regard time as a commodity: Time can be gained, lost, spent, wasted, or saved. In this orientation, time is linear, with events happening one after another. In general, monochronic cultures value punctuality, completion of tasks, and adherence to schedules. For instance, most college staff and faculty in the United States maintain a monochronic orientation to time. Classes, meetings, and office appointments start when scheduled. Faculty members see one student at a time, hold one meeting at a time, and keep appointments except when faced with an emergency. Typical family problems are considered poor reasons for not fulfilling academic obligations—for both faculty and students.

By contrast, people with a **polychronic** orientation conceptualize time as more holistic, perhaps more circular: Many events can happen at once. U.S. American businesspeople often complain that meetings in the Middle East do not start "on time," that people socialize during meetings, and that meetings may be canceled because of personal obligations. Often, tasks are accomplished because of personal relationships, not in spite of them.

Schedules are less important than personal obligations in polychronic cultures. Sandra discovered this when she was an international student in India. She did not have a computer and had to use the university computer room. So she arrived there at 8 A.M., but the room was not open. An assistant told her to come back at 9 A.M. She went back at 9 A.M., but the room was still not open. She asked the same person and he said to return at 12 P.M.—but the room was still not open then. Later she found out that the schedule for the computer room depended on the schedule and the varying obligations of the computer lab director. It sometimes opened at 3 P.M., and other times she had to come back the next day. While this may seem inconvenient to a monochronic-oriented person, a polychronic person takes a more flexible approach and understands that keeping a strict schedule should not be the most important obligation in life.

Many international business negotiations, technical assistance projects, and team projects fail because of differences in time orientation. International students and business personnel often complain that U.S. Americans seem too busy and too tied to their schedules; they suggest that U.S. Americans do not care enough about relationships and about the personal aspects of living. An international student of ours complained, "It is so hard to get used to the fast pace of college life here. It seems that people are too busy to enjoy other people and relationships; they are just anxious and always worried about being on time and getting things done."

These differences in time orientation can be particularly consequential in contemporary work life, where technology makes it possible to be "plugged-in"

Surf's Up!

Take a test to assess the degree to which you have a monochronic or poly-chronic approach to time at www.innovint .com/downloads/mono _poly_test.php. Think about occasions when your views on time might have created communication challenges in your encounters with others.

twenty-four hours a day, seven days a week. Workers are often expected to be available to coworkers, clients, and customers at work in another time zone, even if they are off the clock.[19] This presents a challenge for many workers—how to balance personal time and work time. In Chapter 11, we'll discuss more about the important role that time orientations play in business contexts, particularly during international negotiations.

Some ethnic groups in the United States may also have a polychronic time orientation. Chicano/a college students often find that their family and social obligations, viewed as very important at home, are not as important at the university. As one student, Lucia, said, "It's hard to make sure everyone in my family is taken care of and to get my school work done at the same time. Sometimes I have to take my grandmother to the doctor, go grocery shopping with my mom, help my aunt with her Medicare problems, and still somehow find the time to attend class and get my homework done."

The implications for intercultural misunderstandings between people with these different time orientations are significant. In technical assistance projects overseas, for example, coworkers with different time orientations can become very frustrated with one another, as revealed in this summary of how monochronic Western workers and polychronic workers from Madagascar (Africa) viewed each other.[20]

Monochronics on Polychronics	*Polychronics on Monochronics*
They never plan for the future.	They are always in a hurry.
They are losing time and money.	They don't give priority to the art of living.
They fail to plan and so cause problems.	They are obsessed with money.
	They do not give priority to people.

It takes a great deal of patience and cross-cultural understanding to work together in these situations.

Silence   As we noted in Chapter 5, cultural groups may vary in the relative emphasis placed on speaking and on **silence**. In most U.S. American contexts, silence is not highly valued. Particularly in developing relationships, silence communicates awkwardness and can make people feel uncomfortable. One of the major reasons for communicating verbally in initial interactions with people is to reduce uncertainty. In U.S. American contexts, people employ active uncertainty reduction strategies, such as asking questions. However, in many other cultural contexts, people reduce uncertainty by more passive strategies, such as remaining silent, observing, and perhaps asking a third party about someone's behavior. And silences can be as meaningful as language. Some of the early investigations of silence did not fully value the communicative importance of silence in many different cultures, including those in the United States. It is worthwhile for us to rethink the way we view silence, to see it not "as an absence, but, rather, as a fullness of opportunity for being and learning."[21]

Surf's Up!

Nonverbal behaviors that are not offensive in your own culture may be seen as rude in other cultures. Visit this website (www.cba .uni.edu/Buscomm/ nonverbal/Culture.htm) to learn more about cultural variations in nonverbal behaviors.

particularly to understand the worlds humans create within silence. What role does silence play in your life? What does it mean when you (or your friends or family) are silent?

Communication scholar Kris Acheson acknowledges that silence in the United States has often been associated with negative, unhealthy relationships, or with disempowerment, when women and/or minorities feel their voices are not heard. However, she tells us that U. S. Americans increasingly recognize the positive and sometimes powerful uses of silence in certain contexts. For example, nurses and doctors are encouraged to honor silent patients and learn to employ silence in their ethical care; young people are advised to seek out silence in their lives for the sake of health and sanity, to even noiseproof their homes in an attempt to boost health.

In business contexts, sometimes keeping quiet is the best strategy and talking too much can kill a business deal. In education, teachers can create a space for understanding rather than counterarguments by asking for silent reflection after comments or performances. Finally, she admits that in some U. S. contexts, like politics and law, silence is still seen as completely negative; pleading the fifth equates silence with guilt and silence by politicians is often viewed as too much secrecy.[22] However, in many cultural contexts, silence is viewed rather positively. For example, silence in Japan is not simply the absence of sound or a pause in the conversation that must be filled. Silence can convey respect for the person who has spoken, or it can be a way of unifying people. Silence in Japan has been compared to the white space in brush paintings or calligraphy scrolls: "A picture is not richer, more accurate or more complete if such spaces are filled in. To do so would be to confuse and detract from what is presented."[23]

People from Finland also value silence in certain contexts. For example, researchers have described the *Asaillinen* (matter of fact) nonverbal style among Finnish people. This style involves a rather fixed and expressionless face and a belief that talkativeness is a sign of unreliability. Silence, on the other hand, for Finns reflects thoughtfulness, appropriate consideration, and intelligence—particularly in public discourse, or in educational settings, like a classroom.[24]

Silences can have many meanings in various contexts. In a classic study on the rules for silence among the Western Apache in Arizona, researcher Keith Basso identified five contexts in which silence was appropriate: meeting strangers, courting, seeing friends after a long absence, being with people who are grieving, and getting cursed out. Some of these patterns hold true for other Native American groups, like the Diné and the Yaqui, as well. Being shy around strangers is directly related to the belief that forming social relationships is a serious matter that calls for caution, careful judgment, and plenty of time.

Basso and others hypothesize that the underlying commonality in all social situations is that participants see their relationships in these contexts as ambiguous or unpredictable, and silence is an appropriate response to uncertainty and unpredictability. He also hypothesizes that this same contextual rule may apply to other cultural groups. It is also possible that in many communities silence is associated not just with uncertainty, but also with social situations in which a known and unequal distribution of power exists among participants.[25] For example, in work contexts in Japan, being silent and listening very respectfully to one's boss would be the appropriate response, whereas a U.S. American supervisor might admire the subordinate who "speaks right up."

Silence can be tricky in intercultural encounters. It can be useful when trying to sort out uncertainty in intercultural interactions because it gives one time to think through attributions. However, silence is not only a function of conversation, but an expression of culture and identity; in intercultural context, however, it may be confused with a lack of communication competence. This was the case for Japanese students studying in an Australian university. Japanese students used silence, as they would in Japan, as a strategy to save face (to avoid making mistakes when speaking English) or to be polite (to not offend the professor or other students by contradicting them). However, their silence was negatively evaluated by Australian lecturers who interpreted the silence as students' lack of engagement and a reflection on the professors' teaching expertise.[26]

A similar study shows how Chinese students' use of silence in U.S. classrooms demonstrated their Chinese cultural identities (showing politeness and respect). However, this study showed how students could, with support and encouragement from professors, reconstruct their identities and develop intercultural competence by adapting somewhat to the cultural expectations of the U.S. classroom context.[27]

Cultural Variation or Stereotype?

As noted previously, one of the problems with identifying cultural variations in nonverbal codes is that it is tempting to overgeneralize these variations and to stereotype groups of people. Table 6.1 lists some cultural variations in nonverbal behaviors, but we must be careful not to assume that every member of that cultural group exhibits the same nonverbal behaviors, nor that we don't have to consider the context in which these nonverbal behaviors may be used.

For example, we have to be very careful when comparing Japanese and Western attitudes toward silence. Those familiar with life in Japan have observed that the television is on nonstop in many Japanese homes, and Zen gardens offer tape-recorded messages about the beauty to be seen. So, although silence might be a cultural ideal, things may differ in practice. In specific situations, such as mother–daughter relationships, there may be more emphasis on silence than in comparable U.S. American situations. Still, we should take these warnings about the dangers of overgeneralizations seriously.[28]

Cultural variations are tentative guidelines that we can use in intercultural interaction. They should serve as examples, to help us understand that there is a great deal of variation in nonverbal behavior. Even if we can't anticipate how someone's behavior may differ from our own, we can be flexible when we do

Info Bites

How attracted we are to someone is largely based on nonverbal communication. Did you know that we are attracted to others whose natural odor is genetically different from ours? Each of us has an MHC, or Major Histocompatibility Complex, a dense set of genes that determines our odor type. In order to produce the most genetically fit offspring, we are attracted to others whose MHC is genetically different from ours. We usually emphasize the role of cultural differences in intercultural encounters, and don't consider the role of biological differences. Smell is one case where differences are essential! Visit http://dsc.discovery.com/videos/science-of-sex-appeal/ to watch videos about sexual attraction and nonverbal communication.

TABLE 6.1 Interesting Nonverbal Behaviors

Brazil: The Brazilian considers the OK sign in the United States (made with the thumb and forefinger) as obscene.

China: Chinese always use both hands when passing a gift or food.

Kenya: Pointing with an index finger is very insulting.

Samoa: It is rude for a person standing to sway while having a conversation.

Fiji: Crossed arms is a sign of respect when talking.

Italy: The American gesture for one (raising the index finger) means two in Italy.

Greece and Turkey: When saying "no," it is expressed with a small nod of the head upward.

Japan: Laughter may signify embarrassment instead of amusement in certain situations.

Thailand: Thais believe a spirit lives at the doorsill of a house, so one never pauses on the doorsill.

Source: Selling Destinations: Geography for the Travel Professional, 4th ed., by M. Mancini, 2003, Clifton Park, NY: Thomson/Delmar Learning.

Info Bites

If you are standing in the doorway to a home or office, are you inside or outside? Germans consider the doorway part of the interior space, so an intrusion into these areas will cause problems. By contrast, in an Arab country, it is perfectly acceptable to push and elbow someone out of a desired spot in a public place. How do you think a typical German tourist would fare in Egypt?

encounter differences in, say, how close a person positions himself or herself, uses eye contact, or conceptualizes time.

Prejudice is often based on nonverbal aspects of behavior. That is, the negative prejudgment is triggered by physical appearances or physical behavior. For example, even college students' evaluations of professors' teaching may be subtly influenced by their professors' physical appearances. A recent research study showed that college students consistently rate less attractive professors as less skilled in teaching. Perhaps more interesting was that students rated both female and minority professors lower overall than their White, male peers. As one psychologist explained, "It just shows that white, native-speaking males are still the norm for professors in students' eyes."[29]

Teachers also may be influenced by the physical appearance of their students. Some educators suggest that decisions to place African American students in special education classes may be partially related to administrators' negative evaluations of their posture and walk. When African American high school students don't walk the typical "White walk" (erect posture and steady stride), and instead deliberately swagger with bent posture, head tilted to one side, and one foot dragging, White teachers tend to perceive them as aggressive, low achievers and potential candidates for special education programs. In fact, 21 percent of African Americans are in special education even though they represent only 16.8 percent of the U.S. public school population.[30] Similarly, immigrant Asian children and some Asian Americans are sometimes negatively evaluated and discriminated against because of their cultural practice of remaining quiet in the classroom to show respect for the teacher.[31]

An extreme example of the importance of physical appearance in expressions of prejudice is hate crimes. For example, in fall 2005, in Marysville,

Cultures differ widely in the systems of nonverbal symbols that they use. This woman wears a tear-drop bindi. People use many other non-verbal symbols to mark their cultural identities, including attire, hairstyles, jewelry, and tattoos.

California, Daniel J. Farris, 18, was charged with assault with a deadly weapon, causing pain, suffering, or injury to an elder or dependent adult, and hate crime for allegedly beating an elderly Black man while yelling racial slurs.[32]

As in many other instances of hate crimes, the victim's appearance was more significant than his specific cultural heritage. From these kinds of experiences with prejudice, people start to develop "a map" that tells them where they belong and where they are likely to be rejected. Victims can often spot prejudicial behavior and people with surprising accuracy. In an interesting study, Blacks were able to detect prejudiced people (identified previously by objective survey measurement) after only 20 seconds of observation, with much higher accuracy than Whites.[33] For this reason, members of minority groups may avoid places where and situations in which they do not feel welcome.

In addition to triggering prejudice, nonverbal messages also can communicate it, often in very subtle ways—like averting one's gaze, withholding a smile, or leaning one's body away. Because there is no explicit verbal expression of prejudice, the interpretation of these nonverbal behaviors is left to the person receiving the communication.

Sociologist Allan Johnson compiled the following list of nonverbal behaviors that can be interpreted as prejudicial:

- Not looking at people when we talk with them
- Not acknowledging people's presence, but making them wait as if they weren't there

- Staring as if to say "What are you doing here?" or stopping the conversation with a hush they have to wade through to be included in the smallest way

- Not listening or responding to what people say; drifting away to someone or something else

- Avoid touching their skin when giving or taking something

- Watching them closely to see what they're up to

- Avoiding someone walking down the street, giving them a wide berth when passing, or even crossing to the other side[34]

DEFINING CULTURAL SPACE

What are cultural spaces, and what do they have to do with intercultural communication? Cultural space relates to the way communication constructs meanings of various places. For example, at the beginning of this book, we provided some background information about ourselves and the cultural places where we grew up. These particular cultural spaces are important in understanding our identities. There is nothing in the rolling hills of Delaware and Pennsylvania or the red clay of Georgia that has biologically determined who Judith and Tom are. However, our identities and our views of ourselves are formed, in part, in relation to cultural places—the mid-Atlantic region for Judith and the South for Tom. Each region has its own histories and ways of life that help us understand who we are. Our decision to tell you something about the cultural spaces we grew up in was meant to communicate something about who we think we are.

The meanings of cultural spaces are dynamic and ever changing. Therefore, the Delaware that Judith left behind and the Georgia that Tom left behind are no doubt much different now. In addition, the relations between people's cultural spaces and identities are negotiated in complex ways. Thus, because someone is from India does not mean that his or her identity and communication practices are always and only "Indian." Let's look at some specific cultural spaces that we can all identify with—our homes and our neighborhoods.

Cultural Identity and Cultural Space

Home Cultural spaces are important influences on how we think about ourselves and others. One of the earliest cultural spaces we experience is our **home**—the immediate cultural context for our upbringing. As noted previously, nonverbal communication involves issues of status, and the home is not exempt from issues of status. For example, the social class of an American home is often expressed nonverbally: from the way the lawn is cared for, to the kinds of cars in the driveway, to the way the television is situated, to the kinds of furniture in the

What Do You Think?

How we dress in large part determines how people view and feel about us. How much can a person guess about you by what you wear? For example, how does your appearance communicate your nationality? How might your appearance be viewed by people from other cultures?

home. These signs of social class are not always so obvious for all social class positions, but they often provide important clues about social class.[35]

Even if our home does not reflect the social class we wish to be in, we often identify with it strongly. We often model our own lives on the way things were done in our childhood homes. Although this is not always the case, the home can be a place of safety and security. African American writer bell hooks remembers:

> When I was a young girl the journey across town to my grandmother's house was one of the most intriguing experiences. . . . I remember this journey not just because of the stories I would hear. It was a movement away from the segregated blackness of our community into a poor white neighborhood [where] we would have to pass that terrifying whiteness— those white faces on porches staring down on us with hate. . . . Oh! that feeling of safety, of arrival, of homecoming when we finally reached the edges of her yard.[36]

"Home," of course, is not the same as the physical location it occupies, nor the building (the house) on that location. Home is variously defined as specific addresses, cities, states, regions, and even nations. Although we might have historical ties to a particular place, not everyone feels the same relationship between those places and their own identities.

Some people have feelings of fondness for the region of the country where they grew up. Another writer talks about his relationship to his hometown in South Carolina:

> Now that I no longer live there, I often think longingly of my hometown of Charleston. My heart beats faster and color rushes to my cheek whenever I hear someone mentioning her; I lean over and listen, for even hearing the name casts a spell. Mirages rise up, and I am as overcome and drenched in images as a runner just come from running. I see the steeples, the streets, the lush setting.[37]

But others feel less positive about where they come from. A writer who grew up in Texas expresses his ambiguous feelings about the state: "What I feel when I fly from California to Texas must be what an expatriate from any country feels returning to his childhood home. . . . Texas is home, but Texas is also a country whose citizenship I voluntarily renounced."[38] The meanings of Texas no longer "fit" this writer's sense of who he is or who he wants to be.

The relationships between various places and our identities are complex. These three writers have different feelings about their "home," which highlights the complexity that exists between identity and location. Where you come from and where you grew up contributes to how you see yourself, to your current identity. Many people experience ambivalence about the regions of the country where they grew up. They may have fond memories, but they may now also see the area in a new way—as perhaps provincial, or conservative, or segregated.

Surf's Up!

Explore the Handspeak website (www.handspeak.com). Take the tour and find out how to say "Hello," "Good-bye," and "Friend" in American Sign Language (ASL). How is sign language similar to and different from other forms of nonverbal communication?

Many neighborhoods are marked by their ethnic and religious character. While there may have been laws that created these kinds of neighborhoods in the past, what are the advantages and disadvantages of sustaining these neighborhoods today?

What Do You Think?

According to research, people treat those whom they consider attractive or beautiful more favorably than those whom they consider ugly or unattractive. Standards of beauty vary widely across cultures, but there is also evidence that people with the most symmetrical faces are most likely to be considered beautiful across cultures, regardless of supposed racial or cultural markers of beauty. Is beauty truly in the eye of the beholder?

Neighborhood   One significant type of cultural space that emerged in U.S. cities is the **neighborhood,** a living area defined by its own cultural identity, especially an ethnic or racial one. Cities typically developed segregated neighborhoods, reflecting common attitudes of prejudice and discrimination, as well as people's desire to live among people like themselves. Malcolm X, in his autobiography, tells of the strict laws that governed where his family could live after their house burned down: "My father prevailed on some friends to clothe and house us temporarily; then he moved us into another house on the outskirts of East Lansing. In those days Negroes weren't allowed after dark in East Lansing proper . . . where Michigan State University is located."[39]

The phenomenon of "Whites-only" areas has been very common in U.S. history. These types of neighborhoods are good examples of how power influences intercultural contact. The segregation of African Americans was not accidental. Beginning in 1890 until the late 1960s (the fair-housing legislation), Whites in America created thousands of Whites-only towns, commonly known as "sundown towns." This was a reference to the signs often posted at their city limits that warned, as one did in Hawthorne, California, in the 1930s: "Nigger, Don't Let The Sun Set On YOU In Hawthorne." In fact, during that 70-year period a majority of incorporated places (in the United States) kept out African Americans.[40] In these segregated neighborhoods, certain cultural groups defined who got to live where and dictated the rules by which other groups had to live. These rules were enforced through legal means and by harassment. For Malcolm X and bell hooks, these lines of segregation were clear and unmistakable. One of our older students also recalls these times:

I lived 9 of my first 12 years in Miami, Florida, where segregation and discrimination were a way of life. Schools and housing were segregated, and "colored" people had to ride at the back of the bus. . . . When I was about 7 or 8, I saw a man get hit by a car as he was crossing the street. They called an ambulance, but when it came they wouldn't take the man to the hospital because they had sent the wrong "color" of ambulance. I don't remember if the man was Black or White; I only recall how angry I was. . . . Later we moved to California, where segregation of Whites and Blacks was accomplished covertly by "White flight"—when African Americans moved into a neighborhood, most of the Whites moved out.

In San Francisco, different racial politics constructed and isolated Chinatown. Until racial covenants were lifted in 1947, Chinese Americans were forced to live in Chinatown. The boundaries that marked the acceptable place for Chinese Americans were clear and were carefully guarded through violence:

The sense of being physically sealed within the boundaries of Chinatown was impressed on the few immigrants coming into the settlement by frequent stonings which occurred as they came up Washington or Clay Street from the piers. It was perpetuated by attacks of white toughs in the adjacent North Beach area and downtown around Union Square, who amused themselves by beating Chinese who came into these areas. "In those days, the boundaries were from Kearny to Powell, and from California to Broadway. If you ever passed them and went out there, the white kids would throw stones at you," Wei Bat Liu told us.[41]

In contrast to Malcolm X's family being excluded from living in East Lansing, the Chinese of San Francisco were forced to live in a marked-off territory. Yet another system of segregation developed in Savannah, Georgia, around 1900. There, Chinese immigrants were advised by other Chinese Americans to live apart from each other, rather than settle in ethnic enclaves, because of the negative experiences of residents of Chinatowns in San Francisco and New York.[42] They felt that creating a Chinatown would increase anti-Chinese sentiment, as well as make them easier targets for anti-Chinese discrimination.

Historical forces and power relations have led to different settlement patterns of other cultural groups in ethnic enclaves across the U.S. landscape. Many small towns across the Midwest were settled by particular European groups—for example, in Iowa, Germans in Amana, Dutch in Pella, and Czechs and Slovaks in Cedar Rapids. Cities, too, have their neighborhoods, based on settlement patterns. For instance, South Philadelphia is largely Italian American, South Boston is largely Irish American, and Overtown in Miami is largely African American. Although it is no longer legal to mandate that people live in particular districts or neighborhoods based on their racial or ethnic backgrounds, the continued existence of such neighborhoods underscores the importance of historical influence.

Info Bites

Research reports that deaf babies "babble" with hand gestures in the same way that hearing babies babble with vocal sounds. Why do you think nonverbal communication is so necessary before (and after) we have the ability to communicate verbally? If nonverbal communication is universal, why are there cultural variations? (SOURCE: *The Nonverbal Communication Reader,* p. 54)

Regionalism Ongoing regional conflicts, expressions of nationalism, ethnic revivals, and religious strife point to the continuing struggle over who gets to define whom. Such conflicts are hardly new, though. In fact, some cultural spaces, such as Jerusalem, have been ongoing sites of struggle for many centuries. Similarly, during the 20th century, Germany and France fought over Alsace-Lorraine, and both the Germans and the Czechs claimed the Sudetenland region. Other areas have retained their regional identities despite being engulfed by a larger nation—for example, Scotland and Wales in Britain, the Basque region in both Spain and France, Catalonia in Spain, Brittany and Corsica in France, and the Kurdish region in both Turkey and Iraq. Although regions may not always be clearly marked on maps of the world, many people identify quite strongly with particular regions.

Regionalism—loyalty to some area that holds cultural meaning—can take many different forms, from symbolic expressions of identification to armed conflict. Within the United States, people may identify themselves or others as southerners or midwesterners. People from Montreal might identify more strongly with the province of Quebec than with their country, Canada. Similarly, some Corsicans might feel a need to negotiate their identity with France. Sometimes people fly regional flags, wear particular kinds of clothes, celebrate regional holidays, and participate in other cultural activities to communicate their regional identification. But these expressions of regionalism are not always simply celebratory, as the violent conflicts in Kosovo, Chechnya, Eritrea, Tibet, and East Timor indicate. The idea of national borders may seem simple enough, but they often ignore or obscure conflicting regional identities. To understand how intercultural communications may be affected by national borders, we must consider how issues of history, power, identity, culture, and context come into play.

Cyberspace **Cyberspace**—Another set of familiar cultural spaces are found on the Internet and in mobile communication technologies. People meet and interact with each other in real time in **MMOGs:** (Massively Text-based Multiplayer Online Games) and virtual worlds like *Second Life*. These spaces are primarily for recreational purposes and people can assume their own or another identity. There are other Internet spaces, like discussion boards, where people connect for fun, to gain information, or to experience a supportive community (e.g., an online group where Japanese elderly meet for support or a bulletin board where gay, lesbian, and transgendered people can offer support and exchange useful information). Increasingly, blogs are spaces where people connect. According to recent statistics, there are now about 70 million blogs worldwide and bloggers collectively create almost one million posts every day.[43] People blog for many reasons, but often to connect with others, to test ideas or "muse," and as a community forum.[44] For example, religious blogs are increasingly popular—a place where individuals can express their thoughts and feelings about their own personal faith and connect with others with similar beliefs or to a wider public audience.[45] Social networking sites (SNS) are another type of virtual space where young people especially interact.[46]

Communication scholars have investigated how these virtual spaces affect the communication that occurs there. Some suggest that this disembodied communication and lack of shared reality, a kind of "absent presence," can lead to social isolation[47]; other experts think that mobile communication may result in a psychological "emptying out" of public space, where people's bodies are present, but personalities are engaged elsewhere (on cell phones, PDAs, etc.), resulting in the stress of always being somewhere else no matter where one might be physically.[48] However, still others suggest that virtual spaces offer a different cultural space for interacting and that cyber relationships are formed, maintained, and dissolved in much the same way as offline relationships.[49] What do you think? We'll explore cyber relationships further in Chapter 9.

Changing Cultural Space

Traveling   What happens when people change cultural spaces? Traveling is frequently viewed as simply a leisure activity, but it is more than that. In terms of intercultural communication, **traveling** changes cultural spaces in a way that often transforms the traveler. Changing cultural spaces means changing who you are and how you interact with others. Perhaps the old saying "When in Rome, do as the Romans do" holds true today as we cross cultural spaces more frequently than ever. However, this is not always easy to do. After traveling to Morocco, our student Jessica described the nonverbal behavior of some of the U.S. American students she was with:

What Do You Think?

How does a salesperson read others' body language? Check out this website (www .positiveresults.com/ articles/body_language .asp) to see the major areas of body language that salespeople usually observe.

> We were informed before the trip that women in Morocco dress differently, that they cover practically every inch of their bodies. We were not expected to do that, but we were told to dress appropriately, in pants or a skirt that covered our legs and a shirt with sleeves. It felt like a slap in the face when I saw two girls on the trip in cut-off jean shorts and tight tank tops that showed their midriffs. They even had the nerve to ask our tour guide why the Moroccan women were shouting "shame" and casting evil looks.

Should people alter their communication style when they encounter travelers who are not in their traditional cultural space? Do they assume that the travelers should interact in the ways prescribed by their own cultural space? These are some of the issues that travel raises; we address these issues in Chapter 10.

Migration   People also change cultural spaces through **migration** from a primary cultural context to a new one. Migration, of course, involves a different kind of change in cultural spaces than traveling. With traveling, the change is temporary and, usually, desirable. It is something people seek out. By contrast, people who migrate do not always seek out this change. For example, many people were forced from their homelands of Rwanda and Bosnia and had to settle elsewhere. Many immigrants leave their homelands simply to survive. But they often find it difficult to adjust to the change, especially if the language and customs of the new cultural space are unfamiliar. That is, they may suffer culture shock, as described in Chapter 4. As one recent immigrant to the United States

What Do You Think?

Blogs, short for weblogs, have become a popular online place for people to journal their experiences and share information about their lives. From blogs about politics and photography to those about food and mothering, blogs create a space where people can freely express their identity and culture. How can you use a blog to tell others about yourself? How can you read others' blogs as a way of learning about cultural groups different from your own? If you want to start reading blogs, you may want to begin with *Time* magazine's top 25 blogs at www.time.com and search "Top 25 Blogs."

describes it, "I myself experienced such shock after arriving in the United States. The people's language and behavior were the first aspects that made me feel insecure and disoriented. The stress I experienced caused sleeplessness and a feeling of being lost."

Even within the United States, people often find it difficult to adapt to new surroundings when they move. Tom remembers how northerners who moved to the South often were unfamiliar with the custom of banks closing early on Wednesday or with the traditional New Year's Day foods. And ridiculing or ignoring the customs of their new cultural space simply led to further intercultural communication problems.

The Dynamic Nature of Cultural Spaces

The dynamic nature of cultural space stands in sharp contrast to more traditional Western notions of space, which promoted land ownership, surveys, borders, colonies, and territories. No passport is needed to travel in the current dynamic cultural space, because there are no border guards. The dynamic nature of current cultural spaces underscores their relationship to changing cultural needs. The space exists only as long as it is needed in its present form.

Phoenix, Arizona, for example, which became a city only in the past few decades, has no Chinatown, no Japantown, no Koreatown, no Irish district, no Polish neighborhood, and no Italian area. Instead, people of Polish descent might live anywhere in the metropolitan area but congregate for special occasions or for specific reasons. On Sundays, the Polish Catholic Mass draws worshippers from throughout Phoenix. When people want to buy Polish breads and pastries, they can go to the Polish bakery and also speak Polish there. Ethnic identity is only one of several identities important to these people. When they desire recognition and interaction based on their Polish heritage, they can fulfill these desires. When they seek other forms of identification, they may go to places where they can be, say, Phoenix Suns fans or art lovers. Ethnic identity is neither the sole factor nor necessarily the most important factor at all times in their lives. The markers of ethnic life in Phoenix are the urban sites where people congregate when they desire ethnic cultural contact. At other times, they may frequent other locations to express other aspects of their identities. In this sense, this contemporary urban space is dynamic and allows people to participate in the communication of identity in new ways.[50]

As noted, the rise of the Internet has added a new dimension to the creation of cultural spaces. We can now enter (virtually) a number of spaces where we can communicate in ways that express different aspects of our cultural identities. Our physical space or location is no longer the most significant barrier to communicating with others who share our cultural identities. Because we are communicating in cyberspace, we are no longer bound by our physical bodies. We can "pass" as men or women, members of many different religious and ethnic communities, or people with different political perspectives or sexualities. While it is still difficult to communicate in languages we do not speak, the Internet even makes some rudimentary translation sites available. Many people, however, have no interest in enacting identities with which they do not identify. Why communicate about lacrosse, for example, if you would prefer to spend time communicating about your auto that reflects your identity? Cyberspace pushes the boundaries of what cultural space is, how quickly cultural spaces can shift, and how quickly we can take control over who we are and where we are, whenever we wish.[51]

SUMMARY

In this chapter, we examined both nonverbal communication principles and cultural spaces. Nonverbal communication, which operates at a subconscious level, is learned implicitly and can reinforce, substitute for, or contradict verbal behaviors.

Nonverbal behaviors can communicate relational meaning, status, and deception. Nonverbal communication is influenced by culture, although many cultures share some nonverbal behaviors. Methods of nonverbal communication include eye contact, facial expressions, gestures, time orientation, and silence. Sometimes cultural differences in nonverbal behaviors can lead to stereotyping of other cultures.

Cultural space influences cultural identity. Cultural spaces relate to issues of power and intercultural communication. Homes, neighborhoods, regions, nations, and cyberspace are all examples of cultural spaces. Two ways of changing cultural spaces are travel and migration. Current cultural spaces are dynamic, accommodating people of different cultural identities who coexist.

BUILDING INTERCULTURAL SKILLS

1. Become more conscious of your nonverbal behavior in intercultural encounters. Practice your encoding skills. You can do this by noting the nonverbal behaviors of others—their facial expressions, gestures, eye contact, and so on. Check to see if their nonverbal communication is telling you that they understand or misunderstand you.

2. Become more aware of others' nonverbal communication. What messages are they sending? And how do you react to those messages? Think about when you are uncomfortable in intercultural encounters. Is your discomfort due to the nonverbal messages others are sending? Are they violating the rules you're used to? Standing too close, or too far away? Touching too much, or not enough? Talking too loudly, or too softly?

3. Practice your decoding skills. Check out your perceptions of others' nonverbal behavior. Are you accurate, or do you misread their nonverbal cues? Are they misunderstanding when you think they are understanding? Are they happy when you think they are upset?

4. Expand your nonverbal communication repertoire. Practice new nonverbal behaviors. Try varying your posture, facial expressions, and eye contact.

5. Be flexible and adaptable in your nonverbal communication in intercultural encounters. Try synchronizing your behavior to that of others, which usually communicates that you feel good about your relationship. If others stand with their arms folded, do the same. If they stand closer than you're used to, don't move away. If they use more eye contact, try to do the same.

6. Become more aware of your prejudicial assumptions based on nonverbal behavior. When you have a very negative reaction to others, check out the basis for these assumptions. Is it simply because of the way they look? Give them another chance.

ACTIVITIES

Nonverbal rules: Choose a cultural space that you are interested in studying. Visit this space on four different occasions to observe how people there interact. Focus on one aspect of nonverbal communication, such as eye contact or personal space. List some rules that seem to govern this aspect of nonverbal communication. For example, if you are focusing on personal space, you might describe, among other things, how far apart people tend to stand when conversing. Based on your observations, list some rules about proper (expected) nonverbal behavior in this cultural space. Share your conclusions with the class. To what extent do other students share your conclusions? Can we generalize about nonverbal rules in cultural spaces? What factors influence whether an individual follows unspoken rules of behavior?

ENDNOTES

1. Smith, R. J., & Tyson, A. S. (2005, March 7). Shootings by U.S. at Iraq Checkpoints Questioned Page. *Washington Post*, p. A01. retrieved March 17, 2008 from http://www.washingtonpost.com/wp-dyn/articles/A12507-2005Mar6.html

2. Knapp, M. L., & Hall, J. A. (2005). *Nonverbal communication in human interaction.* (6th ed.). Belmont, CA: Wadsworth.

3. Knapp & Hall (2005).

4. Knapp & Hall (2005).

5. Jones, S. E., & LeBaron, C. D. (2002). Research on the relationship between verbal and nonverbal communication: Emerging integration. *Journal of Communication, 52,* 499–521.

6. Lock, C. (2004, July 31). Deception detection. *Science News, 166,* 72–73; Vrij, A. (2004). Why professionals fail to catch liars and how they can improve. *Legal and Criminological Psychology, 9,* 159–181.

7. Montepare, J. M. (2003). Evolution and nonverbal behavior: Adaptive social interaction strategies. *Journal of Nonverbal Behavior, 27,* 141–143; Patterson, M. L. (2003). Commentary: Evolution and nonverbal behavior: Functions and mediating processes. *Journal of Behavior, 27,* 201–207.

8. Ekman, P., & Keltner, D. (1997). Universal facial expressions of emotion: An old controversy and new findings. In *Segérstrâle & Molnár, pp. 27–46.* See also Galati, D., Sini, B., Schmidt, S., & Tinti, C. (2003, July). Spontaneous facial expressions in congenitally blind and sighted children aged 8–11. *Journal of Visual Impairment and Blindness, 97,* 418–428.

9. Montepare, J. M. (2003). Evolution and nonverbal behavior: Adaptive social interaction strategies. *Journal of Nonverbal Behavior, 27,* 141–143; Patterson, M. L. (2003). Commentary: Evolution

and nonverbal behavior: Functions and mediating processes. *Journal of Nonverbal Behavior, 27,* 201–207.

10. Alberts, J., Nakayama, T. K., & Martin, J. N. (2007). *Human Communication in society.* Boston: Allyn-Bacon.

11. Andersen, P. A., Hecht, M. L., Hoobler, G. D., & Smallwood, M. (2002). Nonverbal communication across cultures. In W. B. Gudykunst & B. Mody (Eds.), *Handbook of international and intercultural communication* (2nd ed., pp. 89–106). Thousand Oaks, CA: Sage.

12. Andersen, Hecht, Hoobler, & Smallwood (2002).

13. Fattah, H. M. (2005, May 1). Why Arab men hold hands. *The New York Times,* Week in Review, Section 4, p. 2.

14. Knapp, M. L., & Hall, J. A. (2001). *Nonverbal communication in human interaction.* Belmont, CA: Wadsworth.

15. Archer, D. (1997). Unspoken diversity: Cultural differences in gestures. *Qualitative Sociology, 20,* 79–105.

16. Norwegians confused by Bush "horns" salute. (2005, December 1). *USA Today.* Retrieved from http://www.usatoday.com/news/washington/2005-01-21-bush-norwegians_x.htm?csp=34&POE=click-refer

17. Archer (1997), p. 87.

18. Hall, E. T. (1959). *The silent language.* New York: Doubleday; Hall, E. T. (1976). *Beyond culture.* New York: Doubleday.

19. Macduff, I. (2006). Your pace or mine? Culture, time, and negotiation. *Negotiation Journal, 22*(1), 31–45.

20. Dahl, O. (1993). *Malagasy meanings: An interpretive approach to intercultural communication in Madagascar.* Stavanger, Norway: Center for Intercultural Communication, p. 66.

21. Covarrubias, P. (2007). (Un)Biased in Western theory: Generative silence in American Indian communication. *Communication Monographs, 74*(2), p. 270.

22. Acheson, C. (2007). Silence in dispute. In C. S. Beck (Ed.), *Communication Yearbook 31* (pp. 2–59), New York: Lawrence Erlbaum Associates.

23. Condon, J. (1984). *With respect to the Japanese.* Yarmouth, ME: Intercultural Press, p. 41.

24. Carbaugh, D., & Berry, M. (2001). Communicating history, Finnish and American discourses: An ethnographic contribution to intercultural communication inquiry. *Communication Theory, 11,* 352–366; Sajavaara, K., & Lehtonen, J. (1997). The silent Finn revisited. In Jaworski (Ed.), *Silence: Interdisciplinary perspectives* (pp. 263–283). New York: Mouton de Gruyter.

25. Basso, K. (1970). "To give up on words": Silence in Western Apache culture. *Southwestern Journal of Anthropology, 26,* 213–230; Braithwaite, C. A. (1990). Communicative silence: A cross-cultural study of Basso's hypothesis. In D. Carbaugh (Ed.), *Cultural communication and intercultural contact* (pp. 321–327). Hillsdale, NJ: Erlbaum.

26. Nakane, I. (2006). Silence and politeness in intercultural communication in university seminars. *Journal of Pragmatics 38,* 1811–1835.

27. Liu, J. (2002). Negotiating silence in American classrooms: Three Chinese cases. *Language and Intercultural Communication, 2*(1), 37–54.

28. Mosbach, H. (1988). The importance of silence and stillness in Japanese nonverbal communication: A cross cultural approach. In F. Poyatos (Ed.), *Cross cultural perspectives in nonverbal communication* (pp. 201–215). Lewiston, NY: Hogrefe.

29. Montell, G. (2003, October 15). Do good looks equal good evaluations? *Chronicle of Higher Education.* Retrieved from http://chronicle.com/jobs/2003/10/2003101501c.htm

30. Neal, L. V. I., McCray, A. D., & Webb-Johnson, G. (2001). Teachers' reactions to African American students' movement styles. *Intervention in School and Clinic, 36,* 168–174.

31. Matthews, R. (2000). Culture patterns of South Asian and S.E. Asian Americans. *Interventions in School and Clinic, 36,* 101–105.

32. *Hatewatch for the Record.* (n.d.). Southern Poverty Law Center. Retrieved from http://www.splcenter.org/intel/hatewatch/fortherecord.jsp

33. Richeson, J., & Shelton, J. N. (2005). Brief report: Thin slices of racial bias. *Journal of Nonverbal Behavior, 29,* 75–86.

34. Johnson, A. G. (2001). *Privilege, power and difference.* Thousand Oaks, CA: Sage.
35. Fussell, P. (1983). *Class.* New York: Summit Books.
36. hooks, b. (1990). *Yearning: Race, gender, and cultural politics.* Boston: South End Press, p. 41.
37. Greene, H. (1991). Charleston, South Carolina. In J. Preston (Ed.), *Hometowns: Gay men write about where they belong* (pp. 55–67). New York: Dutton.
38. Saylor, S. (1991). Amethyst, Texas. In J. Preston (Ed.), *Hometowns: Gay men write about where they belong* (pp. 119–135). New York: Dutton.
39. X, Malcolm, & Haley, A. (1964). *The autobiography of Malcolm X.* New York: Grove Press, pp. 3–4.
40. Loewen, J. (2005). *Sundown towns: A hidden dimension of American racism.* New York: New Press.
41. Nee, V. G., Nee, B. D. B. (1974). *Longtime Californ': A documentary study of an American Chinatown.* Boston: Houghton Mifflin, p. 60.
42. Pruden, G. B., Jr. (1990). History of the Chinese in Savannah, Georgia. In J. Goldstein (Ed.), *Georgia's East Asian connection: Into the twenty-first century: Vol. 27. West Georgia College studies in the social sciences* (pp. 17–34). Carrollton: West Georgia College.
43. State of the Blogosphere / 2008. (2008). Technorati.com. Retrieved December 13, 2008 from http://technorati.com/blogging/state-of-the-blogosphere/
44. Nardi, B. A., Schiano, D. J., & Gumbrecht, M. (2004). *Blogging as social activity, or, would you let 900 million people read your diary?* Proceedings of the 2004 ACM conference on Computer supported cooperative work (pp. 222–231). Chicago, Illinois. Retrieved February 2, 2009 from http://home.comcast.net/~diane.schiano/CSCW04.Blog.pdf
45. Cheong, P. H., Halavais, A., & Kwon, K. (2008). The chronicles of me: Understanding blogging as a religious practice. *Journal of Media and Religion, 7,* 107–131; Cheong, P., & Poon, J. (In press). Weaving webs of faith: Examining Internet use and religious communication among Chinese Protestant transmigrants. *Journal of International and Intercultural Communication.*
46. boyd, d. m. & Ellison, N. B. (2007). Social network sites: Definition, history, and scholarship. *Journal of Computer-Mediated Communication, 13*(1), 210–230.
47. Gergen, K. J. (2002). The challenge of absent-presence. In J. Katz & M. Aakhus (Eds.), *Perpetual contact: Mobile communication, private talk, public performance* (pp. 223–227). Cambridge, UK: Cambridge University Press.
48. Katz, J. E. (2007). Mobile media and communication: Some important questions. *Communication Monographs, 74*(3), 389–394.
49. Boase, J. (2008). Personal networks and the personal communication system. *Information, Communication & Society, 11*(4), 490–508.
50. Drzewiecka, J. A., & Nakayama, T. K. (1998). City sites: Postmodern urban space and the communication of identity. *Southern Communication Journal, 64,* 20–31.
51. Strate, L., Jacobson, R. L., & Gibson, S. L. (Eds.), *Communication and cyberspace: Social interaction in an electronic environment.* Cresskill, NJ: Hampton Press.

CHAPTER SEVEN

Popular Culture and Intercultural Communication

STUDY OBJECTIVES

After reading this chapter, you should be able to:

1. Define popular culture.
2. Identify some types of popular culture.
3. Describe characteristics of popular culture.
4. Explain why it is important to understand popular culture in intercultural communication.
5. Discuss why people consume or resist specific cultural texts.
6. Understand how cultural texts influence cultural identities.
7. Discuss how cultural group portrayals in popular culture forms influence intercultural communication.
8. Suggest effects of the global domination of U.S. popular culture.

KEY TERMS

cultural identities
cultural imperialism
cultural texts
culture industries
electronic colonialism

folk culture
media imperialism
popular culture
reader profiles

My dad's profession is very demanding, and he travels all across the world for it. When I was around 10 years old, my dad decided to take me with him on a business trip to Tel Aviv, Israel. . . . One day I went with my cousins to one of their friend's house. When I met their friends, they seemed wary of me, and I could tell I was being talked about in Hebrew, which made me pretty uneasy. Though, everything changed when I saw they had a Super Nintendo system. While their friends didn't speak English, the international language of gamers was our medium, even though it wasn't verbal. While we couldn't speak the same language, the international allure of video games allowed us to get closer and to become friends. I became closer with my cousins through this, along with their friends, and was very popular by the end of my trip. I learned that while we may have different cultures or speak different languages, we're a lot more similar than we think.

—Andrew

Our student, Andrew, found a way to connect across language differences by playing video games with some Israeli youth. Sometimes popular music or movies from the United States, video games from Japan, or sports can help people bridge cultural and linguistic differences, as these forms of culture can cross international boundaries. As people purchase these cultural products, we can see that cultures are different, but that they share popular culture products that can be a way to connect them with others. These are complex relationships that highlight the importance of thinking about this kind of culture when we think about intercultural communication.

Culture is central to intercultural communication, but we often overlook some of the meanings of culture in everyday life. One kind of culture that is often overlooked by intercultural communication scholars is popular culture. But popular culture plays a very important role in how we understand the world, helping us reinforce our sense of who we are and confirming our worldviews.

Neither Tom nor Judith has ever been to Cuba, Kenya, Brazil, Nigeria, India, Russia, or China. Yet all of these places, and many more, evoke images of what it is "really" like to be there. We derive images about these places from the news, movies, television shows, advertisements, and other kinds of popular culture. Sometimes we feel as if we've been somewhere when we watch the Travel Channel. And when people actually visit Paris, or Honolulu, or Tokyo, they might exclaim that it looks just like it does on television! Obviously, not all of this "information" in popular culture is up-to-date and accurate. Some popular culture images reinforce stereotypes of other cultures, while other images challenge those stereotypes. In this chapter, we examine the role that popular culture plays in building bridges in, as well as barriers to, intercultural communication.

POPULAR CULTURE AND INTERCULTURAL COMMUNICATION

We can experience new places by traveling and by migrating. But there will always be places around the world that we have not visited and where we have not lived. Most of us do not even make it around the globe.

So what do we know about places we have never been, and how do we acquire this "knowledge"? Much of what we know about these places probably comes from popular culture—the media outlets of television, music, videos, and magazines that most of us know and share. And how does this experience of places traveled to only through popular culture affect intercultural communication?

The complexity of popular culture is often overlooked in our society. People express concerns about the social effects of popular culture—for example, the effects of television violence on children or the relationship between heterosexual pornography and violence against women. Yet most people look down on the study of popular culture, as if there is nothing of significance to learn there. This attitude can make it difficult to investigate and discuss popular culture.

As U.S. Americans, we are in a unique position in relationship to popular culture. Products of U.S. popular culture are well known and widely circulated around the globe. Many U.S. film, music, and television stars, such as Beyoncé, Brad Pitt, Angelina Jolie, Colin Farrell, and Jennifer Lopez, are also popular outside the United States, creating an uneven flow of **cultural texts**— cultural artifacts that convey norms, values, and beliefs—between the United States and other nations. Scholars Elihu Katz and Tamar Liebes note the "apparent ease with which American television programs cross cultural and linguistic frontiers. Indeed, the phenomenon is so taken for granted that hardly any systematic research has been done to explain the reasons why these programs are so successful."[1]

By contrast, U.S. Americans are rarely exposed to popular culture from outside the United States. Exceptions to this largely one-way movement of popular culture include foreign performers who sing in English, such as ABBA, Björk, Shakira, Golden Earring, and Celine Dion. Consider how difficult it is to find foreign films or television programs throughout most of the United States. The apparent imbalance of cultural texts globally not only makes U.S. Americans more dependent on U.S.-produced popular culture but also can lead to cultural imperialism, a topic we will discuss later in this chapter.

Pop Culture Spotlight

Popular culture from the United States is widely circulated around the globe, but there are several recent examples of other countries influencing pop culture within the United States. Did you know that *American Idol* is actually based on a popular British television show called *Pop Idol? Pop Idol* has been adapted for television audiences in many other countries such as Canada, India, Singapore, Germany, Poland, Iceland, Armenia, Bulgaria, and Brazil. What countries gave us shows such as *Ugly Betty, Kath and Kim,* and *Big Brother?*

The study of popular culture has become increasingly important in the communication field. Although intercultural communication scholars traditionally have overlooked popular culture, we believe that these forms of culture are significant influences in intercultural interaction. In this chapter, we explore some of these influences.

WHAT IS "POPULAR CULTURE"?

Sometimes it may seem obvious what constitutes **popular culture** and what does not. For example, we often consider soap operas, reality television shows, and romance novels to be popular culture, while symphonies, operas, and the ballet are not. Popular culture often is seen as populist, in that it includes forms of contemporary culture that are made popular by and for the people through their mass consumption of these products. As John Fiske, professor of communication arts, observes:

> To be made into popular culture, a commodity must also bear the interests of the people. Popular culture is not consumption, it is culture—the active process of generating and circulating meanings and pleasures within a social system: culture, however industrialized, can never be adequately described in terms of the buying and selling of commodities.[2]

In his study of popular Mexican American music in Los Angeles, ethnic studies professor George Lipsitz highlights the ways that marginalized social groups are able to express themselves in innovative, nonmainstream ways. In this study, he demonstrates how the "popular" can arise from a mixing and borrowing from other cultures. He suggests that "the ability of musicians to learn from other cultures played a key role in their success as rock-and-roll artists."[3] Here, as elsewhere, the popular speaks to—and resonates with—the people, but it speaks to them through many cultural voices. Lipsitz continues:

> The marginality of Chicano rock-and-roll musicians has provided them with a constant source of inspiration and a constant spur toward innovation that gained them the attention of mainstream audiences. But this marginal sensibility amounts to more than novelty or personal eccentricity; it holds legitimacy and power as the product of a real historical community's struggle with oppression. . . . As Chicano musicians demonstrate in their comments about their work, their music reflects a quite conscious cultural politics that seeks inclusion in the American mainstream by transforming it.[4]

Intercultural contact and intercultural communication play a central role in the creation and maintenance of popular culture. Yet, as Lipsitz also points out, the popular is political and pleasurable, which opens new arenas for complicating the ways we might think about popular culture.

Thus, popular culture can be said to have four significant characteristics: (1) It is produced by culture industries, (2) it is different from **folk culture,** (3) it is

What Do You Think?

According to the U.S. Census Bureau's May 2006 official statistical estimates, there are 42.6 million "Hispanics or Latinos" residing in the United States. How do federally funded organizations such as the Census Bureau's use of statistical evidence support or subvert media messages such as the "Latin explosion"? Which aspects of Latino/a culture are apparent in the works of individual entertainers such as Christina Aguilera, Marc Anthony, Jennifer Lopez, and Shakira? What marks their music, style, and/or identity as Latino/a? (SOURCE: *Annual Estimates of the Population by Sex, Race and Hispanic or Latino Origin for the United States: April 1, 2000 to July 1, 2005,* Population Division, U.S. Census Bureau. Release Date: May 1, 2006)

Pop stars, like Rihanna, often enjoy worldwide popularity. Although she is from Barbados, she moved to the United States, and the popularity of U.S. popular culture products can launch many careers. This has important implications for both individuals and cultures worldwide.

everywhere, and (4) it fills a social function. As Fiske points out, popular culture is nearly always produced by what are called **culture industries** within a capitalist system that sees the products of popular culture as commodities to be sold for profit. The Disney Corporation is a noteworthy example of a culture industry because it produces amusement parks, movies, cartoons, and a plethora of associated merchandise. As shown in Table 7.1, culture products can be imported from other countries.

Folk culture refers to the traditional rituals and traditions that maintain cultural group identity. Unlike popular culture, folk culture is typically not controlled by any industry and is not driven by a profit motive. For example, the celebration of Oktoberfest in Germany is laden with rituals that vary from one region to another. While these rituals may be open to outsiders, they express and confirm cultural identity and group membership.

TABLE 7.1 U.S. Television Shows Imported from Other Countries

While many television shows from the United States are popular in other countries, sometimes U.S. television shows borrow ideas from other countries. Here are some examples:

Kath and Kim—Australia

American Idol—Great Britain

Ugly Betty—Colombia

Big Brother—the Netherlands

More recently, communication scholars Joshua Gunn and Barry Brummett have challenged the notion that there is an important difference between folk culture and popular culture. They note that scholars "write as if there is a fundamental difference between a mass-produced and mass-marketed culture and a more authentic 'folk' culture or subculture. Such a binary is dissolving into a globally marketed culture. A few remaining pockets of folk culture remain here and there: on the Sea Islands, in Amish country, in departments of English. The rest of folk culture is now 50% off at Wal–Mart."[5] In the new context of globalization, whatever happened to folk traditions and artifacts? Have they been unable to escape being mass-produced and marketed around the globe?

Popular culture also is ubiquitous. We are bombarded with it, every day and everywhere. On average, U.S. Americans watch more than 40 hours of television per week. Movie theaters beckon us with the latest multimillion-dollar extravaganzas, nearly all U.S.-made. Radio stations and TV music stations blast us with the hottest music groups performing their latest hits. And we are inundated with a staggering number of advertisements and commercials daily.

It is difficult to avoid popular culture. Not only is it ubiquitous, but it also serves an important social function. How many times have friends and family members asked about your reactions to recent movies or television programs? What kind of reaction would you get if you said, "I don't watch television"? Communication scholars Horace Newcomb and Paul Hirsch suggest that television serves as a cultural forum for discussing and working out our ideas on a variety of topics, including those that emerge from television programs.[6] We see how others feel about various issues—from gay marriage to immigration to school shootings—and how we feel about them as they are discussed on television. These forums include daytime and late-night talk shows, news programs, and situation comedies, among many others. Television, then, has a powerful social function: to serve as a forum for social issues.

In their study on print news coverage, communication scholars Dreama Moon and Tom Nakayama analyzed newspaper accounts of the murder of Arthur "J. R." Warren in West Virginia.[7] Although the small town where he was murdered did not have a local paper, they found that the media coverage did highlight significant differences in how African Americans, gays and lesbians, and White heterosexual residents experienced and perceived everyday life and tolerance in the small West Virginia town. Through the media, African Americans and gays and lesbians were able to offer an alternative view that differed from the dominant view of idealized small-town life. Again, newspapers served as a forum for discussion of this tragic event.

In contrast, not all popular culture may serve as a forum for public deliberation. In his study of baseball tributes in ballparks after the attacks of September 11, 2001, Michael Butterworth found that these rituals tended to discourage expression of opinions that differed from a nationalistic patriotism at the expense of democratic deliberation. Butterworth describes these baseball tributes and

Info Bites

Scholar Raymond Williams argued that popular culture is important to study because in one week we are exposed to more stories and dramas in the media than Europeans a thousand years ago would have been exposed to in their entire lives.

notes: "If baseball can be understood as a representative institution of American democratic culture, then the ways in which it performs (or fails to perform) democratically merit scrutiny and criticism. In the aftermath of unprecedented tragedy (for Americans), baseball could have been a site not only for communal healing but also for productively engaging the pluralism that the game does or should represent."[8] Baseball tributes, then, are a form of popular culture that do not serve a cultural forum for the democratic exchange of ideas.

The ways in which people negotiate their relationships to popular culture are complex. It is this complexity that makes understanding the role of popular culture in intercultural communication so difficult. Clearly, we are not passive receivers of this deluge of popular culture. We are, in fact, quite active in our consumption of or resistance to popular culture, a notion that we turn to next.

U.S. POPULAR CULTURE AND POWER

My roommate Aaron and I took the two Japanese students to the Memorial Union to play pool. They seemed really excited and interested in all my questions or comments. . . . It was my belief that the Japanese people were very shy and quiet. However, these girls proved me wrong. They were somewhat shy, but most of the time they were laughing and having a good time. . . . They told me what kind of stereotypes they had about America. They told me that they thought everyone ate junk food and that there were a lot of criminals. I think most of these impressions are mainly due to the media portrayal of our country in Japan. I think most movies overly illustrate America's fast-paced life, which involves fast food.

—Charlie

One of the dynamics of intercultural communication that we have highlighted throughout this text is power. In considering popular culture, we need to think about not only the ways that people interpret and consume popular culture but also the ways that these popular culture texts represent particular groups in specific ways. If people largely view other cultural groups through the lens of popular culture, then we need to think about the power relations that are embedded in these popular culture dynamics.

Global Circulation of Images/Commodities

As noted previously, much of U.S. popular culture is circulated worldwide. For example, U.S.-made films are widely distributed by a culture industry that is backed by considerable financial resources. Some media scholars have noted that the U.S. film industry earns far more money outside the United States than from domestic box-office sales.[9] This situation ensures that Hollywood will continue to market its films overseas and that it will have the financial resources to

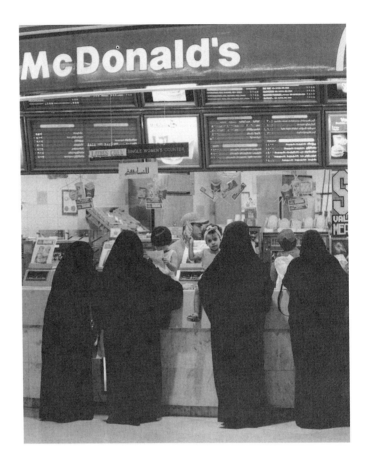

McDonald's has adapted to different cultures. For example, women in Dhahran, Saudi Arabia, must wait for their orders at the single women's counter. Cultural adaptation is an important phenomenon in the exportation of U.S. popular culture.

do so. For example, as of April 25, 2006, the blockbuster *Star Wars: Episode III—Revenge of the Sith* had earned over $380 million in the United States but had earned more than $462.6 million from the rest of the world.[10]

Many other U.S. media are widely available outside the United States, including television and newspapers. Cable News Network (CNN) is widely available around the world. MTV also broadcasts internationally. And the *International Herald Tribune*, published jointly by the *New York Times* and the *Washington Post*, is available in many parts of the world. The implications of the dominance by U.S. media and popular culture have yet to be determined, although you might imagine the consequences.

Recently, however, the emergence of Aljazeera, the news channel based in Qatar, has begun to offer a different voice in international news. Given the recent focus on the Arabic-speaking world, Aljazeera's perspective has taken a particularly significant place. As they describe themselves: "With more than 30 bureaus and dozens of correspondents covering the four corners of the world Aljazeera has given millions of people a refreshing new perspective on global events."[11]

The French will launch a similar CNN-type news channel that is focused on providing an alternative view to the BBC, CNN, and Aljazeera. Given the recent tensions between France and the United States over the invasion of Iraq, a French government official noted, "France may see things differently and we feel it is important that we get our message across."[12] Although informally referred to as "CNN à la française," this new "channel would promote a vision of a 'multipolar' world that is not dominated by one superpower, such as the United States."[13] This new channel will not initially be available in the United States, but it hopes to expand from Europe, Africa, and the Middle East to Asia, South America, and the United States later. This will allow the French to compete with CNN, the BBC, and Aljazeera as international broadcasting networks to promote their view of the world.

Popular Culture from Other Cultures

Although U.S. popular culture tends to dominate the world market, not all popular culture comes from the United States. The popularity of some contemporary culture is limited to particular cultures, while other forms of popular culture cross into a more international market. For example, the James Bond books and movies have roots in Britain, but the famous character has been exported to the United States. In their study of the James Bond phenomenon, scholars Tony Bennett and Janet Woollacott note that in the Bond film *License to Kill* "the threat to the dominance of white American male culture is removed not by a representative of that culture, and certainly not by a somewhat foppish English spy, but by the self-destruction of the forces ranged against it."[14] The appropriation of the British character into U.S. ideological and economic terrain complicates arguments about the dominance of U.S. popular culture products.

The popularity of Japanese anADMIN anime or cartoons reflects another non-U.S. popular culture phenomenon. Anime clubs have emerged across the United States and around the world. The fascination with anime highlights the ability of non-U.S. popular culture to become popular internationally. Although many people think of anime as children's cartoons, "most anime tells sophisticated stories with complex characters aimed at adults."[15] Yet, "like so many cultural phenomena, anime is not just about anime itself, but about a subculture that's grown up enough to find some mainstream acceptance but is often still misunderstood."[16] The way that Japanese popular culture is imported into the United States is reflected in the development of anime clubs, websites, meetings, and other social activities.

More recently, with wide praise and some condemnation of the movie, *Slumdog Millionaire*, "a rags-to-riches story set partly in the slums of Mumbai, is this year's sleeper hit. With a modest budget of $15 million, it's gone on to earn nearly $100 million worldwide. Critics have awarded it top prizes at the Golden Globes, and the film [was named Best Picture at the Academy Awards]. But back in India, the movie has become a cultural lightning rod, attracting protests and charges of 'slum voyeurism.' A lawsuit alleges it defames Mumbai's urban

This photo shows a protest in India where the successful *Slumdog Millionaire* movie is showing. Does it matter who profits from such images of third-world slums?

poor, and many take offense at the appearance of 'dog' in the title."[17]   While this movie may appear to be a product of India, its origins are more complex.

As one *Newsweek* writer commented, "Despite appearances, *Slumdog* is a British production. It was produced by Christian Colson, directed by Danny Boyle (*Trainspotting*) and, though based on Indian author Vikas Swarup's novel *Q&A*, scripted by Simon Beaufoy—all of whom are white and sure bets for Oscar nominations. Meanwhile, out of the sprawling cast, only Dev Patel has a shot."[18] Thus there is some concern that this British film benefits from exploiting the economic situation in Mumbai and selling scenes of poverty around the world for the entertainment of others. This concern is related to the issues of cultural imperialism that we turn to next.

Cultural Imperialism

It is difficult to measure the impact of the U.S. and Western media and popular culture on the rest of the world. But we do know that we cannot ignore this dynamic. The U.S. government in the 1920s believed that having American movies on foreign screens would boost the sales of U.S. goods. The U.S. government worked closely with the Hays Office (officially, the Motion Picture Producers and Distributors of America) to break into foreign markets, most notably in the United Kingdom.[19]

The discussions about **media imperialism** (domination or control through the media), **electronic colonialism** (domination or exploitation utilizing technological forms), and **cultural imperialism** (domination through the spread of cultural products), which began in the 1920s, continue today. These are three of

What Do You Think?

What do the entertainment rating systems mean to you? Can you identify the differences between a teen-rated (13+) and a mature (17+) video game? Log onto www.esrb.org and you can search games by rating, platform, and content to better understand how rating systems work.

TABLE 7.2 Top Ten Grossing Movies Worldwide

 1. *Titanic* (1997)
 2. *The Lord of the Rings: The Return of the King* (2003)
 3. *Pirates of the Caribbean: Dead Man's Chest* (2006)
 4. *The Dark Knight* (2008)
 5. *Harry Potter and the Sorcerer's Stone* (2001)
 6. *Pirates of the Caribbean: At World's End* (2007)
 7. *Harry Potter and the Order of the Phoenix* (2007)
 8. *Star Wars: Episode I—The Phantom Menace* (1999)
 9. *The Lord of the Rings: The Two Towers* (2002)
10. *Jurassic Park* (1993)

Source: Internet Movie Database. Last updated March 2, 2009. From: http://www.imdb.com/boxoffice/alltimegross?region=world-wide

the terms that are often used to discuss the larger phenomenon of one culture dominating another, typically through economic domination and the infusion of cultural products that change the cultural values of the recipient culture. While media imperialism emphasizes this domination through media systems, electronic colonialism draws attention to the technological means of domination. Table 7.2 shows ten top-grossing movies worldwide, but note how many of them are U.S.-made. The interrelationships among economics, nationalism, and culture make it difficult to determine how significant cultural imperialism might be. The issue of cultural imperialism is complex because the phenomenon of cultural imperialism is complex. In his survey of the cultural imperialism debates, scholar John Tomlinson identified five different ways of thinking about cultural imperialism: (1) as cultural domination, (2) as media imperialism, (3) as nationalist discourse, (4) as a critique of global capitalism, and (5) as a critique of modernity.[20] Tomlinson's analysis underscores the interrelatedness of issues of ethnicity, culture, and nationalism in the context of economics, technology, and capitalism. Because economic, technological, and financial resources are not equally distributed around the world, some ethnic, cultural, and national groups face more difficulty in maintaining their identities and traditions. To understand the concerns about cultural imperialism, therefore, it is necessary to consider the impact of U.S. American popular culture. There is no easy way to measure the impact of popular culture, but we should be sensitive to its influences on intercultural communication.

Many cultural groups around the world worry about the impact of cultural imperialism. The government of Quebec, for example, is very concerned about the effects of English-language media on French Canadian language and culture. The French have also expressed concern about the dominance of U.S. popular culture and its impact on French society. Yet the popularity of U.S. popular culture products, such as *Law & Order*, *24*, and Janet Jackson CDs and videos, outside the United States reinforces particular notions of romance, masculinity,

What Do You Think?

Concerns over pornography are not new, but the Internet has provided a new communication medium for the distribution and viewing of pornography. Recently, China has criticized some Internet providers such as Google and noted that: "Searching for images results in an enormous number of vulgar, pornographic sites. Google, receiving notice, did not undertake any effective measures." How effective can China be in resisting pornography that is available over the Internet? What other ideas or images might cause concern that cross national borders through the Internet? Are there ideas or images that you resist on the Internet? (SOURCE: Bradsher, K. "China criticizes Google and others on pornography." *New York Times*, January 5, 2009, Retrieved March 2, 2009 from: http://www.nytimes.com/2009/01/06/world/asia/06pornography.html?partner=rss&emc=rss)

friendship, and happiness and promotes often idealized images of where U.S. Americans live and what kinds of commodities they purchase.

Yet, we must also remember that viewers are active agents and it is not always clear that they are dominated by imported images. In a recent study on this tension between global networks and local networks, Jonathan Cohen examines the situation in Israel. He examines Israel's 99 channels and identifies six different ways that these channels function in the global and local environment. He then notes: "Foreign television is often thought to be harmful because it separates people from their national communities,"[21] but he warns that we should not so easily view foreign television in this way. He doesn't think it is yet clear that watching U.S. television shows "like *Sex and the City* or *The Apprentice*, weakens viewers' connections to Israeli culture or strengthens them by providing a stark contrast to viewers' lives."[22] Cohen is emphasizing that we cannot assume that people who watch certain shows are passive viewers. The influence of media is more complex than a simple imposition of meaning from abroad.

Popular culture plays an enormous role in relations among nations worldwide. It is through popular culture that we try to understand the dynamics of other cultures and nations. Although these representations are problematic, we also rely on popular culture to understand many kinds of issues: the conflicts in Bosnia-Herzegovina and Kosovo; the murders of homeless children in Brazil; the rise of nationalism in Hawaii, Quebec, and Eritrea; and the tensions between India and Pakistan. For many of us, the world exists through popular culture.

CONSUMING AND RESISTING POPULAR CULTURE

We navigate our ways through the numerous popular culture choices. After all, as Australian scholar Nadine Dolby notes, "Popular culture, at the end of the 20th century, is a key site for the formation of identities, for the ways in which we make sense of the world, and locate ourselves within it."[23] In order to maintain our identities, as well as to reshape them, we often turn to popular culture. At times, we seek out cultural texts; at other times, we try to avoid certain texts.

Consuming Popular Culture

Faced with such an onslaught of cultural texts, people navigate their ways through popular culture in quite different ways. Popular culture texts do not have to win over the majority of people to be "popular." In fact, people often seek out or avoid specific forms of popular culture. For example, romance novels are the best-selling form of literature, but many people are not interested in reading these novels. Likewise, whereas you may enjoy watching soap operas or professional wrestling, many people find no pleasure in those forms of popular culture. We are bombarded every day with myriad popular culture texts. We actively seek out and choose those texts that serve our needs. Often people in our social groups participate in particular forms of popular culture, and so we feel that we should participate as well.

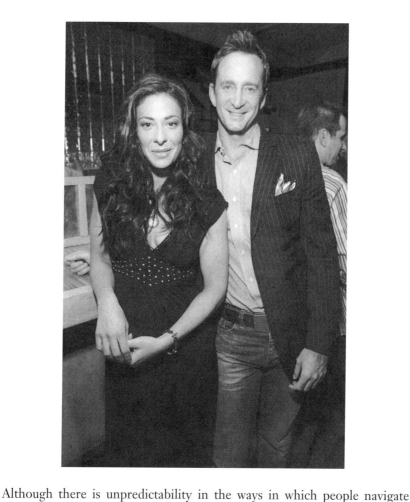

What Not to Wear, hosted by Stacy London and Clinton Kelly, is currently a very popular TV show. Why might some viewers be attracted to such a show and others resist it? How might consuming or resisting such a show be related to one's cultural identity?

What Do You Think?

The Real World has been a staple at MTV for 17 years with its most recent season in *The Real World–Cancun*. By mixing people with diverse backgrounds, lifestyles, and interests, MTV has been able to draw viewers to see how these people interact, get along, and engage in conflict. How "real" is this kind of reality television? What kinds of connections do you see between reality TV and intercultural communication? What draws viewers to this kind of programming?

Although there is unpredictability in the ways in which people navigate popular culture, certain patterns are evident. Advertising departments of popular magazines even make their **reader profiles** available to potential advertisers. These portrayals of readership demographics indicate what the magazine believes its readership "looks" like. Although reader profiles do not follow a set format, they generally give the average age, gender, individual and household incomes, and other pertinent data about their readers. For example, the reader profiles of *BusinessWeek*, *GQ*, *Cosmopolitan*, and *Maxim* should not look alike, as they are targeting different groups.

Other popular culture industries likewise attempt to market their products to particular audiences. The advertisements you see during the Super Bowl are not always the same ones you will see on MTV or during beauty pageants. While demographic information alone will not predict which forms of popular culture a particular person will consume, certain trends in popular culture consumption usually can be identified. For example, the type of consumers who might be interested in *Blue's Clues*, as opposed to MTV's *Road Rules*, should be fairly evident.

The recent rise of reality television shows has again sparked debates about the consumption of these cultural texts and the type of cultural identity they reinforce. The enormous popularity of some of these shows, including *American Idol, The Surreal Life, Survivor,* and *Project Runway,* point to their importance in our society. But what is it about these shows that we enjoy? Why do we consume them? A writer for *Time* magazine asks, "Isn't there something simply wrong with people who enjoy entertainment that depends on ordinary people getting their heart broken, being told they can't sing or getting played for fools?"[24] There are no easy answers, of course, and we do not know what meanings people are drawing from reality TV. But perhaps we do enjoy a critique of our mainstream cultural values: "Companies value team spirit; *Survivor* says the team will screw you in the end. The cult of self-esteem says everybody is talented; *American Idol's* Simon Cowell says to sit down and shut your pie hole. Romance and feminism say a man's money shouldn't matter; *Joe Millionaire* waged $50 million that they're wrong."[25] The popularity of these shows points to some cultural needs that are being fulfilled. Why do you think so many reality TV shows are popular? What kind of cultural identity might be served by these shows?

The important point here is that popular culture serves important cultural functions that are connected to our **cultural identities**—our view of ourselves in relation to the cultures we belong to. We participate in those cultural texts that address issues that are relevant to our cultural groups, for example, by offering information and points of view that are unavailable in other cultural forums. They also tend to affirm, by their very existence, these other cultural identities that sometimes are invisible or are silenced in the mainstream culture. Some cultural texts focus on issues relevant to people in particular religious, ethnic, regional, political, and other contexts.

Readers actively negotiate their way through cultural texts such as magazines, consuming those that fulfill important personal and social needs. Sometimes popular culture can also be an arena where people consume these products but as a way to empower their identities rather than simply affirm them. For example, in Iran, there has been much discussion and concern over the attendance of women at soccer games. Consuming this type of popular culture challenges traditional gender roles in Iranian society, as these women fans sometimes celebrate alongside males. In 1998, many women did not stay home to watch the Iranian team qualify for the World Cup on television. In this kind of participation in sports culture, "Iranian women seem to be using football to invert patriarchal mores."[26] By consuming this type of popular culture, Iranian women are working toward recreating what gender means and how it functions in Iranian society. Think about the various television programs, movies, mass market paperbacks, and tabloids that flood the cultural landscape. The reasons that people enjoy some over others cannot easily be determined.

Resisting Popular Culture

At times, people actively seek out particular popular culture texts to consume. At other times, they resist cultural texts. People often resist particular forms of popular culture by refusing to engage in them. For example, some people feel the need to avoid television completely; some even decide not to own televisions. Some people refuse to go to movies that contain violence because they do not find pleasure in such films. These kinds of conscious decisions are often based on concerns about the cultural politics at work.

In a recent study on media consumption practices among members of the Church of Jesus Christ of Latter-day Saints (Mormons), there was significant resistance to Hollywood and television texts. Three media practices were identified in this study: "resistant readings of media texts that focus on the immoral nature of Hollywood and television personalities; a demarcation of the sanctity of the home and the media as an outside threat to their religiosity; and finally practices of program avoidance or resistance in some instances."[27] By resisting the messages of popular culture, their religious identity can be reaffirmed. For example, those who did watch some *Jerry Springer* shows felt the shows served as "a lens into the outside world of those who do not practice family values."[28] Some church members simply avoided certain shows once they were seen as threatening to their religious identity.

Another form of resistance can focus on popular culture products as places where societal members engage with these products to encourage consumers to rethink their relationship to popular culture. For example, many people have very different feelings about the doll, Barbie. Barbie, as a product, is now fifty years old. While Barbie is not a person with a birthday, she is said to turn 50 in 2009. *New York Times* writer, Rob Walker, noted:

> Barbie's durability as a subject to be interpreted is remarkable. There are books like M. G. Lord's "Forever Barbie" and the essay collection "The Barbie Chronicles"; the "Barbie Nation" documentary; the artist Tom Forsythe's "Food Chain Barbie" series, featuring photos of disrobed Barbies in a blender, a skillet, and oven-baked enchiladas; and countless academic deconstructions. A memorable study by British researchers a few years ago suggested that even little girls who owned boxes of Barbies eventually expressed "violence and hatred" toward the doll, as one scholar put it, manifested in burning, smashing or microwaving.[29]

One artist, Margaux Lange, takes Barbie dolls and cuts them up in various ways. She then uses these Barbie parts to make jewelry. As you might guess, "Some Barbie fans, however, find her jewelry off-putting."

Additionally, people resist popular culture because of the impact that outside cultural influences might have on a nation. For example, recently, "Iran's prosecutor general railed on Sunday against the invasion of Barbie, Batman, Spider-Man, and Harry Potter and demanded that the country's young be protected against them."[30] Protecting children is often used in discussions about the impact of popular culture. In this case, resistance can be on a national level, rather than an individual level.

Pop Culture Spotlight (cont.)
- *Blubber,* by Judy Blume
- *Revolting Rhymes,* by Roald Dahl
- *Halloween ABC,* by Eve Merriam
- *A Day No Pigs Would Die,* by Robert Peck
- *Heather Has Two Mommies,* by Leslea Newman
- *Christine,* by Stephen King
- *I Know Why the Caged Bird Sings,* by Maya Angelou

(SOURCE: From onlinebooks@ pobox.upenn.edu [List provided by Greenwood Press])

Resistance to popular culture can be related to a number of other identities; unlike members of the Church of Jesus Christ of Latter-day Saints, however, the motivation behind this resistance emerges more from how others might view their group. For example, consider the show *Trading Spouses: Meet Your New Mommy*, which often brings mothers from wealthy families into the homes of less fortunate families and vice versa. This type of home switching raises many questions about how those in differing socioeconomic classes are represented in popular culture. Sometimes other social differences are emphasized, such as religious differences, on this television show. Concerns about the stereotyping and images that would occur from media images have motivated resistance. People resist popular culture in many ways, and organizations have emerged to monitor media images and coverage. For example, Media Action Network for Asian Americans (MANAA) monitors anti-Asian images in the media and organizes resistance to them. Gay and Lesbian Alliance Against Defamation (GLAAD) serves a similar function by focusing on gay and lesbian media images. Both groups also praise positive and accurate depictions of their social identities. There are many other groups serving similar functions. Resistance, then, can happen on an individual level or a social level. You may choose not to watch a particular television show, or you may work with others to picket studios, boycott advertisers' products, or resist particular media images in more public ways.

REPRESENTING CULTURAL GROUPS

A White student pointed out that his difficulty in answering questions about Latino culture was due to lack of knowledge. Growing up in an all-White town, he had never had any contact with Latinos. Based on what he knew from TV, he had negative feelings about their culture. This all changed when he came to college and had his own experiences. I thought this was interesting because I didn't think an all-White place existed in America.
                                                                    —Adam

As noted at the beginning of this chapter, people often are introduced to other cultures through the lens of popular culture. And these introductions can be quite intimate. For example, through movies, the audience sees and enters the private lives of people they do not know, in ways they never could as tourists.

Yet, we must also think about how these cultural groups are portrayed through that lens of popular culture. Not everyone sees the portrayal in the same way. For example, you may not think that the TV show *Desperate Housewives* represents quintessential U.S. American values and lifestyles. But some viewers may see it as their entree into the ways that European Americans live.

Because some groups are not portrayed as often in popular culture, it is easier to stereotype them. Conversely, some groups are portrayed so often in popular culture that it is difficult to stereotype them. For example, White Americans are portrayed as heroes and villains, as good people and bad people, as responsible and irresponsible, as hardworking and lazy, as honest and dishonest.

To understand other cultures and groups, and their experiences, we can investigate their representations in popular culture. For example, U.S. Americans seldom learn about the Navajo code talkers, who played an important role in World War II. Serving as Marines during the war, the Navajo code talkers utilized the Navajo language to devise an unbreakable code. And by creating a GI Joe doll, called "Navajo GI Joe," the culture industry ensured that this history would not be forgotten. As Sam Billison, one of the Navajo code talkers, observed, "This will let people know about the code talkers. I think it's really going to put us on the map."[31] In this way, popular culture representations can increase a group's visibility in society.

Migrants' Perceptions of Mainstream Culture

Ethnographers and other scholars have crossed international and cultural boundaries to examine the influence of popular culture. In an early study, Elihu Katz and Tamar Liebes set up focus groups to see how different cultural groups viewed the TV show *Dallas*: "There were ten groups each of Israelis, Arabs, new immigrants to Israel from Russia, first and second generation immigrants from Morocco, and kibbutz members. Taking these groups as a microcosm of the worldwide audience of *Dallas*, we are comparing their readings of the program with [those of] ten groups of matched Americans in Los Angeles."[32]

Katz and Liebes found that the U.S. Americans in Los Angeles were much less likely to perceive *Dallas* as portraying actual life in the United States. By contrast, the Israelis, the Arabs, and the array of immigrants were much more inclined to believe that this television show was indeed all about life in the United States. Katz and Liebes note: "What seems clear from the analysis, even at this stage, is that the non-Americans consider the story more real than the Americans. The non-Americans have little doubt that the story is about 'America'; the Americans are less sure."[33] The results of this study are not surprising, but we should not overlook what we can learn about the intercultural communication process. We can see that these popular culture images are often influential in constructing particular ways of understanding cultural groups other than our own.

Another study that focused on immigrants to the United States found similar results.[34] Researchers asked female Korean immigrants why they preferred watching Korean TV shows (which they had to rent at the video store) to U.S. American TV shows. The women pointed out that, because of the cultural differences, the Korean TV shows were more appealing. Yet, as one respondent noted,

> I like to watch American programs. Actors and actresses are glamorous, and the pictures are sleek. But the ideas are still American. How many Korean women are that independent? And how many men commit incest? I think American programs are about American people. They are not the same as watching the Korean programs. But I watch them for fun. And I learn the American way of living by watching them.[35]

The Barbie doll, a popular cultural product, is displayed at her 50th birthday celebration in 2009. Some people embrace her and some reject her. What are some of the ways that people resist this image of female beauty?

Here, both consumption of and resistance to U.S. American popular culture are evident. This woman uses U.S. American television to learn about the "American" way of living, but she prefers to watch Korean shows because they relate to her cultural identity.

The use of popular culture to learn about another culture should not be surprising. After all, many teachers encourage their students to use popular culture in this manner, not only to improve their language skills but also to help them learn many of the nuances of another culture.

Popular Culture and Stereotyping

Intercultural communication still has a long way to go in this country. With so many different races being American, why do we still only picture white skin/blond hair/blue eyes as American? —Cindy

In what ways does reliance on popular culture create and reinforce stereotypes of different cultures? As noted at the outset of this chapter, neither Judith nor Tom has had the opportunity to travel all over the world. Our knowledge about other places, even places we have visited, is largely influenced by popular culture. For people who do not travel and interact in relatively homogeneous social circles, the impact of popular culture may be even greater.

There are many familiar stereotypes of ethnic groups represented in the media. Scholar Jack Shaheen, who is of Lebanese descent, went in search of "real" Arabs after tiring of the way Lebanese and other Arabs were portrayed in the media—as oil billionaires, mad bombers, and sexy belly dancers. According to Shaheen, "Television tends to perpetuate four basic myths about Arabs: they are all fabulously wealthy; they are barbaric and uncultured; they are sex maniacs with a penchant for white slavery; and they revel in acts of terrorism."[36] Shaheen describes other common untruths—for example, that all Iranians are Arabs and that all Arabs are Muslims.

Communication scholar Lisa Flores describes the portrayal in television documentaries of Mexicans responding to natural disasters. According to Flores, news programs often show Mexicans as resilient, patient, faithful, and rather passive—and therefore as somehow acceptable. Yet we are also encouraged to feel pity for them; the inference is that they need White America's assistance to cope with these natural disasters. In turn, this feeds into the stereotype that Mexicans are not sufficiently hardworking, honest, or driven to become "Americans." In her study, Flores connects these images of Mexicans to portrayals of Mexican Americans as not quite U.S. American, "although the difficulty in becoming American is posited as not a lack of choice, but lack of ability."[37]

African American women also have been portrayed stereotypically on TV, especially in the 1950s and 1960s, when the roles they held were secondary—for example, as domestics. Scholar Bishetta Merritt also reminds us of the African American female characters who often appear as background scenery in prime-time TV: the person buying drugs, the homeless person on the sidewalk, the hotel lobby prostitute. Merritt points out that these women still project images, even if they aren't the focus.[38] Merritt explains:

> If the majority of black women the television audience is exposed to are homeless, drug-addicted, or maids, and if viewers have no contact with African American women other than through television, what choice do they have but to believe that all women of this ethnic background reflect this television image? . . . It is, therefore, important, as . . . the population of this country includes more and more people of color, that the television industry broaden the images of African American women to include their nuances and diversity.[39]

What about those ethnic groups that simply don't appear except as infrequent stereotypes: Native Americans and Asian Americans? How do these stereotypes influence intercultural interaction? Do people behave any differently if they don't hold stereotypes about people with whom they are interacting? Two communication researchers, Valerie Manusov and Radha Hegde, investigated these questions in a study in which they identified two groups of college students: those who had some preconceived ideas about India and those who didn't.[40] It turns out that the preconceived ideas were fairly positive. Manusov and Hegde then asked all of the students to interact, one at a time, with an international student from India who was part of the study. When the students with preconceptions talked with the Indian student, they interacted differently from those who had no expectations. Students from the former group relied less on small talk, covered more topics, and asked fewer questions within each topic. Overall, their conversations more closely resembled those between

Info Bites

Are you interested in knowing what the most popular movies are in the United States? How about internationally? Check out the following charts of top-five box-office films, both national and international: **USA Box Office:** 1. *Titanic* (1997), 2. *The Dark Knight* (2008), 3. *Star Wars* (1977), 4. *Shrek 2* (2004), 5. *E.T. the Extra-Terrestrial* (1982). **Non-USA Box Office:** 1. *Titanic* (1997), 2. *The Lord of the Rings: The Return of the King* (2003), 3. *Pirates of the Caribbean: Dead Man's Chest* (2006), 4. *The Dark Knight* (2008), 5. *Harry Potter and the Sorcerer's Stone* (2001). (Source: http://www .boxofficemojo.com/alltime/)

people who know each other. The students with the preconceptions also were more positive about the conversation.

What can we learn from this study? Apparently, having some information and positive expectations may lead to more in-depth conversations and positive outcomes than having no information. But what happens when negative stereotypes are present? It is possible that expectations are fulfilled in this case, too.

Let's look at the ongoing controversy over the use of the logo of the University of North Dakota's Fighting Sioux. In August 2005, the National Collegiate Athletics Association (NCAA) placed a "ban on Indian imagery that it considers 'hostile or abusive'" in postseason play.[41] The University of North Dakota (UND) is 1 of the 18 institutions listed by the NCAA that would be impacted by this decision. While the university is appealing this ban, many people are embracing the logo and others are actively resisting it.

Let's look at how this logo creates strong feelings on both sides and how people are responding to the NCAA decision. There is mixed reaction to the meaning of the way the logo is used. Among American Indians as well there is disagreement about the use of the logo. It is important to recognize that all members of any cultural group have diverse reactions to popular images. For example, not all women are offended by the Hooters restaurant/bar chain that features scantily clad female servers. Some women, however, do not like the way that women are represented at Hooters.

If we focus on the role that this mascot's imagery may play into stereotyping American Indians, we can see some of the elements that influence the impact of this popular image. American Indians are a relatively small segment of the population. At UND, there were 378 American Indian students out of 12,954 students in the 2005–2006 academic year.[42] They were the largest minority group at UND, but only about 3 percent of the student population. The U.S. census taken in 2000 showed that 642,200 people live in the state of North Dakota and 31,329 are American Indian or about 4.9 percent of the population.[43] To whom, then, is this logo communicating? Which groups have a dominant voice in how the logo is interpreted? Think about who is communicating with whom. What kind of power differential is at work here when primarily non-American Indians choose and circulate these images to mostly non-American Indians?

UND's web page describes the image in this way: "Since the early 1930s, the University of North Dakota athletic teams have been known as the Fighting Sioux and have used an American Indian head representation as their symbol. UND officially adopted the name 'Fighting Sioux' in honor of the first inhabitants of the region and some of the American Indian tribes of the state."[44] The president of the university, Charles Kupchella, says, "I don't have a clue why anyone would take offense to something done respectfully and clearly meant as an honor."[45]

As we noted earlier in this book, we need to consider history as one important frame that helps us understand how meaning is created. The history of American Indian imagery is reflected in distorted media images: "The

Pop Culture Spotlight

Consider controversies over sport mascots such as the NCAA's or the American Baseball Association's use of American Indian symbols and imagery. What do these symbols reveal about the ways cultures are represented in popular culture? Sports such as basketball and baseball serve as hallmarks of great American pastimes and as such are relevant to examine for the ways American pop culture fosters static images of what other cultures "look" like.

Hollywood Indian is a mythological being who exists nowhere but within the fertile imaginations of its movie actors, producers, and directors."[46] How might these other distorting images influence the reading of this logo?

Finally, it is also important to try to understand what it is like to be at UND and listen to the experiences of people there. One professor highlights this aspect of the controversy: "'Unless you're here, you don't know what it's like and how nasty it can get,' said a psychology professor, Doug McDonald, who is Sioux. 'I've had students in my office in tears because of the harassment we get.'"[47] The logo and associated meanings (e.g., the sale of "Sioux-per dogs") create an environment in which some students clearly see negative stereotyping.

SUMMARY

In this chapter, we focused on popular culture, one of the primary modes of intercultural experience. The images produced by culture industries such as film and television enable us to "travel" to many places. We rely heavily on popular culture as a forum for the development of our ideas about other places. For example, many people who have never been to China or studied much about the Chinese economic system have very strong ideas about the country and its economy based on news reports, films, documentaries, and so on.

It is significant that much of our popular culture is dominated by U.S.-based cultural industries, considering how we use popular culture as a form of intercultural communication. Not all popular culture emerges from the United States, but the bulk of it does. And it contributes to a power dynamic—cultural imperialism—that affects intercultural communication everywhere.

Popular culture has four important characteristics: it is produced by culture industries; it is distinct from folk culture; it is ubiquitous; and it serves social functions. Individuals and groups can determine the extent to which they are influenced by popular culture. That is, we may choose to consume or resist the messages of popular culture. Our cultural identities play a significant role as we navigate our way through popular culture. Popular culture also helps us understand other cultural groups. We tend to rely more heavily on media images of cultural groups we have little or no personal experience with, but stereotyping can be a problem here.

A great deal of popular culture is produced in the United States and circulated globally. The imbalance in the exchange of American popular culture and other popular culture texts has raised concerns about cultural imperialism.

BUILDING INTERCULTURAL SKILLS

1. Be a reflective consumer of popular culture. Be conscious of the decisions you make about which popular culture texts you choose. Think about why you choose certain television shows, magazines, and other cultural texts. Try

reading magazines or watching films or TV shows that you normally would not to expand your intercultural communication repertoire.

2. Be aware of how popular culture influences the formation of your cultural identity and worldviews. Be conscious of how popular culture images create or reinforce your views about other places and other people, as well as yourself and your immediate environment.

3. Be aware of how media portrayal of different cultural groups might influence your intercultural interactions with those groups. How might others see you?

4. Think about how you might resist popular culture and when you should do so. Do you talk back to the TV when news is framed in a particular way? Do you notice who gets to speak and who is interviewed, as well as who is not allowed to speak?

5. Think about how you might be an advocate for those whose voices are not heard in popular culture. How might you help challenge imbalances in popular culture?

ACTIVITIES

1. *Popular culture:* Meet with other students in small groups, and answer the following questions:

    a. Which popular culture texts (magazines, TV shows, and so on) do you watch/buy, and why?

    b. Which popular culture texts do you not like and not watch/buy, and why? Discuss why we like certain products and not others. For example, do some products reinforce or support our worldviews? Do they empower us in some way? Enlighten us?

2. *Ethnic representation in popular culture:* Keep a log of your favorite TV shows for one week. Answer the following questions for each show, and discuss your answers in small groups.

    a. How many different ethnic groups were portrayed?

    b. What roles did members of these ethnic groups have?

    c. What ethnic groups were represented in the major roles?

    d. What ethnic groups were represented in the minor roles?

    e. What ethnic groups were represented in the positive roles?

    f. What ethnic groups were represented in the negative roles?

    g. What types of roles did women have?

    h. What kinds of intercultural interactions occurred?

    i. What were the outcomes?

    j. How do the roles and interactions support or refute common stereotypes of the ethnic groups involved?

ENDNOTES

1. Katz, E., & Liebes, T. (1987). Decoding *Dallas:* Notes from a cross-cultural study. In H. Newcomb (Ed.), *Television: The critical view* (4th ed., pp. 419–432). New York: Oxford University Press.

2. Fiske, J. (1989). *Understanding popular culture.* New York: Routledge, p. 23.

3. Lipsitz, G. (1990). *Time passages: Collective memory and American popular culture.* Minneapolis: University of Minnesota Press, p. 140.

4. Lipsitz (1990), p. 159.

5. Gunn, J., & Brummett, B. (2004). Popular culture after globalization. *Journal of Communication, 54*, 707.

6. Newcomb, H., & Hirsch, P. M. (1987). Television as cultural forum. In Newcomb.

7. Moon, D. G., & Nakayama, T. K. (2005). Strategic social identities and judgments: A murder in Appalachia. *Howard Journal of Communications, 16*, 1–22.

8. Butterworth, M. (2005). Ritual in the "church of baseball": Suppressing the discourse of democracy after 9/11. *Communication & Critical/Cultural Studies, 2*, 122.

9. Guback, T. (1969). *The international film industry: Western Europe and America since 1945.* Bloomington: Indiana University Press. See also Guback, T., & Varis, T. (1982). *Transnational communication and cultural industries.* Paris: UNESCO.

10. *Revenge of the Sith.* (2006). Lee's Movie Info. Retrieved from http://www.leesmovieinfo.net/wbotitle.php?t=2594&section=2&format=4

11. About Aljazeera. (2003). *Aljazeera.* Retrieved from http://english.aljazeera.net/NR/exeres/5D7F956E-6B52-46D9-8D17-448856D01CDB.htm

12. Wilshire, K. (2003, March 30). Chirac demands France create a rival to CNN. (London) *Daily Telegraph.* Retrieved from http://www.telegraph.co.uk/news/main.jhtml?xml=/news/2003/03/30/wchirc30.xml

13. Louet, S. (2005, November 30). "French CNN" seen operational by end of 2006. *Reuters Business Channel.* Retrieved December 3, 2005, from http://today.reuters.com/business/newsArticle.aspx?type=media&storyID=nL30762703

14. Bennett, T., & Woollacott, J. (1987). *Bond and beyond: The political career of a popular culture hero.* New York: Methuen, pp. 293–294.

15. Hung, M. (2001, August 2). Tooned into anime. *Houston Press.* Retrieved from http://www.houstonpress.com/issues/2001-08-02/feature.html/1/index.html

16. Hung (2001, August 2).

17. Zakaria, F. (2009, January 30). Slum voyeurism? *Newsweek.* Retrieved January 30, 2009 from: http://www.newsweek.com/id/182341

18. Setoodeh, R. (2009, January 10). And the Oscar doesn't go to . . . *Newsweek.* Retrieved January 30, 2009 from: http://www.newsweek.com/id/178869

19. Nakayama, T. K., & Vachon, L. A. (1991). Imperialist victory in peacetime: State functions and the British cinema industry. *Current Research in Film, 5*, 161–174.

20. Tomlinson, J. (1991). *Cultural imperialism.* Baltimore: Johns Hopkins University Press, pp. 19–23.

21. Cohen, J. (2005). Global and local viewing experiences in the age of multichannel television: The Israeli experience. *Communication Theory, 15*, 451.

22. Cohen (2005), p. 451.

23. Dolby, N. (1999). Youth and the global popular: The politics and practices of race in South Africa. *European Journal of Cultural Studies, 2*(3), 296.

24. Poniewozik, J. (2003, February 17). Why reality TV is good for us. *Time*, p. 67.

25. Poniewozik (2003, February 17), pp. 66–67.

26. Fozooni, B. (2008). Iranian women and football. *Cultural Studies, 22*, 114–133.

27. Scott, D. (2003). Mormon "family values" versus television: An analysis of the discourse of Mormon couples regarding television and popular media culture. *Critical Studies in Media Communication, 20*(3), 325.

28. Scott (2003), p. 328.

29. Walker, R. (2009, January 22). Deconstructing Barbie. *New York Times.* Retrieved January 30, 2009 from: http://www.nytimes.com/2009/01/25/magazine/25wwln-consumed-t.html?_r=1

30. van Gelder, L. (2008, April 28). Iran versus Barbie. *New York Times*. Retrieved January 30, 2009 from: http://www.nytimes.com/2008/04/28/arts/28arts-IRANVERSUSBA_BRF.html?scp=7&sq=barbie&st=cse

31. G. I. Joe doll salutes Code Talkers. (2000, March 4). *The Arizona Republic*, p. E9.

32. Katz & Liebes (1987), pp. 419–432.

33. Katz & Liebes (1987), p. 421.

34. Lee, M., & Cho, C. H. (1990, January). Women watching together: An ethnographic study of Korean soap opera fans in the U.S. *Cultural Studies*, *4*(1), 30–44.

35. Lee & Cho (1990), p. 43.

36. Shaheen, J. G. (1984). *The TV Arab*. Bowling Green, OH: Bowling Green State University Press, p. 4.

37. Flores, L. (1994). *Shifting visions: Intersections of rhetorical and Chicana feminist theory in the analysis of mass media*. Unpublished dissertation, University of Georgia, p. 16.

38. Merritt B. D. (2000). Illusive reflections: African American women on primetime television. In A. González, M. Houston, & V. Chen (Eds.), *Our voices* (3rd ed., pp. 47–53). Los Angeles: Roxbury.

39. Merritt (2000), p. 53.

40. Manusov, V., & Hegde, R. (1993). Communicative outcomes of stereotype-based expectancies: An observational study of cross-cultural dyads. *Communication Quarterly*, *41*, 338–354.

41. Borzi, P. (2005, November 26). A dispute of great spirit rages on: North Dakota fights to keep a logo: Indians consider its use profane. *New York Times*, p. B15.

42. *2005–2006 student body profile*. (n.d.). University of North Dakota. Retrieved from http://www.und.edu/profile/

43. Ogunwole, S. U. (2002). *The American Indian and Alaska Native population: 2000*. Retrieved from http://www.census.gov/prod/2002pubs/c2kbr01-15.pdf

44. *History of the fighting Sioux names*. (n.d.). University of North Dakota. Retrieved from http://www.universityrelations.und.edu/logoappeal/history.html

45. Quoted in Borzi (2005, November 26), p. B16.

46. Jojola, T. (1998). Absurd reality II: Hollywood goes to the Indians. In P. C. Rollins & J. E. O'Connor (Eds.), *Hollywood's Indian: The portrayal of the Native American in film*. Lexington: University Press of Kentucky, p. 12.

47. Quoted in Borzi (2005, November 26), pp. B15–B16.

8

Culture, Communication, and Conflict

STUDY OBJECTIVES

After reading this chapter, you should be able to:

1. Identify and describe the characteristics of intercultural conflict.

2. Define interpersonal conflict and its characteristics.

3. Identify five different types of conflict.

4. List the basic principles of nonviolence.

5. Suggest some ways in which cultures differ in their views toward conflict.

6. Understand how people come by their conflict strategies.

7. Identify and describe four styles for dealing with intercultural conflict.

8. Discuss the relationship between ethnicity, gender, and conflict communication.

9. Define social movements.

10. Explain why it is important to understand the role of the social and historical contexts in intercultural conflicts.

11. Discuss some suggestions for dealing with intercultural conflicts.

KEY TERMS

accommodating style
anti-Americanism
conflict
direct approach
discussion style
dynamic style
emotionally expressive style
engagement style
incompatibility
indirect approach
intercultural conflict
interdependent
intermediary
international conflict
interpersonal conflict
mediation
pacifism
political conflict
religious conflict
restraint style
social conflict
social movements

One thing we can be sure of is that conflict is unavoidable. Conflicts are happening all around the world, as they always have, and at many different levels. For example, conflicts can happen on the interpersonal level, called **interpersonal conflict,** which was the case for our student Joy, who described a recent conflict with her boyfriend. Joy is from a midwestern, third-generation Scotch-Irish family. Her boyfriend's family is first-generation Filipino/a. Cultural differences between the groups often cause conflict and misunderstanding. The most recent conflict occurred when Joy's family discovered that her step-grandmother was very sick with cancer. Joy described her boyfriend's reaction when she told him this news on the telephone:

> He really said nothing. His first reaction was "Oh," and then he went on with whatever he was doing at the time. I was shocked. I couldn't believe that he had been so insensitive to me and my family. I was furious, but he saw nothing wrong in what he had done. . . . We managed the conflict by arguing and talking . . . [and then] discussed what we were both angry about . . . and then agreed to try to be more aware of the differences we both have in regards to certain situations and to meet each other halfway, not just blame each other.

What Do You Think?

What types of conflict do you find to be the most difficult to negotiate? Do you approach conflicts with your partner, your coworkers, friends, and parents in different ways? Are there patterns in the ways you deal with conflict? If conflicts are inevitable, why do we sometimes avoid them with certain people in our lives?

Conflict can also happen on a societal level, also known as **political conflict.** For example, environmentalists and developers may disagree on the importance of economic interests, as is the case in the Northwest United States. For many years, loggers and environmentalists have been at odds; the logging industries claim that logging is necessary to provide products, jobs, and economic growth. Environmentalists claim logging should be restricted or eliminated in places where it causes damage to mountains, rivers, and animal populations.[1]

Cultural conflicts can also occur on the international level, or **international conflict.** The recent disagreement between France and the United States over the invasion of Iraq led to some strong feelings on both sides of the Atlantic. In the United States, some school exchange trips involving French students were canceled. A teacher in Philadelphia sent an e-mail to the French families to tell them the exchange was canceled: "The main reason for this is that we do not feel that we can ensure a truly comfortable or hospitable stay for your students as the anti-French sentiment here in the U.S. is very strong."[2] The anti-French sentiment and the cutting of ties through an e-mail shocked "the French parents who decided to inform the American embassy and the Minister of Foreign Affairs."[3] The larger international conflict between the United States and France affects more everyday interactions between U.S. Americans and French, as in the case of these schoolchildren.

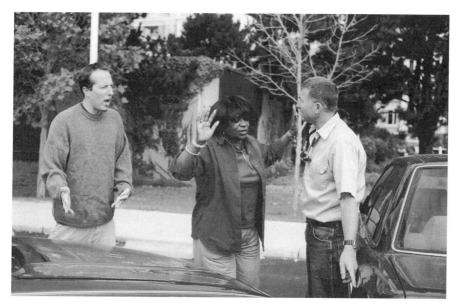

Some conflicts are managed by mediators, who help disputants resolve their differences. Mediators may be used informally, as in auto accidents, or more formally, as when lawyers are consulted in divorce or real estate disputes.

Conflict may also arise from mediated communication. U.S. television, film, and other media have dominated the world market for many years. Many people in other countries feel that this cultural dominance stunts their economic growth and imposes U.S. cultural values, which has led to resentment and conflict.[4] Many Canadians, for example, believe that it has been difficult for their country to develop a distinct Canadian cultural identity since it is so heavily influenced by U.S. cultural products. But this resentment has lessened somewhat in recent years with the increasing number of Canadian celebrities who have contributed to U.S. popular culture—for example, Martin Short, Michael J. Fox, Mike Myers, Shania Twain, Dan Aykroyd, Jim Carrey, and Peter Jennings.

In this chapter, we identify characteristics of intercultural conflict, as well as different types of conflict and conflict styles. We also examine how cultural background can influence conflict management and discuss guidelines for engaging in intercultural conflict. Finally, we look at societal forces that influence intercultural conflict.

As you think about intercultural conflict, consider the role of communication in these situations. While communication differences can sometimes be the cause of intercultural conflict, particularly in interpersonal situations, communication is often not the clear cause of conflicts on international or societal levels. International conflicts can be ignited by struggles over resources, such as oil, food, or water. Yet, communication can often play important roles in how the conflict is played out. Communication can exacerbate the conflicts or help to reduce the conflicts.

CHARACTERISTICS OF INTERCULTURAL CONFLICT

Conflict is usually defined as involving a perceived or real **incompatibility** of goals, values, expectations, processes, or outcomes between two or more **interdependent** individuals or groups.[5] A good example of intercultural conflict can be seen in the *maquiladoras*—sorting or assembly plants along the Mexican–U.S. border. Because Mexicans and U.S. Americans work alongside one another, intercultural conflict inevitably occurs.[6] For example, some Mexican managers think that the U.S. American managers are rude in their dealings with each other and with the workers. While both Mexican and U.S. American managers have common goals, they also have some different expectations and values, which leads to conflict. The Mexican managers expect the U.S. American managers to be more polite and to value harmony in their relationships. The U.S. American managers expect the Mexicans to be more direct and honest and to not worry so much about the "face" and feelings of other managers and workers. These conflicts have roots in the history of U.S.–Mexican relations, a history characterized by economic and military domination on the part of the United States and by hostility and resentment on the part of Mexico.

What are characteristics of **intercultural conflict**? How does intercultural conflict differ from other kinds of conflict? One unique characteristic is that intercultural conflicts tend to be more ambiguous than intracultural conflict. Other characteristics involve language issues and contradictory conflict styles.

Ambiguity

There is often a great deal of ambiguity in intercultural conflicts. We may be unsure of how to handle the conflict or of whether the conflict is seen in the same way by the other person. And the other person may not even think there is a conflict. In Joy's case presented at the beginning of the chapter, she and her boyfriend both admitted the conflict; that was the first step in resolving it.

However, often when we encounter ambiguity, we quickly resort to our default style of handling conflict—the style we learned in our family. If your preferred way of handling conflict is to deal with it immediately but you are in a conflict with someone who prefers to avoid it, the conflict may become exacerbated as you both retreat to your preferred styles. Thus, the confronting person becomes increasingly confrontational, while the avoider retreats further.

Language Issues

The issues surrounding language may be important ones. Language can sometimes lead to intercultural conflict, and it can also be the primary vehicle for solving intercultural conflict. This was true for Jodi, a student of ours, who described a recent conflict she had with some fellow workers:

> I work in a restaurant where the kitchen employees are mostly of Mexican descent. Some of the men would make inappropriate comments in

What Do You Think?

In the news we often find evidence of conflicts between different nations and nation-states such as India and Pakistan, Israel and Palestine, and others. Media coverage of these conflicts is not the only form of war in our daily lives. How might war metaphors be a part of your argument style in conflict situations? How do metaphors such as "advancing an argument," "putting up a front," "giving your best shot," "being off target," or "shooting down a point" help or hinder conflict resolution?

Spanish. I chose to ignore it, but my method of resolving the conflict was not beneficial. It just resulted in my feeling uncomfortable. Finally, I decided to take the initiative. I used my Spanish speaking skills to let the employees know I could understand them—somewhat. Then I decided to make an effort to greet them whenever I came into contact with them. I found that they are much more friendly. This was the best approach to take, and it yielded good results.

However, when you don't know the language well, it is very difficult to handle conflict effectively. At the same time, some silence is not necessarily a bad thing. Sometimes it provides a "cooling off" period during which the participants can calm down and gather their thoughts. This was our student Dotty's experience with her host family in France. Initially, she was experiencing culture shock and was not getting along with her host "brother." So she told her host family to go out without her because she wasn't feeling well. She recalls: "I spent the afternoon and evening walking along the beach and exploring the forest. This allowed relations to continue, but it gave time to work things out. I felt good about the time out. It all turned out well, but it required some time and patience."

Contradictory Conflict Styles

Intercultural conflict also may be characterized by contradictory conflict styles. In the *maquiladoras*, the biggest difference between U.S. Americans and Mexicans seems to be in the way U.S. Americans express disagreement at management meetings. The Mexican managers tend to be more indirect and more polite in conflict situations, whereas the U.S. American managers prefer to confront conflict directly and openly. These very different styles in handling conflict cause problems in the workplace and sometimes lead to more conflict.

CONFLICT TYPES AND CONTEXTS

Perhaps if everyone agreed on the best way to view conflict, there would be less of it. The reality is that different approaches to conflict may result in more conflict. In this section, we identify five different types of conflict and some strategies for resolving them.

Types of Conflict

Common categories of conflict include affective conflict, conflict of interest, value conflict, cognitive conflict, and goal conflict.[7] Affective conflict occurs when individuals become aware that their feelings and emotions are incompatible. For example, suppose someone finds out that his or her romantic feelings for a close friend are not reciprocated. Their different levels of affection may lead to conflict.

A conflict of interest describes a situation in which people have incompatible preferences for a course of action or plan to pursue. For example, one student

Surf's Up!

Consider the implications that stereotypes about women drivers, the elderly, Arab Americans, and Asian Americans might have for conflicts occurring while driving. Go to the website http://roadragers.com/ and take a survey to analyze your driving style.

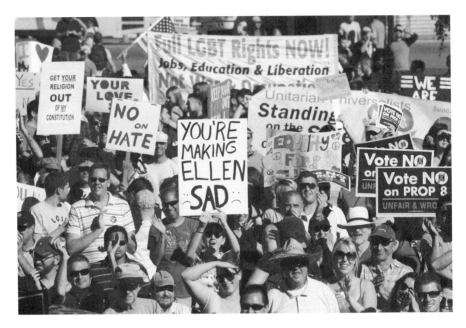

Nonviolent confrontation provides an opportunity for social change. People who protest peacefully can highlight injustices and lend credibility to social movements.

Surf's Up!

Do you know the style of conflict negotiation that best describes you? Access www .personalitytest.net/ and find out more about how personality type and conflict negotiation coincide. (SOURCE: Personality Test Center © 2000–2005)

of ours described an ongoing conflict with an ex-girlfriend: "The conflicts always seem to be a jealousy issue or a controlling issue, where even though we are not going out anymore, both of us still try to control the other's life to some degree. You could probably say that this is a conflict of interest."

Value conflict, a more serious type, occurs when people have differing ideologies. For example, suppose that Ruben and Laura have been married for several months and are starting to argue frequently about their views on when to start their family and how to raise their children. Laura believes strongly that one parent should stay at home with the children when they are small, so she would like to wait until they have saved enough money and she can stop working for a few years. Ruben wants to have children immediately but does not want Laura to stop working; he thinks their children will do fine in day care. This situation illustrates value conflict.

Cognitive conflict describes a situation in which two or more people become aware that their thought processes or perceptions are in conflict. For example, suppose that Marissa and Derek argue frequently about whether Marissa's friend Bob is paying too much attention to her. Derek suspects that Bob wants to have sex with Marissa, but Marissa doesn't agree. Their different perceptions of the situation constitute cognitive conflict.

Goal conflict occurs when people disagree about a preferred outcome or end state. For instance, consider the decision that Rodrigo and Jason had to make when Rodrigo was offered an upper management position in a state over 1,500 miles away from their home. Moving meant that Jason had to give up his job and move away from his family, but it also meant that Rodrigo would have the position he wanted and they would be living in the city they had always hoped for.

The Importance of Context

How we choose to manage conflict may depend on the particular context or situation. For example, we may choose to use discussion style when arguing with a close friend about serious relational issues in a quiet movie theater. By contrast, we may feel freer to use a more confrontational style at a political rally.

Nikki, a student with a part-time job at a restaurant, described an experience she had in serving a large group of German tourists. The tourists argued with her about the bill, claiming that they had been overcharged. Nikki explained that a 15 percent service charge had been added. The Germans thought that she had added the tip because they were tourists; they hadn't realized it was the policy when serving large groups. Nikki explained that she was much more conciliatory when dealing with this group in the restaurant than she would have been in a more social context. She thought the Germans were rude, but she practiced good listening skills and took a more problem-solving approach than she would have otherwise.

One of our students, Courtney, recounted a conflict she had when one of her friends made the college football team. She told him he had "natural talent," and he thought she was being racist because he was Black. Even though Courtney didn't mean to be racist, we can only understand the conflict within the historical context of White–Black relations in the United States; as he told her, he gets these kinds of comments a lot. Thus, the conflict context can be viewed in two ways: (1) in terms of the actual situation in which the conflict happens and (2) as a larger societal context. We'll discuss the larger societal context of conflict later in the chapter.

Info Bites

Active listening is a three-step process suggested by interpersonal communication scholars to help reduce conflict. It includes paraphrasing the other person's ideas, expressing understanding of them, and then asking questions about them. From an intercultural perspective, why would this process be helpful?

CULTURAL INFLUENCES ON CONFLICT MANAGEMENT

A key question is this: Is open conflict good or bad? That is, should conflict be welcomed because it provides opportunities to strengthen relationships? Or should it be avoided because it can only lead to problems for relationships and groups? Another key question is this: What is the best way to handle conflict when it arises? Should individuals talk about it directly, deal with it indirectly, or avoid it? Should emotions be part of the conflict resolution? Are expressions of emotions viewed as showing commitment to resolving the conflict at hand? Or is it better to be restrained and solve problems by rational logic rather than emotional expressiveness? Also consider the following questions: How do we learn how to deal with conflict? Who teaches us how to solve conflicts when they arise? How we answer all of these questions depends in large part on our cultural background and the way we were raised.

Family Influences

The ways in which people respond to conflict may be influenced by their cultural background. More specifically, most people deal with conflict in the way they learned while growing up—their default style. Conflict resolution strategies usually relate to how people manage their self-image in relationships. For example, they may prefer to preserve their own self-esteem rather than help the other person "save face." Or they may prefer to sacrifice their own self-esteem in order to preserve the relationship.

We tend to prefer a particular conflict style in our interactions for many reasons. A primary influence is our family background; some families prefer a particular conflict style, and children come to accept this style as normal. For example, the family may have settled conflict in a direct, confrontational manner, with the person having the strongest argument (or the biggest muscle) getting his or her way.

Sometimes people try very hard to reject the conflict styles they saw their parents using. For example, suppose that Maria's parents avoided open conflict and never discussed what was bothering them. Their children learned to avoid conflict and become very uncomfortable when people around them use a more expressive style of conflict management. Maria has vowed she will never deal with conflict that way with her own children and has tried very hard to use other ways of dealing with conflicts when they do arise in her family. It is important to realize that people deal with conflict in a variety of ways and may not have the same reasons for choosing a certain style.

Family conflict can also arise from generational differences in immigrant families that reflect intercultural differences. In Europe, the focus is sometimes on "Muslim girls who are harassed or punished for being too Western. Latifa Ahmed, 25, arrived in the Netherlands from Morocco when she was 8. As she grew up near Amsterdam, her family turned against her because she preferred to be with her Dutch classmates.

"They were bad, they were infidels, I was told," she said. "My parents and my brothers started hitting me." Latifa, who lived at home until she was 23, said, "I was going crazy from all the fights and the lies, but I was afraid to run away and lose my family."[8]

Other immigrant families may have conflicts over arranged marriages, dating, and other cultural expectations that may highlight differences between the country of origin and the new homeland.

Two Approaches to Conflict

There are at least two primary ways that you can approach conflict. You can be either direct or indirect, and you can be either emotionally expressive or restrained.[9] The way you approach conflict probably depends on your cultural background and the way you were raised. Let's look at each of these two dimensions more closely.

Direct and Indirect Conflict Approaches This **direct/indirect approach** to conflict is similar to the direct/indirect language dimension we discussed in Chapter 5. There it was applied specifically to language use, whereas here it represents a broader conflict resolution approach. Some cultural groups think that conflict is fundamentally a good thing; these groups feel that it is best to approach conflict very directly, because working through conflicts constructively results in stronger, healthier, and more satisfying relationships. Similarly, groups that work through conflict can gain new information about members or about other groups, defuse more serious conflict, and increase group cohesiveness.[10]

People who take this approach concentrate on using very precise language. While they may not always feel comfortable with face-to-face conflict, they think that it's important to "say what's on your mind" in a conflict situation. The goal in this approach is to articulate the issues carefully and select the "best" solution based on an agreed-upon set of criteria.

However, many cultural groups view conflict as ultimately destructive for relationships. For example, many Asian cultures, reflecting the influence of Confucianism and Taoism, and some religious groups in the United States see conflict as disturbing the peace. For instance, most Amish think of conflict not as an opportunity for personal growth, but as a threat to interpersonal and community harmony. When conflict does arise, the strong spiritual value of **pacifism** dictates a nonresistant response—often avoidance or dealing with conflict very indirectly.[11]

Also, these groups think that when members disagree they should adhere to the consensus of the group rather than engage in conflict. In fact, members who threaten group harmony may be sanctioned. One writer gives an example of a man from the Maori culture in New Zealand who was swearing and using inappropriate language in a public meeting:

> A woman went up to him, laying her hand on his arm and speaking softly. He shook her off and continued. The crowd now moved back from him as far as possible, and as if by general agreement, the listeners dropped their gaze to their toes until all he could see was the tops of their heads. The speaker slowed, faltered, was reduced to silence, and then sat down.[12]

These people tend to approach conflict rather indirectly. They concentrate on the meaning that is "outside" the verbal message and tend to be very careful to protect the "face" of the person with whom they disagree. They may emphasize vagueness and ambiguity in language and often rely on third parties to help resolve disagreements. The goal in this approach is to make sure that the relationship stays intact during the disagreement. For example, they may emphasize the past history of the disputants and try to build a deeper relationship that involves increased obligation toward each other.

Emotional Expressiveness/Restraint Conflict Style   A second broad approach to conflict concerns the role of emotion in conflict. People who value intense and overt displays of emotions during discussion of disagreement rely on the **emotionally expressive style.** They think it is better to show emotion during disagreement than to hide or suppress feelings; that is, they show emotion through expressive nonverbal behavior and vocalization. They also think that this outward display of emotions means that one really cares and is committed to resolving the conflict. In fact, one's credibility is based on the ability to be expressive.

Pop Culture Spotlight

Cultural traditions such as those found in martial arts customs in many Eastern traditions seem to teach ways of responding to aggression that avoid conflict or limit violence. How do films that center on the 9/11 attacks on America such as *Fahrenheit 9/11* (2004), *United 93* (2006), and *World Trade Center* (2006) fuel or de-escalate support for U.S. retaliation?

On the other hand, people who believe in the **restraint style** think that disagreements are best discussed in an emotionally calm manner. For these people, it's important to control and internalize one's feelings during conflict and to avoid nonverbal emotion. They are uncomfortable with emotional expression and think that such expressions may hurt others. People who use this approach think that relationships are made stronger by keeping one's emotions in check and protecting the "face" or honor of the other person. Credibility is demonstrated by maintaining tight control over one's emotions.

These two approaches to conflict resolution reflect different underlying cultural values involving identity and preserving self-esteem. In the more individualistic approach that sees conflict as good, the concern is with individuals preserving their own dignity. The more communal approach espoused by both Amish and Asian cultures and by many other collectivist groups is more concerned with maintaining harmony in interpersonal relations and preserving the dignity of others. For example, in classic Chinese thought, social harmony is the goal of human society at all levels—individual, family, village, and nation.[13]

Intercultural Conflict Styles

Surf's Up!

The success of the recent fiction novel and movie *The Da Vinci Code* asks audiences to question what it would mean if Jesus and Mary Magdalene were married, as well as the role of women in spirituality. The implications of the film have angered many Catholic and evangelical leaders who have called the film both blasphemous and a conspiracy. What is this conflict about? Why are many officials so upset about the success of this book and film?

It is possible to combine the four dimensions discussed and come up with four different conflict resolution styles that seem to be connected to various cultural groups: the discussion style, the engagement style, the accommodating style, and the dynamic style.[14]

The **discussion style** combines the direct and emotionally restrained dimensions and emphasizes a verbally direct approach for dealing with disagreements—to "say what you mean and mean what you say." People who use this style are comfortable expressing disagreements directly but prefer to be emotionally restrained. This style is often identified as the predominant style preferred by many White Americans, as well as Europeans, Australians, and New Zealanders. This approach is expressed by the Irish saying, "What is nearest the heart is nearest the mouth."

The **engagement style** emphasizes a verbally direct and confrontational approach to dealing with conflict. This style views intense verbal and nonverbal expression of emotion as demonstrating sincerity and willingness to engage intensely to resolve conflict. It has been linked to some African Americans and Southern Europeans (France, Greece, Italy, Spain), as well as to some people from Russia and the Middle East (Israel). This approach is captured in the Russian proverb, "After a storm, fair weather; after sorrow, joy."

The **accommodating style** emphasizes an indirect approach for dealing with conflict and a more emotionally restrained manner. People who use this style may be ambiguous and indirect in expressing their views, thinking that this is a way to ensure that the conflict "doesn't get out of control." This style is often preferred by American Indians, Latin Americans (Mexicans, Costa Ricans), and Asians. This style may best be expressed by the Swahili proverb, "Silence produces peace, and peace produces safety," or by the Chinese proverb, "The first to raise their voice loses the argument."

In this style, silence and avoidance may be used to manage conflict. For example, the Amish would prefer to lose face or money rather than escalate a conflict, and Amish children are instructed to turn the other cheek in any conflict situation, even if it means getting beat up by the neighborhood bully.

Individuals from these groups also use **intermediaries**—friends or colleagues who act on their behalf in dealing with conflict.[15] For example, a Taiwanese student at a U.S. university was offended by the People's Republic of China flag that her roommate displayed in their room. The Taiwanese student went to the international student advisor and asked him to talk to the U.S. American student about the flag. People who think that interpersonal conflict provides opportunities to strengthen relationships also use **mediation**, but mainly in formal settings. For instance, people retain lawyers to mediate disputes, hire real estate agents to negotiate commercial transactions, and engage counselors or therapists to resolve or manage interpersonal conflicts.

What are the basic principles of nonviolence applied to interpersonal relations? Actually, nonviolence is not the absence of conflict, and it is not a simple refusal to fight. Rather, it involves peacemaking—a difficult, and sometimes very risky, approach to interpersonal relationships. Individuals who take the peacemaking approach (1) strongly value the other person and encourage his or her growth, (2) attempt to de-escalate conflicts or keep them from escalating once they start, and (3) attempt to find creative negotiation to resolve conflicts when they arise.[16]

It is often difficult for people who are taught to use the discussion or engaging style to see the value in the accommodating style or in nonviolent approaches. They see indirectness and avoidance as a sign of weakness. However, millions of people view conflict as primarily "dysfunctional, interpersonally embarrassing, distressing and as a forum for potential humiliation and loss of face."[17] With this view of conflict, it makes much more sense to avoid direct confrontation and work toward saving face for the other person.

The **dynamic style** uses an indirect style of communicating along with a more emotionally intense expressiveness. People who use this style may use strong language, stories, metaphors, and use of third-party intermediaries. They are comfortable with more emotionally confrontational talk and view credibility of the other person grounded in their degree of emotional expressiveness. This style may be preferred by Arabs in the Middle East.

Cautions about Stereotyping   As with any generalization, however, it must be remembered that all conflict resolution styles can be found in any one cultural group, and while cultural groups tend to prefer one style over another, we must be careful not to stereotype. Also, these cultural differences may depend on a number of factors, including (1) whether regions have been historically homogeneous and isolated from other cultures, (2) the influence of colonization, and (3) the immigration history of different cultural groups. For example, there is much more African influence in the Caribbean (compared to Central and Latin America), resulting in a more direct and emotionally expressive approach (engagement style) than in Mexico—which has maintained a more indirect and emotionally restrained approach (accommodation style). And there is a great variety of cultures within the African continent, accounting for tremendous variation in conflict resolution styles.[18]

Gender, Ethnicity, and Conflict

Our gender and ethnicity may influence how we handle conflict. Men and women in the United States seem to have different communication styles. These different ways of communicating sometimes lead to conflict and can influence how men and women handle conflict. One problem area involves what is known as "troubles talk." For example, women typically make sympathetic noises in response to what a friend says, whereas men may say nothing, which women interpret as indifference. Or women commiserate by talking about a similar situation they experienced, whereas men follow rules for conversational dominance and interpret this as stealing the stage. And in telling stories, men tend to be more linear, whereas women tend to give more details and offer tangential information, which men interpret as an inability to get to the point.[19]

Men and women also talk about relationships in different ways. Women may express more interest in the relationship process and may feel better simply discussing it. But men are more oriented toward problem solving and may see little point in discussing something if nothing is identified as needing fixing.[20]

How does ethnic background affect the way males and females deal with conflict? In one study, when African Americans, Asian Americans, White Americans, and Mexican Americans were asked to describe how they dealt with conflicts they had had with a close friend, they gave different kinds of answers.[21] African American males and females generally said they used a problem-solving approach. One respondent said, "I told him to stay in school and that I would help him study." Another explained, "We decided together how to solve the problem and deal with our friend."

White males and females generally seemed to focus on the importance of taking responsibility for their own behavior. Males mentioned the importance of being direct, using expressions like "getting things in the open" and "say right up front." Females talked about the importance of showing concern for the other person and the relationship and of maintaining situational flexibility. One woman explained, "She showed respect for my position and I showed respect for hers." By contrast, Asian Americans generally used more conflict-avoiding strategies than did White Americans.[22]

Mexican American males and females tended to differ in that males described the importance of talking to reach a mutual understanding. One man wanted to "make a better effort to explain"; another said that he and his partner "stuck to the problem until we solved it together." Females described several kinds of reinforcement of the relationship that were appropriate. In general, males and females in all

What Do You Think?

The recent reports about U.S. government offices and officials wiretapping and tracking communications of U.S. journalists under the 2001 Patriot Act have fueled a lot of public discussion about what is considered public and private information. The reports have also fueled a discussion about what is protected speech in times of domestic and international crisis. What sorts of information should be protected? When, if at all, does the state have the right to be listening?

groups described females as more compassionate and concerned for feelings, and males as more concerned with winning the conflict and being "right."

In their study of African American and European American women's views on workplace conflict, communication scholars Lynn Turner and Robert Shuter found that African American women viewed workplace conflict more negatively, more passively, and with less optimism about a positive resolution than European American women.[23]

In any case, it is important to remember that, while ethnicity and gender may be related to ways of dealing with conflict, it is inappropriate and inaccurate to assume that any one person will behave in a particular way because of his or her ethnicity or gender.

Religion and Conflict

Religious differences also can be an important source of conflict. Religious beliefs are often a source of very strongly held views that can cause **religious conflict** with others who may not share those views. Recently, for example, Rev. Fred Phelps of Westboro Baptist Church in Kansas and his followers have been protesting at the funerals of soldiers who have died in Iraq and Afghanistan. In order to communicate their religious views, they have been attending soldiers' funerals with protest signs: "'Thank God for Dead Soldiers,' read one of their placards. 'Thank God for I.E.D.'s,' read another, a reference to the bombs used to kill service members in the war. They want to drive home their point—that God is killing soldiers to punish America for condoning homosexuality."[24] Various state legislatures and Congress are considering laws against this type of religious expression at military funerals. In this case, religious differences are the source of the conflict. While not all people read the Bible in the same way, these religious differences can influence how people interpret these military deaths and how we should appropriately respond.

A little farther west, in Utah, conflicts between Mormons and non-Mormons are not uncommon. The *Salt Lake Tribune* noted that "It is nothing new for protesters to loiter near the LDS Conference Center and Salt Lake Temple." Within a historical context, the anti-Mormon views of Latter-day Saints (LDS) by other Christian groups are nothing new. Pressured to leave New York, Ohio, Missouri, and later Illinois before settling in Utah, Mormon history points to many anti-Mormon incidents, including the murder of the founder, Joseph Smith, in Illinois. The semiannual LDS General Conference in Salt Lake City continues to draw protesters, including "a small coterie of self-described Christian preachers." Some of their protests included displaying "in disrespectful and vulgar ways, some of the intimate, sacred temple garments worn by LDS women." This kind of conflict may provoke the LDS members into responding, which may escalate the conflict.[25]

Religious conflicts are not always nonviolent. Throughout European history, for example, the persecution of Jews often has been violent; recall, for instance, the atrocities of the Inquisition and the Holocaust. Religious conflicts between Catholics and Protestants also have been a mainstay of the conflict in Northern Ireland.

Info Bites

Did you know that the United States currently has a shortage of qualified nurses to staff U.S. hospitals? Part of proposed 2006 immigration legislation expedites visas for non-U.S. nurses to work in the United States. This may, however, be at the detriment of the nations those nurses are leaving—mostly from India and the Philippines—which also need qualified nurses. Is this the beginning of a new global health concern?

Value Differences and Conflict Styles

Another way of understanding cultural variations in intercultural conflict resolution is to look at how cultural values influence conflict management. Cultural values in individualistic societies differ from those in collectivist societies. Individualistic societies place greater importance on the individual than on groups like the family or professional work groups. Individualism is often cited as the most important European American value, as can be seen in the autonomy and independence encouraged in children. For example, children in the United States may be encouraged to leave home at age 18, and older parents often prefer to live on their own rather than with their children. By contrast, people from collectivist societies often live in extended families and value loyalty to groups.

These contrasting values may influence communication patterns. Thus, people from individualistic societies tend to be more concerned with preserving their own self-esteem during conflict, tend to be more direct in their communication, and tend to adopt more discussion conflict styles. By contrast, people from collectivist societies tend to be more concerned with maintaining group harmony and with preserving the other person's dignity during conflict. They may take a less direct conversational approach and adopt accommodating and engaging conflict styles.[26]

In their study on differences between conflict styles between individualists and collectivists, communication scholars Deborah Cai and Edward Fink studied preference for five different conflict styles: avoiding, obliging, integrating, compromising, and dominating.[27] They found that "different cultural orientations were associated with different meanings that people ascribe to ways of handling conflict."[28] The only conflict style that was interpreted similarly between individualist and collectivist cultural orientations was the dominating style in which your own interests are more important than the other person's.

How people choose to deal with conflict in any situation depends on the type of conflict and on their relationship with the other person. For example, in conflicts involving values and opinions, the Japanese may use the accommodating style more with acquaintances than with close friends. By contrast, they may use discussion conflict styles more with close friends than with acquaintances. In conflicts of interest, they may use a dominating style more with acquaintances than with close friends.[29] This suggests that, with people they don't know very well and with whom harmony is not as important, the Japanese use discussion or accommodating styles. However, with close friends, the way to maintain harmony is to work through the conflict using a discussion style.

MANAGING INTERCULTURAL CONFLICT

Productive versus Destructive Conflict

Given all the variations in how people deal with conflicts, what happens when there is conflict in intercultural relationships? One option involves distinguishing between productive and destructive conflict in at least four ways.[30] First, in productive conflict, individuals or groups try to identify the specific problem; in destructive conflict, they make sweeping generalizations and have negative attitudes. For example, in an argument, one shouldn't say, "You never do the dishes," or "You always put me down in front of my friends." Rather, one should state the specific example of being put down: "Last evening when you criticized me in front of our friends, I felt bad."

Second, in productive conflict, individuals or groups focus on the original issue; in destructive conflict, they escalate the conflict from the original issues and anything in the relationship is open for reexamination. For example, guests on talk shows discussing extramarital affairs might start by citing a specific affair and then expand the conflict to include any number of prior arguments. The more productive approach would be to talk only about the specific affair.

Third, in productive conflict, individuals or groups direct the discussion toward cooperative problem solving ("How can we work this out?"); in destructive conflict, they try to seize power and use threats, coercion, and deception ("Either you do what I want, or . . .").

Finally, in productive conflict, individuals or groups value leadership that stresses mutually satisfactory outcomes; in destructive conflict, they polarize behind single-minded and militant leadership. In many political conflicts, such as those in the Middle East, people seem to have fallen into this trap, with leaders unwilling to work toward mutually satisfactory outcomes.

Competitive versus Cooperative Conflict

As you can see, the general theme in destructive conflict is competitive escalation. Conflict often spirals into long-term negativity, with the conflicting parties establishing a self-perpetuating, mutually confirming expectation. As one writer

What Do You Think?

Writing in 2001 about contemporary global wars, Arundhati Roy expresses: "People rarely win wars; governments rarely lose them. People get killed. Governments molt and regroup, hydra-headed" (p. 126). Is this true? Can you think of contemporary conflicts where her statement holds true? (Source: *Power Politics*, by A. Roy, 2001, Cambridge, MA: South End Press)

The "Truth and Reconciliation" hearings in South Africa were founded on a notion of forgiving—but not forgetting. The hearings provided a forum for South Africans to recount and admit to the injustices and violence of apartheid and move toward national healing.

notes, "Each is treating the other badly because it feels that the other deserves to be treated badly because the other treats it badly and so on."[31]

How can individuals and groups promote cooperative communication in conflict situations? According to Morton Deutsch, the general tone of a relationship will promote certain processes and acts.[32] For example, a competitive atmosphere will promote coercion, deception, suspicion, rigidity, and poor communication; a cooperative atmosphere will promote perceived similarity, trust, flexibility, and open communication. The key here is that this atmosphere needs to be established in the beginning stages of the relationship or group interaction. It is much more difficult to turn a competitive relationship into a cooperative one once the conflict has started to escalate. Our colleague Moira remembered a potential conflict during her first week at a new job and how she tried a cooperative approach:

> One of the staff members, Florence, seemed very cool to me. All the other staff members welcomed me to the organization; Florence never said a word. Then we had a misunderstanding about a project we were working on together, and it looked as if things could escalate into a big conflict. I decided that I really didn't want to get off on the wrong foot with her. So I took a deep breath, took a step back, and tried to get things off on a better foot. She had remarked that she was worried about her son, who was having problems in school. I had found a tutor for my son, who also had problems. So I decided to share this with her. We found that we had a lot in common. I found that she wasn't aware that she was being cool; she was just worried about a lot of family problems. We got the work thing cleared up, and we're actually pretty good friends now. I'm really glad I didn't let things escalate.

Exploration is essential in developing a cooperative atmosphere. Exploration may be done in various ways in different cultures, but it has several basic steps: (1) The issue is put on hold, (2) both parties explore other options, or (3) they delegate the problem to a third party. Blaming is suspended, so it's possible to come up with new ideas or positions. "If all conflicting parties are committed to the process, there is a sense of joint ownership of the recommended solution. . . . [M]oving toward enemies as if they were friends exerts a paradoxical force on them and can bring transcendence."[33]

UNDERSTANDING CONFLICT AND SOCIETY

To fully understand intercultural conflict, we need to look beyond individuals who may be in conflict. Many intercultural conflicts can be better understood by looking at the social, economic, historical, and political forces. Figure 8.1 shows the location of many armed conflicts around the world.

Social and Economic Forces

Social conflict results from unequal or unjust social relationships between groups. Consider, for example, the social conflict in northern Wisconsin between

Info Bites

Ruben, an American engineer for a technology company in Italy, was frustrated by the communication styles he ran into in Italy. For example, when he explained a new procedure, it was part of the cultural norms to always answer "Yes" to questions like "Do you understand?" When people didn't understand and mistakes occurred, conflict erupted. If you were Ruben, what would you have done to either resolve these conflicts or stop them before they start?

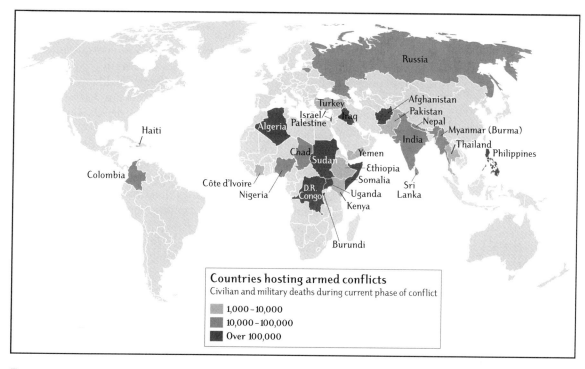

Figure 8.1   Hot spots of conflict in 2008. There are currently many countries that have conflicts. Conflicts are not unusual, but common around the world.

Source: http://www.ploughshares.ca/imagesarticles/ACR08/poster2008.pdf

many Whites and Native Americans over fishing rights. Much of the media attention focused only on the intercultural conflicts between particular individuals, but these individual conflicts were only the tip of the iceberg.[34] The economy in this part of Wisconsin is heavily dependent on tourism and fishing. Many Whites accused the Anishinabe (Chippewa) of overfishing, causing an economic downturn in the area and leading to uneasy social relationships. A treaty signed in 1837 had given the Anishinabe year-round fishing rights in exchange for the northern third of Wisconsin. Recognizing these social, economic, and historical contexts is necessary to understanding the current conflict.

Historical and political forces also are sources of conflict. Many international conflicts have arisen over border disputes. For example, Argentina and the United Kingdom both claimed the Malvinas (or Falkland) Islands in the South Atlantic, which led to a short war in 1982. Disputes between France and Germany over the Alsace-Lorraine region lasted much longer—from about 1871 to 1945. Similar disputes have arisen between Japan and Russia over islands north of Japan. The historical reasons for such conflicts help us understand the claims of both sides.

Info Bites

In February 2005 King
Gyanendra of Nepal
seized control of the state
insisting that he could
control and squelch the
Maoist revolt that has
been waging throughout
Nepal for nearly 10 years.
After nearly a year of the
king's control, Nepali citizens took to the streets of
the capital, Katmandu, in
protest, insisting that the
king restore democratic
power to the elected rep-
resentatives. While many
citizens died in these
protests, in April 2006
Gyanendra restored
power to the legislative
body. Might we think
about this as a social
movement? Do protests
work this effectively in all
cultures? What is the role
of protest in the United
States?

Some conflict may be due to political or cultural differences, but other conflicts occur during **social movements,** in which individuals work together to bring about social change. These individuals often use confrontation as a strategy to highlight the injustices of the system. So, for example, when African American students in Greensboro, North Carolina, sat down at Whites-only lunch counters in the 1960s, they were pointing out the injustices of segregation. Although the students were nonviolent, their actions drew a violent reaction that, for many people, legitimized the claims of injustice. Similarly, the women's suffrage movement in the United States was not an individual effort, but a mass effort to win the right to vote. Indeed, many contemporary social movements involve conflicts, including movements against racism, sexism, and homophobia; movements to protect animal rights, the environment, free speech, and civil rights; and so on. College campuses are likely locations for much activism.

There is, of course, no comprehensive list of existing social movements. They can arise and fall apart, depending on the opposition they provoke, the media attention they attract, and the strategies they use. To stimulate social change, social movements need confrontation to highlight whatever perceived injustice is being done and to open the way for social change to halt the continuation of this injustice.

Confrontation, then, can be seen as an opportunity for social change. In arguing for a nonviolent approach to working for change, Dr. Martin Luther King, Jr., had this to say:

> Nonviolent resistance is not a method for cowards; it does resist. . . . [It] does not seek to defeat or humiliate the opponent, but to win his friendship and understanding. The nonviolent resister must often express his protest through noncooperation or boycotts, but he realizes that these are not ends themselves; they are merely means to awaken a sense of moral shame in the opponent.[35]

Although nonviolence is not the only form of confrontation employed by social movements, it has a long history—from Mahatma Gandhi's struggle for India to gain independence from Britain, to the civil rights struggle in the United States, to the struggle against apartheid in South Africa. And images of the violent confrontations with nonviolent protesters tended to legitimize the social movements and delegitimize the existing social system. For example, the televised images of police dogs attacking schoolchildren and riot squads turning fire hoses on protesters in Birmingham, Alabama, in the 1950s and 1960s swung public sentiment in favor of the civil rights movement.

Some social movements have also used violent forms of confrontation. Groups such as Action Directe in France, the Irish Republican Army, the environmental group Earth First!, and independence movements in Corsica, Algeria, Kosovo, and Chechnya have all been accused of using violence, which tends to result in their being labeled as terrorists rather than simply protesters. Even the suggestion of violence can be threatening to people. For example, in 1964, Malcolm X spoke in favor of civil rights: "The question tonight, as I understand it, is 'The Negro Revolt and Where Do We Go from Here?' or 'What Next?' In my little humble way of understanding it, it points toward either the ballot or the bullet."[36] Malcolm X's rhetoric terrified many U.S. Americans, who then refused to give legitimacy to his movement. To understand communication practices such as these, it is important to study the social context in which the movement operated.

Many conflicts are fueled by economic problems, which often find their expression in terms of cultural differences. Many people find it easier to explain economic troubles by pointing to cultural differences or by blaming cultural groups. The recent worldwide financial crisis may precipitate increased tension and conflict between cultural groups. Economic concerns have given rise to some protests in Europe, but only those in Britain have risen to a serious level:

> Yet for all the economic pain, the social and political fallout from deglobalisation has not yet been severe. Protests may still come. Or maybe national governments are absorbing most of the ire. In December, Greece saw riots after a police bullet killed a teenager. In France, unions brought over 1m people onto the streets for a one-day strike, and a riot in Latvia over economic policy ended in more than 100 arrests. But only in Britain, where workers have picketed refineries and power stations over the hiring of foreigners, has protest had a very anti-global tone.[37]

The economic decline of Ireland, Iceland, Latvia, as well as Britain, among many others worldwide, has pushed people to reconsider their participation in globalization. Yet, so far, the protests have not turned to blaming others. Perhaps as we have become a more global village, people feel more interconnected to others than ever before. As the economy continues to decline around the world, pay attention to the way that communication is used to bring people together or create divisions based on cultural differences. Cultural differences may not be the cause of the economic troubles, but they have been used in the past to help explain financial crises.

Historical and Political Forces

Although as children we may have learned that "Sticks and stones may break my bones, but names will never hurt me," we know that derogatory words can be a source of many intercultural conflicts. Many derogatory words gain power from their historical usage and the legacy of oppression that they reference. As noted in Chapter 3, much of our identity has historical roots. It is only through understanding the past that we can understand what it means to be a member of a

Pop Culture Spotlight

Of the four most popular professional sports in the United States—baseball, football, basketball, and hockey—which one do you think promotes the most open interpersonal conflict in general: among players, and between players and referees or umpires? Why? Which promotes the least? Why? Which have the best and worst cultures for solving conflicts once they begin?

particular cultural group. For example, understanding the history of Ireland helps us understand the meaning of Irish identity.

Sometimes ongoing tensions between groups is not limited to those groups and draws in others. For example, the conflict between the Israelis and the Palestinians is not limited to those two groups. The history of this part of the world, the role of religious differences, and the contemporary issues fueling the conflict all work together to ensure that the conflict draws in others.

In January 2009, the Turkish Prime Minister walked out of a global economic summit after criticizing Israel's military attack on Gaza (in response to rockets being fired into Israel): "The dispute about Israel's offensive against Hamas took place at a panel discussion Thursday. It ended when Erdogan told Israeli president Shimon Peres: 'You kill people,' and then stalked off the stage." This confrontation has led to celebration of his criticism when he arrived back in Turkey: "Thousands of jubilant Turks welcomed their prime minister home on Friday, thronging the airport and later chanting "Turkey is proud of you!" after he publicly confronted the Israeli president over the Gaza war."[38] He also won praise from the Iranian president: "Iranian President Mahmoud Ahmadinejad has lauded Turkish Prime Minister Recep Tayyip Erdogan for taking a stand against Israel's war on the Palestinians of Gaza."[39]

Historically, however, Turkey and Israel have been allies and Turkey has increasingly played a mediator role among various players in the Middle East: "Although Mr. Erdogan has strongly criticized Israel's Gaza offensive, his country and Israel have long enjoyed close diplomatic relations. With its strong relations with the militant group Hamas, which controls Gaza, Mr. Erdogan's Justice and Development Party has played a growing role mediating among Israel, Syria, Lebanon, and the Palestinians."[40] This recent spat may put that mediator role in question in the future. These conflicts did not emerge from interpersonal conflicts among the current inhabitants; rather, in large part, they represent reenactments of conflicts grounded in the history of conflicts in the Middle East between Arabs and Jews. The contemporary participants are caught in a historical web pitting cultural identities against one another. In fact, these dynamics are at work all around the world. Historical antagonisms become part of cultural identities and cultural practices that place people in positions of conflict. Whether in the Middle East, Northern Ireland, Rwanda, Uganda, Nigeria, Sri Lanka, East Timor, Kosovo, or Chechnya, we can see these historical antagonisms lead to various forms of conflict.

Another type of political influence on intercultural conflict is **anti-Americanism.** Anti-Americanism refers to the ideas, feelings, and sometimes actions against the United States—most often against the U.S. government, although it can also refer to the culture and people. Anti-Americanism has a very long history and it is complicated by the economic, military, and political differences between the United States and other nations around the world. Anti-Americanism can affect intercultural interaction on many levels—from the interpersonal to the social—and you may want to reflect on the potential for conflict that may arise. How well do you understand anti-Americanism and what is the best way to deal with it?

This photo shows Israeli President Shimon Peres and Turkish Prime Minister Tayyip Erdogan in conflict at a 2009 global economic summit. Erdogan walked off the stage after saying to Peres "You kill people."—referring to Israeli incursions in Gaza. This conflict is not an interpersonal conflict between Erdogan and Peres and can only be understood in terms of the history of international relations and Middle Eastern conflicts.

Anti-Americanism is complex because it is a unifying perspective that crosses many cultures in ways that many cultural values do not: "loathing for America is about as close as we can get to a universal sentiment: it is the one dynamic that unites fundamentalists and liberals, Arabs and Latin Americans, Asians and Europeans, and even the overshadowed Canadians, with the rest of the world."[41] This shared vision is not simply a political game, or a way of distancing oneself from U.S. foreign policy as it might have once been. As one British writer notes: "Today, however, when I talk with friends and relatives in London, when I visit Europe, the anti-Americanism is more than just sardonic asides, rueful Monty Python–style jibes, and haughty intimations of superiority. Today something much more visceral is in the air. I go to my old home and I get the distinct impression that . . . people really *loathe* America somewhere deep, deep in their gut."[42]

Recent foreign policy decisions by the U.S. government have reinvigorated these anti-American sentiments that have simmered for years. Whatever you may feel about U.S. foreign policy, think about how these policies impact other people around the world. While it may not be easy to avoid the kinds of conflict that arise due to anti-Americanism, ignorance of how U.S. foreign policy impacts others around the globe is not a helpful place to start understanding the

What Do You Think?

Much of the social conflict about nonsanctioned border crossing along the U.S.–Mexico border is not because of political or economic reasons, but because of environmental concerns. What happens to our understanding of human life when environmental concerns are prioritized above humanitarian concerns? Is this an appropriate prioritization? If so, why? What role does the environment play in contemporary international conflicts?

perspective of others. Whether you agree or disagree with some of the overseas activities of the U.S. government, your own personal beliefs may not always matter in avoiding anti-Americanism.

When people witness conflict, they often assume that it is caused by personal issues between individuals. When we reduce conflict to the level of interpersonal interaction, we lose sight of the larger social and political forces that contextualize these conflicts. People are in conflicts for reasons that extend far beyond personal communication styles.

So how do we escape the historical, political, and social forces that entrap us in conflict? Today, forgiveness is the strategy being used around the world to break the trap of conflict. Yet, forgiving is not easy, as we can see in the case of the conflicts in Northern Ireland:

> Thirty-three years after Sam Malcolmson was shot by an Irish Republican Army gunman, the wound in his side is still open and leaking fluid. He has to change the dressing constantly. He takes morphine four times a day for blinding pain caused by bullet shards lodged in his spine. . . .
>
> "People tell me I should forgive and forget so we can all move on," said Malcolmson, who was a 22-year-old police recruit when the IRA ambushed him in 1972. "They are asking an awful lot.". . .
>
> The British government is asking for such forgiveness on the grounds that it will help seal the peace in Northern Ireland after more than three decades of sectarian violence.[43]

Yet, the British government feels forgiveness is essential to building a lasting peace there. As you can see, it isn't always easy to move on from conflict, but it can help avoid future conflicts and future pain for others who follow.

SUMMARY

In this chapter, we identified several characteristics of intercultural conflict: ambiguity, language issues, and contradictory conflict styles. There are different types of conflict relating to interests, values, and goals, and to cognitive and affective factors. There are also different conflict styles, including discussion style which is direct and emotionally restrained, the engagement style which is direct and confrontational, the accommodating style which is indirect and emotionally restrained, and the dynamic style which is indirect and emotionally intense. Some cultural groups use intermediaries to resolve conflict.

We also outlined two very different cultural approaches to conflict: conflict as productive versus conflict as destructive. In most U.S. contexts, conflict is seen as ultimately positive, offering opportunities for personal growth. In contrast, many Asian cultures and some ethnic groups within the United States view conflict as ultimately destructive and harmful to relationships. Gender and ethnicity can influence conflict style preferences. For example, people from individualistic cultures may tend to use discussion style, whereas people from collectivist cultures may prefer the accommodating or dynamic style. However, the type of conflict and the relationship of the disputants also influence these tendencies.

Finally, we highlighted productive versus destructive and cooperative versus competitive approaches to conflict and discussed the importance of social, economic, historical, and political forces in understanding conflict and society. Conflicts arise against the backdrop of existing social movements—for example, in reaction to racism, sexism, and homophobia. Some social movements use nonviolent means of dealing with these conflicts; others confront conflict with violence.

BUILDING INTERCULTURAL SKILLS

1. Stay centered and do not polarize. This means moving beyond traditional stereotypes and either-or thinking. It is important, though difficult, to avoid explaining the other person's motives as simple while seeing your own as complex. Try to see both sides, and be open to a third, centered perspective that may bring a new synthesis into view.[44] It's OK to get angry, but it's important to move past the anger—to refrain from acting out feelings.

2. Maintain contact. This does not mean that you have to stay in the conflict situation. Sometimes we need to walk away for a while. However, do not cut off the relationship. Attempt a dialogue rather than isolating yourself from or fighting with your opponent. Unlike normal conversation, dialogue is slow, careful, full of feeling, respectful, and attentive.[45] Dialogue offers an important opportunity for coming to a richer understanding of your own intercultural conflicts and experiences.

3. Recognize the existence of different styles. Conflict is often exacerbated because of the unwillingness of partners to recognize style differences, which often have cultural origins. Failure to recognize cultural differences can lead to negative evaluations of partners.

4. Identify your preferred style. Although we may change our way of dealing with conflict, based on the situation and the type of conflict, most of us tend to use the same style in most situations. It is also important to recognize which conflict styles "push your conflict button." Some styles are more or less compatible, and it's important to know which styles are congruent with your own.

5. Be creative and expand your repertoire. If a particular way of dealing with conflict is not working, be willing to try a different style. In most intercultural communication, adaptability and flexibility serve us well, and conflict communication is no exception. This means that there is no so-called objective way to deal with conflict. Recognizing this condition may promote conflict resolution.

6. Recognize the importance of context. It is important to understand that larger social, political, and historical contexts give meaning to many types of conflict. Conflict arises for many reasons, and it would be misleading to

think that all conflict can be understood solely within the interpersonal context. And once you understand the contexts that frame the conflict, whether cultural, social, historical, or political, you will be in a better position to conceive of possibilities for resolution.

7. Be willing to forgive. This means letting go of—not forgetting—feelings of revenge.[46] This may be particularly useful in intercultural conflict.[47]

ACTIVITY

Cultures in conflict: In groups of four, select two countries or cultural groups that are currently or have historically been in conflict. Divide each group of four into pairs, and have each pair research the conflict from the perspective of one of the two cultural groups. Using library and community resources, including interviews with cultural members, outline the major issues and arguments of the assigned culture. Explore the role of cultural values, political contexts, and historical contexts in the conflict. Be prepared to present an oral or written report of your research.

ENDNOTES

1. Hymon, S. (2003, January 14). Firm's logging degrades rivers, increases floods, state study says. *Los Angeles Times*, p. B7.
2. Woodall, M. (2003, June 11). E-mail galls French school. *The Philadelphia Inquirer.* Retrieved from http://www.philly.com/mld/inquirer/living/education/6059080.htm
3. Dupont, T. (2003, June 3). Des lycéens de Carcassonne victims de la francophobie américaine. *Transfert* (Paris). Retrieved from http://www.transfert.net/a8904. ("The French parents who decided to inform the American embassy and the Minister of Foreign Affairs")
4. Delgado, F. (2002). Mass-mediated communication and intercultural conflict. In J. N. Martin, T. K. Nakayama, & L. A. Flores (Eds.), *Readings in intercultural communication* (2nd ed., pp. 351–359). Boston: McGraw-Hill.
5. See Hocker, J. L., & Wilmot, W. W. (2000). *Interpersonal conflict* (6th ed.). New York: McGraw-Hill; Cupach, W. R., & Canary, D. J. (1997). *Competence in interpersonal conflict.* New York: McGraw-Hill.
6. Lindsley, S. L., & Braithwaite, C. A. (1996). You should "wear a mask": Facework norms in cultural and intercultural conflict in *maquiladoras. International Journal of Intercultural Relations, 20,* 199–225.
7. Cole, M. (1996). *Interpersonal conflict communication in Japanese cultural contexts.* Unpublished dissertation, Arizona State University, Tempe.
8. Simons, M. (2005, December 29). Muslim women in Europe claim rights and keep faith. *New York Times*, p. A3.
9. Hammer, M. R. (2005). The Intercultural Conflict Style Inventory: A conceptual framework and measure of intercultural conflict approaches. *International Journal of Intercultural Relations 29*(6).
10. Filley, A. C. (1975). *Interpersonal conflict resolution.* Glenview, IL: Scott, Foresman.
11. Kraybill, D. (1989). *The riddle of Amish culture.* Baltimore: Johns Hopkins University Press.
12. Augsburger, D. (1992). *Conflict mediation across cultures.* Louisville, KY: Westminster/John Knox Press, p. 80.
13. Ting-Toomey, S., & Oetzel, J. G. (2002). Cross cultural face concerns and conflict styles: Current status and future directions. In W. B. Gudykunst & B. Mody, *Handbook of international and intercultural communication* (2nd ed., pp. 143–165). Thousand Oaks, CA: Sage. See also Ting-Toomey, S. (Ed.). (1994). *The challenge of facework: Cross cultural and interpersonal issues.* Albany: State University of New York Press.

14. Hammer, R. (2003). *The Intercultural Conflict Style Inventory: Individual profile and interpretive guide*. N. Potomac, MD: Hammer Consulting Group, LLC.
15. Ting-Toomey, S., Yee-Jung, K. K., Shapiro, R. B., Garcia, W., Wright, T. J., & Oetzel, J. G. (2000). Ethnic/cultural identity salience and conflict styles in four U.S. ethnic groups. *International Journal of Intercultural Relations, 24,* 47–81.
16. Hocker, J. L., & Wilmot, W. W. (1991). *Interpersonal conflict* (3rd ed.). Dubuque, IA: Brown.
17. Kim, M-S. (2002). *Non-Western perspectives on human communication.* Thousand Oaks, CA: Sage, p. 63.
18. Hammer, M. R. (2004) *Intercultural Conflict Style Inventory, Facilitators Manual.* Hammer Consulting Group, LLC 267 Kentlands Boulevard, PMB 705, N. Potomac, MD 20878.
19. Tannen, D. (1986). *That's not what I meant! How conversational style makes or breaks relationships.* New York: Ballantine Books. See also Tannen, D. (1990). *You just don't understand: Women and men in conversation.* New York: Morrow.
20. Wood, J. T. (1994). *Gendered lives: Communication, gender, and culture.* Belmont, CA: Wadsworth.
21. Collier, M. J. (1991). Conflict competence within African, Mexican, and Anglo American friendships. In S. Ting-Toomey & F. Korzenny (Eds.), *Cross-cultural interpersonal communication* (pp. 132–154). Newbury Park, CA: Sage.
22. Ting-Toomey et al. (2000), pp. 47–81.
23. Turner, L. H., & Shuter, R. (2004). African American and European American women's visions of workplace conflict: A metaphorical analysis. *Howard Journal of Communications, 15,* 169–193.
24. Alvarez, L. (2006, April 17). Outrage at funeral protests pushes lawmakers to act. *New York Times,* p. A14.
25. The other cheek. (2003, October 19). *The Salt Lake Tribune,* p. AA1.
26. Ting-Toomey, S., Gao, G., Trubisky, P., Yang, Z., Kim, H. S., Lin, S. L., et al. (1991). Culture, face, maintenance and styles of handling interpersonal conflicts: A study in five cultures. *International Journal of Conflict Management, 2,* 275–296; Ting-Toomey, S. (1997). Intercultural conflict competence. In Cupach & Canary, pp. 120–147. See also Trubisky, P., Ting-Toomey, S., & Lin, S. L. (1991).The influence of individualism-collectivism and self monitoring on conflict styles. *International Journal of Intercultural Relations, 15,* 65–84; Nadler, L. B., Nadler, M. K., & Broome, B. J. (1985). Culture and the management of conflict situations. In W. B. Gudykunst, L. Stewart, & S. Ting-Toomey (Eds.), *Communication, culture, and organizational processes* (pp. 77–96). Beverly Hills, CA: Sage.
27. Cai, D. A., & Fink, E. L. (2002). Conflict style differences between individualists and collectivists. *Communication Monographs, 69,* 67–87.
28. Cai & Fink (2002), p. 83.
29. Cole (1996).
30. Augsburger (1992), p. 47.
31. Deutsch, M. (1987). A theoretical perspective on conflict and conflict resolution. In D. Sandole & I. Sandole-Staroste (Eds.), *Conflict management and problem solving.* New York: New York University Press, p. 41.
32. Deutsch, M. (1973). *The resolution of conflict: Constructive and destructive processes.* New Haven, CT: Yale University Press.
33. Hocker & Wilmot (1991), p. 191.
34. Hall, B. "J." (1994). Understanding intercultural conflict through kernel images and rhetorical visions. *International Journal of Conflict Management, 5*(1), 62–86.
35. King, M. L., Jr. (1984). Pilgrimage in nonviolence. In J. C. Albert & S. E. Albert (Eds.), *The sixties papers: Documents of a rebellious decade* (pp. 108–112). New York: Praeger. (Original work published in 1958).
36. X, Malcolm. (1984). The ballot or the bullet. In Albert & Albert, pp. 126–132. (Original work published in 1965).
37. Turning their backs on the world. (2009, February 19). *The Economist.* Retrieved March 2, 2009 from: http://www.economist.com/world/international/displaystory.cfm?story_id=13145370

38. Turkish leader hailed at home after Israel spat. (2009, January 30). *MSNBC*. Retrieved January 30, 2009 from: http://www.msnbc.msn.com/id/28934392/

39. Iran lauds Erdogan's protest in Davos. (2009, February 1). *Tehran Times*. Retrieved January 31, 2009 from: http://www.tehrantimes.com/index_View.asp?code=188218

40. Bennhold, K. (2009, January 29). Leaders of Turkey and Israel clash at Davos panel. *Washington Post*. Retrieved January 31, 2009 from: http://www.nytimes.com/2009/01/30/world/europe/30clash.html?scp=2&sq=erdogan&st=cse

41. Sardar, Z., & Davies, M. W. (2002). *Why do people hate America?* New York: Disinformation Company, p. 195.

42. Abramsky, S. (2004, July 23). Waking up from the American dream. *The Chronicle of Higher Education*, p. B9.

43. Sullivan, K. (2005, December 7). In Northern Ireland, forgiveness is a bitter pill. *The Washington Post*, p. A19.

44. Augsburger (1992), p. 66.

45. See Hocker & Wilmot (1998), p. 266.

46. Lulofs, R. S. (1994). *Conflict: From theory to action*. Scottsdale, AZ: Gorsuch Scarisbrick.

47. Augsburger (1992), p. 66.

CHAPTER NINE

Intercultural Relationships in Everyday Life

STUDY OBJECTIVES

After reading this chapter, you should be able to:

1. Identify and describe the benefits and challenges of intercultural relationships.

2. Understand the role that similarities and differences play in intercultural relationships.

3. Identify cultural differences in relational communication.

4. Identify and describe issues in intercultural friendships, intercultural romantic relationships, and gay relationships.

5. Describe how computer mediated communication (CMC) can both facilitate and hinder intercultural relationships.

6. Understand how society influences intercultural relationships.

KEY TERMS

complementarity	intercultural relationships
compromise style	intimacy
consensus style	obliteration style
contact hypothesis	physical attraction
friendship	romantic relationships
gay relationships	similarity principle
intercultural dating	submission style

A student of ours named Erich worked on campus at the Memorial Union, where most of his coworkers were from India. This multicultural working environment raised several interesting issues for Erich:

> One thing I realized was the fact that similarity played a big role in the integration of the Indian students. After sitting down and talking, difficult at first, we realized that we were all university students, working together, and this opened up lines of communication and sped up the integration process. After one semester, we were all integrated and had a new batch of students show up. This time we knew how to help them and ourselves feel more comfortable.

Another student, Susie, and the guy she was dating were both raised in the southwestern United States, but their cultural backgrounds differed. Susie had a middle-class Mexican cultural background that was very family-oriented. Her parents were always involved in and showed great concern for all her decisions in life. As she explained it, "With a Mexican father of three girls, it was a very protective environment." Her boyfriend had been raised in a working-class suburb by an Asian mother and German father who were not as intimately involved in his activities. Thus, school and education were his highest priority. According to Susie,

> The relationship experiences were very interesting as we both learned about our cultural traits and norms. I enjoyed learning about and understanding his environment even as he began to experience and understand the environment I was raised in. It was a continuous learning process for both of us.

Think about your friends, classmates, and coworkers, all of whom may differ from you in terms of age, physical ability, ethnicity, religion, class, or sexual orientation. How did you get to know them? Perhaps in the workplace, as Erich did, or in a romantic relationship, as Susie did. Maybe you met and developed a relationship online. Do your intercultural relationships differ from those characterized by cultural similarity? How do intercultural relationships form? Do intercultural relationships online develop differently from offline relationships? How are these relationships influenced by society? Are they supported or discouraged by local institutions like schools, churches, and synagogues? What are some strategies you can use to build better intercultural relationships—at school, at work, and at play?

In this chapter, we explore the benefits and challenges of intercultural relationships. We then discuss different kinds of intercultural relationships, including friendships and romantic relationships. We also examine the role society

Info Bites

Did you know that in 1966 NBC shocked audiences when *Star Trek* episode 67, "Plato's Stepchildren," aired. In this episode, Captain Kirk, a white man, and Lieutenant Uhura, a black woman, kissed each other, creating what now is considered the first interracial kiss in television history.

plays in intercultural relationships. Finally, we talk about strategies to build solid intercultural relationships and alliances.

BENEFITS OF INTERCULTURAL RELATIONSHIPS

Most people have a variety of **intercultural relationships** that span differences in age, physical ability, gender, ethnicity, class, religion, race, and nationality. Take Maria, for example, a student who works part time in a resort as a bartender. Her coworkers are ethnically diverse—Latinos/as, Whites, and African Americans. The clientele is international—Europeans, Asians, and South Americans who come to the resort to play golf and relax. One of her good friends is an older woman, Linda, a neighbor who is disabled with severe emphysema. Maria and Linda watch TV and fix meals together. Maria's Black friend Shawna is dating Jurgen, an international student from Germany, and all three enjoy rollerblading and hiking together. Maria's family is Catholic, but her sister married Jay, who is Jewish. Maria's parents had difficulty accepting Jay at first, but eventually they became more accepting, especially after the grandchildren were born.

As this example shows, intercultural relationships can encompass many kinds of cultural differences and offer many rewards and opportunities. The key to these relationships is often an interesting balance of differences and similarities. While Maria's friends are diverse, she has many things in common with each one—rollerblading with Shawna and Jurgen, watching TV and preparing gourmet meals with Linda, building ties with her sister's family. Through all these relationships, Maria and her friends and acquaintances learn about each other's different worlds.

The benefits of such relationships include (1) learning about the world, (2) breaking stereotypes, and (3) acquiring new skills. In intercultural relationships, we often learn specific information about unfamiliar cultural patterns and language. For example, Anneliese, a graduate student who lived in Guatemala, explained that she learned a new way of looking at time, that "meeting at nine o'clock" might mean 9:30 or 10:00, not because someone forgot or wasn't "on time," but because there was a completely different definition for "9:00." She also learned a different language than the Spanish she had learned in the university setting.

We may also learn more about what it really means to belong to a different culture. For example, recall how Susie learned something about what it meant to grow up in a different class and ethnic environment through her relationship with her boyfriend. A romance or close intercultural friendship may be a way to bring abstractions like "culture" or "race" to life.[1]

We may learn something about history. Another one of our students, Jennifer, told us how she learned more about the Holocaust from her Jewish friends and about the "Middle Passage" from her African American friends. This is a kind of "relational learning," learning that comes from a particular relationship but generalizes to other contexts. While Jennifer learned something specific about Jewish and African American history, she also learned the importance of

Info Bites

There are magazines devoted to exploring issues of intercultural and interracial relationships, including *New People, Interracial Classified, Small World,* and *Interrace Magazine.* Based on your study of intercultural communication, what kinds of issues do you think these magazines should address?

Relationships often are formed because of proximity. That is, we are attracted to people who live near us and who work, study, and worship with us. How many friends do you have who are culturally different from you?

different ethnic histories and is now more curious to learn about the histories of other ethnic groups. Relational learning is often much more compelling than knowledge gained from books.

Intercultural relationships also can help break stereotypes. Another student, Andy, told us he used to think that Mexicans were lazy. He formed this opinion from media images, discussions with friends, and political speeches about immigration in the Southwest. However, when he met and made friends with immigrants from rural Mexico, his opinion changed. He saw that the everyday life of his friends was anything but easy. They had family responsibilities and sometimes worked two jobs to make ends meet.

We also often learn how to do new things in intercultural relationships. For example, through her friendships with students in the United States and abroad, Judith has learned to make paella (a Spanish dish) and *nopalitos con puerca* (a cactus-and-pork stew), to play bridge in French, and to downhill ski. Through intercultural relationships, newcomers to the society can acquire important skills. Andy's immigrant friends often asked him for help with unfamiliar tasks like buying car insurance or shopping at supermarkets. And when Tom first moved to France, his new French friends helped him navigate the university cafeteria.

In short, intercultural communication can lead to a sense of connection with others and can establish a lifelong pattern of communicating to bridge differences. For example, yet another student, Jessica, recounts how an encounter with an international exchange student led to a lifetime interest in intercultural relations. It all began when she was a first-year high school student.

> My best friend's older sister had just gotten back from Germany and brought home an exchange student. My one memory of my first encounter with Edith, the exchange student, happened at breakfast one morning after a sleep-over party. We were going to make waffles, and Edith didn't know what waffles were. I loved explaining them to her and telling her about different syrups and then learning about the different foods she ate in Germany. It was so fun to talk to her.

Three years later, Jessica went on the same exchange program to New Zealand:

> What an amazing experience. Not only did I get to stay with a family that had three girls, one my age, but I also learned about the Maoris, the first people to inhabit New Zealand. I developed a lifelong relationship with my host family and relished learning the differences and similarities between our cultures. I have fond memories of sitting up late at night drinking tea, not coffee, with my New Zealand mother. We would talk for hours. This was a powerful learning experience.

This led to still more intercultural experiences and relationships:

> My exchange sister came home with me, and the other seventeen delegates in the program also brought their exchange sisters or brothers home from all over the world. Talk about a salad mix of cultures. We took various trips for six weeks. It was so exhilarating.
>
> Although my experiences have for the most part been overseas, I feel they have opened a window for me. My worldview has gone from just me to phenomenally huge. I see things from other people's point of view; I actually try to see things in a different light. I have my experiences with people from other cultures to thank.

What Do You Think?

The Friendship Force International website (www.friendshipforce.org/) says, "Friendship Force International is a nonprofit organization dedicated to the principle that each person can make a contribution to global goodwill. Home hospitality—the heart of a Friendship Force exchange—provides the opportunity for people of different countries and cultures to connect at a personal level." How important are intercultural friendships in today's world? Do you agree they are the key to global goodwill and world peace?

CHALLENGES IN INTERCULTURAL RELATIONSHIPS

While intercultural relationships can enrich our lives and provide tremendous benefits, they can also present several challenges, including motivation; differences in communication styles, values, and perceptions; negative stereotypes; anxiety; affirming another's cultural identity; and the need for explanations. Let's look at each of these in turn.

Motivation

Perhaps the most fundamental challenge in intercultural relationships is motivation. In order to build relationships across cultural boundaries, there has to be a desire. There are increasing opportunities to meet people from other cultures through the Internet, and increasing cultural diversity in many schools and workplaces, and yet a recent survey shows that today's first-year college students have less interest in meeting people who are different from them.[2] In surveys, young people repeatedly say that they are open to intercultural romantic relationships and yet for some groups, the rate of intercultural dating is approximately the same as it was 20 years ago.[3] What do you think motivates people to pursue (or not pursue) intercultural relationships?

Differences in Communication Styles, Values, and Perceptions

A second challenge is that intercultural relationships, by definition, are often characterized by cultural differences in communication styles, values, and perceptions. These dissimilarities probably are most noticeable in the early stages of the relationship, before people get to know each other on a more personal, individual level. For example, an American couple was a bit offended when some of their Chinese friends—whom they had met only recently—asked them how much they paid for their car or their house. They didn't realize that these are commonly expected questions in China, and if you don't want to answer them, you can just change the topic. One of our Chinese students noticed this cultural difference in communication "rules":

> I recently bought a car, and when I mentioned it to my Chinese friends, all of them asked how much it cost and told me whether or not they thought it was a good deal. However, when I told my American friends about my car, they asked about the make, the model, the year, everything except the price!

However, once some commonality is established, these cultural differences may have less effect because all relationships become more individualized as they move to more intimate stages. For example, when Agusia first met Angelina in a class project, all they knew about each other was that Angelina was a Latina and that Agusia grew up in Poland. But as they got to know each other, they found out they both had small daughters, were active in their Catholic churches, and were social work majors. As they got to be good friends and learned about what they shared and how they differed, the cultural differences became less important.

As Angelina and Agusia found out, there is an interplay of both differences and similarities in intercultural relationships. The differences are a given, and the challenge often is to discover and build on the similarities. These similarities may consist of common interests and activities, common beliefs, or common goals.

Negative Stereotypes

A third challenge in intercultural relationships is negative stereotyping. As discussed in Chapter 2, stereotypes are a way of categorizing and processing information, but they are particularly detrimental when they are negative and held rigidly. These mainstream ideas and stereotypes can be powerful and persistent. Sometimes it takes conscious effort to detect the stereotypes we hold in everyday life and to find information that counteracts them.

One suggestion is to detect when you are "thinking under the influence" (TUI) of prejudices or stereotypes. Notice when you feel surprised by someone "different," because this can often signify a negative assumption or stereotype. A communication colleague, Brenda Allen, gives two examples of TUI "aha" moments.

> A panelist on a program I attended was a wheelchair user who also was hearing impaired. When she made several witty comments, I noticed that her sense of humor amazed me. As I questioned my feelings, I realized that I assumed she would have a gloomy outlook on life because of her disabilities. Aha! I was TUI of the prejudicial notion that disability is a state of being doomed. . . .
>
> Recently an elderly man slowly boarded a bus I was riding on. After he sat down, he began to talk with another older man. As I eavesdropped on their conversation, I was impressed with how articulate they were, especially after the first man said he was 90 years old. I had assumed that both men would have limited communication competence. Aha! I was TUI of a stereotype of aging as decline.

Allen goes on to wonder if other people write these men off as "over the hill" and how many of us miss rich opportunities to interact with someone "different" because of TUI.[4]

Anxiety

A fourth challenge in intercultural relationships involves overcoming the increased anxiety commonly found in the early stages of the relationship. (Some anxiety always exists in the early stages of any relationship.) This anxiety stems from fears about possible negative consequences of our actions. We may be afraid that we will look stupid or will offend someone because we're unfamiliar with that person's language or culture. For example, our student Sam has a lot of friends who speak Spanish at home, and he has studied Spanish for five years in high school and college. But when he visits with his friends' families, he's often anxious about speaking Spanish with them. He's afraid he'll say something stupid or reveal his ignorance in some way.

Differences of age are not usually cause for discomfort, but relationships that span differences in physical ability, class, or race may engender more anxiety. Caterina described for us the last meeting of an interracial discussion group.

> We really did make great connections and friendships in our time together, based on intelligence and honor. It was great to see that some of the girls who initially spoke of their discomfort around others who are different from them spoke out and informed us they were not as scared anymore. They gave up their fear and took a great step forward, one that I hope they will remember always.

Info Bites

Yasuko Kanno, in her book *Negotiating Bilingual and Bicultural Identities: Japanese Returnees Betwixt Two Worlds* (Erlbaum, 2003), describes bilingual and bicultural identities: "bilingual individuals position themselves between two languages and two (or more) cultures, and incorporate these languages and cultures into their sense of who they are." In the United States the number of bicultural or bilingual people is rapidly increasing. Some experts believe that these people can play a key role in facilitating intercultural communication in many contexts.

As this statement suggests, people face a kind of "hurdle" in developing intercultural relationships, and once they pass that hurdle, it's much easier to develop other intercultural relationships.[5]

The level of anxiety may be even higher if people have negative expectations based on previous interactions or on stereotypes.[6] For example, some White and African American students seem to have more difficulty discussing intercultural issues with each other than they do with international students, perhaps because of negative stereotypes held by both groups. By contrast, intercultural interactions in which there are few negative expectations and no history of negative contact probably have less anxiety associated with them. For example, one student tells of traveling to New Zealand as an 18-year-old on a sports team. He had no negative preconceptions about New Zealanders and no real language barrier. While he experienced a little anxiety at the beginning, he quickly found similarity with people he met, and it was "truly an unforgettable experience."

Affirming Another Person's Cultural Identity

A fifth challenge in intercultural relationships is affirming the other person's cultural identity. This means that we need not only to recognize that the other person might have different beliefs, perceptions, and attitudes, but also to accept those characteristics as an important part of the other's identity.[7]

However, this is often difficult, especially for majority group individuals. There is often a tendency for members of the majority culture to assume their attitudes, beliefs, and behaviors are the norm and that the minority member should adapt to them.[8] For example, a college student, Andrea, had a good friend Sherry who is Filipina and tended to have a collectivistic approach to friendship. When the two friends went to Europe, Sherry had a last-minute emergency and needed to borrow $600 from Andrea. From Sherry's perspective, lending money was a natural thing for friends to do and was not that unusual. But Andrea had a tough time getting over the fact that Sherry took it so matter of factly, did not thank Andrea profusely, and did not repay it immediately. This aspect of Sherry's identity was a difficult thing for Andrea to accept and is still a barrier in their friendship.

The Need for Explanations

Finally, intercultural relationships often present the challenge of having to explain things. Intercultural relationships can be more work than in-group relationships and can require more "care and feeding" than do those relationships between people who are very similar. A lot of the work has to do with explaining—explaining to themselves, to each other, and to their respective communities.[9]

First, in some way, consciously or unconsciously, we ask ourselves what it means to be friends with someone who is not like us. Do we become friends out of necessity, or for our job, or because everyone around us is different in some way? Do we become friends because we want to gain an entree into this group for personal benefit or because we feel guilty?

Info Bites

While the divorce rate of the United States is disputed, many estimate that it is around 50 percent. The divorce rate in Japan is approximately 27 percent, while India is approximately 1 percent, and Australia is about 40 percent. How do you think culture influences whether couples get divorced? (SOURCE: http://www.divorcerate.org/)

Intercultural relation-ships present both opportunities for and challenges to commu-nication. They can also reflect an inter-esting balance of similarities and dif-ferences. In what ways might these young women be similar, and in what ways might they be different?

Second, we explain things to each other. This process of mutual clarification is one of the healthiest characteristics of intercultural relationships. Judith recalls her Algerian friends explaining that they really thought their sisters and moth-ers were treated better in some ways than women are treated in the United States. For example, they explained that no woman would be expected to raise children by herself in Algeria, as is commonly practiced in the United States. They felt sorry for single mothers in the United States who often struggle on their own to raise children. Judith grew to understand that situations can be viewed in very different ways and to realize that others can interpret things very differently.

People who cross cultural boundaries and form close relationships with individuals who are, say, much older or of a different ethnicity often have to explain this to their respective communities. For example, in the film *Naturally Native*, three Native American sisters have different views on being Indian. The oldest sister, Karen, doesn't understand why her youngest sister can't be more Indian, why she wants to go outside her group to find friends, and why being Indian isn't more important to her.

Note that usually the biggest obstacles to boundary-crossing friendships come not from minority communities but from majority communities. This is because those in the majority, such as Whites, have the most to gain by maintaining social inequality and are less likely to initiate boundary-crossing friendships. By contrast, minority groups have more to gain. Developing intercultural relationships can help them survive and succeed, particularly economically and professionally.

In intercultural relationships, individuals recognize and respect the differences. In these relationships, we often have to remind ourselves that we can never know exactly what it is to walk in another person's shoes. Furthermore, those in the majority group tend to know less about those in minority groups than vice versa. As one of our White students told us, thanks to intercultural relationships with other students, she "was able to hear several examples of true stories of discrimination that Hispanic people go through on a daily basis. I never really thought any of that existed anymore. I don't know why, but their stories really impacted me, and made me much more aware of the hardships that minorities have to go through. It was a real learning opportunity." Overall, intercultural friendships, while challenging, add a special richness to our lives. To be successful, they require "mutual respect, acceptance, tolerance for the faux pas and the occasional closed door, open discussion and patient mutual education; all this gives crossing friendships—when they work at all—a special kind of depth."[10]

FOUNDATIONS OF INTERCULTURAL RELATIONSHIPS

How do we come to know people who are different from ourselves? Some relationships develop simply because of circumstances—for example, when students work together on a course project. Some relationships develop because people come into contact with each other on a frequent basis: for example, neighbors in dorms or apartments. Others develop because of a strong **physical attraction** or because of similar interests, attitudes, or personality traits. And sometimes relationships develop between dissimilar people simply because they are different. Paradoxically, there seems to be some truth to both "Birds of a feather flock together" and "Opposites attract."

Similarities and Differences

An awareness of the importance of both similarities and differences is at the heart of understanding intercultural relationships. According to the **similarity principle,** we tend to be attracted to people whom we perceive to hold attitudes similar to ours in terms of politics, religion, personality, and so on.[11] And there is evidence that this principle holds for many cultural groups.[12] Finding people who agree with our own beliefs confirms those beliefs. After all, if we like ourselves,

Pop Culture Spotlight

Could Hollywood be changing its tune in being more willing to show intercultural or interracial relationships? *ER, Grey's Anatomy, My Name is Earl, Lost,* and *Will & Grace* have all featured interracial couples. The movie *Hitch* featured Will Smith (African American) and Eva Mendez (Latina) as an interracial couple in the lead roles. (SOURCE: http://racerelations.about.com/od/raceinthemovies/a/ictvscreen.htm)

we should like others who share our views. Thus, individuals may explicitly seek partners who hold the same beliefs and values due to deep spiritual, moral, or religious convictions. For example, our student Christine, who is Greek Orthodox, has decided that she'll seek a marriage partner who shares her religious beliefs and values. Also, if we're friends with people who are like us, we can better predict their behavior than if they are different from us.

In addition, the similarity principle seems to reinforce itself. Not only do we like people we think are similar to us, but we also may think that people we like are more similar to us than they actually are. Similarity is based not on whether people actually are similar, but on the perceived (though not necessarily real) recognition or discovery of a similar trait. This process of discovery is crucial in developing relationships. In fact, when people think they're similar, they have higher expectations about future interactions.[13]

But we may also seek out people who have different personality traits and therefore provide balance, or **complementarity,** in the relationship. For example, an introverted individual may seek a more outgoing partner, or a spendthrift may be attracted to an individual who is more careful with money.

Some individuals are attracted to people simply because they have different cultural backgrounds. Intercultural relationships present intriguing opportunities to have new experiences and to learn new ways of looking at the world. And whether (and when) we seek out people who are different from or similar to ourselves may be due partly to our own experiences. For example, when Judith was in college, she wanted to socialize with international students because she was intrigued by their backgrounds and experiences. Growing up, Judith had had little opportunity to be with people who were different from her. By contrast, Tom sought out other Asian Americans when he was in college because he had had little prior opportunity to be around Asian Americans.

U.S. Americans tend to accept some relationships of complementarity more than others. For example, it's more acceptable to date international students than to date across class lines. So, intercultural relationships are characterized by both similarities and differences. Although we may be attracted initially by differences, some common ground or similarity must be established if the relationship is to develop, flourish, and be mutually satisfying over time.[14]

Cultural Differences in Relationships

Friendships   How are **friendships**—personal, nonromantic relationships with culture-specific overtones—formed? What are the characteristics of a friend? How do these notions vary across cultures? For some people, a friend is someone to see or talk with occasionally and someone to socialize with—go to lunch or a movie, discuss interests, and maybe share problems. These casual friendships may not last if one person moves away. But other people view friendship much more seriously. For these people, friendships take a long time to develop, include many obligations (perhaps lending money or doing favors), and last a lifetime. Some differences in relationship expectations can be seen in Table 9.1.

What Do You Think?

How would (or did) your family respond to your being in an intercultural romantic relationship? If you are the product of an intercultural relationship, do you think that would make your family more or less accepting?

TABLE 9.1 Some Interesting Cultural Variables in Relationships

Brazil: To be invited to a Brazilian's home is an honor. Guests are expected to stay for many hours rather than stop for a brief visit.

China: Face-saving is extremely important in China. Chinese always avoid embarrassing situations and help one another save face and retain self-respect.

France: When the French greet people, they tend to be formal. Titles such as Monsieur, Madame, and Mademoiselle are often used. If they know the person, they may give the traditional kiss by the cheek/air.

Spain: The Spanish often invite guests to their home out of courtesy. One should wait until the host insists to accept the invitation.

Germany: Germans tend to be formal. They do not use first names unless they know the person very well.

Egypt: Always use titles such as Doctor or Professor to address people.

Kenya: The Kenyans socialize at the end of the meal, not before the meal.

Greece: Avoid overpraising any item in a Greek home because the host may feel obligated to present it as a gift later.

Source: Selling Destinations: Geography for the Travel Professional, 4th ed., by M. Mancini, 2003, Clifton Park, NY: Thomson/Delmar Learning.

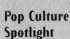

Pop Culture Spotlight

Author Zadie Smith writes about an enduring friendship between the families of a middle-aged, working-class, White Englishman named Archie and his best friend Samad, a Muslim Bengali immigrant, who are living in North London. *White Teeth* explores intercultural marriage and friendship in contemporary society, locating and weaving together postcolonial narratives of the Caribbean, India, and Britain. One of the characters in the novel, Irie, who is the daughter of Archie and his 19-year-old Jamaican wife, wishes for a time when "roots" no longer matter in relationships and society.

The term *friend* may have different meanings for different cultural groups. For example, in the United States, the term applies to many different kinds of relationships. In contrast, in India and in many other countries, the concept is defined more narrowly. Shyam, a student from India, described the difference between friendship in the United States and friendship in India:

[Americans] try to have a lot of friends; they don't meet the same people again and again all the time. . . . In India close friends are together most of the time, day after day after day hanging out together. My impression is, Americans probably don't do that; they try to meet different people.[15]

What most people in the world consider simply a friend is what U.S. Americans would consider a "close friend." A German student explained that in Germany one can hardly call somebody a friend even if he or she has known that person for over a year. Only if one has a "special emotional relationship" can he or she view that person as a friend.[16] For most U.S. Americans, the special emotional relationship would be reserved for a close friend.

Europeans are often amazed at the openness and informality of Americans and how quickly they can form friendships. In contrast, Europeans are not so quick to invite people into their home and do not necessarily introduce their friends to other friends. While in America, a friend of a friend is practically your own friend, Europeans see friendship as much more of an exclusive club.[17]

The upshot is that Americans often come across as forward, intrusive, and overbearing. They sometimes embarrass their European acquaintances by their openness and by how quickly they reveal things about themselves. As one Polish man visiting the United States observed:

> I discover I am learning many intimate details of the personal lives of the people I have just met. I find myself a bit embarrassed, but I doubt that they are. They become my friends so quickly, and as quickly they begin to share their problems with me. . . . In America, when one meets someone, he or she immediately becomes a friend.[18]

It's possible that this American informality and openness may drive Europeans to be even more reserved and distant. It might be better for Americans to give their European acquaintances more time to open up and initiate **intimacy,** and they should be careful not to interpret European reserve as lack of warmth.

Sometimes this openness and informality can be interpreted negatively. For example, international students in the United States often remark that U.S. American students seem superficial. That is, they welcome interactions with strangers and share information of a superficial nature—for example, when chatting at a party. When some international students experience these types of interactions, they assume that they have become "close" friends. But then they discover that the U.S. American students consider them to be merely acquaintances. A student from Singapore described her relationships with American students:

> I learned in the first couple months that people are warm yet cold. For example, I would find people saying "Hi" to me when I'm walking on campus or asking me how I am doing. It used to make me feel slighted that even as I made my greeting back to them, they are already a mile away. Then when real interaction occurs, for example, in class, somehow I sense that people tend to be very superficial and false. Yet they disclose a lot of information, for example, talking about personal relationships, which I wasn't comfortable with. I used to think that because of such self-disclosure, you would share a special relationship with the other person, but it's not so because the same person who was telling you about her personal relationship yesterday has no idea who you are today. Now I have learned to not be offended or feel slighted by such incidents.

The differences in the openness and informality of Americans compared to Europeans may have something to do with the different histories and geography. Early Americans had to reach out to people they didn't know, whether they wanted to or not; when people move to a new place, they don't have the luxury of keeping distant. For Europeans, whose populations are much denser and who have a history of invasions and wars from close neighbors, a certain caution and formality seems understandable.[19]

There are also both similarities and differences between Japanese and U.S. American students with regard to friendships.[20] In general, young people in both countries seem to be attracted to people who are similar to them in some way, and they use the same words to describe characteristics of a friend: trust, respect, understanding, and sincerity. However, they give these characteristics different

Pop Culture Spotlight

Have you seen either the movie or the television show *The Odd Couple?* How does the friendship between Felix, the neat freak, and Oscar, the slob, resemble an intercultural friendship?

priority. For Japanese students, togetherness, trust, and warmth are the top characteristics; for U.S. American students, understanding, respect, and sincerity are most important. These preferences may reflect different cultural values: The Japanese value relational harmony and collectivism, whereas the U.S. Americans value honesty and individuality. For many U.S. Americans, relationships are based on and strengthened by honesty, even if the truth sometimes hurts. In general, Japanese college students seem to disclose less about themselves to friends than do Americans.[21]

Hispanic, Asian American, African American, and Anglo American students hold similar notions about two important characteristics of close friendship: trust and acceptance. However, whereas Latino/a, Asian American, and African American students report that it takes, on average, about a year to develop a close friendship, Anglo Americans report that it takes only a few months. And each group may emphasize a slightly different aspect of friendship. For example, Latinos/as emphasize relational support; Asian Americans emphasize a caring, positive exchange of ideas; African Americans emphasize respect and acceptance; and Anglo Americans emphasize recognizing the needs of individuals.[22]

Romantic Relationships   There are also similarities and differences in how **romantic relationships** are viewed in different cultures. In general, most cultures stress the importance of some degree of openness, involvement, shared nonverbal meanings, and relationship assessment in romantic relationships. However, there are some differences. In general, U.S. American students emphasize the importance of physical attraction, passion, love, and autonomy, reflecting a more individualistic orientation. Thus, togetherness is important as long as it doesn't interfere too much with one's own freedom. Practicing openness, talking things out, and retaining a strong sense of self are strategies for maintaining a healthy intimate relationship.

But many other cultural groups emphasize the acceptance of the potential partner by family members as more important than romantic or passionate love, reflecting a more collectivist orientation.[23] For example, our student Mark described the experience of meeting his fiancée Elea's Greek American parents for the first time:

> It was the inevitable "meeting the parents" that posed the greatest conflict in this relationship. At home, they spoke Greek, ate only Greek food, went to a Greek Orthodox church, and lived under traditional, conservative, old-country rules. In this meeting, what ended up causing difficulties for me was a cultural handicap in interpreting their messages. I could listen politely and answer respectfully, yet I could not understand their stories and how they related to me. I sensed they were probing for some key to my values and integrity. They asked questions about my intentions toward their daughter, my goals in life, and my family's background.
> I sensed that there were "right" and "wrong" answers, and I grew anxious without their cultural answer key.

Pop Culture Spotlight

In the film *A Bronx Tale*, an Italian American boy and an African American girl fall in love. Although their communities have a history of violent interactions, the young lovers still try to see each other. But as the boy becomes more deeply involved in his community's gang, learning the ropes and getting to know the people, he pulls back from the relationship. How do your intercultural relationships affect your connections with your own culture?

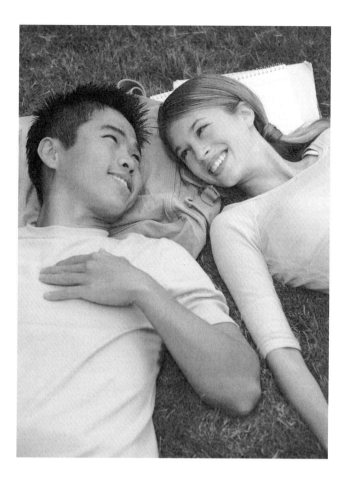

Intercultural relationships can provide a window into different ways of living and thinking. They can also lead to a sense of connection with others and help establish a lifelong pattern of communication across differences.

Mark went on to say that he was still learning about their culture and values: "Years into this relationship, I am continually developing a sense of the values, philosophies, and methods that drive the culture, the questions, and the stories of my parents-in-law."

The U.S. American emphasis on individual autonomy in relationships can be problematic. Trying to balance the needs of two "separate" individuals is not easy, and extreme individualism makes it difficult for either partner to justify sacrificing or giving more than he or she is receiving. All this leads to fundamental conflicts as partners try to reconcile the need for personal freedom with marital obligations. In fact, one study indicated that people with extremely individualistic orientations may experience less love, care, trust, and physical attraction with their partners in romantic relationships. These problems are less common in more collectively oriented societies.[24]

Gay Relationships   We have far more information about heterosexual friendships and romantic relationships than about **gay relationships,** or same-sex romantic relationships. But we do know that homosexuality has existed in every society and in every era. And while we in the United States tend to have fairly rigid categories ("heterosexual," "bisexual," "homosexual," and so on), cross-cultural and historical studies show a great deal of variety in how intimate human relations are carried on. For example, although sexual relations among the ancient Greeks occurred between persons of the same gender, there is no evidence that they were systematically differentiated from others or made into a uniform category. For another example, traditional Mojave Indians recognize gay individuals as being unique, "two spirit persons." A special ceremony in late childhood marks a transition into the third-gender role. The child is then recognized as a two spirit person, usually accepted by the parents who supported him. This acceptance of homosexuality was the product of a long cultural history that involved myth and ceremonial initiation.[25]

In many cultures, people engage in activities that would be considered homosexual in the contemporary United States, but are not regarded as such in their culture. They may regard themselves as "straights" or just "human beings" who on occasion participate in gay encounters. They simply might be unwilling to identify themselves with a category term such as *homosexual*.

Gay relationships may be intracultural or intercultural. Although there are many similarities between gay and straight relationships, they also differ in at least four ways: their views on intimacy, the role of sexuality, conflict management strategies, and the importance of close friendships. First, U. S. gay males tend to seek emotional support from same-sex friendships, whereas straight males, socialized toward less self-expression and emotional intimacy, turn to women for emotional support—often a wife or female romantic partner, rather than a same-sex friend.

This was not always the case in the United States. And in many countries today, male friendships are similar to romantic love relationships in that men feel free to reveal to their male friends their deepest feelings and may show physical affection by holding hands. In this instance, same-sex friendships and romantic love relationships may involve expectations of undying loyalty, devotion, and intense emotional gratification.[26] This seems to be true for men in gay relationships; they tend to seek emotional support from same-sex friendships.[27] But this does not seem to apply for straight women and lesbians. That is, both gay and straight women seek intimate friendships with women more than with men.

Second, the role of sexuality also may differ in heterosexual relationships and in gay friendships. In heterosexual relationships, friendship and sexual involvement typically are mutually exclusive; the sex thing always seems to "get in the way." Friendships between straight men and women can be ambiguous because of the sex thing. This ambiguity does not hold in gay relationships. Gay friendships often start with sexual attraction and involvement but persist even after sexual involvement is terminated.

Third, while relationship satisfaction is about the same for both straight and gay couples, there seem to be some differences in the area of conflict management. Overall, gay and lesbian couples seem to manage conflict better than

What Do You Think?

Propositions 8 in California and 101 in Arizona were passed in 2008, defining marriage in those states as a union between a man and a woman. Do you think this is going to lead to greater or lesser acceptance of gay relationships in those states? In the United States? Should gay couples have the same rights as straight couples?

straight couples. They use more affection and humor and fewer hostile emotional tactics during conflict, and they are more positive after a disagreement. They tend to emphasize power-sharing and fairness; their partners' positive comments have more impact on feeling good, while their negative comments are *less* likely to produce hurt feelings.[28]

Finally, close friendships may be more important for gay people than for straight people. Gay people often suffer discrimination and hostility from the straight world.[29] In addition, they often have strained relationships with their families. For these reasons, the social support they receive from friends in the gay community can play a special role. Sometimes friends fill in as family, as one young man explained:

> Friends become part of my extended family. A lot of us are estranged from our families because we're gay and our parents don't understand or don't want to understand. That's a separation there. I can't talk to them about my relationships. I don't go to them; I've finally learned my lesson: family is out. Now I've got a close circle of good friends that I can sit and talk to about anything. I learned to do without the family.[30]

In the United States, there is little legal recognition of permanent gay and lesbian relationships. At the time of this writing, only six states offer spousal rights to same-sex couples—Vermont, Connecticut, California, New Hampshire, New Jersey, and Oregon. Only Massachusetts issues marriage licenses to same-sex couples. Hawaii, Maine, Washington, and the District of Columbia offer some spousal rights for same-sex couples. Most U.S. states prohibit same-sex marriage.[31] The federal government has also passed the Defense of Marriage Act, which allows states to not recognize same-sex marriages registered in other states. These political and legal actions influence how gay and lesbian relationships develop and how they are terminated in the United States. When straight people end marriage relationships, there is often a delay, due to family and social pressures, religious beliefs, custody battles, and so on. However, some gay relationships probably terminate much more quickly, because they are not subject to these pressures. This also may mean that, even though they are shorter-lived, gay relationships are happier and more mutually productive.[32]

Some countries, however, do recognize same-sex relationships and so create a different environment for gay and lesbian relationships. For example, King Sihanouk has recently supported gay marriages in Cambodia.[33] In the Netherlands, Belgium, Spain, and Canada, gay and lesbian couples are allowed to marry with all the same legal rights and responsibilities as heterosexual marriage.[34] In many European countries (and also Australia and New Zealand) gay relationships are recognized as legal "partnerships"; in some of these countries (e.g., Denmark, Finland, Iceland, Norway, and Sweden) same-sex couples are provided rights similar to those enjoyed by married couples. In other countries (Czech Republic, France, Germany, Luxembourg, Norway, Sweden, and Switzerland) the rights of these partnerships are somewhat more restricted, pertaining to health and medical benefits and financial rights (tax status, inheritance).[35]

Surf's Up!

Erving Goffman argues that we present ourselves in terms of social roles, much like the roles an actor plays. We have different roles for different situations, and Goffman says that trying to keep them straight involves "impression management." Go to this website to learn more about Goffman's ideas: http://en.wikipedia.org/wiki/Impression_management. Do you ever have trouble keeping your different roles straight?

However, in many places in the world, the social contexts are much more problematic for gay partners in permanent relationships. Regardless of one's position on the desirability of gay and lesbian marriage, it is important to understand how society can influence same-sex relationships.

RELATIONSHIPS ACROSS DIFFERENCES

Communicating in Intercultural Relationships

Intercultural relationships among people from different cultures may be similar to intracultural relationships in many ways. But some unique themes related to issues of competence, similarity, involvement, and turning points can guide our thinking about communicating in these relationships.[36]

Competence   It is important to have language skills in intercultural interactions. Even when people speak the same language, they sometimes have language difficulties that can prevent the relationship from flourishing. There are four levels of intercultural communication competence: (1) unconscious incompetence, (2) conscious incompetence, (3) conscious competence, and (4) unconscious competence.[37]

Unconscious incompetence reflects a "be yourself" approach in which an individual is not conscious of cultural differences and does not see a need to act in any particular way. Sometimes this works. However, being ourselves works best in interactions with people who are very similar to us. In intercultural contexts, being ourselves often means that we're not very effective and we don't realize our ineptness. For example, a few years ago, high-ranking government officials from Rwanda visited an American university to participate in an agricultural project. The Americans dressed informally for the meeting and did not pay attention to the seating arrangement. In Rwanda, however, the seating arrangements in meetings indicate rank and are very important. Thus, the Rwandans were insulted by what they perceived to be rudeness on the part of the Americans, although they said nothing. The Americans, by "being themselves" and being oblivious to Rwandan cultural preferences, were unconsciously incompetent.

At the level of conscious incompetence, we realize that things may not be going very well in the interaction, but we're not sure why. Most of us have experienced intercultural interactions in which we felt that something wasn't quite right but we couldn't figure out what it was. For example, in the movie *Gung Ho*, Michael Keaton's character, trying to save a failing auto plant in the Midwest, travels to Japan to try to interest Japanese businessmen in a joint venture. He shows up late to the meeting, speaks informally, and makes jokes. The businessmen do not respond, sitting with stony expressions on their faces. Keaton's character realizes things aren't going well, but he doesn't recognize that he is insulting them by being so informal.

As instructors of intercultural communication, we teach at a conscious, intentional level. Our instruction focuses on analytic thinking and learning. This

Sharing a common goal or working on a common task, as these workers are doing, can help facilitate intercultural relationships. Sometimes intercultural alliances are formed when people share common interests, beliefs, and goals.

describes the level of conscious competence. Reaching this level is a necessary part of the process of becoming a competent communicator. However, reaching this level is necessary but not sufficient.

Unconscious competence is the level at which communication goes smoothly but is not a conscious process. You've probably heard of marathon runners "hitting the wall," or reaching the seeming limits of their endurance, and then, inexplicably, continuing to run past this point. Communication at the level of unconscious competence is like this. We cannot reach this level by consciously trying; rather, we achieve it when the analytic (conscious, rational) and holistic (unconscious, intuitive) parts of our brains are functioning together. When we concentrate too hard or get too analytic, things don't always go easier.

You've also probably had the experience of trying unsuccessfully to recall something, letting go of it, and then remembering it as soon as you're thinking about something else. This is what unconscious competence involves—being well prepared cognitively and attitudinally, but knowing when to "let go" and rely on your holistic cognitive processing.

Similarity While dissimilarity may account for an initial attraction between two people, it is very important to find and develop some similarity that transcends the cultural differences. For example, shared religious beliefs can help establish common bonds, as can shared interests in sports or other activities, or similar physical appearances, lifestyles, or attitudes.[38] When our student Jaclyn was 15, her family hosted a student from France for the summer. She automatically assumed that they wouldn't have anything in common and that the French student would be "uncool." However, Jaclyn was wrong, and they got to be good friends: "It turned out that we both liked the same music and the same groups. We both learned a lot about each other and each other's cultures. I even decided to start learning French. To this day we keep in touch through e-mail."

Involvement   All relationships take time to develop, but it is especially important to make time in intercultural relationships. This is one aspect of involvement. Intimacy of interaction is another element of involvement, as are shared friendship networks. Sharing the same friends is often more important for international students than the host country students because they have left their friends behind. Our student Dotty recalled introducing her friend Sung Rim to her other friends:

> I actually felt a little nervous about introducing my friends to her. I wasn't sure how well they would communicate with her. It was fine, though, and I think she felt at ease. She mostly just listened to the conversation. I could tell she was listening and trying to understand. We would try to talk slower so she could feel comfortable to participate and we made some plans to get together after finals. I would like to continue to really get to know her.

Turning Points   There are often significant events that relate to perceived changes in the relationship—turning points that move the relationship forward or backward. For example, asking a friend to do a favor or to share an activity might be a turning point. And if the other person refuses, the relationship may not develop beyond that point. Likewise, self-disclosure may reveal similarities and move a relationship to a new level. For example, in conversation, two professors found that they had similar ideas about communicating and teaching in the classroom. They also discovered that they both came from working-class families and that religion played a strong role in their childhood. But a turning point in their relationship came when one professor revealed that she was gay. Her friend recalled, "As a heterosexual I had never before given much thought to sexual orientation or gays 'coming out of the closet.' Thanks to Anna, I have become far more sensitive and enlightened."[39]

The process of dealing with differences, becoming involved by finding similarities, and moving beyond prejudice was summed up by a U.S. American student talking about her relationship with a Singaporean friend:

> We just had different expectations, different attitudes in the beginning, but at the end we were so close that we didn't have to talk about it. . . . After we erased all prejudices, that we thought the other person has to be different, after we erased that by talking, we just understood each other.[40]

Intercultural Dating

Intercultural dating involves the pursuit of an intercultural romantic relationship. Why do some people date interculturally and others not? The reasons people give for dating within and outside their own ethnic group are very similar: They are attracted to the other person, physically or sexually. However, the

Pop Culture Spotlight

On the show *Momma's Boy,* mothers help their sons choose a potential partner. Regarding who her son could date, JoJo Bojanowski's mom said, "I just can't see that white/black thing—I just can't have a black girl." She also went on to say that her son could not date a girl who is Jewish, Muslim, Asian, comes from a divorced home, or is anything other than White. The potential dates were outraged by what they perceived to be ignorant and racist comments. Watch JoJo's mom at: http://popwatch.ew .com/popwatch/2008/ 12/mommas-boys-the .html reasons people give for not dating someone within or outside their own ethnic group are often very different. One reason given for not dating someone within the ethnic group is lack of attraction; reasons given for not dating outside the ethnic group include not having an opportunity and not having thought about it.[41]

In one survey, 77% of those surveyed said it's all right for Blacks and Whites to date each other—up from 48% who felt this way in 1987. The young are the most accepting; 91% of the people questioned, who were born after 1976, said that interracial dating is acceptable—compared with 50% of the oldest generation.[42] This survey showed that attitudes are more tolerant, but do people's behaviors match their attitudes? The answer to this seems to depend on at least five different factors: gender, ethnicity, diversity of social environment, diversity of friendship network, and diversity of parents' friendships. First, most studies show that men are more likely than women to date interculturally—reflecting their greater power and ability to choose romantic partners. Males may also be less inclined to heed parents' disapproval. Second, people of color are more likely to date interethnically than Whites. Whites are the least likely to date outside their ethnic/racial group and Latinos/as are the most dated ethnic group. This probably reflects family and societal disapproval of black-white relationships and higher tolerance for other pairings (White–Latino/a, Latino/a–Black, Black–Asian, etc.).[43]

Third, people are more likely to date someone from another cultural group if they have contact with people from different cultures—if their neighborhood, schools, and churches are culturally diverse.[44] However, even more important is the diversity of friendship network, a fourth influence. That is, it isn't enough just to *be around* people who are culturally different—one must form friendships in order to develop romantic relationships. Friends may introduce you to potential romantic partners, and having their approval probably helps sustain the intercultural relationship. Having a diverse set of friends, then, is more important than being in a diverse environment in general.[45]

Having a diverse set of friends and romantic relationships may be difficult in some instances. Most people, by the time they reach adolescence, have been taught that it is better to date within one's own ethnic and racial group. This seems to be especially true for Whites and Blacks. A very recent national survey found that young white and black students who dated interracially were likely to encounter disapproval, ranging from very subtle to overt hostility from their peers—often from students of the same race. Whites and Blacks who dated Asian-Americans and Latinos did not encounter such disapproval.[46]

Parents play an important role in whether their children date interculturally.[47] A fifth influence on the decision to date interculturally is the ethnic diversity of parents' friends. It's possible that the initial decision to date interculturally may depend on one's friends. However, the decision to *continue* dating probably depends on the attitudes and, more important, on the *behavior* of one's parents. In other words, the deciding influence isn't whether parents are accepting of intercultural dating, but whether they have diverse friendships. It's not what the parents say that is influential, but what they do.[48]

Info Bites

Stanford University sociologist Michael Rosenfeld calculates that more than 7 percent of America's 59 million married couples in 2005 were interracial, compared to less than 2 percent in 1970. Did you know that until June 12, 1967, it was illegal in Virginia (and 13 other states) for Whites and Blacks to marry? The ban against miscegenation (interracial sexual relationships) was enforced in 30 U. S. states until the 1950s. It was challenged in Virginia by Mildred and Richard Loving who had been married in 1958 in Washington, DC, where interracial marriages were permitted. Upon their return to Virginia a group of police officers invaded their home in hopes of finding them in the act of sex. They were charged and sentenced to prison time, which would be suspended if they agreed to leave the state. They moved to Washington, DC, and in 1963 the ACLU filed a motion on their behalf. Finally, in 1967 the Supreme Court declared that Virginia's anti-miscegenation law was unconstitutional, thereby ending all race-based legal restrictions on marriage in the United States. (SOURCE: http://www.msnbc.msn.com/id/18090277/)

On the other hand, parents can pass on their negative attitudes about intercultural dating to their children. Women are particularly prone to pressure from parents. As one Latina woman said, "It would be hard to date interethnically because my parents wouldn't agree with it and neither would my [H]ispanic friends." A White woman expressed similar feelings: "It would be difficult for me to date someone of another ethnicity. Not because of any prejudices I have but because I come from a family that doesn't approve of that. My grandparents (on both sides) look down on dating other races and my father isn't too crazy about it."[49] The parents often reflect the general societal sentiment. And, indeed, a major reason people give (especially Whites) for not dating interethnically is negative social pressure.[50] Later in the chapter, we'll discuss the impact of societal influence on intercultural relationships.

Intercultural Marriage

There has been a steady increase in the number of intercultural marriages over the past 20 years, and the opposition to such marriages seems to be in a continuing decline, so much so that one scholar refers to it as a "love revolution."[51] In fact, more than one-fifth of all American adults say they have a close relative who married someone of a different race.[52] Blacks are twice as likely (37 percent) as Whites (17 percent) to have an immediate family member in an interracial marriage; Hispanics, at 27 percent, fall in the middle of these two groups. The most common type of interracial couple in 2000 was a White husband married to an Asian American wife.[53] However, not all intercultural marriages are accepted. While there seems to be little opposition to a German American marrying an Italian American, there is still some resistance to interreligious marriages. Some Jewish, Christian, and Muslim parents object to their children marrying outside their faith. Religion often plays an important role in decisions about intercultural dating and marriage. For example, studies have shown that more religious Christians tend to favor dating and marrying within one's own racial group.[54] Similarly, many Muslim-Americans feel the same, although it can be the source of conflict sometimes between first-generation and second-generation Muslim immigrants, as interracial marriages among second-generation Muslims are becoming increasingly common. As one young Muslim, Nora, describes it,

> It's so hard to marry [someone] of your same race. We're in America, we go to school with . . . different people our entire lives. And then parents . . . say . . . "I don't care if you've been friends with white, black, red, whatever, brown [Muslims]. Those are not people that you can fall in love with."[55]

However, the real division seems to lie in crossing racial lines. There is still a fair amount of resistance to interracial marriages, with Whites being the least accepting—at 52 percent approval, compared to 85 percent of Blacks who approve of interracial marriage.[56]

Robyn Preston-McGee, who is white, recounts her family's reaction to her marrying her husband who is African American:

> When my husband and I finally decided to take the plunge after dating for four years, we eloped. I think deep down we were worried about the "if anyone here can show just cause" part. My father's side of the family was horrified, my mother's tolerant, but not overjoyed. When my grandmother showed our wedding photo to a family member, they asked, "What nationality is he?" Perhaps they were hoping she would respond with the more exotic-sounding "Nigerian" or "Haitian." Nope. Just plain ol' African-American. My marriage and the subsequent birth of my daughter solidified my father's "disownership" of me. . . . All of this is not to whine about the opposition I've faced for marrying the person I married. . . . But when my white students, for example, joyously remark that "racism is a thing of the past," I ask them to consider how their own parents would react if they brought home a black person to marry. A flash of awareness comes across their faces . . . and I already know their answer.[57]

What are the major concerns of couples who marry interculturally? Their concerns, like those of dating couples, often involve dealing with pressures from their families and from society. In addition, intercultural couples face the issue of raising children. Sometimes these concerns are closely related. Although many couples are concerned with raising children and dealing with family pressures, those in intercultural marriages must deal with these issues to a greater extent. They are more likely to disagree about how to raise the children and to encounter opposition and resistance from their families about the marriage. They are also more likely to have problems related to values, eating and drinking habits, gender roles, attitudes regarding time, religion, place of residence, stress, and ethnocentrism.[58]

Of course, every husband and wife develop their own idiosyncratic way of relating to each other, but intercultural marriage poses consistent challenges. Most couples have their own systems for working out the power balance in their relationships, for deciding who gives and who takes. As shown in Table 9.2, there are four common styles of interaction in intercultural marriages: submission,

What Do You Think?

Are interreligious relationships intercultural relationships? Are they easier or harder to develop than interracial relationships? Does it depend on how important religious faith is to the people involved?

TABLE 9.2 Four Styles of Interaction in Intercultural Marriages

	Accept		
		Submission	Consensus
Partner		Compromise	
		Obliteration	Submission
	Ignore		Accept
		Self	

Adapted from Romano, D. (1997). *Intercultural marriage. Promises and pitfalls* (2nd ed.). Yarmouth, ME: Intercultural press.

There are many different definitions and meanings related to marriage relationships. For example, gay marriages are very controversial in the United States but they are legally recognized in other countries such as the Netherlands, Belgium, and parts of Canada.

compromise, obliteration, and consensus. Couples may adopt different styles depending on the context.

The **submission style**, the most common style, occurs when one partner accepts the culture of the other partner, abandoning or denying his or her own. The submission may occur only in public; in their private life, the relationship may be more balanced. But this style rarely works in the long run. People cannot erase their core cultural background, even though they may try.

With the **compromise style**, each partner gives up some parts of his or her culturally bound habits and beliefs to accommodate the other. Although this may seem fair, it really means that both people sacrifice important aspects of their life. For example, the Christian who gives up celebrating Christmas for the sake of a Jewish spouse may eventually come to resent the sacrifice.

With the **obliteration style**, both partners deal with differences by attempting to erase their individual cultures. They may form a new culture, with new beliefs and habits, especially if they live in a country that is home to neither of them. In fact, this might seem to be the only way for couples whose backgrounds are completely unreconcilable to survive. However, because it's difficult to be completely cut off from one's own cultural background, obliteration is not a particularly good long-term solution.

The style that is the most desirable, not surprisingly, is the **consensus style**, one based on agreement and negotiation. It is related to compromise in that both partners give and take, but it is not a tradeoff. It is a win–win proposition. Consensus may incorporate elements of the other models. Thus, on occasion, one spouse might temporarily "submit" to the other's culture. One of our Navajo (Diné) students described how she adapts somewhat to her husband's more traditional culture when his mother comes to visit by letting his mother cook breakfast.

> I am half Native American and half Irish. Though I was raised on the reservation, I attended school in town and was taught to try to adapt to the "outside" world. Because of this I was often accused of trying too hard to "be white."
>
> I never realized how drastic these differences were until after I got married. My husband, who is full Native American, grew up on an isolated reservation and in a home where his mother woke up at 6 each morning to make breakfast for the family.
>
> My husband got used to me not doing this and seemed OK with it, but the first time his parents came to visit, boy did I hear about it! His mom was so upset with me. We explained my point of view to her but it didn't really help. Whenever she comes over now, she gets up early and makes breakfast.

True consensus requires flexibility and negotiation.

The challenges can be especially difficult for the spouse who is living in the foreign country. The one who is speaking the other language may be put in a weaker position, especially during times of conflict.[59] A Belgian wife describes her frustration during times of conflict with her Finnish spouse:

> I get very angry and frustrated when I am trying to explain something and he doesn't understand me, or misunderstands me. Then I feel: how can you be so stupid. However, I know very well that the fault is in me, because I just can't say it so well, but still it makes me so furious that he doesn't understand me.[60]

This wife felt welcomed and excluded at the same time living in the home country of her spouse. It had an important impact on her self-concept and identity:

> In the beginning I felt accepted; people spoiled me and invited me with open arms. However, I have my frustrations to find my identity here. I often think back at what kind of person I had become if I would've stayed there. . . . I experience myself as an international person, as a citizen of the world. I don't really belong here, if I go back I don't belong there, but I belong enough here and enough there to be actually happy.[61]

Couples who are considering permanent intercultural relationships should prepare carefully for the commitment by living together, spending extended time with the partner's family, learning the partner's language, studying the partner's religion, and learning the partner's cuisine. For example, a student named Vicki dated and eventually married Hassan, a graduate student from Morocco. Before marrying, they spent time in Morocco with his family; Vicki even lived with his family for six months while Hassan was still in the States.

What Do You Think?

Nowadays, with the development of Internet and online chatting tools, people can form intercultural friendships or romantic relationships via the Internet. Some people argue that it is impossible to establish a meaningful relationship with somebody you only meet online, whereas others believe that online relationships are not that different and it is easier for you to "be yourself" online. What do you think?

They knew it was important for her to get to know his family and cultural background, as he had learned about her and the American culture. Couples who marry interculturally should also consider legal issues like citizenship, children's citizenship, finances and taxation, ownership of property, women's rights, divorce, and issues regarding death.

A recent study of intercultural marriages, some based on religious and some on ethnic/racial differences, found that these differences did indeed lead to conflict, but that communication played an important role in the success of these relationships. That is, open communication about the differences helped promote relationship growth. If partners were able to understand, appreciate, and integrate each other's similarities and differences, they would be able to use these in an enriching manner.[62]

Internet Relationships

Do intercultural relationships develop differently in computer mediated communication (CMC) contexts like the Internet? One might argue that there are aspects of CMC that are both a help and a hindrance in intercultural relationships. The Internet gives us the opportunity to communicate and develop relationships with people who are very different from ourselves. We can communicate with people in other countries as easily as talking to our next-door neighbors. One of our students, Mariana, described her experience of getting to know Charlotte, a Finnish student, during a virtual team project in one of her classes:

> Although we're separated by oceans and many miles, we share the same daily activities and understand each other quite well. What I enjoyed most about this experience was that even after this project Charlotte and I will be friends. We've already contacted each other on *Facebook* and sent messages. Besides focusing on the course project, I've gotten to know a lot about my partner's studies in school and her personal life.

A second way that CMC facilitates intercultural communication is that it can filter out much of the information we base first impressions on—physical attractiveness, gender, age, and race. While we may find it helpful to have information about people's characteristics, this information sometimes causes prejudice and discrimination. For example, when Mariana and Charlotte communicated during the class project, they didn't know each other's height, race, or age—unless they chose to tell each other. Our Internet interactions may be freer of the tendency to stereotype or discriminate against someone based on those physical characteristics. But can these relationships survive face-to-face meetings? The answer depends on whether one has engaged in honest self-disclosure, communicated one's "true self," and established solid commonality. Thus, an online relationship that is based on "mutual self-disclosure and common interests rather than superficial features such as physical attraction, provide[s] a more stable and durable basis for the relationship . . . [which] enables it to survive and flourish once those 'gates' do come into operation when partners meet in person."[63]

TABLE 9.3 Social Networking Sites (SNS) Growth by Worldwide Region*

	Unique Visitors		
	Jun-07	**Jun-08**	**Percent Change**
Worldwide	**464,437**	**580,510**	**25%**
Asia Pacific	162,738	200,555	23%
Europe	122,527	165,256	35%
North America	120,848	131,255	9%
Latin America	40,098	53,248	33%
Middle East–Africa	18,226	30,197	66%

*June 2008 vs. June 2007, Total Worldwide Audience, Age 15+, Home and Work Locations

Source: comScore Press Release (2008, August 12). Social Networking Explodes Worldwide as Sites Increase their Focus on Cultural Relevance. Retrieved February 18, 2009 from http://www.comscore.com/press/release.asp?press=2396

How does CMC impact existing relationships? Many of our friendships are now maintained through both online and offline interaction. For example, most Social Networking Sites (SNSs) like *Facebook* and *MySpace* are used to maintain existing offline relationships or solidify offline connections, as opposed to meeting new people.[64] As shown in Table 9.3, SNSs are popular all around the world. According to comScore, Inc., the total of worldwide SNS visitors in 2008 was almost 600,000; *Facebook* and *MySpace* are both marketing aggressively internationally. *Friendster* is popular in the Pacific; *Orkut* in Brazil and India; *Mixi* in Japan; *LunarStorm* in Sweden; *Grono* in Poland; *hi5* in many countries in Latin America, South America, and Europe; *Bebo* in the United Kingdom, New Zealand, and Australia; and *Cyworld* in Korea. Some SNSs are aimed at diverse audiences, while others function to connect people of similar language, racial, sexual, religious, or nationality-based identities and interests. Whatever the particular audience, they present endless opportunities to develop and maintain intercultural relationships.[65]

As we consider intercultural relationships in cyberspace, whether local or global, what are the aspects of CMC that make intercultural communication more difficult? For one thing, CMC filters out nonverbal cues (facial expressions, gestures, and so on) that help us interpret the tone of what the writer is saying (using sarcasm, jokes, and so forth). This filtering can present many possibilities for misunderstanding in an intercultural communication situation, particularly if one speaker is writing in a language that is not his or her first language. When humor is misunderstood, it often takes complicated explanations to clarify.[66] As one communication professor discovered:

> One of the students in my online course made a remark meant to be slightly sarcastic and humorous, about one of the group projects he was involved in for our course. However, the remark was perceived by some of

the international members of his group to be in poor taste. Some thought it very rude and insulting. Others just found it childish. It took almost half the semester to figure out what had gone wrong, why the remark was mis-understood and to get things back on a good footing. I can't imagine it would have taken even half that long if the interaction had been face to face instead of on the Internet.

Sometimes problems caused by language differences are exacerbated because one or both interactants may not be aware of the problem, since confusion or misunderstanding is generally shown nonverbally—by a quizzical look or a raised eyebrow. Online communicators may have to work a little harder to make sure they understand each other and to give the other some leeway in expressing dif-ferent cultural values and communication styles.

One CEO responsible for virtual teams reported misunderstandings between Israelis and U.S. Americans during e-mail exchanges. Americans thought the Israelis a bit rude and Israelis thought the Americans a bit superfi-cial. As it turns out, Israelis, whose speaking style is often characterized as very direct and low-context, found it odd that the Americans would add "niceties" to their e-mails like "Thanking you in advance for . . .," The Israelis responded "What are they thanking me for? I haven't done anything yet." After this was brought to their attention, all team members agreed to be more tolerant and to accept this small cultural difference in e-mail etiquette.[67]

In addition to misunderstanding due to lack of nonverbal cues, intercultural CMC can also lead to misunderstandings based on different contexts and forms for Internet usage. For example, in some countries people are charged by the minute for their Internet use, so their messages might naturally be shorter and to the point, leading some U.S. Americans to conclude that they are abrupt or rude.

Dating websites continue to flourish; according to one survey, 37 percent of single American Internet users who are looking for a romantic partner have gone to a dating website.[68] Some focus on bringing people together from specific religious backgrounds (e.g., JDate.com, for Jewish singles, CatholicMingle .com) or specific ethnic/racial groups (e.g., InterracialSingles.net, BlackSingles .com, LatinSinglesConnection.com). Sites like lavalifePRIME.com, BOOMj .com, and PrimeSingles.net are among those offering social networking for older singles. In one study, people around 40 years of age were the most active online daters, probably because it is relatively difficult for people of this age group to find a romantic partner using more traditional strategies.[69] Also, younger people are increasingly using *Facebook* and *Facebook's* new online dat-ing applications—Are You Interested and Meet New People—to find roman-tic partners.[70] As noted above, there are advantages to online relationships: you can meet more people, and first impressions are not based solely on physical attributes. But there are still some dangers—the user puts personal information in a relatively public place, and because of characteristics of the Internet—anonymity and filtering of cues—people can present false information about themselves (e.g., marital status, age, and even gender).

SOCIETY AND INTERCULTURAL RELATIONSHIPS

Finally, it is important to consider how society views and influences interpersonal relationships. Why do some people marry outside their racial or ethnic group more than others? For example, 50 percent of Native Americans marry outside their racial group, while only 25 percent of Asians do.[71] Of course, people marry outside their group for love. But in a racist society, one could argue, this "love" cannot be free from societal thinking. Therefore, these relationships can never be equal, because the partners will always be seen by themselves and by society as unequal.

For example, the official 2000 Census shows that Black men are 2.8 times more likely to marry outside their racial group—predominantly to White women—than Black women. Asian women are 2.4 times more likely to marry outside their group, predominantly to White men.[72]

These statistics reflect a great deal of frustration for African American women and Asian American men. The statistics also beg the question of why this is the case. Why do so few African American women and Asian men marry outside their racial group? One answer might be that society, the media, and individuals reinforce a negative image of both groups.

One young Taiwanese American who attended a dinner/discussion event, "Mating and Dating in the Asian American Community," said, "we're at the bottom of the pile, right along with black women." Lakshmi Chaudhry, an Indian American who attended the dinner, recounts:

> The rage among the men in that room was palpable as they spoke of a lifetime of sexual invisibility in a culture that constructs them as either effeminate or repulsive. . . . The sexual marketplace is a minefield for people of color. Our choice of bed partners is defined by a racial hierarchy that places Anglos squarely at the top. They determine who's hot and who's not. . . . Asian men, unfortunately don't cut it.[73]

And we can see how Hollywood movies reinforce this negative image by consistently pairing Asian women with Anglo men rather than Asian men. For example, in *Shanghai Knights*, actress Fann Wong is paired up with Owen Wilson instead of Jackie Chan, who is conveniently cast as her brother. As Chaudhry describes it, "Hollywood's message is unmistakable: No women for the Asian guy." Asian women have a better shot at connecting with Anglos, but it comes at a price. They are often stereotyped as exotic and expected to be deferring and serve White men. One of our Japanese graduate students recounted her experience in dating a White American:

> Everything went fine at the beginning. My English was not good, so he would help me with different things, and I thought that he was very nice and good to me. . . . When I didn't speak English well, he had the control in our relationship and he could manipulate information around me, for example, if his friends said something he didn't want me to understand, he didn't translate it for me and kept it secret from me. . . . [A]fter I started

understanding English and American culture more, I gained more power and he lost his power. When we were fighting, we were actually negotiating our power relation, and when it changed so significantly that the relationship was no longer worth it for either of us, our relationship was over.

Chaudhry summed up her feelings on the issue:

A chirpy white woman I once met at an airport lounge said to me, "I don't care about race when it comes to dating. It's all about chemistry." Smug in her liberal credentials, she didn't understand that color-blind attraction is a racial privilege. . . . [I]n a world still defined by racial division, there is no such thing as just plain old chemistry.

It is important to consider intercultural relationships within the society in which they develop. Because of societal pressures, interracial couples especially find that they have to develop strategies for dealing with the outside world. If they have internalized the negative images of the other group, they may feel like they're "sleeping with the enemy" or feel cut off from their own ethnic group. They may develop ways of ignoring those who see every problem as racial, and they may turn to each other for support and strength—seeing their home as a refuge from an often hostile society.[74]

How can society promote satisfying relationships between people from different cultures? Just putting people together is not the answer. Policies based on this notion, like busing to desegregate schools, have not resulted in desired outcomes. Another answer is the **contact hypothesis,** the notion that only under very specific conditions do intercultural contacts result in positive and tolerant attitudes toward the other groups.[75] While this contact hypothesis can be applied to intercultural contact in general, it is very useful in explaining patterns of interethnic dating and marriage. In the dating and marriage context, the contact hypothesis asserts that the chance for members of different groups to intermarry depends mainly on their opportunities to meet and interact socially—in cooperative (not competitive) situations, where members of both groups have equal status and hold common goals. In addition, knowing just one individual from another group as an acquaintance is not sufficient. Interracial tolerance occurs only when Blacks and Whites of equal status share a wide variety of contacts; when the contact is intimate, personal and friendly, and ideally involves several individuals of the other group. In other words, intercultural friendships and relationships occur when the conditions of encounter promote friendly interaction.

As a society, which institutions or contexts promote these types of opportunities for interracial contact? Neighborhoods? Educational institutions? Churches, synagogues, and other places of worship? The workplace? From very recent research, it appears that *integrated* religious institutions and educational institutions provide the best opportunities for intercultural friendships and the best environment to improve attitudes about interracial marriage.[76] For example, a study of six California State University campuses found that the students on these campuses interacted equally, in interracial and intraracial encounters.[77] These campuses are very diverse; no one ethnic or racial group is a majority. On the other hand, neighborhoods and workplaces do not seem to provide opportunities for the *kind* of contact (intimate, friendly, equal status interaction) that clearly facilitates intercultural friendships.[78]

SUMMARY

In this chapter, we discussed intercultural communication in relationships with people who are both similar to and different from ourselves. Through intercultural relationships, we can acquire specific and general knowledge beyond our local communities, break stereotypes, and acquire new skills. But developing relationships with people who are different from ourselves requires us to be motivated; to deal with differences in communication styles, values, and perceptions; to avoid the tendency to stereotype; to cope with the anxiety that sometimes accompanies these relationships; to try to confirm the other's cultural identity; and to explain to ourselves and others.

We also discussed the foundations of intercultural relationships and the cultural variations in how relationships develop. Two principles—similarities and differences—seem to operate for most people in most cultures, in that individuals are simultaneously drawn to the similarities and the differences of other people. Gay relationships are similar in many ways to heterosexual relationships, but they differ in some aspects. In gay relationships, friendship and sexual involvement are not mutually exclusive, as they tend to be for heterosexuals. Gay men seem to seek more emotional support from same-sex friends than heterosexual men do. Gay couples seem to manage conflict better than straight couples. Friendships may play a special role in gay relationships because the individuals often experience strained relationships with their families.

Finally, we described how communication in intercultural relationships involves issues of competence, involvement, and similarity and hinges on turning points. Intercultural dating and marriage, particularly in the United States, are still not very common and are often disapproved of by family and society. Computer mediated communication can both facilitate and hinder intercultural relationships. Society can influence our relationships in important ways, helping or hindering us in exploring and developing intercultural relationships.

BUILDING INTERCULTURAL SKILLS

1. Be aware of the complexities of communicating across cultures and of power issues. The goal is to find a way in which we can work toward unity based on "conscious coalition, of affinity, of political kinship," in which we all win.[79]

   Intercultural friends recognize and try to understand how ethnic, gender, and class differences lead to power differentials, and to manage these power issues. They also recognize that history is seen as more or less important by those who are more and those who are less powerful. Finally, they value differences and affirm others as members of culturally different groups.

2. Recognize the value of building coalitions. Coalitions can develop from the multiple identities of gender, sexual orientation, race, physical ability, region, religion, age, social class, and so on. Become involved in whatever way you can in your immediate spheres—of friendships and activities—and cultivate emotional interdependence with others.

3. Look to role models for how to be an effective agent of change. Perhaps you can find these role models in the lives of those around you or in literature or those who have gone before us. Be aware that it's easy to get overwhelmed and feel a sense of despair or powerlessness in working to improve things. Identify your strengths, and use them. Thus, if you're a parent, talk to your children about intercultural issues and building bridges and coalitions between cultural groups. If you have a job, talk to your coworkers. If you are an extrovert, use your people skills to gather others together for dialogues on cross-cultural awareness and understanding. If you are an employer, identify who is missing from your workforce. What are you doing about it?

ACTIVITY

1. *Intercultural relationships:* Think about all your friends, and make a list of those to whom you feel close. Identify any friends on the list who are from other cultures. Then answer the following questions, and discuss your answers with other class members.

   a. Do people generally have more friends from their own culture or from other cultures? Why?

   b. What are some of the benefits of forming intercultural friendships?

   c. In what ways are intercultural friendships different from or similar to friendships with people from the same culture?

   d. What are some reasons people might have for not forming intercultural friendships?

ENDNOTES

1. Brislin, R. W. (1983). The benefits of close intercultural relationships. In S. H. Irvine & J. W. Berry (Eds.), *Human assessment and cultural factors* (pp. 521–538). New York: Plenum.
2. Farrell, E. (2005, February 4). More students plan to work to help pay for college. *The Chronicle of Higher Education*, pp. A1, A34.
3. Clark-Ibanez, M. K., & Felmlee, D. (2004). Interethnic relationships: The role of social network diversity. *Journal of Marriage and Family, 66*, 229–245.
4. Allen, B. J. (2004). *Difference matters: Communicating social identity.* Long Grove, IL: Waveland Press.
5. Brislin (1983), pp. 521–528.
6. Stephan, W. G. (1999). *Reducing prejudice and stereotyping in schools.* New York: Teachers College Press.

7. Collier, M. J., & Bornman, E. (1999). Core symbols in South African intercultural friendships. *International Journal of Intercultural Relations, 23,* 133–156.
8. Chen, L. (2002). Communication in intercultural relationships. In W. B. Gudykunst & B. Mody (Eds.), *Handbook of international and intercultural communication* (2nd ed., pp. 241–257). Thousand Oaks, CA: Sage.
9. Pogrebin, L. C. (1992). The same and different: Crossing boundaries of color, culture, sexual preference, disability, and age. In W. B. Gudykunst & Y. Y. Kim (Eds.), *Readings on communicating with strangers* (pp. 318–336). New York: McGraw-Hill.
10. Pogrebin (1992), p. 318.
11. Byrne, D. (1971). *The attraction paradigm.* New York: Academic Press. See also Byrne, D., & Blaylock, B. (1963). Similarity and assumed similarity of attitudes between husbands and wives. *Journal of Abnormal and Social Psychology, 67,* 636–640.
12. Osbeck, L. M., & Moghaddam, F. M. (1997). Similarity and attraction among majority and minority groups in a multicultural context. *International Journal of Intercultural Relations, 21,* 113–123. See also Tan, D., & Singh, R. (1995). Attitudes and attraction. *Personality and Social Psychology Bulletin, 21,* 975–986.
13. Duck, S., & Barnes, M. K. (1992). Disagreeing about agreement: Reconciling differences about similarity. *Communication Monographs, 59,* 199–208. See also LaGaipa, J. J. (1987). Friendship expectations. In R. Burnett, P. McGee, & D. Clarke (Eds.), *Accounting for relationships* (pp. 134–157). London: Methuen.
14. Hatfield, E., & Rapson, R. L. (1992). Similarity and attraction in close relationships. *Communication Monographs, 59,* 209–212.
15. Gareis, E. (1995). *Intercultural friendship: A qualitative study.* Lanham, MD: University Press of America, p. 96.
16. Gareis (1995), p. 128.
17. Storti, C. (2001). *Old world, new world: Bridging cultural differences: Britain, France, Germany and the U.S.* Yarmouth, ME: Intercultural Press.
18. Storti (2001), p. 68
19. Storti (2001).
20. Barnlund, D. S. (1989). *Communication styles of Japanese and Americans: Images and reality.* Belmont, CA: Wadsworth.
21. Kito, M. (2005). Self-disclosure in romantic relationships and friendships among American Japanese college students. *Journal of Social Psychology, 14,* 127–140.
22. Collier, M. J. (1991). Conflict competence within African, Mexican and Anglo American friendships. In S. Ting-Toomey & F. Korzenny (Eds.), *Cross cultural interpersonal communication* (pp. 132–154). Newbury Park, CA: Sage. See also Collier, M. J. (1996). Communication competence problematics in ethnic friendships. *Communication Monographs, 63,* 314–346.
23. Gao, G. (1991). Stability of romantic relationships in China and the United States. In Ting-Toomey & Korzenny, pp. 99–115. See also Sprecher, S., Aron, A., Hatfield, E., Cortese, A., Potapova, E., & Levitskaya, A. (1994). Love: American style, Russian style, and Japanese style. *Personal Relationships, 1,* 349–369. And see Kito (2005).
24. Dion, K. K., & Dion, K. L. (1991). Psychological individualism and romantic love. *Journal of Social Behavior and Personality, 6,* 17–33. See also Dion, K. K., & Dion, K. L. (1993). Individualistic and collectivistic perspectives on gender and the cultural context of love and intimacy. *Journal of Social Issues, 49,* 53–59.
25. Herdt, G. (1997). *Same sex, different cultures: Exploring gay and lesbian lives.* Boulder, CO: Westview Press.
26. Hammond, D., & Jablow, A. (1987). Gilgamesh and the Sundance Kid: The myth of male friendship. In H. Brod (Ed.), *The making of masculinities: The new men's studies* (pp. 241–258). Boston: Allen & Unwin.
27. Nardi, P. (1999). *Gay men's friendships: Invincible communities.* Thousand Oaks, CA: Sage.
28. Gottman, J., & Levenson, R. (2004). 12-year study of gay & lesbian couples. Retrieved January 29, 2009 from http://www.gottman.com/research/gaylesbian/12yearstudy

29. Nakayama, T. K. (1998). Communication of heterosexism. In M. L. Hecht (Ed.), *Communication of prejudice* (pp. 112–121). Thousand Oaks, CA: Sage.

30. Nardi, P. M. (1992). That's what friends are for: Friends as family in the gay and lesbian community. In K. Plummer (Ed.), *Modern homosexualities: Fragments of lesbian and gay experience* (pp. 108–120). New York: Routledge.

31. Same-sex marriage, civil unions, and domestic partnerships (2009, February 18). The New York Times online. Retrieved February 18, 2009 from http://topics.nytimes.com/topics/reference/timestopics/subjects/s/same_sex_marriage/index.html

32. Patterson, C. (2000). Family relationships of lesbians and gay men. *Journal of Marriage and the Family, 62*, 1052–1069.

33. Cambodian king backs gay marriage. (2004, February 20). *BBC News*. Retrieved from http://news.bbc.co.uk/2/hi/asia-pacific/3505915.stm

34. Knox, N. (2005, August 11). Religion takes a back seat in Western Europe. *USA Today*, p. 01a.

35. Cole, D. (2001, July 31). Germany opens door to gay marriage. *Agence Presse*. Retrieved from http://www.gfn.com/archives/story.phtml?sid=9975. See also Fish, E. (2005). The road to recognition: A global perspective on gay marriage. *Harvard International Review, 27*, 32–35. And see ILGA Europe website, http://www.ilga-europe.org/europe/issues/marriage_and_partnership

36. Sudweeks, S., Gudykunst, W. B., Ting-Toomey, S., & Nishida, T. (1990). Developmental themes in Japanese–North American relationships. *International Journal of Intercultural Relations, 14*, 207–233.

37. Howell, W. S. (1982). *The empathic communicator.* Belmont, CA: Wadsworth.

38. Graham, M. A., Moeai, J., & Shizuru, L. S. (1985). Intercultural marriages: An intrareligious perspective. *International Journal of Intercultural Relations, 9*, 427–434.

39. Allen, B. J. (2004). Sapphire and Sappho: Allies in authenticity. In A. González, M. Houston, & V. Chen (Eds.), *Our voices: Essays in culture, ethnicity and communication* (4th ed., pp. 198–202). Los Angeles: Roxbury.

40. Quoted in Gareis (1995), p. 136.

41. Martin, J. N., Bradford, L. J., Drzewiecka, J. A., & Chitgopekar, A. S. (2003). Intercultural dating patterns among young white U.S. Americans: Have they changed in the past 20 years? *Howard Journal of Communications, 14*, 53–73.

42. Kreager, D. A. (2008). Guarded borders: Adolescent interracial romance and peer trouble at school. *Social Forces, 87*(2), 887–910; Levin, S., Taylor, P. L., & Caudle, E. (2007). Interethnic and interracial dating in college: A longitudinal study. *Journal of Social and Personal Relationships, 24*(3), 323–341.

43. Clark-Ibanez & Felmlee (2004); Moore, R. M. (2000). An exploratory study of interracial dating on a small college campus. *Sociological Viewpoints, 16*, 46–64.

44. Martin et al. (2003).

45. Clark-Ibanez & Felmlee (2004).

46. Kreager (2008).

47. Mills, J. K., Daly, J., Longmore, A., & Kilbride, G. (1995). A note on family acceptance involving interracial friendships and romantic relationships. *Journal of Psychology, 129*, 349–351; Moore (2000).

48. Clark-Ibanez & Felmlee (2004).

49. Clark-Ibanez & Felmlee (2004), p. 300.

50. Clark-Ibanez & Felmlee (2004).

51. Root, M. P. P. (2001). *Love's revolution: Interracial marriage.* Philadelphia: Temple University Press.

52. Lee, S. M., & Edmonston (2005). New marriages, new families: U.S. racial and Hispanic inter-marriage. *Population Bulletin, 60*(2).

53. Taylor, Funk, & Craighill (2006).

54. Yancey, G. (2008). Homogamy over the net: Using internet advertisements to discover who interracially dates. *Journal of Social and Personal Relationships, 24*(6); 913–940.

55. Grewal, Z. A. (2009). Marriage in colour: race, religion and spouse selection in four American mosques. *Ethnic and Racial Studies, 32*(2), 323–345.

56. Jacobson, C. K., & Johnson, B. R. (2006). Interracial friendship and African Americans' attitudes toward interracial marriage. *Journal of Black Studies, 36*, 570–584; Johnson, B. R., &

Jacobson, C. K. (2005). Context in contact: An examination of social settings on Whites' attitudes toward interracial marriage. *Journal of Social Psychology, 68,* 387–399.

57. Preston-McGee, R. (2008, September 30). Interracial marriage: Yes, it's still hard. Retrieved January 30, 2009 from http://www.alternet.org/sex/100981/interracial_marriage:_yes,_it's_still_hard/

58. Romano, D. (1997). *Intercultural marriage: Promises and pitfalls* (2nd ed.). Yarmouth, ME: Intercultural Press.

59. Cools, C. A. (2006). Relational communication in intercultural couples. *Language and Intercultural Communication, 6*(3&4), 262–274.

60. Cools (2006).

61. Cools (2006).

62. Reiter, M. J., & Gee, C. B. (2009). Open communication and partner support in intercultural and interfaith romantic relationship: A relational maintenance approach. *Journal of Social and Personal Relationships. 25*(4), 539–599.

63. McKenna, Green, & Gleason (2002), p. 24.

64. boyd, d. m., & Ellison, N. B. (2008). Social network sites: Definition, history, and scholarship. *Journal of Computer-Mediated Communication, 13*(1), 210–230; Ellison, N. B., Steinfeld, C., & Lampe, C. (2007). The benefits of Facebook "Friends": Social capital and college students' use of online social network sites. *Journal of Computer-Mediated Communication, 12*(4), 1143–1168.

65. boyd & Ellison (2008); Swartz, J. (2008, February 10). Social Networking Sites going global. USA Today online. Retrieved February 17, 2009 from http://www.usatoday.com/money/industries/technology/2008-02-10-social-networking-global_N.htm

66. St. Amant, K. (2002). When cultures and computers collide: Rethinking computer-mediated communication according to international and intercultural communication expectations. *Journal of Business and Technical Communication, 16,* 196–214.

67. Snyder, B. (2003, May). Teams that span time zones face new work rules. *Stanford Business.* Stanford Graduate School of Business website. Retrieved from http://www.gsb.stanford.edu/news/bmag/sbsm0305/feature_virtual_teams.shtml

68. Madden M., & Lenhart A. (2006). *Online dating.* Washington, DC: Pew Internet & American Life Project.

69. Facenda, V. L. (2008, March 31). Chemistry.com reinforces formula with $40M effort. *Brandweek,* 10644318, 49 (13), p. 17; Jayson, S. (2008, June 2). Singles find love after 45. *USA Today,* Life Section p. 01d. Retrieved December 6, 2008 from http://login.ezproxy1.lib.asu.edu/login?url=http://search.ebscohost.com.ezproxy1.lib.asu.edu/login.aspx?direct=true&db=aph&AN=J0E375610119608&site=ehost-live; Valkenburg, P. M., & Peter, J. (2007). Who visits online dating sites? Exploring some characteristics of online daters. *Cyberpsychology & Behavior, 10*(6), 849–852.

70. Krauss, A. (2008, February 20). Piggybacking on Facebook. The New York Times Online. Retrieved February 25, 2009 from http://query.nytimes.com/gst/fullpage.html?res=9C05E6D81431F933A15751C0A96E9C8B63

71. Lind (2003, June 16).

72. Taylor, Funk, & Craighill (2006).

73. Chaudhry, L. (2003, February 3). Chemistry isn't color-blind. *AlterNet.org.* Retrieved from http://www.alternet.org/story.html?StoryID=15090

74. Foeman, A., & Nance, T. (2002). Building new cultures, reframing old images: Success strategies of interracial couples. *Howard Journal of Communications, 13,* 237–249.

75. Pettigrew, T. F. (1998). Intergroup contact theory. *Annual Review of Psychology, 49,* 65–85.

76. Johnson & Jacobson (2005).

77. Cowan, G. (2005). Interracial interactions of racially diverse university campuses. *Journal of Social Psychology, 14,* 49–63.

78. Johnson & Jacobson (2005).

79. Kivel, P. (1996). *Uprooting racism; How White people can work for racial justice.* Gabriola Island, British Columbia: New Society, pp. 204–205.

CHAPTER TEN

Intercultural Communication in Tourism Contexts

STUDY OBJECTIVES

After reading this chapter, you should be able to:

1. Describe variations in host attitudes toward tourists.

2. Identify and describe characteristics of tourist–host encounters.

3. Describe ways in which tourists can learn about the cultures they visit.

4. Understand the various communication challenges that tourists encounter.

5. Identify cross-cultural differences in social norms and expectations encountered by tourists.

6. Understand the role culture shock might play in a tourism experience.

7. Describe the language challenges that tourists might face.

8. Understand how social and political contexts influence tourism encounters.

KEY TERMS

authenticity	retreatism
boundary maintenance	revitalization
eco-tourism	socially responsible
host	tourism
medical tourism	staged authenticity
resistance	tourist

Since the beginning of time, humans have been traveling in ever-widening patterns about the earth. From the days of early explorers, who traveled on foot and by boat, to modern roamers, who travel by car and plane, there has been an increase in travel and tourism. The World Tourism Organization estimates that almost 100 million people crossed international borders in 2008—more than 2 million a day. In fact, travel and tourism is one of the world's largest industries, generating almost $856 billion in 2007.[1]

Almost all of us have been tourists or will be someday. Being a tourist may involve travel to another region of the United States, like a visit to Disneyland or a trip to the Amana colonies in Iowa, or an international trip like those taken by many college students. It may involve a bus trip in Europe, visiting seven countries in seven days, or an **eco-tourism** cruise to remote areas in Australia or Indonesia that emphasizes appreciation for and conservation of the environment. One of the fastest growing types of tourism is **medical tourism;** thousands of people travel to places like Thailand, Indonesia, and Malaysia every year to take advantage of medical care at prices much lower than those in their home countries. For example, Alice Conway was with a tour group in Thailand when two people in their group needed medical attention. Alice reported that the medical care they received was efficient, of high quality, and relatively inexpensive. On arrival at Bangkok Adventist hospital, they discussed their problems with the English speaking hospital staff and, after a few tests, they were both treated—one for a minor ear condition and the other with a treatable case of salmonella (he was afraid he had malaria). While they did not travel to Thailand specifically for medical procedures, Alice reported:

> If Bangkok Adventist was any indication, it was easy to see why Thailand is a mecca of medical tourism. Aside from being one of the cleanest and most efficient hospitals any of us had ever been to, it was also one of the least expensive by far. The whole bill for a check up, lab tests, and meds at a world class hospital: less than $50.[2]

Another type of tourism is cultural and heritage tourism, which focuses on the arts, history, and unique cultural aspects of a location.[3] In this type of tourism, travelers experience rituals, festivals, and celebrations of local cultures (e.g., the annual Navajo Nation fair held every August in Window Rock, Arizona). Tourists soak up the history of a location by visiting battlefields, historic districts, reenactments of historical events, museums, and so on (e.g., Colonial Williamsburg in Virginia—the restored 18th-century town where museum workers in costume tell the stories of the men and women of the 18th-century city). For some, learning about the cultural and historical backgrounds of the peoples and places they visit enhances the enjoyment of their travels.[4]

Info Bites

Few places on earth can match Madagascar as an ecotourism destination. Almost 70 percent of Madagascar's animals are found only in this island nation, from the beautiful Parson's chameleon to the panda-like indri that perches in the treetops. Madagascar lies just off the east coast of Africa in the Indian Ocean, and traveling by air to get there does generate greenhouse gases. However, ecotourism trade benefits the environment and the economy in Madagascar where the government gives 50 percent of revenue to neighboring communities. The government there is in the middle of tripling the size of its national park system, which is just in time because ecotravel is growing three times as fast as the entire tourism industry. (Source: Walsh, B. (2008). Madagascar goes green. *Time, 172*(18). p. 70.)

TABLE 10.1 World's Top 10 Tourism Destinations in 2008

1. France	6. United Kingdom
2. Spain	7. Germany
3. United States	8. Ukraine
4. China	9. Turkey
5. Italy	10. Mexico

Source: Tourism Highlights, 2008 edition. Published by the UNWTO (World Tourism Organization). Retrieved February 9, 2009, from http://www.hotelnewsresource.com/pdf8/UNWTO123008.pdf

Table 10.1 shows the top 10 world tourist destinations in 2008. In any case, tourism contexts provide rich opportunities for intercultural encounters.

These encounters may be positive, as was our student Sarah's experience when she traveled to Italy with her senior class. She gained a great appreciation for the art and history of Italy and an admiration for the bilingual Italians she met. It was the first time she had been out of the country and didn't know what to expect:

> I remember getting off the plane and being in awe of my surroundings. During our two-week stay, we traveled to Rome, Venice, Assisi, and the Padua. I learned a lot about the Italian culture during those two weeks, but the one thing that stood out in my mind was that most of the Italians we met spoke English, while hardly any of us could speak Italian.

Some cultural groups desire only limited contact with the outside world, often restricted to business transactions. This is the case for many Mennonites and Amish. Here, a Mennonite girl sells cheese in Chihuahua, Mexico.

In contrast to Sarah's experience, some tourist encounters are tinged with resentment and power differentials, as in Charles's experience:

> I will never forget the trip I took with some of my work friends to Mexico. I remember crossing the border from the U.S. Nogales to Mexico's Nogales, and immediately being overtaken by the stark differences such as the changes in the quality of sidewalks as well as streets that seemed to be so close together. A couple of my friends seemed to take these visible differences as reinforcement of a belief that we were somehow better than the people that lived in the "Mexican" Nogales. It was night when we arrived and men with flyers and stuff to sell were everywhere. My friend John actually started making fun of the guys who were trying to give us flyers. He snatched the flyer and threw it back at the man, and that's when I saw the looks on the other Mexican men's faces. Even though we were here legally, the resentment in their eyes made me feel as if I were an illegal. As we turned the corner I heard one of the men grumble "Arrogant Americans." Had the men only pretended not to speak English to play into our stereotypes? Should we really have crossed the border in the first place—especially if we were only there to check out the Mexican clubs?

All of this has implications for intercultural communication. What are typical intercultural encounters in tourist contexts? How do cultural differences influence communication in these contexts? How do societal structures influence tourist encounters? How do politics and economic events impact tourist encounters? How can communication be improved in these contexts? These are some of the questions we'll be tackling in this chapter. First, we describe some tourist experiences that lead to particular kinds of host–tourist interaction. Then we discuss the communication challenges in tourist contexts and some of the societal impacts of tourism. Finally, we look at some skills that can help us communicate better in tourist contexts.

INTERCULTURAL COMMUNICATION AND TOURISM

Several different groups come into contact in tourism contexts—the tourists themselves, businesses/service providers in the host culture, and members of the host culture community. First, there are the **tourists**—the visitors to another region. Tourists may have different motivations for visiting. For example, history buffs might travel to Gettysburg, Pennsylvania, as a way to experience what they've read in history books. Culture-seekers who are fascinated by different ways of life might enjoy socializing and meeting new people, or they may want to seek out their own ethnic and cultural roots. Tourists could include religious pilgrims or people simply seeking recreation or adventure. A recent type of traveler is the ecotourist, who wishes to see and protect endangered species of flora or fauna. Finally, status-seekers are those tourists who want to travel to the most expensive and exotic

What Do You Think?

According to U.S. State Department statistics during the 2008 fiscal year, over 16 million Americans were issued valid U.S. passports (http://travel.state.gov/passport/services/stats/stats_890.html). However, Americans are often criticized for having little knowledge of other countries and limited travel experiences. Consider the following: (1) If you had the chance to give a short presentation about another country, which would you select? (2) What information about that country and people do you think would be important to highlight? (3) What does this scenario tell you about your understanding of nations outside the United States?

locations.[5] Tourists also come from a variety of socioeconomic backgrounds, from the college student backpacker on a limited budget to the status-seeker who travels first class. Second, there are the businesses/service providers. These are the people who serve in the tourist industry—hotel workers, tour guides, waiters, and so on. And finally, there is the **host,** or residents of the tourist region, and the host community may have varying attitudes toward the tourists.

Tourism can bring benefits to host communities; local businesses prosper because of tourism, and interaction with tourists can promote a sense of cultural pride and provide a window to the outside world for local residents.[6] However, there can be negative impacts as well, especially in small, less economically developed communities. Tourism can result in increased crime, traffic problems, disruption of family life, alcohol and drug problems, crime, and sexual promiscuity.[7] Many small Mexican beachfront communities have experienced these negative effects as thousands of people from the United States and Europe flood their towns each winter.

Another negative outcome of tourism occurs when cultural groups feel that they are merely products to be purchased by tourists—resulting in a loss of cultural traditions and damaged self-esteem.[8] For example, the Alarde fiesta in Fuenterrabia, Spain, was an annual celebration for 350 years until local officials decided that the celebration should be held twice a year—to attract more tourists. Residents quickly lost their passion for this cultural celebration and within only 2 years, insisted on being paid to participate because their former celebration was now an obligation.[9] For another example, when luxury tour groups and young travelers began visiting communities in rural New Guinea, the residents' cultural identity was negatively impacted; they began to see themselves through the tourists' eyes as "native," "backward," and uncivilized.[10]

In order to minimize these negative impacts, some tourism experts have proposed strategies that emphasize positive economic, social, cultural, and environmental impacts in the tourist industry—called **socially responsible tourism.** For people who manage and sell tourist experiences, it means providing rewarding holiday experiences for tourists while enabling local communities to enjoy a better quality of life and conserving the natural environment.[11] Many tourists support this move; in addition to simply enjoying travel, they want to learn more about the host country, meet local people, and reduce the environmental and social impact of their visit.

Attitudes of Hosts toward Tourists

Coping with tourists can be a complex process for people in host countries. The attitudes of residents may range from retreatism, to resistance, to boundary maintenance, to revitalization and adoption.[12] Some communities that are not enthusiastic about tourism may simply practice **retreatism,** or avoiding contact with tourists. This may occur especially in places where the economy has become dependent on tourism but the community feels invaded by tourists. The downside of tourism can include crowded streets, transportation, and shops. High demand during tourist season results in high prices of food and other items and can lead to overcharging of locals and tourists alike. Scarce resources like water and sanitation systems may come under pressure, and tourists may unknowingly insult local sensibilities. For example, locals in small Mediterranean villages are often shocked and feel violated by the scantily clad tourists who walk the streets of their conservative villages or go topless on their beaches. Or in one village in Greece, residents were appalled at visitors sleeping in their churches. "They went there with their sleeping bags, they used this holy place for camping. Now we keep all the churches locked during the summer and the keys are kept by a neighbor."[13]

This sense of invasion may result in locals finding ways to keep their everyday life hidden from the eyes of the tourists. They may go so far as to change the language or the dates of community events to ensure that these events are for locals only. For example, locals in Sardinia were advised to use the term *Sagra* rather than *Fiesta* in advertising their village festivals since fewer non-Italians would recognize the term *Sagra*. On the Greek island of Skyros, locals wait until the tourist buses leave the annual feast of their Saints before they celebrate the "real feast." They can then relax, eat, drink, and sing together, away from the curious eyes of the tourists.

Another example of retreatism happens in a small village in Norway, where residents complain that tourists feel free to walk into their yards and peer into their "quaint" houses. And in Malta, a local family discovered two German tourists peering into their home. This curious couple, who came to the village with a tour, simply opened the glass inner door and walked into the family's brightly lit front room. To cope with this and to protect their privacy, the family felt like they had to close the wooden outer door that was previously always left open.[14]

Similar situations occur when U.S. tourists visit American Indian reservations. They sometimes violate the pueblo residents' boundaries for personal space by touching them, or picking up residents' babies without permission. In addition, tourists are often impatient with American Indians' approach to time; in one instance, tourists complained about the length of a Hopi special event because they weren't able to complete their rushed tourist itinerary—revealing the clash between the Anglo value of efficiency with the Hopi commitment to a less linear, more "in the moment" approach to time.[15] When people feel so invaded, they may resort to forms of **resistance** to tourist intrusions. Resistance may take fairly passive forms like grumbling and gossiping about tourists or creating denigrating stereotypes about difficult tourists. For example, stereotypes about arrogant Germans, complaining Dutch, and stingy Swedes abound in many Mediterranean tourist locales.

Resistance can also include more assertive forms, as when Mexican resort staff occasionally pretend not to speak English to rude tourists or in mild harassment of female tourists. Making fun and using ridicule are also forms of resistance, as in this encounter between a tourist and an American Indian:

> A lady was examining the silver balls on a squash blossom necklace. She turned to Cippy Crazyhorse and in a slow, overemphasized fashion intended for someone who does not really understand English she asked "Are these hollow?" Cippy promptly replied "Hello" and warmly shook her hand. Again the lady asked "Are they hollow" pronouncing the words

What Do You Think?

James Clifford, in the essay "Traveling Cultures" (in *Cultural Studies*, Routledge, 1992), argues that when we travel we are involved in many more relationships than we might think—with maids, bellhops, guides, and so on. If you have traveled to other countries for vacations, what different kinds of people did you depend on that you were perhaps unaware of?

even more theatrically this time. Cippy cheerily responded with another "Hello." This went on a few more times, by which time everyone around was laughing, until eventually the lady herself saw the joke.[16]

When locals feel pushed beyond their limit by tourism, they may even resort to organized protest or even violence. For example, when locals on Skyros, a small Greek island, first encountered topless tourists sunbathing, they were appalled, called the police, and eventually designated one beach that would be used by topless tourists. Sometimes reactions can be even more dramatic and violent. In one incident, a French tourist was stoned to death by the villagers of San Juan Chamula in Chiapas, Mexico, for photographing their carnival. And in another case, a furious Navajo (Diné) man shot out the tires of a tourist's car when the tourist barged into his hogan to photograph his family eating there.[17]

Boundary maintenance to regulate the interaction between hosts and tourists is a common response among certain cultures within the United States, like the Amish, Hutterites, or Mennonites, that do not really desire a lot of interaction with tourists. The Amish in these communities may interact with tourists on a limited level, but they maintain a distance from outsiders and often will turn their backs to cameras. They take no pictures themselves and do not appreciate anyone photographing them. They base their objection on the second commandment in the Bible (Exodus 20:12: "Thou shalt not make unto thee any graven image . . ."). They learn to ignore or endure the tourists' gaze and the insulting photography, and to go on with their lives.[18]

In Lancaster County, Pennsylvania, where many Amish and Mennonites live, there are many commercial simulated cultural experiences, like "Amish Village" or "Amish Farm and Home," in which actors play Amish characters and educate tourists about Amish culture. In this way, a boundary is retained between the real Amish and the tourists. However, this boundary is breaking down somewhat as many Amish feel forced to leave their community. Due to escalating land values caused by development, many young Amish can no longer afford to buy or work farms when they marry and so cannot continue the tradition of Amish farming communities. Therefore, many Amish are leaving the Lancaster area and relocating where land is cheaper. Those who stay depend more and more on tourism and interact more directly with tourists—turning their homes into bed and breakfast inns and selling quilts, crafts, and Amish food.

A final response of host to tourists is **revitalization** and adoption. Some communities have been revitalized economically by embracing tourism—like colonial Williamsburg and many towns in New England that feature colonial architecture. Communities may decide to actively invest money to draw tourists or may be more passive, accepting the tourism but maintaining boundaries. Some communities wholeheartedly embrace tourism and welcome interaction with tourists, accepting tourism as part of their social and cultural fabric. For example, towns like Tombstone, Arizona, and seasonal beach and ski towns capitalize on tourism.

What Do You Think?

When we speak of vacationing or traveling, we often think of going out of the country, or at least to some resort location. Have you thought about what you can do in and around your state? The U.S. government has collected all of the states' tourism pages and put them in one location. Check it out at www.usa.gov/Citizen/Topics/Travel_Tourism/State_Tourism.shtml

By marketing their culture, local residents sometimes rediscover their own history and traditions and begin to realize their own worth. They may establish museums for tourists, and they learn about their own traditions. Or they may set up heritage parks, festivals, and handcraft markets that lead to preservation of the local culture. In some poor areas with declining populations, tourism can have the effect of revitalizing the area and halting the depopulation.

However, residents often do not share equally in the profits from revitalization and marketing of culture. In poor areas, the tourism potential is often first discovered and initiated by outsiders, who reap most of the profits, as is the case in Hawaii:

> [T]ourism has only brought the same kinds of low paying menial, dead-end jobs that have always been the lot of local workers. The setting of a luxury hotel may be worlds away from the sugar plantation, but in terms of the degradation and oppression of human labor, it is probably a good deal worse.[19]

Of course, there can be a variety of responses within the same community. There may be some residents who prefer to retreat and limit their interaction with tourists, while others may embrace tourism and welcome the visitors. This can cause conflicts in communication among community members.

Characteristics of Tourist-Host Encounters

Whatever the attitude of the host community toward the tourists, most intercultural contact between host and tourist is very limited. These interactions are short term and transitory, commercialized, and involve unbalanced power dynamics.[20] For example, consider Sena's tourist experience in Manipur, India. When she returned, she talked with her friends about the treatment of women in Manipur. She said that the women she met were more similar to Western women—in the clothing they wore and the jobs they had—compared with women in other parts of India. Her experiences with Manipuri women were, however, only surface level. If she had stayed longer and learned more about the culture, she might have discovered that although Manipuri women have some freedom socioeconomically and educationally, when it comes to decision making, an important responsibility, a woman's domain is confined to the domestic sphere.

As Sena's experience illustrates, most tourism encounters, by definition, are short term and transitory. Tourists rarely stay in one place for long and often have very little interaction with people in the host country. In fact, one writer observes that tourists on tour buses rolling through a country are really watching a silent movie, with the tour guide supplying the soundtrack.[21] This means that most contact between tourists and hosts or service providers will be quite brief, as in the preceding example. In these brief encounters, long-lasting impressions can be made based only on the tourists' anecdotal experiences. Since many tourists are in the host country for a limited time, they lack both knowledge of local customs and the motivation to gain a deep understanding of

Pop Culture Spotlight

When travel isn't possible, sometimes the next best thing is a movie. Have you ever noticed that locations in Hollywood films have the power to inspire travel? Consider such films as *Ocean's Eleven* (glitzy Las Vegas), *Memoirs of a Geisha* (Kyoto, Japan), *Lost in Translation* (Tokyo, Japan), and *Amélie* (Paris, France).

the culture. Therefore, their impressions are based on superficial knowledge and have the potential to perpetuate stereotypes or misperceptions.[22]

Second, most host–tourist interactions are commercialized. This commercializing of interpersonal relationships has had dramatic effect in some developing countries where generous hospitality is the norm; people often invite visitors, even strangers, for meals and to participate in community life. They may even offer gifts as part of the hospitality. With the development of a tourism industry, these goods and services that used to be part of people's personal and social lives are commercialized and offered as products to be bought by tourists.[23] So these brief, superficial interactions are predictable and ritualistic and offer few opportunities for tourists to engage in genuine social interactions with local people.

The final characteristic of tourist–host communication is the unbalanced nature of the interaction. First, host and tourist have very different views on the meaning of tourism. For tourists, "tourism" means playtime, a break from the normal work routine, a quest for novelty, and an escape from the mundane life at home. However, for many of the hosts whose jobs rely on tourism it can mean exhausting menial work, family stress, and the commercialization of their culture. Also, tourists, hosts, and service providers often have different socioeconomic backgrounds, with the tourists more economically and socially privileged than those with whom they interact. While the tourists may be disadvantaged in not knowing the local language, in general, they are in the privileged position of "buying" the hosts' services. Depending on the strength of the local economy, the locals' very survival may depend on the tourists' purchases. How does this imbalance affect communication between host and tourist? For one thing, those with less power in general often feel they have to accommodate to the more powerful.[24] For example, hosts must learn the tourists' language(s) or risk losing out on economic benefits; they might feel pressure to deliver the most desirable products and services. But perhaps most important, they may experience a feeling of being patronized, of not being recognized as on the same level with tourists—in all aspects of the tourist encounter, from the language they speak, to the way they are treated in the commercial transactions involving souvenirs, lodging, and other goods and services. However, many factors influence the imbalance between tourist and host. An interaction between a middle-class English businessperson on holiday in Spain with a local restaurant manager does not represent a huge power differential. However, the relationship is still unbalanced due to the commercial nature of the interaction.[25]

The extremes of these imbalanced relationships are represented in tourism in developing countries, or in previously colonized countries where the legacy of colonialism still lingers.[26] For example, one study of backpacking in Asia showed the tremendous power of Western backpackers. These backpackers determine which locations and communities will profit from tourism, and they make demands on locals to deliver the kind of experience they want in their backpacking adventure—often at the expense of the local backpackers' preferences.[27] Western backpackers are not necessarily interested in authentic relationships with people in countries they visit, but rather see them only as a group of people who happen to inhabit an exotic place they are "collecting." This kind of tourism can be seen as a type of "colonial" encounter with Third World people.[28] This can be seen in real-life conversation when you hear people ask travelers, "So how many countries have you been to?"[29]

The United Nations has focused on tourism as one way to address the severe economic imbalances in some developing countries (2.5 billion people live on less than US$2 a day). In 46 of the 49 least developed countries, foreign tourism is already one of the main sources of income. The United Nations STEP program (Sustainable Tourism, Eliminating Poverty), in cooperation with local governments, businesses, and communities, has identified more than 150 potential projects to boost tourism in 30 of the poorest countries.[30]

Given the economic imbalance of so many tourist encounters, when is contact between locals and tourists likely to result in more positive feelings and good communication between hosts and tourists? When is the outcome more likely to be negative? As you might expect, when tourists are friendly and respectful and demonstrate interest in a country and culture (beyond an interest in the beaches and recreational sites), local residents perceive tourists to be more like guests, develop pride in their culture, and are more likely to welcome interaction with tourists. Also, when tourists take opportunities for more extensive interaction with locals, there is the possibility of mutual understanding and even lasting friendships.

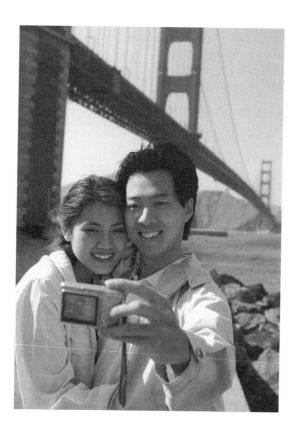

Interactions between tourists and members of the host culture often are superficial and transitory. Taking a picture of themselves in front of a tourist attraction, like this couple is doing, is a common tourist practice; however, interacting with U. S. Americans would reveal far more about U. S. culture.

On the other hand, when tourists visit historically unfriendly places (like U.S. Americans visiting the Middle East), have little prior knowledge of the culture, and have only superficial encounters with hosts, outcomes of tourist–host encounters are likely to result in negative attitudes and reinforced stereotypes. Negative outcomes are also more likely where there are major differences in religious or cultural values (for example, Western tourists in Muslim countries who violate norms of female modesty or prohibition of alcohol). In addition, economic differences can also lead to negative outcomes, as when rich tourists to developing countries display little regard for their hosts. This can lead to resentment and unwillingness to communicate on the part of hosts, and tourists then learn less about the host culture than they might have otherwise.[31]

Cultural Learning and Tourism

Some tourist–host encounters do go beyond the superficial confines of the tourist role. This may happen unexpectedly when sharing food, holding a long conversation, or simply participating in a meaningful slice of the local culture. A Canadian student described just such an incident:

> One of my best experiences occurred in Antilles, France, where we met a young Dutch couple. They were interested in getting to know us because we were Canadians. They were going to Monte Carlo the next day and asked us to go along. We squeezed into a tiny convertible Renault and spent a marvelous day visiting and learning about the country. Between Dutch, French, and English we managed to understand one another. It was a fantastic experience to get to know them.[32]

And one can learn something about the local culture even in a short time. As an Australian traveler writes: "My impression of England is that everywhere people seemed to be valued for their own sake rather than from a materialistic, functional point of view. There seemed to be less sex role differentiation than in Australia."[33]

However, as we suggested in Chapter 1 it is important to recognize that your opportunities for intercultural learning and what you learn may depend on your social and economic position in society. If you are middle class, you may be privileged to travel and experience new cultures and places in a way that others are not. At the same time, this recognition of privilege may not be always easy or comfortable. In traveling to developing countries, you may wonder if you are reproducing historical colonial economic relationships. How does this learning affect your communication in tourist–host encounters?

COMMUNICATION CHALLENGES IN TOURISM CONTEXTS

Being a student of intercultural communication in tourism contexts provides many interesting communication challenges, including the four described below: (1) searching for authenticity, (2) following the social norms and expectations of

What Do You Think?

Tourists often face challenges to their accepted cultural beliefs and ways of life. Have you considered the differences in attitudes about family, religion, and sexual orientation that might create real issues for those traveling and engaging in intercultural encounters? Consider the complexities of traveling for pleasure to places that are not safe spaces for lesbian, transgendered, transsexual, and gay tourists. What can we learn from news accounts of antigay protests and acts of violence such as the 2006 attack on two gay tourists in St. Martin? Two men who were traveling with a lesbian cruise company were beaten and hospitalized. The event sparked controversy between gay and lesbian rights' groups and St. Martin media outlets. (Source: http://travel2 .nytimes.com/2006/04/30/ travel/30transgays.html) the host country, (3) dealing with culture shock, and (4) rising to the challenges of a foreign language. Let's examine each of these challenges in turn.

The Search for Authenticity

The issue of **authenticity** is often a challenge in tourist–host encounters. Many tourists feel it is important that they experience the "real" cultural traditions of a visited community—not a simulated or a "Disneyfied" experience. They want a unique experience: something very different from their own mundane cultural life.[34] Host communities, then, sometimes feel they have to present the tourists with experiences that are exotic and appeal to tourists—sometimes requiring that they alter the reality of their everyday cultural life.[35] For example, residents of a local New Guinea community changed their cultural performances to conform to tourist expectations: they shortened their performances; scheduled performances at times when light was better for taking photographs; and modified their handicrafts so they were small enough for tourists to pack in their suitcases.[36] In other instances, locals change their dress and daily routines to appear more quaint, primitive, and authentic.

The challenge for host communities, especially those involved in cultural tourism, is to maintain a balance between presenting their cultural traditions in a way that maintains their value for the community, while still appealing to tourist tastes. The search for authenticity also involves challenges for the tourists. Tourists can mistakenly believe that they have seen the authentic culture—when in fact the locals have altered their cultural traditions in order to please tourists—presenting what some scholars call **staged authenticity**.[37] For example, consider the American Indians who perform their dances in traditional dress and sell their handiwork at tourist centers in the Midwest and Southwest. While the dances may be somewhat authentic, they are only a small part of the American Indian experience and the dress is worn only on special days. However, since many tourists see only this one aspect of the Indian culture, they may think they have seen how the Indians "really live" but in reality have very incomplete, and rather stereotypical, notions of the everyday lives of local Indians. Creating this staged authenticity for tourists can also have negative impacts on the host community members since they are forced to offer a representation of themselves that is not authentic.[38]

Unknowingly, the tourist's search for authenticity can create the very conditions that he or she was trying to avoid—an "inauthentic" cultural experience. So as a tourist, you might remind yourself that *all* societies evolve and change; no group (including your own) stays the same; and it is rather ethnocentric to prefer that others in less developed communities remain in a less technologically advanced and primitive state.[39] Another reminder is that local hosts are people just like you, meeting the challenges of everyday living and not historical objects, whose cultural life exists only for the tourists' pleasure and purchase.

Social Norms and Expectations

There are many cultural norms that have implications for intercultural communication between tourists and hosts. Some of the most relevant are norms about public social behavior, shopping, and communication style.

Comportment on the Street   As we saw in Chapter 6, norms regarding nonverbal behavior vary dramatically from culture to culture. And expectations about comportment in the street are no exception, ranging from very informal, as in the United States, to more formal, as in many countries. Sometimes the norms are related to religious beliefs and traditions, as with Muslims, Amish, and others whose religion dictates one's appearance.

Cultural norms also dictate how people interact with each other in public. In some cultures, strangers are expected to greet each other and interact in the streets. For example, in Egypt and many North African countries, there is a great deal of interaction in the streets, with shopkeepers greeting everyone and children interacting with strangers, especially tourists. In the United States, strangers may interact in some public contexts, such as in a line at a checkout counter, on an airplane, or at a sporting event. And people may smile at strangers. However, in some countries, such as those in Europe, there is much less smiling at strangers. In Japan, there is very little interaction, verbal or nonverbal, among strangers in public.[40]

Of course, the type of interaction that occurs in public depends on many things, including the size of the town and cultural expectations for male–female interaction. Our student Shannon described an experience she had when she and her mother were visiting Mexico:

Info Bites

Travelers visiting famous churches in Italy, like the Sistine Chapel in Rome or the Duomo in Florence, are required to dress in a certain way. Women must put on a dress, and men must wear pants. Guidebooks suggest that women carry around a lightweight dress in a backpack that they can quickly slip on over their more casual clothes.

> As we were walking along the streets, window shopping, several groups of men were whistling and shouting things at us. We were both extremely offended. As we were eating lunch, we asked our waiter about this. We wanted to know if they were being rude or making fun of us. He informed us that it was actually a compliment. The way we reacted was not productive, and we realized that we were just not accustomed to this.

This same kind of interaction is expected in many other cultures that value open appreciation of (mainly) women's appearance. French women comment that they feel invisible in the United States, that no one notices them, unlike in France, where appreciation is expressed more openly.

Shopping   Communication norms involved in shopping also vary from culture to culture. One shopping norm has to do with touching merchandise. In the United States, shoppers are expected to touch the merchandise and try on clothing before making a purchase. However, in many cultures, one does not touch merchandise and tries on clothing only if one is almost certain to buy. This is true in most countries in Europe. Similarly, in Japan, the relationship between customers and shop clerks is very businesslike. People speak only when necessary.

Many tourist groups depend on a tour guide while exploring unfamiliar lands. The tour guide becomes the "culture broker" for the group, interpreting the language, history, and cultural traditions of the host country.

Shop clerks say only "thank you" and customers don't talk with clerks except when ordering. However, in the United States, shop clerks are expected to talk with customers, starting with "How are you?" and "Did you find everything?" and so on. Sometimes customers even talk about their private lives with cashiers at grocery stores, which never happens in Japan.

A second shopping norm has to do with bargaining. Expectations about bargaining also vary from culture to culture. In most transactions in the United States, for example, the price for the merchandise is set and is not negotiated. However, in many countries, shoppers are expected to bargain; through the act of bargaining, people are connected. Some tourists find this very challenging and, given the differences in resources between tourist and host, confusing. Should one enter into the bargaining process as part of adapting to local customs, or should one simply pay the stated price, given the fact that the tourist often has more resources? A student visiting Mexico described this dilemma after she was approached by street vendors who seemed tired of what they were doing: "Their voices are weary of the effort to persuade. I feel uncomfortable and out of place in this environment. The uneasiness and suspicions concerning business relationships vie with my feelings about humanity. This lingers on with me and I am left confused."[41] We feel uncomfortable with our First World status only when we are confronted with another's poverty, which highlights the economic disparity between tourists and hosts.

Culture Shock

As we discussed in Chapter 4, being in new cultural contexts can often lead to culture shock and feelings of disorientation. Of course, sometimes tourists have so

What Do You Think?

What political implications does one have to consider before embarking on a trip to another country? Crossing the border to Mexico, many travelers are met by merchants who follow them down the street offering lower and lower prices for their products. In many other countries such as Haiti and Laos, the American dollar will "go a long way." What ethical considerations (such as exploitation) might you bring up in class about traveling to nations that do not have the same economic standing as the United States?

Some tourist experiences represent a prepackaged version of national or regional history, such as this reenactment of these 18th-century colonial activities—lace-making in Independence Mall in Philadelphia. How might colonial history be presented differently from the viewpoints of American Indians or slaves?

Pop Culture Spotlight

Movies are one vehicle by which we learn about intercultural travel. But movies obviously do not give us the big picture of another country and often portray the "exotic" in ways that make the film more exciting. Consider what movies such as *Mission Impossible 3,* the *Kill Bill* series, *Braveheart,* and the *Pirates of the Caribbean* series tell us (and don't tell us) about other places and people.

little contact with the host culture that there is little opportunity for culture shock. The degree of culture shock may also depend on how different the host culture is from the tourist's home culture. For example, when our student Jordan visited Canada with his grandparents, he experienced very little culture shock because the language was the same (they visited English-speaking areas of Canada). He experienced very little culture shock when he visited Austria with his church choir as well. The little sightseeing he did was by bus with other members of the choir and with an English-speaking tour guide. The group ate all its meals together and stayed in the same hotel. So he actually had very few intercultural encounters.

By contrast, when he visited Vietnam with his father, who had been there during the war, he experienced quite a big culture shock: "It was so hot, I couldn't understand a word that was said, and the food was strange. I thought it would be easier, since I had already been abroad before, but it was hard." Indeed, the physiological aspects of traveling can be troublesome for tourists. On short-term trips, one's body doesn't have the time to adjust to new climate conditions or new foods or eating customs. And feeling fatigued or under the weather often can affect communication with others.

Keep in mind that it is the tourist who is experiencing the culture shock; the problem is not the culture itself. However, tourists who experience culture shock often take it out on the host community. For example, they may get angry with servers for not serving food fast enough, or complain about the smells or sights, or take a prejudicial or patronizing attitude toward the local culture. This behavior also presents a challenge for members of the host culture. When presented with rude behavior, it is difficult for them to remember that the tourist who is complaining about the service actually may be expressing general frustration, may be suffering from culture shock, or may simply be fatigued.

Perhaps it is not just the tourist who experiences culture shock, for the host population can suffer the same shock. The encounters might be stressful for both because both tourist and host are being confronted with new values and behaviors and uncertainty. They are both required to accommodate, to some extent, the other group. Both hosts and tourists probably experience more shock when they have limited previous intercultural experience.[42]

Language Challenges

Language is often a problem for tourists. One cannot learn all the languages of cultures where one might visit in a lifetime, and it can be frustrating not to be able to understand what is being said. It is often part of culture shock. As our student Laura explained:

> When I went to Hermosillo, I definitely felt a huge dose of culture shock. I remember trying to talk to my host sister through the use of Spanish-English dictionaries and a bit of sign language. This experience was very tough. I remember trying to act friendly and saying "hello" to several Mexican students. They would look at me like I was crazy and often offer no response. I felt very stupid when I couldn't understand what people were saying while speaking Spanish.

The expectations of various host cultures regarding language also may differ. Sometimes tourists are expected to get along using the host language, but other cultures provide more language assistance for travelers. Our student April was 16 when she took a trip to France with a group from her high school, while a group of French students visited her hometown. It was not exactly an exchange program because they weren't touring each other's schools or community, but there would be one dinner with prominent townspeople in their respective communities. She recalled the experience:

> The first day we arrived, everyone spoke in English. We got to our hotel, and everything there had English writing. Since none of us spoke fluent French, an English speaker accompanied us, happily translating for us. I thought it was a wonderful trip.

However, when she got back home, she discovered that the French students had had quite a different experience:

> They were expected to know English, so nobody from my school district bothered to get an interpreter. They had to rely on the fluent English speakers of their own group to do even the most simple things like ride the bus. At the dinner my town hosted, the English-speaking French students had to interrupt their meal to translate to the other students. I am sure when they returned they could not have had many good things to say about my town.

Info Bites

How far will your money go in another country? Before you travel, you may want to familiarize yourself with the exchange rate and how much things cost in the country you will visit. Go to www.xe.com for a currency exchange calculator.

SOCIAL AND POLITICAL CONTEXTS OF TOURISM

We also need to consider the social, political, and environmental impacts on tourism. As the events of 9/11 attested, political events can impact the tourism industry dramatically. This terrorist act had far-reaching effects, including decline in profits for airlines, hotels, and other parts of the tourism industry; increases in security; and a fear of flying for many people. And the events did not affect just the United States; there was also a global downturn in international travel. Travel confidence was gradually restored, but it was further dented by terrorist attacks in Riyadh, Casablanca, Jakarta, and Mumbai in 2003, and in Mumbai again in 2008.

Political instability can have devastating consequences for tourism. For example, one of the seven wonders of the world, Victoria Falls—an awesome mile-long, 350 foot high falls—is now rarely seen by tourists in Zimbabwe, Africa. Not long ago, the hotels there were full and people were thriving. However, disputed elections, political violence, inflation of 231 million percent, and food shortages have resulted in fewer tourists and a huge drop in tourism revenue for the people there. On the other hand, Zambian towns on the other side of the falls (a less compelling view) have seen a sharp rise in tourism, and people there are thriving.[43]

Even the perception of political trouble can affect tourism. For example, the tourism industry in Pakistan has been severely affected by terrorism, as foreign countries and international airlines have branded Pakistan an "unsafe destination." The same is true for India, an important tourist destination for many, which had a long history of political stability. But after terrorist attacks on one of the leading tourist hotels in Mumbai, tourism plummeted.[44]

Economic downturns can also wreak havoc on tourism. The 2008 world economic crisis resulted in tourism coming to a standstill in many regions of the world. During tough times people tend to save their cash to cover the essentials (food, shelter, family necessities) and spend less on vacations and leisure travel. As oil and gas prices rise, airline travel becomes prohibitively expensive and people even forego long-car-ride vacations, taking different types of travel vacations—perhaps camping instead of staying at hotels or driving instead of flying. Some destinations may flourish in bad economic times. One county in Michigan hoped to profit from high gas prices in summer 2008. Muskegon, a county just outside Chicago, was hoping that Chicagoans would spend less money on gas and vacation at Muskegon's lakeside attractions rather than travel farther north to popular waterfront resorts.[45]

Different regions of the world are affected in different ways during economic downturns. Tourism in Europe and Asia was hardest hit in 2008, but some regions saw little downturn—some destinations in Latin America (notably Honduras, Nicaragua, Panama), Uruguay in South America, Republic of Korea, Indonesia, India, Egypt, Lebanon, Jordan, Morocco, and Turkey. Surprisingly, tourism remained strong in the Middle East, Africa, and the Americas. The tourism businesses that survive and thrive in economic downturns are those that can adapt.[46]

Many health experts are concerned about the possibility of a pandemic of bird flu. According to a 2009 World Health Organization report, this flu has now killed at least 254 people in more than 15 countries. So far most of the people who have contracted the disease have had direct contact with sick birds. There has been some human-to-human spread, but it has been vey limited and unsustained.[47] However, if the virus mutates to a strain that can be transmitted easily among humans, travelers crossing national borders will be in key positions to transmit the flu. Governments may have to close borders; people may stay home out of fear. According to the secretary-general of the UN World Tourism Organization, Francesco Frangialli, "Travel and tourism will be the [carrier] and the victim."[48]

We also need to mention the enormous effects of natural disasters on travel and tourism. In addition to the devastating loss of life and human suffering, the Asian tsunami in December 2004 and Hurricane Katrina in the southeastern United States in August 2005 caused widespread economic distress.

Prior to the hurricanes, 10 million tourists visited New Orleans each year and spent almost $5 billion. After the hurricanes, the tourism industry lost $15 million per day. Hotels and jobs were gone, and people left. Fortunately, the tourism industry has revived. According to a recent report, New Orleans saw 7.1 million visitors in 2007, and total tourism spending is back up to 2004 figures: $4.8 billion.[49]

More recently, a devastating earthquake in the Chinese province of Sichuan, in May 2008, left 88,000 dead or missing. The earthquake site has now become a tourist destination. As a sort of pilgrimage, people are visiting the town of Beichuan, where 15,000 people died, and city officials have decided to leave the town the way it is—with bodies untouched under the wreckage—as a memorial. The townspeople are turning to tourism as a way to get back on their economic feet. Disaster survivors set up stalls selling videos and photos of the disaster. Many used to work in a toy factory, but that is gone now and it's difficult to find jobs. One young tourist climbed over railings in high heels to pose for a photo in front of the devastation, saying that she wanted to take home photos to show her family, "I want a picture for a memento." Local officials hope that tourists like this will contribute at least 20 percent of the county's future GDP, up from 8 percent before the earthquake.[50]

While the travel industry concentrates primarily on the economic impacts of the industry, we should also explore the many implications for intercultural communication. These political, health, and economic events can lead to an atmosphere of fear of each other and fear of traveling to certain areas of the world, which can lead to a lack of opportunity for understanding and empathy for others.

SUMMARY

In this chapter, we addressed the intercultural communication issues that are relevant in tourist contexts. It's important to learn more about communication aspects of cross-cultural tourism encounters, especially given the increase in travel and the enormous amount of money spent on tourism each year.

We also described the various types of host attitudes toward tourists. Host communities may resist tourist encounters, retreat from them, maintain some

Surf's Up!

Today's traveler has a lot more to think about when deciding to travel for business or pleasure. Safety is becoming a major concern for anyone planning a trip overseas. Check out the U.S. State Department website, which publishes detailed safety protocols and tip sheets designed to assist travelers in facing issues of security abroad (http://travel.state.gov/travel/tips/brochures/brochures_1231.html). The site also includes links to safety advisories for specific countries. It might be interesting to look at the link "Tips for Travelers to the Middle East & North Africa." In thinking of the social and political contexts of tourism, how might you compare these tips to, for example, tips for avoiding buying phony souvenirs? What do these bits of information tell us about the importance of intercultural communication in today's world?

boundaries, or actively seek them out. Tourist–host encounters often are short term, commercialized, and involve an unequal power dynamic.

We identified some of the communication challenges in these encounters, including the search for authenticity, differing social norms, culture shock on the part of the tourist, and language issues. Finally, we explored some of the social, political, and environmental impacts on tourism like 9/11, the possible bird flu pandemic, the China earthquake, and Hurricane Katrina.

BUILDING INTERCULTURAL SKILLS

1. Gather knowledge about the culture that you would like to visit, even if you would be there for only a short time. Having some information about the places you are visiting communicates respect for the local culture and customs.

2. Learn a few words of the language—again, even if you visit for only a short time. Locals tend to respect the traveler who tries to communicate something in the local language. At least learn how to say "Please" and "Thank you."

3. Learn something about the local customs that may affect your communication. What are the local religious holidays? For example, Ramadhan, celebrated in many Muslim countries, falls on different days each year and is a time of fasting by day and feasting at night. In many Muslim countries, it is considered very impolite to eat in public during the day. Learn something about the social norms for public dress, behavior, and comportment.

4. Observe. Perhaps this is the primary skill to practice, especially for many Americans who are used to acting or speaking first when presented with ambiguous or unfamiliar situations. There's a piece of advice for travelers to Africa that could apply anywhere: "Keep quiet. Listen and observe behavior before offering an opinion."[51] As a Swahili proverb says, "Travel with open eyes and you will become a scholar."[52] This underscores the importance of observation before speaking. If you're not sure of appropriate behavior, observe others.

5. Practice staying flexible and tolerating ambiguity. In traveling, the cardinal rule is to be flexible. You often don't know exactly how things are going to turn out. Your communication in encounters with local people and service providers will always be more effective and enjoyable if you remain flexible.

6. Be reflective. If you take the time to learn about the cultural practices of the host community, you will also likely learn much about yourself and your culture. With this greater awareness of different and similar approaches to time, family, work, play, and interpersonal relationships, you are in a better position to interpret tourist encounters. Self-reflexivity also allows you to recognize the importance of your own "location" in the historical, geopolitical tourist context.

ACTIVITIES

1. *Tourist websites:* Go to various tourist websites (for example, www.visit.hawaii.org or www.visitmississippi.org or www.state.nj.us/travel). Analyze these sites for cultural aspects of their marketing strategies. For example, which cultural groups are they targeting? How many and which languages are available on these websites?

2. *Newspaper travel sections:* Go to the travel section in a Sunday newspaper. Read some of the travel advice or articles about other places. What kind of cultural information is presented? Who is the intended audience of the articles? How are the host communities portrayed? As welcoming tourists? As retreating from tourists? As maintaining boundaries?

ENDNOTES

1. World Tourism Highlights 2008. UN publication. Retrieved October 15, 2008 from http://www.unwto.org/facts/eng/highlights.htm

2. Conway, Alicia B. (2008, July 2). Boston Globe online. Medical Tourism. Retrieved January 31, 2009 from http://bostonglobe.longjaunt.com/photos/2008/07/02/medicaltourism/; Medical tourism remains robust despite economic gloom. (2009, January 30). Retrieved January 31, 2009 from http://www.bernama.com/bernama/v5/newsbusiness.php?id=386728

3. Richter, L. K. (2005). The politics of heritage tourism development. In G. Corsane (Ed.), *Heritage, museums and galleries: An introductory reader* (pp. 257–271). New York: Routledge; Timothy, D. J., & Boyd, S. W. (2003). *Heritage tourism.* London & New York: Prentice Hall.

4. Bean, S. R., & Martin, J. N. (2006). Touring culture(s): Intercultural communication principles and international tourism. In M. B. Hinner (Ed.), *FreibergerBeiträge zur interkulturellen und Wirtschaftskommunikation, Band 2* [A Forum for General and Intercultural Business Communication]. Frankfurt am Main, Germany: Peter Lang.

5. Mancini, M. (2004). *Selling destinations: Geography for the travel professional* (4th ed.). New York: Delmar Learning.

6. Smith, V. L., & Brent, M. (2001). *Hosts and guests revisited: Tourism issues of the 21st century.* Elmsford, NY: Cognizant Communication Corporation.

7. Kariel, G. H., & Kariel, P. E. (1982). Socio-cultural impacts of tourism: An example of the Austrian Alps. *Human Geography, 64*(1), 1–16; King, B., Pizam, A., & Milman, A. (1993). Social impacts of tourism: Host perceptions. *Annals of Tourism Research, 20,* 650–665.

8. Burns, P. (2004). Introduction: Tourism and social identities. *Tourism, Culture & Communication, 5,* 1–2.

9. Greenwood (1989), as discussed in Timothy & Boyd (2003).

10. Bruner, E. (1991). Transformation of self in tourism. *Annals of Tourism Research, 18,* 238–250.

11. *Responsible tourism handbook: A guide to good practice for tourism operators.* (2003). Greening the WSSD. Retrieved February 7, 2006, from http://www.eldis.org/fulltext/tourismhandbook.pdf

12. Boissevain, J. (1996). Introduction. In J. Boissevain (Ed.), *Coping with tourists: European reactions to mass tourism* (pp. 1–26). Providence, RI: Berghahn Books.

13. Zarkia, C. (1996). Philoxenia receiving tourists—but not guests—on a Greek island. In J. Boissevain (Ed.), *Coping with tourists: European reactions to mass tourism* (pp. 143–173). Providence, RI: Berghahn Books, p. 167.

14. Boissevain (1996), p. 8.

15. Hall, E. T. (1981). *Beyond culture.* Garden City, NY: Anchor Press; Laxson, J. D. (1991). How "we" see "them" tourism and Native Americans. *Annals of Tourism Research, 18,* 365–391.

16. Boissevain (1996), p. 15.

17. Boissevain (1996), p. 21.
18. Denlinger, M. (1993). *Real people: Amish and Mennonites in Lancaster County, Pennsylvania.* Scottdale, PA: Herald Press.
19. Kent, N. (1977). A new kind of sugar. In B. R. Finney & K. A. Watson (Eds.), *A new kind of sugar: Tourism in the Pacific.* Santa Cruz, CA: Center for South Pacific Studies, p. 182.
20. Bean & Martin (2006).
21. Leclerc, D., assistant professor, Department of Recreation, Management, and Tourism, Arizona State University, Tempe.
22. Ooi, C.-S. (2002). *Cultural tourism and tourism cultures: The business of mediating experiences in Copenhagen & Singapore.* Herndon, VA: Copenhagen Business School Press.
23. Berno, T. (1999). When a guest is a guest: Cook islanders' view of tourism. *Annals of Tourism Research, 26*(3), 656–675.
24. Allen, B. J. (2004). *Difference matters: Communicating social identity.* Long Grove, IL: Waveland Press.
25. Bean & Martin (2006).
26. Aitchison, C., MacLeod, N., & Shaw, S. (2000). *Leisure and tourism landscapes: Social and cultural geographies.* London: Routledge; Mowforth, M., & Munt, I. (1997). *Tourism and sustainability: New tourism in the Third World.* London: Routledge.
27. Teo, P., & Leong, S. (2006). A postcolonial analysis of backpacking. *Annals of Tourism Research, 33*, 109–131.
28. Pratt, M. (1992). *Imperial eyes: Travel writing and transculturation.* London: Routledge.
29. Bean & Martin (2006).
30. Sustainable Tourism—Eliminating Poverty. UN World Tourism Organization. Retrieved November 13, 2008 from http://www.unwto.org/step/about/en/step.php?op=1
31. Reisinger, Y., & Turner, L. W. (2003). Cross-cultural behavior in tourism. Oxford; Butterworth Heinemann.
32. Pearce, P. L. (1982). *The social psychology of tourist behavior.* New York: Pergamon Press, p. 127.
33. Pearce (1982), p. 134.
34. MacCannell, D. (1973). Staged authenticity: Arrangements of social space in tourist settings. *American Journal of Sociology, 79*(3), 589–603.
35. Timothy & Boyd (2003).
36. Bruner (1991).
37. MacCannell (1973.)
38. Bean & Martin (2006).
39. Sheperd, R. (2002). Commodification, culture and tourism. *Tourist Studies, 2*,(2), 183–201.
40. See Hall, E. T., & Hall, M. R. (1990). *Understanding cultural differences.* Yarmouth, ME: Intercultural Press. See also Barnlund, D. C. (1989). *Communication styles of Japanese and Americans: Images and reality.* Belmont, CA: Wadsworth.
41. From a student journal compiled by Jackson, R. M. (1992). *In Mexico: The autobiography of a program abroad.* Queretaro, Mexico: Comcen Ediciones, p. 73.
42. Reisinger & Turner (2003), p. 159.
43. Brulliard, K. (2009, January 31). Troubled Zimbabwe loses tourist bright spot. StarTribune.com. Retrieved February 5, 2009 from http://www.startribune.com/world/ 38722512.html?elr=KArksLckD8EQDUoaEyqyP4O:DW3ckUiD3aPc:_Yyc:aUUsZ
44. Ghauri, I. (2009, January 20). *Daily Times.* Terrorism severely affected tourism in Pakistan. Retrieved February 5, 2009 from http://www.dailytimes.com.pk/default.asp?page=2009% 5C01%5C20%5Cstory_20-1-2009_pg7_21; Moodie, M. (2008, November 27). Mumbai terrorist attacks and Thai political protests paralyse tourism sector. Retrieved February 9, 2009 from http://www.moodiereport.com/document.php?c_id=23&doc_id=19258
45. Alexander, D. (2008, May 25). Gas prices may help spark tourism here. Muskegon Chronicle online. Retrieved February 9, 2009 from http://blog.mlive.com/chronicle/2008/05/high_gas_ prices_may_help_spark.html
46. Beirman, D. (2008, October 15). Tourism and the Global Economic Crisis of 2008. ETurboNews. Retrieved February 5, 2009 from http://www.eturbonews.com/5604/ tourism-and-global-economic-crisis-2008; International Tourism challenged (2009, January 27).

World Tourism Organization press release. Retrieved February 5, 2009 from http://www.unwto.org/media/news/en/press_det.php?id=3481&idioma=E

47. Cumulative Number of Confirmed Human Cases of Avian Influenza A/(H5N1) Reported to WHO. (2009, February 5). Retrieved February 9, 2009 from http://www.who.int/csr/disease/avian_influenza/country/cases_table_2009_02_05/en/index.html; Key facts about Avian influenza. Centers for Disease Control. Retrieved February 9, 2009 from http://www.cdc.gov/flu/avian/gen-info/facts.htm

48. Haberkorn, J. (2006, April 13). Tourism industry ponders bird flu. *The Washington Times.* Retrieved from http://www.washingtontimes.com/business/20060412-091608-5731r.htm

49. New Orleans Tourism Industry Report (2008, August 29). Retrieved February 9, 2009 from http://www.neworleansonline.com/pr/releases/releases/Katrina3rdAnniversary_2ndQuarterTourismReportTWO.pdf

50. Lim, L. (2009, February 5). Tourists flock to quake-ravaged region of China. National Public Radio. Retrieved February 5, 2009 from http://www.npr.org/templates/story/story.php?storyId=98518404

51. Richmond, Y., & Gestrin, P. (1998). *Into Africa: Intercultural insights.* Yarmouth, ME: Intercultural Press, p. 227.

52. Richmond & Gestrin (1998), p. 227.

CHAPTER ELEVEN

Intercultural Communication and Business

CHAPTER OUTLINE

STUDY OBJECTIVES

After reading this chapter, you should be able to:

1. Describe how demographic changes influence intercultural communication in business contexts.

2. Identify and describe the role of power in intercultural business contexts.

3. Identify the primary work-related values.

4. Discuss how work-related values influence intercultural business encounters.

5. Discuss the role of language and communication style in intercultural business.

6. Give an example of how rules for business etiquette vary from culture to culture.

7. Understand how diversity, prejudice, and discrimination play out in various domestic and global business contexts.

8. Describe the impact of social and political events on business encounters.

KEY TERMS

affirmative action (AA)
Americans with
  Disabilities Act (ADA)
collectivist
equal employment
  opportunity (EEO)

facework
international negotiation
multinational

It is possible that for many people, particularly in the United States, the workplace presents the most opportunities for intercultural encounters. Indeed, the business context presents many opportunities and challenges for intercultural communication. Often the challenges are introduced by language differences. One of our students works in a bilingual (Spanish/English) company that recently changed health care providers. As a result, the many benefits changes (physician networks, benefits, copays, and so on) had to be communicated accurately to both English- and Spanish-speaking employees. Our student recounted the frustration of trying to ensure that all technical terms were communicated properly in both languages.

Sometimes cultural differences surface in the form of lack of knowledge and stereotyping, as Kaori, one of our graduate students, experienced when she worked for a Japanese American boss at a small company in the United States. Her boss was born and raised in the United States and never lived in Japan.

> One day, we had very important clients from Japan. As we got seated around the table, my boss offered them beer. Yes, beer, during the business meeting! They politely declined his offer, but he insisted that we had beer, saying he knows that Japanese people drink alcohol when they do business. I had no idea where he got that information from, but the Japanese businessmen didn't want beer, so we did not drink during the meeting.

Many of us actually have experience in dealing with cultural differences in a business context—perhaps from working in a restaurant with a multicultural kitchen and serving staff, or perhaps in a business that exports or communicates frequently with overseas clients and consumers. In this chapter, we address intercultural communication issues that arise in both domestic and international cultural settings.

THE DOMESTIC AND GLOBAL ECONOMY

Domestic Growth

As we noted in Chapter 1, there is increasing demographic diversity in the United States, and so the workforce is becoming increasingly diverse as well. The new workers will be older, more likely to be female, and more ethnically diverse than the current workforce.[1] According to recent reports, the Latino/a consumer market in the United States is actually as big or bigger than the GDP (gross domestic product) of Mexico or Canada, and the number of Latino/a-owned companies has been growing at three times the national average, producing nearly $222 billion in revenue.[2] The growth of both Black and Hispanic buying power is predicted to outpace that of Whites, which is projected to be 128 percent.[3]

What Do You Think?

If you had to guess, which companies do you think would be rated the most ethical and socially responsible? Starbucks, perhaps? Or maybe Whole Foods Market? Actually, neither of these companies ranks in the top 10 of *Business Ethics* magazine's "100 Best Corporate Citizens." Intel was number one in 2008, but also ranking in the top ten are Eaton, Nike, Bank of America Corp., and Deere and Co. What sorts of stakes do these high-tech companies have in social and environmental responsibility? Why should these big corporations care?

Businesses are also starting to realize the enormous buying power of people with disabilities as people with disabilities have discretionary spending power of $220 billion annually.[4] For example, improved advertising images and improved access to advertising by deaf people led to changes in consumer behavior. When closed captioning became widely available to deaf television viewers in 1980, 73 percent of deaf people switched to a brand that had television ad captioning. This is an important statistic, for according to government estimates, at least 23 million Americans have hearing impairments.[5] Of the 70 million families in the United States, more than 20 million have at least one member with a disability; with these numbers, advertisers are starting to understand how important it is to tap into that market.[6]

Women also have more buying power today than ever before, and as a group, they influence 80 percent of all vehicle purchases in the United States. In 2003, women spent about $55 billion of the $100 billion spent in the U.S. consumer electronics market. In fact, they initiate nearly 75 percent of electronics purchases on their own or with a spouse.[7] Women are playing an increasingly important role in business leadership. According to the Center for Women's Business Research, 10.1 million firms are owned by women (50 percent or more), employing more than 13 million people, and generating $1.9 trillion in sales as of 2008.[8] This increasing diversification in both the workplace and the consumer market has tremendous implications for intercultural communication.

Global Growth

As shown in Table 11.1, global markets (importers, exporters) are now more connected than ever. According to business experts, globalization used to mean that business expanded from richer countries to developing countries, but global businesses in

TABLE 11.1 The Top 10 Importer/Exporter Countries to the United States in 2007

International trade is very important to the U. S. economy. Note the countries to which the United States exports most of its goods and the countries from which it imports most of its goods.

EXPORTS TO:	EXPORTS FROM:
1. Canada	1. China
2. Mexico	2. Canada
3. China	3. Mexico
4. Japan	4. Japan
5. United Kingdom	5. Germany
6. Germany	6. United Kingdom
7. South Korea	7. South Korea
8. Netherlands	8. France
9. France	9. Venezuela
10. Taiwan	10. Taiwan

This abandoned customs building on the France-Belgium border shows how moving goods across borders has become easier due to the creation of the European Union.

many developing countries, like China and India, are growing rapidly. For example, a Chinese computer-maker (Lenovo) bought IBM's personal computer business in 2005; Lenovo had the right to use the IBM brand for five years but dropped it two years ahead of schedule, because Lenovo was so confident in its own brand. It had revenues of $16.8 billion in 2007. One of the Chinese computer innovations is an "express repair" button that recovers a computer system within 60 seconds of a crash, especially important in countries where energy sources are unreliable. Another example is Safaricom, Kenya's most popular cellphone company—it raised $800 million in the biggest IPO yet in sub-Saharan Africa in 2008. There is also the Tata Group, an Indian conglomerate, which paid Ford $2.3 billion for two car businesses: Jaguar and Land Rover. Inbev, a Brazilian beer giant, bought Anheuser-Busch in 2008 to become the world largest brewer. The interconnectedness of these global markets is also dramatically shown in the current global economic downturn. The housing slump in the United States is connected to the worldwide credit crisis, the declining value of the U.S. dollar, and fluctuating oil prices.[9]

As discussed in Chapter 1, a lot of debate exists about the pros and cons of the rampant globalization that is now occurring. However, one thing is certain: we have to agree with the authors of *Workforce 2020:* "The rest of the world matters to a degree that it never did in the past. We can no longer say anything sensible about the prospects for American workers if we consider only the U.S. economy. . . . Fast-growing Asian and Latin American economies present us with both opportunities and challenges."[10] The international market has become especially attractive as communication and transportation costs have plummeted; in the case of the Internet, the communication costs are almost zero. And in both domestic and international settings, intercultural encounters occur.

What Do You Think?

Did you know that there is a movement in certain parts of Africa, Asia, the Caribbean, and the United Kingdom to ban skin-whitening products? These products (often referred to as bleaching creams) are sometimes used to cover or clear away age or liver spots in North American cultures. However, in places like Japan, Thailand, and China, where pale skin is a symbol of beauty, there is a history of using substances like licorice and aloe vera to lighten the skin. In Africa and the Caribbean, many Black women attempt to lighten their skin to improve status, thinking that they appear less threatening or more attractive to the opposite sex. (SOURCE: A. Holloway, 2003, *Canadian Business, 76,* p. 72)

POWER ISSUES IN INTERCULTURAL BUSINESS ENCOUNTERS

Intercultural communication occurs in many different types of business settings, including domestic contexts with multicultural workforces and international contexts. Elements of power exist in almost every business encounter. Some power comes from political and economic strength. Consider the common practice of outsourcing American jobs to India. While we often see the benefits in cheaper products for U.S. Americans (along with the loss of jobs), we rarely consider the effects of this practice on Indian culture. And yet, as one of our Indian students explains, the pressure to meet expectations of powerful American **multinational** corporations has led some Indians to change their language and cultural practices:

> Just about 20 years ago in India there weren't many English schools. Now, call centers and other IT help desk jobs from U.S. American companies are fortifying a prospering Indian economy. As a result, people have started to put their kids in English schools rather than just native language schools. So many people now "proudly" say their kids don't read/write native language but they read/write English, American English. Any time you talk to a customer service representative in the U.S., there are good chances you are talking to someone in India.

He worries about the effect of these economic opportunities (and pressures), how they might change the cultures and languages of India:

> People in India believe that learning American English is necessary not only to get a job at the call center but also to succeed in life, to compete in the world and be a ready world citizen. Which to me somewhat makes sense but I worry about how my heritage will be carried on once everyone becomes "Americanized." There are nearly 118 languages and many dialects now spoken in India. I ponder how we will pass on a culture once we lose complete knowledge of it.

Intercultural communication occurs in encounters with superiors, subordinates, and peers, and with customers and clients. Power is also evident in these encounters. Although customers and workers come from diverse cultures, management ranks and boardrooms remain almost exclusively White male enclaves. These numbers reflect the relative power of these particular racial, ethnic, and gender groups in the U.S. In 2004:

> African-Americans made up about 13.8% of the U.S. workforce, but were just 6.5% of managers; Hispanics were 11.1% of the workforce and 5% of the managers. Whites, by contrast, made up 69% of the workforce, but 84.5% of managers and dominate even more among top managers. Just 7.9% of top earners at Fortune 500 companies are women.[11]

Those with the most privilege in business contexts may be unaware of the extent to which their positions afford them power. However, business experts suggest that truly effective leaders realize that in order to be successful in a diverse global marketplace, power needs to be shared. One such expert reported the following example:

> Take the experience of a CEO at Frito-Lay: After a white boss addressed a group of black managers—standing a few feet above them on some patio steps at the company headquarters—he received an email from a worker who compared the experience to being addressed by a slave owner on a plantation. Rather than dismiss or ignore the message, the boss took her comment to heart. He understood that employees from different backgrounds may have wide ranging associations and that in turn led him to the practice of having his top executives sponsor different employee affinity groups so they could become more attuned to the differences.[12]

As companies do more and more business around the world, top executives realize that diversity isn't simply a matter of doing what is fair or good public relations; it's a business imperative. They know they need a workforce that reflects the changing demographics of their customers. Rather than trying to hire a certain number of African Americans or Hispanics and then encouraging these groups to blend together and conceal their differences, they're trying to tap into the differences to capture new business and increase the bottom line. There's evidence that this diversity can pay off in profits. For example, in 2004 about one percentage point of Frito-Lay's profit came from new products inspired by diversity efforts: guacamole-flavored Doritos chips and Gatorade Xtreme, aimed at Hispanics; Mountain Dew Code Red, which appeals to African Americans; and a newly launched wasabi-flavored snack aimed at Asians.[13]

In addition, new businesses in developing countries are increasingly headed mostly by non-White men or women. In the Arab world, there's a misconception that women don't participate in the workplace. As one CEO said, "If you want to compete globally you have to understand that 80% of the globe isn't white and 50% isn't male."[14]

Power relations can also play out on a more interpersonal level. For example, Francine, a student of ours, described an intercultural encounter with the manager, who happened to be from Syria, of the health club where she worked: "He was very rude and disrespectful to me. He humiliated me in front of other members and refused to give me any information in order to contact the corporate office." She described how she tried to resolve the conflict, but she felt very dominated by the manager. She speculated that the root of the conflict might lie in cultural differences in communication style. He had a very forceful, expressive way of speaking, and she interpreted this very negatively, although it may have been perfectly appropriate conduct in his culture.

Communication across power divides can be very difficult, particularly when there is a cultural difference in how power is viewed or how power distance, as explained in Chapter 2, is expressed. Cultural groups that believe in high power distance feel that an organization functions best when differences in power are clearly marked. That is, bosses act like bosses and workers act like workers, and there is no confusion about which is which. For example, in the Indian workplace subordinates are to "defer to their boss, to always be polite and respectful, and never openly offend, challenge, correct, or otherwise disagree with their superior."[15] Francine may have been in a similar situation. Her boss may have been emphasizing the power difference between himself and Francine, expecting the same kind of deference from her.

By contrast, cultural groups that believe in low power distance (as in most U.S. contexts) feel that power differences, though very real, should be minimized and that an egalitarian view is best. For example, in the Icelandic workplace superiors are less autocratic and there is a friendly and relaxed atmosphere between superiors and subordinates. "Icelandic managers consult their superiors rather more than those in other low-power-distance countries, probably because they see them more as colleagues than as bosses."[16] In intercultural business situations, varying values concerning power dynamics and different behavioral expectations can result in communication challenges for bosses and subordinates alike.

COMMUNICATION CHALLENGES IN BUSINESS CONTEXTS

There is a lot of discussion recently whether rampant globalization is resulting in a global business culture where national cultural differences do not matter as much as they used to. Most experts conclude that this is not happening, that there are very few instances where culture does not matter at all.[17] In fact, communication challenges in business contexts can reflect cultural differences in work-related values, language issues, communication styles, and business etiquette, as well as issues related to diversity, prejudice, and discrimination.

Work-Related Values

Individualism versus Collectivism   One of the value differences that affects intercultural communication in business contexts is the distinction between individualism and collectivism. As discussed in Chapter 2, many cultures (such as most U.S. cultures) are individualistic, while others (such as many cultures in Asia and in Central and South America) are **collectivist**—that is, they place more importance on the individual in relation to groups. How does this difference play out in work situations?

In countries with individualistic views, workers are expected to perform certain functions with clearly defined responsibilities; a clear boundary exists between their job and another person's job. In collectivist countries like Japan, the opposite is true. That is, Japanese organizations do not necessarily define the precise job responsibilities assigned to each individual; rather, it's the job of a work unit, a section, or a department.[18] The same is true for many Latin

American and southern European cultures, as well as many Asian countries, like China and India, in which people are much more apt to help one another at work and to see less rigid lines between tasks.[19] These cultural differences in values can present challenges to workers and management. For example, Roberto, a manager from Colombia, has a high collectivist work and communication style. He encourages his subordinates to fill in for each other when they can, he tries to preserve the harmony of the work team, and he is careful not to criticize workers in front of their peers. He prefers to talk with them one on one in private or to communicate through a third person if there is a conflict situation. This style sometimes clashes with that of other managers, who have a more individualistic orientation. They think he is too lenient with his staff and sticks up for them too much.

There are some cultural groups, like the Greeks, for whom individualism in the workplace may be even more developed than in the United States. Thus, most Greeks strongly prefer not to work for a large company. About half the labor force is self-employed, and 90 percent of businesses have fewer than 10 employees. Greeks are not accustomed to working in teams—unless the team happens to be the family. Indeed, the concept of family often extends to the workplace. As one observer noted, "Greek managers sometimes use the term *nikokyris* to describe their job, which means that they see themselves as the head of the family, the one who takes care of family matters."[20]

These value differences are not always hard and fast; international business experts acknowledge that, with globalization, many of these differences are blurred. For example, young business workers in Asia and other parts of

Surf's Up!

Have you ever thought of owning your own business? This can be difficult for some. In particular, many women face challenges in getting key investors to take their ideas seriously. Woman Owned is an online resource and community that assists women in working through all of the steps of starting and owning a business. Check it out at www .womanowned.com.

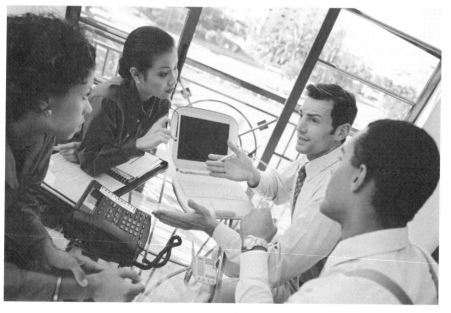

Working on projects in groups is very common in business settings. Although this diverse project group may have more cultural gaps to work through than a more homogeneous group, the potential benefits of diverse viewpoints are significant. What do the nonverbal cues tell you about this group's communication?

the world are blending traditionally collectivist practices with more individualistic beliefs.[21] As we have stressed throughout this book, it is important to always remember that cultures are complex and heterogeneous and that our cultural generalizations should always be open to change.

Work and Material Gain   Most Americans think that hard work is a virtue that will eventually pay off. To the people of many other cultures, however, work is a necessary burden. Australians, for example, admire the "bludger"—the person who appears to work hard while actually doing little.[22] Most Mexicans consider work a necessary evil, needed to earn enough money to live and, if possible, to have enough left over to enjoy the really important things in life: family and friends.[23] And some Europeans share the Mexican attitude toward work. A business consultant describes one Italian worker's impressions of Germans:

> He liked Germany, but found the Germans very *lineare*, meaning direct, purposeful, and efficient. *"Lineare"* is not a compliment. It characterizes a one-dimensional person, while Italians feel it is important to develop the whole person, not just the work side. I said I thought the Americans were probably just as bad as the Germans, but he shook his head and grinned. "Worse," he said, "much worse."[24]

Cultural groups that see work as having a low priority believe that, because work is necessary and takes up most of the daylight hours, ways should be found to make it more agreeable by creating a convivial workplace.

The different attitudes toward work can lead to intercultural communication conflicts in the workplace. This was the case when U.S. Americans, Japanese, and Saudi Arabians worked together on a major project in Tokyo. As one writer observed,

> When the American and Saudi managers went to Japan to meet with the Japanese engineers, the cross-cultural problems between the Saudis and Japanese were instant, dramatic and chronic. The Saudis stood too close, made intense eye contact and touched the Japanese. On top of that, the Saudis were enjoying Tokyo's sights. Their leisurely approach clashed with the Japanese work ethic—the Japanese concluded they weren't serious about the project. The tension escalated until Americans became the buffers between the Saudis and Japanese.[25]

Related to attitudes toward work is the variation in views toward business in general. Not everyone sees business as an academic subject. For example, the British don't quite accept that business is something a person would actually study the way one has to study subjects such as biology or statistics. According to the British, business is not a real field or profession, and one simply needs a few months to get the hang of it. While this has begun to change in the era of globalization, it is still an attitude held by some, particularly the upper class, who were taught that there is something vulgar about wealth. In 1996, while there were 80,000 MBAs graduating in the United States, Oxford awarded its first

Pop Culture Spotlight

The movie *WALL-E* takes place approximately 700 years in the future. It is about a cleaning robot whose purpose is to clean the earth, after the humans have left to live in space, because the earth has become "overrun with garbage and devoid of plant and animal life, the legacy of years of environmental degradation and thoughtless consumerism." Do you feel your behaviors and buying choices have consequences? Why or why not? (Source: http://www.imdb.com/title/tt0910970/synopsis)

Cultural norms regarding space and privacy in business contexts vary from culture to culture. How might this business space be set up differently if it were in the United States?

MBA degrees ever—to 49 graduates. As further evidence of this attitude toward business, the Oxford University administrators rejected a controversial $34 million gift from a Saudi entrepreneur to build a school of business.[26]

Quality versus Efficiency

Another conflict in work-related values is based on the relative value placed on quality versus efficiency and practicality. For most Americans, efficiency and getting the job done for the lowest cost are the ultimate goals. However, people in many different cultures hold different views. For example, the French are more interested in designing. There is a notion among the French that in business one should not worry so much about whether a product is competitive as long as it is well designed. They feel that if the product is well designed and elegant, it will be competitive.

Germans insist on quality, as both producers and consumers. Quality may come at a high price, but the German view is that people will pay for the best quality and that as a worker it's important to do the best job on principle. In German and American work settings, conflict can arise when Americans would rather produce something expediently than elegantly (or exquisitely).

These differences in priorities can lead to intercultural conflict. For example, Pam (an American) and Andre (a Frenchman) argue about whether to redesign an existing product or get it to market sooner in order to beat their competition. Andre insists that it is worth taking the time to make a sleeker, more elegant design. Pam appeals to profit motive, timeliness, and competence—not persuasive arguments in Andre's world.

Pop Culture Spotlight

Attitudes about the workplace vary from culture to culture and can vary even more from city to city or business to business. But sometimes it is possible to see how workplace experiences overlap within a culture, as many Americans seemed to empathize with the characters in the 1999 movie *Office Space*. The protagonists in the film confront the sometimes dull routines of U.S. corporate culture and parody the plight of workers whose 8-to-5 workday often consists of monotonous tasks they are forced to complete within the limits of a small office cubicle. One of the movie's biggest moments is when the major characters beat a malfunctioning fax machine to death out of frustration. The film is often seen as a metaphor for working-class lives.

One might explain these U.S. business values partly by the fact that the United States is a young country and that we have less appreciation for history and time. We feel pressured by time, because we don't think we have much of it, whereas for European businesses, 5 years is not long, and many European businesses routinely plan 10 and 20 years ahead. Also, U.S. Americans historically have placed more emphasis on the practical aspects of products. In the history of the European settlers, things had to be done expediently, and there was little time to tinker with perfection.[27]

Task versus Relationship Priority   A related value has to do with whether the highest priority is placed on relationships or on task completion. In most work contexts in the United States, the most important thing is to accomplish the task. It is not necessary to like the people one works with. However, in many cultures, work gets done because of relationships. This seems to be the case in China where personal relationships are vital for business success. The importance of personal relationships is such that there is a special term, *guanxi*, which means a personal bond or connection that goes beyond social and cultural connections. The Chinese do not differentiate business from friendship, so in order to be successful in business, personal relationships (*guanxi*) must be developed.[28] Cultural differences in task versus relationship priorities can cause much frustration in international work settings.

For example, as one of the top salespeople at his U.S. firm, Tom was asked to head up a presentation to a Latin American company. He arrived, ready to explain his objectives to the marketing rep sent to meet him at the airport. But the rep was continually changing the subject and asking personal questions about his family and his interests.

> [Tom] was informed that the meeting was arranged for several days later and his hosts hoped that he would be able to relax a little first and recover from his journey, perhaps see some sights and enjoy their hospitality. . . . During the next few days, Tom noticed that though they had said they wanted to discuss details of his presentation, they seemed to spend an inordinate amount of time on inconsequentials. This began to annoy Tom as he thought that the deal could have been closed several days earlier.[29]

This was a classic case of culture clash. Tom's top priority was to accomplish the task; his counterparts' top priority was to establish a good relationship so that the work could get accomplished. These different priorities also show up in the multicultural workplaces of the United States. Some people work better if they have a good relationship; others merely want to get the task done. Our student Karla observed this in her job:

> Currently, I work in a restaurant with many people who are from Mexico. After working with them, I have come to realize that they have very different attitudes about work from what I am used to. While teamwork is

always stressed at my job, these workers actually do look out for the best interests of one another. It is a great learning experience for me to work side by side with them and to learn about their work ethics.

Language Issues

Language issues can come into play in various ways in business contexts. One of our students, Robert, who worked for a cellular telephone company, described a language problem he experienced one day when he had two customers who spoke only Spanish:

> What I understood was that their cell phone was not working. I couldn't tell the exact problem because they didn't speak English. We both became very upset, since neither of us spoke the language of the other. I ended up having to get our Spanish customer service rep on the phone to help bridge the communication gap between the two of us. This was definitely productive, because we were able to figure out the problem and resolve the situation with little hassle from that point on. I was glad in the end that I could help, but was also very frustrated because I needed outside help. It was a very uneasy feeling: to stand face to face with someone and have no idea what they are talking about and not being able to communicate with them.

International business is sometimes conducted in English even when none of the participants speak English as a first language. For example, a recent study identified communication challenges faced by Icelandic companies doing business in Spain, France, and India.[30] The Icelanders conducted business in all three countries in English and each country's setting presented particular language challenges. In India, accent was a problem. Even though both Icelanders and Indians spoke English fluently, Icelanders have a Scandinavian accent and the Indians have different accents depending on their first language. (There are 18 official languages in India.)[31] Communicating with the Spanish and the French posed different challenges. Icelanders are less reticent about using English than their French and Spanish counterparts, because of the almost universal practice of studying foreign language in Icelandic schools. They found that their French and Spanish counterparts were often reluctant to explicitly discuss misunderstandings or problems that arose. If they did not understand something the Icelanders said, they would not immediately ask for clarification, but would carry on with the work (in some cases even avoiding the Icelanders); the language problem only became evident later, when projects were not completed on time or other difficulties arose. The Icelanders weren't sure if this reticence to speak up was because of their discomfort with speaking English, or because of a preference for a more indirect or high-context communication style.[32] This example also points to a common problem in intercultural communication—one cannot always be sure of the cause of the problem! Increasingly, international business travelers have to deal with a medley of languages.

What Do You Think?

In 1993, the U.S. National Basketball Association (NBA) included just five non-U.S. players. By 2008, however, there were 76 players from 31 different countries. How many of these players can you name? Taking into consideration the ways in which new technology allows for greater access to U.S. media, why might the NBA be reaching out to international players?

Many cultures emphasize the importance of building strong relationships in effective business endeavors. What do the nonverbal gestures and facial cues tell you about the relationships among these four businessmen?

The same can be true in domestic business situations. With the growing cultural diversity in the workplace comes linguistic diversity. To make working with a multilinguistic workforce easier, don't assume that, just because people are speaking a language other than English, they are talking about you. This may be a common reaction when those around us are speaking a language we don't understand, but it's egocentric and erroneous. Generally, people speak the language they feel most comfortable with. Laura, one of our students, experienced this firsthand:

> When I was working in a restaurant, I was constantly hearing my name being spoken in Spanish conversations. It was very frustrating to have people talking about me when I had no clue what they were saying. Finally, I was standing next to a friend who speaks both English and Spanish, and I heard my name again in conversation. When I asked my friend why people were always talking about me, he gave me a blank look. I told him one of the staff had just said my name. He laughed and said, "No, no, they said '*La hora*'" (per hour). We both had a good laugh, and now I know that wages, not me, are a popular subject.

A second suggestion in working with a multilinguistic workforce is to speak simple, but not simpleminded, English. A non-native speaker can better understand language that is spoken slowly and clearly, and that includes no big words. For example, use "letter" instead of "communication" and "soon" instead of "momentarily." However, don't be condescending in tone and don't raise your voice. In addition, don't crowd too much into one sentence, and pause between sentences. It's probably best to avoid slang and jargon and be careful with jokes.

Many times humor is based on puns and word play, which seldom translate into another language; what one culture considers funny, another might consider not funny, or even rude or crude. Finally, be culturally sensitive. The more you know about the cultures of others, the easier it will be for you to speak with a foreigner who knows only a little of your language. For example, just knowing that most Asians value formality and hierarchy would help you in interacting with Japanese or Chinese people, even if you only know a few words of their language.[33]

As more and more business interaction occurs online, it is worth considering special language issues in cyberspace. Some of the guidelines given above also work online (e.g., using simple language, avoiding jargon and jokes).[34] Additionally, communicating by e-mail may be preferred when there are language challenges, because it allows speakers the time to craft their messages and eliminates misunderstandings due to accent or other paralinguistic cues.[35]

Another potential language issue involves communication between deaf and hearing people. For example, Linda, a sales associate, is deaf in one ear. When customers ask her for assistance, she may not hear them, and they sometimes interpret her behavior negatively.

Communication Styles

Several elements of communication style, as introduced in Chapter 5, are especially relevant in business contexts. These include indirect versus direct, high versus low context, and honesty versus harmony.

Indirect versus Direct   Exchange of information is important in many work settings, especially when a problem exists and information is needed to solve it. People with a direct communication style simply ask for information from the appropriate person. However, a person with an indirect style might not feel comfortable giving the information, particularly when a problem exists and there is a need to save face. How do you obtain information when no one is speaking up? One way is to watch how others who are respected get information from one another and how they get it from you. Observe how subordinates, supervisors, and colleagues give and obtain information, since the approach may vary with an individual's status or relationship.[36]

In general, to have good intercultural business communication, people need to slow down and "sneak up" on information. Many Europeans don't get right to the point. For example, even at a business meeting in a restaurant, the French want to enjoy their dinner. Africans, too, are suspicious of U.S. American directness. In fact, in African business settings, intermediaries often are used to smooth business dealings. One foreign worker was puzzled when a Kenyan coworker complained to him at length about the behavior of someone outside the office. At first, the foreigner couldn't understand why his colleague was complaining so much about an outsider's behavior, but he eventually realized that the Kenyan was trying to explain indirectly what he should be doing.[37]

High/low context communication   Closely related to indirect/direct communication is the notion of high- and low-context style. As discussed in Chapter 5, low-context communicators (most U. S. Americans) prefer to make information very explicit—expressed in *words*. On the other hand, high-context communicators (many Asians and Africans) prefer to communicate more of the message *nonverbally* or *contextually*. This difference can result in challenging business encounters. Remember our earlier example of the Icelandic company with subsidiaries in France, Spain, and India? The Icelanders (mostly low-context communicators) ran into problems in communicating with the French, Spanish, and Indians. For example, the majority of the conversations between Icelandic and French employees were by phone which excludes most of the nonverbal (high-context) communication cues, such as hand gestures, facial expressions, and body movements. This lack of nonverbal cues was very challenging for the French, who prefer a high-context communication style. Moreover, most French people, like other high-context communicators, prefer to communicate face-to-face, believing that it is the best way to build a trusting relationship with people. In the Icelandic-French business venture, there were a lot of sensitive issues being dealt with (e.g. having to lay off employees, adopting a new computer system, and entering new markets) that required cooperation between the two cultural groups. The French found it difficult to build effective, trusting relationships with the Icelanders because of the lack of opportunities to communicate face-to-face.[38]

Honesty versus Harmony   Honesty is not always the best policy in intercultural business contexts, as noted in Chapter 5; form and social harmony may be more highly valued. For example,

> Koreans take considerable care not to disturb one's *kibun*, the sense of harmony or "wellness," in a person. They will hold back or delay or "adjust" bad news to avoid upsetting a person's *kibun*. This is not considered dishonest; the *kibun* takes priority over accuracy. It is rare for anyone to give bad news in the morning. No matter how urgent the matter may appear, the news is likely to be given in the afternoon, so the recipient can recover his *kibun* at home.[39]

Relational harmony is also important in China and, in fact, sets the standard for communicators. Communication scholar Wen Jia puts it this way:

> The kind of communication behavior best at creating and sustaining harmony is regarded as the most effective and most competent communication in Chinese culture.[40]

The focus here is not on truth, per se, but on achieving harmony. Achieving relational harmony in China and many other Asian countries includes the notion of **facework**, especially the importance of saving another's face. U. S. Americans tend to focus on saving their own face—maintaining self-pride, reputation, and credibility. However, for many Asians, the concept of saving face is more about interdependence, achieving *mutual* honor and respect, not focused just for the individual but for the larger group, the family, or organization.[41] In a business context, this may mean allowing other persons room to maneuver, and not saying the unvarnished truth.

As one experienced businessman said, "Everywhere you go, except in Europe and Australia, people will tell you what they think you want to hear." This means that if you ask people for directions and they don't know the way, they will give you directions anyway simply to make you happy. Thus, in these contexts, you need to ask questions in such a way that the other person can't really figure out what you want to hear. Even better, you need to engage the other person in a conversation such that the information you need simply "falls out."

There are also cultural variations in how truth is defined. In many businesses in Asia, there are a number of behaviors that would be considered acceptable everyday practices, whereas in the United States they would be regarded as deceptive, perhaps even unethical. For example, Japanese refiners signed a contract to buy sugar from Australia for $160 a ton, and when world prices dropped, they refused to pay. The Australians thought that "a deal is a deal." The Japanese, much more context-sensitive, thought that the changing circumstances allowed for changes in agreement.[42]

Business Etiquette

Business etiquette varies from culture to culture and is related to the differences in values and communication styles discussed previously. In general, most cultural groups tend to be more formal in business contexts than Americans are. For instance, most Europeans greet each other formally with a verbal greeting and a handshake. In fact, in Germany, as many as 20 minutes daily may be devoted to shaking hands, at the beginning of the day and again at the end.[43]

Similarly, Latin Americans attach great importance to courtesy. A well-mannered person is described as *muy educado* in Mexico, and a prescribed set of behaviors is expected in business settings, including ritual handshaking with and greeting of staff members each morning. The same is true in many African countries. There, high-level officials and business executives expect to be treated with the solemnity and respect due their position. Protocol must be observed; in many countries, at official dinners, no one eats or drinks until the higher-ranking people do, and no one leaves before the highest-ranking guests do so.

In general, when conducting business in most cultures, one should be very careful to avoid excessive familiarity, especially in initial meetings; this means no slouching, putting one's feet up on a desk, or lounging in general.[44] This emphasis on formality can extend to language use. For example, the formal form of "you" (*Usted*) is always used in business contexts in Spanish-speaking Central and South America, except with personal friends. And it is considered proper to address a person by his or her title.[45] The French also do not like informality, the use of first names, or anything that smacks of familiarity or lack of respect. In particular, they "object to hearty backslapping, joking or teasing behavior, or

Info Bites

How do U.S. corporations negotiate dealings with Chinese companies? In her 1999 book *Flexible Citizenship*, Aihwa Ong explains the relative difficulty non-Chinese businesspeople face as Chinese flows of capital are increasingly reliant on a system of "Chinese fraternity" throughout Greater China. How might non-Chinese businesspeople meet this challenge? (SOURCE: *Flexible Citizenship: The Cultural Logics of Transnationality,* by Aihwa Ong, 1999, Durham, NC: Duke University) any kind of phony chumminess."[46] This is also true in business settings in Francophone Africa, where language is more formal and flowery, and titles are necessary—for example, *Monsieur Ministre* or *Conseiller*, or *Monsieur le Directeur* or *Monsieur le Président*.

Etiquette is a traditional value that pervades French society, and business etiquette is symbolized by properly engraved business cards, giving a professional title and academic credentials. But the Japanese may have perfected business card etiquette. When people present cards to a Japanese business professional, they hold the card with both hands so that the other person can read it, and then bow and give their name. If they are presenting cards to several people, they start with the highest ranking. Similarly, in the People's Republic of China, when people receive someone else's card, they should use both hands, bowing and thanking the person for the opportunity to meet him or her. It is considered rude to put the card away immediately.[47] Business cards also are important in most African business settings, and the more elaborate the better; the fancy cards indicate that you want to stay in touch.[48]

International Negotiation

What happens when people from different national and ethnic cultures engage in business negotiations? Negotiating is a special communication task that occurs when business groups have both common interests in working together and conflicting interests which may prevent them from working together. Negotiation is the process of resolving the conflicts to a mutually satisfactory end.[49] There is abundant evidence that the cultural differences identified earlier (differences in work-related values, communication styles, and even business etiquette) have an impact on negotiation processes and outcomes. However, there are no comprehensive lists that identify all cultural patterns, and negotiators often find themselves relying on stereotypes and preliminary data. Here are some of the basic dimensions of **international negotiations** that may be impacted by cultural differences.[50]

Cultural groups may differ in their view of *the basic concept of the negotiation process*. Some cultural groups may view negotiation as one party gaining at the expense of the other, while others see it as a process where parties place different values on each of the issue being negotiated and can then find effective trade-offs with each other. For example, Chinese and Turks tend to see the negotiation process as a win-lose situation. Other countries, like the United States and Scandinavian countries, view it as a process of effective compromises.[51]

Cultural groups may differ in the *task or relationship priority*: either a focus on the specific project at hand, where negotiators spend most time exchanging information regarding various alternatives (relationship is considered unrelated to task), or a focus on the relationship between the two parties. Many cultural groups have the second priority—that good relationships between the parties are essential. Remember our earlier discussion of *guanxi*—the Chinese notion of connection or relationship-building? One of the foremost Western experts on

Chinese negotiating style, Lucian Pye (1992), noted early on the importance of relationships in negotiations with the Chinese: "The driving purpose behind much of Chinese negotiating tactics is the goal of creating a relationship, characterized as friendship, in which the American partner will feel strong and imprecisely limited bonds of obligation."[52] Once a business relationship is established, Chinese believe that the relationship is "on" even when negotiation isn't active. They are also thrown off sometimes by the North American practice of using lower-level people for preliminary discussion and then sending in top-level people to sign the contract.[53] This exaggerated sense of friendship obligations can be confusing and frustrating to U. S. American negotiators.[54]

However, it may be that U. S. American negotiators are recognizing how important relationships are to some cultural groups. In a recent study, researchers selected negotiators from four countries representing four major regions of the world (United States, Mexico, Finland, Turkey) and asked them about their priorities in international negotiations.[55] They found that negotiators from all four countries, including the United States, agreed that it was important to build trust and friendship with members of the other team. Both Turks and U. S. Americans thought it was also important to focus on task, while Finns were highly focused on building relationships.

There may be a *difference in the basis of trust*. One side may believe that the other party will fulfill obligations because of a signed contract (trust is external to relationship), or because of the relationship between the two parties (trust is internal to relationship). In the study mentioned above, both U. S. and Mexican negotiators thought that relationships were the basis for building trust. Again, the researchers suggest that this may reflect a growing emphasis in U. S. businesses on developing and maintaining long-term relationships with suppliers and customers.

Finally, there may be cultural differences in the *preferred form of agreement*. One side may prefer agreement based on formal written contracts while the other side may prefer an informal agreement based on the historical and social context of the relationships. Finally, all countries expect and depend on written agreements—so, one implication of the study findings is that negotiators should realize that the goals of a signed contract and of building a relationship are not necessarily mutually exclusive.

Intercultural Relationship Building

As we have seen, so many cultures emphasize the importance of relationships in effective business endeavors that a general guideline for intercultural business success might be: learn how to develop good relationships.[56] What are some suggestions for developing good communication and business relationships? A recent study asked this question of business managers in different countries around the world and found some interesting results.[57] The managers all reported that relationships were important, though individualists (e.g. Europeans, New Zealanders, South Africans) tended to see relationships as central to achieving business goals, whereas collectivists (e.g. Chinese, Indians) saw relationships as more worthy just in themselves. They gave many suggestions for building relationships—getting to know colleagues and clients in one-on-one or larger meetings. They emphasized two important general processes, building trust and reciprocal behavior, which varied along cultural lines. For example, New Zealander and South African managers take an egalitarian, informal, direct approach ('old-mate' networking system) to developing business contacts and then follow up, keeping in touch in more impersonal public meetings. They use a direct but flexible communication style, founded on a win-win approach. This direct, informal style to relationship building is also embraced by many North American business people.

On the other hand, Chinese managers emphasize the need for building *guanxi*, offering assistance often in indirect ways through a third party, and then building the relationship to a friendship—always on an interpersonal one-to-one basis. This more indirect, interpersonal style is embraced by business people from many Asian and Latin/South American countries. They prefer building relationships one-on-one, and are always careful to respect hierarchy. In most intercultural business relationships, it's important to pay attention to people's places in the hierarchy and to recognize and respect symbols of authority, to know whose views may carry more weight and whose opinions must be asked before decisions are made. A senior manager in Japan, for example, is not considered just a manager by a new recruit. The new recruit looks up to the senior manager as his teacher. Similarly, German managers have enormous power—they are in charge of their departments, and employees generally accept the authority and don't argue. These examples show how specific strategies may vary from culture to culture, but the fundamental value of strong relationships is seen as crucial to effective business encounters the world over.

Diversity, Prejudice, and Discrimination

You may never have the occasion to hand out business cards in a multinational context overseas, or engage in international business negotiation, but you still may have to address issues of diversity in the U.S. workplace. It may be interesting to identify cultural differences in workplace communication styles and values, but the real challenge is knowing how to work with these differences in a productive way. Unfortunately, not all differences are seen as "equal," and certain communication styles often are viewed negatively and can lead to prejudice and discrimination.

As discussed in Chapter 5, the language and communication style of those holding the most power is often the desired form of communication, and business contexts are no exception. Until recently, in most U.S. organizations, there was one dominant culture with a corresponding style of communication—White, Anglo Germanic, mostly Protestant, and male. In terms of communication and values, this means it was individualistic and emphasized directness, honesty over harmony, and task completion over relationship building. Individuals who held other values and used different communication styles often didn't fit in—or worse, were not hired or promoted.

In a classic book on management written in 1938, Chester Barnard observed that the key function of the business executive was the ability to get along and "fit in" with others in the workplace. A requirement for fitting in with others, according to Barnard, was shared "education, experience, age, sex, race, nationality, faith, politics, and very specific personal traits as manners, speech, personal appearance, etc."[58] Unfortunately, these traits are sometimes still required for those who want to succeed in the workplace, which can make it difficult for women, minorities, and international workers who do not possess these attributes.

Sometimes prejudice and discrimination are based on personal characteristics like names. The discrimination may begin even before one is hired. For example, employers may be more likely to interview job applicants with names like Smith and Jones than Mohamed or Farrah. As discussed in Chapter 6, some discrimination is based on physical appearance. For example, Muslim American women have reported discrimination based on their wearing of head coverings. Throughout 1,400 years of Muslim history, most Muslim women have covered their heads—an expression of their belief in the importance of modesty. They believe that covering the hair with scarves and veils brings respect and protection. Muslim women in America who wear head coverings do this as a conscious expression of their commitment to the teachings of the Qurán. However, this practice has led to prejudice and discrimination. For example, a Muslim woman was sent home from her job as a security guard when her supervisor told her to remove her head covering, as it was not part of her uniform—which she was not told during her employment interview. In northern Virginia, JC Penney fired a Muslim teenage worker when she refused to take off her scarf while working. Orthodox Jews share a similar belief and a similar practice, but have not faced as much discrimination.[59] The difference in the treatment between U.S. American Jews and Muslims shows how political and historical factors influence communication in business contexts—discussed later in the chapter.

Discrimination may also be based on skin color. When David Price, Harvard MBA graduate and African American, got a big marketing job in 1981, he was told he had to go through an interview with the person he'd be reporting to—just as a formality. His new boss told him bluntly that his father had taught him three things: Don't trust people with facial hair, don't trust people from Ivy League schools, and don't trust Black people. He told Price, "I've got this fundamental bias, but I think I'm being straight up with you, so that's what you're up against."[60]

More recently, when Karen Thomas was working at a large financial services firm, she was asked to help some managers on a project. She obliged by giving some suggestions on how to improve an important presentation. "I was so naïve to believe they wanted my input," she says. "They said 'Oh, OK, could you type this up for me?'"[61]

Things are different now: There are fewer cases of such blatant discrimination in the workplace, and yet it still exists. Business experts say that discrimination based on race and gender now exists more at higher levels of organizations where criteria for advancement are more subjective—where it depends more on who you know, than on your specific job skills.[62]

This discrimination may be one explanation for the problem of retention of minority workers in high-level jobs. In a study of a law firm where 100 percent of African American lawyers left the firm to seek employment elsewhere, interviewers discovered that there was a consistent pattern of very subtle marginalization and alienation from White colleagues. The African American lawyers all recounted being ignored by White lawyers who were too busy to advise them, but not too busy to assist other White junior colleagues. The African American Lawyers were also not invited to professional or social engagements with White colleagues.

What is interesting is that while the African American lawyers saw the pattern of discrimination from their vantage point, none of the White lawyers did—each just saw his or her *individual action* as a minor lack of courtesy. The White lawyers became defensive when asked to explain their lack of interest and missed appointments—and recited their credentials as "good" White people who "belong to the ACLU" and who have a Black friend or even a distant relative "who is married to one."[63] It is these types of small, seemingly unimportant actions (from the Whites' point of view) that help maintain the structural inequality in the workplace. The resulting discrimination and prejudice have led, among other things, to diversity training and **affirmative action (AA)** policies—statutes that direct companies to hire a certain percentage of women and minorities.

Most organizations define diversity as having the right racial composition and think that if they get the right racial composition, then everything is fine. Experts say that diversity should be much more than that. Diversity should be used as a resource to be more effective as a business.[64] In order to achieve this, diversity expert R. Roosevelt Thomas Jr. says corporations must do two things. First, they have to discard the assimilation myth—the idea that everyone should share the same cultural practices. This is an outdated notion. On the other hand, organizations don't want balkanization, where women employees work with women customers and Blacks go after Blacks. Rather, organizations should learn to leverage the differences—develop an environment where employees are able to serve customers different from themselves, and also where employees aren't afraid to share perspectives that are unique to them.

Second, management (and workers) need to separate job requirements from personal preferences. Thomas says that corporations need to be clear about what the *requirements* are to succeed at their company. In hiring practices and in work situations, we might encounter people who don't meet our preferences, like playing golf or being married; but the question should be, *do they meet the requirements?* Can I work with people who are qualified that are not like me? Thomas explains what this means:

> If you're in a historically homogeneous organization and you find an influx of both genders and multiple races, if you don't work diligently to be clear about requirements, people that violate these will be excluded

even though they're qualified. As a rule, I tell people to practice "foxhole diversity." Let's pretend the enemy is active all around and I've got to find people to be in the foxhole with me. I don't have to ask too many questions. Does the candidate have all of his or her faculties? Does the person have a gun? Can they shoot? That's about it. I don't care where they went to school, their religion or their sexual preference. Can they do the job? If you're on a basketball team and you only pass to someone of your own race, then there's going to be a problem.[65]

Some minorities and women are grateful for the emphasis on diversity and the implementation of affirmative action policies. Our colleague Marie, for example, had this to say:

I know that the only reason the company hired me for my first job was that I am a woman. I was the first woman in the department, and they were under a lot of pressure to hire me. And they should have been under pressure, and they were right to hire me. I was qualified for the job, but they wouldn't have given me the chance if it weren't for AAP. In my next job, I was also an affirmative action hire, because the company needed more women at senior levels. I also realize that I, along with other White women, have actually benefited more than women of color have from AAP.

But other women and minorities, while grateful for a chance to compete, are troubled by the question of whether they are viewed as having been given advantages. Anna, a successful businesswoman, observes:

I have worked in corporate America for 11 years. In my current management position, I am responsible for promotions and staffing in two departments. We were deciding promotional moves when the director asked where we were in terms of affirmative action for a particular department. I was floored. Though I was aware of what affirmative action was and why it existed, it was my first experience in seeing how it could affect people positively or negatively. We had ranked potential candidates based on productivity and results. This was a tough experience in that I started to doubt my own self-worth. Even though I have won awards and received recognition for my accomplishments, I still had to wonder if that was truly the only variable in their decision to promote me.

For many people, affirmative action is troublesome. Although affirmative action policies began as a way to address past discrimination, the focus now is on reverse discrimination, with majority members claiming that they are being disadvantaged by affirmative action.[66] Anna describes her struggles in dealing with affirmative action issues in her position as manager:

It is a thorny issue for people in positions of power also, particularly for minorities. I am now in a position to train employees whom I see as potential management candidates. I have struggled with how to balance this idea of affirmative action when picking my candidates. I don't want to be perceived as someone who gives special privileges to minorities. And I don't want to be perceived as a minority who ignores affirmative action policies. When it comes to intercultural communication, whether you are from a minority or dominant culture, you will encounter such issues. In this time of my life, I only want to try to make a difference.

Companies have many reasons for addressing affirmative action and diversity issues.[67] There may be moral grounds—a need to address the long history of racism, sexism, and conflictual intergroup relations in the United States. There may be a feeling that it is the responsibility of those who have benefited from this historical pattern to begin to "level the playing field." However, more often it is legal and social pressures—in the form of **equal employment opportunity (EEO)** laws, affirmative action (AA), and the **Americans with Disabilities Act (ADA)**—that cause companies to address affirmative action issues. For example, the ADA requires employers to make "reasonable" accommodations for employees and potential employees with disabilities. It also requires that public accommodations, buildings, transportation, and telecommunications be accessible to people with disabilities, as when Wal-Mart, the world's largest retailer, was sued in California for gender discrimination. The class action lawsuit may finally come to involve 500,000 women workers—the largest sex discrimination suit ever. Those who brought the lawsuit contended that women have not been given equal job assignments and that their career opportunities have not been the same as for men. They also felt that there has been inequality in training and compensation.[68]

Finally, companies may address issues of multiculturalism and diversity because they think it will have an impact on their bottom line—profit. And this does seem to be the case. A number of studies show that companies that value, encourage, and ultimately include the full contributions of all members of society have a much better chance of succeeding—and profiting.[69]

SOCIAL AND POLITICAL CONTEXTS OF BUSINESS

It is important to consider the social and political contexts of business and to think about how social and political events can affect business encounters. For example, the terrorist acts of 9/11 had a tremendous effect on business encounters both domestically and internationally. This event triggered loss of confidence and a downturn in the stock market, and many travel-related businesses lost money and were forced to lay off workers. Social events like the SARS medical scare in the summer of 2003 also had a tremendous impact on business. Companies canceled business trips and conventions in Asia and Canada. Again, this had a ripple effect, and many businesses outside of travel and tourism were impacted.

These and other recent events impact intercultural encounters. There are lost opportunities for contact, fear of contact, and suspicion about people from

What Do You Think?

On May 1, 2006, thousands of immigrants and immigrants' rights supporters across the nation did not go to work but took to the streets in a protest that was dubbed "A Day Without Immigrants." What are the cultural elements involved in these demonstrations? How did these protests impact businesses? Do corporations have an ethical responsibility to allow employees to participate in a protest? How might these events affect intercultural communication among various racial/ethnic groups in the workplace?

the Middle East and Asia. After 9/11, there were also many examples of discrimination and prejudice toward Middle Easterners. For example, after 9/11, people who simply appeared to be Middle Eastern were sometimes denied boarding on airplanes or were refused service in businesses. During the SARS scare, some people refused to interact with or sit close to people who appeared to be from Asia. Business declined in Chinatown, and incidents of harassment were reported.[70]

We might also consider how the recent national discussion on immigration reform affects intercultural communication in U.S. businesses. On May 1, 2006, thousands of immigrants and supporters participated in a nationwide event called "A Day Without Immigrants." Organizers asked immigrants and supporters to show their economic muscle by boycotting all aspects of commerce—including going to work and school—as a protest against the proposed immigration reform. The new policies proposed included legislation making illegal entry into the United States a felony, and proposals to deport all illegal immigrants (some 11–12 million) back to their country of origin. Thousands of Latinos/as stayed home from school and work. In Los Angeles and other cities, many businesses closed, either to show their alliance or because they did not have enough workers to sustain daily business.[71]

Some Americans are confident that the nation's economy and culture can absorb the immigrants. For example, immigration scholar Alan Kraut says, "I see immigrants as people who are coming to the United States to cast their lot with Americans. What we hear from some quarters is that these immigrants are somehow different, the notion that they will not assimilate. I think that expresses far too little faith in the power of American culture."[72] Others say that the economy cannot absorb the new workers. Mark Krikorian, executive director of the Center for Immigration Studies, counters: "It's not 1910 anymore. We have an economy that doesn't offer the same kind of upward mobility for people with low education." He continues, "We've changed, not the immigrants."[73] While it is not clear what impact the walkouts and demonstrations have had on the U.S. economy, immigration issues affect intercultural business relations between immigrants and native-born citizens. If immigration policies are tightened and hiring illegal immigrants becomes a felony, some fear that employers may be afraid to hire immigrants, leading to more unemployment among immigrants. Increased anti-immigrant feelings may lead to increased discrimination against Latinos/as in the workplace.

Some African Americans are resentful of the economic progress made by recently arrived Latinos/as; they see the loosening of immigration policies as going against their interests, as it results in more competition for lower-paid jobs sought by some African Americans. As described in Chapter 1, these challenges are not unique to the United States. European countries, like France and Germany, are also experiencing challenges of large groups of immigrants from poorer countries. Thus, it is important to remember that each intercultural encounter occurs in a social and political context that goes beyond the few individuals involved.

SUMMARY

In this chapter, we looked at some of the communication issues in intercultural business settings. Intercultural communication is becoming increasingly important in business due to increasing domestic diversity and the expansion of global markets.

We also described the various kinds of intercultural encounters that occur in various business settings. Intercultural encounters can occur between subordinates and superiors or among peers. Power differentials often complicate intercultural work encounters.

Finally, we addressed several communication challenges in business contexts: cultural differences in work-related values and communication style, in language use, and in norms of business etiquette. These cultural differences can influence important business processes—such as international negotiation and relationship-building. These differences can also lead to prejudice and discrimination if only one dominant style is accepted in an organization.

BUILDING INTERCULTURAL SKILLS

1. Try to identify the ways in which your workplace is diverse. Are there differences in race, ethnicity, gender, age, and physical ability? Are there different values and communication styles that accompany this diversity?

2. Try to identify the different cultural values in your workplace. What are the dominant values that are expressed in your workplace? Are these similar to those values you were raised with? Or are they in conflict with your own values? Or in conflict with values of other employees? Are there communication style differences in your workplace?

3. If you are dealing with a multilingual workforce, remember to practice good language skills: Speak slowly, use everyday language, and avoid jargon. Also try paraphrasing.

4. Be flexible; try to see other people's point of view. Practice being patient. Sometimes a diverse workplace requires more empathy and understanding than a monocultural setting, and this takes time to achieve.

5. Be an advocate for people who are not being treated fairly in the workplace. Are the legal standards (EEO and ADA laws) being met?

ACTIVITIES

1. *Newsworthy businesses:* Watch the news for international coverage of business events. What kinds of businesses are newsworthy? What kinds of business events are considered important? Which countries' economies are

considered most interesting? Are we more interested in learning about business etiquette in England or Japan than in Kenya or Egypt?

2. *Business media:* Look at business magazines such as *Wall Street Week* or *Forbes*. How much focus is there on diversity issues in American businesses? How much of the coverage is on the dominant culture values and communication style? How many stories are there about women and minorities in the business world?

3. *State websites:* Look at a state website (such as www.yesvirginia.org). Analyze the site for cultural benefits for locating in Virginia. To which cultural groups are the appeals pitched? Is any attention given to attracting a diverse workforce?

ENDNOTES

1. Scommegna, P. (2003). U.S. growing bigger, older and more diverse. Population Reference Bureau. Retrieved from http://www.prb.org/Template.cfm?Section=PRB&template=/Content Management/contentDisplay.cfm& contentID=10201

2. King, K. (2007, October 1). Hispanic entrepreneurship, buying power on the rise. CNN .Com/US. Retrieved November 3, 2008 from http://www.cnn.com/2007/US/10/01/hispanics .economy/index.html

3. Humphreys, J. M. (2004). The multicultural economy 2004: America's minority buying power. *Georgia Business and Economic Condition, 64,* 1–28. Retrieved from http://www.selig.uga.edu/ forecast/GBEC/GBEC043Q.pdf. See also Miller, S. Minority buying power expected to rise. *The Washington Times.* Retrieved from http://www.washingtontimes.com/functions/print.php? StoryID=20030824-110947-6770r

4. Corkery, M. (2005, November 14). A special effort. *Wall Street Journal,* p. R8.

5. Haller, B. (2001, February 18). Disability and advertising. *The Baltimore Sun.* Retrieved from http://www.towson.edu/~bhalle/dis-advert.html

6. Corkery (2005, November 14).

7. Palmer, I. L. (2000, August 21). Why women love sport-utility vehicles. Retrieved from http://4wheeldrive.about.com/gi/dynamic/offsite.htm?site=http://www.edmunds.com/news/ feature/general/42997/article.html. See also Jones, C. (2003, January 11). Electronics experts tout power of women consumers. Reviewjournal.com. Retrieved from http://www.reviewjournal.com/ lvrj_home/2003/ Jan-11-Sat-2003/business/20453578.html

8. Women own 20% of $1 million plus businesses. Center for Women's Business Research website. Retrieved November 3, 2008 from http://www.nfwbo.org/index.php

9. Bishop, M. (2008, September 20). A bigger world: A special report on globalization. *The Economist, 388*(8598), 1–26; *World Economic Situation and Prospects 2008 update* (United Nations publication, Sales No. E.08.II.C.2). Retrieved February 18, 2009 from http://www.un.org/esa/policy/ wess/wesp2008files/wesp08update.pdf

10. Judy, R. W., & D'Amico, C. (1997). *Workforce 2020.* Indianapolis: Hudson Institute. See also Kikoski, J. F., & Kikoski, C. K. (1999). *Reflexive communication in the culturally diverse workplace.* Westport, CT: Praeger, p. 3.

11. Hymowitz, C. (2005, November 14). The new diversity. *Wall Street Journal,* p. R1.

12. Chozick, A. (2005, November 14). Beyond the numbers. *Wall Street Journal,* p. R4.

13. Chozick, (2005, November 14), p. R4.

14. Hymowitz (2005, November 14), p. R1.

15. Storti, C. (2007). *Speaking of India: Bridging the communication gap when working with Indians.* Boston, MA: A Nicholas Brealey Publishing Company.

16. Eyjolfsdottir, H. M., & Smith, P. B. (1996). Icelandic business and management culture. *International Studies of Management & Organization, 26*(3), 61–72.

17. Kanungo, R. P. (2006). Cross culture and business practice: are they coterminous or cross-verging? *Cross Cultural Management: An International Journal, 13*(1), 23–31; Leung, K., Bhaga, R. S., Buchan, N. R., Erez, M., & Gibson, C. B. (2005). Culture and international business: recent advances and their implications for future research. *Journal of International Business Studies, 36,* 357–378.

18. Fatahi, K. (1996). *International management: A cross-cultural and functional perspective.* Upper Saddle River, NJ: Prentice Hall.

19. Bhasin, B. B. (2007). Succeeding in China: Cultural adjustments for Indian businesses. *Cross Cultural Management: An International Journal, 14*(1), 43–53.

20. Broome, B. J. (1996). *Exploring the Greek mosaic: A guide to intercultural communication in Greece.* Yarmouth, ME: Intercultural Press, p. 86.

21. Bhasin (2007); Negi, V. S. (2007, October 30). Cultural challenges in cross border mediation. Law and technology resources for legal professionals. Retrieved October 8, 2008 from http://www.llrx.com/features/crossbordermediation.htm; Shim, Y.-J., Kim, M-S., & Martin, J. N. (2008) *Changing Korea: Understanding culture and communication.* New York: Peter Lang.

22. Fatahi (1996), p. 168.

23. Kras, E. S. (1989). *Management in two cultures: Bridging the gap between U.S. and Mexican managers.* Yarmouth, ME: Intercultural Press, p. 46.

24. Copeland, L., & Griggs, L. (1985). *Going international: How to make friends and deal effectively in the global marketplace.* New York: Random House, p. 13.

25. Copeland & Griggs (1985), p. 112.

26. Storti (2001).

27. Storti (2001).

28. Bhasin (2007); Zhu, Y., Nel, P., & Bhat, R. (2006). A cross cultural study of communication strategies for building business relationships. *International Journal of Cross Cultural Management, 6*(3), 319–341.

29. Brislin, R. W., Cushner, K., Cherrie, C., & Yong, H. (1986). *Intercultural interactions: A practical guide.* Beverly Hills, CA: Sage, p. 154.

30. Kristjánsdóttir, E. S., & Martin, J. N. (In press). A case study in intercultural management communication: Icelandic managers and French, Spanish and Indian employees. In M. Hinner (Ed.), *Freiberger Beiträge zur interkultrellen und Wirtschaftskommunikation* (Vol 3). Frankfurt am Main, Germany: Peter Lang.

31. Storti, C. (2007). *Speaking of India: Bridging the communication gap when working with Indians.* Boston, MA: Nicholas Brealey Publishing.

32. Kristjánsdóttir & Martin (In press).

33. Beamer, L., & Varner, I. (2007). *Intercultural communication in the global workplace,* 4th ed. Boston: McGraw-Hill.

34. St. Amant, K. (2002). When cultures and computers collide: Rethinking computer-mediated-communication according to international and intercultural communication expectations. *Journal of Business and Technical Communication, 16,* 196–214.

35. Osman, G., & Herring, S. (2007). Interaction, facilitation, and deep learning in cross-cultural chat. A case study. *Internet and Higher Education, 10,* 125–141; Thompson, L., & Ku, H-Y. (2005). Chinese graduate students' experiences and attitudes toward online learning. *Educational Media International, 42*(1), 33–47.

36. Brislin et al. (1986), p. 101.

37. Richmond, Y., & Gestrin, P. (1988). *Into Africa; Intercultural insights.* Yarmouth, ME: Intercultural Press, p. 129.

38. Kristjánsdóttir & Martin (In press).

39. Copeland & Griggs (1985), p. 105.

40. Jia, W. (2008). Chinese perspective on harmony: An evaluation of the harmony and the peace paradigms, *China Media Research, 4*(4), p. 25.

41. Jia, W. (1997–98). Facework as a Chinese conflict-preventive mechanism: A culture/discourse analysis. *Intercultural Communication Studies*, 7(1), 43–61; Ting-Toomey, S., & Oetzel, J. G. (2002). Cross-cultural face concerns and conflict styles: Current status and future directions. In W. B. Gudykunst & B. Mody (Eds.), *Handbook of international and intercultural communication* (pp. 143–164). Thousand Oaks, CA: Sage.

42. Begley, S. (2003, March 28). Science Journal: East–West differences challenge assumptions about human thinking. *Wall Street Journal* (Europe), p. A5. See also Kim, M-S. (2002). *Non-western perspectives on human communication*. Thousand Oaks, CA: Sage.

43. Hall, E. T., & Hall, M. R. (1990). *Understanding cultural differences*. Yarmouth, ME: Intercultural Press, p. 64.

44. Richmond & Gestrin (1998), p. 134.

45. Kras (1989), p. 36.

46. Hall & Hall (1990), p. 116.

47. Business card etiquette. (1998). *International business resources on the WWW*. Michigan State University Center for International Business Education and Research. Retrieved from http://ciber.bus.msu,edu/busres/channel/businesscard.html

48. Richmond & Gestrin (1998), p. 132.

49. Beamer, L., & Varner, I. (2007). *Intercultural communication in the global workplace*, 4th ed. Boston: McGraw-Hill.

50. Metcalf, L. E., Bird, A., Peterson, M. F., Shankarmahesh, M., & Lituchy, T. R. (2007). Cultural influences in negotiations: A four country comparative analysis. *International Journal of Cross Cultural Management*, 7(2): 147–168.

51. Metcalf, Bird, Peterson, Shankarmahesh, & Lituchy (2007); Negi, S. (2007, October 30).

52. Pye, L. W. (1992). *Chinese negotiating style: Commercial approaches and cultural principles*. New York: Quorum, p. 103.

53. Beamer & Varner (2007).

54. Fang, T. (1999). *Chinese business negotiating style*. Thousand Oaks, CA: Sage.

55. Metcalf, Bird, Peterson, Shankarmahesh, & Lituchy (2007).

56. Hinner, M. B. (2005). General Introduction: Can quality communication improve business relationships? In M. B. Hinner (ed.), *Freiberger Beiträge zur interkultrellen und Wirtschafts- kommunikation* (Vol 1: pp. 15–40). Frankfurt am Main, Germany: Peter Lang.

57. Zhu, Nel, & Bhat (2006).

58. Barnard, C. (1938). *The functions of an executive*. Cambridge, MA: Harvard University Press, p. 224. Quoted in Kikoski & Kikoski (1997), p. 14.

59. McCloud, A. B. (1995–1996). American Muslim women and U.S. society. *Journal of Law and Religion*, 12, 51–59.

60. Trottman, M. (2005, November 14). A helping hand. *Wall Street Journal*, p. R5.

61. Preciphs, J. (2005, November 14). Moving ahead but slowly. *Wall Street Journal*, p. R3.

62. Preciphs (2005, November 14), p. R4.

63. Pierce, J. L. (2003). "Racing for innocence": Whiteness, corporate culture, and the backlash against affirmative action. In A. W. Doane & E. Bonilla-Silva (Eds.), *White out: The continuing significance of racism* (pp. 199–230). New York: Routledge, p. 213.

64. Chozick (2005, November 14).

65. Chozick (2005, November 14), p. R4.

66. Little, B. E., Murry, W. D., & Winbush, J. C. (1998). Perceptions of workplace Affirmative Action Plans. *Group and Organization Management*, 23(1), 27–47.

67. Ferdman, B. M., & Brody, S. E. (1996). Models of diversity training. In D. Landis & R. Bhagat (Eds.), *Handbook of intercultural training* (2nd ed., pp. 282–305). Thousand Oaks, CA: Sage.

68. Wal-Mart Class website, http://www.walmartclass.com/walmartclass94.pl. See also Featherstone, L. (2004). *Selling women short: The landmark battle for women's rights at Wal-Mart*. New York: Basic Books.

69. Hayles, R. (1996). What do racism and sexual harassment cost your business? *Cultural Diversity at Work*, 9, 1.

70. *SARS and Accusations of Discrimination.* Wikipedia. Retrieved from http://en.wikipedia.org/wiki/SARS_and_accusations_of_racial_discrimination
71. Thousands march for immigrant rights. (2006). *CNN.com.* Retrieved from http://www.cnn.com/2006/US/05/01/immigrant.day/index.html
72. Hutcheson, R. (2006, April 3). A nation of immigrants, with mixed feelings. *The Philadelphia Inquirer*, p. A01.
73. Hutcheson (2006, April 3), p. A01.

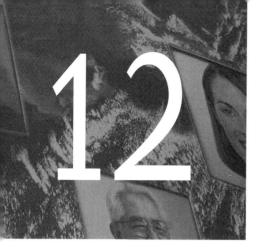

CHAPTER TWELVE

Intercultural Communication and Education

STUDY OBJECTIVES

After reading this chapter, you should be able to:

1. Understand the role of culture in setting educational goals. Note how colonization influences educational goals and curricula. Explain how colonization might influence study-abroad programs.

2. Understand the ways that different cultural groups were educated and the purposes of those different experiences. Be able to identify the educational goals of Indian schools, historically Black colleges and universities, and women's colleges.

3. Explain how different cultural role expectations can influence classroom communication. Note that different cultures may use different grading systems.

4. Explain how power differences can influence communication in educational contexts.

5. Describe the complexities of affirmative action and reverse discrimination.

6. Understand how cultural identities are formed in the educational process.

7. Be able to describe some social issues that arise in education.

KEY TERMS

Afrocentric	international students
colonial educational system	learning styles
	reverse discrimination
Eurocentric	study-abroad programs
HBCUs	teaching styles

Honestly, if it weren't for my travels, I don't think I would be the person I am today. When you travel abroad, you leave your comfort zone, and everything that makes you feel safe is left behind. You have to face challenges by yourself, and when you succeed, your confidence goes up, and so does your feeling of independence. You start thinking of different possibilities that, if it weren't for your travels, you would have never considered.

—Kyle Castanon[1]

Kyle's experience in another country is reflected in many similar stories from students who have had international experiences. If an important goal of education is to make a change in the lives of students, then international education is one of the most successful experiences where this can happen. Education can play a key role in developing culturally competent, global citizens; however, simply studying another culture does not necessarily develop intercultural competence.

One common approach to studying other cultures has been to focus on studying the language and literature of another culture. In studying French, Judith and Tom both learned the grammar and vocabulary of French and read many classic French works of literature, such as Albert Camus' *L'Étranger* (*The Stranger*), Émile Zola's *Germinal*, as well as some of the short stories of Guy de Maupassant. While this approach to French language and culture was followed by many students, and can form the foundation for future intercultural experiences, both Judith and Tom found that the intercultural competence they developed to cross between U.S. and French cultures did not occur in those classrooms.

In their work on intercultural education, Janet Bennett and Riika Salonen note that "being global citizens—seeing ourselves as members of a world community, as well as participants in our local contexts, knowing that we share the future with others—requires powerful forms of intercultural competence."[2] But the intercultural competence to learn how to communicate effectively with others who have very different experiences—in our society and around the globe—is not easily taught. We do not often learn to listen to the voices of others in our own society, much less those from around the world. We may sit next to others in class who have very difference experiences, but how much do we really understand these differences?

Education is an important context for intercultural communication, since students and teachers come from a variety of cultural backgrounds and bring a variety of expectations to the classroom. Educational institutions may be structured differently within different cultures, but they remain one of the most important social institutions for advancement in any society. If educators and students communicate in ways that are not sensitive to cultural differences in the educational institution, these same institutions may end up reproducing the social inequality of U.S. society. As noted in the report *Workforce 2020*, "The disparity between whites and minorities in college attendance is actually increasing."[3] Despite the reduction in barriers to college admissions based upon race, minority enrollments are decreasing. Improved intercultural communication practices can only help alleviate this problem. Further, many students are **international students,** meaning that they come to the United States or go abroad to study. In this chapter, we explore intercultural communication issues in the educational context.

EDUCATIONAL GOALS

What is the purpose of education? As noted previously, education is widely perceived to be an important avenue for advancement in society. After all, if you cannot read or write, it is difficult to succeed in this society. Yet, beyond the basic skills of reading, writing, and arithmetic, we need to think about the educational goals that various cultures establish. For example, what kinds of knowledge does an Italian need to acquire to succeed in Italian society? What kinds of things should a South Korean student study to prosper in South Korean society? How might these things differ from what U.S. American students need to study to advance in their society?

There is no universal curriculum that all students follow. Thus, clearly, it's more important for Brazilians to know the history of Brazil than it is for Indonesians. Not surprisingly, educational goals for different cultural groups are largely driven by members' need to know about themselves and their society. For example, students in France study French geography and learn that "La Manche" separates France from Britain; students in Britain study their island's geography and learn that the "English Channel" separates Britain from France. We are all taught to look at the world through our own culture's framework. Thus, in the United States, we call that body of water the "English Channel," just as the British do, because of our common language and historical ties. Our education necessarily frames our worldviews and our particular ways of knowing.

Education, however, is not driven simply by the desire to teach and learn about ourselves. In colonial contexts, for example, the colonial power often imposed its own educational goals and system upon the colonized. In so doing, this **colonial educational system** served educational goals that differed from what the colonized might have valued. Thus, "in colonial and neocolonial historical situations, a hierarchy of cultural importance and value is imposed by the colonising power, both on the conquered indigenous societies, and on the white agents of colonial oppression themselves."[4] Within educational institutions, this meant that students were expected to study Bach, Beethoven, and Debussy rather than their own culture's music; to read Chaucer, Shakespeare, and Milton instead of their native literature; and so on. This displacement of educational goals had a tremendous impact upon the ways that these former colonial societies were formed. The path to success involved embracing and understanding the colonizer's culture, history, literature, and society rather than the native one.

What Do You Think?

The May 2000 issue of *Spectra,* the professional publication of the National Communication Association, ran an advertisement for a teaching job at Sultan Qaboos University in Oman. The ad promised "tax-free salaries ... paid travel, free and good housing ... and end-of-contract gratuity." Assuming you had the credentials, would you take the job? Why or why not?

Many universities attract students from all over the world and so are common sites for intercultural interaction. Thus, many U.S. American students study abroad, just as many international students come to the United States to study. Cultural differences can impact what happens in the classroom.

You might be surprised to learn that your educational experience reflects America's colonial legacy. Despite the popular claim that we are a multicultural society with immigrants from all over the world, we tend to value European writers, artists, and histories more than, say, Asian writers, artists, and histories. For example, you learned more about the medieval period than the Heian period. The United States began as 13 colonies, and the reverberations of this colonial history persist in our educational goals today—to the benefit of some people and the detriment of others.

STUDYING ABROAD

We encounter cultural differences in education in a variety of contexts. While you may be most familiar with the traditional U.S. classroom setting, this is

TABLE 12.1 Open Doors 2008: Report on International Educational Exchange

TOP 20 LEADING PLACES OF ORIGIN OF INTERNATIONAL STUDENTS, 2006/07 & 2007/08

Rank	Place of Origin	2006/07	2007/08	2007/08 % of Total	% Change
	World Total	**582,984**	**623,805**	**100.0**	**7.0**
1	India	83,833	94,563	15.2	12.8
2	China	67,723	81,127	13.0	19.8
3	South Korea	62,392	69,124	11.1	10.8
4	Japan	35,282	33,974	5.4	−3.7
5	Canada	28,280	29,051	4.7	2.7
6	Taiwan	29,094	29,001	4.6	−0.3
7	Mexico	13,826	14,837	2.4	7.3
8	Turkey	11,506	12,030	1.9	4.6
9	Saudi Arabia	7,886	9,873	1.6	25.2
10	Thailand	8,886	9,004	1.4	1.3
11	Nepal	7,754	8,936	1.4	15.2
12	Germany	8,656	8,907	1.4	2.9
13	Vietnam	6,036	8,769	1.4	45.3
14	United Kingdom	8,438	8,367	1.3	−0.8
15	Hong Kong	7,722	8,286	1.3	7.3
16	Indonesia	7,338	7,692	1.2	4.8
17	Brazil	7,126	7,578	1.2	6.3
18	France	6,704	7,050	1.1	5.2
19	Colombia	6,750	6,662	1.1	−1.3
20	Nigeria	5,943	6,222	1.0	4.7

Source: Institute of International Education website, http://opendoors.iienetwork.org/?p=131534

Surf's Up!

Howard University is one of the most famous historically Black colleges and universities. It has traditionally encouraged students to study abroad to see through the eyes of other people and experience different ways of living. The International Exchange Program at Howard University suggests that students of engineering or architecture study in Germany where they experience advances in both disciplines. Students of history, political science, or biology might be interested in studying in Africa, the Middle East, or South America where America will direct or redirect its initiatives in the future. What do you think are the most appropriate places for you to study abroad? What kinds of things are you expected to learn when studying abroad? (SOURCE: Howard University website, http://www.howard.edu/rib/StudyAbroad/index.htm)

not the only educational context. Many students become "international students" by studying in another country. You may have encountered international students in your classes (see Table 12.1), and you may know American students who have gone abroad to study and to experience another culture. In fact, many universities offer **study-abroad programs** to give their students international experiences. However, study-abroad opportunities are not equally available or taken advantage of by all students. Most are White, as shown in Table 12.2. Because the cultural norms in different educational settings vary widely, international students engage directly in issues relevant to intercultural communication.

TABLE 12.2 Ethnicity of U.S. Students Who Studied Abroad, 2006-2007

Although race/ethnicity is not a requirement for studying abroad, why do you think that White Americans and Asian Americans study abroad at higher rates than their demographic proportion of U.S. society? Why are other groups at lower rates?

RACE/ETHNICITY	
Caucasian	81.9%
Asian American/Pacific Islander	6.7
Hispanic American	6.0
African American	3.8
Multiracial	1.2
Native American	0.5

Similarly, the number of women who study abroad far exceeds men. Why do you think this might be?

SEX	
Female	65.1%
Male	34.9

Source: Institute of International Education website, http://opendoors.iienetwork.org/?p=131562

History plays an important role in these students' experiences, as do the educational systems they enter. Many students from former European colonies study at institutions in the former colonizing nation. For example, Indonesian students may study in the Netherlands, Indian students may study in Britain, and Lebanese students may study in France. Belgians sometimes point out that the second largest Congolese city is Louvain-la-Neuve, where the Francophone (French-speaking) Université Catholique de Louvain is located. When Tom asked students from the Congo why they came to Belgium, which once colonized the Congo, to study, they pointed out that the Belgian educational system is structured similarly to their own and that they learn French in school. Therefore, they can move easily between institutions in the two nations. Because of the history of Belgium's colonization of the Congo, these intercultural connections remain vibrant. Notably, fewer students from the Congo attend the Katholieke Universiteit Leuven in Belgium; this university is located across the Belgian linguistic border in Leuven, where Flemish, not French, is spoken. Again, history is very important in understanding intercultural relations and intercultural communication.

As the global economy changes, where students go to study and which languages they choose to study also changes. As you can see from Table 12.3, the number of U.S. students going to study in China has grown by an extraordinary 90 percent. As China grows economically, the importance of understanding

TABLE 12.3 Open Doors 2008: Report on International Educational Exchange

TOP 20 DESTINATIONS OF U.S. STUDY ABROAD STUDENTS, 2005/06 & 2006/07

Rank	Destination	2005/06	2006/07	2006/07 % of Total	% Change
	World Total	**223,534**	**241,791**	**100.0**	**8.5**
1	United Kingdom	32,109	32,705	14.6	1.9
2	Italy	26,078	27,831	12.5	6.7
3	Spain	21,881	24,005	10.7	9.7
4	France	15,602	17,233	7.7	10.5
5	China	8,830	11,064	4.9	25.3
6	Australia	10,980	10,747	4.8	−2.1
7	Mexico	10,022	9,461	4.2	−5.6
8	Germany	6,858	7,355	3.3	7.2
9	Ireland	5,499	5,785	2.6	5.2
10	Costa Rica	5,518	5,383	2.4	−2.4
11	Japan	4,411	5,012	2.2	13.6
12	Argentina	2,865	3,617	1.6	26.2
13	Greece	3,227	3,417	1.5	5.9
14	South Africa	2,512	3,216	1.4	28.0
15	Czech Republic	2,846	3,145	1.4	10.5
16	Chile	2,578	2,824	1.3	9.6
17	Ecuador	2,171	2,813	1.3	29.6
18	Austria	2,792	2,810	1.3	0.6
19	New Zealand	2,542	2,718	1.2	6.9
20	India	2,115	2,627	1.2	24.2

Source: Institute of International Education website, http://opendoors.iienetwork.org/?p=131556

Chinese culture and language becomes increasingly vital. This phenomenon is not limited to the United States, as European students are also turning to Chinese. "In France, 12,000 secondary students are now studying it. Ten years ago, there were only 2,500."[5] As the market for those with knowledge of Chinese culture and language grows, those with additional skills (e.g., engineering, business) may be highly in demand. Studying abroad can help you learn so much more than you could ever learn in a classroom in your home institution that many students are taking the opportunity to go abroad.

When the University of Southern California decided to stop teaching German, many people were alarmed at the trend that may be forming over which languages should be prioritized. Howard Gillman, dean of USC's College

This photo of the segregated Monroe School in Topeka, Kansas, was taken in 1949. In 1954, in *Brown v. Board of Education of Topeka,* the Supreme Court declared such segregation to be unconstitutional. How do you think integration changes the educational process? As you look around your classroom, how integrated is your educational experience?

of Letters, Arts and Sciences, is quoted as saying, "There was a time when, because of world events, the study of German and Russian and a few other languages and cultures struck us as really central. We now have a much broader perspective in the world." In this new world that we now live, the university should also shift its attention to this "broader perspective."[6]

Part of this broader view means that the university "wanted to shift resources away from European languages to Asian languages like Chinese and Japanese. The decision was made in view of the growing importance of Asia for the American economy generally and the economy in Los Angeles specifically".[7] Not only are universities responding to our changing global environment, students are also shifting their language studies. Enrollments are sharply rising in Arabic, Chinese, Japanese, and Korean, while "as a share of total language course enrollments, the percentage studying Spanish, French, and German declined from 74.4 percent in 2002 to 71.3 percent in 2006".[8] As you watch the world changing, which languages do you think will become more important in the future? Which languages will become less important?

Although we cannot predict the future, especially what kinds of international relations may or may not develop, China looks to be a powerhouse in the future. What other languages may become important? What will happen with Russia? Will it become an economic powerhouse? Or will capitalism falter there? Should you study Arabic? Will the Middle East become even more important in the future as oil becomes scarce? Or will alternative fuels decrease our relationships there? How might you best position yourself to work in this new global environment?

CULTURALLY SPECIFIC EDUCATION

Also relevant to intercultural communication is the historical rise and development of educational institutions geared toward various cultural groups. For example, the Morrill Act of 1890 established what are today known as **HBCUs,** or historically Black colleges and universities. Alabama State, Delaware State, South Carolina State, Tennessee State, Grambling State, and Howard are all examples of HBCUs. Debates over the purpose of these educational institutions reflect the cultural attitudes inherent in education. For example, rather than being routes for empowering African Americans, some critics charged that these educational institutions focused on creating subservient Black workers in a White-dominated society. A century ago, for example, the famous Black educator Booker T. Washington pushed for the study of industrial arts and vocation training, as "no race can prosper till it learns that there is as much dignity in tilling a field as in writing a poem."[9] After all, one writer noted, "Black colleges, which in many cases were little more than secondary schools, received unequal funding from state or, under land-grant provisions, federal sources."[10] And this inequality only served to perpetuate the historical inequality between Whites and Blacks—a sad legacy that persists to this day.

Other educational institutions were established for White women, such as Mississippi University for Women (MUW) and Texas Women's University, and for Native Americans, such as the College of the Menominee and Diné College. The White women's colleges were established for reasons quite different from those for establishing the Native American colleges. But in each case, education was intimately related to a specific culture and served different purposes for different students. In the same sense, your own cultural identity is reflected in your educational choices and experiences.

Not all of these colleges and universities have retained their original missions, yet many continue to draw the students for whom they were originally established. Chartered in 1884, the Mississippi University for Women was "the first state-supported college for women in America." Almost a hundred years later, it changed its policies and began to admit both women and men.[11] Today, MUW's mission statement reflects its traditional emphasis: "Admitting men since 1982, MUW still provides a high quality liberal arts education with a distinct emphasis on professional development and leadership opportunities for women."[12]

The educational experiences of minority and majority students in these institutions are not necessarily the same as those of students in institutions that were initially established for White males, such as Georgia Tech. Georgia Tech has long since departed from its original charter as the university's website boasts: "Women students were admitted in 1952, and in 1961 Georgia Tech became the first university in the Deep South to admit African American students without a court order."[13] The student experiences at these different kinds of institutions reflect these different histories, different student composition, and different social contexts, as well as institutional goals.

Info Bites

Historically, American Indians were placed in many boarding schools across the country for cultural assimilation into White society. White people thought forced assimilation in boarding schools would be the best solution to American Indian problems. This forced cultural assimilation caused many cultural struggles for both teachers and students. Boarding schools served as a site for both cultural loss and cultural persistence of the Native American people. Check this website for more information about these schools: http://xroads .virginia.edu/~HYPER/ INCORP/Native/school .html.

There are many other kinds of educational institutions that no longer exist but whose reverberations are still felt. For example, "Indian schools" were established to assimilate Native American children to White American society by educating them off reservation in boarding schools. In Phoenix today, there is a main artery called "Indian School Road," along which the Phoenix Indian School once sat. In writing about an Indian school in Oklahoma, K. Tsianina Lomawaima tells us that "although Chilocco was closed in 1980, it persists as a social reality today in many communities across Oklahoma,"[14] in that many alumni continue to gather regularly. Indeed, because in these schools "acculturation and assimilation into the dominant White society remained the explicit goal of policy and practice,"[15] it is hardly surprising that the education that these students received after being separated from their families and communities "had a tremendous impact on language use and retention, religious conservatism and conversion, attitudes toward education and feelings of self-esteem, to name but a few influences."[16]

The effects of education reverberate across generations, because once languages, customs, traditions, and religions are lost it is difficult, if not impossible, for subsequent generations to recover them. Education is very influential in maintaining or irreparably altering various cultural communities.

More recently, driven by other pressures, discussions have begun over the education of immigrant children. Unlike earlier segregated schools, immigrant children are entering school systems under pressure from the U.S. federal government's No Child Left Behind program, which mandates that all students become literate. This is a particular challenge for schools with immigrant students who have had little formal schooling in their native languages. The problem for educators is that they "must help students with little formal schooling read, write, and do math at the same level as the kids who arrive at school as kindergartners fluent in English."[17] Some school districts have developed separate programs with strategies designed to help these students. Some schools have hired bilingual teachers to help students learn English, as well as their other lessons. In Crete, Nebraska, for example, a meatpacking plant has drawn many immigrant workers and their families. This influx of new residents has changed the school, but also brought in more state aid to help hire bilingual teachers: "While the percentage of minority students rose from 5 percent to 35 percent in 10 years, Crete school superintendent John Fero said state aid covered the additional costs for bilingual teachers and other expenses."[18] In contrast to that approach, other places, such as Arizona, forbid the teacher explaining words or concepts—even if the teacher does know the word in another language, since "By state law, their teacher cannot teach in any language but English."[19] In 2000, Arizona voters passed Proposition 203, "the most restrictive English-only education law in the country and prohibited textbooks, materials, bulletin boards, or teaching in any language but English."[20] Debates continue to focus on the best approach to help nonnative English speakers in the educational system. There are no easy answers, but these issues confronted U.S. Americans in the past and the way that they handled those

These students are viewing their grades publicly posted on a bulletin board in a glass case outside their classroom. In the United States grades are considered private information.
Do you think grades should be public or private?

issues continues to reverberate today. How will the decisions made today impact us in the future?

Religious educational institutions are another site where cultural values can influence the educational experience. At Stonehill College, a private Catholic institution in Massachusetts, Katie Freitas, a student, decided to make condoms available to students. She and some classmates made boxes of condoms available in the dormitories on campus. The college removed them because it was against college policy to distribute birth control on campus. The college's spokesman, Martin McGovern, said, "We make no secret of our religious affiliation, and our belief system is fairly straightforward. We don't expect everyone on campus to agree with our beliefs, but we would ask people, and students in particular, to respect them."[21] Some people have sided with the students and their interest in promoting safe sex practices. Some people have sided with the institution because the students chose to attend a Catholic college.

Similarly, a student who completed all of the coursework for an undergraduate degree has been denied this degree due, in part, to the publication of a calendar. Chad Hardy has lost his appeal to Brigham Young University for his degree. Mr. Hardy published a calendar, "Men on a Mission," that features shirtless Mormon men who have returned from missions around the world. His "diploma was withheld by BYU last fall after he was excommunicated from the Church of Jesus Christ of Latter-day Saints, which owns and runs the school." The Dean of Students Vernon L. Heperi "called the calendar offensive and disrespectful because it depicts missionaries in an 'inappropriate light.'"[22] While his excommunication and the calendar underscore a clash of values between

Info Bites

It wasn't until 1934 that discussions of Native American culture were permitted in schools sponsored by the Bureau of Indian Affairs. Previously, the policy of the federal government had been "full assimilation and eradication of Indian culture." (SOURCE: http://www.oiep.bia.edu/)

Mr. Hardy and this church, this case may lead you to think about the values that different institutions hold. Some religious groups have established educational institutions to further their values in the educational context. Like gender and race, religion can also shape the educational experiences of students.

INTERCULTURAL COMMUNICATION IN EDUCATIONAL SETTINGS

Much of our communication behavior in the classroom is not interpreted in the way we intend it by people from different cultural backgrounds. Education is deeply embedded in culture, and our expectations for the educational process are a part of our culture. The roles that we enact in the classroom are very much a part of the cultural influences on education. Let's look at how these roles can differ.

Roles for Teachers and Students

When Tom taught at a Francophone university in Belgium, another professor gave him a helpful cultural tip: "In Belgium, students don't answer the professor's questions, even if they know the answer. In the United States, American students answer the professor's questions, even if they don't know the answer." This cultural generalization was helpful to Tom as he navigated the role of professor in this different context. Although he did ask questions throughout the term, the lack of discussion in the classroom was understandable. Because he was concerned about imposing his own cultural framework on the Belgian students, Tom did not push them to participate in discussions, nor did he demand that they answer his questions. As the term progressed, some of the students began to speak more in class, even as Tom felt that he was moving toward more of a lecture format. The classroom became a site for negotiation of these cultural differences.

These kinds of cultural differences can create confusion in the classroom for students and teachers. Note the following example from the Netherlands:

> When Setiyo Hadi Waluyo came from his native Indonesia to study at Wageningen Agricultural University here, he was shocked by what he saw. Time and again a professor would ask a question, a student would answer, and the professor would say, "You're absolutely right!"
>
> "I felt: What's going on here?" recalls Mr. Waluyo. "The students know more than the professors?"[23]

The culture clash over **learning styles** (the different ways that students learn in different cultures) and **teaching styles** (the styles that instructors use to teach) is common as students increasingly travel to study in other cultures. Often we are unaware of our cultural assumptions about education until we are confronted with different ways of learning. In a recent study focusing on Chinese students who were studying at a university in New Zealand, scholar Prue Holmes found that the Chinese students learned to adapt to the New Zealand classroom communication

What Do You Think?

Did you know that U.S. university professors and teaching associates who are women or people of color (or both) consistently get lower marks in their teaching evaluations than their White male counterparts? Think about your classes and instructors. How do you evaluate their performance at the end of the semester? Do the expectations vary depending on the instructor's identity? How does power play into the dynamics of evaluation?

styles which included interrupting, asking, and challenging the material. They found much guidance from other international students who helped them adapt, but they still found it difficult to engage in intercultural communication with New Zealand students.[24] Think about the assumptions you have concerning how your instructors should behave. Perhaps you think that instructors should set time aside in class for discussion of the material, or that students should be allowed to say what they think about the readings, or that grading should be done "on a curve." In many universities, for example, students are assigned books to read before the end of the term and take one exam at the end of the term, rather than getting a structured reading list and assignments along the way.

Grading and Power

When Tom taught at a Francophone Belgian university, he was surprised when the instructors posted the exam grades in a large glass case in the main hall of the building. The exam scores were posted by name, alphabetically. The students would crowd around the list and some would exclaim in joy at their scores, while others would be comforted by their friends when they saw their scores. In the United States, posting grades in this manner would be a violation of the Family Educational Rights and Privacy Act of 1974, also known as the Buckley Amendment. Students' grades are considered private information.

   When you think about grades, how important are they? Should grades be private or public information? Different cultures feel differently about grades and you should not assume that everywhere is the same. How important are grades? What do they mean in our culture? What do your grades communicate to others?

   As in any other social setting, the classroom is embedded with cultural expectations about power relations. While there may always be a power difference in the communication between instructors and students, this difference can be greater or lesser in various cultures. In the United States, for example, the relationships between instructor and students tend to be less formal than in other cultures. Michael, a student of ours, recalled the following intercultural conflict, which reflects this power difference:

> While on a study-abroad program in Malaysia, I received what I thought was an unfair grade on a paper. As I discussed my unhappiness in his office, the teacher became increasingly angry that I was commenting about his grading in his office. In the heat of the argument, I was threatening to report him to the school's governing board, and he was threatening to get me kicked out of the school! Obviously, this conflict spiraled way out of control. . . . Several red flags were telling me that intercultural differences were at play. . . . In his culture, students are disrespectful when they question teachers' decisions. In my culture, questions show that you are paying attention. I chose to explain my actions to the teacher, and we were able to put out the fire. We refocused on communication behaviors and ended in a win/win situation: I got a better grade, and he received more respect.

What Do You Think?

What are the major issues that international students face in a different educational system? Many U.S. American students want to go to England or Ireland where they may not encounter language barriers. Do you think language is the biggest barrier to studying abroad? What are the benefits of living in a place where a non-English language is spoken? Find more information at the website www .studentsabroad.com/ adviceforparents.html. Think about what kind of experiences would be the most valuable to studying abroad and what kind of things need to be taken care of living abroad?

Michael's experience highlights the role that culture plays in the educational process. The relationship between instructor and student is not uniform around the world. Michael's decision to discuss these cultural differences openly with his instructor in Malaysia was helpful in resolving this situation. Cultural differences often cause intercultural conflicts simply because the individuals involved fail to confront those differences.

Notions of "fair" and "unfair" are culturally embedded as well. Our grading system is far from universal. Different cultures use different ways of evaluating student work. When Tom taught in Francophone Belgium, he was familiar with the grading system, as it is the same grading system used in French universities, where the highest grade (which is almost never given) is 20. In most U.S. colleges and universities, the highest grade, which is expected to be given to a number of students in every class, is an A.

Grading scales differ around the world and it is not always easy to know what a particular grade means. In South Africa, in grades 4–6, students are graded on a scale of 1 to 4, and 4 is the highest grade. But in grades 7–9, students are graded on a scale of 1 to 7, and 7 is the highest grade.[25] There are no easy ways to understand different grading systems, but the World Education Service's website has a converter that lends insight into different systems at: www.wes.org/gradeconversionguide. You can see that a "1" would be a very good grade in Germany, but a very poor grade in Switzerland. Do not assume that all grading scales are the same, nor that the highest grades are always given in a class. In some cultures, there is no grading "on a curve."

Admissions, Affirmative Action, and Standardized Tests

Debates over university admissions are not new. Because university resources are expensive and limited, admissions to universities are competitive. The University of Bristol in the United Kingdom faces such competition, receiving "about 39,000 applicants for 3,300 undergraduate places each year."[26] The high costs of university education eventually led to the closing of the Université de Kinshasa in the Congo.[27]

Because of the economic importance of university degrees, admissions are important in empowering and disempowering cultural groups. Thus, many people struggled to break down barriers to university admissions that were based on nonacademic factors such as race. The University of Tennessee reflects many of these tensions, as "Black undergraduates were not admitted until 1961; the first black faculty member was appointed in 1964."[28] Those explicit barriers to admission have long been dismantled. Today, universities do not deny admission based on race. Arizona State University has a nondiscrimination statement that, in part, says, "Discrimination is prohibited on the basis of race, color, religion, national origin, citizenship, sex, sexual orientation, age, disability, and special disabled veteran, other protected veteran, newly separated veteran, or Vietnam era veteran status."[29]

In order to overcome some of the historical as well as contemporary reasons that have led to student bodies that do not reflect the demographic profiles of society at large, the civil rights movement led to the establishment of affirmative action policies. These policies encouraged institutions to act affirmatively to ensure a more representative student body. As a part of this movement, questions were raised about the ability of institutions to measure "merit," particularly on standardized tests. How do we know who is more qualified to be admitted? Recently questions have been raised about the ways that equal opportunity is thwarted by privileging children of alumni in the admissions process. Given the historical barriers that prevented some cultural groups from attending some colleges and universities, how might the children of alumni not reflect society at large?

Across the Atlantic, the prestigious *Institut d'études politiques* in Paris has established what some have called a French affirmative action program and what the French refer to as *zone d'éducation prioritaire*, or ZEP. Students from disadvantaged backgrounds are "offered counseling, special courses, and visits to Sciences Po's campus."[30] This way of acting affirmatively has recently withstood a court challenge. The court did not question the principle of the program but has instructed the institution to modify and to clarify some of its regulations. According to government commissioner Jean-Pierre Demouveaux, however, there was no opposition from the court to creating "a path for access to high school students from socially disadvantaged backgrounds."[31] The principle behind ZEP is to integrate all sectors of society into French society.

More recently, concern over admissions policies also have shifted to the admissions criteria themselves and the ways that they favor some cultural groups over others in admissions. The emergence of the notion of **reverse discrimination,** or policies that disadvantage Whites and/or males, has become a rhetorical strategy to argue for more spaces for those dominant groups. The University of Michigan recently won a Supreme Court battle to include race as one of many factors in its admissions decisions. The university has posted a website that explains the two related court cases and their current admissions policies at www.umich.edu/~urel/admissions/.

Other universities also face similar concerns. The University of Utah recently has come under scrutiny for the admissions practices of its medical school. The dean of the medical school noted that there is a misperception "that white male applicants experience reverse discrimination, despite the fact that the medical school is 87 percent white and 65 percent male."[32] Yet Utah's "controversy, which isn't nearly over and done, stems from accusations by some state legislators of 'reverse discrimination' at the medical school against 'white, Mormon males.'"[33] Similar concerns about reverse discrimination have arisen at other universities as well.

Part of the criteria in U.S. undergraduate admissions may include the Scholastic Aptitude Test (SAT). In developing the "new SAT," some groups will likely benefit over others:

> Girls tend to outperform boys on writing exams, so their overall scores could benefit from the addition of the new writing section. Boys usually score higher on the math section, but the new exam will contain fewer of

the abstract-reasoning items at which they excel. The elimination of analogies may exacerbate the black-white SAT score gap, since the gap is somewhat smaller on the analogy section than on the test as a whole.[34]

Concern over the value of trying to predict academic success led the president of the University of California to recommend that the SAT no longer be used in admissions to its eight undergraduate campuses. In announcing his recommendation, he noted that "minorities are concerned about the fact that, on average, their children score lower than white and Asian American students." While there may be myriad reasons for this disparity in scores, he also noted that the "strength of American society has been its belief that actual achievement should be what matters most. Students should be judged on the basis of what they have made of the opportunities available to them."[35] Changes to the SAT may help mitigate some of the problems with the test, but it still remains notoriously difficult to predict academic success.

More recently, changes in the student body profile have led some admissions officers to give preference to men over women. Preferential admissions are not only about racial differences. As the dean of admissions at Kenyon College in Gambier, Ohio, noted in reviewing one woman's application, "Had she been a male applicant, there would have been little, if any, hesitation to admit. The reality is that because young men are rarer, they're more valued applicants. Today, two-thirds of colleges and universities report that they get more female than male applicants, and more than 56 percent of undergraduates nationwide are women."[36] Given these demographics, some admissions officers have chosen to give preference to male applicants. While this dean acknowledges this preferential treatment, she also notes, "I admire the brilliant successes of our daughters. To parents and the students getting thin envelopes, I apologize for the demographic realities."[37] What do you think about this kind of preferential treatment? How do admissions officers judge the merits of any applicant? How should colleges admit students? There are no easy answers to this question, but whatever decisions are made are likely to impact how our culture develops and the kinds of intercultural interaction that will ensue.

COMMUNICATION, EDUCATION, AND CULTURAL IDENTITY

A Navajo student shared a cultural myth/experience that people from her tribe are all familiar with. Apparently, people in her tribe have encountered "beings" called skin chasers. They are beings that have the face of a human but the body of an animal. They appear in the evening, but not to everyone. She received feedback from her teacher, who said in so many words that it couldn't be true. The Navajo student was really upset that [the teacher] could pass judgment and in her eyes ridicule something that was so sacred to her tribe and cultural background.   —Mona

This photo of a classroom at the Carlisle Indian Industrial School in Carlisle, Pennsylvania, was taken around 1902. Carlisle was one of many "Indian schools" that attempted to "civilize" their students by eradicating tribal identities, languages, and religions. What ramifications might this educational process have for contemporary Native Americans?

Mona's story strikes at the heart of the debates over cultural identity, education, and the role of communication in reinforcing or challenging identities. Education itself is an important context for socialization and empowerment. Education professor Ann Locke Davidson observes:

> Education is popularly conceptualized as one factor integral to achieving the economic parity and geographic dispersal presumed basic to integrating diverse citizens into American society. Yet, while it is clear that education improves individual chances for social mobility, it is equally apparent that schools work less well for impoverished African American and Latino school children.[38]

Similarly, Mona's story about her Navajo (Diné) friend demonstrates the alienation that students from other cultures may experience in the classroom.

We often like to think that education provides equal opportunities for all students, but inequities in the paths that students follow reflect differing patterns of treatment. These experiences are powerful forces in the shaping of their identities, and students are very attuned to these forces. One Mexican American high school student, Sonia, notes about her White teachers:

> It's probably in the way they look at you, the way they talk, . . . like when they talk about the people who are going to drop out. And then Mr. Kula, when he's talking about teenage pregnancy or something like that, he

What Do You Think?

Did you know that corporal punishment in schools is legal in many areas within the United States? According to CNN, in 2007 more than 200,000 students were spanked or paddled in schools within the United States. Currently, twenty-two states allow some form of corporal punishment in schools. For more information regarding corporal punishment within the United States visit www.stophitting .com/index.php?page= statesbanning. Globally, over 100 countries do not prohibit the use of corporal punishment in schools. Cases range from pinching and slapping on the back of the head to more severe cases of spanking, paddling, and caning. For more information on global corporal punishment within schools visit www. internationalcap.org/ abuse_statistics.html. Do you think corporal punishment in schools is necessary? If so, why and when is corporal punishment in schools necessary? If not, what other forms of punishment would be more appropriate in the context of education?

turns around and looked at us. It's like, he tries to look around the whole room so we won't notice, but like he mostly tries to get it through our heads. . . . Sometimes I think he's prejudiced.[39]

Sonia, like other students, develops her identity within this educational context. Because her experience is shared by other students who are also of Mexican descent, it is a shared cultural experience that shapes a cultural identity. It is not simply an individual identity.

Even teachers who are not overtly racist may not have received the kind of education necessary to incorporate materials into the curriculum that reflect the diversity of their students. Nor have they been able to develop this curriculum. Education professor Henry Giroux tells us that, "despite the growing diversity of students in both public schools and higher education, there are few examples of curriculum sensitivity to the multiplicity of economic, social and cultural factors bearing on a student's educational life."[40]

Think about your own education. How much did you learn about the history of other cultural groups in the United States or elsewhere? How much literature did you read that was written by authors from a range of cultural backgrounds? How much art and music were you exposed to that came from non-Western cultures?

This issue about the key role of education in creating our identities was highlighted by James Loewen's best-selling book *Lies My Teacher Told Me*.[41] In this book, Loewen underscores the ways that U.S. students are taught about the past by reviewing U.S. history textbooks for high schools. He points out the misinformation, as well as blind patriotism, in recounting many historical events. Although this approach to U.S. history may encourage U.S. students to be loyal citizens, it does little to help them understand the importance of history to their identities, as well as the real importance of understanding the past.

The United States is not alone in shaping history to build particular cultural identities. In 2005, "anti-Japanese demonstrations in China—over Japanese school textbooks allegedly glossing over wartime atrocities—spark heated press comment in both countries."[42] Japan has come under critique for the content of its history textbooks as well, particularly by South Korea and China. Both of these nations experienced Japan's militarism prior to Japan's pacifism after World War II. Yet, Chinese, Koreans, and Japanese all recognize the key importance of education and what is taught in building national identities: "Their students learn history through government-approved textbooks that are, especially with nationalism rising in all three countries, useful tools in shaping national identities. Since the textbooks require the central government's imprimatur, they are taken as a reflection of the views of the current leaders."[43] Yet, these countries are not the only ones that teach history to their students.

After the attacks on September 11, 2001, Saudi Arabia came under attack for its educational content, as a number of the terrorists came from that nation. In light of that background, "the government has faced significant pressure from both inside and outside the country to change its schools."[44] Yet a review of these textbooks released in 2006 found that "a sample of official Saudi textbooks for Islamic studies used during the current academic year reveals that, despite the Saudi government's statements to the contrary, an ideology of hatred toward Christians and Jews and Muslims who do not follow Wahhabi doctrine remains in this area of the public school system. This indoctrination begins in a first-grade text and is reinforced and expanded each year, culminating in a 12th-grade text instructing students that their religious obligation includes waging jihad against the infidel to 'spread the faith.'"[45] If you are interested in reading more about the report from Freedom House, see the web page at www.freedomhouse.org/religion/.

While we have looked only at the United States, Japan, and Saudi Arabia, many of these trends in history education are probably not unique to these three countries. Think about what you were taught in school and how that might influence how you see the world. How might the education that others have received shaped their worldviews in ways that might create intercultural barriers as you encounter others from around the world? Since we cannot agree about the past, you can see how it would be impossible to create history textbooks that could be used around the world. This is an educational issue that is likely to continue to impact intercultural relations.

SOCIAL ISSUES AND EDUCATION

With the recent election of Barack Obama, the first African American president, a new round of discussions has emerged about how we deal with racial issues in education. Should we continue to teach *The Adventures of Huckleberry Finn* and *To Kill a Mockingbird*? And this "debate hasn't been limited to literature either: in the past few weeks alone, National Public Radio, many African American blogs, and talk-show host Michael Baisden all led discussions questioning whether we still need Black History Month."[46] On the one hand, the election of the first African American president is a significant sign that older ways of thinking about race are changing. Perhaps this moment does mean that we need to re-examine how we teach and learn about literature and history.

On the other hand, the election of Obama does not mean that older ways of thinking about race have simply disappeared. In March 2009, Dartmouth College became the first Ivy League school to hire an Asian American president, when they hired Dr. Jim Yong Kim. One day later, an anonymous e-mail was sent out over a campus listserv. *The Boston Globe* reports that:

> The anonymous e-mail referred to Dr. Jim Yong Kim, a Korean-born Harvard medical school professor and global health pioneer, as a "Chinaman" and went on to bemoan the loss of another "hard-working American's job" to "an immigrant willing to work in substandard conditions at near-subsistent wage."

What Do You Think?

Since the 1980s, spurred by the writings of people like E. D. Hirsch, Alan Bloom, and William Bennett, conservatives have increasingly stressed the importance of teaching Western civilization classes. These efforts are in response to the attempt to broaden the curriculum to include the histories of other cultures. If you've taken a Western civilization class, what did you think of it? What did it teach you?

"Unless 'Jim Yong Kim' means 'I love Freedom' in Chinese, I don't want anything to do with him," the e-mail said. "Dartmouth is America, not Panda Garden Rice Village Restaurant."[47]

While educational institutions can be places of international, interracial, and intercultural contact, these contacts do not necessarily lead to increased intercultural competence. Some students "who see culture as a barrier tend to deny, resist, or minimize differences" while "those who see culture as a resource tend to accept and appreciate difference."[48] As the world grows smaller, it is important to strive to become a global citizen by profiting from your interactions with others who are different. Education is one crucial site where this can happen.

As noted previously, the development of educational institutions, as well as the educational process itself, is deeply embedded in any culture. As students and instructors meet in the classroom, cultural differences can lead to misunderstandings in communication. There is, of course, no way to escape the history of education and the ways this history has created cultural expectations about what should happen in the educational process. Nor is this a call to find a way to escape education. After all, you are pursuing education in an educational institution, and as authors of this book, we also have a role in the educational institution. In any case, there are some social issues that we should consider as they bear upon intercultural communication.

First, it is important to recognize that the educational process reflects cultural power. The things we study (and do not study), the way we communicate in the classroom, the relationships between students and instructors—all involve issues of power. How do we determine what gets studied and what does not in various courses? Whose communication style sets the tone in the classroom? Why are interactions between students and instructors always embedded in a hierarchical relationship? The answers to these questions all have to do with power issues, and it is important to recognize that everyone's culture is not treated the same in the curriculum.

Second, it is important to recognize that the structure of educational institutions, as opposed to the people in them, often plays a significant role in the way that power functions. Thus, we need to understand how the educational system empowers some over others—and how this happens because of the way the system is set up. For example, some colleges require history or literature courses, but the history and literature that they teach might be **Eurocentric,** focusing on European or Western views of history and literature. By taking a Eurocentric approach, these courses reinforce a particular worldview that challenges some student identities more than others. As noted earlier in the book, we are often taught the history of our state or nation. Clearly, however, this approach to education can create barriers to intercultural communication.

One response to this problem is to teach **Afrocentric** history,[49] which centers on the African rather than the European experience and exposes African American students to an entirely different view of the world and their place in it. Of course, as sociologist James Loewen notes, "To be sure, the answer to

Thanksgiving is an important U.S. holiday. The educational process is important in instilling a sense of the significance of this holiday. Thanksgiving is not seen as a "White" holiday in the way that Kwanzaa, Lunar New Year, and other holidays are seen as ethnically specific. Why do you think it is important for us to view Thanksgiving as a national holiday instead of a holiday for Whites?

Eurocentric textbooks is not one-sided Afrocentric history, the kind that has Africans inventing everything good and whites inventing slavery and oppression."[50] These curriculum innovations are vital to the self-esteem, cultural identity, and empowerment of all students, but schools don't seem to know how to teach in ways that are more inclusive and that are fair to all cultural groups. As James Loewen says about U.S. history, "Students will start learning history when they see the point of doing so, when it seems interesting and important to them, and when they believe history might relate to their lives and futures. Students will start finding history interesting when their teachers and textbooks stop lying to them."[51]

Finally, as education professor William Tierney suggests, "Our colleges and universities need to be noisier—in the sense that honest dialogue that confronts differences is good. To be sure, we must not drown out other voices. . . . We must work harder at developing dialogues of respect."[52] To accomplish this, we must be willing to point out cultural differences that are creating problems in the educational process. Only by talking about these differences and the reasons for them can we begin to change the educational process. We have to create an environment in which cultural differences are assumed to exist and are discussed. We need to move away from an environment in which culture is assumed to be irrelevant since everyone shares the same culture.

In her study of racism in higher education, communication professor Jennifer Simpson concludes, "'Racism is not a theory.' It is not an easy lesson for white people to learn. It is also a difficult lesson for groups of people in higher education to learn, as we cling to safe and predictable routes to knowledge.

Changes in the classroom and in higher education are not easy either. They will come only with costs, heavy at times."[53] Whether or not we are ready to undertake the difficult work ahead of us to ensure that education is for everyone, whatever their background, remains to be seen. It is important to be aware that not everyone shares the same culture and has the same orientation to learning and teaching.

SUMMARY

In this chapter, we looked at some of the challenges that cultural differences bring to the educational process. Because education is a process of socialization and enculturation, it is relevant to intercultural communication. Different cultures have different educational goals. The curricula in some nations do not reflect their own cultures, but instead focus on the European cultures of their former colonizers. Some culturally specific educational institutions may have different educational goals from other institutions. Both teachers and students enact cultural roles in the educational setting. Even grading is cultural, in that all educational systems do not use the same grading system. And varying admissions policies, sometimes discriminatory, have important historical and contemporary implications for intercultural relations. Standardized tests, part of the admission procedures, have sometimes contained implicit cultural biases.

We also examined the ways that communication in education can influence the cultural identities and self-esteem of students. Some instructors may knowingly or unknowingly communicate their cultural biases in the classroom. Finally, the issue of Eurocentric versus Afrocentric approaches to history and the need for more dialogue in the classroom highlight the social relevance of education.

BUILDING INTERCULTURAL SKILLS

1. Be more sensitive to the ways that your educational curriculum reinforces or challenges your culture and cultural identity. Think about how it might not function in the same way for other students. How is the education you receive targeted toward the majority of students at your college? How is bias reflected in the history you are taught, the literature you are assigned, the music and art you experience, and the social issues you study?

2. Be aware of the cultural nature of the expectations you have for educational roles. If you sense that someone is not acting as a "student" should or as an "instructor" should, how much of this feeling is due to cultural differences?

ACTIVITIES

1. *Maps and worldviews:* Look at a map of the world. Unless you are looking at a "Peters Projection" map, you will notice that the equator is not in the middle of the map, even if it does run around the middle of the world. Why

is the equator not in the middle of the map, and what kinds of worldview might this map be projecting?

2. *Culture and the curriculum:* Find an old college catalog from your school or another one. Look for courses that were taught then but that are less important or nonexistent today. Were there courses in home economics? Whom were these for? What assumptions did such courses make about socialization? How about industrial arts? What languages were taught then, and which ones are taught today? What cultural needs did education fulfill?

ENDNOTES

1. Castanon, K. (2002). Quoted in GLOBE students abroad—In their own words. *Global Learning Options for a Broader Education, International Education, California State University, Long Beach.* Retrieved March 6, 2009 from: http://www.csulb.edu/divisions/aa/iec/globe/abroad/index.html

2. Bennett, J. M., & Salonen, R. (2007, March/April). Intercultural communication and the new American campus. *Change,* pp. 46–50.

3. Judy, R. W., & D'Amico, C. (1997). *Workforce 2020: Work and workers in the 21st century.* Indianapolis: Hudson Institute, p. 116.

4. Docker, J. (1995). The neocolonial assumption in university teaching of English. In B. Ashcroft, G. Griffiths, & H. Tiffin (Eds.), *The post-colonial studies reader* (pp. 443–446). New York: Routledge.

5. Hennebelle, I. (2006, April 20). Mon avenir, c'est . . . du chinois! *L'Express,* p. 80. (In France, 12,000 secondary students are now studying it. Ten years ago, there were only 2,500.)

6. Das Ende for German at USC. (2008, April 11). *Inside Higher Education.* Retrieved March 7, 2009 from: http://www.insidehighered.com/news/2008/04/11/german

7. Brockmann, S. (2009, March 6). The study of foreign languages should not be a zero-sum game. *The Chronicle of Higher Education.* Retrieved March 3, 2009 from: http://chronicle.com/weekly/v55/i26/26a03301.htm

8. More students, more languages. (2007, November 14). *Inside Higher Education.* Retrieved March 7, 2009 from: http://www.insidehighered.com/news/2007/11/14/languages

9. Washington, B. T. (1971). The Atlanta Exposition address, September 1895. In A. Meier et al. (Eds.), *Black protest thought in the twentieth century* (2nd ed., pp. 3–8). Indianapolis: Bobbs-Merrill, p. 5.

10. Goodenow, R. K. (1989). Education, Black. In C. R. Wilson & W. Ferris (Eds.), *Encyclopedia of southern culture* (Vol. 1). New York: Anchor Books, p. 253.

11. *MUW history.* (n.d.). Mississippi University for Women. Retrieved from http://muw.edu/aboutmuw/history.php

12. *Mission/Purpose.* (n.d.). Mississippi University for Women. Retrieved from http://muw.edu/aboutmuw/mission.php

13. *About Tech.* (n.d.). Georgia Institute of Technology. Retrieved from http://www.gatech.edu/about/history.html

14. Lomawaima, K. T. (1994). *They called it Prairie Light: The story of Chilocco Indian School.* Lincoln: University of Nebraska Press, p. 160.

15. Lomawaima (1994), p. 3.

16. Lomawaima (1994), p. xv.

17. Aratani, L. (2006, May 29). Older students who need basics pose challenge. *The Washington Post,* p. B2.

18. Bauer, S. (2006, May 31). Nebraskans show immigration frustration. *The Washington Post.* Retrieved June 1, 2006, from http://www.washingtonpost.com/wp-dyn/content/article/2006/05/31/AR2006053100335.html

19. Bland, K. (2006, February 26). State struggles to help English-learners achieve. *The Arizona Republic.* Retrieved June 1, 2006, from http://www.azcentral.com/specials/special24/articles/0226ellday1blomo0226.html

20. Kossan, P. (2006, February 28). English-only immersion debated for schools. *The Arizona Republic.* Retrieved June 1, 2006, at http://www.azcentral.com/specials/special24/articles/0228ellprimer0228.html

21. Schworm, P. (2009, March 5). Catholic college bars student's free condoms. *The Boston Globe.* Retrieved March 7, 2009 from: http://www.boston.com/news/local/massachusetts/articles/2009/03/05/catholic_college_bars_students_free_condoms/

22. No degree for creator of Mormon calendar. (2009, March 2). *The Houston Chronicle.* Retrieved March 3, 2009 from: http://www.chron.com/disp/story.mpl/bizarre/6290585.html

23. Burton, B. (2000, February 25). Preventing culture clashes: Learning styles, food, and dorm life challenge foreign students in Holland. *The Chronicle of Higher Education*, p. A56.

24. Holmes, P. (2005). Ethnic Chinese students' communication with cultural others in a New Zealand university. *Communication Education, 54,* 289–311.

25. National policy on assessment and qualifications for schools in the general education and training band. (n.d.) Department of Education, Republic of South Africa. Retrieved on March 7, 2009 from: http://www.education.gov.za/Curriculum/GET/doc/ANatioanalPolicy.pdf

26. Bristol denies admissions bias. (2003, February 26). *BBC News.* Retrieved from http://news.bbc.co.uk/2/hi/uk_news/education/2798507.stm

27. Juakali, K. (2001, December 19). L'Université de Kinshasa ferme ses portes. *Afrik.com.* Retrieved from http://www.afrik.com/article3775.html

28. Brief historical sketch of the University of Tennessee. (n.d.). University of Tennessee. Retrieved from http://web.utk.edu/~mklein/brfhist.html

29. Equal Employment Opportunity/Affirmative Action Policy. (n.d.). Arizona State University. Retrieved from http://www.eoaa.asu.edu/Pres%20EOAA%20policy%20statement.html

30. Bollag, B. (2003, November 7). French court upholds landmark program of affirmative action in college admissions. *The Chronicle of Higher Education.* Retrieved form http://chronicle.com/prm/daily/2003/11/2003110703n.htm

31. Laronche, M. (2003, November 7) Sciences-Po condemned to review the method of its ZEP conventions. *Le Monde.* Retrieved from http://www.lemonde.fr/web/recherche_articleweb/1,13-0,36-341087,0.html?query=sciences+po&query2=&booleen=et&num_page=1&auteur=&dans=dansarticle&periode=30&ordre=pertinence&G_NBARCHIVES=796331&nbpages=2&artparpage=10&nb_art=11

32. Betz, L. (2002, Summer). True admissions. *Continuum Magazine.* Retrieved from http://www.alumni.utah.edu/continuum/summer02/andfinally.htm

33. Keller, R. H., & Keller, D. R. (2003, October 19). Machen's bane: Just who gets into medical school at the U? *The Salt Lake Tribune*, p. AA7.

34. Cloud, J. (2003, October 27). Inside the new SAT. *Time*, 49–50.

35. Atkinson, R. C. (2001, February 18). Standardized tests and access to American universities. Robert H. Atwell Distinguished Lecture. 83rd Annual Meeting of the American Council on Education. Washington, DC. Retrieved from http://www.ucop.edu/pres/comments/satspch.html

36. Britz, J. D. (2006, March 23). To all the girls I've rejected. *New York Times*, p. A25.

37. Britz (2006, March 23), p. A25.

38. Davidson, A. L. (1996). *Making and molding identity in schools: Student narratives on race, gender, and academic empowerment.* Albany: State University of New York, p. 22.

39. Davidson (1996), p. 128.

40. Giroux, H. A. (1996). Is there a place for cultural studies in colleges of education? In H. A. Giroux, C. Lankshear, P. McLaren, & M. Peters (Eds.), *Counternarratives: Cultural studies and critical pedagogies in postmodern spaces.* New York: Routledge, p. 50.

41. Loewen, J. W. (1995). *Lies my teacher told me: Everything your American history textbook got wrong.* New York: New Press.

42. China, Japan eye textbook tension. (2005, April 11). *BBC News*. Retrieved May 23, 2006, from http://news.bbc.co.uk/2/hi/asia-pacific/4432535.stm

43. Onishi, N. (2005, April 17). In Japan's new texts, lessons in rising nationalism. *New York Times*. Retrieved May 23, 2006, from http://www.nytimes.com/2005/04/17/weekinreview/17onishi .html?ex=1271390400&en=60e4a68bc70713c4&ei=5090&partner=rssuserland&emc=rss

44. Fattah, H. (2006, May 24). Don't be friends with Christians or Jews, Saudi texts say. *New York Times*, p. A10.

45. Shea, N. (2006, May 21). This is a Saudi textbook. (After the intolerance was removed.) *The Washington Post*, p. B1.

46. Samuels, A. (2009, March 9). Rethinking race in the classroom. *Newsweek*, pp. 52–53.

47. Jan, T., & Schworm, P. (2009, March 7). Campus insider: Racist e-mail rocks Dartmouth campus. *The Boston Globe*. Retrieved March 7, 2009 from: http://www.boston.com/news/local/ breaking_news/2009/03/campus_insider_3.html

48. Bennett & Salonen (2007), p. 48.

49. Loewen (1995), p. 302.

50. Loewen (1995), p. 302.

51. Loewen (1995), p. 311.

52. Tierney, W. G. (1997). *Academic outlaws: Queer theory and cultural studies in the academy*. Thousand Oaks, CA: Sage.

53. Simpson, J. (2003). *I have been waiting: Race and U.S. higher education*. Toronto: University of Toronto Press, p. 196.

Intercultural Communication and Health Care

STUDY OBJECTIVES

After reading this chapter, you should be able to:

1. Understand the importance of communication in health care delivery. Describe some of the ways that communication can be overlooked and how this might impact the delivery of medical services.

2. Explain some of the intercultural barriers to effective health care. Explain the ways that some cultural groups have been or continue to be treated in the health care system. Describe how prejudicial attitudes can influence health care delivery.

3. Explain how religious or spiritual beliefs may be important in effective health care delivery. Describe some of the ways that health care professionals can deal with religious and spiritual beliefs. Discuss the ethical implications of some of the ways that health care professionals deal with religious or spiritual beliefs.

4. Explain how power differences can influence health communication.

5. Identify the four frameworks that physicians might use in communicating about a patient's health.

6. Describe the role of ethics committees. Describe some of the complex issues to be dealt with in making ethical health care decisions.

KEY TERMS

AIDS
alternative medicine
benevolent deception
biologically based practices
complementary medicine
contractual honesty
energy medicine
ethics committees
euthanasia
fat acceptance movement
health care professionals
HIV
manipulative and body based practices
medical jargon
medical terminology
mind-body medicine
prejudicial ideologies
religious freedom
religious history
strict paternalism
Tuskegee Syphilis Project
unmitigated honesty

The longer I stay in the U.S., the more differences I find between American and Chinese health care practices. For instance, some elderly people spend the rest of their lives in nursing homes even if they have children, and that seems to be commonly acceptable. However, in China, children have the responsibility to take care of their elder parents. Sending one's parents to nursing homes, although not illegal, is considered by the general public as a very bad practice. Another difference I found is that, in the U.S., abortion is a very controversial topic; however, in China, it's commonly considered just as a medical practice, and is not associated with moral judgments in general.

—Lan

Lan's experience with cultural differences in health care is instructive in how we think about health care more generally. While we may often think of health care as a scientific or medical issue, health care and communication are also deeply embedded in culture.

What you have learned about intercultural communication has important applications in the health communication context. As the U.S. population ages and new medical technologies are developed, health care will become even more significant in our lives. Health care has also become increasingly controversial as more and more managed care corporations have entered the market. Within this changing context, as the U.S. population becomes increasingly diverse, U.S. Americans are beginning to seek out health care from a variety of sources—from traditional Western practitioners to more "exotic" Eastern practices.

In this chapter, we discuss some of the reasons communication about health has become more important and some of the ways you might navigate this communication context. Not only patients, but **health care professionals**—including physicians, nurses, physical and occupational therapists, and medical technicians—can come from a variety of cultural backgrounds. Intercultural communication and misunderstandings in health communication arise daily in this context.

THE IMPORTANCE OF COMMUNICATION IN HEALTH CARE

Intercultural communication is increasingly relevant in the health communication context for a number of reasons. First, as our population becomes increasingly diverse, complexities arise in communicating about health issues. Not only are health care professionals communicating with people

Info Bites

Alternative forms of medicine are finding more widespread acceptance within the United States. In 2008, The Center for Life opened at The University of New Mexico in Albuquerque. The Center for Life offers what they term "complementary medicine," which includes both Eastern and Western medical practices. According to *Frontline*, 30 percent of Americans use alternative forms of therapy, and *Discovery Health* reported that in 1997 alone Americans spent over $30 billion of their own money on complementary or alternative forms of medicine. For an overview of the debate surrounding alternative forms of medicine, visit PBS at: www.pbs.org/ wgbh/pages/frontline/ shows/altmed/.

TABLE 13.1 Home Countries of Foreign Doctors

About 23% of all physicians in the United States were educated abroad. Here is a list of the top 10 countries that send physicians to the United States. How might intercultural communication be important here?

1. India—19.5%	6. Dominican Republic—2.5%
2. Pakistan—11.9%	7. Syria—2.5%
3. Philippines—8.8%	8. United Kingdom—2.4%
4. Ex-USSR—3.1%	9. Germany—2.3%
5. Egypt—2.6%	10. Mexico—1.8%

Source: http://www.mdgreencard.com/situation.html

Surf's Up!

Did you know that you can major in health communication? Health communication covers a variety of issues such as patient–physician communication, health communication in organizations, social support, and health promotion. In a culturally diverse setting, how should we approach these issues?

from differing cultural backgrounds, but these same patients are communicating with nurses, doctors, and other health care professionals from differing cultural backgrounds. Table 13.1 shows some of the diversity of cultural backgrounds of U.S. physicians. And in some cultures, there may be certain stigmas associated with communicating about health issues, making it difficult to discuss these concerns. For example, in some cultures, subjects such as mental illness, AIDS, bird flu, sexually transmitted diseases, impotence, and abortion are not easily broached.

Second, health care professionals and patients may not realize the importance of communication. This oversight may seem incidental to medical training and treatment, but the reality is, much medical practice, particularly diagnosis, relies heavily on patient communication. In many ways, this shortcoming in health care reflects a Western cultural phenomenon, "due partly to the belief that the biomedical model of health care—the predominant model in Western societies—is based on a range of predominantly physical procedures (physical examination, physical manipulation, injections, etc.) rather than communication between two parties."[1] In other words, Western physicians tend to rely heavily on physical symptoms to evaluate illness, rather than communicating with patients about what they are experiencing.

However, good communication is crucial to quality health care. Health care providers ask questions to diagnose problems, to help patients understand the treatment, and so on. And patients come to health professionals to seek treatment and ask questions. But even native English speakers complain about the use of **medical jargon**—potentially confusing or difficult-to-understand medical terminology—by physicians. In trying to understand more about a patient's family history, doctors commonly ask a number of questions about the health of family members. In the following example, the use of jargon results in miscommunication:

DOCTOR: Have you ever had a history of cardiac arrest in your family?

PATIENT: We never had no trouble with the police.[2]

While the term "cardiac arrest" may not seem like medical jargon to the physician or to you, the patient clearly did not understand it. The dialogue continues:

DOCTOR: How about varicose veins?

PATIENT: Well, I have veins, but I don't know if they're close or not.[3]

If English speakers have trouble with common medical terms, health care professionals need to be especially careful using these terms. For those patients who are communicating in a second language, **medical terminology**—scientific language used by doctors to describe specific medical conditions—can be particularly confusing. And when cultural misunderstandings arise, it can lead to inadequate treatment.

Third, and probably the most obvious barrier to health services, are language barriers. Some health care providers ask their bilingual employees to serve as interpreters to patients who do not speak English. In a case cited in New York City, for example, when a "Spanish-speaking hospital receptionist refused to interpret during her lunch hour, doctors at St. Vincent's Staten Island Hospital turned to a 7-year-old child to tell their patient, an injured construction worker, that he needed an emergency amputation."[4] Language issues can create problems in health care, not only in hospitals, but also in pharmacies. A study done by pediatricians in the Bronx section of New York City found that "pharmacies often used computer programs to translate prescriptions. Only one pharmacy employed a Spanish-speaking pharmacist that could check the translations."[5] This raises even more issues with language barriers in health care. As the authors of this study noted, "we visited one of the large chain pharmacies, and discovered that the computer could not translate some commonly used terms, such as *dropperful*, or *for thirty days*."[6] Many hospitals rely on their workers or bilingual children of patients to help translate. At one California hospital, "there have often been no Hmong-speaking employees of any kind present in the hospital at night. . . . Sometimes not even a child is available. Doctors on the late shift in the emergency room have often had no way of taking a patient's medical history. . . . I asked one doctor what he did in such cases. He said, 'Practice veterinary medicine.'"[7] There are no easy answers to many of these concerns, given the numerous languages spoken in the United States and around the world, but awareness of these issues may lead to innovative ways of dealing with language differences.

Fourth, health care providers and patients alike may operate out of an ethnocentric framework without realizing it. Assumptions about health care often have cultural roots. Consider the following example: Setsuko, a Japanese woman now living in the United States, had to spend several months in the hospital for a chronic illness. She became extremely depressed, to the point of feeling suicidal. Whenever the staff would ask her how she was doing, Setsuko would answer that she was fine. Based on this lack of communication, the nursing and medical staff were unaware of her depression for weeks. It was not until she began to exhibit physical signs of depression that she was offered a psychiatric consultation. The problem was that Setsuko was culturally conditioned to be a good patient by not making a fuss or drawing attention to herself or embarrassing her

Patients and health care providers come from a variety of cultural backgrounds with differing assumptions about health care and the proper roles of doctors and nurses. These cultural differences can influence the health care patients receive. Health care providers need to be sensitive to these cultural differences in providing health services.

family with complaints about being depressed, so she always reported that she was fine. Although the psychiatrist tried to explain that in this context a "good patient" was expected to discuss and report any and all problems or symptoms, Setsuko still had to work to redefine her cultural role as a good patient in order to receive better health care. In this case, both the health care providers and the patient struggled to negotiate a more effective communication framework to ensure better treatment.

Fifth, treating patients is not always a matter of communication between the physician and the patient. While one-to-one communication generally works well in Western cultures, which are more oriented to individualism, other cultures may focus more on the family's role in health care. Thus, communication between the physician and the patient is only one element in the communication process. Unfortunately, most health communication research has limited itself to the physician–patient relationship. Laurel Northouse, a nursing professor, and Peter Northouse, a communication professor, note: "This lack of systematic study of professional-family interaction is symptomatic of the lack of importance that health professionals have traditionally attributed to this relationship in health care."[8]

This cultural bias in thinking about the role of the family in health care can lead to problems. Consider the case of the Samoan man hospitalized with a gunshot wound. Throughout the day, more and more family members gathered in the waiting room. Because there were so many extended family members, hospital personnel asked them to wait in the main lobby. The family members became increasingly irate because they wanted to see the patient as a large group, but the hospital had a policy of only three visitors at a time. Tensions between the family and the staff continued to escalate until a hospital administrator, sensitive to cultural differences, made a special exception and allowed large groups of family members to visit the patient.

A similar cultural pattern occurs in Iranian culture, where families may be seen as ignoring or violating hospital visiting hours, which can create conflict with the hospital staff. This cultural pattern emerges from a cultural duty to be there for the patient:

> Iranians are very sociable, and hospital visits to friends or relatives are considered a moral duty. Visitors come in large number, bring sweets, flowers, and gifts. It is a time to socialize and to keep the patient company, and most hospitalized Iranians enjoy having large numbers of noisy visitors. In Iranian culture it is considered shameful to leave a loved one alone in the hospital without visitors.[9]

If hospital staff understand this cultural difference in health care, it might help avoid cultural conflicts with the patient's family. Given the importance of the family in the overall health care of the patient, cultural accommodation might be seen as one way of nursing the patient to better health.

Families, of course, can provide very important support to a patient as she or he recovers. Their role is even more important after the patient returns home. But this means that the family must receive adequate information about the patient's condition. In turn, this means that health care professionals must be sensitive to cultural differences and must adapt their communication accordingly.

Finally, some work has begun to show the importance of community involvement in health care. In their work on community-based health communication, communication scholars Leigh Arden Ford and Gust Yep found that a community-oriented approach often works much better than a focus on individuals. Part of this effectiveness emerges when community health workers "become catalysts for change. Through their public health and communication network role enactments, they promote community organizing efforts and enable individual empowerment. Significantly, community health workers empower themselves as they become a means to empowerment for individuals, families, neighborhoods, and communities."[10] This community-based approach seems to work in Haiti, where Dr. Paul Farmer of Partners in Health focused on "community-based solutions to its health problems. That meant, for example, training local residents as doctors, technicians and outreach workers who could diagnose and treat their neighbors."[11] A focus on community as a foundation for health care is quite different from a more traditional focus on the individual, but it seems to work.

INTERCULTURAL BARRIERS TO EFFECTIVE HEALTH CARE

In Chapter 3, we discussed the importance of history in intercultural communication. Let's look at some of these historical dynamics as they influence health care today. This is important because the history of medicine guides how different cultural communities may relate to health care.

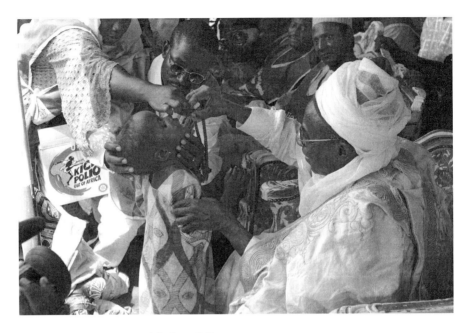

These doctors are vaccinating children against polio, despite rumors in some countries that polio vaccines were a conspiracy to sterilize children. What might have happened in the past to lead to such fears?

Historical Treatments of Cultural Groups

First, historically, widespread ideologies about different cultures have fostered differential treatment for some groups, especially racial and ethnic minorities, by medical professionals. As sociologist Chris Shilling writes, "Historically, the negative construction of black bodies has made them targets for a variety of moral panics surrounding health and disease."[12] In the past, medical conclusions about alleged racial difference have justified a number of deplorable social practices, from slavery, to colonization, to immigration restrictions.[13]

This differential treatment has caused some cultural groups to be justifiably suspicious of contemporary health care. For example, the infamous **Tuskegee Syphilis Project,** conducted by the U.S. Public Health Service on unsuspecting African Americans in Tuskegee, Alabama, over a 40-year period, spurred some of these concerns.[14] In this study, Black patients who sought out medical care for syphilis were instead given placebos (sugar pills), but were not told that they were part of a study, simply to establish an experimental control group. The purpose of the study was to explore how syphilis spreads in a patient's body and how it spreads in a population. Periodic reports were published in medical journals, but the Centers for Disease Control received only one letter from a physician raising ethical concerns. The study was finally halted, not by the medical community, but only after a public denouncement by Senator Edward Kennedy in Congress. Unfortunately, it's hardly surprising that such a study was not conducted on wealthy White Americans in Beverly Hills.

The Tuskegee Syphilis Project, among other studies and projects, has reinforced suspicion about the medical community from many marginalized communities. This "mistrust of the medical system by some African Americans has

Info Bites

The National Minority AIDS Council (NMAC) is a national organization "dedicated to developing leadership within communities of color to address the challenges of HIV/AIDS" (see also www.nmac.org/home/). Based on your study of intercultural communication, what kinds of issues do you think this organization should address?

been identified as a barrier to optimal health care and participation in clinical trials."[15] In a recent study on perceptions of trust in medical care, differences in trust emerged between White and Black respondents. These researchers found that "African Americans have been shown to have greater awareness of the documented history of racial discrimination in the health care system than white Americans, and this greater awareness of historical discrimination has been associated with less trust of clinical and research institutions. This is consistent with our finding of greater concern among African Americans about the potential for harmful experiments being performed in hospitals."[16] Given this horrible history, how might health care providers work with African Americans to gain their trust? Given the "alarming inequities in health outcomes between different racial and ethnic groups in the United States," it is important that we focus on "the development of strategic, adaptive, and sensitive health communication across a range of communication channels and media" to enhance the health of all of us.[17] The rise of **AIDS** (acquired immune deficiency syndrome) and **HIV** (human immunodeficiency virus) in the late 20th century provoked new fears among gays and minorities that the medical community would again provide differential treatment. As Jeffrey Levi, an AIDS and health policy consultant, argues:

> Homophobia was not introduced into the health-care system with the AIDS epidemic. Rather, its long-standing legacy of discrimination and exclusion has resulted in the creation of a separate health-care system within the gay community, a health-care system that responded to this new crisis immediately, saving countless gay lives—and heterosexual lives as well—while the government-sponsored system floundered, unable to find the will or the funds to operate.[18]

The slow response to the AIDS epidemic by the federal government has been widely discussed and critiqued.[19] In his analysis of public discourses about AIDS, Larry Gross, a communication professor, concludes that "AIDS thus taught two lessons. First, a disease that strikes gay people (and people of color, and drug users, and poor people) will not receive adequate attention. Second, people will begin to pay attention when famous and important people are involved."[20] Thus, the HIV/AIDS epidemic highlighted the traditional lack of trust between the health care system and minority communities.

Prejudicial Ideologies

Second, **prejudicial ideologies**—sets of ideas based on stereotypes—about various cultural groups affect both health care professionals and patients. These attitudes can present significant barriers to intercultural communication. Consider the following case: A social worker in one of the nursing units was recording information on a patient's chart when she overheard staff members discussing a patient who had recently been admitted to the unit. They were not certain if the patient was Chinese, Taiwanese, or Vietnamese. The head nurse called the supervisor of international services, who helped clarify that the patient was

Taiwanese and so needed a Taiwanese-speaking interpreter. As they continued to discuss the patient, one staff member said, "So she doesn't speak any English at all? How does she get along in this country if she can't speak English?" Another staff member responded, "She doesn't need to get along here. They are all on welfare."[21] Given our concern with the kinds of health care received by members of nonmainstream cultural groups, these comments take on even more significance than simply being prejudicial. Such attitudes may influence the quality of health care that patients receive. And health care professionals are hardly immune to prejudice. Attending nursing school or medical school does not purge feelings of homophobia, racism, sexism, and other kinds of prejudice.

Patients, too, often enter the health care system with prejudicial attitudes. Tom's brother-in-law, for example, a physician in North Carolina, often encounters patients who prefer not to be treated by doctors who are "Yankees." He is frequently asked, "Where are you from?" which suggests that regional differences remain barriers. Because he is from California, these patients consent to his treatment; after all, he is not a "damn Yankee." Regional identities can influence whether people trust medical professionals.

Because of this mistrust, many people prefer to obtain a significant amount of their medical information from their own communities. For example, in the case of AIDS, many gay men turned to the gay community for information on the latest experimental drugs and treatments. In the South, some low-income Whites believe that Prozac is addicting despite scientific evidence to the contrary. However, because Prozac is seen as addictive within this community, patients often refuse to take the drug when it is prescribed. The point here is that people may turn to their own communities out of mistrust of medical professionals. Sometimes these communities can provide significant alternative health care, as in the case of gay men and AIDS; other communities, however, can provide misinformation.

Currently, the ongoing effort to wipe out polio continues, but it has encountered a major setback with the belief that polio vaccinations are meant to sterilize children, as well as the spread of polio in areas that are very difficult for health care workers to reach. The earlier success in eliminating polio may be difficult to continue:

> The decline from 350,000 new cases in 1988 (when the goal of rapid polio eradication was first declared) to 2,000 cases now (chiefly in Nigeria, India, Pakistan and Afghanistan) looks like a near victory. But the final stretch is the hardest . . . . The fighting in Afghanistan and Pakistan has hampered vaccination programmes there. So have rumours among Muslims in northern Nigeria that the vaccination programme was in fact a conspiracy to sterilise children. That allowed the polio virus to strengthen and spread. The Nigerian strain may have now reached a dozen other countries.[22]

Because of these fears about the vaccines, polio may spread, rather than face elimination. Yet, why would people be afraid of a conspiracy to sterilize children? What might have happened in the past to lead to such fears?

RELIGION AND HEALTH CARE

Even when they are not facing serious illness or death, many people turn to religion or spirituality to help them try to understand the complexities of life.[23] When they are ill, however, some people are driven to seek answers to questions that science cannot always answer. While some people turn to spiritual healing, others prefer to combine their spiritual beliefs with traditional medical care. Sometimes spirituality and/or religion can be helpful in the healing process; other times, it may be helpful in facing death.

The role of religion and spirituality in health care is still a controversial topic, but today "more than half of the med schools in the country" offer courses in religion and spirituality, "up from just three a decade ago."[24] Yet the role of religion and spirituality in health care raises a number of issues about ethical ways to approach the topic of incorporating health practices into existing beliefs and helping patients avoid any pressure they may feel about their beliefs. It is also important for health care professionals to avoid imposing their beliefs on patients. One example of such an error is when a "doctor told his patient that 'if she was right with God, she wouldn't be depressed.'"[25] Needless to say, health care professionals should not assume that all patients share their beliefs, as people around the world hold a wide range of spiritual views.

Yet, accommodating for religious differences can be an important part of effective health care. Consider the following example:

> Dr. Susan Strangl, a family-medicine doctor at UCLA, [had] a Muslim patient who needed medication but was observing Ramadan and couldn't drink or eat during the day. After taking a **religious history**—routine for all hospitalized patients at UCLA—Strangl chose a once-a-day medication that could be taken after sundown. "If we hadn't talked about it, I would have written him a prescription for four times a day and he would not have taken it," she says.[26]

While religious and spiritual beliefs vary widely, Drs. Koenig, McCullough, and Larson attempted to survey the studies available in this area and compiled the *Handbook of Religion and Health Care*. Our understanding of the role of religion and spirituality in health still leaves us with many unanswered questions, but they do recommend seven specific strategies for physicians and other health care professionals in dealing with patients:[27]

- Take a religious history.
- Support or encourage religious beliefs.
- Ensure access to religious resources.
- Respect visits by clergy.
- View chaplains as part of the health care team.
- Be ready to step in when clergy are unavailable.
- Use advanced spiritual interventions cautiously.

What Do You Think?

Should hospitals provide interpreters for their patients who do not speak English? If so, for all languages or only a few? If you were vacationing in, say, Italy and had to go to the hospital, would you expect someone at the hospital to speak English? What about Mongolia, which gets very few English-speaking tourists?

Some of these suggestions may be difficult for health care professionals to follow, particularly when they are followers of different religions, hold different spiritual beliefs, or are atheists or agnostics. Patients also may not want to discuss such topics. One physician, "Dr. Jim Martin, head of the American Academy of Family Physicians, teaches residents to take spiritual histories, but 'if a patient flinches, we don't go there.' And if a patient says faith or spiritual beliefs are not important, 'we check that box and move on.'"[28]

Some physicians, however, argue against some of the previously suggested guidelines. For example, Dr. Richard P. Sloan of the Columbia-Presbyterian Medical Center cautions against praying with patients: "It confuses the relationship. It may encourage patients to think a prayer is going to somehow improve their well-being. It certainly will improve their spiritual well-being but there's no evidence it's going to improve their health." His biggest concern about health care professionals engaging in religious issues is "Manipulation of **religious freedom.** Restriction of religious freedom. Invasion of privacy. And causing harm. It's bad enough to be sick, it's worse still to be gravely ill, but to add to that the burden of remorse and guilt for some supposed failure of religious devotion is unconscionable."[29] While some health care professionals may believe that spiritual beliefs or religious beliefs can help patients be healthier, Dr. Sloan notes, "The question is if religion is demonstrably efficacious, if it really influences longevity, morbidity and mortality, and the quality of life, why don't the insurance companies get in on it?"[30] The point here is that there is no easy list of ways to deal with cultural differences and religious differences in health care. Issues of ethics, however, should always be at the forefront of considerations. Communication about these issues can be key to unraveling the ethical issues at hand.

Many health care professionals may not be aware of the diversity of religious and spiritual beliefs around the world. How can studying religious and cultural differences be helpful to health care professionals? How can health care professionals communicate respect for others' religious or spiritual beliefs without compromising their own beliefs? How assertive should patients be about asking health care professionals to accommodate their religious or spiritual beliefs? Health care professionals should also be aware that some patients may fear getting inferior care if they do not share the dominant religious beliefs. How might patients and health care professionals assure each other in this context? All of these questions are at the forefront of the debate about the role of religious or spiritual beliefs in health care.

Cultural Influences on Approaches to Medicine

Different cultures bring different perspectives on our health—how we stay healthy, as well as how we fall ill. You may have heard many cultural stories in your own home about staying healthy or ways to avoid illness. Some people are told that wearing a hat in cold weather is important because the head loses an enormous amount of heat, when in reality, any exposed parts of your body are places

What Do You Think?

Currently, obesity is measured according to Body Mass Index (BMI), which is calculated by dividing weight by height in inches squared. What is your BMI? Is this a fair measure or are there other factors that should be considered? Using BMI statistics, the National Center for Health Statistics estimates that of U.S. adults 20 years and older 32.7 percent are overweight, 34.3 percent are obese, and 5.9 percent are extremely obese. What would other cultures think of the use of BMI as a measure of overall health?

where heat is lost. If you wear a swimsuit in cold weather, for example, the exposed parts of your body will release heat at the same rate as the head. Some people are told to eat chicken soup when they are ill, because chicken soup is a cure. For others, boiling citrus in water is a drink to help cure various illnesses.

There are also many cultural differences about what might be considered something that needs medical attention. Increasingly, in the United States, for example, the loss of hair on men is seen as something that may require medicines, such as Rogaine (minoxidil) to help correct this "problem." The television show, *Nip/Tuck*, highlights the use of medicine to solve other "problems" that may not be considered health-care problems in other cultures. For example, is the need for breast augmentation a cultural issue? Or a health issue? Or both?

Lots of attention has been focused on obesity in the United States. Cultural attitudes about weight have changed over the years in the United States, as well as in cultures around the world. Once seen as a sign of wealth, today obesity is seen as a sign of medical disorder in need of medical treatment. The debates over weight and what should be acceptable have been at the forefront of the **Fat Acceptance Movement**, a social movement that works to end discrimination against overweight people and the assumption that they are necessarily unhealthy or in need of medical treatment.

In the United States and many other westernized nations, the dominant model of medicine is based on biomedical science. All other approaches fall under the term, **alternative medicine**. There is no comprehensive list of other ways of thinking about medicine and health, but some of the major approaches to alternative medicine include homeopathy, naturopathy, and traditional Chinese medicine. Acupuncture is one approach used in traditional Chinese medicine, and many patients report that it does work for them. The use of herbs is another aspect of traditional Chinese medicine. There are many other approaches that developed in China and are widely accepted in many Asian cultures.

There are too many other approaches to medicine that would fall under alternative medicine than we can list here, but they are also seen as equally valid approaches to health care. These other approaches are sometimes referred to as "complementary and alternative medicine." Currently, the National Institute of Health has a unit called the National Center for Complementary and Alternative Medicine that is focused on other approaches to health. There are many different approaches to health that are not considered traditional medicine. They have been categorized into four major approaches: (1) mind-body medicine, (2) biologically based practices, (3) manipulative and body-based practices, and (4) energy medicine.[31]

Mind-body medicine focuses on using the mind to influence the body. Some of these approaches include patient-support group therapy, meditation, and prayer. **Biologically based practices** refers to the use of products found in nature as therapy. Some of these approaches include the use of herbal therapies, dietary supplements, and other natural products. **Manipulative and body-based practices** refers to the use of massage or chiropractic approaches to health. **Energy medicine** focuses on the use of energy fields to foster health.

When used, in any combination, in conjuction with traditional Western medicine, these alternative approaches are considered to be **complementary medicine**. Some health care providers accept a complementary approach, while others feel negatively about alternative medicine.

POWER IN COMMUNICATION ABOUT HEALTH CARE

There is often an imbalance of power in health communication situations. We examined the role of power in Chapter 2, but let's take a look at how it might function in communication in the health care context.

Imbalances of Power in Health Communication

Communication between physician and patient is often marked by an imbalance in power with regard to medical knowledge and access to treatment. Patients, for example, may not have access to drugs without a written prescription from a physician. In order to get that prescription, the patient must rely on the physician, who has the power to prescribe drugs. Physicians in HMOs (health maintenance organizations), which are increasingly common in the United States, can elect to refer or not refer patients to specialists. Physicians have power over patients in other ways as well. For example, they can recommend certain treatments (and not others), order medical tests, and otherwise determine what kind of treatment the patient receives.

What Do You Think?

Before children played "doctor" or "nurse," perhaps they played "healer." The ways in which people care for the sick and dying in society have varied across cultures and throughout history. The doctors of Western society today attribute many remedies to the cultural healers of yesterday. So, why is it that contemporary science seems to want to divorce itself from folk or ancient traditions?

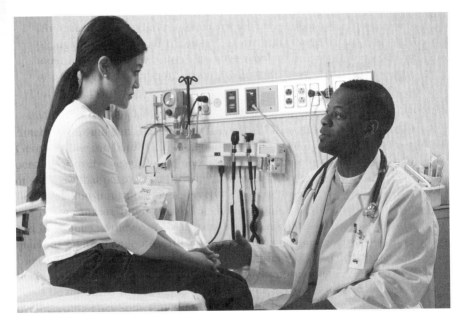

Physician–patient communication reflects the power imbalance built into the health care structure in the United States. Physicians' power over patients includes medical knowledge and access to treatment, prescriptions, and tests.

This power imbalance is built into the health care structure in the United States, but physician–patient communication also reflects these power differences. For example, if Judith goes to see a physician for the first time, the physician may introduce herself by saying, "Hi Judith, my name is Doctor Tyndall." What would happen if Judith were to respond, "Hi Lisa, my name is Doctor Martin"? Some physicians would be amused, but others would be irritated by the perceived effort to challenge the power imbalance.

Note also the potential confusion of patients when they meet Dr. Tyndall. Who is Dr. Tyndall? Is she an intern? A staff physician? What role does she play in providing health care? And how many other health care professionals will the patient see today? Because patients may encounter many health care workers in a single day, cultural differences in communication may be exacerbated. The process of negotiating cultural differences may be especially difficult for the patient because each communication interaction may be brief.

Health Care as a Business

It is important to remember that the health care industry in the United States is a huge business. The implications for patients have been the subject of heated public debates over the allocation of health care resources. One controversial issue is whether HMOs ration health care resources; obtaining such resources often is not easy or automatic.

The continuing rapid rise in health care costs in the United States does not appear to have any easy answers. The National Coalition on Health Care reports that:

> In 2008, total national health expenditures were expected to rise 6.9 percent—two times the rate of inflation. Total spending was $2.4 TRILLION in 2007, or $7900 per person. Total health care spending represented 17 percent of the gross domestic product (GDP). U.S. health care spending is expected to increase at similar levels for the next decade reaching $4.3 TRILLION in 2017, or 20 percent of GDP.[32]

A different way of looking at rising health care costs is to see that: "Health care is expected to account for $1 of every $5 spent in the United States in another decade."[33] If health care costs continue to skyrocket, what will happen to the availability of health care resources?

Patients from countries where health care is provided by the government may be confused by the private health care system in the United States. U.S. Americans, too, can become lost in the maze of rules and regulations governing the access to specialists and special treatments. Because there is a power imbalance at work here, patients need to recognize that HMOs are businesses. It may not be enough simply to ask for many medical services, particularly higher-priced treatments.

For example, Didier, a French patient who needed extensive occupational therapy after an accident, did not understand why the number of occupational

Pop Culture Spotlight

According to The American Society for Aesthetic Plastic Surgery, there were 11.7 million cosmetic procedures in 2007. The popular cable television show *Nip/Tuck* is based on the plastic surgery phenomenon, involving a fictitious partnership based in Miami, Florida. The website for the show www.fxnetworks.com/shows/originals/niptuck/aboutTheShow.php even allows viewers to submit photos for critique by the *Nip/Tuck* community. Why are Americans obsessed with body image? How does your cultural background impact your version of the "ideal" body image? How might these differences impact communication between different cultural groups?

therapy hours was so limited, especially after his physician told him he would need much more therapy before returning to work. It was only after Didier realized that his HMO was a business that he began to pester the HMO for more hours; in France, this service is provided by the government. Eventually, the HMO consented to more therapy. But Didier believes that it was only after the cost associated with his relentless pestering threatened to exceed the cost of the therapy that the HMO consented to the additional therapy. Thus, patients have to realize that they are the objects of a cost–benefit analysis and that they have to insist on getting access to health care resources.

At the time of this writing, President Obama has just become president and he has indicated his desire to invoke health care reform. His call for changes in the ways that health care is managed in the United States has drawn a range of supporters who are "calling for fast action on the issue from the Obama Administration":

> What could unite the American Medical Assn., the lobbying arm of the pharmaceutical industry, Regence BlueCross BlueShield, and the Service Employees International Union (SEIU) in a common cause? Surprisingly, health-care reform.[34]

The specific reforms to the current health care system are far from agreed upon. Whatever changes do occur will change the way that U.S. Americans view health care and its status as a for-profit system.

Intercultural Ethics and Health Issues

What are the ethics of health care communication? In the physician–patient relationship, the physician has far more information than the patient, and the ethics are complicated, particularly in intercultural situations. With regard to communication ethics in health care, physicians can give information about the patient's health within four general frameworks: (1) strict paternalism, (2) benevolent deception, (3) contractual honesty, and (4) unmitigated honesty.[35]

Strict paternalism reflects a physician's decision to provide misinformation to the patient when the physician believes it is in the best interests of the patient. If a patient has terminal cancer, for example, the physician may not feel it would be helpful to tell the patient that he or she has high blood pressure as well. **Benevolent deception** occurs when the physician chooses to communicate only a part of a patient's diagnosis. For example, a patient might be told that she or he has cancer and that treatments are available, but not be told that the prognosis is very poor. **Contractual honesty** refers to the practice of telling the patient only what she or he wants to hear or to know. For example, if a patient says, "I only want to hear about the treatments available to me, but not my chances of survival," a physician may choose to follow the patient's wishes. Finally, **unmitigated honesty** refers to when a physician chooses to communicate the entire diagnosis to a patient. Some health care professionals prefer this communication route as a protection against lawsuits. However, some patients

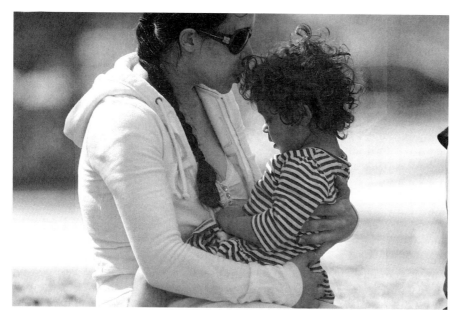

Medical technology allowed Nadya Suleman to have octuplets, in addition to the six children she already had. Some people criticized her for this decision. Is it anyone else's business how many children a woman has? What are health care ethics issues in this case?

are put off by the bluntness of this approach. For instance, if a physician told a patient that some very expensive and painful treatments were available but the patient probably wouldn't survive anyway, that patient might be justifiably upset.

The fear of malpractice suits guides many decisions related to ethics. Sometimes health care organizations use **ethics committees**—often staffed by health care professionals, religious leaders, and social workers—to help make decisions about ethics.[36] In the intercultural context, these decisions can be complex. In some cultures, the family is intimately involved in the health care and medical treatment of its members. In other cultures, medical information is confidential and is given only to the patient, unless he or she is incapacitated or incapable of understanding. Knowing the appropriate way to communicate with patient and family is not easy. For example, some patients may not want their families involved in their care if they have a miscarriage, are suffering from colon-rectal cancer, or are depressed. And many medical procedures are very controversial, even among members of the same culture.

Recently, the birth of octuplets to Nadya Suleman, also known as "octomom," who already had six children, has raised the issue of ethics in the use of in vitro fertilization. "The American Society for Reproductive Medicine, a leading organization in the field of reproductive medicine, recommends that a woman under the age of 35 should have no more than two embryos implanted by way of in vitro fertilization (IVF)."[37] Since Suleman's physician implanted more than two embryos, questions about the ethics of this decision have arisen. Also, people have raised ethical questions about her ability to provide for her fourteen children. Many people have very strong feelings about her decision to have fourteen children. What do you think was the right thing for the physician to do? What should Nadya Suleman have done? Is it anyone else's business if she decides to have as many children as she wishes? How do you decide on the ethics in this case?

In some religious systems, **euthanasia,** which involves ending the life of a terminally ill patient, is seen as suicide and therefore is unacceptable. In other religions, euthanasia is acceptable for terminally ill patients. Key issues include how much control a patient should have in this situation, how much power a physician should have if his or her ethical framework differs from the patient's, and how much power the state should have in making laws preventing or permitting euthanasia.

SUMMARY

In this chapter, we examined a number of issues relevant to intercultural communication and health care. Intercultural communication is becoming more important in health care as the population becomes more culturally diverse. Communication is vitally important to the functioning of health services, and this communication is not simply between patient and physician.

We also looked at barriers to effective health care. The history of differential medical treatment and medical studies has created mistrust among some cultural groups. The Tuskegee Syphilis Project and the AIDS epidemic are two examples of how and why groups can come to mistrust the health care system. Many health care providers and patients also hold prejudicial ideologies that can create barriers to effective treatment and to the provision of health care resources. In addition, religious beliefs can also present communication and health care challenges.

Finally, we turned to the issue of power in health communication. There is an imbalance of power between physician and patient, as well as an imbalance of power between patients and the health maintenance organizations. Four ethical approaches to health issues are strict paternalism, benevolent deception, contractual honesty, and unmitigated honesty.

BUILDING INTERCULTURAL SKILLS

1. Reflect on the history of your own family and traditional health care. Do you have many family members who are health care professionals? Did you grow up going to the doctor frequently? How much trust do you have in physicians?

2. Think about how you communicate to others in health care situations. As a patient, do you realize the importance of your communication to the physician or nurse in the diagnosis and treatments you receive? How might you better communicate your health situation to health care professionals? What kinds of cultural attitudes about various health issues do you hold that could be barriers to more effective communication? For example, have you been raised to be ashamed to ask questions about certain parts of your body?

3. Think about how health care professionals communicate with you. If you have a serious illness that may require much interaction with a physician, for example, is this someone whom you can trust?

4. Think about how health care professionals might encourage more open communication from patients so that they can receive better health care.

ACTIVITIES

1. *The media and health care:* Watch the news media for coverage of health issues as they relate to the most affected cultural groups. For example, is AIDS still framed as a "gay disease"? Is the hanta virus portrayed as a Navajo illness? In what ways does the conflation of the cultural group with the disease create misunderstandings?

2. *Communication about health care:* Talk to a health care professional about his or her experiences with cultural differences in communication. What were the main problems in the communication process? What suggestions might you make to avoid these problems in the future?

ENDNOTES

1. Pauwels, A. (1995). *Cross-cultural communication in the health sciences.* South Melbourne, Australia: Macmillan Education Australia, p. 3.
2. Pauwels (1995), p. 94.
3. Pauwels (1995), pp. 94–95.
4. Bernstein, N. (2005, April 21). Language barrier called health hazard in E.R. *New York Times,* p. B8.
5. Sharif, I., Lo, S., & Ozuah, P. O. (2006). Availability of Spanish prescription labels. *Journal of Health Care for the Poor and Underserved, 17*(1), 67.
6. Sharif et al. (2006), p. 67.
7. Fadiman, A. (1997). *The spirit catches you and you fall down: A Hmong child, her American doctors, and the collision of two cultures.* New York: Farrar, Straus and Giroux.
8. Northouse, L. L., & Northouse, P. G. (1998). *Health communication: Strategies for health professionals.* Stamford, CT: Appleton & Lange, p. 103.
9. Bahjati-Sabet, A., & Chambers, N. A. (2005). People of Iranian descent. In Waxler-Morrison, N., Anderson, J. M., Richardson, E., & Chambers, N. A., *Cross-cultural caring: A handbook for health professionals* (pp. 127–161.). 2nd ed. Vancouver: University of British Columbia Press.
10. Ford, L. A., & Yep, G. A. (2003). Working along the margins: Developing community-based strategies for communicating about health with marginalized groups. In T. L. Thompson, A. M. Dorsey, K. I. Miller, & R. Parrott (Eds.), *Handbook of health communication* (pp. 241–261). Mahwah, NJ: Erlbaum, p. 253.
11. Arnst, C. (2006, May 29). Health as a birthright. *BusinessWeek,* p. 20.
12. Shilling, C. (1993). *The body and social theory.* Newbury Park, CA: Sage, p. 58.
13. See, for example, Gilman, S. L. (1985). *Difference and pathology: Stereotypes of sexuality, race and madness.* Ithaca, NY: Cornell University Press; Gilman, S. L. (1988). *Disease and representation: Images of illness from madness to AIDS.* Ithaca, NY: Cornell University Press; Harding, S. G. (Ed.). (1993). *The "racial" economy of science: Toward a democratic future.* Bloomington: Indiana University Press; Harding, S. G. (1998). *Is science multicultural? Postcolonialism, feminisms, and epistemologies.* Bloomington: Indiana University Press; Mondimore, F. M. (1996). *A natural history of homosexuality.* Baltimore: Johns Hopkins University Press; Stoler, A. L. (1995). *Race and the education of desire.* Durham, NC: Duke University Press.

14. Solomon, M. (1985). The rhetoric of dehumanization: An analysis of medical reports of the Tuskegee Syphilis Project. *Western Journal of Speech Communication, 49,* 233–247.

15. Scherer, C. W., & Juanillo, N. K., Jr. (2003). The continuing challenge of community health risk management and communication. In Thompson, Dorsey, Miller, & Parrott, p. 228.

16. Boulware, L. E., Cooper, L. A., Ratner, L. F., LaVeist, T. A., & Powe, N. R. (2003, July–August). Race and trust in the health care system. *Public Health Reports, 118,* 363–364.

17. Kreps, G. L. (2006). Communication and racial inequalities in health care. *American Behavioral Scientist, 49,* 1–15.

18. Levi, J. (1992). Homophobia and AIDS public policy. In W. J. Blumenfeld (Ed.), *Homophobia: How we all pay the price* (pp. 217–232). Boston: Beacon Press, p. 217.

19. For some of these discussions, see, for example, Patton, C. (1990). *Inventing AIDS.* New York: Routledge; Patton, C. (1996). *Fatal advice: How safe-sex education went wrong.* Durham, NC: Duke University Press; Shilts, R. (1987). *And the band played on: Politics, people and the AIDS epidemic.* New York: St. Martin's Press.

20. Gross, L. (1993). *Contested closets: The politics and ethics of outing.* Minneapolis: University of Minnesota Press, p. 34.

21. Northouse & Northouse (1998), pp. 288–289.

22. So near, so far. (2009, January 22). *The Economist.* Retrieved January 30, 2009 from: http://www.economist.com/world/international/displaystory.cfm?story_id=12972597

23. Aldridge, D. (2000). *Spirituality, healing and medicine: Return to the silence.* Philadelphia: Jessica Kingsley.

24. Kalb, C. (2003, November 10). Faith & healing. *Newsweek,* p. 44.

25. Kalb (2003, November 10), pp. 55–56.

26. Kalb (2003, November 10), p. 54.

27. Koenig, H. G., McCullough, M. E., & Larson, D. B. (2001). *Handbook of religion and health.* Oxford: Oxford University Press.

28. Kalb (2003, November 10), p. 54.

29. Sloan, R. P. (2003, November 10). 'Religion is a private matter.' Interview with C. Kalb. *Newsweek,* p. 50.

30. Sloan, R. P. (2000, January/February). Religion, spirituality and medicine. *Freethought Today.* Retrieved from http://www.ffrf.org/fttoday/jan_feb00/sloan.html

31. National Center for Complementary and Alternative Medicine. (2007, February). What is CAM? National Institutes of Health. Retrieved March 5, 2009 from: http://nccam.nih.gov/health/whatiscam/overview.htm

32. National Coalition on Health Care. (2009). Health insurance costs. Retrieved February 2, 2009 from: http://www.nchc.org/facts/costs.shtml

33. Health care costs will continue their brisk climb. (2007, February 21). MSNBC. Retrieved February 2, 2009 from http://www.msnbc.msn.com/id/17249734/

34. Arnst, C. (2009, February 2). Health reform: Stumbling blocks still remain. *BusinessWeek,* pp. 60–61.

35. Pauwels (1995), p. 272.

36. Kreps, G. L., & Kunimoto, E. N. (1994). *Effective communication in multicultural health care settings.* Thousand Oaks, CA: Sage, pp. 67–69.

37. Stateman, A. (2007, February 9). The octuplet mom speaks, and questions grow. *Time.* Retrieved March 5, 2009 from: http://www.time.com/time/nation/article/0,8599,1877962,00.html

Glossary

accommodating style Emphasizes an indirect approach for dealing with conflict and a more emotionally restrained manner.

adaptors Gestures related to managing our emotions.

affirmative action (AA) Statutes that attempt to stop discrimination by encouraging the hiring of minorities and women.

Afrocentric An orientation toward African or African American cultural standards, including beliefs and values, as the criteria for interpreting behaviors and attitudes.

age identity The identification with the cultural conventions of how we should act, look, and behave according to our age.

AIDS Acquired immune deficiency syndrome; a disease caused by a virus, HIV, transmitted through sexual or blood contact, that attacks the immune system. (See **HIV**.)

alternative medicine A medical approach that goes against the norms of the medical establishment. It can incorporate holistic medicine, spirituality, and/or non-Western wellness philosophies.

Americans with Disabilities Act (ADA) A law requiring that places of business make "reasonable" accommodations for employees with physical disabilities.

anti-Americanism Negative ideas, feelings, and sometimes actions against the United States, most often the U.S. government.

argot A nonstandard way of communicating that separates insiders from outsiders of a coculture.

assimilable The degree of participation in a type of cultural adaptation in which an individual gives up his or her own cultural heritage and adopts the mainstream cultural identity.

authenticity In tourism, the search for "real" cultural experiences very different from the tourist's everyday life.

back translation The process of translating a document that has already been translated into a foreign language back to the original language—preferably by an independent translator.

benevolent deception Withholding information from a patient, ostensibly for his or her own good.

bilingual Able to speak two languages fluently or at least competently.

bilingualism The ability to speak two languages.

biologically based practice Use of products found in nature to provide therapy.

blog Web log; website, like a journal, maintained by an individual with regular entries of commentary, descriptions of events or other material such as graphics or video.

boundary maintenance The regulation of interaction between hosts and tourists.

class identity A sense of belonging to a group that shares similar economic, occupational, or social status.

class structure The economic organization of income levels in a society; the structure that defines upper, middle, lower, and other social classes.

cocultural group Nondominant cultural groups that exist in a national culture—for example, African American or Chinese American.

code switching Changing from one language or communication style to another.

collectivism The tendency to focus on the goals, needs, and views of the ingroup rather than individuals' own goals, needs, and views. (Compare with **individualism**.)

colonial education system Schools established by colonial powers in colonized regions. They often forbade the use of native languages and discussion of native cultures.

colonial histories The histories that legitimate international invasions and annexations.

communication A symbolic process whereby reality is produced, maintained, repaired, and transformed.

communication style The metamessage that contextualizes how listeners are expected to accept and interpret verbal messages.

complementarity A principle of relational attraction suggesting that sometimes we are attracted to people who are different from us.

compromise style A style of interaction for an intercultural couple in which both partners give up some part of their own cultural habits and beliefs to minimize cross-cultural differences. (Compare with **consensus style, obliteration style,** and **submission style.**)

conflict The interference between two or more interdependent individuals or groups of people who perceive incompatible goals, values, or expectations in attaining those ends.

consensus style A style of interaction for an intercultural couple in which partners deal with cross-cultural differences by negotiating their relationship. (Compare with **compromise style, obliteration style,** and **submission style.**)

constructive identity An identity that is actively negotiated from various cultures in contact and that often creates feelings of a new multicultural identity.

contact cultures Cultural groups in which people tend to stand close together and touch frequently when they interact—for example, cultural groups in South America, the Middle East, and southern Europe. (See **noncontact cultures.**)

contact hypothesis Intercultural contacts can result in more positive and tolerant attitudes toward other cultural groups, but only under very specific conditions.

context The physical or social situation in which communication occurs.

contractual honesty Telling a patient only what he or she wants to know.

core symbols The fundamental beliefs that are shared by the members of a cultural group. Labels, a category of core symbols, are names or markers used to classify individual, social, or cultural groups.

cosmopolitans People who view themselves as citizens of the world and are responsible to each other.

cross-cultural trainers Trainers who teach people to become familiar with other cultural norms and to improve their interactions with people of different domestic and international cultures.

cultural contact When two or more cultures come together, sometimes on an individual basis, but often through larger social migrations, wars, and other displacements.

cultural group histories The history of each cultural group within a nation that includes, for example, the history of where the group originated, why the people migrated, and how they came to develop and maintain their cultural traits.

cultural identities Who we are as influenced by the cultures to which we belong.

cultural imperialism Domination through the spread of cultural products.

cultural space The particular configuration of the communication that constructs meanings of various places.

cultural texts Cultural artifacts (magazines, TV programs, movies, and so on) that convey cultural norms, values, and beliefs.

culture Learned patterns of behavior and attitudes shared by a group of people.

culture industries Industries that produce and sell popular culture as commodities.

culture shock A relatively short-term feeling of disorientation and discomfort due to the lack of familiar cues in the environment.

cyberspace The electronic medium of computer networks, in which online communication takes place.

deception The act of making someone believe what is not true.

demographics The characteristics of a population, especially as classified by age, sex, and income.

diaspora A massive migration, often caused by war or famine or persecution, that results in the dispersal of a unified group.

diasporic histories The histories of the ways in which international cultural groups were created through transnational migrations, slavery, religious crusades, or other historical forces.

direct approach Emphasizes that conflict is fundamentally a good thing and should be approached head on.

discrimination Behaviors resulting from stereotypes or prejudice that cause some people to be denied equal participation or rights based on cultural group membership (such as race).

discussion style Combines the direct and emotionally restrained dimensions and emphasizes a verbally direct approach for dealing with disagreements.

dynamic style Uses an indirect style of communicating along with a more emotionally intense expressiveness.

eco-tourism Tourism of sites of environmental or natural interest.

electronic colonialism Domination or exploitation utilizing technological forms.

emblems Gestures that have a specific verbal translation.

embodied ethnocentrism Feeling comfortable and familiar in the spaces, behaviors, and actions of others in our own cultural surroundings.

emotionally expressive style Conflict style where intense and overt displays of emotions are valued during discussion of disagreements.

encapsulated identity An identity that is torn between different cultural identities and that often creates feelings of ambiguity.

enclaves Regions that are surrounded by another country's territory; cultural minority groups that live within a larger cultural group's territory.

energy medicine Use of energy fields as an approach to health.

engagement style Emphasizes a verbally direct and confrontational approach to dealing with conflict.

equal employment opportunity (EEO) Laws against discrimination in the workplace.

equivalency An issue in translation, the condition of being equal in meaning, value, quantity, and so on.

ethics Principles of conduct that help govern behaviors of individuals and groups.

ethics committees Groups that provide guidance in making health care decisions; usually composed of health care professionals, administrators, lawyers, social workers, members of the religious community, and patient representatives.

ethnic histories The histories of ethnic groups.

ethnic identity A set of ideas about one's own ethnic group membership; a sense of belonging to a particular group and knowing something about the shared experience of the group.

ethnocentrism An orientation toward one's own ethnic group; often a tendency to elevate one's own culture above others.

Eurocentric The assumption of the centrality or superiority of European culture.

euthanasia The ending of the life of a terminally ill patient.

eye contact A nonverbal code that communicates meanings about respect and status and often regulates turn taking during interactions.

facework Specific communication strategies used to maintain our own face or other people's faces.

facial expressions Facial gestures that convey emotions and attitudes.

family histories The body of knowledge shared by family members and the customs, rituals, and stories passed from one generation to another within a family.

folk culture Traditional culture that is not practiced for financial profit.

friendship A personal, nonromantic relationship that has culture-specific definitions.

gay relationships Same-sex romantic relationships.

gender histories The histories of how cultural conventions of men and women are created, maintained, and/or altered.

gender identity The identification with the cultural notions of masculinity and femininity and what it means to be a man or a woman.

gestures Nonverbal communication involving hand and arm movements.

globalization The increasing tendency toward international connections in media, business, and culture.

global nomads People who grow up in many different cultural contexts because their parents relocated.

global village A term coined by Marshall McLuhan in the 1960s that refers to a world in which communication technology links people from remote parts of the world.

grand narrative A unified history and view of humankind.

HBCUs Historically Black colleges and universities.

health care professionals Physicians, nurses, and all the other medical staff with whom patients in the health care system come into contact.

heterogeneity Consisting of different or dissimilar elements.

hidden histories The histories that are hidden from or forgotten by the mainstream representations of past events.

high-context communication A style of communication in which much of the information is contained in the contexts and nonverbal cues rather than expressed explicitly in words. (Compare with **low-context communication.**)

HIV Human immunodeficiency virus. (See **AIDS.**)

home The immediate cultural context for our upbringing; where we have lived.

Homo narrans A Latin term used to describe the storytelling tendencies of human beings.

host Residents of a tourist region.

hyphenated Americans Americans who identify not only with being American citizens but also with being members of ethnic groups.

identity The concept of who we are. Characteristics of identity may be understood differently depending on the perspectives that people take (for example, social psychological, communication, or critical perspectives).

illustrators Gestures that go along with and refer to speech.

immigration Movement to a new country, region, or environment to settle more or less permanently.

improvised performance A way of thinking about intercultural interaction in which two people are making up a performance as they go along.

incompatibility A state of incongruity in goals, values, or expectations between two or more individuals.

indirect approach Emphasizes that conflict should be avoided.

individualism The tendency to emphasize individual identities, beliefs, needs, goals, and views rather than those of the group. (Compare with **collectivism.**)

intellectual histories Written histories that focus on the development of ideas.

intercultural communication The interaction between people from different cultural backgrounds.

intercultural conflict The perceived or real incompatibility of goals, values, or expectations between two parties from different cultures.

intercultural dating The pursuit of a romantic intercultural relationship.

intercultural relationships Relationships that are formed between individuals from different cultures.

interdependent A state of mutual influence; the action or behavior of one individual affecting the other person in a relationship.

interlanguage The form of language that emerges when a nonnative speaker overlaps his or her native grammar or structure onto another language.

intermediary In a formal setting, a professional third party, such as a lawyer, real estate agent, or counselor, who intervenes when two parties are in conflict. Informal intermediaries may be friends or colleagues who intervene.

international conflict Conflict that occurs on the international level, often between nations.

international negotiation The process of two national groups (who have common and conflicting interests) resolving conflicts to a mutually satisfactory end.

international students Students attending high school or college in another country. (See **study-abroad programs.**)

interpersonal allies People, often friends, who work for better interpersonal and intergroup relations.

interpersonal conflict Conflict that occurs between individuals rather than groups or nations.

interpretation The process of verbally expressing what is said or written in another language.

intimacy The extent of emotional closeness.

labels Terms used to refer to people's identities.

language A means of communication using shared symbols.

language acquisition The process of learning language.

language policies Laws or customs that determine which language will be spoken when and where.

learning styles The different ways students learn in different cultures.

low-context communication A style of communication in which much of the information is conveyed in words rather than in nonverbal cues and contexts. (Compare with **high-context communication.**)

macrocontexts The political, social, and historical situations, backgrounds, and environments that influence communication.

majority identity development The development of a sense of belonging to a dominant group.

manipulative and body based practices Use of massage or chiropractic approaches to health.

maquiladoras A Mexican term indicating assembly plants or factories (mainly of U.S. companies) established on the U.S.–Mexico border and using mainly Mexican labor.

masculinity/femininity value A cultural variability dimension that concerns the degree of being feminine—valuing fluid gender roles, quality of life, service, relationships, and interdependence—and the degree of being masculine—emphasizing distinctive gender roles, ambition, materialism, and independence.

media imperialism Domination or control through media.

mediation The act of resolving conflict by having someone intervene between two parties.

medical jargon Medical terminology, especially that which is confusing or difficult for the layperson to understand.

medical terminology A set of scientific words and phrases used by doctors to precisely describe illness.

melting pot A metaphor that assumes that immigrants and cultural minorities will be assimilated into the U.S. majority culture, losing their original cultures.

migrating When an individual leaves the primary cultural context in which he or she was raised and moves to a new cultural context for an extended period of time.

mind-body medicine Healing that focuses on use of the mind to influence the body.

minority identity development The development of a sense of belonging to a nondominant group.

MMOGs (Massively Text-based Multiplayer Online Games) Participants interact with environments, objects, and other participants.

mobility The state of moving from place to place.

monochronic An orientation to time that assumes it is linear and is a commodity that can be lost or gained.

multicultural identity A sense of in-betweenness that develops as a result of frequent or multiple cultural border crossings.

multilingual The ability to speak more than two languages fluently or at least competently.

multinational Companies that have operations in two or more nations.

multiracial and multicultural people People whose heritage draws from more than one racial or cultural group.

national history A body of knowledge based on past events that influenced a country's development.

national identity National citizenship.

neighborhood Living area defined by its cultural identity, especially an ethnic or racial one.

noncontact cultures Cultural groups in which people tend to maintain more space and touch less often than people do in contact cultures. Great Britain and Japan tend to have noncontact cultures. (See **contact cultures.**)

nonverbal codes Systems for understanding the meanings of nonverbal behavior, including personal space, eye contact, facial expressions, gestures, time orientation, and silence.

nonverbal communication Communication through means other than language—for example, facial expressions and clothing.

obliteration style A style of interaction for an intercultural couple in which both partners attempt to erase their individual cultures in dealing with cultural differences. (Compare with **compromise style, consensus style,** and **submission style.**)

pacifism Opposition to the use of force under any circumstances.

perception The process by which we select, organize, and interpret external and internal stimuli to create our view of the world.

personal identity A person's notions of self.

personal space The immediate area around a person, invasion of which may provoke discomfort or offense.

phonology The study of speech sounds.

physical ability identity A knowledge of self based on characteristics related to the body, either more permanent or temporary—for example, sight, hearing, and weight.

physical attraction Sexual desire based on the appearance of another.

political conflict Conflict that happens at the societal level over political issues.

political histories Written histories that focus on political events.

polychronic An orientation to time that sees it as circular and more holistic.

popular culture Forms of contemporary culture that are made popular by and for the people through their mass consumption of these products. Those systems or artifacts that most people share and that most people know about, including television, music, videos, and popular magazines.

postcolonialism An intellectual, political, and cultural movement that calls for the independence of once colonized states and also liberation from colonialist ways of thinking.

power A state of differential levels of societal and structural privilege.

power distance A cultural variability dimension that concerns the extent to which people accept an unequal distribution of power.

pragmatics The study of how meaning is constructed in relation to receivers and how language is actually used in particular contexts in language communities.

prejudice An attitude (usually negative) toward a cultural group based on little or no evidence.

prejudicial ideologies Sets of ideas that rely on stereotypes.

racial and ethnic identity Identifying with a particular racial or ethnic group. Although in the past racial groups were classified on the basis of biological characteristics, most scientists now recognize that race is constructed in fluid social and historical contexts.

racial histories The histories of nonmainstream racial groups.

reader profiles Portrayals of readership demographics prepared by magazines.

regionalism Loyalty to a particular region that holds significant cultural meaning for that person.

regulators Gestures used to guide the flow of a conversation, especially for turn taking.

relational messages Messages (verbal and nonverbal) that express how we feel about others.

relativist position The view that the particular language we speak, especially the structure of the language, shapes our perception of reality and cultural patterns. (Compare with **nominalist position** and **qualified relativist position**.)

religious conflicts Conflicts that arise from strongly held views and religious beliefs.

religious freedom The ability to practice one's religion without fear; a concern among health care professionals who worry about engaging in religious issues.

religious histories Bodies of knowledge containing the items of faith and that faith's prescriptions for action that have been important for a cultural group.

religious identity A sense of belonging to a religious group.

resistance Avoiding intrusions; may take fairly passive forms or more assertive forms.

restraint style Conflict style where disagreements are best discussed in an emotionally calm manner.

retreatism The avoidance of tourists by hosts.

revitalization The economic benefits associated with tourism in certain areas.

romantic relationships Intimate relationships that comprise love, involvement, sharing, openness, connectedness, and so on.

self-awareness Related to intercultural communication competence; the quality of knowing how you are perceived as a communicator, as well as your strengths and weaknesses.

self-reflexivity A process of learning to understand ourselves and our own position in society.

semantics The study of words and meanings.

sexual orientation histories The historical experiences of gays and lesbians.

silence The absence of verbal messages.

similarity principle A principle of relational attraction suggesting that we tend to be attracted to people whom we perceive to be similar to ourselves.

social conflict Conflict that arises from unequal or unjust social relationships between groups.

social histories Written histories that focus on everyday life experiences of various groups in the past.

socially responsible tourism Tourism that emphasizes positive economic, social, cultural, and environmental impacts from the tourism industry.

social movements Organized activities in which individuals work together to bring about social change.

social positions The places from which we speak that are socially constructed and thus embedded with assumptions about gender, race, class, age, social roles, sexuality, and so on.

social roles Roles we enact that are learned in a culture—for example, mother, big brother, and community leader.

socioeconomic class histories Bodies of knowledge relating to a group's relationship to social class and economic forces.

source text The original language text of a translation. (See also **target text**.)

staged authenticity When local people alter their cultural performances to meet tourist expectations, the resulting representation of the local culture is not authentic.

status The relative position an individual holds in social or organizational settings.

stereotypes Widely held beliefs about a group of people.

stereotyping The use of stereotypes.

strict paternalism A physician's provision of misinformation for the supposed benefit of the patient.

study-abroad programs University-sponsored programs that give course credit for study in other countries.

submission style A style of interaction for an intercultural couple in which one partner yields to the other partner's cultural patterns, abandoning or denying his or her own culture. (Compare with **compromise style, consensus style,** and **obliteration style**.)

syntactics The study of the structure, or grammar, of a language.

target text The new language text into which the original language text is translated. (See also **source text**.)

teaching styles The different ways teachers teach in different cultures.

third culture style A new communication style that results from two people trying to adapt to each other's styles.

tourists Visitors to another country or region.

translation The process of producing a written text that refers to something said or written in another language.

traveling The changing of cultural spaces through locomotion.

Tuskegee Syphilis Project A government-sponsored study of syphilis in which treatment of the disease was withheld from African American males for the purpose of establishing an experimental control group.

U-curve theory A theory of cultural adaptation positing that migrants go through fairly predictable phases (excitement/anticipation, shock/disorientation, and adaptation) in adapting to a new cultural situation.

uncertainty avoidance A cultural variability dimension that concerns the extent to which uncertainty, ambiguity, and deviant ideas and behaviors are avoided.

universalist position An ethical approach that emphasizes the similarity of beliefs across cultures—for example, killing within the group or treason.

unmitigated honesty A physician's communication of the entirety of a medical diagnosis to a patient.

values A system for viewing certain ideas as more important than others.

verlan A French form of argot in which the syllables in words or the words are often reversed.

Whiteness The associations having to do with the identities of White people.

worldview Underlying assumptions about the nature of reality and human behavior.

Photo Credits

Index